Springer Texts in Business and Economics

Springer Texts in Business and Economics (STBE) delivers high-quality instructional content for undergraduates and graduates in all areas of Business/Management Science and Economics. The series is comprised of self-contained books with a broad and comprehensive coverage that are suitable for class as well as for individual self-study. All texts are authored by established experts in their fields and offer a solid methodological background, often accompanied by problems and exercises.

Phillip Anthony O'Hara

Principles of Institutional and Evolutionary Political Economy

Applied to Current World Problems

Phillip Anthony O'Hara
Global Political Economy Research Unit
Perth, WA, Australia

ISSN 2192-4333 ISSN 2192-4341 (electronic)
Springer Texts in Business and Economics
ISBN 978-981-19-4157-3 ISBN 978-981-19-4158-0 (eBook)
https://doi.org/10.1007/978-981-19-4158-0

© The Editor(s) (if applicable) and The Author(s), under exclusive license to Springer Nature Singapore Pte Ltd. 2022, corrected publication 2023
This work is subject to copyright. All rights are solely and exclusively licensed by the Publisher, whether the whole or part of the material is concerned, specifically the rights of translation, reprinting, reuse of illustrations, recitation, broadcasting, reproduction on microfilms or in any other physical way, and transmission or information storage and retrieval, electronic adaptation, computer software, or by similar or dissimilar methodology now known or hereafter developed.
The use of general descriptive names, registered names, trademarks, service marks, etc. in this publication does not imply, even in the absence of a specific statement, that such names are exempt from the relevant protective laws and regulations and therefore free for general use.
The publisher, the authors, and the editors are safe to assume that the advice and information in this book are believed to be true and accurate at the date of publication. Neither the publisher nor the authors or the editors give a warranty, expressed or implied, with respect to the material contained herein or for any errors or omissions that may have been made. The publisher remains neutral with regard to jurisdictional claims in published maps and institutional affiliations.

This Springer imprint is published by the registered company Springer Nature Singapore Pte Ltd.
The registered company address is: 152 Beach Road, #21-01/04 Gateway East, Singapore 189721, Singapore

Preface

My studies into the specific concepts and principles of political economy *started* with the work of Nicholas Kaldor on the irrelevance of equilibrium economics, then progressed to Dale Bush's principles of institutional change; Charles Wilber's holistic economics; Gunnar Myrdal's circular and cumulative causation; Karl Marx's principle of contradiction; Thorstein Veblen's "habits, institutions, and instincts"; Joan Robinson's concepts of historical time, surplus, and development; Joseph Schumpeter's creative destruction, innovation, and surplus value; Ron Stanfield's notions of the economic surplus, culture, and the nurturance gap; Bill Dugger's concepts of institutional economics; Marilyn Power's social provisioning framework; J.M. Keynes's notions of aggregate demand and uncertainty; David Gordon's social structures of accumulation; Michel Aglietta's Regulation Approach; Karl Polanyi's *disembedded* economy and the double movement; Marilyn French's gendered history of the world; and Immanuel Wallerstein on hegemony and uneven development.

Later, I studied carefully the concepts of path dependence, complexity, emergence, heterogeneous groups and agents, uncertainty and effective demand, historical specificity and evolution, the community's stock of knowledge, vested interests v. the common good, endogenous money, and modern monetary theory. More recently, I have studied Mario Bunge's scientific philosophy, emergence, and complexity, plus Fernand Braudel's events, conjunctures, and long durations. Of course, I have also studied works and traditions closely linked to *all* the above ideas and scholars.

This book is written for students and scholars of political economy, institutional and evolutionary themes, interdisciplinary approaches, public policy, global political economy, and history of political economy (HPE). It takes ideas from HPE (including the most recent history) to scrutinize current real-world problems. The "core general principles," *in aggregate,* used in this book, including "historical specificity and evolution," "hegemony and uneven development," "circular and cumulative causation," "contradiction," "heterogeneous groups & agents," "uncertainty," "innovation," and "policy & governance," have been termed by some scholars "O'Hara's principles of political economy." There are also some other associated principles and concepts utilized, where appropriate, for scrutinizing various core current problems of the world. Furthermore, these core general and associated principles and concepts are situated within the framework of a whole corpus of contemporary principles of institutional and evolutionary political economy.

Historically, the first real-world complex problem I analyzed through the use of some of these concepts and principles was the rise and fall of institutional waves of expansion and decline of US, regional and global capitalism, in the light of late-1940s–2000s boom and collapse. This was documented in several papers and books. Then I scrutinized the problems of terrorism and the war on terrorism, followed by climate change, AIDS-HIV, the subprime crisis—GFC, financial crises, the nurturance gap, corruption, AI and robotics, and the coronacrisis. I had carte blanche to study what I wanted to, so I decided to spend my research time scrutinizing the major problems of the world. I hope it has helped others understand these anomalies; it has done good service to my brain (kept it working well).

I will be continuing this work of understanding core concepts and principles of political economy, especially with an institutional and evolutionary context, and applying them to major world problems. I am also writing a global history of the world, among other projects. It seems to be a useful and creative thing to do. If any reader of this work has ideas to assist in conceptualizing and studying world problems, please do contact me. I always need to balance scholarly work with things to help other parts of my body and mind, such as singing, dancing, exercising, travelling, relating, practicing yoga-nidra, eating good food, and linking to nature, which in turn helps me do the work. I recommend this "double movement" to others.

People who helped me on specific chapters are acknowledged in a note to each chapter just before the References. More generally, I would like to make special mention here, with thanks for the exquisite encouragement and advice provided (variously: early on, later, always), by Ron Stanfield, Bill Dugger, Rhoda O'Hara, John Davis, Kosta Josifidis, Svetlana Chandler-Kirdina, Wolfram Elsner, Ian Kerr, Andrew Brennan, Howard Sherman, Cecilia Winters, Allen Oakley, Geoffrey Harcourt, Baidyanath Ghosh, Michael McLure, and Albert Schweinberger. I also wish to thank the help provided by the Springer Nature editorial staff, Lucie Bartonek, and Aarthi Padmanaban, especially on the agreement and final-draft-of-manuscript issues, and S. Ramabrabha on production and final checking of manuscript.

Perth, WA, Australia
ohara.gperu@gmail.com

Phillip Anthony O'Hara

Copyright Acknowledgments

Some of the chapters of this book were originally published in journals and edited books. Most have been edited, revised and extensively updated for this book. The following is a list of the previous publications, and where relevant the copyright acknowledgments that I have been asked to provide. Full bibliographical details are (also) provided as footnote/references to the respective chapters in this book. I wish to thank the various parties for allowing me to use copyright material in this current book.

An earlier version of Chap. 2 was originally published as Chapter 12: Phillip Anthony O'Hara (2019) "History of Institutional Economics," in Ajit Sinha & Alex M. Thomas (Editors), *Pluralist Economics and Its History*, London & New York: Routledge (Taylor & Francis Group), pp. 171–190. Licensor: INFORMA UK LIMITED. Reproduced with permission of the licensor through PLSclear. Pluralistic Economics and Its History - 1st Edition - Ajit Sinha - Al (routledge.com)

An earlier version of Chap. 3 was originally published as: Phillip Anthony O'Hara (2007), "Principles of Institutional-Evolutionary Political Economy—Converging Themes from the Schools of Heterodoxy," *Journal of Economic Issues*, 41(1)(March 2007): 1–42. Thanks go to the Association for Evolutionary Economics (AFEE), which holds exclusive copyright to the article, for permission to revise the article for inclusion in this book. https://doi.org/10.1080/00213624.2007.11506993

An earlier version of Chap. 4 was originally published as: Phillip Anthony O'Hara (2021), "Global Coronavirus Pandemic Crisis and Future Crisis Prevention," *Panoeconomicus*, 68(5)(Dec 2021): 587–623. Thanks go to the copyright holder, the Association of Economists of Vojvodina and the Serbian Association of Economists—Kosta Josifidis, as well as the Public Knowledge Project—for permission to revise this paper for inclusion in this book. http://panoeconomicus.org/index.php/jorunal/article/view/1550/676 [sic]

An earlier version of Chap. 5 was originally published as: Phillip Anthony O'Hara (2009), "Political Economy of Climate Change, Ecological Destruction and Uneven Development," *Ecological Economics*, 69(2)(15 Dec 2009): 223–234. Licensor: Elsevier B V Company. Reproduced with permission of the licensor through PLSclear. https://doi.org/10.1016/j.ecolecon.2009.09.015

An earlier version of Chap. 6 was originally published as: Phillip Anthony O'Hara (2014), "Political Economy of Systemic and Micro-Corruption Throughout the World," *Journal of Economic Issues,* 48(2)(June 2014): 279–308. Thanks go to the Association for Evolutionary Economics (AFEE), which holds exclusive copyright to the article, for permission to revise the article for inclusion in this book. https://doi.org/10.2753/JEI0021-3624480203

An earlier version of Chap. 8 was published as: Phillip Anthony O'Hara (2012), "Principles of Political Economy Applied to Policy and Governance: Disembedded Economy, Contradictions, Circular Cumulation and Uneven Development," *Journal of Economic and Social Policy,* 15(1)(2012): 1–37. The journal was an open access repository, where authors retain copyright to their authored works.

An earlier version of Chap. 9 was published as: Phillip Anthony O'Hara (2009), "Money, Credit and Finance in Political Economy: National, Regional and Global Dimensions," in *Handbook of Pluralistic Economics Education,* edited by Jack Reardon. London & New York: Routledge (Taylor & Francis Group), pp.230–255. Licensor: INFORMA UK LIMITED. Reproduced with permission of the licensor through PLSclear. The Handbook of Pluralist Economics Education - 1st Edition - Jack Re (routledge.com)

Chapter 10 was originally published as: Phillip Anthony O'Hara (2004), "The War on Terrorism, Political Economic Contradictions and Policy Issues," in *Global Political Economy and the Wealth of Nations: Performance, Institutions, Problems and Policies.* London & New York: Routledge (Taylor & Francis Group), 2004, 302–324. Licensor: INFORMA UK LIMITED. Reproduced with permission of the licensor through PLSclear. Global Political Economy and the Wealth of Nations: Performance, Insti (routledge.com)

An earlier version of Chapter 11 was published as: Phillip Anthony O'Hara (2022), "AIDS and HIV," in *International Encyclopedia of Public Policy: Volume 1, Global Governance and Development,* edited by P.A. O'Hara. Perth, Australia: Global Political Economy Research Unit (GPERU), pp. 1–16. As stated in the *IEPP*, Vol 1, p. 11, *"Contributors have copyright © to their individual articles."* http://pohara.homestead.com/Encyclopedia/Volume-1.pdf

An earlier version of Chap. 12 was originally published as: Phillip Anthony O'Hara (2014), "Political Economy of Love: Nurturance Gap, Disembedded Economy and Freedom Constraints Within Neoliberal Capitalism," *Panoeconomicus,* 61(2): 161–192. Thanks go to the copyright holder, the Association of Economists of Vojvodina, the Serbian Association of Economists—Kosta Josifidis, as well as the Public Knowledge Project—for permission to revise this paper for inclusion in this book. www.doiserbia.nb.rs/img/doi/1452-595X/2014/1452-595X1402161H.pdf

About the Book

Principles of Institutional and Evolutionary Political Economy: Applied to Current World Problems presents the major concepts and principles of political economy, and then applies these principles to major socioeconomic and politico-economic problems of the world. After a historical survey of institutional and evolutionary concepts and principles, the author outlines the contemporary conceptual edifice of principles, and then applies core ones to major problems of the world. Some of the problems analyzed include the coronavirus crisis, climate change, corruption, AI and robotics, and policy and governance. The book then scrutinizes money and financial crises, terrorism and the war on terrorism, HIV-AIDS, and the nurturance gap. This is the very first volume to *explicitly* study the major historical and contemporary principles of institutional and evolutionary political economy as well as to *explicitly* apply these in detail to many major world problems. It has been written for students and scholars of political economy, global political economy, public policy, and institutional and evolutionary studies.

Contents

1 Introduction 1
   1.1   Concepts and Principles 1
   1.2   Principles and Problems of the World: The Chapters 8
   References 15

2 History of Concepts and Principles 19
   2.1   Introduction 20
   2.2   Proto-Institutional and Evolutionary Science 22
   2.3   Principles of Thorstein Veblen 23
   2.4   Keynes, Schumpeter & Later Evolutionary-Institutional
         Scholars 27
   2.5   Contemporary Institutional and Evolutionary Political
         Economy 32
   2.6   Conclusion 38
   References 39

**3 Contemporary Institutional and Evolutionary Concepts
and Principles** 45
   3.1   Introduction 46
   3.2   Historical Specificity; Hegemony and Uneven
         Development 49
         3.2.1   Evolution of Capitalism, Trust, Uneven
                Development 50
   3.3   Heterogeneous Groups and Agents 56
   3.4   Circular and Cumulative Causation (CCC) 60
         3.4.1   CCC, Emergence and Complexity 65
   3.5   Contradictory Dynamics 68
   3.6   Uncertainty 71
   3.7   Innovation 73
   3.8   Policy and Governance 75
         3.8.1   Progressive Agenda for Change 76
         3.8.2   Trust, Community and Destructive Creation 76
         3.8.3   Entropy, Precautionary Principle and Minimal
                Dislocation 77

	3.9 Concepts and Principles in This Book	78
	3.10 Conclusion	80
	References	82
4	**Global Coronavirus Pandemic Crisis**	**89**
	4.1 Introduction	90
	4.2 Political Economy of the Coronavirus Pandemic	91
	4.3 Historical Evolution of the Global Coronavirus Crisis	93
	4.4 Heterogeneous Groups and Agents	101
	4.5 Circular & Cumulative Causation and Contradictions of Coronacrisis	108
	4.6 Uncertainty and the Pandemic	114
	4.7 Preparedness Policies, Uncertainty and the Future	117
	4.8 Conclusion	122
	References	123
5	**Climate Change**	**129**
	5.1 Introduction	130
	5.2 Historical Specificity of Climate Change	131
	5.3 Contradictions of Climate Change	138
	5.4 Uneven Development of Climate Change	143
	5.5 CCC and Uncertainties of Climate Change	149
	5.5.1 Shared Socioeconomic Pathways (SSPs)	153
	5.5.2 Cascading Tipping Points	155
	5.6 Conclusion	157
	References	159
6	**Corruption**	**165**
	6.1 Historical Specificity of Corruption	166
	6.2 Contradictions of Corruption, Heterogeneous Groups and Uneven Development	173
	6.3 Uneven Development of Corruption	182
	6.4 Conclusion	190
	References	191
7	**Artificial General Intelligence and Autonomous Humanoid Robotics**	**195**
	7.1 Introduction: '*hetero autonomia humanio roboto*'	196
	7.2 Artificial Intelligence and Robotics in Historical Perspective	199
	7.3 CCC: Philosophy & Micro-Meso A(G)I Political Economy Principles	205
	7.4 Contradictions Between the Two Main Schools of A(G)I	216
	7.5 Neurobiological Political Economy Design Principles of Brain-Body-Environment Interaction for Embodied Cognition AGI-AHR	221

	7.6	Conclusion	240
	References		244
8	**Policy and Governance**		251
	8.1	Introduction	252
	8.2	Science of Provisioning	253
	8.3	Disembedded Economy	253
	8.4	Contradictions	260
	8.5	Circular and Cumulative Causation	266
	8.6	Uneven Development	269
	8.7	Conclusion	272
	References		273
9	**Money and Credit Circuits, Cycles and Crises**		277
	9.1	Introduction	278
	9.2	Waves and Phases of Industrial-Financial Capitalism	279
	9.3	Dynamic Circuit of Money Capital	284
	9.4	Endogenous Versus Exogenous Money and Credit	286
	9.5	Financial Instability Hypothesis	290
	9.6	Global Money, Payments and Prices	293
	9.7	Chartalism and Modern Monetary Theory	297
	9.8	Conclusion	300
	References		301
10	**Terrorism and the War on Terrorism**		307
	10.1	Introduction	308
	10.2	Contemporary Terrorism: Nature and Trends	309
	10.3	Terrorism: Low Fatality Risk, High System Risk	311
	10.4	Technology Promotes Terrorism	315
	10.5	Attempt to Reestablish Strategic US Hegemony Encouraged Terrorism	317
	10.6	Global Deregulation Expands Terrorism and Radical Islam	319
	10.7	Policy Issues and Measures	321
	10.8	Conclusion	325
	References		326
11	**HIV and AIDS**		329
	11.1	Introduction	330
	11.2	Social History of HIV-AIDS	330
	11.3	Natural History of HIV	332
	11.4	Global Distribution of HIV-AIDS	333
	11.5	Details of Natural History of HIV: Heterogeneous Groups	335
	11.6	Natural History of HIV-AIDS in Individuals: Heterogeneous Groups and Contradictions	337
	11.7	Cofactors and Causal Controversy: Contradiction and Heterogeneous Groups and Agents	340

	11.8	Crisis in Social Reproduction During High Trajectory Period	343
	11.9	Governance Policies and Innovation	346
	11.10	Conclusion	348
	References		348
12	**Love Capital and the Nurturance Gap**		**351**
	12.1	Introduction	352
	12.2	Historical Specificity of Love: Collectivist and Individualistic Economies	355
	12.3	Circular and Cumulative Causation: Love Styles and Core Factors	357
	12.4	Contradictions of Love Styles: General and Within Neoliberal Capitalism	367
		12.4.1 Contradiction Between Markets and Nurturance	370
		12.4.2 Contradiction Between Individual and Society	371
		12.4.3 Contradiction Between Love Freedom and Constraint	372
	12.5	Love Phases Through Path Dependence, Evolution and Instability	374
	12.6	Conclusion	379
	References		380
13	**Conclusion**		**385**
	References		388

Correction to: Principles of Institutional and Evolutionary Political Economy C1

Glossary 389

Name Index 419

Subject Index 425

About the Author

Phillip Anthony O'Hara has a PhD in political economy, held a personal chair at Curtin University, and is currently director of the Global Political Economy Research Unit (GPERU) in Perth, Australia. He specializes in studying concepts and principles, major problems of the world, institutional change and adjustment, global political economy, history of the world, and scholarly biography. He has published more than 100 articles in refereed journals and edited books as well as 14 volumes of books and special issues of journals, was president of the Association for Evolutionary Economics (AFEE), and is currently on the editorial or international advisory boards of the *Review of Evolutionary Political Economy*, *Panoeconomics*, *the International Journal of Pluralism and Economics Education*, and *Terra Economicus*. His major books include (among others) the two-volume *Encyclopedia of Political Economy*, the four-volume *International Encyclopedia of Public Policy*, and *Growth and Development in the Global Political Economy* as well as *Global Political Economy and the Wealth of Nations*. He has won many awards for his research, including 'Journal Article of the Year' and 'Book of the Year', from the European Association for Evolutionary Political Economy (EAEPE) and also from Curtin Business School.

Abbreviations

AGI	Artificial general intelligence
AHR	Autonomous humanoid robotics
AI	Artificial intelligence
AIDS	Acquired immunodeficiency syndrome
AMAZ	Amazon rainforest
AMOC	Atlantic meridional overturning circulation
APG	Alpine glaciers
AWIS	Arctic winter ice sheet
ASSI	Arctic summer sea ice
AWIS	Arctic winter ice sheet
AZ	Astra-Zeneca
BOE	Bank of England
BWS	Bretton Woods System
CC	Coronacrisis
CCC	Circular and cumulative causation
CESM	Mario Bunge's framework of system components (C), environments (E), structures (S), and mechanisms (M)
CPI	Corruption Perceptions Index
CPSP	Core, periphery, semi-periphery
COP26	26th UN Climate Change Conference of the Parties (COP26) in Glasgow on 31 October–13 November 2021
COVAX	COVID-19 Vaccines Global Access
CS	Cytokine storm
EAIS	Eastern Antarctic ice sheet
EIU	*Economist* Intelligence Unit
ENR	El-Nino regime
EU	European Union
FAO	Food and Agricultural Organization
FIH	Financial instability hypothesis
FPE	Feminist political economy
FPEs	Feminist political economists

GFC	Global financial crisis
GHG	Greenhouse gas
GHGs	Greenhouse gasses
GHSI	Global Health Security Index
GIS	Greenland ice sheet
GOFAI	Good old-fashioned AI
HIV	Human immunodeficiency virus
HRW	Human Rights Watch
I-E	Institutional and evolutionary
IE	Institutional and evolutionary
IEPE	Institutional and evolutionary political economy
IEPEs	Institutional and evolutionary political economists
IMF	International Monetary Fund
IMS	Indian monsoonal system
IPCC	Intergovernmental Panel on Climate Change
JHU	John Hopkins University
LAC	Latin America & the Caribbean
LGBT	Lesbian, gay, bisexual, and transsexual (people or movement)
LPI	Living Planet Index
KWS	Keynesian Welfare State
MENA	Middle East and North Africa
MIT	Massachusetts Institute of Technology
MMT	Modern Monetary Theory
NA	North America
NBF	Northern boreal forests
NEP	Northeast permafrost
NPF	Northern permafrost
NTI	Nuclear Threat Initiative
PE	Political economy
PKI	Post-Keynesian institutionalism
RCP	Representative Concentration Pathways
SEG	Social, environmental, and governance ethic/stakeholders
SSA	Sub-Saharan Africa
SSA	Social structure(s) of accumulation
SSP	Shared Socioeconomic Pathway(s)
TB	Tuberculosis
TCR	Tropical coral reefs
UK	United Kingdom
UNAIDS	Joint United Nations Programme on HIV/AIDS
UNDP	United Nations Development Program
UKIPO	UK Intellectual Property Office
VOC	Variant of concern
VOI	Variant of interest

WB	World Bank
WAMS	West African monsoonal system
WHO	World Health Organization
WMO	World Meteorological Organization
WWF	Worldwide Fund for Nature

The original version of this book has been revised "due to corrections mentioned in the Front Matter, Chapters 1, 2, 3, 9 and the Back Matter." The correction to this book can be found at https://doi.org/10.1007/978-981-19-4158-0_14

Introduction 1

Abstract

This introduction defines and outlines the nature of the core major concepts and principles of institutional and evolutionary political economy, and provides a summary of the chapters which apply the principles to core global problems. We outline the nature of the chapters on the history and the contemporary concepts and principles. Then we summarise the chapters on major global problems including the coronacrisis, climate change, corruption, AI and robotics, policy and governance, financial instability and crises, terrorism and the war on terrorism, AIDS-HIV plus love and the nurturance gap.

Keywords

Institutional & evolutionary · Political economy · Concepts and principles · Coronacrisis · Climate change · Corruption · Artificial intelligence · Policy & governance · Financial instability & crises · Terrorism · AIDS & HIV · Love & nurturance gap

1.1 Concepts and Principles

This is the first time a volume or volumes have been published on *specific substantial sets* of contemporary principles and concepts of institutional and evolutionary political economy (IEPE). It is also the first time a volume or volumes have emerged applying such *specific substantial principles* and concepts to numerous current world problems in some detail. This is also the first of three books on such political economy principles and concepts applied to global, regional and national problems and issues. The three books are loosely tripled and parallel, but marketed as separate volumes, as they do deal with somewhat different problems and use variably

© The Author(s), under exclusive license to Springer Nature Singapore Pte Ltd. 2022, corrected publication 2023
P. A. O'Hara, *Principles of Institutional and Evolutionary Political Economy*, Springer Texts in Business and Economics,
https://doi.org/10.1007/978-981-19-4158-0_1

different methods to deal with the issues. *This* first volume, *Principles of Institutional and Evolutionary Political Economy: Applied to Current World Problems* (O'Hara 2022b), includes two chapters on concepts and principles; followed by nine chapters where concepts and principles are applied to current world problems; then a Conclusion and a Glossary.

The two introductory chapters on principles and concepts include one on the history (Chap. 2 below) and one on the contemporary state of play (Chap. 3). Chapters 4, 5, 6, 7, 8, 9, 10, 11 and 12 apply such principles and concepts to problems such as the coronacrisis and preparation for the next such crisis (Chap. 4), climate change (Chap. 5), corruption (Chap. 6), AI and robotics (Chap. 7), policy and governance (Chap. 8), money, financial instability and crises (Chap. 9), terrorism (Chap. 10), AIDS-HIV (Chap. 11) and love and the nurturance gap (Chap. 12). A Conclusion follows (Chap. 13) along with a Glossary.

The second volume, *Long Wave Institutional Dynamics and Political Economy Crises of Capitalism: Principles, Social Structures of Accumulation and Empirics* (O'Hara 2023) (my third book on '*SSAs*'), applies the principles and concepts to the uneven and structural crisis tendencies of capitalism during the 1780s–2020s, paying special attention to the period of the 1940s–2020s. Here we apply some core principles to historical-institutional long waves; survey the crises as they are situated in phases and stages of capitalist development; apply the principles to geopolitical conflict, GFC and coronacrisis; and scrutinize long-wave '*SSAs*' associated with China and the USA. This volume will be published soon after the first.

The third volume, *Advances in Political Economy Principles: Applied to Current World Problems*, provides much more detail on the principles and concepts, as we have *complete chapters* on each substantive core general principle/concept of (1) historical specificity and evolution; (2) circular and cumulative causation; (3) contradiction; (4) heterogeneous groups and agents; (5) economic surplus; (6) power, hegemony and uneven development; (7) uncertainty; (8) innovation, (9) policy and governance, plus others. Then we variously apply some of the principles/concepts to problems/issues of (10) crime and injustice, (11) waves of climate change, (12) crises and cycles, (13) geopolitical power and rivalry, (14) humanoid robotics, (15) neuroscience, (16) innovation and development, (17) trust, sociality and community, (18) cosmology and planetary settlement, plus (19) state and politics. The third volume has a way to go before publication (O'Hara Forthcoming).

I began working on the principles of political economy in the 1980s, when I included two chapters on principles in my PhD; one chapter mainly on the principles of 'holism (circular and cumulative causation), contradiction and evolution'; and the other on 'instrumental and ceremonial functions of institutions' (see O'Hara 1992). Then I started the *Encyclopedia of Political Economy* (2 vols), where the main objective was to detail the concepts/principles with applications to the main problems of the world (O'Hara 1999). My understanding of such principles and their application was greatly advanced by the collaborative work of this encyclopedia, which included around 300 scholars worldwide.

1.1 Concepts and Principles

Then I published *Marx, Veblen and Contemporary Institutional Political Economy: Principles and Unstable Dynamics of Capitalism* (O'Hara 2000), which won the Gunnar Myrdal Award for Book of the Year, from the European Association for Evolutionary Political Economy (EAEPE). An Elgar reviewer of my manuscript suggested I publish some of the chapters in refereed journals first, and then modify and extend/link them for the book, which I did. This was a very good way of getting comments on the chapters, seeing how they are received after publication, and getting more involved in political economy networks and associations. It was an extended version of my PhD, with more detail on the principles and much more extensive details on the empirics of the institutions and their transformation over time. The method of publishing in journals and then rewriting/extending/linking for the books is one I have continued to pursue in this current volume.

Neoliberalism and globalisation were advancing rapidly around the world during the 1990s and 2000s, and during 1998 I started the Global Political Economy Research Unit (GPERU) as a vehicle through which to analyse some of these trends and apply some of the principles to core problems of the world. These included more intense economic crises; declining levels of trust and community in many regions; climate change and declining biodiversity; terrorism and the war on terrorism; AIDS and HIV; governance and policy; money, credit and finance; the rising power of emerging economies; the WTO, IMF and transnational systems of production and distribution; world poverty, disease and hunger; plus ethnic tensions and anomalies. Numerous political economy principles and concepts were useful to the task. The outcome of this research was two books, *Global Political Economy and the Wealth of Nations: Performance, Institutions, Problems and Policies* (O'Hara 2004a) and *Growth and Development in the Global Political Economy: Social Structures of Accumulation and Modes of Regulation* (O'Hara 2006); the latter winning the *Book of the Year Award* from Curtin Business School (CBS). Later a four-volume *International Encyclopedia of Public Policy* brought to the fore a global collaborative body of work involving around 200 scholars scrutinizing these problems, concepts and principles (O'Hara 2011a).

It was out of this milieu of neoliberal globalization and networks of scholars that I realised how important the principles and concepts are for focusing on global, regional, national and subnational problems. I started again crafting papers on the contemporary principles of political economy in the mid-to-late 2000s, with special reference given to institutional and evolutionary perspectives. These papers were sympathetically refereed and eagerly snapped up by various editors and refereed journals. So I continued writing on the principles and they continued to be in high demand (e.g., O'Hara 2007a, b, 2008a, 2009a, 2019, 2022c). Then I set myself the task of applying some of the core general principles to major problems of the world, such as climate change, the global financial crisis, corruption, terrorism, uneven development, artificial intelligence, HIV, nurturance gap, and the coronacrisis (e.g., O'Hara 2008b, 2009a, b, c, 2012, 2014a, 2021a). Others have applied what have *collectively* come to be called "O'Hara's principles" to problems of elephant poaching and ivory trafficking (Brennan and Kalsi 2015) plus global growth waves (Samudro 2012), and Gandhian thought (Ghosh 2003, 2007, 2012).

Before I outline the chapters of this volume, I must explain my use of the notions of principles and concepts. Over the years I have scrutinized dozens of books and articles that have the words 'principles' and 'concepts' in the title. To my dismay, in the vast majority of cases, authors do not explain what is meant by the terms, and the vast majority do not even mention the words 'principle' and/or 'concept' (meaningfully) in the main text of the book/article. For instance, this is the way Nils J. Nilsson (1982), *Principles of Artificial Intelligence* and Daniel Fusfeld (1988), *Economics: Principles of Political Economy*, deal with principles (but note: Fusfeld's work as a whole has been a major influence on my scholarship).

Therefore, we need to gain an idea of what concepts and principles are and how they interrelate. The *Oxford English Dictionary* defines a concept as "an *idea* or mental image which corresponds to *some distinct entity* or class of entities, or to its essential features, or determines the application of *a term* . . ., and thus plays a part in the *use of reason* or language" (OED 2017a; emphases added). In essence then a concept is the process of using reason to develop a specific idea about some class or entity or a feature or application of this class or entity. In social and institutional economics, William Dugger (1989, 1995) and Ron Stanfield (2011), for instance, have been especially productive in developing political economy concepts. Undertaking the festschrifts for Stanfield (O'Hara 2011b) and Dugger (O'Hara 2022c) enhanced my understanding of concepts majorly.

The *Oxford English Dictionary* defines a principle, as "a *fundamental truth* or proposition that serves as the *foundation for a system* of belief or behavior or for a *chain* of reasoning", and "a general scientific *theorem or law* that has *numerous* special applications *across a wide field*" (OED 2017b; emphases added). A principle is thus a general, fundamental truth, law or theorem about a system or a chain of reasoning with applications to a wide area of behavior or thought. In institutional-evolutionary political economy, principles have been developed by, for instance, Dale Bush (1987), Daniel Fusfeld (1988), and Phillip O'Hara (1994, 2007b), for scholarly analysis.

Thanks to Ian Kerr (2021), I have come to believe that, firstly, a concept can be incorporated into a principle, mainly by using it in a generalization or in a prescription/injunction (a law or instruction); secondly, an important concept is normally embedded in a specific principle; and thirdly to transform a concept into a principle one must engage in promulgation, put into effect, this injunction. These three 'rules', what we may call "Kerr's rules of concepts and principles", have been incorporated into the concepts/principles in this chapter and the book as a whole.

I wish to add a fourth point, that there are various types of concepts and principles, especially relating to scope. Some are narrow and some are wide and some in between these extremes. The concepts and principles that especially concern me in this book are what I would call "core, general" ones; one might also call them "primary" ones. I distinguish them from *more specific* ones, from the viewpoint of this study, which can be examined *under the umbrella of* the core general principles/concepts. In different contexts, these more specific ones may be reset as primary ones, depending on the task at hand.

1.1 Concepts and Principles

In this context, I am reluctant to cite *one* concept/principle as *the* core one for IEPE, and emphasise the point just made that one can rearrange the list (see Table 3.1 below) to emphasise some rather than others, or add others where necessary, depending on the core objectives of the analysis. For instance, some heterodox scholars cite the *concept/principle of social provisioning* as the defining aspect of their type of economics (heterodox, feminist, institutionalism), but I believe that while this does have advantages (specifically defining the field; having a concept that is so wide it defines everything one is interested in), there are costs associated with it, as there are with the approach taken in this book.

Numerous concepts and principles are scrutinized in this volume. But when dealing with contemporary problems of the world, one has to be succinct and certain principles and concepts come to the fore much more than others. These main ones are what I call the *Eight Core General Concepts and Principles of IE Political Economy* examined in many chapters of this book, which include (1) historical specificity; (2) hegemony and uneven development; (3) heterogeneous groups and agents; (4) circular and cumulative causation; (5) contradiction; (6) uncertainty, (7) innovation, (8) those associated with policy and governance. Here I explain briefly what these concepts and principles are, as well as provide a comment on other concepts relevant to the frame of each of them (more specific ones). Developing these concepts and principles has mainly been inspired by the institutional and evolutionary influences of Thorstein Veblen, Karl Marx, Joseph Schumpeter, J.M. Keynes, Charlotte Perkins Gilman, and their followers, plus of course the scholars already mentioned above (e.g., in the 'Preface').

The *concept of historical specificity* states that an examination of history and context provides crucial insights into core elements of every world problem and issue, especially regarding waves, cycles, stages, phases, stylized facts, evolutions and metamorphoses. The *principle of historical specificity* states that political economy must utilise an examination of history and context so as to comprehend and provide policy advice for understanding such issues and ameliorating such problems. Under the umbrella of this core general principle/concept, the current study from time to time deals with more specific concepts (and possible principles) that are inextricably related to history, such as historical time, evolution, realism, culture-institutions-habits, phases/stages of change, blind drift, social provisioning, path dependence, and stylized facts.

Closely linked to historical specificity is the *concept of hegemony and uneven development*, the idea that there are differential power relations within and between nations and regions, which often manifest in one core nation or region having overriding dominance. Some of these nations and areas are called the core, the most dominant; some are in the semi-periphery, of medium dominance; and some reside in the periphery and have the least power. The *principle of hegemony and uneven development* states that to fully comprehend most core problems of the world, political economists need to scrutinise these uneven power relations in some depth. Under the umbrella of this core concept/principle are others such as capitalist world-system; core, periphery, semi-periphery (CPSP); production, commercial, financial and military dominance (PCFMD); international regimes (and accumulation regimes); trust, cooperation and conflict; and power and authority (hard-soft).

The *concept of heterogeneous groups and agents* states that the world (and possibly the universe) and its areas comprise various agents that are grouped into species, genders, ethnicities, classes, age, plus other groupings, which enables political economy to understand and provide policy advice for various problems and issues. The *principle of heterogeneous groups and agents* states that scholars must utilise such groupings and agents for understanding core problems and issues and also for moderating such problems. This core general concept/principle is closely linked to such concepts (and possible principles) as agency/structure, gender, class, ethnicity, nationality, species, age, other groupings, trust, enabling myths/ emulation, and inequality of income, wealth and power.

The *concept of circular and cumulative causation* includes two major subcomponents. The first is circular causation, in which problems and issues are determined by complex multi-factor causation through interdependency between major elements. The second is cumulative causation, namely, that these multicausal elements typically multiply or amplify the causal process as they merge together as the ongoing dynamics is of a higher order of magnitude than the singular elements in isolation. The *principle of circular and cumulative causation* states that political economy must utilise this concept in order to properly understand and ameliorate the problems of the world. This core general concept/principle is closely linked to concepts (and potential principles) such as multifactor approach, interdependence, circular economy, emergence, complexity, multiplication/amplification, inequality, aggregate demand, economic surplus, plus positive (and negative) feedbacks.

The *concept of contradiction* draws attention to various complex potential and actual conflicts within and between various processes of the political economy, some of which are systemic institutional dynamics, others more regional, meso- and micro-anomalies, while others link to various heterogeneous groups and agents. This concept originally emanated from Georg Wilhelm Friedrich Hegel, Karl Marx and Joseph Schumpeter (creative destruction), and the main systemic contradictions are those associated with Karl Polanyi's notion of the disembedded economy and the double movement, Veblen's idea of the vested interests versus the common good, and Marc Tool's/Dale Bush's instrumental and ceremonial functions of institutions. The *principle of contradiction* states that political economy must study these contradictions in order to comprehend the workings of the world's major problems and processes, including providing (systemic) policy advice. This core general concept/principle is closely linked to issues of power and authority, plus more specific contradictions, concepts, and principles associated with capital and labor; finance and industry; monopoly and competition; urban and regional; capital and state; capital v. ecology; ethnic group v. ethnic group; men v. women; and so on.

The *concept of uncertainty* is the idea that the major contradiction of capitalism is that between various long-term horizons through which investment goods are planned and created, and the shorter horizon within which these capital goods are variously financed through debt, equity and bonds; and it is through this temporal mismatch that economic and financial cycles, crises and instabilities of capitalism typically emerge. Uncertainty also (in a related context) is associated with the issues described by Marx/Engels and Schumpeter about global capitalism being an inherently revolutionary system that castes aside all fetters to its progress in promoting new products, processes, markets, sources of raw material, and organisations while it forever destroys old jobs, industries, cultures, ecologies and ways of life in the search for profits and accumulation. The *principle of uncertainty* states that one must study the processes leading to uncertainty so as to understand and provide policy advice for moderating un(der)employment, cycles, crises, cultural decline, climate change, psychological malaise, and other instabilities. This concept/principle is also linked to other concepts (and potential principles) such as the circuit of money capital, prevailing business climate, expectations, cycles, waves and crises, recessions and depressions, aggregate effective demand, endogenous money and credit, financial instability hypothesis, modern monetary theory (MMT), and fictitious capitals.

The *concept of innovation* in this book draws on the idea that to solve world problems it is usually necessary to engage in innovation, that is, to 'do something different in socioeconomic life' (to paraphrase Schumpeter 1911), that is thought to be useful in reducing the anomalous nature of the various world problems. Such innovations can vary considerably, from, for instance, applying certain ideas, (re)-forming specific organisations, developing new methods of doing things, and applying specific policies. The *principle of innovation* states that it is necessary to innovate to solve world problems; and that one is required to analyse how these new ways of doing things can impinge on the problems at hand. Sometimes these new ways of doing things are a revitalisation of old ways that have been ignored or underplayed, or need to be modified somewhat, and sometimes it involves something quite new or reconstructed, in order to ameliorate the anomaly; and sometimes it involves applying a (new) principle, or a series of principles, to the problem, that have not been applied to the problem before (or for a long time). Under the umbrella of innovation are the concepts (and potential principles) of creative destruction; the community's joint stock of knowledge, information, skills and intelligence; new products, processes, raw materials, markets and organisations; artificial intelligence; social conditions of innovation; mutation, variation and selection; and intellectual property.

The *concept of policy and governance* is the idea that it there are specific organisational tools available for use to potentially improve the community's standard of living, quality of life, ecological diversity, biological health, culture and generally to moderate or ameliorate pressing world problems in the immediate, medium and long-term. The *principle of policy and governance* states that one should variously use these organisational tools to deal with such anomalies, standards, qualities, diversities, ecologies and cultures. Under the umbrella of this concept/principle are such specific concepts (and potential principles) as social provisioning; quality of life; participatory democracy; community protection; functional finance; fiscal and monetary policy; agreements, accords and contracts; cultural diversity; and climate change mitigation and adaptation.

The best way to study social, economic and political problems and systemic policies is to utilise all of these *core general* concepts/principles since they provide a different but in aggregate more *comprehensive* and *broad* (i.e., holistic) *vision* of the anomalies. Most of the problems examined in this book start with the background history, hegemony and uneven development patterns to contextualise or situate the anomalies within historical time. Then we often scrutinise the heterogeneous groups and agents involved in the generation of problems and the way in which these problems are induced by and also affect various groupings and individuals. Next we typically study the contradictions involved in the generation of anomalous processes, and the circular and cumulative fashion in which their dynamics usually manifest through time. Often we supplement the study of such problems by seeing how contradictions that operate in a circular and cumulative fashion generate varying degrees of uncertainty, especially regarding climate change, crises, and changes in the prevailing business climate. Various types of innovations and governance measures are then introduced that relate to the problem at hand, especially those that seek to promote social provisioning in its various forms.

In Chapters 4, 5, 6, 7, 8, 9, 10, 11 and 12 dealing with the world problems, we commence with the most recent historically pressing global crisis, the coronavirus pandemic,[1] then go on to study climate change, corruption, AI-robotics for assisting the elderly plus other uses, policy-governance, financial instability and crises, terrorism, HIV and the nurturance gap. These are explained briefly in the next section.

1.2 Principles and Problems of the World: The Chapters

I knew I would have to write a chapter, chapter two below, on the history of institutional and evolutionary principles, after I had written most of the chapters for this current book. So I took the opportunity of doing this when Ajit Sinha asked me to write a chapter on institutional and evolutionary themes for his book on the history of pluralistic economics (O'Hara 2019). A rewritten and extended version of this work is included here as Chap. 2, where I trace the principles to the physiocrats and the classical economists, and then proceed to emphasise the importance of Marx, Veblen, Schumpeter, Keynes, and their followers to the extent that they emphasise specifically institutional and evolutionary themes. I see Veblen as the prototypical institutional-evolutionary scholar, who, usually unwittingly, developed the principles of historical specificity and evolution; the culture-institutions-habits-individuals nexus; heterogeneous groups and agents; hegemony and uneven development; cumulative causation; contradiction; plus innovation and systemic policies.

---

[1] Another world problem emerging will likely be more significant than the coronacrisis, namely, a possible world war (or a long-term geopolitical conflict), in the light of the Ukraine conflict, the potential for further European wars, and conflict in the Asia-Pacific region. In this context, see the book by C.W. Mills (1958), *The Causes of World War Three*. This wide-ranging geopolitical conflict is analysed in O'Hara (2023).

Then I go on to explain the importance of scholars such as John Commons, Charlotte Gilman, Wesley Mitchell, Clarence Ayres, Gunnar Myrdal, J.K. Galbraith, Joan Robinson, Nicholas Kaldor, Paul Baran, Paul Sweezy, Regulation and social structure of accumulation scholars, post-Keynesian institutionalists, as well as various feminists, neo-Schumpeterians, and complexity thinkers who take an institutional-evolutionary line of inquiry.

A very early version of Chap. 3 (O'Hara 2007b) became one of the most downloaded formally published papers of mine, the lead paper in the *Journal of Economic Issues* for that year, and perhaps my most influential. In it I lay the foundations for institutional-evolutionary principles emanating from Veblenians, post-Keynesian institutionalists, radical-institutionalists, progressive Schumpeterian institutionalists, global political economists, complexity scholars, and evolutionary feminists, among others. The chapter is structured according to the eight core general concepts/principles outlined above. We summarize the main literatures and issues associated with each of the major concepts/principles.

This chapter firstly scrutinizes world problems discussed therein via the concepts/principles of historical specificity and hegemony/uneven development as we briefly survey the world from the late 1700s through to the 2020s (Sect. 3.2). In Sect. 3.3 we explain the third core general concept/principle of heterogeneous groups and agents as it links to world problems. Section 3.4 examines CCC, including Kaldor, Myrdal, complexity and emergence, providing links to world problems. Section 3.5 scrutinises the concept/principle of contradiction, including general and specific contradictions, and how they help explain world problems. Section 3.6 examines world problems vis-à-vis the concept/principle of uncertainty, applied to money, crises and systemic disarray. Section 3.7 applies world problems to the concept/principle of innovation associated with creative destruction and the community's joint stock of knowledge. Lastly Section 3.8 analyses the concept/principle of policy and governance, including different styles of IEPE, in the context of policies linked to world problems.

The general nature of these concepts and principles is thus outlined in these two chapters (2 and 3), even though they are mostly historically contingent and subject to modification on the basis of new insights and empirical evidence. The task ahead is to apply them to contemporary problems and issues. I wanted to publish this book in the shadows of a new global crisis. So when the coronacrisis emerged, deepened and then mellowed in some areas, then rose again, this was a perfect opportunity to write a chapter on a crucial current world problem and get the volume ready for the publisher. Two days after I finished what was later to become Chap. 4 on the coronacrisis, I sent it to selected scholars and quickly got offers of publication (O'Hara 2021a). This Chap. 4 benefits from additional updates, rewrites and comments from scholars. (Acknowledgements for each chapter are included as a note just before the "References" section.)

I start the pandemic chapter by reviewing five core papers on the political economy of the coronacrisis, which gives readers a good idea of where I am comparatively situated. Then I use the principle/concept of historical specificity and evolution to follow the emergence, development and transformation of the coronacrisis globally in terms of cases, deaths, waves and uneven developments. This is followed by an analysis of the role of heterogeneous groups and agents in terms of how the crisis affected and was affected by different genders, classes, ethnicities, ages, other agents, species/variants, institutions and vaccines. The CCC and contradiction section scrutinises the four main conflicting forces impacting on the crisis: humans v. coronavirus; neoliberalism v embeddeness; hegemony v. development; and science v. misinformation. Then the principle of uncertainty is applied to socioeconomic activity during the coronacrisis as well as to crisis preparedness and policies relevant in the past and into the future. I believe that this chapter is a classic example of how to apply institutional-evolutionary principles to current world problems.

Chapter 5 examines another crucial, even more important anomaly, climate change. The first major draft was published in *Ecological* Economics (O'Hara 2009b) and won two awards, one for *Journal Article of the Year*, from EAEPE, and the other *Journal Article of the Year* from CBS. It has been extensively rewritten and updated on the basis of more recent evidence and studies, which reinforce the paper's major thesis. I received more personal comments on this published paper than any other written by me. They all said my results were too radical. Now it is clear that my conclusions are mainstream. I said essentially that we should aim for an increase in global mean temperature of 1.5 °C or less by 2100 rather than 2.0 °C or more (since the start of industrialization) and that tipping points and points of no return are more extreme than (previously) expected and happening now rather than simply in the future. In this chapter I make the point that 1 °C is too high but should be (at the very maximum) the aim of climate policy to 2100, mainly due to the interdependent and cumulative nature of the tipping points that are already likely operating, and/or very soon will be impacting majorly on the climate and various species of the world.

To make these points I start out with the principle of historical specificity and evolution, examining climate change over successive waves of Earth's history, including the current one during the anthropocene. Then the industrial revolution is set within the context of the ecological circuit of social capital, and the social and political change required for transcending the circular treadmill of production. The principle of contradiction examines the extensive social costs of business and consumers receiving free resources from nature, as competition requires successive exhaustion of resources to generate profits and products. Uneven development demonstrates that the periphery and to some degree semi-periphery are subject to major costs of climate change, while core nations of advanced capitalism have set up structures for receiving cheap resources from poorer ones. It is thus easier for the core to adapt to climate change because of these structural inequities. CCC and uncertainty apply perfectly to climate change as non-linear threshold effects and exponentially expanding processes lead to very serious wild-fires, extensive heatwaves, floods, hurricanes, rising sea-levels and droughts especially in the northern hemisphere, around the tropics, plus other areas. The path dependence of *tipping pints* and especially *points of no return* require serious institutional transformations along with major innovations to moderate and adapt to climate change that go well beyond the context of the recent COP26 Glasgow conference.

Chapter 6 is a revised and updated version of my Presidential Address to the Association for Evolutionary Economics (AFEE), presented in Philadelphia (O'Hara 2014a). The background to the paper was that I have been harassed and intimidated by several vested interests, going back to 2001 and forward to the present, and I was interested in whether their actions constituted specific forms of corruption or other forms of illegal acts. Another context was that I had been teaching about money laundering and tax evasion and wanted to situate that within broader issues of corruption. Also, I was very interested in what appeared to be extensive corruption not only by so-called policy makers but also their private sector colleagues, in Africa, the Middle East, Latin America, and one would also have to include the advanced capitalist world as well.

I was thus very motivated to get to the bottom of the corruption issue. Through the principle of historical specificity I advanced the thesis that we should go back to the works of Socrates, Plato and Aristotle (as is often the case among corruption scholars), as well as Veblen, and view corruption as abuses of power against the common good in favour of vested interests. The principle of contradiction thus viewed various styles of corruption employed by the vested interests around the world, such as "influence, haven and speculative market corruption" in the US and UK; "elite cartels corruption" in Botswana and Greece; "oligarchs and clan corruption" in India, Russia and Pakistan; and "official Moguls corruption" in China, Egypt, and Nigeria. Then I employed the principle of uneven development to scrutinise various forms and degrees of corruption and found high levels in the core, semi-periphery and periphery.

Chapter 7 arose out of the *inadequate resources* given to caring for the elderly throughout the world, and also the general interest of having intelligent robots that can communicate with humans, and greater agency in enhancing quality of life. One of the (anonymous) readers of this paper said that it is a classic example *par excellence* of applying political economy principles to current issues and problems. I got excited about this topic because the 'new AI' of embodied cognition scholars has been applying principles to intelligent robot design, which are in parallel with the principles of political economy. So I tried to ascertain the main principles of 'old AI', classic computational systems, and then to critically evaluate the power and contradictions within and between each school in promoting general intelligence among robots. I complete the paper by outlining eight neurological political economy design principles of brain-body-environment interaction for generating embodied cognition robotic intelligence, that are based on CCC, emergence and complexity. Briefly these involve the use of neurological design principles such as the body-brain-environment interface, memory triad, functional specialisation and integration, overlapping functions, Hebbian learning, spatial-spectral temporal perception, and the dynamic core and consciousness. (These issues are developed further in a book I am writing on 'robots with general intelligence'.)

Chapter 8 on policy and governance, starts with Polanyi's principle (contradiction) of the disembedded economy, and how this relates to cycles and waves of policy-making concerning the double movement and the relationship between formal markets, reciprocity, redistribution and householding (as well as informal community markets). Then we scrutinize the principle of contradiction, paying attention to the importance of capital-labor relations, the finance-industry dichotomy, monopoly versus competition, profit and the environment, plus individual versus society. Thereafter the principle of circular and cumulative causation is linked to social and production aspects of complex systems of political economy. And lastly we examine the principle of uneven development and how crucial this is to policy-making institutions as the world undergoes asymmetries of financial instability, climate change and wave dynamics. Core principles thus provide a good grounding for general policy purposes when activist governance measures are required to improve human and environmental provisioning.

Chapter 9 emerged from an invitation I received from Jack Reardon to write a chapter in a book on pluralistic economics, and based on 30 years of teaching and researching about money, credit and finance I decided to write on institutional-evolutionary perspectives of money, financial instability and crises (O'Hara 2009c). Recently a publisher read the chapter and asked me to write a book detailing the issues and problems involved in modern money and finance. The paper as updated here starts off by arguing for a perspective that synthesises the work of Marx, Veblen, Keynes and Schumpeter on money, credit and finance, including updates to the present. It develops a dynamic, processual investigation of the phenomena through an extended social circuit of money capital, from which emerges prospective yield (Keynes), surplus value (Marx, Schumpeter), intangible capital (Veblen) and/or profit, interest and rent. It situates money and finance in history through the waves of socioeconomic evolution through time, and the successive financial institutional innovations and crises that have occurred. It then outlines the concepts of endogenous money and financial instability, paying attention to the cat-and-mouse game between central banks and financial institutions and the movement from (Hyman Minsky's notions of) hedge to speculative and Ponzi finance over the Juglar cycle (and long wave). This is linked to what Charles Kindleberger (and his cowriter) states is the most extreme period of financial crashes and crises in the history of capitalism during the 1980–2010s. Then after discussing the international financial system and the Davidson Proposal for reform, it outlines the central tenets of modern monetary theory (MMT), for which the coronacrisis has been seen as a testing ground for its principles, including a sympathetic and critical view of the concepts of Chartalism, functional finance, taxes-drive-money and the bond market.

Chapter 10 deals with principles applied to terrorism and the war on terrorism; an anomaly political economy has tended to evade. Soon after the so-called "9/11" (2001) attacks on the World Trade Centre (in New York City) and the Pentagon (near Washington DC), I was on study leave in Los Angeles, Japan and France. At UCLA I found 'all the journals in the world' with their first issues on the terrorist attacks and the war on terrorism, which I read quickly and wrote a paper which I presented in Santa Monica and Boston. Some other political economists and myself were seriously engaged in research on this topic but found few outlets. One editor I spoke to (a specialist on equilibrium) said briefly, after perusing the paper for a few seconds, that it was more politics than economics. One international journal of political economy refuse(d) to consider papers on these subjects (point blank). I fail to understand, how political economists can ignore crucial global and regional problems such as this, and basically leave it to international relations journals to analyse it. In the meantime I published my first paper on it in O'Hara (2004b) and my second in a book edited by Wolfram Elsner and Hardy Hanappi (O'Hara 2008b). I came back to the article to revise it for the Chapter, and decided that 9/11 was such an iconic series of events, including the aftermath and the wars in Iraq and Afghanistan, that I should more or less keep it as it is. (It does also provide insights into other terrorist attacks and the general so-called 'war on terrorism'.)

This chapter situates the problem historically, defines terrorism, provides examples, and then deals with four main contradictions affecting the situation, especially regarding the relatively 'isolated' attacks in New York and near Washington DC (and later, London, Bali, Paris, Boston, Sydney, Auckland, and so on). The first contradiction is that such attacks constitute relatively low risks of fatality for specific individuals compared with car accidents, suicide, murder and TB, but also a high apparently system (social) risk which often lead people to become fearful and intimidated in a circular and cumulative fashion. The second contradiction is that technology can both enhance the human condition as well as, when used by terrorists as a form of sabotage, substantially reduce the quality of life of the community. The third contradiction is that the strategic use of such terrorists (such as the *Mujahideen*) by the US to fight the Soviets in Afghanistan led to the emergence of a power vacuum during the early 1990s onwards which *Al Qaida*, the *Taliban* and other groups used to enhance their strategic ambitions. And the fourth contradiction is that global deregulation and neoliberalism led to greater uneven development throughout the world as well as lax regulations that enhanced the ability of terrorists to form financial and social networks to plan successful attacks on the West.

Then I propose innovations and policies relating to each contradiction to deescalate the power of such *jihadis*. These include public education programs on terrorism, and consequence management on the ground; circuit breakers, supply buffers, microbe attack preparation, and alternative nodes to reduce the extent of technological centralization; the deepening of multilateralism, greater linkages to Islamic cultures, and dialogue with Islamic powers; a new balance between regulation and freedom to reduce cyber-terrorism, terrorist movements, and their access to finance; plus the promotion of progressive counter-forces such as Islamic political economy.

Biology, evolution and ecology have major space in this book, since they variously arise in chapters on the coronacrisis, climate change, robotics and artificial intelligence, plus AIDS-HIV. This of course is no surprise to those who know the origins of the circuits of social capital (circuits of the blood), the notion of the circulation of capital, the principle of circular and cumulative causation, the circular economy, entropy, and a host of other notions scrutinised in this book (O'Hara 2009d). Indeed, since political economy is essentially an interdisciplinary, multidisciplinary and/or transdisciplinary study of the world (see O'Hara 2021b on these), it variously incorporates numerous disciplines and sub-disciplines into its edifice. The reasons for this, as Mario Bunge (2016) stressed, is that major world problems can only be studied and hopefully solved and rectified by utilising multiple (inter)disciplines. These problems of the world do not, therefore, have disciplinary limits, if one is serious about understanding and 'doing something about them'.

It is in this context that we introduce Chapters 11 (AIDS-HIV) and 12 (Love). Ever since the 1980s I had wanted to study AIDS and HIV, since I thought, as with other problems of the world, if I am to live in this world, and have the time to study its problems, I should understand them, regardless of their nature or texture. As I began to read on HIV-AIDS it became *screamingly* obvious how political economy principles are relevant. As a result I wrote a long article on this subject for my 4-volume *International Encyclopedia of Public Policy* (O'Hara 2022a), as well as a relatively short paper for the *Journal of Economic Issues* (O'Hara 2007b).

Chapter 11 thus starts out with the principle/concept of historical specificity as it charts the evolution of AIDS-HIV from an obscure disease-virus in small pockets of western Africa to a global Pandemic in every area of the world, and eventually increasing human resistance through a declining trajectory of its incidence. Then the principle of heterogeneous groups and agents is used to explain how the disease tends to inflict especially homosexuals (men in the west) and heterosexuals (especially women in Africa); those with malnutrition, established ailments, and lower literacy (especially in Africa); plus injectors of drugs and sex-workers. In addition, the virus itself includes numerous agents, those which tend to be more virulent (HIV-1) and less virulent (HIV-2), in addition to those with varying degrees of virulence (numerous variants with differential virulence). The principle of contradiction was easy to relate to HIV-AIDS because as soon as one understands the disease-virus the core contradiction becomes glaringly obvious. The core contradiction (put simply) is that the HIV virus exploits the limits of the human immune system by enhancing human immune activation, resulting in fewer CD4 helper-cells but more CD8 killer cells (during the latently period), and when CD4 cells decline to below 200/µL AIDS diseases become (more) manifest as CD8 cells also decline and HIV-1 viruses replicate much faster potentially resulting in death (without effective intervention) through usually several opportunistic infections. This leads to explaining the process using the principle of CCC, or multivariant causality, as HIV tends to be promoted by unprotected sex, needle and fluid exchanges, HIV viral strain, and other microbes, while the extent of AIDS diseases is also dependent upon genetics, nutrition, socioeconomic group, and drugs. Linking both sides of HIV-AIDS together without effective intervention leads to the amplified nature of the diseases (for a time) as the latency period evolves to full blown AIDS. I finish the paper by dealing with issues of socioeconomic reproduction and governance.

Chapter 12 is on the political economy of love, intimacy and passion. Since my PhD I have been writing papers on family and community relations, among other institutions such as the state, production-distribution, world economy and finance. The first paper I wrote on 'family and community' was about household labor and its role in stimulating long wave upswing in the US during the 1950s and 1960s, followed by its relative demise as upswing led to downswing into the 1970s, 1980s and 1990s (O'Hara 1995). This paper won the 1995 *Journal Article of the*

Year Award from CBS. When rewriting on a similar topic in the 2000s (O'Hara 2004a) for my second long waves and institutional performance book (O'Hara 2006) I expanded the view to include degrees of social trust, inequality and instability in the community (especially in the USA). Then I read the magisterial paper by my colleagues Ron and Jackie Stanfield (1997) about 'where has love gone' in the age of neoliberalism and globalisation. This led me to write this chapter on the political economy of love, naturally utilising the principles of political economy in the process. Other factors also influenced the nature of the journal article (O'Hara 2014b) which eventually was transformed into the chapter, include the work of my student Caitriona Jones who wrote an essay applying Minsky's financial instability hypothesis to relationships; plus the nature of my own relationships; and the declining trust and sociality I could see around me.

The chapter critically evaluates the forms of love capital being accumulated by people in capitalist economies. We start by situating love historically in the neoliberal culture and then examine the six main love styles as well as the five critical factors through the process of circular and cumulative causation. We then scrutinise the contradictions of neoliberal capitalism involving the nurturance gap, disembedded economy and freedom constraint which inhibit the generation of holistic love capital. The path dependent nature of love is then linked to relational phases and instabilities, especially involving serial monogamy in the United States. What emerges is a comprehensive and wide-scope view of problems involved in stimulating holistic love capital in the contemporary environment. (Very recently, I noticed an Italian author has published a book, with an English translation, where she discusses explicitly my concept of "love capital", and uses it as the main title of her book; see Jennifer Guerra 2022).

Chapter 13, the Conclusion, summarises the book as a whole and situates the main conclusions within the context of further volumes of political economy principles and applications emerging in the short and long-term future. A Glossary follows.

It leaves me to say that I hope you enjoy this book, as it has been written to be lucid and readable, although at times it will be intense. I also hope you will provide me with comments, reviews and other forms of feedback to improve the second edition as well as the science of political economy as a whole. You may also seek out the second volume on long waves, crises and institutional-based performance, and later the third volume providing more detail on the concepts-principles and further applications to world problems.

References

Brennan, Andrew John, and Jaslin Kaur Kalsi. 2015. Elephant Poaching & Ivory Trafficking Problems in Sub-Saharan Africa: An Application of O'Hara's Principles of Political Economy. *Ecological Economics* 120: 312–337.

Bunge, Mario. 2016. *Between Two Worlds: Memoirs of a Philosopher-Scientist*. Geneva: Springer.

Bush, Paul Dale. 1987. Theory of Institutional Change. *Journal of Economic Issues* 21 (3): 1073–1116.

Dugger, William M. 1989. Radical Institutionalism: Basic Concepts. In *Radical Institutionalism: Contemporary Voices*, ed. W.M. Dugger, 5–24. Westport: Greenwood Press.
———. 1995. Veblenian Institutionalism: The Changing Concepts of Inquiry. *Journal of Economic Issues* 29 (4): 1013–1027.
Fusfeld, Daniel. 1988. *Economics: Principles of Political Economy*. 3rd ed. Boston: Scott, Foresman & Co.
Ghosh, Baidyanath. 2003. *Gandhian Political Economy: Genesis, Principles and Development*. PhD Thesis. Global Political Economy Research Unit, Curtin Business School, Perth, Australia.
Ghosh, Baidyanath. 2007. *Gandhian Political Economy: Principles, Practice and Policy*. Aldershot, UK: Ashgate Publishing.
Ghosh, Baidyanath. 2012. *Beyond Gandhian Economics: Towards a Creative Deconstruction*. New Delhi: Sage Publications.
Guerra, Jennifer. 2022. *Love Capital: A Manifesto for Political and Revolutionary Eros*. Milan: Bompiani Publishers. Translated from the Italian by Alice Kilgariff.
Kerr, Ian Alexander. 2021. *Relationship Between Principles and Concepts*, Draft Note, 14 November.
Mills, C. Wright. 1958. *The Causes of World War Three*. New York: Ballantine Books.
Nilsson, Nils J. 1982. *Principles of Artificial Intelligence*. San Francisco: Morgan Kaufman.
O'Hara, Phillip Anthony. 1992. *A Critical Analysis of the Reproduction of Institutions Within Capitalism: Integrating Macroinstitutional Themes from Marxist and Institutionalist Political Economy*. PhD Thesis. University of Newcastle, New South Wales, Australia. Supervisor: Professor Allen Oakley.
———. 1994. Methodological Principles of Institutional Political Economy: Holism, Contradiction and Evolution. *Methodus: Bulletin of the International Network of Economic Method* 5 (1): 51–71.
———. 1999. *Encyclopedia of Political Economy*. 2 Vols. London/New York: Routledge. Paper Edition 2001. (Chinese Edition Published 2010.)
———. 2000. *Marx, Veblen and Contemporary Institutional Political Economy: Principles and Unstable Dynamics of Capitalism*. Aldershot: Edward Elgar.
———, ed. 2004a. *Global Political Economy and the Wealth of Nations: Performance, Institutions, Problems and Policies*. London/New York: Routledge.
———. 2004b. The War on Terrorism, Political-Economic Contradictions and Policy Issues, In P.A. O'Hara (2004a), pp. 303–324.
———. 2006. *Growth and Development in the Global Political Economy: Social Structures of Accumulation and Modes of Regulation*. London/New York: Routledge.
———. 2007a. Principles of Institutional-Evolutionary Political Economy: Converging Themes from the Schools of Heterodoxy. *Journal of Economic Issues* 41 (1): 1–42.
———. 2007b. Heterodox Political Economy Specialization and Interconnection–Concepts of Contradiction, Heterogeneous Agents, Uneven Development. *Intervention. Journal of Economics* 4 (1): 103–124.
———. 2008a. Can the Principles of Heterodox Political Economy Explain its Own Re-emergence and Development? *Beyond the Horizon* 16 (4): 260–278.
———. 2008b. A New Global Military-Terrorism-Hegemony Social Structure of Accumulation for Long-Wave Upswing? In *Varieties of Capitalism and New Institutional Deals: Regulation, Welfare and the New Economy*, ed. Wolfram Elsner and Hardy Hanappi, 159–180. Cheltenham: Edward Elgar.
———. 2009a. Political Economy of Climate Change, Ecological Destruction and Uneven Development. *Ecological Economics* 69: 223–234.
———. 2009b. Money, Credit, and Finance in Political Economy National, Regional, and Global Dimensions. In *The Handbook of Pluralistic Economics Education*, ed. Jack Reardon, 230–255. Oxford/New York: Routledge.
———. 2009c. The Global Securitized Subprime Market Crisis. *Review of Radical Political Economics* 41 (3): 318–334.

———. 2009d. Современные принципы неортодоксальной политической экономии. *Вопросы теории* 12: 38–57.

———. (2011a) *International Encyclopedia of Public Policy.* 4 Vols. Perth: GPERU. [Some of these articles have been re-written to keep up-to-date]. http://pohara.homestead.com/Encyclopedia/Volume-1.pdf, http://pohara.homestead.com/Encyclopedia/Volume-2.pdf, http://pohara.homestead.com/Encyclopedia/Volume-3.pdf, http://pohara.homestead.com/Encyclopedia/Volume-4.pdf.

———. 2011b. Stanfield's Concepts of Social and Political Economy: Introduction to the Special Issue. *Forum for Social Economics, 40*(1), 1–6. https://www.tandfonline.com/doi/abs/10.1007/s12143-010-9068-3.

———. 2012. Principles of Political Economy Applied to Policy and Governance: Disembedded Economy, Contradictions, Circular Cumulation and Uneven Development. *Journal of Economic and Social Policy* 15 (1): 1–38.

———. 2014a. Political Economy of Systemic and Micro-Corruption Throughout the World. *Journal of Economic Issues* 48 (2): 279–307. https://doi.org/10.2753/JEI0021-3624480203.

———. 2014b. Political Economy of Love: Nurturance Gap, Disembedded Economy and Freedom Constraints within Neoliberal Capitalism. *Panoeconomicus* 61 (2): 161–192. https://doi.org/10.2298/PAN1402161H.

———. 2019. History of Institutional Economics. In *Pluralistic Economics and Its History*, ed. Ajit Sinha and Alex M. Thomas, 171–190. London/New York: Routledge.

———. 2021a. Global Coronavirus Pandemic Crisis and Future Crisis Prevention. *Panoeconomicus* 68 (5): 587–623. http://panoeconomicus.org/index.php/jorunal/article/view/1550/676.

———. 2021b. Objectives of the *Review of Evolutionary Political Economy*'s 'Manifesto' and Editorial Proposals on World Problems, Complex Systems, Historico-Institutional and Corruption Issues. *Review of Evolutionary Political Economy* 2 (2): 359–387. https://doi.org/10.1007/s43253-021-00040-9.

———. 2022a. HIV and AIDS. In *International Encyclopedia of Public Policy: Volume 1*, ed. P.A. O'Hara, 1–12. GPERU: Perth. http://pohara.homestead.com/Encyclopedia/Volume-1.pdf.

———. 2022b. *Principles of Institutional and Evolutionary Political Economy: Applied to Current World Problems.* Springer.

———. 2022c. Integrating Dugger's Concepts with O'Hara's Principles to Advance Social and Institutional Economics. *Forum for Social Economics* 51 (1): 9–40. https://doi.org/10.1080/07360932.2018.1467332.

———. 2023. *Long Wave Institutional Dynamics and Political Economy Crises of Capitalism: Principles.* Social Structures of Accumulation and Empirics: Springer.

———. Forthcoming. *Advances in Political Economy Principles: Applied to Current World Problems.*

OED. 2017a. Concept. In *Oxford English Dictionary.* Oxford: Oxford University Press.

———. 2017b. Principle. In *Oxford English Dictionary.* Oxford: Oxford University Press.

Samudro, Bhimo Rizky. 2012. *A Political Economy Analysis of Uneven Global, Regional, National and Sub-National Performance 1950-2010.* Degree of Doctor of Philosophy (PhD) Thesis. School of Economics and Finance, Curtin University, Perth, Australia.

Schumpeter, Joseph. 1911. *Theory of Economic Development: An Inquiry into Profits, Capital, Credit, Interest, and the Business Cycle.* Cambridge, MA: Harvard University Press. 1934.

Stanfield, James Ronald. 2011. Some Social Economics Concepts for Future Development. *Forum for Social Economics* 40 (1): 7–18. https://www.tandfonline.com/doi/abs/10.1007/s12143-010-9065-6.

Stanfield, James R., and Jaqueline B. Stanfield. 1997. Where Has Love Gone? Reciprocity, Redistribution, and the Nurturance Gap. *Journal of Socio-Economics* 26 (2): 111–126. https://psycnet.apa.org/doi/10.1016/S1053-5357(97)90028-7.

History of Concepts and Principles

2

Abstract

The purpose of this chapter is to *outline* the history of institutional and evolutionary core general concepts and principles. We commence with the institutionalist tendencies of the physiocrats in the 1700s through to the classical economists and Karl Marx of the 1800s, and onto the 'founding father' of evolutionary-institutionalism, Thorstein Veblen, in the late 1800s and early 1900s. This is followed by the contributions of Joseph Schumpeter and John Maynard Keynes, then IEPE perspectives of John Commons, Wesley Mitchell, Clarence Ayres, Charlotte Perkins Gilman, later contributions of Gunnar Myrdal, J.K. Galbraith, Joan Robinson, Nicholas Kaldor, Paul Baran & Paul Sweezy, and others in the mid-to-later twentieth century. Contemporary evolutionary-institutionalists associated with the Association for Evolutionary Economics (AFEE) and the European Association for Evolutionary Political Economy, along with complexity, neo-Schumpeterian and feminist scholars, among others, are additionally explored; plus a short discussion of the so-called new institutional economics.

Keywords

Historical specificity · Concepts & principles · Karl Marx · Thorstein Veblen · J.M. Keynes · Joseph Schumpeter · Feminists · European scholars · Japanese scholars · Neo-Schumpeterian school · Hegemony & uneven development · Complexity & emergence · Institutions & habits · Heterogeneous groups & agents · Circular & cumulative causation · Contradiction · Uncertainty · Innovation · Policy & governance

© The Author(s), under exclusive license to Springer Nature Singapore Pte Ltd. 2022, corrected publication 2023
P. A. O'Hara, *Principles of Institutional and Evolutionary Political Economy*, Springer Texts in Business and Economics,
https://doi.org/10.1007/978-981-19-4158-0_2

2.1 Introduction

The purpose of this chapter is to *outline* the history of institutional and evolutionary core general concepts and principles. We commence with the tendencies of the physiocrats in the 1700s through to the classical economists and Karl Marx of the 1800s, and onto the 'founding father' of institutional and evolutionary themes, Thorstein Veblen, in the late 1800s and early 1900s. This is followed by the contributions of Joseph Schumpeter and John Maynard Keynes, then the perspectives of John Commons, Wesley Mitchell, Clarence Ayres, Charlotte Perkins Gilman, plus the later contributions of Gunnar Myrdal, J.K. Galbraith, Joan Robinson, Nicholas Kaldor, Paul Baran and Paul Sweezy, in the mid-to-late twentieth century. Contemporary Veblenian institutionalists associated with the Association for Evolutionary Economics (AFEE) and the European Association for Evolutionary Political Economy and other allies, such as neo-Schumpeterians and evolutionary feminists, are additionally explored, along with new institutional economics.

The philosophy of science that institutional-evolutionary scholars employ is realistic, materialistic, pragmatic and systemically policy-oriented. It seeks to understand the world as it exists and as it has evolved and changed, keeping 'close to the ground', yet also seeking a wide vision, and trying to generalise about the structure and dynamics of real social economies evolving through historical time. It essentially tries to comprehend the changing ways of life that groups of people operate within economic systems to solve problems that emerge in the process of engaging in production, distribution, exchange and socioeconomic reproduction.

This generates a broad view of institutional-evolutionary trends, starting with the *principle of historical specificity and evolution*, where every serious problem or topic is required to be embedded in an historical inquiry into its emergence and evolution, since much can be learned from historical and cultural analysis. This is especially the case for phases and stages of development and evolution, the relationship between culture and scholarship, social provisioning, path dependence and hysteresis. The history of institutional and evolutionary political economy (IEPE), broadly conceived, illustrates how the origins of the school start with the Physiocrats, the classical economists and Karl Marx, through the earlier cultural origins of capitalism.

Institutional-evolutionary science did not formally emerge until Veblen's work on institutions, habits and evolution at the turn of the nineteenth into the twentieth century, during the time of the development of corporate capitalism, imperialism and financial dominance of industry. This immediately led to a flurry of new scholars taking on the task of developing the new school and impacting on policy through, for instance, the New Deal in the USA. But it took until the long boom of capitalism of the 1950s and 1960s for the formal inception of an association of mostly Veblenian scholars to be formed—the Association for Evolutionary Economics (AFEE [1965])—which continues even now to generate creative institutional scholarship,

2.1 Introduction

in the *Journal of Economic Issues*. Into the 1980s and 1990s other trends developed, including the emergence of groups and/or journals that take an institutional-evolutionary stance in Europe, Japan, Latin America and several other areas as well; while even orthodoxy recognised the importance of institutions, which stimulated the development of various forms of 'new institutionalism'. Special mention should be given to the European Association for Evolutionary Political Economy (EAEPE) and their newly developed *Review of Evolutionary Political Economy,* for the type of analysis developed in this book.

This history of institutional and evolutionary political economy also follows the evolution of several other principles of inquiry that are institutional-evolutionary in their origin. For instance, the *concept/principle of the nexus between institutions, habits and individuals* is linked to various institutional-evolutionary scholars, but which had its origins in the work of Veblen. This broad principle links several levels of analysis to form a multilayered framework. More delimited in scope is the *concept/principle of heterogeneous groups and agents*, which Veblen (unwittingly) utilised to recognise the different roles played in the social economy, and the differential capabilities, skills and backgrounds of players in the institutions. Another high point of theory that formally started with Veblen, but which either in name or function was also associated with numerous other scholars who took an institutional-evolutionary direction, is the *concept/principle of circular and cumulative causation* (CCC), including the notion of interdependency between spheres, emergence-complexity, and amplified impact of changes.

The *concept/principle of contradiction* is linked to various forms of political economy, including especially Veblenian institutionalism, some neo-Marxists, some feminists, neo-Schumpeterians, and post-Keynesian institutionalists, through the conflicts and instabilities associated with the institutionalised anomalies between capital and labour, industry and finance, men and women, monopoly and competition, nation versus nation, business versus the environment, individual versus society, ethnic group versus ethnic group, and capital versus state/citizens. This is closely linked with the concept/*principle of uncertainty*, which was implicitly developed by Marx, Schumpeter and Karl Polanyi but explicitly by Keynes and several others. It states that political economists should study the uncertain dynamics of especially capitalism as it generates creative destruction, disembedded tendencies, debt finance for long-term projects plus global expansion into other markets, cultures, and production-distribution systems.

The IEPE *concept/principle of innovation* is important and relates to the methods of the great political economists to enhance the human and ecological condition. It can of course relate to organisational, technological and social new ways of doing things, including ways of absorbing the economic surplus through the sales effort, finance and policy (discussed further below). We also include the *concept/principle of uneven development and hegemony*, developed by numerous schools of institutional and evolutionary political economy (starting with Veblen), as it applies to nations and regions, through which IEPEs need to analyse ways in which global powers establish dominance and whence elites benefit from the global source of power, and how associated anomalies can be ameliorated. In addition, several schools and trends in IEPE seek to develop principles and concepts that are appropriate for inclusion in decision-making through various organisations. In this context, the *concept/principle of policy and governance* states that political economists should investigate problems and their solution through improvements to social provisioning, standard of living, quality of life, effective climate change mitigation and adaptation and other means via governments, civil society groups, research bodies, and corporations.

We reveal which *major* institutional-evolutionary scholars wittingly or unwittingly utilise or develop these concepts/principles as the chapter evolves, and which deviate from them somewhat and why.

2.2 Proto-Institutional and Evolutionary Science

The first generation of proto-institutional-evolutionary scholars included the physiocrats and some of the classical economists. The physiocrats, most notably François Quesnay (1694–1774) and his *Tableau économique* ('graphic representation'), were active especially in France during the 1700s, and sought to comprehend the dynamics of the advanced economy of the time through the circuit of relationships between farmers (the productive class), landowners and the unproductive classes (industrialists, merchants and craftsmen). This first major model of the economy, the *Tableau*, was institutional-evolutionary in the sense of being *realistic* and concentrating on the dominant sectors and classes of the economy evolving through historical time at the macro, meso and micro levels. This circuit of economic relations was probably fairly representative of the economy of its time, when agriculture in France was much more productive of the economic surplus than the manufacturing sector.

As productive agriculture *started* to promote industry and market capitalism, Adam Smith (1723–1790), much influenced by the Physiocrats, emerged as a proto-institutional-evolutionary scholar in the sense that he placed a good deal of emphasis on historical specificity and the evolution of the institutions. It is also true, most notably, that he was the first to specifically illustrate what scholars would later call the concept/principle of circular and cumulative causation (CCC) in the generation of the economic surplus. In this, productive investment in agriculture (sector I) can stimulate cheap and steady supply of inputs to industry (manufacturing; sector II), which in turn through greater division of labour and higher wages can stimulate trade (sector III), expanding competition in foreign markets, thus increasing the potential surplus that can be used for further productive investment and expansion of the division of labour (see Prue Kerr 1993). Crucial for Smith were the interdependencies between sectors and the articulated development of the whole economy, in *The Wealth of Nations* (1776); as well as the role of ethics, trust and association in the *Theory of Moral Sentiments* (1759).

Thomas Malthus (1766–1834), especially in his *Principles of Political Economy* (1820), was also a proto-institutional-evolutionary scholar in the sense that he scrutinised the distribution of the product between the major classes of capitalism, and explained how the economic surplus is generated through the process of effective demand interacting with production to realise value on the market. David Ricardo (1772–1823), notably in his *Principles of Political Economy and Taxation* (1817), had threads of institutional-evolutionary themes in his method as he sought to comprehend the role of value, classes, distribution of income, accumulation, surplus and machinery. Simonde de Sismonde's (1773–1842) *New Principles of Political Economy* (1819) was very influential and presaged Marx in developing, in embryonic form, the concepts of historical specificity, periodic crises, contradiction, surplus value, social class and socioeconomic policy.

As industrial capitalism expanded and evolved further throughout the 1800s, Karl Marx (1818–1883) deepened the institutional-evolutionary theme in political economy (see John Elliott 1978). In a whole series of innovative volumes, especially the 1857–1858 *Grundrisse,* and the three volumes of *Capital* (I: production [1867]; II: circulation [1887]; III: profit/competition/credit [1892]), he was an (unwitting) institutional-evolutionary scholar because, firstly, he analysed the evolution of institutions, especially those of 'capitalism', from the primitive phases of (a) mercantilism (simple commodity production) through to (b) manufacture (handicraft workers under one roof), and then onto capitalism proper through (c) competitive machine production (wage labour under the regime of capital), and onto (d) largescale industry (greater concentration). These phases differ, of course, from area to area or nation to nation. He was, secondly, also an institutional-evolutionary scholar because he illustrated the workings of CCC whereby the economic surplus is produced, demanded and then reproduced through time within the institutions of the circuit of social capital. His third institutional-evolutionary thread was his tendency to be realistic in his analysis of the major heterogeneous agents and classes of capitalism, especially in his work on the different types of workers, industrial capitalists, money capitalists, merchants and others such as bookkeepers and transporters (O'Hara 2016). Lastly, he was institutional-evolutionary in the sense of developing a realist and materialist account of the rise and periodic as well as systemic decline of the institutions of capitalism; as well as the contradictory manifestation of the anomalous dichotomies of the capitalist system through recession, depression, cycles and evolutionary transformation.

2.3   Principles of Thorstein Veblen

Thorstein Veblen (1857–1929) is the 'father' of institutional-evolutionary science, through the development of a highly original theoretical schema, and under the influence of Darwinian evolution, pragmatism, the German historical school and Marxism (see Anderson 1932–33; Tilman 1996; O'Hara 2002). Veblen sought to develop a social and political economy of capitalism in tune with the latest phase of its evolution *a la* imperialism, the robber barons, finance capital, and corporate capitalism around the turn of the nineteenth into the twentieth century. His first book, *The Theory of the Leisure Class: An Economic Study of Institutions* (1899), was an innovative, self-conscious attempt to develop an institutional and evolutionary science. Veblen was an institutional and evolutionary scholar, firstly, since he placed the economy firmly within a historical context; this is the *principle of historical specificity and evolution*. He studied the evolution of society from its primitive barbarian roots to the emergence of agriculture, then handicraft, later industrial capitalism, and still later the dominance of business. He concentrated on the capitalism of his day, especially that of US capitalism at the turn of the twentieth century (1895–1905), and later on through to the early 1920s. *The Leisure Class* and most of his other works centred on how the economic surplus (net output) once produced by industry is often wasted on conspicuous consumption, financial wheeling and dealing, wars and mergers (oligopolies).

A *core concept/principle of Veblen is the system-institutions-habits-individuals nexus* (ontology). Veblen was a systemist; i.e., one who concentrates on various systems of organisation and behaviour. He recognised that there are different *levels* of organisation in the social economy, which all exist emergently or in a *sui generis* fashion. They are qualitatively different, yet interactive, *systems*. At the most general level is [A] the world or planet Earth, including the geopolitical environment (see Veblen 1915, 1917); at a 'lower' level is [B] capitalism, i.e., the system of production and distribution characterised by the existence of classes such as capitalists and workers (of various types) producing output; as well as managers, financiers and bookkeepers, plus consumers and merchants (Veblen 1919); at an even 'lower' level is the [C] micro environment, including the sectoral workings of specific corporations, families, local communities, and ecologies (Veblen 1899, 1904, 1923); and at a 'lower' level still are [D] individual human beings, who exhibit various habits of thought and behaviour (Veblen 1899). These systems are all interconnected, but they operate at different levels and hence are qualitatively novel (i.e., emergent) (see Bunge 1974–1989).

Veblen focussed on all of these systems, but his main concern was to situate national forms of capitalism in a geopolitical, social and environmental setting, with the focus on the dominant institutions of the corporation, family, state and community, and how individuals through groups link into this fabric through their capabilities, skills, habits and instincts (O'Hara 1999b). The core 'thing' for Veblen was that these institutions evolve through historical time, and that we must comprehend their changing form in these different historical contexts. In the process, we must not lose sight of the capitalist system within which the institutions operate, and the nature of the groups and individuals in this nexus of interactions.

For instance, Veblen (1904, 1923) developed the first detailed economic analysis of the corporation, which set the scene for later work, including that of Berle and Means (1932) on ownership and control (see O'Kelley 2011); plus, for instance, much work on economic power (e.g., Galbraith 1983; Tool and Samuels 1989); corporate hegemony (William Dugger 1989); and corporate finance (e.g., Karayiannis and Young 1991).

At the most general of these levels, Veblen (1915, 1917) was the first major political economist to (unwittingly) develop the *concept/principle of hegemonic dominance and uneven development,* as he explored the global and regional evolution of capitalism, at a time when Germany was seeking to replace Britain at the apogee of imperial power. Veblen also utilised the *concept/principle of cumulative causation,* concerning the complex manner in which the institutions of capitalism interact with its various nations, classes, ethnic groups, genders and species (see Berger 2009). Such an interaction is not an equilibrium process, since ceteris paribus conditions do not prevail. Instead, an evolution in one area of the social economy will, more often than not, influence other areas, especially if the initial change is crucial, setting in motion (in many cases) a magnified or amplified impact on the system as a whole. In other words, the micro elements of the social economy (individuals, small groups) impact on the meso elements (sectors, institutions, organisations), which in turn affect the macro and global elements (nations, global system); while reverse causation also occurs as the macro and global constituents impact on the meso and micro levels, and the meso impacts on the micro as well. Each level (micro, meso, macro and global) is qualitatively different, so it is not possible, for instance, to reduce the macro from the meso or micro, or the micro from the macro or meso levels. Because of the *complexity* of the linkages between levels, the total impact of a change involving all levels tends to be magnified and amplified, resulting in qualitative as well as quantitative changes through historical time (emergence) (Bunge 2009).

Veblen also (unwittingly) developed the *concept/principle of heterogeneous groups and agents,* wherein he was interested in the real human dynamics of groups of people and individuals who act out their roles through various norms, mores, agreements, accords and routines. The economy is a complicated system of arrangements comprising numerous roles, positions, strata, rankings, estates, divisions, sectors, institutions, ideologies and belief systems. This complexity manifests itself in various classes of occupations, skills-sets, strata of status positions, and officials. Much of Veblen's institutional-evolutionary scholarship sought to situate these different classes within various institutions that change through time, with a view to comprehending how real people contribute (or otherwise) to the reproduction of the system of arrangements. Veblen thus discussed the role of workers, capitalists, financiers, real estate agents, housewives, clerks and so on within the institutions of the corporation, the financial system, the state, family and world economy set within an ecological and biological environment (Veblen 1899, 1914, 1923).

It is clear that Veblen unwittingly utilised the *concept/principle of contradiction,* under the influence of Marx, socialists and the classical economists, the various historical schools of political economy, and many other works. The main contradiction he examined was that between the 'vested interests and the common man' (Veblen 1919). In his works, the vested interests (elites) of the early twentieth century in the USA, exploited the community's joint stock of knowledge and skills by controlling the main sectors or commanding heights of the economy; especially that of steel, railways, armaments, vehicles, construction and machinery. Corporate mergers, increasing concentration of industry, strategic alliances, interlocking directorships, and political interlocks were the main ways in which the vested interests accumulated power for the realisation of their various aims and objectives. As the twentieth century evolved into the 1920s he saw the formation of a *Great Union of Vested Interests* being created through various accords between business, state and labour. But the overriding power is held by those who control business, since they are better able to exploit the joint stock and manage sabotage (restricting output) through various means of upsetting the industrial system in the pursuit of industrial profit, through periodic redundancies, recessions, depressions plus financial and banking crises.

A core concern of Veblen was thus the contradictory tendency of capitalism towards periodic and structural crises, including financial crises, recessions, depressions, protracted dislocation, systemic bottlenecks, and industrial strife. He sought to comprehend the anomalous workings of the system and to suggest *systemic* means for its amelioration. In *The Vested Interests and the Common Man* (1919) and *Absentee Ownership* (1923), for instance, he set the scene for the coming of the next major crisis. Much of his assessment made use of the distinction (contradiction) between instrumental (productive) and ceremonial (relatively unproductive) activities. The *concept of innovation* was important for Veblen, as he saw changes in the way of doing things as crucial for improvements in the standard of living of the masses. This led to the *principle of innovation*, that in order to moderate social problems one needs to incorporate new knowledge and methods. Also associated with this was his *concept of policy and governance* which concentrated on systemic changes to institutions to ameliorate anomalous functioning. The productive instrumental elements were those of workmanship, knowledge, skills and communication (the community's joint stock) embodied in production, transportation, education and community relations; while the unproductive ceremonial elements comprised much of corporate control, financial dominance of industry, the waste of conspicuous consumption, disinformational advertising, and state spending of armaments for fighting wars for domestic and global business (exploiting the joint stock).

In Veblen's system, three main contradictions (unproductive ceremonial processes) can be seen to have led to the emergence of high levels of unstable finance, waste and sabotage by powerful corporations into the 1920s. The first is the increasing oligopolisation of industry (monopoly capital) which often acted as a barrier to new innovators and productivity. The second is the increasing dominance of finance capital, especially through the debt, equity and capital markets generating unsustainable speculative bubbles. And the third is a combination of advertising and waste in the interests of the conspicuous consumption of the leisure class. He saw the transfer of economic surplus and national income from industry, workers, and community development towards monopolies, finance/real estate and the upper class to be the source of increasingly low productivity, financial instability, and insufficient productive demand (Veblen 1923). In the late 1920s, these three anomalous tendencies merged to cause the greatest crisis in the history of capitalism: the Great Depression of the 1930s.

2.4 Keynes, Schumpeter & Later Evolutionary-Institutional Scholars

The Great Depression, along with two world wars, and recurring crises and instabilities, set the scene for an array of other scholars to contribute to institutional and evolutionary themes (see, e.g., Gruchy 1948, 1972; Mayhew 1987; Hodgson 2004). John Hobson, John Maynard Keynes and Joseph Schumpeter certainly were the most well-known economists to develop certain institutional and evolutionary themes into the early and middle 1900s. Hobson (1858–1940) was a contemporary of Veblen who also authored a book on Veblen (Hobson 1936), and wrote some classic works on imperialism, unemployment and aggregate demand that took an institutional-evolutionary line. His work influenced Keynes, who also found aggregate demand antecedents in the work of Malthus and Marx. Keynes and Schumpeter contributed to the institutional-evolutionary concerns of being realistic, systemic and with a focus on the structural dynamics of capitalism.

Keynes's (1883–1946) major contribution to institutional-evolutionary analysis concerned four themes. The first was in seeing capitalism as an evolutionary system that is subject to changing dynamics, periodic and structural crises, and the need for appropriate structural policies to (partially) rectify the anomalies. The second was the principle of aggregate effective demand (Keynes 1936), which was crucial to capitalism in order to evade and rectify problems of crisis, instability and depression. The third was the concept of uncertainty (Keynes 1937); namely, that industrial investment under capitalism is forever subject to a long-term horizon of prospective yield (relative to supply price), with partial funding of this based on debt-generating instabilities that perpetually subject the system to crises by undermining prospective yield (and increasing supply price). And the fourth was Keynes's monetary theory of production, where money and aggregate demand are not mere veils but actually do impact output (and prices) in the short and long terms. Indeed, it is money and demand that, in Keynes's system, push the system forward and finance both innovation and general production as well as potentially enhancing prospective yield and hence expected profits, but also speculation, crisis and instability.

Schumpeter (1883–1950) had his own themes, buried temporarily by the so-called ('bastard') Keynesian revolution and the neoclassical synthesis. It wasn't until the 1970s that his contributions and influences started to really take off in academic and policy circles; which has continued into the twenty-first century. His institutional-evolutionary themes were similar to those of Marx, Veblen and Keynes in being realistic in his formulations; concerned with the evolutionary dynamics of capitalism through long historical time; and especially being concerned with the cyclical and structural instabilities which he thought would lead capitalism to its grave. He emphasised the generation of surplus value from process, product, raw material, market and corporate forms of innovation. The early business cycle model of *The Theory of Economic Development* (1911) was developed much further in his two-volume work on *Business Cycles* (1939); while the contradiction of creative destruction inherent in innovation and its double movements was enunciated in some detail in his *Capitalism, Socialism and Democracy* (1942).

Schumpeter contributed three main proximate things to institutional-evolutionary themes. The first was the concept, first developed by Marx, that cycles are endogenously generated by the institutions of capitalism; specifically through innovation activated by entrepreneurs or corporations via investment in new techniques, products and organisations. Some of the innovations help to generate short cycles, while others of a more durable and substantial nature engender longer cycles. Secondly, Schumpeter realised, as Marx, Veblen and Keynes had previously, that unproductive finance is a main instigator of amplified cycles, which sets the scene for depression (such as the 1930s and 2008ff). Thirdly, he recognised that capitalism has inherent contradictions that contribute to short, medium and secular crises and instabilities; as well as to its eventual demise. Schumpeter (1942) situated capitalism's demise as being directly related to its successes—creative destruction—as capitalism becomes buoyant through innovation, but also generates counter forces that waste the resources of its success through institutionalising innovation, protecting the system from excesses, and reducing its destructive capabilities. (Oakley 1990; Bloch 2018.)

Keynes and Schumpeter were clearly very important institutional-evolutionary scholars. Also crucial, especially in the interwar, World War II and postwar eras, were John Commons, Wesley Mitchell, Clarence Ayres, John Kenneth Galbraith, and Gunnar Myrdal (see Allan Gruchy 1948, 1972; Geoffrey Hodgson 2004). Commons (1862–1945) was a key member of the "Wisconsin school", and along with some others, made contributions to the New Deal. He developed not only general principles of collective action but also technical analyses of labour relations and public utilities. He was also a systemist in seeing *interconnections* between the relationships activated in the social economy—*the circular economy* (part of CCC)—which led him, especially in his two-volume *Institutional Economics: Its Place in Political Economy* (1934), to centre on transactions, such as those concerning bargaining, managing and rationing; and the nature of the working rules of laws, customs and going concerns, which enable such transactions to be undertaken to varying degrees of success.

Wesley Mitchell (1874–1948) was a student of Veblen at Chicago, and it was Veblen who engendered a lifelong concern in Mitchell with the contradictory and cumulative motion associated with business cycles, which Mitchell developed at the National Bureau of Economic Research (NBER). In numerous books and articles, such as *Business Cycles and Their Causes* (1941), his concern was with the *endogenous contradictions* that engendered rising costs and declining demand during the late upswing in the cycle, especially factors which inhibit the profit of business enterprise. These contradictions tend to become *cumulative* (rather than equilibrium-tending) since the upswing sets in motion various conflicts and bottlenecks that impede continual growth. The downswing itself is also cumulative in that the declining profit and demand endogenously generates heightened uncertainty, leading to recession and often depression. However, forces of the downswing can also endogenously assist the recovery, especially the declining costs and the rising average propensity to consume, which can enable more optimism and thus initiate renewed upswing (negative feedback). For Mitchell, there were multiple types of cycles (or fluctuations, such as short cycles and long waves), in which the phases are interrelated or endogenously generated, and his analysis continues to inform even more contemporary theoretical and empirical analysis of cycles (e.g., Sherman and Kolk 1996).

Clarence Ayres (1891–1972) was the de facto leader of the Texas School (the 'cactus branch'). His main contribution to institutional-evolutionary themes was in reformulating Veblen's basic dichotomy of the *instrumental and ceremonial functioning of institutions* for theory and policy. For Ayres, the progressive instrumental values are those of participation, knowledge, skills and tools (defined broadly) to enhance the enlightenment project of promoting and extending the human condition towards reason and quality of life for the common good. The ceremonial functions, for Ayres, generated an extension of inequality, invidious comparison, and vested interests; basically supporting the elites in their quest for power and dominance over the common people. In a whole series of books, including *The Divine Right of Capital* (1946) and *The Theory of Economic Progress* (1962), Ayres developed his analysis of institutional and evolutionary political economy, involving greater participation of the population in the economy and politics; basically a contemporary New Deal (including a Global New Deal) involving welfare, innovation and inclusion for the greater good.

Gunnar Myrdal (1898–1987) developed what he called "holistic economics" (broad vision, comprehensive) and won a Nobel Prize for his efforts in 1974. His holistic—or systemic—economics was developed in works such as *The Political Element in the Development of Economic Theory* (1930), *An American Dilemma: The Negro Problem and Modern Democracy* (1944: 2 vols), and *Asian Drama: An Inquiry into the Poverty of Nations* (1968: 3 vols). His *first principle of holism or systemism* (see Myrdal 1978) is that the method of institutional economics must be open in the sense of including an array of factors, such as political, economic, cultural and environmental, in the interdisciplinary analysis of social problems. The *second principle is that of a decentered totality,* in which no one basic factor overrides all others in the determination of socioeconomic dynamics and anomalies. Myrdal castigates economic and technological determinism, arguing instead that 'base' and 'superstructure' are interrelated; it is through the multi-factorial approach that social problems should be viewed.

Myrdal's *third principle posits the importance of circular and cumulative causation:* the circular economy again, that every social problem has both a circular form of causation (interdependency) and, more specifically, operates through the process of cumulative causation. Thus business cycles, poverty, inequality and world development should be viewed as being non-equilibrium in motion; subject to feedback processes, amplified or multiplied dynamics, and instability; as well as uneven development. The nature of these cumulations must be empirically scrutinised through an analysis of the interactions between the dominant forces at play in specific instances. In this conceptual revolution he was joined by Nicholas Kaldor (including, among others, his most brilliant paper from the *Economic* Journal; Kaldor 1972; which is a *'must read'*) and later numerous others in the analysis of cumulative dynamics (CCC). The *fourth principle is that of evolution*; that the world and its institutions continually change through long historical time, often in complex ways; sometimes going forward, and sometimes backwards, but always involving qualitatively different outcomes and institutions through various phases of metamorphosis.

John Kenneth Galbraith (1908–2006) was a post-Keynesian institutionalist who followed Veblen in analysing capitalism as an institutionalised system of power. Being a prolific author of dozens of books, his better-known volumes include *American Capitalism* (1952), *The Affluent Society* (1958) and *Economics and the Public Purpose* (1973). His main contribution to IEPE is the *principle of social balance and counterveiling power* (Stanfield 1996), which we interpret as the processes necessary to *moderate the contradictions of corporate capitalism*. For Galbraith, the competitive sector of the economy is dominated by the administered sector, especially the large corporation but also to some degree the state. The large power of the megacorp needs to be balanced by measures to increase the power of the common people. The expansion of automobiles, factories and warehouses especially over the past hundred years needs to be balanced by the collective provision of transportation networks, public transport and pollution control measures. The expansion of urban and city regions requires measures to service and protect these dispersed communities. The explosion of advertising and the consumer revolution needs to be balanced by proper waste disposal and recycling methods. The increasing number of two-wage couples requires appropriate resources to deal with the more complex issue of child support and family protection. Free market political systems tend to generate private affluence but public squaller. However, Galbraith recognised that many 'public services' support corporate interests and hence policy is more complex than the simple contradiction between public and private concerns.

Thus far we have shown that, historically, major IEPEs tended to be males. This was, of course, a time when women were generally restricted to the domain of the household and family, even in western societies. Some females have contributed to IEPE. Robert Dimand, Mary Ann Dimand & Evelyn Forget (2000) document 120 women, born prior to their book being published, who contributed substantially to 'economics'. They worked on topics associated with, e.g., standard economics, statistical analysis, women and the labor force, household labor, development, the rights of women, feminism, and policy. Few have contributed majorly to *explicit* principles of gender, feminism, institutions and evolution. It would be an impossible task to ascertain to what extent they variously contributed to IEPE. The best that can be done, in this short history of IEPE, is to mention a few female social or political economists who especially stand out.

In the book of biographies mentioned immediately above, five women economists who stand out vis-à-vis IEPE include Charlotte Perkins Gilman (1860–1935), Rosa Luxemburg (1871–1919), Ester Boserup (1910–1999), Edith Penrose (1914–1996), and, most famously, Joan Robinson (1903–1983).

Gilman (1898) has been called an institutionalist who made advances in arguing the case for women having an equal role in the wider society through the marketing of household services and the public provision of education, health and other services. Luxemburg (1913) analysed the problems of capitalist accumulation,

2.4 Keynes, Schumpeter & Later Evolutionary-Institutional Scholars

believing that to sustain demand the system requires continual expansion to non-capitalist areas to absorb the surplus. Boserup (1970) was a Marx-Keynes analyst who studied population growth-investment in underdeveloped nations, paying special attention to the reasons why female leadership on farms declined in favour of males, plus the role of aggregate demand in the growth process. Penrose (1959) was a Professor of Political Economy specialising in technological change within corporations, especially the importance of institutions and resources to advance growth and profits.

The *Joan Robinson (1903–1983) Prize* is EAEPE's award for *Book of the Year*, to symbolize her significant contributions to IEPE, through volumes such as *The Economics of Imperfect Competition* (Robinson 1933), *The Accumulation of Capital* (Robinson 1956), *Economic Philosophy* (Robinson 1962) and *Aspects of Development and Underdevelopment* (1979). The *concept of historical time* (Robinson 1980) is a reappearing theme in her works, as she examines growth and development under short, medium and long-run conditions. Time is crucial, for instance, to Robinson's (1962: Ch 5) work on development and underdevelopment, especially investment and uncertainty in the long-term, taking in account an array of factors such as technique, finance, population and cultural institutions (see also Robinson 1979). Other concepts that have a conspicuous presence in her work include uneven development, economic surplus, effective demand, accumulation and technical innovation (Robinson 1979: chs 2, 6).

The above overview of some historically significant female institutional and evolutionary scholars shows that they have contributed in many areas, including gender, occupational roles, uneven development, technological change and conditions underlying socioeconomic performance. The contributions of Robinson, Luxemburg and Penrose variously influenced by Keynesian, Marxian and Schumpeterian (KMS) themes, raises the issue of other scholars worth noting here under KMS influences. Schumpeterian issues are discussed further below, since it developed mostly in the 1970s and after, but here we briefly review the KM work of Kaldor, Baran and Sweezy.

Nicholas Kaldor is obviously the other major scholar in the history of IEPE who stands out, in addition to Gunnar Myrdal (and Veblen), in developing the circular and cumulative concept. Kaldor (1972) merged increasing returns with aggregate effective demand to show an expansion of demand can stimulate growth through increasing returns, and that this becomes a non-equilibrium process as ↑demand→↑output→↓prices→ ↑exports →↑demand generate bouts of expansion. There are, of course, limits to expansion, as he well knew, but in this context David Gordon (1991) said that Kaldor had too much cumulation and not enough contradiction, which is very pertinent to this current book (since we use both these concepts). Kaldor also contributed to the concept of stylized facts, as patterns of empirical dynamics seen through historical time, and especially sought to minimise the use of general equilibrium theory in economics given its irrelevance to the core processes of growth and policy-making.

The other major I-E influence mentioned, Baran & Sweezy (B&S), should not belittle the other *historical* neo-Marxists who have contributed somewhat to I-E political economy. Specifically we are thinking here of Nikolai Bukharin and Rudolf Hilferding. But B&S have an extra-special place among I-E scholars, of which three contributions stand out (Baran 1957; Baran and Sweezy 1966). First is the *concept of the economic surplus*, in its various forms, which has led to stand-out works on ways of utilising the surplus in the development process as it rises through historical time, as a fusion of Marx-Keynes themes (Stanfield 2011). The second is the *concept of historical specificity*, and especially the notion of monopoly capitalism, including the transnational power of the military industrial complex in the process of hegemonic dominance and uneven development. And the third is the *concept of the irrational system*, where B&S argue that utilising the surplus involves much waste, militarism and useless commodities-services that question the legitimacy of capitalist dynamics.

Next we *briefly* review of contemporaneous workings of IEPE especially as it relates to concepts and principles, before we detail the main concepts/principles utilised in this book in Chap. 3.

2.5 Contemporary Institutional and Evolutionary Political Economy

The past half-century has seen the development of various styles of institutional-evolutionary political economy (see O'Hara 1999a, 2007). One broadly follows Veblen as a systemic science of the evolution of power within and between institutions; another follows Schumpeter in being an evolutionary analysis of innovation set especially within corporate systems; a third studies complex systems of institutions and technology via path dependence, lock-in, and non-equilibrium change, economies of scale and positive (and negative) feedback processes; a neo-Marxian group see capitalism as a profit-based system of exploitation evolving through successive phases of institutional change; a feminist evolutionary-institutional inquiry scrutinizes the reproduction of familial, community, state and workplace spheres through the lens of social provisioning; a post-Keynesian institutional view examines the monetary-production economy undergoing periodic bouts of financial instability; and being grafted onto institutional-evolutionary themes is a neoclassical-type vision of property rights and corporate interests, which has occasionally moved in the Veblenian direction ('new' institutionalism).

During the 1960s and 1970s long boom and start of the declining performance of global capitalism, institutional-evolutionary studies went through a revival. This was partly due to the Keynesian welfare state type policies that were instigated during that time, and partly due to the booming university sector, including war veterans but especially the postwar generation which was looking for new and realistic types of economic theory to help explain the problems emerging in the social economy. These problems variously included the Vietnam War, consumerism, pollution, alienation, discrimination, inequality, sexism, exploitation, racism, underdevelopment, and problematic performance. Feeling also that too many institutionalists and their themes were being left out of the pages of the *American Economic Review*, the Wardman Group (see Almeida 2016 for more details on this group) started having "rump sessions" at the annual meetings of the American Economic Association, which eventually helped to form the Association for Evolutionary Economics (AFEE) in 1965, with their *Journal of Economic Issues* commencing publication in 1967. A sister organisation, the Association for Institutionalist Thought (AFIT) emerged in 1979, with the initial aim of to reflect the 'traditional' theory and policy concerns of institutionalism, along the lines of the work of Thorstein Veblen, John Commons, Wesley Mitchell, Clarence Ayres and John Dewey (later it performed much the same role as AFEE, but with annual meetings in the West of the USA).

Institutional-evolutionary science also has a long history in Europe (see Waller 2001), and AFEE members helped to influence the formation of the European Association for Evolutionary Political Economy (EAEPE) during the 1990s, which led to the inception, more recently, of the *Review of Evolutionary Political Economy* (edited by Wolfram Elsner) (see Cincotti et al. 2020; O'Hara 2021 on this journal). Also, most political economy and economics journals publish material on institutions in evolution through time. Numerous other groupings (formal and informal) were organised, such as in Japan as well as Eastern and Central Europe, China and some other Asian countries; while Latin Americans and Australians, as well as others, started to be involved in these institutional-evolutionary trends. For instance, the Japan Association for Evolutionary Economics publishes the *Evolutionary and Institutional Economics Review*.

Generally, institutional-evolutionary political economy seeks to comprehend the dynamics of economic systems, whether they are pre-capitalist socioeconomic formations; or different varieties of capitalism, fascism, socialism, dictatorship, Islamic forms of governance, and any hybrids or new forms that emerge. Within this framework, a key theme of the above scholarly organisations involves investigating the dominant socioeconomic and political institutions of modern capitalism and proposing alternatives or institutional modifications to capitalism. For instance, some varieties of capitalism that currently exist include the (neo)liberal capitalist economies of the USA, UK and Australia (that have been shedding some of their neoliberal garb); the social democratic systems of Canada and Scandinavia; the corporatist types in Germany, Italy and France; the state capitalist economies of China, Vietnam and Russia; and the dependent semi-peripheral systems in Argentina, Brazil and Chile. They also seek to comprehend the different socioeconomic systems that variously operate in the core, semi-periphery and periphery at the global, regional, national and subnational levels; and especially the structural relationships that operate between these systems and which reinforce development and underdevelopment. Some of the evolutionary-institutionalists who sought to comprehend these 'world development' issues include Nobel Laureates W.A. Lewis (1915–1991), Simon Kuznets (1901–1985; a former student of Mitchell), and Gunnar Myrdal; and, more recently, James Dietz, Ilene Grabel, Ha-Joon Chang, Dilmus James and James Cypher (among several others).

Evolutionary-institutionalists also seek to decompose these systems into their meso-components. This has manifested itself, for instance, in papers and books on the historically contingent evolution and transformation of institutional spheres—or institutional regimes—such as the Bretton Woods System (BWS: IMF, WB, etc); the trade regime; the Keynesian-welfare state (KWS); the international and national systems of financial regulation; the corporation; US hegemony (and decline); the system of industrial relations; and the regimes of the family. As the 1950s and 1960s evolved into the 1970s many of these institutions changed and in some cases underwent maturation and decline through the 1980s and 1990s onwards. The development of theory and empirics on *complexity and emergence; varieties of capitalism; experimental techniques; recent advances in extreme nationalism* in many core and semi-peripheral economies (in particular); plus behavioralism and neuroscience; have been other themes in the journals over recent years.

The 'French' Regulation and social structure of accumulation (*'SSA'*) schools studied phases of capitalist performance involving investment, growth and profit (see e.g., O'Hara 2006, 2023). Veblenian evolutionary-institutionalists have made advances in developing (and extending) principles and concepts as applied to the real world (Fusfeld 1988). For instance, radical institutionalists (led by Bill Dugger, Ron Stanfield, Rick Tilman and Ted Wheelwright), instrumental institutionalists (following J. Fagg Foster, Marc Tool and Dale Bush), 'standard' institutionalists (such as Malcolm Rutherford, Warren Samuels and Anne Mayhew), feminist institutionalists (such as Deborah Figart, Janice Peterson, Zdravka Todorova, Mary Wrenn), post-Keynesian institutionalists (following Nicholas Kaldor, Michal Kalecki, Joan Robinson, Hyman Minsky, Dudley Dillard, Wallace Peterson), and European scholars (such as K.W. Kapp, Geoffrey Hodgson, Nathalie Lazaric, Wolfram Elsner, Svetlana Kirdina-Chandler) are just some of the influences advancing the state of evolutionary-institutionalism.

As the postwar era moved into the 1980s–2020s the relative decline, metamorphosis, and/or transformation of these postwar institutional spheres (Samudro 2012; O'Hara 2012a) saw the emergence, dominance, and more recently relative demise of neoliberalism throughout much of the world. Neoliberalism *had* become a growth industry (before the backlash of the GFC and coronacrisis), also impacting on institutional economics as well as the other schools of heterodoxy and other scholarly spheres. This has manifested itself as the emergence and evolution of corporate power (numerous merger waves, strategic alliances and flexible systems of production); financial dominance of industry (successive financial crises); the reconfiguration of the military-industrial state (numerous major wars); capital dominance over labour (stagnating real wages and rising un(der)employment); the rising relative power of Asia (deindustrialisation of much of the core); climate change and declining ecological biodiversity; plus diminishing social/cultural capital in the family and community; which have all became major themes in the evolutionary-institutional literature. Such literature has also come to specialise on the major problems and institutional developments throughout the world; a major achievement in itself.

The *concept/principle of institutionalised culture and evolution* (see Hamilton et al. 2010) has become a major concern through an investigation especially of the rising power of corporate culture. As the power of the corporate sector has risen to new heights so too corporate hegemony has taken hold of other institutions such as the state, the family, finance, educational systems, world economy and industrial relations (Dugger 1989). Through the age of the Internet, corporate objectives and tendencies are more successfully being realised to extend the scope and reach of capital. All businesses and indeed interpersonal relations are developing through the

Internet, as it becomes the main way of communicating in an increasingly global electronic system. Company accounts, financial systems, banking data, personal letters, advertising, sports, music, communication and even research are being conducted through the Internet. Computers, smart phones, robotics, artificial intelligence, medical science, surveillance methods, security systems, financial control systems, production methods, drones, stocktaking, driverless cars, flying taxis, and a host of other activities (including terrorism) are becoming more sophisticated as biotechnology and electronics mature as industries. Evolutionary-institutionalists have been especially interested in these cultural changes, including how workers and management in many sectors are losing employment, while other opportunities arise, as computers and robotics are taking over many of the production, distribution and exchange tasks. (See, e.g., Thierry and Poussing 2010).

The *concept of social provisioning* (SP) has generated swarms of scholarly activity, especially among feminists, institutionalists and general IEPEs. Social provisioning is the notion that political economy should analyse the ways in which cultures can be provided with the means of life, including food, shelter, clothing, education, remuneration, well-being, and how the reproduction *process engages* people within society. SP is especially concerned with ecological cultures of communities. They ask questions such as: How do workers interact on the job? What is the impact on the environment? What contribution do waged and non-waged workers make to the sustenance of the community? How effective is the level of nurturance in the community? How ethical is the circuit of economic relations between households, ecology, business, state, finance, and world economy? (Marilyn Power 2009, 2015.) In citing the provisioning principle, that provisioning should be the starting point of political-economic analysis (Gruchy 1987), William Dugger (1996) uses the associated concepts of historical specificity, cumulative causation, cultural analysis, invidious comparison, power, reproduction and contradiction, among others, in investigating capitalism. (See also Berik and Kongar 2021; Heinz 2020; Jo and Todorova 2018.)

Modern institutional-evolutionary scholars have also advanced an understanding of the ways in which the vested interests—or the Great Union of Vested Interests—exploit the joint stock of knowledge, skills and institutional capabilities. The concept of innovation involved in Veblen's notion of the *community's joint stock of knowledge,* and the exploitation of the joint stock by the ruling classes—a *major contradiction* affecting people's livelihood—advances our understanding of the increasingly unequal share of capabilities, education, norms, mores and etiquette upon which control of productive capital, finance and economic surplus is based (Dugger 1988, 1995, 2019). It also provides a foundation for the vast wastage of socioeconomic resources through spending on capital, goods and services upon which conspicuous consumption, the military-industrial complex, political lobbying and private think tanks are based. This in turn provides a foundation for extensive systemic corruption in the form of institutionalised nepotism, fraud, embezzlement, bribery, state capture and extortion upon which much of the expropriation of the surplus and other resources are dependent (O'Hara 2014).

Among institutional-evolutionary scholars there is much discussion and even dissent on the concept/principle of policy and governance. All seek to advance scholarship at the micro level of how individuals and groups of people can enhance their standard of living and quality of life through expanding their capabilities, skills, resources, networks and relationships. Left institutional-evolutionary scholars tend to promote an egalitarian framework of redistribution to inculcate more participation of the working classes in the economic, social and political framework of the community through a guaranteed minimum income scheme, a comprehensive universal health care system, and free primary, secondary and tertiary education. They also see the need for more democracy in the workplace through the institutionalisation of worker cooperatives, workers being elected to the board of companies, and for fully fledged corporate responsibility to be incorporated in the articles of association as well as the habits and directives of companies. In general, they see the need for checks and balances to reduce negative externalities generated by business, the state and other organisations. They propose balancing material abundance with quality of life, ecological sustainability and standard of living institutional innovations throughout the community (see Stanfield 1995, 2011; Holt and Greenwood 2014). Some such scholars also develop a more reformist program through generous social safety nets, stringent regulations, demand and industry management techniques, and other innovative policies to balance the numerous contradictions of contemporary capitalism (see, e.g., O'Hara 2012a, Olgen 2014).

New institutionalists have an eclectic pedigree, variously including some public choice, Austrian, and neoclassical scholars. It includes (among others) Douglass North, Oliver Williamson, Mancur Olsen, Friedrich Hayek, Elinor Ostrom, Richard Posner and Andrew Schotter. The *Journal of Institutional Economics* provides a good selection of papers by especially new institutionalists. New institutionalists tend to emphasise exogenous preferences rather than endogenous preferences *a la* Veblenians. They tend to centre on the rational choice explanation of individual decisions rather than decisions being affected by the institutional environment as per Veblenians. The individual is thus the centre of their concern, whereas Veblenians believe that the micro, meso, macro and global levels are all emergent (novel). They *tend* to centre on equilibrium rather than circular and cumulative change through long historical time. For new institutionalists, therefore, institutions *tend* to constrain individual choices and involve rules, norms and principles of action that help to structure (but not determine) the preferences of individuals. This is in contrast to the approach of Veblenians who recognised the importance of the institutional environment in not only constraining but also enabling and indeed helping to shape the habits of thought and behaviour of individuals and groups.

Some of these so-called new institutionalists have gone part of the way towards accommodating Veblen's approach, such as Nobel Laureate Douglass North (2005) in his *later* works, who includes analyses of ideology, historical specificity, evolution, path dependence and bounded rationality. Nobel Laureate Elinor Ostrom (2009) has had some influence from 'original institutionalism', including through John Commons' transaction economics; developing the concept of polycentric systems (state, market, community, etc); her analysis of trust, emergence and complexity; and scrutinizing common pool resources; but contra-Veblen she places some emphasis on traditional microeconomic theory, individual agents, and exogenous factors.

Many new institutionalists are far removed from Veblen as they emphasize the concept/principle of private property rights, supporting as they do the power structures of relatively deregulated capitalism. They also tend to have a micro theory of agents within institutions with little regard for system-problems such as insufficient aggregate demand, recurring structural crises and endogenous cycles and waves. Their rational choice framework tends to ignore radical uncertainty, information problems, and historical evolution (Rutherford 1994). Furthermore, they analyse inefficient institutions and emphasise functions rather than being concerned with the contradictions of capitalism. They emphasise transaction costs yet very often underplay the importance of many of the transactions analysed by Karl Polanyi (1944) such as reciprocity, redistribution, informal marketing and householding, which are important to Veblenians.

There are whole groups of IEPE scholars who are more truly evolutionary and perhaps institutional. These groups utilise the concepts of complexity, emergence, path dependence, bounded rationality, positive feedback (and sometimes negative feedback), increasing returns, information contagion, and self-reinforcing mechanisms to examine technology and knowledge, often working through networks of institutions to achieve certain evolutionary processes. They also tend to use systems analysis, heterogeneous agents, routines, universality with context, and stylized facts to understand adaptation in a world of uncertainty. Some of them have direct and indirect links to the Santa Fe Institute, others to the University of Sussex, or Japan, others with close links to the University of Queensland, or Richard Nelson and Stanley Winter, and others with more specific links to EAEPE (Arthur 1994; Foster and Metcalfe 2001; Bettin 2020; Potts 2000; Elsner 2021; Cincotti et al. 2020).

Neo-Schumpeterians and others of an institutional and evolutionary tendency have been scrutinizing the concept of long waves for several decades. The range of such studies include, e.g., Gerhard Mensch (1975) on *Stalemate in Technology*, to Andrew Tylecote (1994) on the interplay of technology and institutions, (a 'Regulationist'-institutionalist?), Chris Freeman (2008) on swarms of innovation and related issues, realistic analyses of waves of innovation of capitalism (e.g., Mandel 1995; Freeman and Louca 2002), plus a new wave of innovation likely being already upon us (Silva and Serio 2016). (See O'Hara 2023.)

Some IEPE neo-Schumpeterians seek to build bridges with other IEPE traditions, while developing their own authentic concepts of creative destruction, swarms of innovation, and novelty. For instance, the *Journal of Evolutionary Economics (JEE)* publishes numerous relevant IEPE papers on such topics as the three dimensional space of the circular economy, going back to the roots of Kenneth Boulding, Herman Daly and Robert Costanza, and linking ecological and evolutionary economics with the micro, meso and macro dimensions of reality (Chizaryfard et al. 2021). There are discussions and agent-based models of consumption and class, including Veblen and bandwagon effects, with an emphasis on micro-meso and macro-evolution through time (Rengs and Wäckerle 2019). Concepts such as democracy, bounded rationality and political and social institutions are also scrutinized in the light of Schumpeter's work on *Capitalism, Socialism and Democracy* (Egidi 2017). If there is one possible critique of the *JEE*, it is its tendency to publish material that abstracts from real historical trajectories and qualitative-informal processes in the institutions.

2.6 Conclusion

This chapter has outlined the history of institutional and evolutionary concepts and principles. It started with the classical economists and Karl Marx, following through to the original work of Thorstein Veblen, the father of IEPE. Then it extended the inquiry to J.M. Keynes, Joseph Schumpeter, Wesley Mitchell, John Commons, Clarence Ayres, K.W. Kapp, Charlotte Gilman, Gunnar Myrdal, J.K. Galbraith, Joan Robinson, and numerous others. We concluded with some discussion of concepts and principles associated with feminists, neo-Schumpeterians, post-Keynesian institutionalists, neo-Marxist institutionalists, new institutionalists and complexity scholars. In all this we sought to trace the historical trajectory of concepts and principles.

Some core general principles stood out in this array of conceptual revolution. For instance, the concept/principle of historical specificity and evolution was seen as crucial, and we utilise it to examine the broad contours of institutional-evolutionary thought through its variegated history. Evolution and transformation are ongoing, since the process of long term historical change is forever impacting on institutions and individuals, and social provisioning, subjecting them to dislocations, which forever require the adjustment of skills, habits and new relationships, and leading to new phases of evolution.

The combined concept/principle of independency (circular) and cumulative causation (CCC) illustrates well the concern for changes that are greater than the initial adjustment that set the process in motion. The concept/principle of heterogeneous groups and agents seeks to inquire into the various groups and different types of individuals, including various segments of workers, capitalists and functionaries; different genders, ethnic groups and species; as well as numerous micro-groups; that interact within the political economy.

The emergent concept/principle of the nexus between system-nation-institutions-individual recognises that there are various levels in the economy, and that each successive level constitutes a qualitatively different movement from micro to meso to macro to global as complexity and emergence come into play.

The concept/principle of contradiction states that there are various conflicts and tensions operating in the system that generate instability, conflict and anomalous reproduction of the system. These manifest in periodic and structural deep recessions, financial crises, social tension, crime, terrorism, war, climate change, and community dislocation. Such contradictions include those between capital and labour; finance and industry; competition and monopoly; men and women; ethnic group versus ethnic group; business and ecology; plus nation versus nation (or region). Such dichotomies need to be in the forefront of inquiry.

The concept/principle of uneven development and hegemony examines the differential power relations between nations and regions of the world as some periodically succeed in achieving world dominance in production, commerce and finance, which should be at centre stage.

The concept/principle of uncertainty was analysed by post Keynesian institutionalists vis-à-vis the mismatch between long-run capital project investment and short-medium term debt; secondly, by Marxists, Polanyists and Schumpeterians in relation to swarms of innovation which caste aside old industries, skills, cultures and ecologies; and thirdly by feminists and social economists who were cognizant of the long-terms costs of insufficient nurturance, distrust and institutionalised discrimination.

Some evolutionary scholars examine the concept/principle of innovation, evolution of corporations and successive streams of product/process innovation focusing on micro-meso structures of the economy. Numerous scholars of a neo-Schumpeterian tendency follow IE themes closely, engaging those with a more explicitly evolutionary and historical perspective. Some neo-Schumpeterians utilise basic IE concepts of path dependency, emergence, complexity, lock-in, positive feedback, non-equilibrium processes, and transformational metamorphosis at the micro-meso-macro and even global levels.

All of these groups played a role in the concept/principle of policy and governance (often used in a 'systemic' sense). But there were some differences between those who saw the need for functional finance, modern monetary theory and social provisioning, and those with a penchant for moderating the level of public goods in the interests of having more of a balance between public and private realms, especially when it comes to education, health, and infrastructure investment.

In Chap. 3, below, we detail the nature of the core IEPE concepts/principles and try to engender a *fairly* catholic or broad church approach to world problems through institutional-evolutionary political economy. Thereafter, in the chapters that follow that one, we apply some of these core general concepts/principles to core world problems emerging especially in recent years.

Acknowledgements I wish to thank the referees, plus Ajit Sinha and Alex Thomas, for comments and inspiration in the development of this paper. An earlier version was published as O'Hara (2019)

References

Almeida, Felipe. 2016. Inside the Organizational Institutions of Institutional Economics: Why Are There Two Institutionalist Associations? *Journal of Economic Issues* 50: 566–574.
Anderson, K.L. 1932–33. The Unity of Veblen's Theoretical System. *Quarterly Journal of Economics* 47: 598–626.
Arthur, W. Brian. 1994. *Increasing Returns and Path Dependence in the Economy*. Ann Arbor: University of Michigan.
Ayres, Clarence. 1946. *The Divine Right of Capital*. Boston: Houghton Mifflin.
———. 1962. *The Theory of Economic Progress*. New York: Shocken.
Baran, Paul. 1957. *The Political Economy of Growth*. New York: Monthly Review Press.

Baran, Paul, and Paul M. Sweezy. 1966. *Monopoly Capital*. New York: Monthly Review Press.

Berger, Sebastian, ed. 2009. *The Foundations of Non-Equilibrium Economics: The Principle of Circular and Cumulative Causation*. London/New York: Routledge.

Berik, Günseli, and Ebru Kongar. 2021. The Social Provisioning Approach in Feminist Economics: The Unfolding Research. In *The Routledge Handbook of Feminist Economics*, ed. Günseli Berik and Ebru Kongar, 3–21. London/New York: Routledge.

Berle, Adolf A., and Gardiner C. Means. 1932. *The Modern Corporation and Private Property*. 2nd ed. New York: Harcourt, Brace and World, 1968.

Bettin, Steffen S. 2020. Electricity Infrastructure and Innovation in the Next Phase of Energy Transition—Amendments to the Technology Innovation System Framework. *Review of Evolutionary Political Economy* 1 (3): 371–395.

Bloch, Harry. 2018. *Schumpeter's Price Theory*. London & New York: Routledge.

Boserup, Ester. 1970. *Women's Role in Economic Development*. London: Allen & Unwin.

Bunge, Mario. 1974–1989. *Treatise on Basic Philosophy*, 8 Volumes. Boston/Dordrecht.

———. 2009. *Political Philosophy: Fact, Fiction and Vision*. New Brunswick: Transaction Publishers.

Chizaryfard, Armaghan, Paolo Trucco, and Cali Nuur. 2021. The Transformation to a Circular Economy: Framing an Evolutionary View. *Journal of Evolutionary Economics* 31: 475–504.

Cincotti, Silvano, Wolfram Elsner, Nathalie Lazaric, Anastasia Nesvetailova, and Engelbert Stockhammer. 2020. Towards an Evolutionary Political Economy: Editorial to the Inaugural Issue of the *Review of Evolutionary Political Economy*. *Review of Evolutionary Political Economy* 1 (1): 1–12.

Commons, John. 1934. *Institutional Economics: Its Place in Political Economy*. New Brunswick: Transaction Publishers, 1990. Two Volumes.

Dugger, William M. 1988. Radical Institutionalism: Basic Concepts. *Review of Radical Political Economics* 20 (1): 1–20.

———. 1989. *Corporate Hegemony*. New York: Greenwood Press.

———. 1995. Veblenian Institutionalism: The Changing Concepts of Inquiry. *Journal of Economic Issues* 29 (4): 1013–1028.

———. 1996. Redefining Economics: From Market Allocation to Social Provisioning. In *Political Economy for the 21st Century: Contemporary Views on the Trend of Economics*, ed. Charles J. Whalen, 31–43. Armonk/New York: M.E. Sharpe.

———. 2019. The Doleful Dynamics of Competition: Inequality and Fakery in Modernity. *Forum for Social Economics* 48 (1).

Egidi, Massimo. 2017. Schumpeter's Picture of Economic and Political Institutions in the Light of a Cognitive Approach to Human Behavior. *Journal of Evolutionary Economics* 27: 139–159.

Elliott, John E. 1978. Institutionalism as an Approach to Political Economy. *Journal of Economic Issues* 12 (1): 91–114.

Elsner, Wolfram. 2021. Collapse: Institutional Decline and Breakdown, Its Endogeneity and Its Asymmetry Vis-a-Vis Emergence: A Theoretical Frame. *Journal of Economic Issues* 55 (1): 79–102.

Foster, John, and J. Stanley Metcalfe, eds. 2001. *Frontiers of Evolutionary Economics: Competition, Self-Organization and Innovation Policy*. Cheltenham: Edward Elgar.

Freeman, Chris. 2008. *Systems of Innovation: Selected Essays in Evolutionary Economics*. Cheltenham: Edward Elgar, 2008.

Freeman, Chris, and Francisco Louçã. 2002. *As Time Goes By: From the Industrial Revolutions to the Information Revolution*. Oxford: Oxford University Press.

Fusfeld, Daniel. 1988. *Economics: Principles of Political Economy*. 3rd ed. Boston: Scott, Foresman & Co.

Galbraith, John Kenneth. 1952. *American Capitalism*. Boston: Houghton Mifflin.

———. 1958. *The Affluent Society*. Boston: Houghton Mifflin.

———. 1973. *Economics and the Public Purpose*. Boston: Houghton Mifflin.

———. 1983. *The Anatomy of Power*. Boston: Houghton Mifflin Company.

References

Gilman, Charlotte Perkins. 1898. *Women and Economics*. Boston: Small. Reprinted New York: Harper & Row, 1966.

Gordon, David M. 1991. Kaldor's Macro System: Too Much Cumulation, Too Few Contradictions. In *Nicholas Kaldor and Mainstream Economics: Confrontation or Convergence*, ed. Edward J. Nell and Willi Semmler, 518–548. New York: St Martins Press.

Gruchy, Allen G. 1948. *Modern Economic Thought: The American Contribution*. New York: Augustus M. Kelley, 1967.

———. 1972. *Contemporary Economic Thought: The Contribution of Neo-Institutional Economics*. Clifton: Augustus M. Kelley.

Gruchy, Allan. 1987. *The Reconstruction of Economics*. New York: Greenwood Press.

Hamilton, David, Glen Atkinson, William Dugger, and William Waller. 2010. *Cultural Economics and Theory: The Evolutionary Economics of David Hamilton*. London/New York: Routledge.

Heinz, Daniel. 2020. Review of *The Routledge Handbook of Heterodox Economics*. Review of Radical Political Economics 52 (2): 350–353.

Hobson, John A. 1936. *Veblen*. Fairfield: Augustus M. Kelley, 1991.

Hodgson, Geoffrey. 2004. *The Evolution of Institutional Economics: Agency, Structure and Darwinism in American Institutionalism*. London/New York: Routledge.

Holt, Richard P.F., and Daphne T. Greenwood. 2014. *A Brighter Future: Improving the Standard of Living Now and for the Next Generation*. Armonk: M.E. Sharpe.

Jo, Tae-Hee, and Zdravka Todorova. 2018. Social Provisioning Process: A Heterodox View of the Economy. In *The Routledge Handbook of Heterodox Economics*, ed. Tae-Hee Jo, Lynne Chester, and Carlo D'Ippoliti, 29–41. Oxon/New York: Routledge.

Kaldor, Nicholas. 1972. The Irrelevance of Equilibrium Economics. *The Economic Journal* 82 (4): 312–337. Reprinted in Nicholas Kaldor, *Economics Without Equilibrium*. Cardiff University: University College Cardiff Press, 1985.

Karayiannis, Anastassios, and Allan Young. 1991. Transitional Economies and the Veblenian Financial Entrepreneur. In *Economies in Transition: Conception, Status and Prospects*, ed. Allan Young, Ivan Teodorovic, and Peter Koveos, 71–86. Singapore: World Scientific Publishing Company.

Kerr, Prue. 1993. Adam Smith's Theory of Growth and Technological Change Revisited. *Contributions to Political Economy* 12: 1–27.

Keynes, John Maynard. 1936. *The General Theory of Employment, Interest and Money*. London: Macmillan.

———. 1937. The General Theory of Employment. *Quarterly Journal of Economics* 14: 109–123.

Luxemburg, Rosa. 1913. *The Accumulation of Capital*. New York: Monthly Review Press, 1951. Translated by Agnes Schwarzschild.

Mandel, Ernest. 1995. *Long Waves of Capitalist Development: A Marxist Interpretation*. London: Verso.

Mayhew, Anne. 1987. The Beginnings of Institutionalism. *Journal of Economic Issues* 11: 971–998.

Mensch, Gerhart. 1975. *Stalemate in Technology: Innovations Overcome the Depression*. Cambridge, MA: Bellinger Book Co, 1979. Translated from the German.

Mitchell, Wesley. 1941. *Business Cycles and Their Causes*. Berkeley: University of California Press.

Myrdal, Gunnar. 1930. *The Political Element in the Development of Economic Theory*. New York: Simon & Shuster, 1969.

———. 1944. *An American Dilemma: The Negro Problem and Modern Democracy*, 2 vols. New York: Pantheon Books.

———. 1968. *Asian Drama: An Inquiry into the Poverty of Nations*, 3 vols. New York: Twentieth Century Fund.

———. 1978. Institutional Economics. *Journal of Economic Issues* 12 (4): 771–783.

North, Douglas. 2005. *Understanding the Process of Economic Change*. Princeton: Princeton University Press.

Oakley, Allen. 1990. *Schumpeter's Theory of Capitalist Motion: A Critical Exposition and Reassessment*. Aldershot, UK: Edward Elgar.

O'Hara, Phillip Anthony. 1999a. *Encyclopedia of Political Economy*, 2 vols. London/New York: Routledge.

———. 1999b. Thorstein Veblen's Theory of Collective Social Wealth, Instincts and Property Relations. *History of Economic Ideas* 7 (3): 153–180. Reprinted in Rick Tilman (ed), *The Legacy of Thorstein Veblen: Volume 3*, 330–358. Cheltenham: Edward Elgar, 2003.

———. 2002. "The Contemporary Relevance of Thorstein Veblen"s Institutional-Evolutionary Political Economy. *History of Economics Review* 35 (Winter): 78–103.

———. 2006. *Growth and Development in the Global Political Economy: Social Structures of Accumulation and Modes of Regulation*. London/New York: Routledge.

———. 2007. Principles of Institutional-Evolutionary Political Economy—Converging Themes from the Schools of Heterodoxy. *Journal of Economic Issues* 41 (1): 1–42.

———. 2012a. Principles of Heterodox Political Economy Applied to Policy and Governance: Disembedded Economy, Contradictions, Circular Cumulation and Uneven Development. *Journal of Economic and Social Policy* 15 (1): 1–38.

———. 2012b. Short-, Long-, and Secular-Wave Growth in the World Political Economy: Periodicity, Amplitude, and Phases for 8 Regions, 108 Countries, 1940–2010. *International Journal of Political Economy* 41 (1): 3–46.

———. 2014. Political Economy of Systemic and Micro-Corruption Throughout the World. *Journal of Economic Issues* 48 (2): 279–307.

———. 2016. The Contemporary Relevance of Karl Marx's Heterodox Political Economy. In *Marx, Veblen, and the Foundations of Heterodox Economics*, ed. Tae-Hee Jo and Fred Lee, 50–78. New York: Routledge.

———. 2019. History of Institutional Economics. In *Pluralist Economics and Its History*, ed. Ajit Sinha and Alex M. Thomas, 171–190. London/New York: Routledge.

———. 2021. Objectives of the *Review of Evolutionary Political Economy*'s "Manifesto" and Editorial Proposals on World Problems, Complex Systems, Historico-Institutional and Corruption Issues. *Review of Evolutionary Political Economy* 2 (2): 359–387.

———. 2023. *Long Wave Institutional Dynamics and Political Economy Crises of Capitalism: Principles, Social Structures of Accumulation and Empirics*. Springer.

O'Kelley, Charles R.T. 2011. Berle and Veblen: An Intellectual Connection. *Seattle University Law Review* 34: 1317–1350.

Olgen, Faruk. 2014. How to Guide the Economy in a Socially Desirable Direction: Lessons from the 2007 Financial Turmoil. *Journal of Economic Issues* 48 (2): 575–583.

Ostrom, Elinor. 2009. *Beyond Markets and States: Polycentric Governance of Complex Economic Systems*. Nobel Prize Lecture in Economics, 8 December. https://www.nobelprize.org/nobel_prizes/economic-sciences/laureates/....

Penrose, Edith. 1959. *The Theory of the Growth of the Firm*. Oxford: Oxford University Press, 1995. (Revised Ed.).

Polanyi, Karl. 1944. *The Great Transformation*. Boston: Beacon Press, 1968.

Potts, Jason. 2000. *The New Evolutionary Microeconomics: Complexity, Competence and Adaptive Behaviour*. Cheltenham: Edward Elgar.

Power, Marilyn. 2009. Global Climate Policy and Climate Change: A Feminist Social Provisioning Approach. *Challenge* 52 (1): 47–66.

———. 2015. Social Provisioning. In *The Elgar Companion to Social Economics*, ed. John B. Davis and Wilfred Dolfsma, 331–344. Cheltenham: Edward Elgar.

Rengs, Bernhard, and Manuel Scholz-Wäckerle. 2019. Consumption & Class in Evolutionary Macroeconomics. *Journal of Evolutionary Economics* 29: 229–263.

Robinson, Joan Violet. 1933. *The Economics of Imperfect Competition*, 2nd ed., 1969. London: Macmillan.

———. 1956. *The Accumulation of Capital*, 3rd ed., 1969. London: Macmillan.

———. 1962. *Economic Philosophy*. London/New York: Routledge. Republished as a Routledge Class 2021 with a Foreword by Sheila Dow.

———. 1979. *Aspects of Development & Underdevelopment*. Cambridge: Cambridge University Press.

———. 1980. Time in Economic Theory. *Kyklos* 33 (2): 219–229.

Rutherford, Malcolm. 1994. *Institutions in Economics: The Old and the New Institutionalism*. Cambridge: Cambridge University Press.

Samudro, Bhimo Rizky. 2012. *A Political Economy Analysis of Uneven Global, Regional, National and Sub-National Performance 1950-2010*. Degree of Doctor of Philosophy (PhD) Thesis. School of Economics and Finance, Curtin University, Perth, Australia.

Schumpeter, Joseph. 1911. *The Theory of Economic Development*. Cambridge, MA: Harvard University Press, 1934.

———. 1939. *Business Cycles: A Theoretical, Historical and Statistical Analysis of the Capitalist Process*. New York: McGraw-Hill.

———. 1942. *Capitalism, Socialism and Democracy*. New York: Harper & Row.

Sherman, Howard J., and David X. Kolk. 1996. *Business Cycles and Forecasting*. New York: Harper-Collins.

Silva, Glessia, and Luiz Carlos Di Serio. 2016. The Sixth Wave of Innovation: Are We Ready? *RAI Revista de Administração e Inovação* 13: 128–134.

Sismonde de, Jean Charles Leonard Simonde. 1819. *New Principles of Political Economy*. London: Transaction Publishers, 1991. Translated by Richard Hyse. Foreword by Robert Heilbroner.

Stanfield, James Ronald. 1995. *Economics, Power and Culture: Essays in the Development of Radical Institutionalism*. New York: St Martins Press.

———. 1996. *John Kenneth Galbraith*. New York: St Martin's Press.

———. 2011. Some Social Economics Concepts for Future Research. *Forum for Social Economics* 40: 7–18.

Thierry, Penard, and Nicholas Poussing. 2010. Internet Use and Social Capital: Strength of Virtual Ties. *Journal of Economic Issues* 44 (3): 569–595.

Tilman, Rick. 1996. *The Intellectual Legacy of Thorstein Veblen: Unresolved Issues*. Westport: Greenwood Press.

Tool, Marc, and Warren J. Samuels, eds. 1989. *The Economy as a System of Power*. New Brunswick: Transaction Publishers.

Tylecote, Andrew. 1994. *The Long Wave in the World Economy: The Present Crisis in Historical Perspective*. London/ew York: Routledge.

Veblen, Thorsten Bunde. 1899. *The Theory of the Leisure Class: An Economic Study of Institutions*. London: Unwin Books, 1970.

Veblen, Thorstein Bunde. 1904. *The Theory of Business Enterprise*. Clifton: Augustus M. Kelley, 1975.

———. 1914. *The Instinct of Workmanship and the State of the Industrial Arts*. New Brunswick: Transaction Publishers, 1990.

Veblen, Thorsten Bunde. 1915. *Imperial Germany and the Industrial Revolution*. New Brunswick: Transaction Books, 1990.

———. 1917. *An Inquiry into the Nature of Peace and the Terms of Its Perpetuation*. Los Angeles: Tutis Digital Publishing, 2008.

———. 1919. *The Vested Interests and the Common Man*. New York: Kelley, 1964.

———. 1923. *Absentee Ownership and Business Enterprise in Recent Times: The Case of America*. New York: Kelley, 1964.

Waller, William. 2001. Institutional Political Economy: History. In *Encyclopedia of Political Economy*, ed. Phillip Anthony O'Hara, vol. 1, 523–528. New York/London: Routledge. Paper Edition.

Contemporary Institutional and Evolutionary Concepts and Principles

3

Abstract

This chapter scrutinizes some major contemporary concepts and principles of institutional and evolutionary political economy (IEPE) that are especially pertinent to this book. The first *core general one* is *historical specificity and evolution*, under the umbrella of which come numerous others, e.g., historical time, scientific realism, culture and institutions, phases and stages, social provisioning, blind drift, path dependence and stylized facts. The second core general one is *hegemony and uneven development*, which has under its wing the concepts of capitalist world-system, absolute and relative hegemony, hegemonic stability thesis, core/periphery/semi-periphery, production, commercial and financial dominance, and so forth. The third core one is *heterogeneous groups and agents*, and under its umbrella come others, e.g., agency and structure, gender, class, ethnicity, age, species, micro agents, and inequality of income, wealth and power. The fourth is *circular and cumulative causation* (CCC), along with interdependency, emergence, complexity, magnification, uneven development, aggregate demand, economic surplus, plus various feedbacks. The fifth is *contradiction*, which includes power and authority, the disembedded economy, vested interested v. common good, instrumental and ceremonial functions, plus a series of more specific contradictions. The sixth is *uncertainty*, with related ones such as the circuit of money capital, endogenous money, prevailing business climate, cycles-waves-crises, financial instability hypothesis, Modern Monetary Theory (MMT) and tipping points. The seventh is *innovation*, with the community's joint stock of knowledge; creative destruction; information, skills and intelligence; new products, processes, materials, etc.; and others, under its umbrella. The eighth is *policy and governance*, which can be forms of innovation, encapsulating the promotion of social provisioning, quality of life, participatory democracy, functional finance, and so on under its umbrella. Throughout we highlight the main concepts and principles used to scrutinize the specific world problems examined in the chapters that follow.

Keywords

Concepts & principles · Historical specificity · Hegemony & uneven development · Heterogeneous groups & agents · Circular & cumulative causation · Contradiction · Uncertainty · Innovation · Policy & governance

3.1 Introduction

IEPE is a research agenda in the process of creation, comprising many different scholars, traditions and schools of thought. The previous chapter has outlined its history and development. It is an attempt to promote some grounding for alternative perspectives of political economy, ones that don't start out with full information, rational agents, and maximizers of utility, profit and personal happiness. Rather, it seeks to embed capitalism, other systems and varieties, as well as core world problems, in history and institutions; hegemony and uneven developments, analyzing core groups and agents, the circular and cumulative nature of world processes, the contradictions that generate and contribute to anomalies, the role played by uncertainty in dynamics, how innovation can contribute to both resolution and anomalies, and how policy and governance can help ameliorate (or in some cases hinder solving) major world problems.

This book is more in keeping with trying to comprehend how to theorize and understand the political economies we live in, as they are imbued with systemic as well as periodic crises, corruption, pandemics, anomalous forms of climate change, terrorism, and interpersonal anomalies. It seeks to be realistic, institutionally grounded, historically contextual, and mainly concerned with dealing with the systemic anomalies that confront us in our daily lives. How do we deal with pandemics? What is corruption and how do we respond when people undertake it? How should we comprehend and tackle climate change? How can we devise robots that interact with people intelligently and assist the aged? How do policy waves evolve through time? What is terrorism and how should we respond to it? What causes and how do we moderate financial crises and recessions? How did HIV-AIDS become a crisis of social reproduction? What is love and the nurturance gap and how can we improve our intimate lives? These questions are the ones we deal with in this book. The main argument is that we do need some concepts and principles to help understand, situate and moderate contemporary world problems.

The first thing to note is that there is a considerable edifice of concepts and principles out there in the I-E political economy environment that will help with the

3.1 Introduction

tasks of developing an interdiscipline that seeks to tackle world problems and anomalies. The purpose of this chapter is to outline such an edifice. But we also want to emphasize that the conceptual edifice utilized in the chapters that follow does not explicitly utilize *all* of this community of knowledge, concepts and principles, but rather selectively chooses concepts and principles directly relevant to the tasks of understanding some crucial world problems. We do nevertheless need to provide some grounding for the broader community of knowledge, even while we also outline the core concepts and principles utilized for our specific tasks in this book.

Much of the broader community or field of concepts and principles are outlined very tersely in Table 3.1.

Note that this table with its 8 core general and 64 specific concepts and principles is a purely synthetic construction, in the sense that it is useful for the task at hand. It is not a foundational structure devoid of flexibility. Indeed, it could be redrawn in a different form, for different purposes. The *core general concepts and principles* in this study could be modified substantially for other purposes. It is to some degree also a product of my intellectual development, and subject to my interpretation of the main concepts/principles of IEPE (for one of the specific tasks of this book).

We will first provide a general outline of what these notions are all about. Throughout we illustrate which of the concepts and principles we choose for this specific study and why. We start with a general view of institutional and evolutionary political economy (IEPE), including a working definition to start the analysis. Let us define it thus:

> IEPE is a realistic, interdisciplinary study of the dynamic structure, evolution and transformation of human action within socioeconomic systems (e.g., varieties of capitalism, socialism, Islamic governance, etc), paying particular attention to the reproduction, functions, contradictions, problems and unstable dynamics of the system and its institutions of production, distribution, and exchange of material and immaterial resources set within a social, ecological and governance environment through historical time.

Central to this view of IEPE is a study that is realistic, interdisciplinary, human-centered, and systems-oriented; and that links human action with structure, reproduction with contradiction, material with immaterial, and social with political as well as ecological. IEPE seeks to develop an analysis that is realistic in the sense of "keeping close to the ground", while also having a wide vision of the world and its problems. Its practitioners tend to scrutinize the institutional culture of the system, the bounded rationality of its agents and groups, the limitations of the human mind, the asymmetric distribution of knowledge and resources, plus human's relative ignorance of the future. Essentially in this book we utilize mostly the concepts/principles listed in the headings of each section of this chapter (and Table 3.1) to analyze major world problems in the chapters that follow.

Table 3.1 8 core general & 64 specific concepts & principles of IEPE

Historical Specificity	Hegemony & Uneven Development	Heterogeneous Groups & Agents [Trust]	Circular & Cumulative Causation [CCC]	Contradiction [Power & Authority]	Uncertainty	Innovation	Policy & Governance
Historical time	Capitalist world-system	Gender	Multifactor method, circular economy	Disembedded economy	Circuit of money capital	Community's joint stock of knowledge	Social provisioning
Scientific realism	Absolute & relative hegemony	Class	Interdependence	Vested interests v. common good	Prevailing business climate	Creative destruction	Standard of living & quality of life
Culture, institutions & habits	Hegemonic stability theory	Ethnicity/nationality	Emergence	Instrumental v. ceremonial functions	Cycles, waves & crises	Information, skills & intelligence	Participatory democracy
Phases & stages of evolution	Core/periphery/semi-periphery (CPSP)	Age	Complexity	Monopoly v. competition	Booms, recessions & depressions	Clusters of innovation	Principles of community health
Social provisioning	Production, Commercial & Financial (PCF) dominance	Species	Multiplication & amplification	Capital v. labor	Endogenous money & credit	Artificial intelligence	Functional finance
Path dependence	International regimes (& accumulation regimes)	Emulation & conspicuous consumption	Effective demand	Industry v. finance	Financial instability hypothesis	Social conditions of innovation	Social, Ecological & Governance (SEG) ethic
Blind drift	Trust, cooperation & conflict	Inequality of income & wealth	Economic surplus	Capital v. ecology	Modern monetary theory	Mutation, variation, & selection	Agreements, accords & contracts
Stylized facts	Power & authority (hard-soft)	Enabling myths & interactive agency	Positive (& negative) feedback	Men v. women	Tipping points	Intellectual property	Climate change: mitigation & adaptation

Source: Some parts are adapted from O'Hara (2022)

3.2 Historical Specificity; Hegemony and Uneven Development

IEPE recognizes there may be general concepts and principles that apply in different historical circumstances, and also some that are universal in some form. What we do in this book is feature the historico-institutional, cultural, geo-political, financial, biological and ecological contexts whereby concepts and principles are applied to real world problems. Some of these concepts and principles may be capable of being contextualized in different socioeconomic systems, but we situate them contemporaneously in the systems investigated. They thus do not constitute a general theory as such, but are applicable to a fairly wide variety of historical contexts, but only in so far as they can be adapted and modified to suit these changing forms of practices and behaviors.

It is for this reason that we posit the very first core general concept and principle as *historical specificity and evolution* (see Mills 1959; Hodgson 2001). Usually historical specificity is mentioned without the *evolution,* but we want to make clear that it is not only historically contextualized but that the institutions, cultures, behaviors and other assets and resources are always in the process of *becoming* through dynamic evolution. So when we mention historical specificity by itself we usually also mean that it is in evolution and continually changing, at different rates and in different forms, through time.

The *concept of historical specificity and evolution* states that IEPE is a substantive study of the temporal movement of social economies through time, especially as they are impacted by waves, cycles, trends, social provisioning, history and evolution. The *principle of historical specificity and evolution* states that political economy should examine these dynamic processes and embed them in theory and applications, so the subjects of investigation are undergoing change, and as historical regularities present stylized facts for review. I-E political economy is thus linked to the historical and cultural fabric of the community, which have relational and open systems linkages. As Karl Polanyi (1968) noted, such concepts and principles are "substantive" in being part of and linking to institutional and temporal processes of the economy.

Even the general characteristics and principles that all systems possess (see Marx 1857–58), which can be useful for scrutinizing problems of the world and devising concepts and principles, emanate from historical analysis, from studying and comparing different systems and theories in historical time. They do not exist in a vacuum. There are also systems, problems, concepts and principles that are different in different contexts and historical time-periods, and that must be considered in an evolutionary fashion as changing through time. To examine problems, concepts and principles devoid of history and evolution makes no sense at all.

Using history to make political economy dynamic is not easy, which may be why some scholars prefer a formal, ahistorical approach, where they recognize the existence of capitalism, but prefer theory or empirics, not apparently needing to embed their work in historical junctures. History is difficult, requiring much reading and synthesis, and situating current processes in a historical framework. Starting with math and a formal approach is thus much easier for some scholars; they can justify it by "being scientific" and "rigorous". However, IEPE needs to be historical, evolutionary, institutional and cultural by its very nature; history is the context in which we live; everything is subject to metamorphosis and transformation; and devoid of realistic changes IEPE runs the risk of being transhistorical.

3.2.1 Evolution of Capitalism, Trust, Uneven Development

IEPE necessarily recognizes the existence of different economic systems and their evolution, metamorphosis and transformation through long periods. Throughout history there have been (and often continue to be) different forms of organization, such as primitive communistic systems, slavery, feudalism, plus mercantile as well as manufacturing forms of capitalism. There is of course an ongoing debate about capitalism's history and when it came into existence. But the broad facts are that society's founded on private profit, private property, complex capitalized industries and liberal institutions tend to develop majorly after mercantilism led much later to political revolutions and thereafter industrial revolutions into the late 1700s and 1800s.

The important thing to IEPE is for the problems of the world to be placed in historical context (see O'Hara 2021). There are many ways of doing this, depending on one's objective and focus. Concentrating on some of the grand masters of the past helps, as their frameworks seldom become obsolete, although it is usually necessary to update their work on the basis of recent changes. Essentially this is what we do in this book (and the others that follow). Thousands of new papers and books emerge every year in political economy, but where they don't rely on the grand masters of the past, these scholars often try and reinvent the wheel, and often insufficiently ground their studies in the community of knowledge that emerged in the past and rolls forward into the future. Ignoring the great masters is often a recipe for myopic vision; re-developing ideas and empirics that have already been well understood; and possibly insufficiently comprehending the material examined.

Some of the styles of historical specificity from the great masters that are often useful include Karl Marx's structural history of capitalism, Thorstein Veblen's phases of evolution of business, Charlotte Gilman's evolutionary approach to the gendered economy; Schumpeter's long waves and cycles of capitalist development; and J.M. Keynes's situating of capitalism as a monetary-production system (his so-called 'general theory' (GT) was probably a GT of capitalism or a certain phase of its evolution). We could also embrace Nicholas Kaldor's stylized facts; Fernand Braudel's events, conjunctures and the *long duree*; Gunnar Myrdal's circular and cumulative approach to poverty and (under)development; Angus Maddison's statistical trends; Gordon Childe's archeology; Immanuel Wallerstein's several instances of hegemony; Marilyn French's historical evolution of gender; Eric Hobsbaum's expansive history of capitalism; Charles Kindleberger's history of financial crises and crashes; and David Christian's big history framework.

The *principle of historical specificity* thus states that writers and editors should [a] embed topics in historical time; [b] scrutinize transformation through evolution and metamorphosis; and [c] utilize some of the great narratives of historical-evolutionary political economy just mentioned. Historical context is necessary for comprehending and moderating the major world problems studied in the chapters that follow.

As O'Hara (2021) points out, history and evolution have relevance for micro, meso, macro and global dimensions of capitalism and other systems. The more expansive our vision of time becomes the more we move from the micro through to the global. In the short-run we may have only prices that change, but in the long-run capital can be expanded, while in the longer-term technology changes majorly, and in the secular period all major institutions and ideologies undergo metamorphosis. Some scholars in IEPE concentrate mainly on the micro and meso, but eventually this needs to be expanded to the macro and global for it to be comprehensive, even if they think their micro-meso context is perfectly adequate for the current task in hand.

Here I show how history is important for contextualizing the problems of the world investigated in this book, and I specifically link this history with the chapters and problems studied in this book, as I peruse the recent history of capitalism up to the present. This is a very brief, terse, history of industrial capitalism introduced merely to link to our problems of the world.

Since the second concept/principle of hegemony and uneven development is an extension of historical specificity this will be intermeshed into the analysis. The concept of hegemony and uneven development draws attention to the differential power relations of the world economy where some nations and areas have predominant power while others have much less ability to produced intended effects; and the principle of hegemony and uneven development states that these power differentials should be a key part of any explanation of the problems of the world.

For many world problems the question of hegemonic dominance is likely to be relevant. The most powerful nation in the world is likely to be implicated in many of the world's problems, and so are those regions supporting them and those trying to eclipse them. For instance, the period of hegemonic dominance during the 1700s was led by the Dutch states, which gradually gave way to British hegemony during the 1800s (1815–1885), and after the inability of Germany to rise to the apogee of nations through two world wars, this gave rise to US hegemony (1940s–1970s), after which absolute dominance declined and gradually China has been attempting to become the hegemon, with quite a degree of success, but still a way to go before it likely becomes supreme. *All of the world's problems studied in this book link directly or indirectly to hegemony, power and uneven development in the global political economy.*

A related form of historical specificity that is likely to be useful in investigating world problems, and certainly in our case, is to scrutinize certain phases of evolution of capitalism. This requires a broad understanding of the changing dynamics of capitalism, its areas and regions, since at least the revolutions of the late 1700s and the industrial revolutions of the 1800s. Immediately below, examples are provided of historical linkages to the problems of the world, in relation to the chapters that follow.

The first major phase of industrial capitalism emerged after the French and American revolutions, which led to rapid industrialization in the UK, and later other advanced nations, from the early 1800s through to later in the century. The European revolutions of the 1830s and 1848 are usually thought of as being involved in a declining era of performance (Hobsbawm 1962: 54), which lasted in many nations until the gold discoveries of the 1850s in Australia and California, and the subsequent development of largescale industry, which propelled relatively good performance until the emergence of what has been called the "Great Depression" of prices and profits during 1876–1896 (Rostow 1940), when there was overproduction relative to demand throughout many nations, and a series of financial crises.

As Veblen showed (1904, 1923), in response to this overproduction and low profits several strategies were implemented to increase profit and growth by especially the advanced nations. During the 1880s to the 1910s, imperialism (including the "scramble for Africa") helped to provide cheap labor, raw materials and a market for commodities; new accounting techniques of markup pricing, advertising, and the merger movement around 1900 helped generate oligopoly profits for many; and the expansion of finance capital, banking finance and credit enabled some expansion of demand and profitability. The recovery during 1897 to 1914 was not a complete success as many crises still ravaged major economies, and it was uneven as Britain and France did not advance as much as Germany and the US.

As van Duijn (1983) shows, what upswing did exist was cut short by the First World War; while the so-called Spanish flu played an associative role (see Chap. 4 on the coronacrisis). Meanwhile the roaring 1920s, experienced by some, was only a short-term lift that generated speculative bubbles and the resulting crash of Wall Street, plus another Great Depression for the whole world during the 1930s. After this the world experienced the devastation (for most) of the Second World War, which (indirectly) benefitted the US and USSR, as afterwards these two nations fought out a cold war during the postwar boom, which saw the greatest period of growth and accumulation in the whole of world history. The US and the USSR developed institutions which led to their effective leadership in the world economy, including 25–30 years of relative prosperity.

Of the two camps, the US led a series of nations and regions into the most successful regime of accumulation or social structure of accumulation in the history of capitalism, through a series of institutions and technological innovations, including Fordism, the Keynesian welfare-state, and the capital-labor consensus, that were to remain successful from the 1940s/1950s until the 1970s. Crucial events of the 1970s indicated declining absolute power of US hegemony, as they lost the Vietnam War, their pegged exchange rate deteriorated and performance dropped majorly for global capitalism. Aliber and Kindleberger (2015) scrutinize what they call the greatest period of financial instability and financial crises in the history of the world economy, during the 1980s to the 2010s (see Chap. 9, below on financial instability and crises).

3.2 Historical Specificity; Hegemony and Uneven Development

Meanwhile most of the Soviet-style systems collapsed during the long wave downswings of the 1970s–1980s, leading to major depression and thereafter a series of autocratic ultra-nationalistic regimes took their place, especially in Russia, Belarus and Hungary. The periphery also took a hit during this period through major debt-crises, especially in Latin America, caused partly by monetarist policies in the US; along with a series of corrupt regimes with little political capital in several nations of Africa, as well as AIDS, which inhibited their standard of living.

Many of the world problems that emerged during the 1970s–1980s through to the present breakdown are due to system-crises and institutional sclerosis that emerged in the West, the East, Africa, and Latin Nations. Neoliberalism took hold of governance institutions on a global scale, especially during the 1980s–2010s, including the role played by the IMF, World Bank and numerous national administrations, leading to policies of reducing the power of labor vis-à-vis capital, deregulating financial and foreign exchange markets, with a renewed dominance of brute individualism and business principles which did everything to exacerbate the nature and depth of periodic crises. As most analysts now recognize, the GFC (2008–2009) and the resultant Eurodebt crises (2010–2014ff), the greatest crises *at that point* since the Great Depression and World War Two, majorly implicated neoliberalism in these series of crises and speculative bubble crashes. Chapter 4, below, on the coronacrisis situates this crisis as well as the GFC in the context of problems of neoliberalism and it being out of fashion and being superimposed by more activist governance. (See O'Hara 2023 for details of the GFC).

There has also been considerable conflict and instability in the world political economy, as there has been during all recent epochs, as a declining hegemon (US) engages in numerous public altercations with a potentially new hegemon (China), involving trade sanctions, new Islands of military-occupational power in the waters around East Asia (for China); virtual takeover of Hong Kong despite the promise of 'one nation but two systems'; the continual threat of invasion of Taiwan; forced labor and concentration camps for certain Islamic minorities in North-West China; and a desire of the US to reverse their flagging global power by 'Making America Great Again', leading to higher tariffs on Chinese goods and a ban on the use of technology that could be used by Chinese intelligence. In this context, we are seeing Russia under threat from an expanding NATO alliance, leading to the war in the Ukraine, and its potential spread further west and even globally. (See O'Hara 2023).

It was in this unstable global environment during the 1980s–2020s that some of the most intense problems studied in this current book emerged throughout the world. Serious environmental problems, which had been in the process of building up since especially the industrial revolution, but which since the 1970s has been escalating majorly, have now come to the point of systemic crisis, yet even with global accord in theory GHG emissions and their stocks continue to rise (see Chap. 5 on climate change).

The terrorist attacks of 9/11 were generated in the aftermath of the war against the Soviets in Afghanistan, and the resulting power vacuum that led to the rise of various *jihadi* groups such as *Al Qaeda*, the Taliban, later Islamic State and several regional affiliates and fellow-travelers (see Chap. 10, below). HIV-AIDS emerged mainly in sub-Saharan Africa (and to some degree in other nations, and more recently especially in Eurasia), where several governance anomalies associated with corruption, insufficiently developed health-care systems due partly to neoliberalism, and inadequate global assistance, led to more global pandemic or epidemic deaths (36 million) than at any time since the so-called Spanish flu of 1919–1922 (see Chap. 11, below on HIV-AIDS).

Since the late 1970s, China has been leading the field of state capitalist development through market reforms, the movement of labor to urban areas and 'partnerships' with transnational corporations (O'Hara 2023); but more recently (since 2021) it has been seeking a double movement readjustment through greater self-reliance, reduced inequality and more business regulation. Meanwhile, Central and Eastern European former 'state capitalist' (i.e., "communist') nations have long 'recovered' from the major disruptions of the 1990s, and now constitute several different styles of governance, ranging from the 'flagrantly autocratic' systems of Russia and Belarus to the 'democratic authoritarian' regimes of Hungary and Poland, to the more reformist styles of the Czech Republic, Slovakia and the Ukraine.

Today, most nations have varying degrees of capitalist development, and there are different varieties of capitalism. There have been the "neoliberal democracies" such as the United States, the UK and Australia; the "social democracies" in Scandinavia; the "corporatist" varieties such as Japan, Germany and Italy; the "state capitalist" dictatorships of China, Russia and Vietnam; and the "emerging" state-capitalist nations of Asia such as Indonesia and Thailand. The experience of the GFC, Eurodebt crisis and Coronacrisis (see Chap. 4) have led to the relative demise of neoliberal doctrine, in the light of successful functional finance, discretionary fiscal and monetary policies, massive handouts to households and business, plus low interest rates (see Chap. 8 on policy and Chap. 9 on money).

A crucial factor exacerbating uneven development at global, regional and local levels is differential levels of social capital; specifically greater inequality and declining levels of trust (O'Hara 2004a). Development scholars and sociologists have been scrutinizing the concept of social capital especially since the 1970s and 1980s. *General s*ocial capital typically includes those durable structures of trust and sociality that help establish networks of relationships and associations within the prevailing culture and which provide considerable public good functions of communication, information, and coordination. Promoting trust within specific groups of classes of people, such as among the upper classes, or within the middle class, spreading benefits within these particular groups, led Pierre Bourdieu (1997) to argue that the asymmetric distribution of 'sectional' social capital is the main factor propelling class distinctions (Christoforou and Davis 2016).

This led Paul Streeton (2002) to argue long ago that social capital can simultaneously be both a stock and a flow in the sense that using it can reproduce it, in a circular and cumulative process. In like measure, the very process of people not trusting each other has the same circular and cumulative impact, but in a downward direction. But, says Streeton, there is also "asocial capital", in the sense that organized groups can use their own very specific internal social capital to destroy more general linkages of trust and sociality in the community. Globalisation (and neoliberalism) has stimulated mainly corporate and market linkages, while reducing reciprocity, redistribution and householding. The result has been growing international inequality and uneven development (Streeton 2002: 18); a theme that now (2022) is a mainstream concern in policy circles and political economy (Piketti 2014, Piketti et al. 2019). Declining *general social trust* increases costs and cases of legality, courts, jails and insurance; lowers the quality and level of information as well as public goods while it enhances individualism; and expands the asymmetry of information between groups, at micro, meso, macro and global levels (Uslaner 2018).

It was found that corruption is rife not simply in Africa, Latin America, Asia and small offshore resorts, which official data reflects, but also in the advanced capitalist economies. Much of this reflects a lack of general social capital, since corruptors often look to family, friends and associates at the expense of strangers (see Chap. 6, below). The development of what Francis Fukuyama (2002) calls a 'two-tiered moral structure" between insiders and outsiders is a common response where people are perceived to be untrustworthy.

This uneven (but persistent) decline in trust has continued through recent decades, with one writer calling it the "Global Trust Crisis" (Ghosh 2020), which is indicative of broader anomalies associated with neoliberalism and globalization, which have lost much legitimacy, and which have a major impact on politics, especially in people's lack of trust in major social institutions such as governments, corporations, the police and the media. The double movement of, on the one hand, more globalization and free markets, in the light of the GFC, deindustrialization and the coronavirus pandemic, led to the rise, on the other hand, of many variously nationalist, communitarian and left-wing governments that want to restore the social fabric with more 'just', 'equitable' and 'fair' policies.

The concept and nature of trust and its insufficiency are crucial to all of the concepts and principles, as well as world problems, examined in this book. It does appear more obviously relevant to Chap. 12, below, on the nurturance gap hypothesis (see also O'Hara 2006, ch 3; 2014). But it certainly raises its head, if indirectly, in Chap. 4 on the coronacrisis as trust in public institutions becomes a major issue; climate change (Chap. 5) involves issues of trust in short-term governments diligently dealing with mitigation and adaptation; Chapter 6 investigates trust issues relating to mega-corruption by public figures and corporate executives engaged in tax evasion; while Chap. 7 on AI and robotics discusses how we can instill trust in/for intelligent robots; Chapter 9 on money and finance points to issues of trust in the financial system; and Chap. 10 on 9/11 and terrorism links to trust vis-a-vis gathering in public places, traveling overseas and even nationally, and electing governments that protect us from flying 'bombs'.

3.3 Heterogeneous Groups and Agents

IEPE has been resolving an old and complex problem that has proved to be a thorny issue throughout its history. This is the problem of individuals and structures. Traditionally, many political economists have ignored individuals in favor of structures such as economic systems, institutions, cultures, ideologies, classes, genders, 'races', and so forth. It is now recognized how critical it is to link agency with structure. Individuals and structures must both be integrated into the analysis. Figure 3.1 illustrates some of the factors that are important in this new agency-structure analysis[1].

The *concept of agency and structure* states that individuals interact with each other and with resources and infrastructures through various networks, social circles, and groups over time in generating socioeconomic processes. Individuals have certain preferences, resources, sentiments and relationships that impact their quality of life and socioeconomic performance. Relational structures and groups also impact on individuals, be they families, classes, gender, ethnicities, institutions, networks and the gene pool. The principle of agency and structure states that IEPE should situate individuals within groups, positing interdependency between agency and structure, creating the 'social individual'. Individual preferences, resources, sentiments and trust are constantly changing, reproducing and modifying through time (Rodrigues 2014). It is also important to differentiate between needs and wants

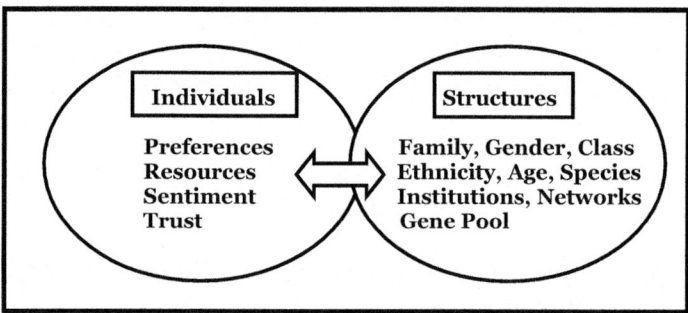

Fig. 3.1 Agency and structure

---

[1] On the relationship between agency and structure, see Hodgson (2004) and Davis (2003). On the issue of Table 3.1 and the IEPE community of concepts and principles, different sets of concepts can be utilized by different groupings of scholars, and agency and structure can be linked into these groupings in different ways. For instance, one recent reference, Tae-Hee Jo et al (2018), attempts to survey the nature of contemporary political economy (heterodox) themes, and a close textual analysis, covering numerous chapters, reveals tentatively, a list of core general concepts from this work. This includes, in possible order of priority: social provisioning, social surplus, effective demand, interactive agency, accumulation regime, circular economy, embeddedness, going concern, power, systemism, and possibly others. It was necessary to scrutinize every chapter of this work to gauge the most important likely concepts in this edited book.

3.3 Heterogeneous Groups and Agents

and to situate these within the context of various subprinciples such as bounded rationality, satiability, growth and interdependence (Lavoie 2004).

Interdependency between individuals, families, online groups, friendships, coworkers, societies, associations, political parties, business groups and so on, is part of *horizontal* emergence-complexity interaction between micro-meso elements of the social economy (see Elder-Vass 2010, 2016). As we see below in the section on CCC and emergence-complexity, IEPE needs to go further by extending micro-meso circles and circuits vertically to the macro and global dimensions of reality, which is where the magnified and accelerating processes come majorly into play.

Crucial to these circles-circuits is the *concept of heterogeneous groups and agents:* There are multiple roles played by agents in the socioeconomic circuits/circles, due to the asymmetric distribution of power, resources, interests and skills. Individual preferences and resources are affected by their institutional, cultural and biological environment, including genetics, family, occupation, income, ethnicity, gender, age, species and class positions. These multiple roles are also affected by corporate, media and party-political institutions. Individuals interact with and are affected by other individuals, friends, family, groups, organizations, systems of belief and valuation.

From this concept we can develop the *principle of heterogeneous groups and agents*, namely, that political economy is required to operationalize this concept, to comprehend its major dynamics and especially the anomalies that emerge through crises, instabilities, and conflicts. This involves, for instance, studying the intergenerational transfer of resources and preferences from parents, family and friends, which is an important determinant of the life possibilities open to people. Class tends to follow family background, as the quality of parental guidance, education, and occupation are fundamentally influenced by the resources on offer to members of families, relations and friendships. The ability of parents to transfer resources to their offspring is a critical determinant of the material and cultural inequities they bring to the future (Bowles et al. 2005). Typically, also, class relations inhibit the realization of potential for a large percent of the population as they have limitations on formal education, travel, trust and networks (Hertel and Groh-Samberg 2019). On the other hand, being a member of the upper classes provides access to a culture of privileges, including status, comfort, and substantial resources throughout life. The existence of multiple class positions makes the analysis more complex and realistic (Resnick and Wolff 2005; Wolff 2019), since heterogeneous roles pervade individual social behavior.

On the interface of classes is the concept of occupation; the role an agent plays in an organization or institution. There exist industrial capitalists, financial capitalists, bankers and entrepreneurs, merchants and traders, accountants and clerks, teachers and professors, managers and CEOs, lawyers and judges, police and social workers, lenders and borrowers, buyers and sellers, lumpens and unemployed, household workers and community carers, electricians and mechanics, computer operators and code-makers, nurses and doctors, laborers and carpenters, and so on. These roles are important to the heterogeneous nature of agents and groups. Many people play multiple roles in shops, corporations, departments, educational institutions, and other organizations. Some are retail managers by day and night club managers by night; others are nurses by day and household workers by night; while others are informal workers in the morning and teachers in the afternoon. Multiple roles are common as part-time (under-)employment becomes widespread.

Ethnicity is also important. Being brought up in a minority group tends to inhibit the ability of people to realize their potential in areas such as occupation, income and networks. Minorities tend to have a higher than average incidence of crime and incarceration, lower educational opportunities, plus smaller income and wealth. In general, their life chances are inhibited due to factors beyond their control. For instance, being part of an indigenous population is a handicap since usually not only one's parents, but also other relatives, friends and neighbors have a reduced ability to participate actively in the economic, political and social affairs of the region, nation and world. When a neighbor or relative becomes more successful they usually move to a "better" suburb or area, thus reducing the extent to which they can function as a role model for others. The negative effect of membership of lower socioeconomic ethnic groups on health and well-being is well known and documented extensively in the literature (e.g., Drentea and Goldner 2006; Abuelgasim et al. 2020).

Gender also impinges on distribution of resources (Peterson and Lewis 1999). Historically, the gender one is born into influences the power one has in socioeconomic life. Throughout much of history – still in many nations – women have looked after the family in the private sphere while men worked in the public sphere of life. This asymmetric distribution of social power usually gave men the capability of determining the nature of the institutions of production, distribution and exchange as well as the shape of the spheres of politics and the world economy. Women may have had some power in the household, but little control over social resources, economic and political power and the shape of the world. In the West, especially, women have been questioning this patriarchal dominance, and some redistribution of income, wealth and power has occurred over the past 60 years. But substantial power differentials still exist, even in the Western world, that continue to impinge on gender access to resources and quality of life (Figart and Warnecke 2013). There are so-called gendered occupations that tend to stratify workers, with women tending to occupy cleaning, teaching, medical and secretarial areas while men occupy manual, building, engineering, managerial and CEO areas. Also, in heterosexual relationships, women tend to perform a double day, where they work for wages and then do most of the household labor, which negatively affects their level of well-being (MacDonald et al. 2005; Lahiri-Dutt and Sil 2014). Married women regularly take time off to care for children while men continue to be remunerated, and when women try to return to work they find employers consider their human capital to have declined since they last earned a wage.

Gender also impinges on sexual preferences and gender identity, which have a greater impact on the social economy than previous decades. This is because, historically quite suddenly, homosexuals have gained legal rights in numerous nations of the world, while transgenders are becoming more visible and also exerting their rights to a greater extent in many nations. This trend for human rights improvements for LGBT persons is likely to expand as more nations and groups successfully advance the civil rights of these and other groups and individuals in the decades to come; with especially more progress being necessary in numerous nations of north and east Africa plus the Middle East (HRW 2022).

Age is another difference involving multiple roles, functions and contradictions between people and other species. People of different ages tend to have varying levels of wealth, health, and happiness, also depending on class, ethnicity and species. Upper and middle class older people tend to have more wealth relative to young cohorts and hence they tend to save more. The saving of older people contributes to a high global savings glut. Lower-working-class and lumpen older people, on the other hand, tend to have very little wealth or saving and often depend upon government pensions or otherwise children or relatives. Elderly people also tend to be inflicted by more underlying health conditions relative to younger groups, especially in the case of the coronavirus, and hence tend to die at higher rates. Globally populations are aging rapidly, even in peripheral nations, potentially leading to 'secular stagnation' of high savers and fewer workers.

Species is another important 'difference' impacting on the political economy. Being the dominant species on Earth, human beings are able to set the tone for (hegemonic) debate, providing the myths and legends that legitimize their power in the ecological environment. But the fact is that planet Earth has been under the sway of a species that has colonized most habitats and destroyed a large proportion of the species. Biodiversity has been declining, especially over the past 200 years when human beings created a system of industrial and commercial power that severely diminished the ability of other species to maintain their stock of genes in the pool of characteristics that determines their ability to reproduce themselves through long historical time. This is a contradictory process, made much worse, especially since the 1970s, as destroying other species and habitats negatively impacts the standard of living and quality of life of humans beings themselves. This is especially pronounced through pollution, global warming, and declining interaction with other species. (See Brennan 2004; FAO 2019). But human beings do not have total dominance as various microorganisms are able to inflict hundreds of millions of deaths upon them through various pandemics, including the current coronacrisis (see Chap. 4, below).

Increasingly one has to consider the role played by machines, be they robots that mechanistically assemble cars, or humanistic robots that can communicate with humans (see Chap. 7, below), or other machines such as computers and smart phones that are used to link to people, groups, places and markets online through the internet. We have the choice between machine or human, be it at supermarkets vis-à-vis checkout operators or self-service checkouts; playing golf at the local course with a friend or online; going to a boutique to buy fashion goods in person or buying online; studying at university in classes or using online lecture notes; and so on.

The institutional and cultural fabric underlying class, occupation, ethnicity, gender, age, species and (intelligent?) machines, undergrid inequality of income, wealth and power in the global, regional, national and local political economies (uneven development). We need to scrutinize micro-meso occupations undertaken by classes, ethnicities, genders, ages as well as robots, computers, machines, the Internet, drones, autonomous vehicles, flying taxis, etc. that assist humans in their work or replace them entirely; and place all this in a national-regional-global context.

The principle of heterogeneous groups and agents is used extensively in this book to investigate major problems of the world. It is used in Chap. 4 to analyze those groups most subject to infection and death during the coronavirus pandemic; the variants of viruses infecting humans; and also those groups using innovation to create effective vaccines and other measures to contain outbreaks. It is especially useful for Chap. 6 on corruption, as we study the various groups involved in promoting the vested interests against the common good by engaging in fraud, embezzlement, state capture, bribery, extortion and nepotism. It is wittingly or unwittingly utilized in studying the other major world problems, such as Chap. 7 to examine the types of humanoid robots and the various schools of AI; Chapter 9 to scrutinize the groups and agents of political economists engaged in comprehending financial crises and instabilities; Chapter 11 to understand the groups that tend to be infected with HIV plus the variants of microbes that infect them; and Chap. 12 on the groups of people adopting certain styles of love involved in the nurturance gap.

3.4 Circular and Cumulative Causation (CCC)

IEPE has been conceptualizing the reproduction processes involved in the production, distribution and exchange of the economic surplus, and the accompanying ravaging of the natural environment and weather systems. It has been detailing the 'circular *stock-flow* of socioeconomic activity' through time and within the institutions. The *concept of the circular economy,* see Fig. 3.2, involves movement,

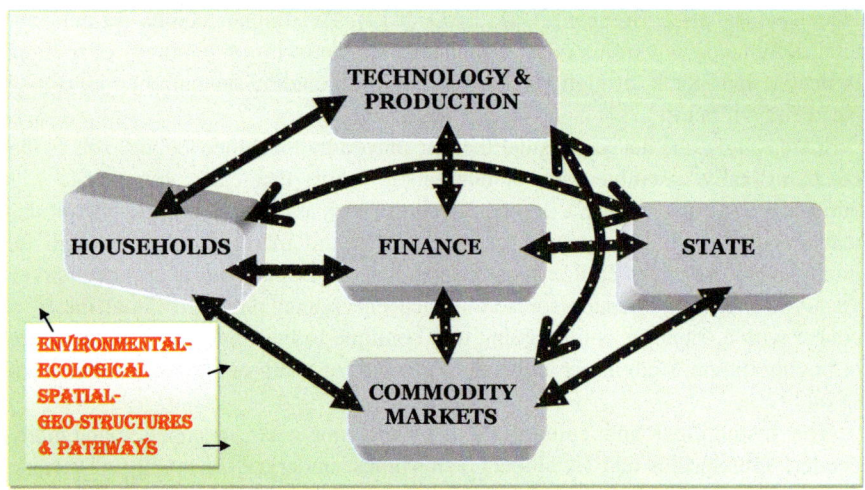

Fig. 3.2 Stocks-circuits of socioeconomic-ecological relations

3.4 Circular and Cumulative Causation (CCC)

dynamics, habits, institutions in motion: the principle that IEPE must comprehend such processes as ongoing relational interactions between people; plus other species, the environment and resources (ecological-spatial-geo-structures and circuits).

The concept of the "institutional-ecological circular stock/flow diagram' (for short) illustrates that there are structural relations organized within institutions, especially households, technology and production systems, financial systems, state and market systems, where socioeconomic activities are arranged through various innovations, habits, rules and roles. A core thing about this institutional structural circuit is the activities undertaken within the institutional systems, but another equally important aspect is the interaction between the systems, including the flow of people, other species, goods, ecological resources, and money between them. The simple *circular flow diagram of economics* tends to under-rate the activities undertaken *within* the systems of institutions-ecology. Figure 3.2 hence emphasizes the activities and relationships within the systems as well as the flows. The arrows represent the flow of goods, people and money/credit and information between the systems, including the crucial role of transportation, ecology, communication, data, information and material resources. The arrows do also illustrate that the sets of systems are not unique in that, essentially they are interdependent: for instance, states also involve technology and production systems, as well as financial systems, households, markets and ecological systems. The same institutional interdependency also applies to the other systems, and also the relationships between global, regional, national and subnational arenas.

From the interactions within and between the various elements of the institutional circuits of socioeconomic relations (an institutional circuit stock/flow diagram) accrues the economic surplus. The *concept of the economic surplus* includes actual, planned and potential versions; but often the actual is defined as the difference between the (necessary) costs of production and the total revenue received. At the macro level it represents conceptually the difference between national income and necessary costs of production (e.g., wages, depreciation, and material inputs). There is a tendency for the economic surplus to increase through history due to advances in technology, skills and aggregate demand. The factors responsible for the generation of the economic surplus (see Chap. 9 for more detail) are potentially multifarious, linking various system-factors, coordinating processes, demand-supply variables, trust, culture, ecological, as well as individual contributions. But there is also a role for exploitation as the vested interests and dominant classes exploit the public goods, organizations, and working classes for their own benefit at the expense of the majority. (O'Hara 2015).

Multi-causal models of symbiotic interaction and feedback are critical to IEPE. Especially important are models involving the *principle of circular and cumulative causation* (CCC) underlying growth, accumulation, and development (Krugman 1991, O'Hara 2008, Berger 2009, Schwardt 2014). Numerous CCC varieties exist, one linking to Kaldorian notions of growth and accumulation; and the other involving Myrdalian analysis of social inequality and institutional change. They both situate the economy within a system of interdependencies between variables and instability of motion.

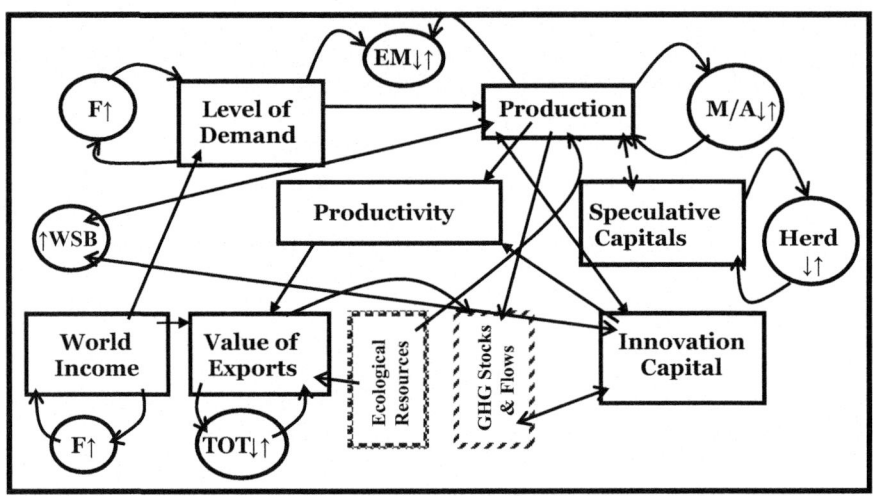

Fig. 3.3 Kaldorian circular & cumulative causation: feedback

For instance, the Kaldor (1966, 1970, 1972) system of CCC can be used to explain the workings of the regime of accumulation in regulation analysis. Consider Fig. 3.3, which examines the workings of aggregate demand, productivity and innovation in mutual interdependency.

Usually the Kaldorian CCC model is used to explain accelerating accumulation and/or decumulation (Pini 1995; O'Hara 1999a). This mode of explanation concentrates on positive feedback among the variables, shown in *black rectangles*, and also ecological linkages (resources and GHG stocks-flows). Aggregate demand, ecological inputs and human labor are the generators that stir the system into motion. Investment, consumption, government spending and net exports represent the monetary (and durable capital) stimuli propelling productivity and innovation. But before investment can be stimulated, minimum levels of stability, certainty, and ecological capacity are required, whereby optimistic expectations of the business climate reproduce high levels of prospective yield into the foreseeable future. In a climate where uncertainty is moderated through institutions, organizations and routines, investment can be generated to propel productivity and innovation.

Productivity expands through economies of scale/scope, learning by doing and ensuring that labor and ecological capitals are extracted through systems of supervision and control, or alternatively through efficiency wages, a positive work environment, and environmental controls. Productivity is also promoted through innovation, which is endogenous to the system as the availability of finance enables entrepreneurs to activate new processes, products, markets, forms of competition and environmental resources. Higher productivity and quality products then stimulate net exports in the world market, leading again to higher levels of demand, investment, growth, and (usually) GHG stocks and flows in a circular and cumulative fashion. 'Downswings' also happen as these CCC processes operate in reverse.

The standard Nicholas Kaldor CCC model, as above, is a positive feedback, self-reinforcing system, which may help explain continuing growth or continuing

3.4 Circular and Cumulative Causation (CCC)

decline, depending on the state of uncertainty, investment and aggregate demand. To transform circular and cumulative dynamics into more (amplified) cyclical dynamics requires the introduction of additional system dynamics feedback processes, through, for instance, business, government (Sterman 2000) or, for instance, cascading tipping points of climate change. This is done by the introduction of feedback loops concerning physical growth, information, decision-rules, and often non-linear climate impacts into the behavioral-institutional relationships and processess (Radzicki and Sterman 1994; Harvey 2021). The introduction of circular loops (circles) in Fig. 3.3 provides a simple example of what happens when such human intervention is introduced, in the form of government, business, and environmental decisions.

Five realistic system dynamics feedback processes are introduced into Fig. 3.3 that are important to IEPE, thus modifying the behavioral relationships underlying the CCC process. First, a system of automatic fiscal stabilizers (F$\uparrow\downarrow$) is introduced in the form of government unemployment and social security payments that are specifically linked to the state of aggregate demand and uncertainty. Secondly, endogenous money and credit (EM$\uparrow\downarrow$) of a structural and accommodative nature are introduced, which provide finance for production, speculative capitals, and innovation. Thirdly, a multiplier and accelerator system is introduced ("M,A$\uparrow\downarrow$"), which introduces the behavior of consumer demand, investment, and stock-inventory adjustment. Fourthly, we introduce a variable degree of herding behavior in the stock market ("Herd$\downarrow\uparrow$"), which is an increasing positive or negative non-linear function of the rate of growth of aggregate demand. Fifthly, a terms of trade effect (TOT$\downarrow\uparrow$) is introduced in the form of the dynamics associated with the Prebisch-Singer hypothesis, impacting on exports. And lastly, an extensive system of investment/disinvestment into GHG-reducing wind turbines, solar panels and batteries (WSB$\uparrow\downarrow$) are introduced into the system of arrangements.

Taken together, these six feedback systems transform cumulative upswing and downswing motion into cycles-waves of prosperity and recession, along with global sea and land temperature changes to mitigate/expand aspects of climate change. System dynamics is a method of illustrating the workings of complex institutional-evolutionary processes in the political economy.

The sub-schools of IEPE, however, do not just specialize in the CCC of growth, (dis)accumulation, cycles/waves, and climate change, somewhat narrowly viewed, but also the social and institutional foundations of development and standard of living. Gunnar Myrdal's (1939, 1944, 1957, 1968, 1978, Nobel Laureate) studies of African Americans, Asian development and institutional economics isolate critical factors of social and cultural change. Myrdal called his institutional method "holistic". Numerous scholars denigrate 'holism' (e.g., Bunge 2000),[2] but not the style enunciated by Myrdal.

---

[2] Mario Bunge (2000), for instance, differentiates holism from systemism and individualism. While he denigrates holism and individualism, he posits systemism as the best form of scientific realism. But his view of holism is not how the scholars mentioned see it. His 'systemism' is our 'holism'.

Holism has a *broad vision* and seeks to be *comprehensive* in its focus. It employs a *big picture* and hones in on specifics without losing sight of the big picture. Holism accords with emergent forms of complexity where [1] 'the whole is greater than the sum of the parts' (due to interdependencies between parts), and [2] 'changes can be so great as to constitute a qualitative, novel, form of phase of evolution' or characteristic (e.g., innovation) of a system. It also posits [3] 'problems are affected majorly by the contradictions that impact the system'. Historically, many other IEPPs have been holists, such as Gruchy (1947), Kapp (1968), Wilber and Harrison (1978), O'Hara (1993), and Baş (2022).

Figure 3.4, illustrates how Myrdal's CCC can be very tersely viewed:

First we examine the purely cumulative dynamics of (social) CCC, then introduce system dynamics feedback loops to enhance the degree of realism of the process. We start, then, by viewing only the linkages between the (round-edged) *rectangles*. Here the general process of acquisition of capabilities is a dominant factor linking interacting factors that influence development. Capabilities are the myriad of abilities that enhance social, economic and political freedom (Sen 1999; Kuhumba 2018): proper nutrition, shelter, clothing, education and emotional development; plus the facilitation of institutions that enhance movement, communication and networks for pursuing life in a complex world. Lack of capabilities lead generally to low income, low or poor employment, deteriorating morale and confidence, and in many cases discrimination, which in turn adversely affect capability levels. Gender, ethnic, class and age discrimination impact negatively on income, morale, employment and skill formation, which in turn generates more discrimination. Low relative and absolute income contribute to capabilities deprivation, shortage of skills, and ultimately more unemployment and underemployment, which negatively affects income. And so on, ad infinitum in a CCC fashion.

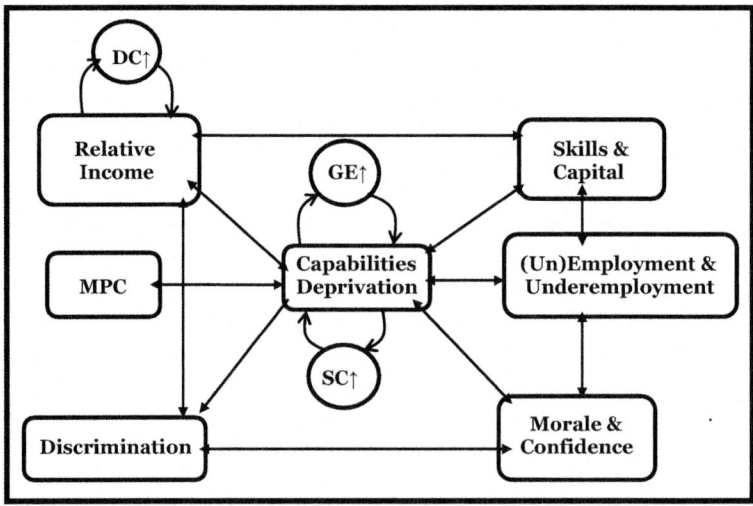

Fig. 3.4 Myrdalian circular & cumulative causation: feedback

3.4 Circular and Cumulative Causation (CCC)

In a system of status emulation, low relative income necessitates a high marginal propensity to consume, since in order to emulate the rich those lower in the pecking order need to spend a greater proportion of their income (Veblen 1899; Duesenberry 1958; Brown et al. 2015). Conspicuous consumption may help these demonstration effects impact on people's social habits and practices. Indeed, *habits* – personal and social - are critical to the whole circuit of reproduction, since they enable skill formation, reduce transaction costs, and provide a form of regularity for moderating levels of uncertainty and instability (Waller 1988). Habits are better if they have an element of potential flexibility, being somewhat adaptable to different situations. The critical habits are those relating to the household, social relations, the work environment, education, waste disposal and thought.

Again, system dynamics stock-flow feedback processes can help add complexity and realism to the social-institutional aspects of CCC. As it currently operates, the social CCC model leads to *greater* relative deprivation of capabilities and capacities. Now we introduce three circular loops, including two "negative feedback" and one "positive feedback" effects, into the model. The first negative feedback factor is a government program of spending on greater educational-ecological knowledge for the lowest classes (GE↑). The second is a government attempt to audit and enhance the social capital of trust and networks of association among the lowest classes; including a system of microfinance to aid fledging business networks among the poorest of the poor, especially for leading-edge green projects (SC↑). The third, positive feedback, variable is an amplification factor associated with conspicuous consumption and general demonstration effects (DC↑), which can *potentially* enhance relative income, well-being and happiness in the consumer society.

The long-term introduction of two negative feedback policy measures can reduce the decumulative capability tendency among the poorest of the poor. The success of the education and social capital policies may enhance the capabilities and hence the skills, capital, ecological knowledge, employment, morale and confidence levels of the very poor. They may succeed in promoting capabilities of the poor, and thus reducing the relative (and absolute) deterioration in the conditions of the very poor. However, the positive feedback associated with conspicuous consumption can have a negative impact by promoting competition and reducing happiness through waste involving invidious distinctions, as people spend more time enhancing their *perceived* relative position in the community, and less time undertaking specifically instrumental activities enhancing their quality of life.

3.4.1 CCC, Emergence and Complexity

CCC, emergence and complexity all involve multi-variant, positive (and negative) feedback, magnified, non-equilibrium, micro-meso-macro-global, non-linear and path dependent dimensions, processes and impacts. They are in the same ontological spectrum of understanding real-world problems. It is thus befitting of IE political economy to merge CC with emergence-complexity as a means of promoting more integration of IEPE themes and concepts. A large-scale project along these lines will need to be generated to accomplish that objective, or at least starting to explore the issue (see O'Hara 2021).

In this context, complexity theory fuses some critical elements, such as evolutionary propositions, endogenous processes, self-reproduction, emergent properties and 'holistic' relationships. These aspects are ideally suited to IEPE since it posits no general equilibrium, a constant flux of variables interacting through historical time, and a transformational reality of change and uncertainty. Of particular interest is the tendency for positive feedback changes in values to have a significant and non-linear impact on the system as a whole, which brings to mind, as mentioned, the CCC analyses of Myrdal and Kaldor; plus K.W. Kapp. And because complexity emphasizes the interdependencies between phenomena, contradictions and paradoxes tend to emerge through institutions and technologies.[3] The system endogenously evolves due to the inherent life of the complex processes involved in real world dynamics. Irreversibility is patterned into the dynamics because the process of change impacts on institutions, technologies and ecologies subject to path dependence (Arthur 1996) and metamorphosis. (See Elsner 2017; Arthur 2021; Colander 2000; Ofori-Dankwa and Julian 2001; Barnes et al. 2004).

The emergence-complexity framework developed by Mario Bunge (1919–2020) is more visionary, contextual and world-problems orientated than some other approaches (Bunge 1974–1989). This is because, firstly, he is a first rate scholar of emergence-complexity, having received numerous awards and honorary doctorates, one of which was the (2014) *Ludwig von Bertalanffy Award in Complexity Thinking*. Secondly, he postulates that the main purpose of scientific realism, his emergent-complexity approach, is to understand and thereby also to *contribute to solving core world problems*. He discounts scholarly discourse that seeks to be uninvolved and aloof from the problems of the world. Thirdly, he recognizes the importance of historical analysis and the need to situate science in history. Hence the notion of *temporal emergence*, that there are different levels involved in history, such as Fernand Braudel's (1950) three tiers of 'events, conjunctures and the long duration'. Most complexity analysts ignore temporal emergence altogether, or introduce it in the most cursory form.

Numerous IEPEs utilize a *critical realistic* view of realism to ground the study. I have found perhaps a better approach to realism (or a different form of critical realism) to be that generated by, again, Bunge, who regarded himself as a *scientific realist*. First and foremost, Bunge's (2016) scientific philosophy advocates systemism, which is based on emergence and complexity, where everything in the world is either a system or part of a system. There are multiple systems in the world, such as physical, chemical, biological, social and technological systems. Systems include interrelated aspects of its parts: at micro levels there are individuals; at meso

---

[3] As Ofori-Dankwa and Julian (2001:416–417) state: Complex[ity] theory is more contradictory and highlights issues of paradox and complexity inherent in studying organizations. . . . Complex[ity] theory . . . is more paradoxical, richly textured, and multifaceted. . . . Theory or research in which scholars attempt to "holistically" describe and understand complicated, multilevel, or multifaceted phenomena is best suited to complex design."

3.4 Circular and Cumulative Causation (CCC)

levels there are institutions, such as corporations, families and technologies; at macro levels are whole national systems; and at the global level there are institutions, individuals, magnified impacts and more destructive creations. Each successively higher level represents a new emergent reality where the individual components interrelate to form this new complex macro-level. Bunge's analysis is realistic in the sense that these realities exist independently of people's consciousness of them. It is also materialistic in that Bunge believes that reality consists entirely of material or concrete 'things' (an important concept for him), such as relationships, institutions, processes, ecologies and objects (Bunge 2003: 172); it does not include spirits, ghosts or mystical phenomena, unless people believe in these in which case 'they' will affect reality.

Bunge always situates emergence-complexity within whole world-systems, including biological, chemical and socioeconomic systems. With this ontology one can isolate socioeconomic systems, including its various micro, meso, macro and global aspects: what is called *vertical emergence*. See Fig. 3.5, for an illustration.

Earlier in this chapter we examined some of the horizontal emergences-complexities involved in heterogeneous groups and agents (especially linked to the work of Elder-Vass). Here we introduce the vertical dimensions. Bunge posited that there are different ontological (vertical) levels in the world, and that they are all both *sui genesis* yet also interactive. Human beings exist in a natural environment, including biological makeup (interactions between genotype and phenotype); and they activate mores, norms and skills through various networks of people (with

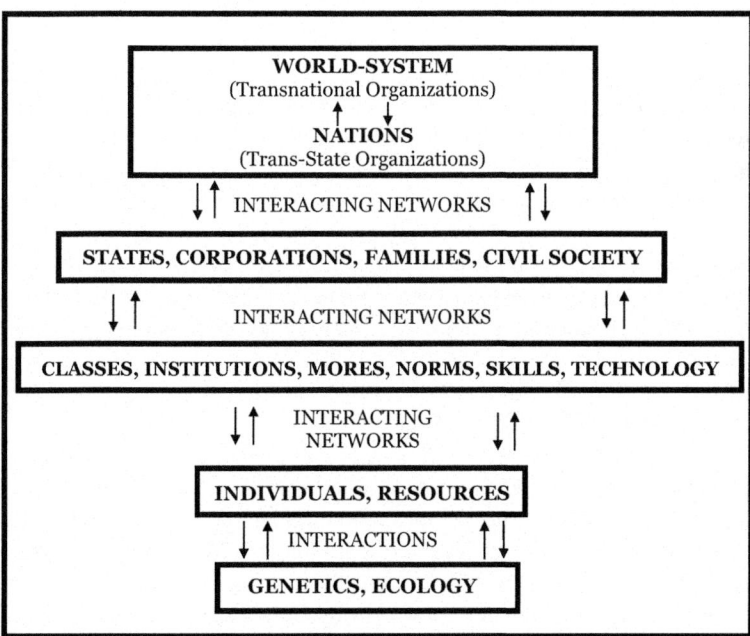

Fig. 3.5 Vertical emergent levels of complexity

resources) within institutions. There are heterogeneous agents and groups within this myriad of associations, which manifest themselves in various roles of a social, political and economic nature; being influenced by gender, ethnic, class, age, species and national characteristics; but also more specific micro roles within the various networks and social circles. These classes, institutions, skills and mores coalesce through various organizations, such as corporations, governance systems, families and civil society groups; which in turn form at a higher emergent level into macro and mega systems such as states, nations and world-systems.

It is thus necessary to scrutinize, or at least to recognize the existence of, all these different levels of qualitatively emergent processes, and to study the various 'mechanisms' at play leading from one level to the next. This is why Bunge recognized the need for an interdisciplinary or even transdisciplinary analysis, since staying at one level leads to partial knowledge. But more importantly, *all major world problems* transcend specific individual "disciplines", because in the real world problems appear at different levels. Hence social issues such as pandemics, unemployment, poverty, inequality, pollution, climate change, corruption, crime, financial instability, discrimination, crises, terrorism, alienation, inflation, and so on, can be viewed at all of these levels. The economic, cultural, political and environmental realms are interrelated and also structurally aligned. The need arises, therefore, to examine the relationships between cultural, political and economic growth-development, and how they change over time (see Bunge 2009). Examining one or even two, such as the micro-meso dimensions, as some do, of these spheres will often lead to a myopic, partial, anomalous vision because the total picture is out of view.

All chapters of this book apply aspects of CCC and emergence/complexity in understanding major world problems. For instance, Chap. 4 uses a model of CCC and contradiction to examine the interrelated factors responsible for the coronacrisis. Chapter 5 uses CCC to investigate factors promoting greenhouse gasses and climate change in a multifactor approach. Chapter 7 utilizes emergence, complexity and CCC to develop core principles of neurobiological political economy and to model the workings of intelligent robots. Chapter 10 uses CCC to analyze the magnified impacts of the network of influences propelling *jihadi* attacks in the light of 9/11. And Chap. 12 uses a CCC and emergence multifactor model to illustrate the various factors leading to holistic love, nurturance and relational attachment.

3.5 Contradictory Dynamics

The *concept of contradiction* is critical for comprehending the endogenous and problematic discontinuities, instabilities, and conflicts of contemporary capitalism, and has its roots in Hegel, Marx plus numerous major IEPE scholars. Social systems generate contradictory relationships that enable and hinder reproduction, even when growth and accumulation are reasonably strong (Harvey 2014; Fraser 2015; O'Hara 2023). The real difficulty is differentiating between contradictions that – on balance and in the long-run – act positively vis-à-vis those which act negatively on the reproduction process as a whole. The most general contradictions analyzed within IEPE include those concerning creative destruction, disembedded economy, instrumental and ceremonial functions of institutions, and the vested interests versus the common good.

It is generally agreed by institutional and evolutionary political economists that the raw workings of capitalism would see a heightening of the cyclical process as well as the pattern of inequality and uneven development. Karl Polanyi (1944) saw this in relation to the *concept of the disembedded economy*, where capitalism in its pure form ravages the social, cultural, and ecological environments in the pursuit of accumulation and profit (Stanfield 1986, 1995). The search for private reward in the form of profit, rent and interest tends to result in the global and regional movement of capital and the destruction of transactions that are not market-oriented. Cultural peculiarities are obliterated, families destroyed, the environment ravaged, and stability upset in the name of progress. The global workings of the capitalist process are thus seen to have a dark side, inextricably linked to creative destruction.

Indeed, the pure market system could not survive and would destroy itself under the impact of its motion. This leads to a "double movement", namely, that for capitalism to be reproduced in an ongoing fashion requires both the propagation of markets as well as the establishment of protective responses such as institutions to sustain the social fabric to reduce uncertainty and promote long-term reproduction of capitalism's conditions of existence. For instance, systems of innovation, market niches, and internal corporate networks are established which create structured environments and potentially embedded processes. But more widely, capitalism requires for its own long-term progress an extensive system of support networks such as forms of reciprocity, redistribution and householding that provide protection against the ravages of pandemics, climate change, financial crises, systemic corruption, wars, un(der)employment, accidents, loneliness, and conflicts.

The disembedded economy is thus a more balanced view of the creative destruction contradiction that Schumpeter (1942) presented in *Capitalism, Socialism and Democracy*, which was implicitly dedicated to Marx. For Polanyi, purely market systems, more fundamentally, would fail to provide the public goods or system-functions required for good levels of long-term growth and accumulation, in addition to standard of living and quality of life. The development of institutions are required for the circuit of capital to adequately solve the system-problems of coordination, management, aggregate demand provision, productivity, climate change, financial crises, corruption, labor power supply, and leadership.

Management is necessary for corporations that seek to moderate the uncertainty of the market and benefit from economies of scale and scope. Due to problems of overproduction and underconsumption, an insufficiency of aggregate demand requires both automatic and (intelligent) discretionary stabilizers and lender of last resort to prevent major dislocation. In order to ensure the extraction of labor effort from workers, systems of corporate organization and supervision have emerged. To ensure the availability of suitable labor power, effective families, schools and universities are necessary. Successful mitigation of greenhouse gas emissions innovations are needed to reduce land, air and sea temperature rises. And to provide leadership for the global system periodically structures of organization and coordination may be useful, preferably in the form of "soft power".

This leads to modern work on the Regulation and social structures of accumulation (*'SSA'*) approaches to institutions in evolution (O'Hara 2000, 2006, 2023). The regulation approach sees the historical tendency for various global, regional and national modes of regulation, comprising both a regime of accumulation and a number of institutional forms (Boyer and Saillard 2002). The *'SSA'* approach takes a similar view to long waves as the Regulation School, although the priority is given to the institutions (Gordon 1998). In both approaches, socioeconomic performance through long-historical time is conditioned by an array of institutional forms built over time. After some decades of relatively strong performance, punctuated usually by periodic mild-medium strength crises and recessions, the contradictions within and between the dominant institutions expand, thus leading to their relative dissolution along with long wave downswing.

Three concepts/principles of institutional change are especially relevant here to the process of institutional change and contradiction (Bush 1999; Bush and Tool 2003). The first is the *concept of ceremonial encapsulation*. This means that progressive change of the social and political economy is inhibited or tempered by the vested interests holding the commanding heights of power. The possession of power gained through struggle, enterprise, privilege, and inheritance can become "locked in" such that changes that enhance development may be inhibited (Papadopoulos 2015). Certain classes, ethnicities, genders and other groups may block social innovations in order to prevent a loss of power and prestige (Adkisson 2004). Such power can be encapsulated in the institutions so that it is perfectly legal, politically acceptable and seen as "natural". The established hegemonic cultural systems of collective behavior are made possible through the workings of certain "enabling myths" that the population come to believe in (Dugger and Sherman 2000, ch 4; Wrenn 2015). They may include the myth that the assertive use of power can justify the ends if it doesn't violate any statute associated with fraud, antitrust, civil and common law.

The second is the *concept of recognized interdependence*, which states that individuals may contribute to progressive institutional change, and manage the ramifications of such change, if they have a broad knowledge about the structure and evolution of the social and natural environment (Elsner 2021). Individuals that are inculcated with the knowledge necessary to comprehend the patterns of interdependency existing within the real world are better able to contribute to and cope with change. In particular, if they are able to understand some of the complexities of institutions and problems involved in change, they may be able to modify their behavior to suit the broader modifications activated. Thus, the supply of information and knowledge has definite public goods type functions that make an argument for universal lower, intermediate and advanced education quite persuasive.

The third is the *concept of minimal dislocation*. This recognizes that the environment within which individuals operate predicates varying levels of uncertainty, lack of information and indecision. It also recognizes the extent to which the parts of the social economy are interdependent and connected. Hence a change somewhere along the line will, with various feedback loops, impact on the other parts of the system. Through the impact of positive-policy loops even progressive changes ('from above') may instigate quite major transformations of the system; leaving many people confused and lacking in resources to cope with the magnitude of the required changes to their lifestyle. The cumulative nature of the changes may create an environment that dislocates many of the necessary and ceremonial parts of the system, thus upsetting reproduction and social provisioning. This could apply to things such as technological and institutional changes, policies concerning transitional economies, social policies, climate change, and the like. Therefore, it is critical when dealing with change to take into account the ability of individuals to adjust and to provide enough resources to aid their adaptation to the new conditions (Spithoven 2021). This can take the form of information, resources and network-generation that make the transition more humane and trustworthy.

Every chapter on world problems in this book deals with contradictions. Chapter 4 on the cornacrisis introduces four contradictions involving (a) humans versus coronaviruses, (b) neoliberalism v. embeddedness, (c) hegemony v. development, and (d) science v. misinformation. Chapter 5 on climate change deals with the contradictions of the circular treadmill of production, social costs of business/consumers, and the increasing entropy of environmental destruction. Chapter 6 on corruption deals mainly with the contradiction of the vested interests versus the common good. Chapter 7 investigates the contradictions between the two major schools of AI and humanoid robotics. Chapter 8 centers on the core policy contradiction of the disembedded economy plus several more specific ones. Chapter 9 on money and credit studies the contradictions involved in the circuit of money capital, fictitious capitals and the periodic escalation of (Minsky's) Ponzi finance. Chapter 10 introduces the contradictions of low fatality rate v. high system risk, technology promoting terrorism, problems of trying to reestablish US hegemony, and how global deregulation expanded the networks of *jihadis*. Chapter 11 studies the contradictions between humans and viruses leading to heightened and then declining HIV infection. And Chap. 12 examines the contradictions between market and nurturance, individualism and society, and love freedom and constraint.

3.6 Uncertainty

History, uneven development, heterogeneous groups, contradictions, circularity and cumulative movements are inherently related and involve uncertainty. All of the concepts and principles form an amalgam of interconnected elements involving imagination, scenario planning and scrutinizing trends of the past to see if they apply into the future, perhaps with modifications appropriate to the changed conditions.

Uncertainty thus naturally emanates from contradictions, cumulation and evolution, and comes directly into IEPE through the writings of J. M. Keynes, Frank Knight, and G.J.S. Shackle. In this context we need to differentiate between risk and uncertainty, since most modern analysts fail to do this, unless they happen to be post-

Keynesian(−institutionalists) (following Keynes (1936, 1937), Knight (1921) and/or Shackle (1972). Risk is where there is the possibility of default and the details of this probability are capable of being scrutinized in detail for purposes of pricing and costing. 'Things' such as car and life insurance, short-term weather forecasting, and horse racing are examples of this. Uncertainty, on the other hand, is where the probabilistic calculation is very difficult because of opaqueness of the data, futurity of the problem, low level information, and limitations of the human mind (Ferrari-Filho and Conceição 2005).

These sort of informational problems are typical of calculations that involve 10 or 20 years into the future, also during the high points of many business cycles when crises often become deeply ingrained in the system, and where, for instance, a core industry is new and little information is available about its future. Keynes specifically considered uncertainty in the light of investment and equity financing. If capitalists raise money as credit in the present for investing in a project that offers potential profits after at least 5 years into the future, because of the lags associated with planning, building, the construction, and so on, then there is a high degree of uncertainty. Investment is usually undertaken at high rates during optimistic business environments and at low rates during pessimistic business climates. But the uncertainty still remains especially if the project is a long-term one.

During high points in most cycles, especially during long wave downswings, an exuberant environment generates much investment but also a rising secondary equity market, and often expanding property, foreign exchange, and labor markets. Numerous business people and others get involved in the buoyant markets, often without adequate cognizance of the underlying uncertainty of rising markets in the face of speculative bubbles and greater likelihood of collapse.

This is typical of the crises in numerous nations during 1974–75, 1980–82, 1987, 1990–92, 1997–98, 2001–02, 2008–2012, and 2020–22. During these booms and associated crashes or recessions many businesses went into bankruptcy because they got caught up in rising markets in the face of crashes and recessions. Periods of high boom to recession are typically when uncertainty is at its apogee, and it is difficult for markets and risk assessment firms to provide proper 'risk' assessments. They are often caught in an exuberant environment assessing 'risk' for firms they provide financial advice to; hence the conflict of interest. It is crucial to have independent financial analysts with the conceptual skills of a political economist, the wisdom of a philosopher, and the technical apparatus of an innovative computer analyst.

This leads to the *concept of endogenous money and credit* where finance is created out of the demand for money characteristic especially of the upper phases of the business cycle (Arestis 1997; Rochon and Rossi 2017). During cycle upswings economic activity expands, along with the need for outside finance. Firms and banks thus engage in greater levels of borrowing and lending, respectively, and if there are severe limits to such finance this usually leads to financial 'innovation' to create instruments and funding opportunities to satisfy demand. Much research has been undertaken by post Keynesian institutionalists on the two main sources of endogenous finance, accommodative and innovative or structural. While the historical weight of argument seems to support business-innovative sources, recent monetary policy interest rate targets lend some credence to accommodative finance; although when interest rates are raised this reduces the degree of accommodation (Rochon and Vernengo 2001).

In this context, Hyman Minsky's (1982) concept of the financial instability hypothesis (FIH) has become a major source of convergence, and Minsky himself saw his analysis as touching various schools of IEPE. The FIH is associated with endogenous finance, conflict between finance and industry, radical uncertainty, and the tendency to financial crises during long wave downswings. The financial instability hypothesis, modern monetary theory (MMT) and functional finance (among other topics) are examined in some detail in Chap. 9 on money-credit circuits, cycles and crises. They have generated much media attention lately and are hence well-known aspects of IEPE outside the interdiscipline (see, e.g., Jeanna Smialek 2022 on MMT). Minsky's endogenous instability method is similar in many respects to the non-equilibrium growth, cycles and crises work of Nicholas Kaldor (1972), David Gordon (1998), Martin Wolfson (1994), Howard Sherman (2003) and Robert Pauls (Forthcoming).

Most chapters dealing with world problems in this book examine uncertainty. Chapter 4 has a section on global uncertainty in the face of the GFC compared with the coronacrisis. Chapter 5 has a section where uncertainty is linked with CCC to scrutinize shared socioeconomic pathways and cascading tipping points in climate change. Chapter 9 deals with uncertainty in the light of the financial instability hypothesis, MMT and financial crises. Chapter 10 links uncertainty especially to the contradiction of terrorism between low fatality risk and high system risk. And Chap. 12 discusses uncertainty in the context of levels of trust, relationship lock-ins and the post-familial family.

3.7 Innovation

It was Schumpeter who developed the concept of innovation, particularly the clustering of innovations (Freeman 2007), more than any other, certainty more than Keynes, yet he failed to link it directly to uncertainty, advocating a similar concept called creative destruction. To comprehend the forward motion of capitalism requires the *principle of the dialectic of innovation and competition* linked to dynamic motion and metamorphosis. Capitalism requires both an active entrepreneurial function and a reactive competitive motion for its inner logic. Continual innovation-competition enables this logic to flow through to growth and accumulation. If innovation is not strong enough accumulation falters due to anomalous productivity and declining expected monopoly rents, while if competition is too strong the monopoly surplus accrues to firms for too short a time, again leading to problems of over-and-under-accumulation. *There are thus relatively narrow parameters that enable capital to operate crisis free.*

The innovation-competition dialectic forces capital to open up new areas for new products and processes through creative destruction set in an environment of instability and change. Uncertainty is thus the normal rule of capital as the development of new combinations is endogenously set in motion by the search for profit at the global level. Searching for profitable opportunities upsets established lines of business, destroys traditional lifestyles, leads people to separate from family and friends, reduces biospheric diversity as the land is cultivated and new firms organized, and periodically leads to un(der)employment as old skills become obsolete.

The very nature of capital creates a movement for the expansion of markets, the introduction of new methods and products and constant interruption of established lines of business. Competition and innovation form a dialectic that compels capital to constantly grow and develop in more nations and geographical areas than ever before (Marx and Engels 1848). New combinations can take at least five main forms, including product and process innovation, new sources of raw materials, the opening up of a new market, and changes in the organization of industry (Schumpeter 1911, 63–66). These can be activated by single entrepreneurs, partnerships, large corporations and production networks. Schumpeter's (1942) later work scrutinized trustified innovation through the corpus of the large corporation, and the contradictions this would likely bring.

Some authors have variously included Knightian uncertainty (Brouwer 2000) and Shacklian uncertainty (Metcalfe 2014) into Schumpeterian themes, while others have incorporated the social elements leading to broad new ways of doing things in economic life (Weber 2007). Some analysts have completely reorganized the (neo-)Schumpeterian principles along the lines of technological, institutional, organizational and social innovation; long-term development; qualitatively stable as well as radical eras of change; nonlinear plus feedback processes establishing discernable patterns of change; path dependence, irreversibility and bounded rationality; systems theory, complexity, and the three pillars of real, money and public sectors; tacit, local and complex future knowledge trajectories; along with heterogeneous agents, public sectors that look to future development, and a thoroughgoing economics that reduces upside and downside uncertainties (Hanusch and Pyka 2007). This approach is skeptical of knowledge being a pure public good, but is dedicated nonetheless to "demand[ing] higher qualities of public goods such as infrastructure, education, basic research, etc. as a condition sine qua non for economic development" (p. 280).

There are numerous I-E political economists who take a broader perspective of innovation, following Veblen, with the concept of the community's joint stock of knowledge. Veblen developed this in works such as *The Theory of the Leisure Class* (Veblen 1899), as well as to some degree in *The Instinct of Workmanship and the State of the Industrial Arts* (Veblen 1914), as well as in *The Vested Interests and the Common Man* (Veblen 1919). There is also some secondary literature on the concept (e.g., O'Hara 1999b; Dugger 2016). Very briefly it states that socioeconomic innovation takes on usually a very wide form, involving changes in the habits and institutions of the community that involve potential long-term livelihood such as peace, social tranquility, communication, knowledge, skills and cooperation. These can also include changes to the material forms of life such as new machines, products and forms of organization that may upset the instrumental functioning of the community. They can also include policies by states, families and corporations that enhance the quality of life and standard of living of the whole community (see, e.g., for theoretical and practical examples, Holt and Greenwood 2014).

There are also intermediate levels of potential improvements involving policy and governance innovation. This involves, for instance, theoretical, institutional and organizational changes and issues relating to constitutions, representation, corruption, property and community power relations (Ball et al. 1989). It also involves policy changes to health, education, infrastructure provision, science and technology, regional development and the environment; and enhanced democratic, participatory and successful policy processes (Brookfield Institute 2018).

The *principle of innovation states* that innovations should be undertaken at all levels—individual, group, institution, civil society, polity, and world levels—to improve the instrumental workings of systems and rectify world problems that impair lives, livelihood and ecological sustainability. Every world problem investigated in this book posits such innovations, whether already in process, reformulated, reset, or to be implemented to reduce the extent of the problem(s).

For instance, Chap. 4 introduces innovations associated with the discovery of vaccines with a high efficacy level; principles of public health; and preparing for the next pandemic. Chapter 5 discusses innovatory planning on climate change in the form of the paradigm of shared socioeconomic pathways. Chapter 6 develops a visionary perspective on corruption in the form of the common good versus the vested interests. Chapter 7 develops the embodied cognition approach to neurological political economy to advance the architecture of humanoid robotics. Chapter 10 introduces several innovations to deal with the threat of terrorism. And Chap. 12 attempts to innovate in political economy by spreading the principles to issues of love and nurturance.

3.8 Policy and Governance

There is some degree of convergence between the sub-schools of IEPE vis-à-vis policy and governance. They all seek a realistic, institutionally rich, dynamic view of the economic process set in a social and ecological environment. Each of them concentrates on special themes while being forced by the weight of evidence and interaction among other scholars to spread beyond this to a broader view of the economy. The interaction between them at conferences, in journals, in the editing of books, and in academic departments has seen much convergence over the past 40 years. Overall, they tend to have an increasingly shared vision of the instituted economy in evolution through historical time.

However, while there is some convergence among IEPEs regarding this dynamic, processual vision about the economy, as we saw in the section above on innovation, there is some divergence among IEPEs when it comes to policy and governance. In a nutshell, neo-Schumpeterians and some other complexity theorists and empiricists would tend to prefer a much smaller government sector than average IEPE scholars. They remain committed to the provision of sound legality, defense, education, health infrastructure, culture and world development (Hanusch and Pyka 2007), but perhaps skeptical regarding some aspects of functional finance, employer of last resort, participatory democracy and general social provisioning. No doubt there are many complexity theorists and empiricists who would extend government to these latter tasks, but the more entrepreneurial-style neo-Schumpeterians, even some who adopt a somewhat holistic position (in our sense), would likely not be in that camp.

3.8.1 Progressive Agenda for Change

Most IEPEs though are likely to support a broadly progressive program that includes a combination of community, workplace, and family participation in matters that affect their lives. In particular, IEPE seeks to promote democratic inclusion for those who have been traditionally denied the power to improve their livelihood beyond the basics. For them it is critical to go beyond mere formal democracy of having the right to be involved in electoral matters to the right of citizens to be actively engaged in the economic process through participatory democracy in the dominant institutions. This involves devolving more power to those who lack adequate resources to become involved meaningfully in the processes of production, distribution, exchange and governance.[4]

Looking at broad governance issues, there are three major areas where many IEPEs are likely to be in broad agreement. The first area concerns the recognition that established governance patterns are endogenously linked to the dominant institutions of the system, and cannot be seen as apart from them as independent umpire. Governance structures and processes are part and parcel of these dynamic and contradictory forces, and hence *to some degree* have difficulty overseeing the social and economic system from above. Current governance processes are thus imbedded in the system of norms, institutions, habits, routines and privileges of the system. This is true regardless of whether governance emanates from governments, corporations, families, or non-government organizations. It is impossible to organize governance in such a way that it operates *above the system* and in abstraction from its many negative (and positive) aspects, especially concerning the vested interests versus the common good. One can *attempt* to gain a broad vision with attention to detail, but it is difficult to eschew preconceptions and vested interests that obscure one's vision, especially in such an uncertain environment where the future intervenes.

3.8.2 Trust, Community and Destructive Creation

The second lesson of governance is that it can reside in any of the institutions, and need not necessarily be activated by government. We need efficient and equitable

---

[4] For instance, historically there have been similarities between egalitarian programs advocated by progressive institutionalistists such as Marc Tool (2001), institutional neo-Marxists Bowles et al. (1990), post Keynesian institutionalists (JPKE 2004–2005), and institutional-radical feminist perspectives on capabilities and entitlements (Feminist Economics 2003). Today these programs need to place much more emphasis on the Green Road (e.g., see Cohen and MacGregor 2022).

institutions concerning households, production, distribution, finance, and the state. We need a whole set of institutions that operate well within the context of the environment in place and emerging in the future. This requires, as we saw above, at the general social level, a high degree of trust, association and community. This is preferable to a system dominated by 'laws, regulations, police and armies' to ensure people do what is required, since these measures are likely subject to abuse, self-interest, corruption and exploitation by the vested interests. We could say that there is *an element* of libertarianism in IEPE, influenced by liberalism and anarchism, given their systematic critique of Stalinism and the Keynesian welfare-regulatory state.

We thus realize more than ever the importance of trust, association and community. Any economy lacking in these qualities is not going to function very well, at least in promoting quality of life and social provisioning. Yet it is difficult to design appropriate policies to these matters, unless, perhaps, they are in the forefront of policy concern, and exhaustively examined with the help of many teams of scholars and practitioners. Much evidence supports the conclusion that the past three decades of capitalist development has seen a shift of resources from *family, society and ecology* to *market, corporation and finance* at all levels (subnational, national, regional and global). In many nations that have been studied, the *rate* of long-term aggregate socioeconomic-ecological performance has not improved since the mid-1970s, and measurement of the social resources that are declining is only beginning (O'Hara 2023). A critical policy issue is thus the need for much better information and surveys on the relative movement of resources from family, society and environment to corporate, market and financial relations, and for the realignment of resources to protect society, health and environment from the market and the treadmill of production.

There are several strands of IEPE that argue this case for economic growth being merely the process of transferring family, society and environmental resources to specific corporations, markets, financial institutions and individuals. These strands include Polanyi's disembedded economy, Marx's notion of destructive creation, the Foster-Bush-Tool theory of instrumental and ceremonial functions of institutions, Edward Nell's theory of transformational growth, and ecological views of strong sustainability. Scholars have been trying to calculate the destruction wrought on social and natural resources to provide a balanced assessment of growth and development (O'Hara 2004b; Menegaki and Tugcu 2016). A policy requirement is for this research to proceed at a faster pace and for the implications to be taken seriously once they are suitably analyzed. These issues are analyzed especially in Chap. 5 on climate change, Chap. 8 on policy, and Chap. 12 on the nurturance gap.

3.8.3 Entropy, Precautionary Principle and Minimal Dislocation

The third area of governance is the *concept of entropy* and the so-called laws of thermodynamics (Georgescu-Roegen 1971, Khalil 2004, Saslow 2020). The first law says that energy can be neither created nor destroyed, while the second says that energy tends to become increasingly unavailable in a closed system. The Earth as a whole is an open system due to the impact of the sun. But nevertheless entropy – the second law – does impact to some critical degree. Economic activity cannot create energy and thus produces negentropy. In essence it destroys environmental resources and biodiversity. The second law also explains the limits of recycling waste. Strong sustainability implies the need for minimum dislocation of ecological resources, rather than trading-off between ecological and durable fixed capital; and to supplement GDP-type figures with measures such as the Index of Sustainable Economic Welfare (ISEW). The precautionary principle recognizes lack of knowledge and uncertainty about changes to the ecological environment vis-à-vis climate change. This has ramifications for advancing the processes of mitigation and adaptation to climate change, in relation to the necessary Green Road style of shared socioeconomic pathway (SSP) (IPCC 2021), examined in Chap. 5.

This raises the issue of the destructive aspect of transformational and disembedded growth requiring resources to support a more gradual process of transition, in order to promote minimum dislocation. Hysteresis and path dependency imply that the traverse between two stable states is affected by the process of adjustment, such that stability may not emerge, due to a considerable period of cumulative motion. In the process, in the downward direction skills are destroyed, families dislocated, regions depressed and communication systems upset while ever-new arrangements are being formed through other skills, institutions, areas and communication systems. In a very practical sense, therefore, it is critical for governments to provide resources in the form of safety nets. With the demise of families, skills and areas, for many people governments are the only other option, despite the limits of governments already mentioned. Neoliberal governments are not likely to provide many such resources because of their closer relationship to business, especially financial and transnational capital. Recent trends have shown neoliberalism to be out of fashion and through the GFC and coronacrisis some progress is being made along these lines to better governance.

These issues of policy and governance are discussed especially in Chap. 4 on the coronacrisis, Chap. 5 on shared social pathways for climate change, Chap. 8 on waves of policy ideology, Chap. 9 on moderating financial crises, Chap. 10 on policies to reduce the threat of terrorism and the war in terrorism, and Chap. 11 on governance measures to tackle HIV-AIDS.

3.9 Concepts and Principles in This Book

Surveying some of the core general and specific concepts and principles of IEPP is a useful task for understanding the interdiscipline. But for studying and comprehending causes and solutions to core global problems we cannot utilize all the concepts and principles examined above (especially all those in Table 3.1). We have to be selective and utilize those that are directly useful to the specific task at hand. The major concepts/principles used in this book to scrutinize the nine global problems detailed in the chapters of this book, Chaps. 4, 5, 6, 7, 8, 9, 10, 11 and 12 below, are shown in Table 3.2.

3.9 Concepts and Principles in This Book

Table 3.2 Concepts & Principles for Explaining World Problems, Overview, Chaps. 4, 5, 6, 7, 8, 9, 10, 11 and 12

Problem/Chapter	Core General Principle 1	Core General Principle 2	Core General Principle 3	Core General Principle 4	Core General Principle 5	Core General Principle 6
Chapter 4: Coronacrisis	Historical specificity	Heterogeneous groups- agents		Contradictions	Uncertainty	Policies & governance/innovation
Chapter 5: Climate change	Historical specificity	Contradiction	Uneven development	CCC	Uncertainty	
Chapter 6: Corruption	Historical specificity	Vested interests v. common good	Uneven development	CCC in uneven development	Heterogeneous groups & agents	
Chapter 7: AI & robotics	Heterogeneous groups & agents	Historical specificity & hegemony	Embodied AI design principles	Contradiction	Neurorobotic design principles	CCC, emergence & complexity
Chapter 8: Policy	Social provisioning	Disembedded Economy & historical specificity	Multiple contradictions	CCC	Uneven development	Historical specificity
Chapter 9: Money & finance	History of waves & phases	Circuit of money capital	Endogenous money & credit	Financial instability hypothesis	Global money	Modern monetary theory (MMT)
Chapter 10: Terrorism	Historical specificity	Contradiction & CCC	Contradict. 1: Technology & CCC	Contradict. 2: Hegemony & uneven development	Contrad. 3: Deregulation & globalization	Policies/Innovations for each contradiction
Chapter 11: HIV & AIDS	Natural history (specificity)	Humans v. virus	CCC	Uneven development	Social reproduction	Policy & governance
Chapter 12: Love	Historical specificity	CCC	Contradict. 1: Markets v. nurturance	Contradict. 2: Individual v. society	Contradict. 3: Freedom v. constraint	Path dependence & evolution

Table 3.2 emphasizes *mostly* the core general concepts and principles that form the basis of the section-titles of this chapter. These core general concepts/principles *form an ensemble* ("a group of items viewed as a whole rather than [just] individually"; Lexico 2022), constituting what Bhimo Samudro (2012), Brennan and Kalsi (2015) and O'Hara (2022) call "O'Hara's principles of political economy". I apply these concepts and principles to the nine critical world problems that follow in the chapters below (see Table 3.1 also). Usually each world problem analyzed deals with the historical evolution of the problem, the role of hegemony and uneven development in its genesis, the heterogenous groups associated with it, the circular and cumulative dynamics of the contradictions, leading to heightened uncertainty, plus the role of innovations and policies.

Often I modify this template when the problem or research process requires it. For instance, such modification occurs in Chap. 8 on policy and governance, where I start with social provisioning and then situate the disembedded economy in historical context, rather than starting with historical specificity per se. Also in this chapter I don't specifically analyse uncertainty as it relates to policy, since it is discussed in a policy context in Chap. 9 on money and financial crises. Chapter 9 deals with the core general principles but is *structured* according to the topic's headings specifically dealing with money and crises. Chapter 10 on terrorism and the war on terrorism deals with core general principles, but is structured, as with Chap. 9, according to key issues relating to the problem; especially the core contradictions. Chapter 12 includes a key section on path dependence, which is under the umbrella of historical specificity. Chapter 2, especially relating to Veblen, includes nine concepts/principles, as one of the umbrella concepts of historical specificity, the nexus between individuals-habits-institutions-culture, is brought more to the fore since it seemed appropriate in the context of the discussion. Note also that in Table 3.1, two concepts, social provisioning and trust, are included under the umbrella of two broad principles, since they are directly relevant to an array of processes relevant to multiple concepts and principles. (Indeed, other concepts/principles are also of this multi-pronged relevance to different core general concepts and principles).

3.10 Conclusion

This chapter has sought to examine some of the major concepts/principles of institutional-evolutionary political economy, and to indicate the direction this book will take on the basis of these concepts/principles. The principles of IEPE are historically contingent, and often take the form of stylized facts and relatively durable propositions that are nevertheless potentially subject to modification on the basis of further investigation. I-E political economy is a realist analysis of the structure, contradictions and unstable reproduction of economic systems, paying particular attention to the link between agency and institutions, habits and instincts in an environment of uncertainty, ignorance and bounded rationality.

3.10 Conclusion

The concept of historical specificity states that history plays a key role in understanding world problems, through the notions of hysteresis, path dependence, phases of evolution, social provisioning and blind drift. IEPE is a realistic view of the evolution and metamorphosis of economic systems, where change is ongoing and principles are always in the process of revision and reassessment in the light of new evidence and developments.

The concept of hegemony and uneven development states that there are major disparities of power in the global political economy, that lead periodically to nations and regions gaining hegemonic power (leading the core), while other areas have much lower levels of authority as part of the periphery and semi-periphery. These asymmetric forces are important in understanding most world problems.

The concept of heterogeneous groups and agents illustrates the heterogeneity of agents, being variously affected by the intergenerational influences of class, ethnicity, gender, age, species as well as other micro-groups/agents. Institutions, habits and culture represent the social cement that condition the often multiple and interlinked roles that agents play in economic life.

The concept of circular and cumulative causation shows that IEPE is a dynamic, circuitous perspective on the world in the process of uneven development and varying levels of divergence due to the asymmetric distribution of information, resources, power and networks. It tends to eschew equilibrium analysis in favor of the complex interplay of endogenous forces operating through interactive and magnified motion.

The concept of uncertainty states that business cycles, waves, climate change and tipping points are typical outcomes of informational anomalies caused by futurity, opaqueness of knowledge and the limitations of the human mind. World problems caused or exacerbated by uncertainty typically include climate change, financial crises, Pandemics, and terrorism. It is thus necessary to analyze uncertainty in order to help ameliorate the anomalies.

The concept of innovation states that clusters of innovation impact through creative destruction giving global capitalism and its components a dynamic yet unstable form of motion. These innovations can help resolve world problems and also generate anomalies from the very process of rapid change and dislocation they embody.

The concept of contradiction is linked to the forces of creative destruction, disembedded economy, vested interests v. common good, as well as the conflict between heterogeneous agents. In association with CCC and uncertainty they play a major role in generating and magnifying crucial world problems, and therefore must be used for understanding them and how to reduce their intensity through historical time.

This is where the concept of policy and governance comes in, since policies can be utilized to moderate the excesses of global capitalism as well as be used through functional finance, participatory democracy, accords and agreements to help solve problems through enhancing the process of social provisioning.

From here we variously utilize these concepts in a principles context, as discussed in Chap. 1, where IEPE requires us to utilize the concepts to understand and work towards ameliorating world problems. In this fashion we study some of the most critical problems of the world, starting with the recent-ongoing coronacrisis, then climate change, corruption, AI-robotics, policy, financial instability and crises, terrorism, HIV-AIDS and the nurturance gap.

Acknowledgements This is a thoroughly revised, updated and reconstructed version of a paper that was originally published in the *Journal of Economic Issues* (O'Hara 2007); in the original version I give thanks to the three anonymous referees, Richard V. Adkisson, Vicki Taggart, John Davis and Ron Stanfield. It was originally presented at a conference at the University of Missouri, Kansas City, and at the ASSAs in Boston.

References

Abuelgasim, Eyad, Li Jing Saw, Manasi Shirke, Mohamed Zeinah, and Amer Harky. 2020. COVID-19: Unique Public Health Issues Facing Black, Asian and Minority Ethnic Communities. *Current Problems in Cardiology* 45 (8): 1–10. https://doi.org/10.1016/j.cpcardiol.2020.100621.

Adkisson, Richard V. 2004. Ceremonialism, Intellectual Property Rights, and Innovative Activity. *Journal of Economic Issues* 38 (2): 459–466.

Aliber, Robert Z., and Charles P. Kindlberger. 2015. *Manias, Panics and Crashes: A History of Financial Crises*. 7th ed. New York: Palgrave Macmillan.

Arestis, Philip. 1997. *Money, Pricing, Distribution and Economic Integration*. London: Macmillan.

Arthur, W. Brian. 1996. *Increasing Returns and Path Dependence in the Economy*. Ann Arbor: University of Michigan Press.

———. 2021. Foundations of complexity Economics. *Nature Reviews Physics* 3 (February): 136–145.

Ball, Terrence, James Farr, and Russell L. Hanson, eds. 1989. *Political Innovation and Conceptual Change*. Cambridge: Cambridge University Press.

Barnes, William, Myles Gartland, and Martin Stack. 2004. Old Habits Die Hard: Path Dependency and Behavioral Lock-in. *Journal of Economic Issues* 38 (2): 371–377.

Baş, İ. Melih. 2022. Editorial. *Holistic Economics* 1 (1): 1.

Berger, Sebastian, ed. 2009. *The Foundations of Non-Equilibrium Economics: The Principle of Circular and Cumulative Causation*. London/New York: Routledge.

Bourdieu, Pierre. 1997. The Three Forms of Capital. In *Education: Culture, Economy and Society*, ed. A.H. Halsey, Hugh Lauder, Phillip Brown, and Amy Stuart Wells, 46–58. Oxford: Oxford University Press.

Bowles, Samuel, David M. Gordon, and Thomas Weisskopf. 1990. *After the Waste Land: A Democratic Economics for the Year 2000*. Armonk/New York: M.E. Sharpe.

Bowles, Samuel, Herbert Gintis, and Melissa Osborne Groves, eds. 2005. *Unequal Chances: Family Background and Economic Success*. Princeton: Princeton University Press.

Boyer, Robert, and Yves Saillard, eds. 2002. *Regulation Theory: The State of the Art*. London/New York: Routledge.

Braudel, F. 1950. Toward a Historical Economics, *Revue Economique*. May: 37–44. Reprinted in F. Braudel (1969) On History. Chicago: University of Chicago Press. Translated by Sarah Mathews.

Brennan, Andrew John. 2004. Environmental Problems of the World: Global Warming and Declining Biodiversity. In *Global Political Economy and the Wealth of Nations: Performance, Institutions, Problems and Policies*, ed. Phillip Anthony O'Hara. London/New York: Routledge.

Brennan, Andrew John, and Jaslyn Kaur Kalsi. 2015. Elephant Poaching & Ivory Trafficking Problems in Sub-Saharan Africa: An Application of O'Hara's Principles of Political Economy. *Ecological Economics* 120: 312–337. https://doi.org/10.1016/j.ecolecon.2015.08.013.

Brookfield Institute. 2018. *Exploring Policy Innovation: Tools, Techniques, and Approaches.* Toronto: Brookfield Institute.

Brouwer, Maria. 2000. Entrepreneurship and Uncertainty: Innovation and Competition among the Many. *Small Business Economics* 15 (2): 149–160.

Brown, Sarah, Daniel Gray, and Jennifer Roberts. 2015. The Relative Income Hypothesis: A Comparison of Methods. *Economic Letters* 130: 47–50. https://doi.org/10.1016/j.econlet.2015.02.031.

Bunge, Mario. 1974–1989. *Treatise on Basic Philosophy.* 8 Volumes. Boston/Dordrecht, NL: Reidel Publishing Company.

———. 2000. Systemism: The Alternative to Individualism and Holism. *Journal of Socio-Economics* 29: 147–157.

———. 2003. *Emergence and Convergence: Qualitative Novelty and the Unity of Knowledge.* Toronto: University of Toronto Press.

———. 2009. *Political Philosophy: Fact, Fiction and Vision.* New Brunswick/London: Transaction Publishers.

———. 2016. *Between Two Worlds: Memoirs of a Philosopher-Scientist.* Geneva: Springer Nature.

Bush, Paul Dale. 1999. Institutional Change and Adjustment. In *Encyclopedia of Political Economy*, ed. Phillip Anthony O'Hara, vol. 1. London/New York: Routledge. Paper edition, 2001.

Bush, Paul D., and Marc Tool. 2003. Foundational Concepts of Instrumentalist Policy. In *Institutional Analysis and Economic Policy*, ed. Marc Tool and Paul Dale Bush. Boston/London: Kluwer Academic Publishers.

Christoforou, Asimina, and John B. Davis. 2016. *Social Capital and Economics: Social Values, Power and Social Identity.* Oxford/New York, Routledge.

Cohen, Maeve, and Sherilyn MacGregor. 2022. *Towards a Feminist Green New Deal for the UK.* Paper for the WBG Commission on a Gender-Equal Economy. Towards-a-feminist-Green-New-Deal-for-the-UK.pdf (wbg.org.uk).

Colander, David. 2000. *The Complexity Vision and the Teaching of Economics.* Cheltenham/Northampton: Edward Elgar.

Davis, John. 2003. *The Theory of the Individual in Economics.* London/New York: Routledge.

Drentea, Patricia, and Melinder A. Goldner. 2006. Caregiving Outside of the Home: The Effects of Race on Depression. *Ethnicity and Health* 11 (1): 41–57.

Duesenberry, James S. 1958. *Business Cycles and Economic Growth.* New York/London: McGraw-Hill.

Dugger, William M. 2016. Technology and Property: Knowledge and the Commons. *Review of Radical Political Economics* 48: 111–126.

Dugger, Willam M., and Howard J. Sherman. 2000. *Reclaiming Evolution: A Dialogue Between Marxism and Institutionalism on Social Change.* London/New York: Routledge.

Elder-Vass, David. 2010. *The Causal Power of Social structures: Emergence, Structure and Agency.* Cambridge: CUP.

———. 2016. *Profit and Gift in the Digital Economy.* Cambridge: Cambridge University Press.

Elsner, Wolfram. 2017. Complexity Economics as Heterodoxy: Theory and Policy. *Journal of Economic Issues* 51 (4): 939–978.

———. 2021. Collapse. Institutional Decline and Breakdown, Its Endogeneity and Its Asymmetry Vis-á-Vis Emergence: A Theoretical Frame. *Journal of Economic Issues* 55 (1): 79–102. https://doi.org/10.1080/00213624.2021.1873048.

FAO (UN Food & Agriculture Organization). 2019. *The State of the World's Biodiversity for Food and Agriculture,* (Eds). J. Bélanger & D. Pilling. FAO Commission on Genetic Resources for Food and Agriculture Assessments. Rome. 572 pp. http://www.fao.org/3/CA3129EN/CA3129EN.pdf.

Feminist Economics. 2003. Special Issue on Amartya Sen's Work and Ideas: A Gender Perspective. *Feminist Economics* 9 (2–3): 1–332.

Ferrari-Filho, Fernando, and Octavio Augusto Camargo Conceição. 2005. The Concept of Uncertainty in Post Keynesian Theory and in Institutional Economics. *Journal of Economic Issues* 39 (3): 579–594. https://doi.org/10.1080/00213624.2005.11506835.

Figart, Deborah M., and Tonia L. Warnecke, eds. 2013. *Handbook on Gender and Economic Life*. Cheltenham: Edward Elgar.

Fraser, Nancy. 2015. Legitimation Crisis? On the Political Contradictions of Financialized Capitalism. *Critical Historical Studies* 2 (2): 157–189.

Freeman, Chris. 2007. A Schumpeterian Renaissance? In *Elgar Companion to Neo-Schumpeterian Economics*, ed. Horst Hanusch and Andreas Pyka, 130–141. Cheltenham: Edward Elgar.

Fukuyama, Francis. 2002. Social Capital and Development: The Coming Agenda. *SAIS Review* 22 (1): 23–37.

Georgescu-Roegen, Nicholas. 1971. *The Entropy Law and the Economic Process*. Cambridge, MA: Harvard University Press.

Ghosh, Indranil. 2020. *The Global Trust Crisis*. https://foreignpolicy.com/2020/01/22/davos-world-leader-trust-institutions-populism-protest/.

Gordon, David M. 1998. *Economics and Social Justice: Essays on Power, Labor and Institutional Change*. Edited by S. Bowles and T. Weisskopf. Cheltenham/Northampton: Edward Elgar.

Gruchy, Allen. 1947. *Modern Economic Thought: The American Contribution*. Clifton: Augustus Kelley. 1967.

Hanusch, Horst, and Andreas Pyka. 2007. Principles of Neo-Schumpeterian Economics. *Cambridge Journal of Economics* 31: 275–289.

Harvey, David. 2014. *Seventeen Contradictions and the End of Capitalism*. Oxford: Oxford University Press.

Harvey, John T. 2021. Feedback Economics: Economic Modeling with System Dynamics. *System Dynamics Review* 37 (4): 363–366.

Hertel, Florian R., and Olaf Groh-Samberg. 2019. The Relation between Inequality and Intergenerational Class Mobility in 39 Countries. *American Sociological Review* 84 (6): 1099–1133. https://doi.org/10.1177/0003122419885094.

Hobsbawn, Eric. 1962. *The Age of Revolution: 1788–1848*. London: Abacus. 1977.

Hodgson, Geoffrey M. 2001. *How Economics Forgot History: The Problem of Historical Specificity in Social Science*. London/New York: Routledge.

———. 2004. *Reconstructing Institutional Economics: Evolution, Agency and Structure in American Institutionalism*. London/New York: Routledge.

Holt, Richard P.F., and Daphne T. Greenwood, eds. 2014. *A Brighter Future: Improving the Standard of Living Now and for the Next Generation*. Armonk/New York: M.E. Sharpe.

HRW (Human Rights Watch). 2022. *World Report 2022: Events of 2021*. New York: HRW.

IPCC (Intergovernmental Panel on Climate Change). 2021. *Climate Change 2021: The Physical Science Basis*. Working Group 1 Contribution To The Sixth Assessment Report of The IPCC. UK: IPCC. (*Draft* report). https://www.ipcc.ch/reports/.

Jo, Tae-Hee, Lynne Chester, and Carlo D'Ippoliti, eds. 2018. *The Routledge Handbook of Heterodox Economics*. New York and London: Routledge.

JPKE. 2004–2005. The Washington Consensus, Neoliberalism and Beyond, Special Issue of the *Journal of Post Keynesian Economics*, 27(2): 187–365.

Kaldor, Nicholas. 1966. *Causes of the Slow Rate of Economic Growth in the United Kingdom*. Cambridge, UK: Cambridge University Press. Reprinted in Nicholas Kaldor, *Further Essays on Economic Theory*. New York: Holmes & Meier Publishers, 1978, 100–139.

———. 1970. The Case for Regional Policies. *Scottish Journal of Political Economy* 27 (3) Reprinted in Nicholas Kaldor, *Further Essays on Economic Theory*. New York: Holmes & Meier Publishers, 1978, 139–154.

———. 1972. The Irrelevance of Equilibrium Economics. *The Economic Journal* 82 (4): 312–337. Reprinted in Nicholas Kaldor, *Economics Without Equilibrium.* Cardiff University: University College Cardiff Press, 1985.

Kapp, K. William. 1968. In Defense of Institutional Economics. *Swedish Journal of Economics* 70 (1): 1–18.

Keynes, John Maynard. 1936. *The General Theory of Employment, Interest and Money.* London: Macmillan.

———. 1937. The General Theory of Employment. *Quarterly Journal of Economics* 51: 209–233.

Khalil, Elias L. 2004. The Three Laws of Thermodynamics and the Theory of Production. *Journal of Economic Issues* 38 (1): 201–226.

Knight, Frank H. 1921. *Rick, Uncertainty and Profit.* New York: Cosimo Classics. 2005.

Krugman, Paul. 1991. Increasing Returns and Economic Geography. *Journal of Political Economy* 99: 484–499.

Kuhumba, Shija. 2018. Amartya Sen's Capability Approach as Theoretical Foundation of Human Development. *Journal of Sociology and Development* 1 (1): 127–145.

Lahiri-Dutt, Kuntala, and Pallabi Sil. 2014. Women's 'Double Day' in Middle-Class Homes in Small-Town India. *Contemporary South Asia* 22 (4): 389–405.

Lavoie, Marc. 2004. Post Keynesian Consumer Theory: Potential Synergies with Consumer Research and Economic Psychology. *Journal of Economic Psychology* 25 (5): 639–649.

Lexico. 2022. *Definition of 'Ensemble'.* ENSEMBLE | Meaning & Definition for UK English | Lexico.com.

MacDonald, Martha, Shelley Phipps, and Lynn Lethbridge. 2005. Taking its Toll: The Influence of Paid and Unpaid Work on Women's Well-Being. *Feminist Economics* 11 (1): 63–94.

Marx, Karl. 1857–58. *Grundrisse: Foundations of the Critique of Political Economy (Rough Draft).* Harmondsworth, Penguin: 1973. Translated with a foreword by Martin Nicolaus.

Marx, Karl, and Friedrich Engels. 1848. *The Communist Manifesto.* Harmondsworth: Penguin. 1967.

Menegaki, Angelika N., and Can Tansel Tugcu. 2016. Rethinking the Energy-Growth Nexus: Proposing an Index of Sustainable Economic Welfare for Sub-Saharan Africa. *Energy Research and Social Science* 17: 147–159. https://doi.org/10.1016/j.erss.2016.04.009.

Metcalfe, Stanley. 2014. *George Shackle and the Schumpeterian Legacy.* University of Graz. Graz Economic Papers, GEP 2014-08. 2014-08.pdf (uni-graz.at)

Mills, C.W. 1959. *The Sociological Imagination.* Harmondsworth: Penguin.

Minsky, Hyman. 1982. *Can "It" Happen Again? Essays on Instability and Finance.* Armonk/New York: M.E. Sharpe.

Myrdal, Gunnar. 1939. *Monetary Equilibrium.* New York: Augustus M. Kelley. 1965.

———. 1944. A Methodological Note on the Principle of Cumulation. In *An American Dilemma: The Negro Problem and Modern Democracy*, ed. Gunnar Myrdal, vol. 2, 1065–1970. New York/London: Harper & Row. Reprinted in Gunnar Myrdal (1958), *Value in Social Theory: A Selection of Essays on Methodology.* Edited by Paul Streeton. London: Routledge and Kegan Paul, 198–205.

———. 1957. Chapter 2: The Principle of Circular and Cumulative Causation. In *Economic Theory and Under-developed Regions*, ed. Gunnar Myrdal, 11–22. London: Methuen & Co Ltd.

———. 1968. Appendix 2: The Mechanism of Underdevelopment and Development and a Sketch of an Elementary Theory of Planning for Development. 1. Circular Causation. In *Asian Drama: An Inquiry into the Poverty of Nations*, ed. Gunnar Myrdal, vol. 3, 1843–1859. Harmondsworth: Penguin Books.

———. 1978. Institutional Economics. *Journal of Economic Issues* 12 (4): 771–783.

O'Hara, Phillip Anthony. 1993. Methodological Principles of Institutional Political Economy: Holism, Evolution and Contradiction. *Methodus* 5 (1): 51–71.

———. 1999a. Political Economy: Major Contemporary Themes. In *Encyclopedia of Political Economy*, ed. P.A. O'Hara, 861–868. London/New York: Routledge. Paper Edition 2001. Chinese Edition 2010.

———. 1999b. Thorstein Veblen's Theory of Collective Social Wealth, Instincts and Property Relations. *History of Economic Ideas* 7 (3): 153–179.

———. 2000. *Marx, Veblen and Contemporary Institutional Political Economy: Principles and Unstable Dynamics of Capitalism*. Cheltenham/Northampton: Edward Elgar.

———. 2004a. A New Family-Community Social Structure of Accumulation for the United States? *Forum for Social Economics* 33 (2): 51–80.

———. 2004b. The Wealth and Welfare of Nations, Continents and Corporations. In *Global Political Economy and the Wealth of Nations: Performance, Institutions, Problems and Policies*, ed. P.A. O'Hara. London/New York: Routledge.

———. 2006. *Growth and Development in the Global Political Economy: Social Structures of Accumulation and Modes of Regulation*. London/New York: Routledge.

O'Hara, Phillip Anthony. 2007. Principles of Institutional-Evolutionary Political Economy—Converging Themes from the Schools of Heterodoxy. *Journal of Economic Issues* 41 (1): 1–42.

O'Hara, Phillip Anthony. 2008. Principle of Circular and Cumulative Causation: Fusing Myrdalisn and Kaldorian Growth and Development Dynamics. *Journal of Economic Issues* 42 (2): 375–387.

———. 2014. Political Economy of Love: Nurturance Gap, Disembedded Economy, and Freedom Constraints Within Neoliberal Capitalism. *Panoeconomicus* 61 (2): 161–192.

———. 2015. Exploitation and Surplus. In *The Elgar Companion to Social Economics*, ed. John B. Davis and Wilfred Dolfsma, 716–734. Cheltenham: Edward Elgar.

———. 2021. Objectives of the *Review of Evolutionary Political Economy*'s 'Manifesto' and Editorial Proposals on World Problems, Complex Systems, Historico-Institutional and Corruption Issues. *Review of Evolutionary Political Economy* 2 (2): 359–387. https://doi.org/10.1007/s43253-021-00040-9.

———. 2022. Merging Dugger's Concepts with O'Hara's Principles to Advance Social and Institutional Economics. *Forum for Social Economics* 51 (1): 9–40. https://doi.org/10.1080/07360932.2018.1467332.

———. 2023. *Long Wave Institutional Dynamics and Political Economy Crises of Capitalism: Principles, Social Structures of Accumulation. Empirics*. Singapore: Springer.

Ofori-Dankwa, Joseph, and Scott D. Julian. 2001. Complexifying Organizational Theory: Illustrations Using Time Research. *Academy of Management Review* 26 (3): 415–430.

Papadopoulos, Georgios. 2015. Expanding on Ceremonial Encapsulation: The Case of Financial Innovation. *Journal of Economic Issues* 49 (1): 127–142. https://doi.org/10.1080/00213624.2015.1013883.

Pauls, Robert. Forthcoming. Capitalist Accumulation, Contradictions and Crisis in China, 1995–2015. *Journal of Contemporary Asia*. https://doi.org/10.1080/00472336.2020.1861640.

Peterson, Janice, and Margaret Lewis. 1999. *The Elgar Companion to Feminist Economics*. Cheltenham/Northampton: Edward Elgar Publishing.

Piketti, Thomas. 2014. *About Capital in the Twenty-First Century*. Cambridge, MA: Belknap Press of Harvard University Press.

Piketti, Thomas, Li Yang, and Gabriel Zucman. 2019. Capital Accumulation, Private Property, and Rising Inequality in China, 1978–2015. *American Economic Review* 109 (7): 2469–2496.

Pini, Poalo. 1995. Economic growth, Technological Change and Employment: Empirical Evidence for a Cumulative Growth Model with External Causation for Nine OECD countries: 1960–1990. *Structural Change and Economic Dynamics* 6 (2): 185–213.

Polanyi, Karl. 1944. *The Great Transformation: The Political and Economic Origins of Our Time*. Boston: Beacon Press. 1957.

———. 1968. The Economy as Instituted Process. In *Primitive, Archaic, and Modern Economies: Essays of Karl Polanyi*, ed. George Dalton. Boston: Beacon Press.

Radzicki, Michael J., and John D. Sterman. 1994. Evolutionary Economics and System Dynamics. In *Evolutionary Concepts in Contemporary Economics*, ed. Richard W. England. Ann Arbor: University of Michigan Press.

Resnick, Stephen, and Richard Wolff. 2005. The Point and Purpose of Marx's Notion of Class. *Rethinking Marxism* 17 (1): 33–38.

Rochon, Louis-Philippe, and Sergio Rossi, eds. 2017. *Advances in Endogenous Money Analysis*. Cheltenham: Edward Elgar.

Rochon, Louis-Philippe, and Matias Vernengo, eds. 2001. *Credit, Interest Rates and the Open Economy: Essays on Horizontalism*. Cheltenham/Northampton: Edward Elgar Publishing.

Rodrigues, João. 2014. Endogenous Preferences and Embeddedness: A Reappraisal of Karl Polanyi. *Journal of Economic Issues* 38 (1): 189–2000.

Rostow, Walt Whitman. 1940. Explanations of the "Great Depression", 1873–96. *Economic History Review* 10 (1): 356–370.

Samudro, Bhimo Rizky. 2012. *A Political Economy Analysis of Uneven Global, Regional, National and Sub-National Performance 1950–2010*. PhD Thesis. Curtin University, School of Economics & Finance, Perth, Australia.

Saslow, Wayne M. 2020. A History of Thermodynamics: The Missing Manual. *Entropy* 22 (1): 1–48. https://doi.org/10.3390/e22010077.

Schumpeter, Joseph. 1911. *The Theory of Economic Development*. Oxford: Oxford University Press. 1938.

———. 1942. *Capitalism, Socialism and Democracy*. New York: Harper & Row. 1975.

Schwardt, Henning. 2014. *Institutions, Technology and Circular and Cumulative Causation in Economics*. London: Palgrave Macmillan.

Sen, Amartya. 1999. *Development as Freedom*. New York: Anchor Books.

Shackle, G.L.S. 1972. *Expectations, Enterprise and Profit*. London: Allen & Unwin.

Sherman, Howard. 2003. Institutions and the Business Cycle. *Journal of Economic Issues* 37 (3): 621–642.

Smialek, Jeanna. 2022. Is This What Winning Looks Like?", *New York Times,* 7 February. https://www.nytimes.com/2022/02/06/business/economy/modern-monetary-theory-stephanie-kelton.html.

Spithoven, Antoon. 2021. Gig Workers and Policies of Minimal Social Dislocation. *Journal of Economic Issues* 55 (2): 516–523. https://doi.org/10.1080/00213624.2021.1919853.

Stanfield, James Ronald. 1986. *The Economic Thought of Karl Polanyi: Lives and Livelihood*. New York: St. Martin's Press.

———. 1995. *Economics, Power and Culture: Essays in the Development of Radical Institutionalism*. New York: St. Martins.

Sterman, John D. 2000. *Business Dynamics: Systems Thinking and Modeling for a Complex World*. London/New York: Irwin/McGraw-Hill.

Streeton, Paul. 2002. Reflections on Social and Antisocial Capital. *Journal of Human Development* 3 (1): 7–22.

Tool, Marc. 2001. *The Discretionary Economy: A Normative Theory of Political Economy*. 3rd ed. New Brunswick/London: Transactions Publishers.

Uslaner, Eric M. 2018. *The Oxford Handbook of Social and Political Trust*. Oxford: Oxford University Press.

van Duijn, J.J. 1983. *The Long Wave in Economic Life*. London: Allen & Unwin.

Veblen, Thorstein. 1899. *The Theory of the Leisure Class*. London: Unwin. 1965.

Veblen, Thorstein Bunde. 1904. *The Theory of Business Enterprise*, 1975. New Brunswick: Transaction Books.

———. 1914. *The Instinct of Workmanship and the State of the Industrial Arts*, 1990. New Brunswick: Transaction Books.

———. 1919. *The Vested Interests and the Common Man ("The Modern Point of View and the New Order")*, 1964. New York: Augustus M. Kelley.

———. 1923. *Absentee Ownership and Business Enterprise in Recent Times: The Case of America*, 1964. New York: Augustus M. Kelley.

Waller, William. 1988. The Concept of Habit in Economic Analysis. *Journal of Economic Issues* 22 (1): 113–126.

Weber, Matthias. 2007. The Neo-Schumpeterian Element in the Sociological Analysis of Innovation. In *Elgar Companion to Neo-Schumpeterian Economics*, ed. Horst Hanusch and Andreas Pyka, 107–129. Cheltenham: Edward Edgar.

Wilber, Charles K., and Robert S. Harrison. 1978. The Methodological Basis of Institutional Economics: Pattern Model, Storytelling, and Holism. *Journal of Economic Issues* 12 (1): 61–89.

Wolff, Richard D. 2019. *Understanding Marxism*. New York: Democracy at Work.

Wolfson, M.H. 1994. *Financial Crises: Understanding the Postwar U.S. Experience*. 2nd ed. Armonk/New York/London: M.E. Sharpe.

Wrenn, Mary. 2015. Immanent Critique, Enabling Myths, and the Neoliberal Narrative. *Review of Radical Political Economics* 48 (3): 252–266. https://doi.org/10.1177/0486613415605074.

Global Coronavirus Pandemic Crisis

Abstract

This chapter undertakes an interdisciplinary analysis of the global coronavirus crisis of 2020–2022, its immediate aftermath and lessons learned, through the use of some core principles of institutional and evolutionary political economy. The principle of historical specificity and evolution examines the background to the emergence of the crisis, plus its evolution and transformation through time. The principle of heterogeneous groups and agents scrutinizes the crisis through the various groups and individuals associated with gender, class, ethnicity, age and species. The principles of circular and cumulative causation (CCC) and contradiction investigate the multiple factors responsible for the crisis and how they interact in determining the depth and recovery from the crisis; while the principle of hegemony and uneven development is also pertinent here. The principle of uncertainty illustrates the changing expectations underlying the business climate and consumer confidence affecting socioeconomic performance, as well as current and future policies associated with health, regulation, budgets and money. We also analyse the coronacrisis through the principles of innovation plus policy and governance. A conclusion follows.

Keywords

Coronacrisis · Principles · Political economy · Historical specificity · Heterogeneous groups & agents · Circular & cumulative causation · Contradiction · Uncertainty · Policy

4.1 Introduction

The coronavirus crisis that beset the world during 2020–2022, and which has dragged on in different forms and degrees ever since, initially threatened to tear the whole world apart, impacting us deeply for years to come. Instead, it majorly affected most areas and nations during 2020, and to varying degrees through the early, middle and especially later months of 2021 (with the Delta variant), and notably during early 2022 (with the Omicron variant), but its impact has been very uneven throughout. The *principle of hegemony and uneven development* implies that the structures of power in the global political economy imbue especially core nations with several advantages with their production networks, commodity chains, policy structures, and financial dynamics, which put them in good stead to fight crises, even though they may not be initially ready for them. This is especially the case under current conditions in which, as the *Economist* (2021a) said, neoliberalism is 'out of fashion', especially among numerous economists and policy-makers. Semi-peripheral and especially peripheral areas have less structural power in the global political economy, which places grave limits on their ability to fight public health, climate change, and most other systemic crises.

All nations were mostly unprepared for a public health crisis that authorities had warned them of, leading to many millions of deaths and hundreds of millions of infections during 2019–2022. However, since the GFC of 2008–2010ff was widely blamed on neoliberal's austerity, low regulation and speculative bubble crashes, this helped especially the advanced capitalist nations fight the coronavirus through crisis measures such as functional finance, widespread handouts to business and workers, massive injections of funds for public health and vaccinations, rental assistance, and low interest rates to stimulate credit multipliers. These crisis measures saw the deep recessions of 2020 reverse to high growth during 2021 and 2022 in most advanced nations, even while infection rates remained high, as well as deaths in many places, as they opened up in especially those nations with relatively high rates of vaccination. Officially, many peripheral and semi-peripheral areas underwent forms of 'economic recovery' during 2021 and 2022, but rates of infection and mortality remained high, yet likely if their citizens were vaccinated the death toll would have declined majorly.

This chapter examines the coronavirus crisis through the lens of certain principles of institutional and evolutionary political economy, including lessons learned from the crisis to prevent another. The principles are methodological devices designed to assist in comprehending holistically ('as a whole') the nature of complex systems dynamics, including crises such as the coronavirus pandemic and potential future crises. The chapter starts with a review of papers that have applied certain political economy principles to the coronavirus crisis. Then we scrutinize further institutional and evolutionary principles, starting with historical specificity and evolution; which follows the background to the emergence of the virus, through to the international transmission of the pandemic, and the differential impact of the crisis throughout the world. This is followed by detail on the heterogeneous groups and agents of human beings, viruses and vaccines that contributed to the differential impact of the crisis and its resolution. We then study the multicausal factors responsible for the crisis and the anomalous dichotomies introducing conflict and instability through the principles of CCC and contradiction; also linked to the principle of hegemony and uneven development. Lastly, we apply the principle of uncertainty to the business climate and consumer confidence leading up to, during and after the immediate crises, plus the way in which uncertainty, innovation and policy & governance principles relate to preparatory and ongoing policies affecting the crisis and how such policies should be structured now and into the future. A conclusion follows.

4.2 Political Economy of the Coronavirus Pandemic

There have been numerous special issues of political economy journals about the coronavirus crisis, such as the *Journal of Australian Political Economy*, the *International Journal of Political Economy*, and the *Review of Political Economy*. There were also a number of conferences on the crisis; for instance, the 2021 conference of the European Association for Evolutionary Political Economy (EAEPE). These special issues and conferences have studied many aspects of the crisis, but none of them, that I have noticed, has investigated it within the framework of several principles of institutional and evolutionary political economy. Hence this chapter. Elsewhere though, some papers have tried to study the crisis within the context of certain political economy concepts or principles, some of which may variously be called neoclassical or Austrian political economy, and others heterodox political economy. In this section we scrutinize the results of five such full-length papers. We start with those that are well removed from the perspective taken up in this chapter, and gradually get closer to those that have a modest resemblance to certain aspects of the perspective enunciated here.

The first is by Peter Boettke and Benjamin Powell (2021), who investigate the COVID-19 pandemic from the view of 'traditional welfare economics'. Using concepts such as markets, pricing mechanisms, costs and benefits, externalities, symmetry (representative agents), and re-selling vaccine rights (onward selling), this chapter argues that governments around the world have not used standard welfare economics to deal with the pandemic. Instead, they argue governments have typically used "command and control" mechanisms of "paternalistic socialism", looking after certain vested interests, overspending, and generally distorting the pattern of economic processes for no good purpose. In places the paper also uses a model of those that are old and those that are young, suggesting that we should enable the economy to function through the use of the young, since the net benefits will be greater than if we tried to protect the old despite the costs. This is a very strange paper, since it appears to be lacking in several key areas: a disregard for the common good, no coherent systemic morality, ignoring functional finance, overemphasising the micro over the meso, macro and global; generally allowing markets to operate irrespective of key areas of market failure and humanistic concerns.

The second paper by Mikayla Novak (2021) uses a strange combination of Austrian theory and practical good sense, which often appear to be in contradiction with each other, to come to conclusions that are similar to the first paper discussed here (above), from which the practical good sense of the real world is quite different. The paper seeks to support voluntarist interaction, typical "liberal" institutions (markets), contractual freedom, property rights protections, freedom of economic entry and exit (p. 6), reducing rent seeking and self-sufficiency (p. 8), and especially inhibiting the centripetal power of the health authorities (p. 9). It also seeks to denigrate government support and regulation of health care services in favour of commercial and economic standards (p. 10) and to inhibit the growth of collective property and monocentric organisation. Eschewing representation agents, on the other hand, it argues that heterogeneous agents that respond quickly to change are a core part of a COVID-19 solution. The use of entrepreneurial action to quickly act on new opportunities such as COVID-19 is important, especially in their responses to the new private sector demands of commercial experimentation. Rather than subsidizing wage-earners to protect them from change, and instead of providing massive government injections of money to put a floor on the downturn, this paper argues that downturns are a good way of reorganising economic relations through agility and a recalibration of economic associations. An alternative policy should be implemented, it is argued, based on the provision of innovative medical treatments, competitive adjustments, more market relations in health care, decentralised community decision-making, and individual liberty.

The final three papers are more in tune with the approach of this current chapter. The third such paper, by Scott Kaplan et al. (2021), is a general paper, and mainly uses a pragmatic and straightforwardly intelligent use of stylized facts to explain aspects of the pandemic. Counter to the first two papers, this one argues that overall there is no *systemic* trade-off between economic activity and public health, since nations that controlled the pandemic had less loss of employment and sales. It also recognises the crucial importance of controlling the disease through the principles of prevention, social distancing, personal protective measures, and international collaboration. It recognises that those who suffered most from the pandemic had pre-existing conditions, were elderly, minorities, and in lower socioeconomic categories. But rather than advocating simply opening up markets to allow the young to benefit vis-à-vis those with pre-existing conditions, it looked more to the common good by advocating more prevention and mitigation as the way forward.

The fourth and fifth political economy papers on the COVID-19 pandemic are *specifically* in synchrony, to some degree, with the principles of this current chapter. The fourth, by Simon Mair (2020), posits an alternative set of principles to challenge neoliberalism in devising solutions to health and ecological problems emerging through the twenty-first century. These principles include but go beyond exchange value to encompass the value of health and ecological sustainability. It also posits the principle that the social economy operates substantively through heterogeneous groups in the ecological community rather than just through markets. The protection of life is said to be a core aspect of an alternative political economy, along with the public provisioning of food, clothing and shelter. In this context, greater attention is said to be required in the provision of public health infrastructure, preventative services, safety nets, health capabilities and capacity, and where necessary imposing lockdowns to protect health value. It calls for multiple forms of value to embed economy within society through the protection of life in general and ecology in particular.

The fifth paper, by Roderick Condon (2020), follows the contours of Jurgen Habermas's communication theory of society in describing the current legitimisation crisis of neoliberalism and the enfolding alternatives of radical pluralism (on the left) and reactionary populism-nationalism (on the right). The author develops a cultural analysis of the crisis of legitimacy and the pandemic, which accords to some degree with institutional and evolutionary political economy. Neoliberalism is said to have lost its legitimacy in the face of the GFC and the pandemic, which has led to two alternative social movements being developed and progressing to condition human behaviour into the future. The first is the pluralistic-democratic movement being followed by the EU (but not all of its constituents) and some other nations, and the second is the developing nationalist-populist trends established by, for instance, former President Donald Trump; Jair Bolsonaro, President of Brazil; Narendra Modi, Prime Minister of India; and Alexander Lukashenko, President of Belarus. Clearly recommending the radical-pluralist movement, Condon outlines a new cultural model to confront the pandemic, including the assertion of collective responsibility for the common good, international cosmopolitanism, recovery funds such as that established with the EU, re-engagement with the WTO, and a global ethics as a countermovement to help solve health, ecology and other problems into the future.

This review of political economy principles papers on COVID-19 has shown the diversity of approaches. The rest of this chapter details core aspects of an institutional and evolutionary approach, especially principles (see Phillip O'Hara 2007a, 2021b, 2022a; Andrew Brennan and Jaslyn Kalsi 2015; Bhimo Samudro 2012), as applied to the COVID-19 pandemic. The third, fourth and fifth papers have some key similarities with this current chapter. But we are more specific in the use of the principles of historical specificity, heterogeneous groups & agents, CCC, contradiction, hegemony/uneven development, uncertainty, innovation and policy/governance.

4.3 Historical Evolution of the Global Coronavirus Crisis

The *principle of historical specificity and evolution* states that world problems and issues should be analysed historically as they evolve through time, and there are many benefits from taking this point of view. Scrutinising the coronavirus crisis historically in general terms involves situating the crisis within the context of history, and doing it specifically involves examining the factors that directly led to its emergence and evolution. The general context deals with previous global pandemics and coronaviruses that have impacted the human population, and what we can and have learnt from these for dealing with the current pandemic. The specific context involves following the evolution of the coronavirus crisis, policy and measures to moderate the pandemic as it changes course from 2020 to 2022 and beyond.

Studies of the coronavirus pandemic must recognise previous pandemics over the past 100 years plus coronavirus infections of varying descriptions. Here we delimit scope to those pandemics that have killed at least one million people per year. Even then, there are finer points of disagreement, especially regarding the suddenness and prolonged nature of some diseases and their degree of globalness (e.g., malaria, TB). As shown in Fig. 4.1, below, there have been at least five pandemics since 1918:

A pandemic is best thought of as a transnational or more specifically a global infection that kills many more than the usual number of people from the so-called "common seasonal influenza" (typically 650,000 in today's terms) on a yearly basis. Five major pandemics have been especially deadly over the past 100 years or so. The mother of them all was the so-called "Spanish Flu", which, in all probability, emerged in the USA, potentially from a military base in Kansas (or North Carolina), and eventually spread to most nations of the world, killing at least 20 million people and more likely 50 million, possibly up to 100 million. The first wave of this (Kansas) H1N1 virus was relatively mild during early 1918, but in late 1918 and into 1919 the second wave was most destructive as it swept across much of the world, especially the USA, Europe, Mexico, New Zealand, Iceland, Iran and Western Samoa (Daniel Flecknoe et al. 2018: 2). Major pandemic factors were the first world-war, especially the movement of military personnel, and the lower resistance of troops on the battle front and in hospitals, although many civilians were killed as well. Wartime secrecy was a core problem as it led to ignorance and inadequate information-sharing among the powers, and hence to the much greater spread throughout the world.

This 'Kansas' pandemic incidence was not limited to the estimated 20–100 m deaths and 500 m infections, but should also include babies not born and not conceived due to dead mothers and fathers, survivors that died of other ailments

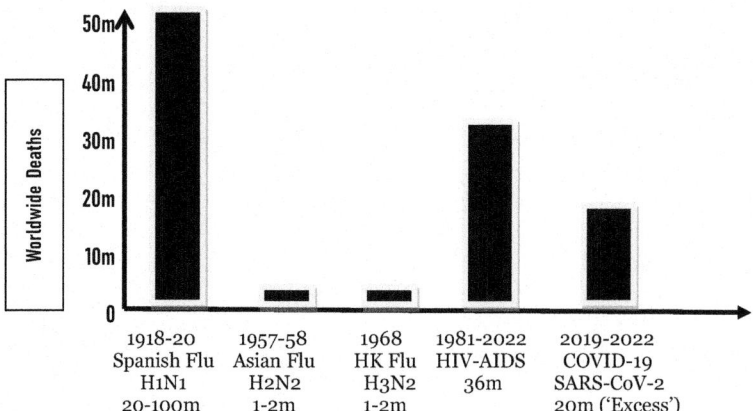

Fig. 4.1 *Some* major pandemics: Past 100 years: Death estimates to 2022. (Source: Adapted & updated from Yen-Chin Liu 2020; *Economist* 2022)

later, and many that survived but were 'much lower achievers' than they otherwise would have been. The 20–100 m deaths also included many that would otherwise have likely died of TB. (Howard Phillips 2014.) It is thus an open question how many were "excess deaths", over-and-above those that would have died in a normal period.

It is perhaps stretching the definition of pandemic to include some of the well-known ones of the 1950s–1970s, since they typically "only" killed 1–2 m people in the space of a couple of years, which is about the number killed from a typical common influenza in 2 years (in today's terms). For instance, the so-called pandemics of the 1950s and 1960s were also "flu" cases, including the so-called "1957–58 Influenza pandemic" and the "1968–70 Hong Kong Flu pandemic". These two global 'pandemics' were closely related as the 1957–1958 one emanated from the H2N2 type virus on mainland China while the 1968–1970 one was caused by H3N2, a co-variant of H2N2, also from China (HK or mainland). They both killed about the same number of people globally, and deaths from both were reduced markedly due to timely efforts to produce an effective vaccine, especially through the efforts of microbiologist Maurice Hilleman and his Team. H2N2 and H3N2 are both avian viruses which can be transmitted directly from birds to humans or through an intermediary.[1]

The HIV-AIDS global pandemic (1981-present) and the Coronavirus-19 pandemic (2020–2021) are the most serious cases to have emerged since the "Kansas" pandemic of 1918–2020. The HIV-AIDS pandemic is an unusual one since there has historically been a large lag (of often 4–20 years) between infection with the HIV retrovirus and the possible onset of morbid AIDS symptoms and death. Global yearly deaths from HIV-AIDS were approximately 350,000 in 1990, rising to just under 2 m in 2005 and then declining to just under 1 m in 2017 (Roser and Ritchie 2021). Now with effective drugs the annual toll is around 700,000 deaths with *cumulative* deaths of around 35 million. No effective vaccine has been developed, but with effective drugs a typical HIV carrier can live almost a normal life, especially in advanced nations (O'Hara 2007b, 2022b).

The latest pandemic, caused by infection with a coronavirus, is the most extreme influenza outbreak since the 'Kansas' flu of 1918–2020. Coronaviruses have been around for centuries or even millions of years, spreading among bats, birds and rats. In the contemporary scene, some coronaviruses are known to produce mild symptoms in humans, while others are much more deadly. Three in particular stand out. The first is severe acute respiratory syndrome (SARS), coronavirus (CoV)—known as SARS-CoV—from the beta coronavirus subgroup (β; lineage B), which caused the influenza variety known as SARS in 2003, and killed 774 people worldwide. The second is Middle East respiratory syndrome coronavirus (MERS-CoV), also from the beta coronavirus subgroup (β; lineage A), which causes

---

[1] The so-called "Russian Flu Pandemic" of 1977 (H1N1 viral strain started in Northern China) and the "Swine Flu Pandemic" of 2009 (H1N1 virus strain from Central Mexico) had a mortality about the same as the yearly common flu, so cannot reasonably be called a pandemic.

MERS influenza, emerging as it did in 2012; which has killed 858 people. (Ahmed Al-Qahtani 2020: 4.) The mortality rate of those with known MERS infections is around 35%. SARS and MERS patients typically experience mild upper respiratory symptoms, possibly leading to pneumonia, and in extreme cases acute respiratory distress syndrome (ARDS) and renal failure.

The third virus, causing the current global crisis, is also a member of the beta coronavirus subgroup (β; lineage B; as with SARS-CoV) and shares 80% of its genome lineage with SARS-CoV. This virus is the first global *coronavirus* pandemic in history, and became known as SARS Coronavirus-2 (SARS-CoV-2), with its accompanying disease termed Coronavirus disease 2019 (COVID-19), which is a type of influenza. It was first identified in Wuhan Province in China in late 2019, with typical symptoms initially including fever, dry cough and malaise, and when more extreme pneumonia, ARDS and potentially single or multifarious organ failures (e.g., pulmonary, renal). It started infecting people at or near the Huanan Seafood Wholesale Market, in Wuhan, China, and spreading nearby and later to other Chinese Provinces, then rapidly throughout the world. The WHO classed COVID-19 as a pandemic on 13 March 2020. During mid-March, Europe was considered the centre of the pandemic, but by late March the United States was cited as a centre of infection. At different times Italy was the 'centre', and later Brazil, then India, followed by Indonesia; and later others that had coped well with the virus were majorly affected (e.g., Thailand, Vietnam).

There is doubt about the origins of the COVID-19 disease, since there is no definitive evidence about whether it started in the Wuhan wet markets (where live, often exotic animals are sold), or close by in Wuhan Province, or perhaps in one of the nearby labs, or from scientists etc. investigating caves or catching bats in the area. Virulent microorganisms often leak from labs. Take the cases of, for instance, the leak of a smallpox virus from a British lab in 1978, the SARS-CoV virus from three separate labs in Asia during 2003–2004, and the H1N1 strain of influenza that spread rapidly in 1977 after leaking from a lab. Strangely, according to *The Economist* (2021b: 52), "Chinese authorities refused requests to provide key epidemiological data on the 174 earliest known cases of COVID-19 in [Wuhan] in December 2019," which prevented key research from being undertaken about the origins of COVID-19.

There is no evidence from the WHO-China Joint Report (2021) on Covid-19 and the WHO-China Joint Mission (2020) on SARS-CoV-2, alluding to informational anomalies about early cases. The first reports the original *clinical diagnosis* of COVID-19 in China was in Wuhan Province, 2 December 2019, but the first *confirmed* case was diagnosed on 8 December 2019. Cases gradually and then rapidly grew, with a major spike on 1 February 2020 for Wuhan at approx. 2000 daily cases and China approx. 4000 daily cases. By 20 February 2020 national cases had dropped to single digits.

The 2021 Joint Report concluded that SARS-CoV-2 had a zoonotic origin, originally from bats, with intermediate host unknown, probably being contracted from the Huanan Wholesale Seafood Market in Wuhan where they sell live animals or closeby. Information on the (then) epidemic was said to have been passed on to the WHO on 3 January 2020, along with the total genome sequence of SARS-CoV-2 on 10 January 2020 (WHO-China Joint Mission 2020: 6). 'Comprehensive Control Measures' were implemented in Wuhan and elsewhere, including application of the core 'principles of public health', including (1) 'aggressive case and contact' tracing, (2) 'isolation and management', and (3) 'extreme social distancing' (p. 10), which led to the number of (official) confirmed cases falling to zero by late February 2020 throughout all of China. Meanwhile infections had spread to all continents and nations.

More recently, evidence is pointing to the Chinese authorities having unduly pressured the visiting team(s) into dismissing the need for further investigation of the origins of the virus. The Head of the WHO investigating team that visited Wuhan in early 2021, Peter Ben Embarek, as well as Tedros Adhanom Ghebreyesus, the Director-General of WHO, have both called for further work on the origins of COVID-19. Others have also called for more studies on the origins of COVID-19, including initially the Australian PM, and the US President who arranged (in May 2021) for a major report to be delivered to him by intelligence officials on its origins 'within 90-days'.

An "Unclassified Report" (ODNI 2021), from the US Director of National Intelligence, issued on 27 August 2021, soon after the official report, based on scientific evidence, concludes that SARS-CoV-2 was not a biological weapon, nor was it genetically engineered, and that Chinese officials were not forewarned of the virus before the initial outbreak of COVID-19. The report put forward 3 hypotheses about its origins. The most likely, H1, supported by 5 sources within the Intelligence Community (IC), was that it was likely caused by natural exposure to an animal infected with the virus or a "close progenitor". The second hypothesis, H2, supported by one IC source, was that it was most likely the result of a laboratory-linked accident, including possibly experimentation, animal handling or sampling by the Wuhan Institute of Virology (WIV). The third Hypothesis, H3, supported by 3 IC sources, was that it was unable to decide whether it had a natural origin or was linked to the WIV, without further information from the Chinese. The global community lacks clinical samples and epidemiological data of the earliest cases of COVID-19. It would thus help prevent further pandemics if more knowledge on COVID-19 origins were available.

COVID-19 is estimated *officially* to have precipitated 6.07 m deaths during 2019–2022 (to date), and therefore is likely to be the third most lethal pandemic this century (if one discounts malaria and TB for not being truly global); with the prime one being the 'Kansas' pandemic of 1918–2020, and the secondary one being AIDS. Table 4.1, below, summarizes global data for COVID-19 waves (major 'ups' and 'downs') of officially confirmed total cases and deaths, plus current wave status:

Current data *confirms* a cumulative 6.07 m official global deaths and 470 m global cases of COVID-19 over 2019–2022. Most cases initially spread to areas of strong tourism and business strength, notably America, Europe and Asia. The number of waves of cases and deaths differ from area to area, but typically deaths lag cases since people get infected before they die of COVID-19 complications. Waves occur due to many factors, such as new variants, vaccines (in some nations),

Table 4.1 Global COVID-19: Waves, *official* cases & deaths; vaccinations; Circa 19 March 2022

Region	Waves: Cases	Cumulative cases OWID [million]	Current wave phase: cases (weekly)	Waves: Deaths	Cumulative deaths: OWID	Current wave: Deaths (weekly)	Partial vaccin. (% Pop)	'Full' vaccin. (% Pop.)	Booster admin. (% Pop.)
World	6	469.71	Downwave	7	6.07 m	Downwave	7	57	19
America	Nth: 6	94.08	Downwave	5	1.40 m	Downwave	Nth: 9	Nth: 62	Nth: 22
	Sth: 4	55.57	Downwave	3	1.27 m	Downwave	Sth: 11	Sth: 72	Sth: 32
Europe	8	171.50	Slight upwave	6	1.75 m	Downwave	3	65	38
Asia	6	132.47	Upwave	4	1.39 m	Downwave	7	66	19
Africa	4	11.46	Downwave	4	0.25 m	Downwave	5	15	1
Oceania	6	4.64	Upwave	5	8456	Upwave	4	62	35

Source: Adapted from raw figures of OWID (2022) (see Mathieu et al. 2021)

4.3 Historical Evolution of the Global Coronavirus Crisis

and countries *recurringly* interspersing freedoms with lockdowns and freedoms (again) followed by more lockdowns. Following this lockdown-freedoms dynamic there are typically a surge of cases and then deaths. However, some areas, especially in advanced nations, have fewer waves of deaths than cases (though aggregate deaths may look high), mainly due to higher vaccinations rates, past immunity, the nature of the mutations, and better health infrastructure. The worst affected by COVID-19 are typically the unvaccinated and those with pre-established medical conditions.

At least three typical styles of COVID-19 waves have emerged in the world relative to confirmed *rates* of cases and deaths per capita, as shown below in Fig. 4.2a–c.

Case A shows how every wave upswing in cases is followed by a wave upswing in deaths, with a lag; and every wave downswing in cases is followed by a wave downswing in deaths. Examples include Russia, Belarus, and Serbia. The final waves for both cases and deaths follow each other in this pattern because efficient vaccination rates are low and hence deaths are still forthcoming at proportionate rates to those of cases. (More recently, with the Omicron variant, both cases and deaths rose and then fell, as per the usual pattern, but we do not know the nature of the next wave, if there is one.)

Case B illustrates nations whose final wave upswing of cases per 100,000 infections is not followed by a similarly intense upwave in deaths, because vaccination/immunity rates are relatively high, the nature of some mutations, and those that die of complications with COVID-19 tend to be not vaccinated/have major pre-existing conditions. Examples include the UK, France and Germany. (This pattern has continued through the Omicron variant waves, as rising cases far outweigh declining deaths.)

Case C exhibits low rates of cases and deaths due to severe lockdowns and social distancing, where waves of cases and deaths occur due to successive bouts of opening up, where eventually a new wave of cases is not followed by major deaths, perhaps due to some degree of natural immunity, vaccinations, the nature of some mutations, and good health-governance systems, especially for those most vulnerable. Examples include Australia and New Zealand. (As they opened up to the ROW

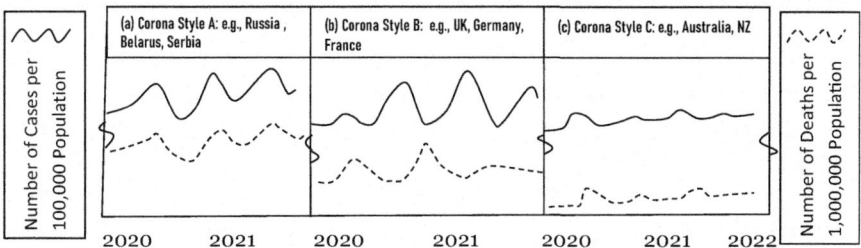

Fig. 4.2 Three styles of COVID-19 waves of cases and deaths. (Source: Synthesized from several data points, OWID (2022) Coronavirus website)

with the Omicron variant, both cases and deaths per capita rose majorly relative to Case B nations.)

These three typical cases likely change over time for specific nations involved. It is usually advanced nations that transition to the stage where case spikes fail to elicit major death spikes (except for those unvaccinated and with pre-existing medical conditions). Less developed nations of especially Africa, but also to some extent certain nations of South East Asia, South Asia, and the Caribbean, have administered few tests and have little capacity for widespread vaccination campaigns. Data for many such areas show far fewer cases/deaths than is likely in reality, as testing is minimal and often there is no data about testing levels. While most developed nations have many more than 100 tests per 100 persons, in Africa there is usually less than 20 tests per 100 persons. Many African nations, such as Tanzania, Cameroon and the Central African Republic, have little data on SARS-CoV-2 tests per unit population. Lacking tests means estimates of cases and deaths are much lower than reality for COVID-19 (WHO 2021a).

This raises the core issue of *excess* deaths (D_{Ex}), defined as the number of deaths in an area during the COVID-19 pandemic (D_p) minus the number of deaths that usually occur in a typical year from all causes (D_{Typ}): $D_{Ex} = D_p - D_{Typ}$. *The Economist*, for instance, uses a model to regularly update estimates of excess deaths. Most nations of the world have official COVID-19 death estimates far lower than the excess deaths above those that usually die in a typical non-pandemic period (e.g., from seasonal influenzas, heart attacks, cancers, etc.). Reasons for this are lack of tests for SARS-CoV-2, inadequate official statistical networks and corruption of the data. Table 4.2, below, includes estimates of excess deaths [D_{Ex}] and official-confirmed data on COVID-19 deaths [D_{Of}] for the world and selected nations (grouped into regions).

This demonstrates five things. The first is that official global data for COVID-19 deaths (6.07 m) understate excess-deaths from the pandemic (20 m) by nearly 14 m. The greater excess deaths are relative to official deaths the greater the undercounting through official figures. The second is that some nations have a close fit between official and excess figures (e.g., Peru, Brazil, Hungary, USA), indicating little undercounting. The third is that numerous nations had a core problem with official figures majorly understating deaths: excess deaths being far greater than official deaths (e.g., Russia, Poland, South Africa, Egypt, Iran; also many other African nations, not shown due to data inadequacies). The fourth is the lack of attention to distributing sufficient numbers of test kits, vaccines, and health infrastructures to nations that have few resources, especially in Africa: resulting in few (valid) figures. And the fifth is that nations with the highest number of total deaths per capita have generally failed to vaccinate their peoples due to governance anomalies (such as Russia, Serbia, Peru).

International organisations, including COVAX, WHO, plus the US government and others, have promised vaccines for especially African nations that are in financial and organisational difficulties in this respect. The crucial task is for this to be activated on the ground urgently before Delta, Omicron and more virulent strains of SARS-CoV-2 mutate even further, before the whole world is able to get to

Table 4.2 *Excess* deaths & *official* COVID deaths (Latest Data Available 21 March 2022[a]), world & 23 nations

Nation	*Excess* deaths (D_{Ex}) per 100,000[a] population mid-point estimate	Cumulative *excess* deaths[a] mid-point estimate	Cumulative *official* COVID deaths (D_{Of})[c]
World	125	20 m (13.8–23.7 m[b])	6.07 m
Peru	651	217,100	212,220
Mexico	475	618,900	292,460
Brazil	354	757,170	649,680
Russia	770	1123.960	324,660
Serbia	779	53,540	13,610
Hungary	444	42,780	41,710
Poland	482	182,110	108,100
South Africa	422	253,200	99,360
Egypt	263	273,680	20,430
Tunisia	54	6500	7160
Italy	319	192,330	137,640
USA	336	1,117,660	921,640
Britain	221	150,510	160,240
France	159	107,270	135,240
Germany	145	121,670	122,820
Iran	315	267,670	137,940
Lebanon	215	14,530	9080
Israel	107	9970	9960
Oman	87	4560	4100
Thailand	85	59,540	22,920
Malaysia	8	2510	26,290
Japan	19	24,350	18,380
Australia	−40	−10,390	1960

Source: Adapted from: [a]*Economist* (2022); [b]Uncertainty Range; [c] OWID (2022)

above 95% (including children) herd immunity through vaccination and previous infection.

4.4 Heterogeneous Groups and Agents

The *concept of heterogeneous groups and agents* involves the existence of species of beings, individuals or agents, which engage in networks of groups and other social organisations. They also have specific genetics, norms, habits and/or tendencies. In the case of the coronavirus crisis they include viruses, other species such as bats and numerous groups of humans, as well as groups of vaccines. The corresponding principle states that we should scrutinise these heterogeneous groups and agents in order to suitably understand core world problems such as the coronacrisis.

The SARS-Coronavirus-2 generates numerous mutations some of which are more virulent than others. Human beings are distinguished vis-a-vis coronavirus infection according to their ethnicity, place of residence, gender, class, age, and other characteristics. Their ability to evade infection and major symptoms depends largely upon which classes they operate within. For instance, regardless of nation, on average those that are elderly, of minority ethnic membership, and of working or lumpen class, tend to have higher rates of infection, lower rates of vaccination, more extreme symptoms and higher rates of mortality than more privileged groups.

Breaking it into components; in terms of age, generally the intensity of symptoms is positively related to age, with successive tipping points coming into play for those that are above-60, above-70, above-80, and above-90. As one ages, the ability of the body to fight invading microorganisms tends to decline markedly as the immune system is often compromised, and the aged tend to have many more pre-existing conditions compared with those that are younger. Hence the original Wuhan-1 virus plus the Alpha, Beta, Delta and Omicron variants generally impact older people much more than the young. But one variant of great concern (Gamma) and one of mere interest (Lambda) have been found to infect youth at a higher rate than the other variants. Currently Omicron has been shown to be much more highly transmissible than all other variants, but proportionately less fatal in relation to Delta.

This raises the second issue: that those—young and old—that have pre-existing conditions tend to be more severely impacted by the coronavirus than those that have no pre-existing conditions. This relates to all pre-existing conditions, the most common being associated with pulmonary, circulatory, psychological, neurological, digestive and reproductive diseases. As mentioned, pre-existing conditions are greater for the "aged" and lower classes; hence their typically higher rate of infection and mortality.

The third subcomponent of coronavirus influenza relates to "minorities": ethnic groups that have fewer opportunities and assets, tend to be subject to the more serious cases of COVID-19, such as serious pneumonia, pulmonary obstruction and organ failure. Such minorities generally have fewer/lower quality assets, knowledge, diet, and more barriers to getting ahead in life, as well as more serious medical conditions.

The fourth subgroup is gender. There is a tendency, overall, for men (per capita cohort) to be more severely affected by coronavirus-2 than women. The likely reasons for this are that men tend to die younger, they have more pre-existing conditions, drink and smoke more, and have worse diets and lifestyles, compared with women.

For instance, a study of 99 confirmed cases of COVID-19 from Wuhan Jinyintan Hospital, by Nanshan Chen et al. (2020), from 1 January to 20 January 2020, found that 51% of these Wuhan inpatients had chronic diseases, but the first two deaths, a 61-year-old man ('patient 1') and a 69-year-old man ('patient 2') 'had no previous chronic underlying disease but had a history of smoking' (p. 5). This is an issue often ignored: that smoking can be a major facilitator of COVID-19 symptoms and indeed mortality. Patient 1 developed severe pneumonia and ARDS and died of a sudden cardiac arrest, while Patient 2 died of pneumonia, septic shock and respiratory failure. Also, apart from generally having a better lifestyle and diet, and typically smoking and drinking less, this paper mentions another *possible* reason why women contract COVID-19 and die less often than men from COVID-19: "The reduced susceptibility of females to viral infections [may in part be due to] protection [given] by [the] X chromosome and sex hormones, which play an important role in innate and adaptive immunity" (p. 6).

Consider also the study by Hector Izurieta et al. (2021) that analysed risk factors for deaths (and hospitalisations) among more than 26 million US medicare beneficiaries. It found that "race, social disparities, old age, and underlying health conditions were associated with a higher risk of COVID-related severe outcomes, including . . . deaths" (p. 945). Pre-existing conditions that tend to heighten COVID-19 death rates include "hypertension, diabetes, obesity, frailty, . . . respiratory diseases, . . . cardiovascular diseases", as well as having a compromised immune system, cognitive impairment, paranoia, congestive heart failure, and pneumonia (p. 947). Native Americans were found to have the highest mortality rate, followed by Hispanics and then blacks; with Asians having the lowest risk along with whites (p. 952). Because women tend to live longer than men there were a greater proportion of them in the study (55.6% women, 44.4% men). The percentage of men in the cohort that died of COVID-19 was 51.5%, compared with women of 48.5% (p. 948). These results were said to be similar to other studies on the subject from the US and other countries.

Heterogeneous groups and agents also relates to microorganisms, other human groups/agents and vaccines. SARS-CoV, MERS-CoV, and SARS-CoV-2 all belong to the batacoronavirus subgroup. A key similarity between SARS-CoV and SARS-CoV-2 lies in the spike protein receptor binding domain, despite some key variations between them. SARS-Cov-2 has a greater reproductive multiplier than SARS-CoV, with elevated viral loads even when hosts are asymptomatic (Al-Qahtani 2020: 14); and a higher stimulation of cytokine inflammation in the host; which helps explain the far greater spread and mortality of the COVID-19 pandemic compared with the earlier SARS-CoV epidemic. (Harapan Harapan et al. 2020.)

The longer the pandemic continued, the greater the spread throughout the world, and the higher the number of mortalities, the more critical was the threat of more virulent strains emerging. WHO (2021b) has differentiated between "Variants of Concern" (VOC) and "Variants of Interest" (VOI). VOC such as Alpha, Beta, Gamma, Delta and Omicron are significantly more virulent than the original SARS-CoV-2 virus. VOI such as Eta, Iota, Kappa and Lambda are of some interest and in need of more research. Table 4.3, below, details core characteristics of the VOC:

Viruses typically mutate through time, with an assessment indicating that SARS-CoV-2 makes "one or two mutations a month" (Jacqui Wise 2021: 2). Such mutations have been assessed as being relatively low, relative to, say, the typical influenza viruses, because of the "proof-reading activity of its replication machinery" (Yongfei Cai et al. 2021: 1). Some of these mutations quickly dissipate, others reproduce quickly. Some are harmless, while others may be highly virulent and lethal. The SARS-CoV-2 virus infects humans through the binding of the RBD

Table 4.3 SARS-CoV-2 variants of concern: Comparison with original

WHO & Pango categories	Nation 1st detected	1st detected	Spike protein mutations (Examples)	Transmission Index vis-à-vis Wuhan-Hu-1
Wuhan-Hu-1 (Orig.)	China	Nov 2019	–	1.00
Alpha (α) B.1.1.7	UK	Sept 2020	N501Y; P681H; A570D	1.82 (43–130%↑)
Beta (β) B.1.351	South Africa	Sept 2020	K417N; E484K; N501Y	1.50 (20–113%↑)
Gamma (γ) B.1.1.28.1 (P.1)	Brazil	Dec 2020	K417T; E484K; N501Y	2.61 (145–176%↑)
Delta (δ) B.1.617.2	India	Dec 2020	L452R; T478K; D614G; E484Q	3.00
Omicron (O) B.1.1.529 (3 Sublineages)	Southern Africa	Nov 2021	60 Mutations, Antibody Resist: G446S; S371L; N440K; Q493R	6.00–9.00

Source: Variously Adapted from WHO (2022), ECDPC (2021), Wiki (2021a), Weilin Zhou and Wei Wang (2021), Elibabeth Mahase (2021), William Harvey et al. (2021), Liu et al. (2021), Chen et al. (2022) and Riediker et al. (2022)

(receptor binding domain) associated with the Spike protein of the virus to the ACE2 (angiotensin-converting enzyme 2) of the human cell. Most of the 'variants of concern' involve mutations of Spike proteins of the virus to enable them to bind to the human ACE2 more effectively. Cai et al. (2021) points out that successive VOCs (now including Alpha, Beta, Gamma, Delta and Omicron) have in aggregate become more significant than the original virus, Wuhan-Hu-1. This is because the variants are able to increase the transmission of the virus to humans, reduce the immune resistance of humans to infection, and promote greater mortality.

The Alpha variant, originating from the UK and spreading throughout the world, involved mutations of the N501Y, P681H, and A570D spike proteins, along with mutations of other parts of the virus. Mutations A570D and P681H enable B.1.1.7 to bind the Spike receptor more effectively to human cells on the ACE2, while mutation N501Y likely enables B.1.1.7 to infect a further range of cells than usual (Cai et al. 2021: 4), thus enhancing transmission by around 82% (43–130%), relative to the original Wuhan virus.

The Beta variant, originating in South Africa and subsequently spreading further, is much more virulent than the Wuhan-Hu-1 variety, but less so than Alpha. It involved mutations of the K417N, E484K and N501Y spike proteins along with several others. Mutation E484K started with Beta and continued through to Gamma. It is a RBD mutation which enhances the ability of the virus to evade neutralising antibodies. Beta has a greater transmission of about 50%, compared with the original virus from Wuhan.

A core difference between Beta and Gamma lies in the K417T mutation of Gamma (instead of K417N). Gamma is of special interest re heterogeneous agents, as *it tends to infect both younger and older groups*, the first SARS-CoV-2 variant of concern to have this characteristic. It is also able to generate about ten times more viral load than the Alpha version. As a result, it has a greater transmission rate than the original Wuhan virus strain of around 161% (145–176%).

Special emphasis has been given to two of the newer VOC strains of SARS-CoV-2, Delta (B.1.617.2) and Omicron (B.1.1.529). The Delta variant originated from India, and has about 200% greater transmission than the original Wuhan virus. This has been of concern to all nations, but especially those lagging in vaccination rates, such as sub-Saharan Africa and parts of Latin America and Asia. Mutations E484Q and L452R enable Delta to evade core antibodies. The Delta period has been termed a "new phase" in the evolution of SARS-CoV-2 and COVID-19, mainly because so many millions have perished worldwide under its onslaught, especially where there are low rates of immunity and pre-established conditions (Kapi Kupferschmidt and Meredith Wadman 2021).

More recently, other strains of the virus have appeared that are 'variants of interest' but may become 'variants of concern' sooner rather than later. One that has now overtaken Delta in terms of transmission in most nations is the Omicron 'variant of concern', which emerged majorly during November 2021, especially from Southern Africa, and which exists in virtually all nations as of March 2022. As Liu (2021) emphasises, the mutations G446S, S371L, N440K, Q493R, especially, enable Omicron to evade antibodies. Omicron lineages have a far greater rate of *transmission* than Delta, some studies suggesting two–to-three times more transmission, depending upon circumstances (Chen et al. 2022; Riediker et al. 2022) and sublineages (Mahase 2022), but likely a much lower rate of *hospitalisation* and especially *death* than Delta. However, because the transmission *rate* is so high, the *aggregate* hospitalisations and deaths are of great concern. Omicron sublineage BA.2 is more transmissible than BA.1. (Other variants are emerging too, such as three types of 'Deltacron'.)

Relative to the *principle of innovation*, other human agents and groups/organisations are of interest, especially those doing path-breaking innovation/research in virology, mass-manufacturing vaccines, vaccine supply coordination, health infrastructures and aggregate demand facilitation. Enormous investments in vaccine development have occurred since the genome for SARS-CoV-2 was isolated, leading to over one hundred potential vaccines being trialled, and over a dozen vaccines being authorized by at least one national regulatory agency. Table 4.4, below, provides summary information about the nature, origin and efficacy of some of the major vaccines currently being used worldwide:

There are four main types of SARS-CoV-2 vaccines (Wiki 2021b). Pfizer and Moderna both contain messenger ribonucleic acid (m*RNA*), designed around a crucial part of the coronavirus called the spike protein, which when injected into human tissue generates an adaptive immune response to seek and destroy the virus. AstraZenaca (AZ), Johnson & Johnson (J&J), and Sputnik are all *viral vector* vaccines, producing an antigen which creates an immune response to the pathogen.

Table 4.4 Major SARS-CoV-2 vaccines: Use and efficacy

Vaccine group/name	Type of vaccine	Nation(s) developing vaccine	Full course infection- & symptom-protection no major P.E.C.	Death prevention efficacy: No major P.E.C.
Pfizer-BioNTech	mRNA Vaccine	Germany/USA	95%	99–100%
Moderna	mRNA Vaccine	USA	95%	99–100%
Oxford-AstraZenaca	Viral Vector	UK/Italy	70%	98–99%
Johnson & Johnson	Viral Vector	USA	66% single dose	97–99%
Sputnik V	Viral Vector	Russia	91% (?)[a]	96–98%? (over-60s?)
Sinavac	Inactivated virals	China	50–91% (?)	95–98%? (over-60s?)

Source: Adapted from Mark Terry (2021)
[a] Inconsistent clinical trial data; *PEC* pre-existing major medical conditions

Sinavac and several others are *inactivated viral vaccines* grown in culture, killed and then promoting a safe immune response.[2]

Evidence for the efficacy of different vaccines varies according to location of study, variant studied, methods used, plus the various age groups, ethnicities, classes, and genders scrutinised. In empirical studies it is often difficult to establish which variant corresponds with which vaccine. What does appear true is that a full course of most of the above vaccines will protect to some degree against hospitalization and more surely death if there are no major pre-existing conditions, especially within 12–16 weeks of inoculation. But since, as mentioned, especially the aged, ethnic minorities and disadvantaged classes have more pre-existing conditions than the young per se, they typically have less protection from vaccines.

Hence, the vaccines have differential average rates of efficacy, within 12–16 weeks of inoculation, even for those with no pre-established major conditions. For instance, before the advent of Omicron a full course of Pfizer or Moderna had an efficacy rate for infection and symptom-protection of about 95%; with death prevention approximating 99–100%. A full course of AZ or J&J provide 66–70% efficacy against infection with significant symptoms and 97–99% of preventing death. There are evidential data limits for Sputnik and Sinavac jabs, but both have possible efficacy against infection and symptoms, although the prevention of hospitalisation/death for the over-65 is unclear.

One empirical UK study attempted to compare the efficacy of the Pfizer, AZ and Moderna vaccines against the Alpha and Delta variants of SARS-CoV-2 (Koen Pouwels et al. 2021). They found they could do this comparison with Pfizer and AZ,

---

[2] There are numerous other types of vaccines, such as *subunit vaccines*, which introduce micro-unit antigens, or fragments of the pathogen, that are able to stimulate an immune response.

but not Moderna, because Moderna wasn't developed when Alpha was a dominant strain. They thus compared Pfizer with AZ during the so-called 'Alpha-dominant period' (1 December 2020 to 16 May 2021) and the 'Delta-dominant period' (17 May to 1 August 2021).

Three main results surfaced. The first was that mean prevention of 'Alpha-SARS-CoV-2' infection was quite high for adults after 14 days of injection with the second dose of Pfizer (78%) and AZ (79%). But for the Delta variety Pfizer (80%) was more effective than AZ (67%) on average. The second result was that, through time, Pfizer and AZ were less effective in preventing infection and symptoms, but still quite effective in preventing hospitalisation and death, unless there were major underlying conditions. The third result is that those vaccinated with Pfizer, AZ and Moderna who become infected have equal viral loads to those who are infected yet unvaccinated, suggesting that they could still pass the virus on to others, and hence pose problems with the so-called potential herd immunity at 95% vaccination/immunity rates.

Since vaccines are less effective over time, especially 2–3 months, various nations have began to institute 'booster-shots' beyond the respective "full dosages" (usually 2 jabs). A major study, undertaken before Omicron emerged, results published in the *New England Journal of Medicine* (Yinon Bar-On et al. 2021), studied Israelis who had received the full 2 jabs of Pfizer vaccine; comprising 1,137,804 people that met the inclusion criteria, all 60 years of age or over that had all received a double dose of Pfizer at least 5 months earlier. Of these, one group had a booster-shot at least 12 days earlier (3rd dose; more men, slightly older) and the other group had not been given a booster (more women, slightly younger). The results were that the non-booster group included 4439 people that contracted SARS-Cov-2 and 294 people with severe illness, while the booster group had 934 infections of COVID-19 and 29 cases of severe illness. In both booster and non-booster groups, many more men and the over-80s became infected and experienced major symptoms. The study concluded that having a Pfizer booster shot increased efficacy from 50% to 95%. The usual caveats applied: more research is needed, how long will efficacy last? Other studies have also supported the efficacy of booster-shots, especially for the elderly and those with established medical conditions (e.g., Matan Levine-Tiefenbrun et al. 2021; Philip Krause et al. 2021).

Especially the elderly and those with established conditions, but also all others, will need to keep taking booster shots into the foreseeable future, including remodelled vaccines for newer variants (such as Omicron), and for *potential* (likely) variants, as the world tries to at least reduce the extent of hospitalisation and deaths if not infection and modest symptoms. If this is successful in the *very long-term* COVID-19 may be considered just another form of influenza (with different variants), with perhaps significant infections and symptoms but low levels of hospitalisation and death. But in the meantime newer strains are emerging; and indeed the condition called 'Long COVID' seems to afflict around 10% of those infected (with Delta), with symptoms such as weakness, tiredness, muscle ache, difficulty concentrating and stress lasting into months and even years (*New Scientist* 2021).

4.5 Circular & Cumulative Causation and Contradictions of Coronacrisis

There are multiple processes leading to the coronacrisis, involving numerous endogenous contradictions that contribute to the transference and spread of the virus, including immunological contradictions propelling magnified results for human beings. These magnified and amplified processes are linked through the *principle of circular and cumulative causation* (CCC), developed by Gunnar Myrdal (1968) and Nicholas Kaldor (1972) (O'Hara 2008); and the *principle of contradiction*, developed by scholars such as Karl Marx (1857–58), David Harvey (2014) and Phillip O'Hara (2006, 2023).

CCC is a multifactor approach that analyses the realistic interdependencies and amplified effects of cofactors through historical time. It seeks to scrutinise processes, how these processes interlink, and how the interlinkages within and between the processes generate multiplier effects beyond the realm of the single variables. Being greater than the sum of the parts, CCC obviously involves complexity, including emergence, where the micro forces combine generating meso influences, while the meso forces multiply to propel macro and global dimensions to the processes. CCC can be viewed from the top down and from the bottom up, plus both in unison. Typically CCC is utilised for understanding and providing structural policy advice for alleviating critical world problems, such as the coronacrisis, climate change, corruption, world hunger and poverty, financial crises and business cycles, and a myriad of other anomalies.

Closely related to CCC is the *principle of contradiction*, which involves certain internally generated dual-interactive anomalies that potentially propel major degrees of instability, conflict and de-synchronization that inhibit socioeconomic performance. Contradictions involve dichotomous forces, some of which are systemic and some macro, meso and micro in nature. The systemic contradictions can be worked up from the micro to the meso and macro through to global forces, and visa versa, with each level involving emergent, multiplied and amplified impacts as we move to more general levels. One such systemic contradiction is associated with Polanyi's concept of the disembedded economy (James Ronald Stanfield 1986); a closely related one is the notion of the vested interests versus the common good (Thorstein Veblen 1919); and another relates to the relative dominance of ceremonial versus instrumental functions of institutions (Marc Tool 2000). Other contradictions that feed into the systemic level include those between capital and labor; finance and industry; gender to gender; ethnic group versus ethnic group; urban and regional; monopoly and competition; and so on. (O'Hara 2001, 2009.)

Merging CCC with contradiction enables us to situate the contradiction factors as CCC processes, as illustrated in Fig. 4.3, below.

The *first* specific coronacrisis contradiction is that *between humans and coronaviruses*. Humans have been in a literal global battle against coronaviruses since possibly late 2019, which questions assumptions about humans being the dominant species on planet Earth. Humans have contributed majorly to declining biodiversity over the past 200 years, and especially over the past 50 years. For

4.5 Circular & Cumulative Causation and Contradictions of Coronacrisis

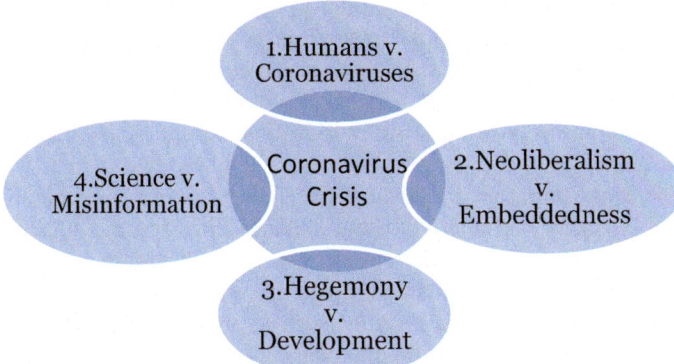

Fig. 4.3 Four contradictory processes impacted by circular & cumulative causation (CCC) dynamics promoting COVID-19

instance, the WWF has estimated a decline in the Living Planet Index (LPI), representing an index of the average abundance of 20,811 populations of 4392 species, from 100% in 1970 to 32% in 2016 (WWF 2020: 16); a drop of 68%. Mostly this is done by a combination of destruction of habitat, consumption, invasive species, and climate change. However, viruses go against this trend since "they constitute the most abundant biological entities and a large reservoir of genetic diversity on Earth" (Daniel de Carcer et al. 2015: 1). Viruses have contributed to the death of likely many hundreds of millions of human beings over the past several hundred years. While the SARS-CoV-2 in a sense contributes to human immunity through activating it, and ensuring that it is capable of keeping the virus in check; especially for the aged, numerous minority groups, others suffering from multiple conditions and unable to fight off the virus, it has contributed up to 24 million (between 14 and 24 m) 'excess' human deaths over 2020–2022 (*Economist* 2022).

Seriously dealing with this contradiction between humans and the SARS-CoV-2 virus involves the principles of public health such as social distancing, reduced travel, wearing of masks, testing for infection, contact tracing, isolating, hospitalisation, and successfully inventing and distributing good vaccines and drugs. Numerous advanced nations have successfully vaccinated the vast majority of their populations by the beginning of 2022; but many underdeveloped and developing nations are unlikely to be fully vaccinated until perhaps the end of 2022 or later. Further virulent mutations will be of concern, as will the need for continual improvement of vaccinations, perhaps indefinitely, since they do not provide long-lasting protection; over time they become less effective. This contradiction is a prime one for humanity to overcome through time.

A core way this contradiction manifests is through the cytokine storm that typically occurs in people vulnerable to coronaviruses due to established medical ailments and immune compromises. These *tend* to include the elderly and others with major medical conditions, such as diabetes, heart and liver disease, circulatory obstruction, psychological anomalies, plus reproductive and respiratory problems. The cytokine storm involves inflammatory responses leading to pain, impaired performance, major disease, established maladies worsening, often leading to death due to organ failures. Inflammation is a normal process of reacting to infection, but it cumulates in the cytokine storm as causation multiplies and amplifies. (Jujun Tang et al. 2020.)

This cytokine storm is a classic CCC process involving potentially four dimensions of factors leading to acute inflammation for the aged and three dimensions for those with chronic disease per se. Both groups often share three dimensions of anomalies. The first is chronic disease (specifics mentioned above). The second is environmental risk factors, such as smoking, substance abuse, poor nutrition, insufficient vitamin D, and social deficits such as inadequate medical infrastructure. The third risk is SARS-CoV-2 specific factors, including, for instance, lower lymphocyte count, excessive C reactive protein, higher levels of cytokines such as interleukin 6, and overabundant chemokines such as CXCL10 and CCL2. Older persons additionally tend to experience a fourth risk, age-related biological changes. (Lolita Nidadavolu and Jeremy Walston 2021.) These aged-specific factors comprise a complex series of processes, including the production of numerous additional inflammatory cytokines, low grade activation of the innate immune system, insufficient clearance of damaged mitochondria, and increased inflammatory signalling (p. e15).

The clinical consequences of this array of multiple factors is often expressed in the COVID-19 cytokine storm, a typically "out of control", disequilibrium, chronic activation of the immune system, variously leading to clinical symptoms such as ARDS, delirium, anorexia, muscle wasting, fatigue, blood clotting, and death. Studies show that the elderly and those with established medical conditions (typically undergoing the cytokine storm) have a far higher mortality rate than the young and the healthy. For instance, as one UK study showed, those "over 65 years old [the group with most established medical conditions] represent 80% of the hospitalizations and have a 23 times higher risk of death than those under 65" (Adriana Pedreanezi et al. 2021: 1567; see also Rajkumar Chinnadurai et al. 2020).

The *second specific coronacrisis contradiction,* between *neoliberalism and more embedded political economy systems,* is an equally challenging conundrum. Neoliberalism includes the institutionalisation of austerity, privatisation, globalization, deregulation, free markets, and often a strong state to enable these processes to thrive (Sumonja 2021). The global financial crisis (GFC) of 2008–2011, and its continuation in various nations thereafter, as well as the coronavirus crisis, have dented the image and dominance of neoliberal policy and ideology (O'Hara 2010, 2011; Geoffrey Gertz and Homi Kharas 2019).

Policy responses to the GFC and the coronacrisis (CC), especially in advanced nations, took the form of functional finance (Abba Lerner 1943), a major principle of embedded systems, which emphasises the results of policy actions in dealing with crises, rather than preconceptions such as balanced budgets and GDP percent limits on deficits. It includes a general proclivity for automatic and countercyclical fiscal and monetary policy, and in CC contexts includes (a) ad hoc handouts to citizens to encourage spending and reduce uncertainty; (b) more extensive unemployment benefit schemes and indeed "government wages" (furlough schemes) for those unable to be employed (fully) by business; (c) money supply providing finance for government, business and consumers, and lower interest rates, to maintain an adequate level of effective demand; and (d) taxation deductions for struggling companies, where taxes are seen not as sources of revenue but aggregate demand regulators. The historical time associated with the CC also saw the greater importance in many advanced nations of targeted public investment in infrastructure, health, education and climate change dynamics.

When the next major crisis emerges functional finance and other non-neoliberal institutions may be further embedded in the institutions of advanced capitalism, at least in dealing with potential crises. Some evidence supports the notion that key elements of the 'economic profession' have rejected neoliberalism (see Gertz and Kharas 2019). But elements of neoliberalism have typically often been maintained in many jurisdictions: such as restoring austerity after crises; privatising health, education, utilities and housing; and maintaining mostly free-wheeling financial systems and decentralised industrial relations systems (David Primrose et al. 2020). Neoliberalism has been questioned and partially de-institutionalised, but not completely replaced by a more embedded system in the vast majority of nations. So this contradiction continues to be played out now and potentially into the immediate future.

A core element of neoliberalism is deregulated globalisation of money, trade and production, tourism, and the integration of corporate networks locally, regionally and internationally, to enable the quickest expansion of both trade, business, and tourism from country to country and from region to region, ultimately encompassing the whole world. The global spread of COVID-19 heightened due to the institutionalisation of these integrated economic relations, commodity chains and production networks. For instance, the KOF Globalisation Index (see Claudius Grabner et al. 2021: 100), comprising trade and finance ('de facto'), for all nations, shows a major increase in the index from 34 to 62 between 1970 and 2016, with some temporary declines during the mid-1980s, early 1990s, and the GFC. The degree of globalisation is positively related to the level of 'complexity' of the economies. While several political forces have seen a decline in globalisation ideology, especially with the rise in extreme nationalism, this has not majorly affected the degree of globalisation at this stage.

However, several developing and underdeveloped nations have less space for policy movement due to path dependent processes, including pre-colonial, colonial, and post-colonial structural anomalies such as corruption, low levels of political capital, plus unsophisticated technological, financial, and fiscal systems, that make it hard to compete with advanced nations in the efficiency with which they tackled the CC.

This leads to the *third specific coronacrisis contradiction* concerning the *principle of hegemonic power and (uneven) development*. Activities that typically dislocate the circular flow of economic activity include geopolitical conflict over trade, borders, airspace, and technology, as well as wars, terrorist attacks, pandemics, and lack of effective leadership. The WHO, for instance, had been attacked by Mr. Trump for being slow to move on the pandemic crisis; as had China where the virus started at or near the Wuhan wet markets. There is an ongoing anomalous relationship between China and the USA and its allies, on several fronts, which has inhibited communication on issues of trade, industry, finance, pandemic and diplomacy; and more recently the invasion of Ukraine by Russia has heightened global and regional disarray. Such factors accelerate uncertainty in the global and regional economies, which has been on the rise, recently since 2018 (see further below), partly due to these conflicts.

A major global contradiction has emerged whereby the advanced economies of Europe, America and parts of Asia have had the *ability* to inoculate the vast majority of their peoples with the major vaccines, and thereby potentially generating herd immunity. But the health and medical services response (not merely the supply of vaccines or tests) for lowly developing or underdeveloping nations of especially Africa, as well as some South Asian, Latin American, and small-island nations, have been dismal. Africa is especially subject not simply to inadequate testing for SARS-CoV-2 and inadequate supply of Covid-19 vaccinations, but a whole array of supply issues associated with hospital infrastructure, staffing, transport and finance, as well as much vaccine hesitancy, leading to major upwaves of infections, hospitalisations and deaths.

This persistent inequity of vaccines, test kits, infrastructure, transport and labor power is correlated with global wealth and income. This does highlight the gross inability of the international agencies and communities to supply infrastructure, services, vaccines and tests according to the principle of the global common good. The same goes for the distribution of COVID-19 drugs, such as casirivimab and indevimab. Most of the markets for such monoclonal antibody drugs emanate from North America and Europe, with very few in less-developed nations, mainly due to the huge expense (*Economist* 2021c). The advanced nations have prioritized their own needs and considered less developed nations when their vaccination rates are looking moderately good. This is contradictory not just for less developed nations, but also for the advanced nations, as failing to look to the common good leads to a greater rate of COVID-19 mutations, especially in places like Africa, which then lead to major COVID-19 case (and usually death) upwaves in virtually all nations. This is what happened with the COVID-19 variants such as Omicron (likely originating in southern Africa), Delta (India), Gamma (Brazil) and Beta (South Africa).

The international organisation, COVAX, as well as many nations especially China and the USA, have provided several hundred million vaccines for distribution to less developed nations. But, as mentioned, this ignores the total supply issue as well as the attitudinal context of the process. China has seen an opportunity to generate further *soft power* through major contributions to the health budgets of many such nations, plus free or subsidized vaccines, hospital machines, masks and the like. Several studies have shown that China's potential hegemonic power has expanded partly due to its accelerated soft power through global assistance especially to developing and underdeveloped nations of Asia, Africa and Latin America (Priya Gauttan et al. 2020). China has also taken serious action to control the virus domestically, which provides them with considerable emulative power in policy and strategy (but not for research on the specific *origins* of the virus). These and other soft power initiatives, such as the Belt and Road Initiative (BRI), are enhancing China's potential hegemonic power (even if the BRI is generating debt problems for recipients in many instances).

This leads to the *fourth specific coronacrisis contradiction,* concerning *science and technology versus disinformation and popular myth.* There seems to be a vast gulf in coronavirus policy and behaviour between groups that are keen on scientific evidence to solve problems, vis-à-vis the principles of innovation and policy/governance, and other groups that eschew science and evidence in favour of their own myths and conspiracy theories. For instance, much of especially Western Europe, Israel, China, Oceania and 'liberals' in the US follow the science as much as feasible. But other groups, closely linked with Mr. Trump, the Brazilian President, to a lesser extent the Indian Prime Minister, and others, often ignore the science. For instance, Mr. Trump gave erroneous recommendations for treating the virus, and the Brazilian President seemed indifferent to hundreds of thousands dying, while the Indian Prime Minister failed to take vaccination seriously, which has led to estimates of over one million excess Indian deaths from the virus (*Economist* 2022).

Disinformation anomalies include various lags, such as that between the first notification of the virus in Wuhan and the flow of data to national and international bodies and agencies. Other informational problems include the anti-science movement, libertarian elements, certain religious groups, Trump supporters, and leaders of other nations (e.g., Brazil, Belarus and India) who discourage mask-wearing, congregate in large masses, contradict the science, and spread conspiracy theories. Much has been documented about these forms of 'misinformation', including specific time-series data on their recurrence through time (see e.g., Sarah Evanega et al. 2020), as well as numerous public demonstrations against lockdowns and mandatory vaccination rules.

These misinformation channels perpetuate certain social habits that have, in normal times, been institutionalised into core aspects of the global, regional, national and local communities. They include shaking hands, hugging, social kissing, congregating in groups, openly coughing and sneezing, driving to friends and relatives places, using much facial expression to convey information, and passing around material objects including food, utensils and commodities. These factors led to the rapid spread of the virus from person to person and from group to group, including from young people to old people who have lower tolerance to the coronavirus. Hence, 'safe COVID practices' usually mean drastic changes in these practices, and often complete cessation, and in extreme cases even between family members (see, e.g., WHO 2021b), at least until core populations have been fully vaccinated/immune. Those who fail to get vaccinated due to misinformation constitute large populations of those infected with SARS-CoV-2, hospitalised, and ultimately dying of the disease.

These four CCC contradictions—human beings v. coronaviruses, neoliberalism v. embeddedness, hegemony v. development, and science v. misinformation—which involve numerous subprocesses, plus related factors, become interlinked and result in multiplier and accelerator trajectories that led to the pandemic and the current estimated 13.8–23.7 million "excess deaths". The core point is that they operate *interdependently*; they are cofactors operating in tandem. The contradiction between humans and viruses created the basic dynamic of disease and death. The contradiction between neoliberalism and embeddedness generated an institutional apparatus more prone to disease and death versus that which protect people from harm. The contradiction between hegemony and development helped engender uneven development of Covid-19 throughout the world. And the contradiction between science and disinformation revealed another duality supporting amplified disease versus community health protection.

All four contradictions, where they promoted disease and death more than community health protection, became multiplied through CCC which led to greater uncertainty throughout the world, although the incidence of such uncertainty varied from place to place, and also through historical time. The nature and pattern of such uncertainty is examined in more detail below.

4.6 Uncertainty and the Pandemic

Political economy, following Frank Knight (1921), John Maynard Keynes (1936, 1937), G.L.S. Shackle (1972) and post-Keynesian institutionalists (PKI), such as Douglas Dillard and Wallace Peterson, *typically* differentiates between risk and uncertainty. Risk is associated with certain deterministic processes that are relatively easy to measure, such as stockmarket volatility, insurance finance, and house price indices; while the concept of uncertainty looks to the future, especially concerning the business climate, and more obtuse calculative processes. Keynes himself saw the dominant contradiction of capitalism as being periodic bouts of extreme uncertainty in the light of 'debt' financing of capital projects those lifecycles spread long into the future. While yields depend upon the current business climate, business expectations become periodically volatile due to the long/short time mismatch, speculative bubbles and supply price rises, causing a crash. Broader measures also impact uncertainty, such as the contradictions examined above.

These broader measures impact on aggregate demand, which is negatively correlated with uncertainty as to the future, rising and falling along with expectations of the current business climate. The principle of uncertainty states that political economy needs to typically analyse uncertainty when trying to solve problems associated with systemic disarray, instability and crises. Few recent scholarly references on uncertainty make reference to the distinction between risk and uncertainty, and those that do have not provided uncertainty data, even if vague and indeterminate, that could be useful for empirics (see Sunanda Sen 2020). Those that have provided indeterminate data relevant to the pandemic fail to distinguish between risk and uncertainty, or deal much with the theory of uncertainly, but nevertheless they have tried to link uncertainty with the pandemic and economic activity.

For instance, surveys undertaken by scholars at the NBER, IMF, Atlanta Fed, Berkeley, and Stanford, have been prolific in generating uncertainty estimates for

4.6 Uncertainty and the Pandemic

many nations of the world, the world as a whole, and also for policy uncertainty. Ahir et al. (2019) develop the broad theory and analysis which is then detailed by teams of researchers. They construct quarterly indices of economic uncertainty for 143 countries from 1996 onwards using frequency counts of "uncertainty" (and its variants) in the quarterly Economist Intelligence Unit (EIU) country reports.

For instance, Fig. 4.4, below, provides estimates, through an index of global uncertainty, for the period 1990–2021.

Figure 4.4 illustrates[3] expansions in global uncertainty in the light of short term factors, such as the corporate crisis, internet crash, terrorist attacks, and associated inception of wars during 2000–2003; the subprime, GFC, and Euro-debt crisis aftermath of 2007–2013; the uncertainties linked to Brexit, the Trump era and other anomalies (including intensified wars in the Middle East and European immigration crises) of 2015–2019; the coronavirus crisis of 2020 and subsequent (uneven and erratic) recovery in many nations during 2021 (plus the heightening of uncertainty during 2022 due to the invasion of Ukraine; data not yet available). The coronacrisis became the most significant short-term socioeconomic disruption (to date, according to available data) over (at least) the past 31 years,[4] generating

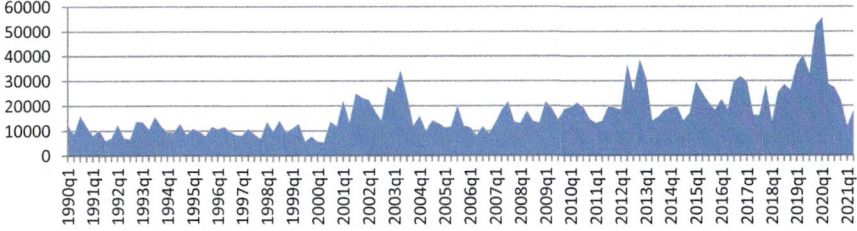

Fig. 4.4 World Uncertainty Index, 1990–2021. (Source: Adapted from the raw dataset which, "should be cited as [Hites] Ahir, [Nicholas] Bloom and [Davide] Furceri, "The World Uncertainty Index", mimeo")

---

[3] See raw data at: https://policyuncertainty.com/wui_quarterly.html The World Uncertainty Index (WUI) is developed by Hites Ahir (IMF), Nicholas Bloom (Stanford) and Davide Furceri (IMF). The EIU reports discuss major political and economic developments in each country, along with analysis and forecasts of political, policy and economic conditions. They are created by country-specific teams of analysts and a central EIU editorial team. To make the WUI comparable across countries, the raw counts are scaled by the total number of words in each report. See also the work of Altig et al. (2020).

[4] Certain structural factors have increased global uncertainty during especially 1999–2021. One core factor is heightening party-political antithesis (and cultural wars) between liberals and populist-nationalist-conservative forces in most regions of the world. For instance, liberals tend to take seriously the science and prudential measures to limit the spread of COVID-19, while populist-nationalist-conservatives have been at the forefront of practices that have led to coronavirus upwaves and heightening deaths, as mentioned. Another structural factor is the heightening conflict between the US and China, which is impacting on numerous areas of the world, in different ways.

high levels of uncertainty that inhibited investment and consumption while necessitating massive government assistance to prevent depression.

For most advanced nations, as economic and health policies have supported low interest rates, furlough schemes, massive injections of funds, extensive vaccination programs, periods of shutdown and opening up, so uncertainty has tended to decline for business, consumers and government as the 2020 crisis moved to recovery in 2021. For the world and its regions the pandemic during 2020 was the worst output reduction since the second-world war and/or the Great Depression of the 1930s. For the USA it was the 'deepest recession' but also the 'shortest recession' since the 1930s–1940s, due to the roaring recovery in late 2000 and 2021 (*Economist* 2021d).

Comparisons for the immediate impact of both the GFC and the coronacrisis on GDP growth are shown below for the World and regions, in Table 4.5, below.

Three stylized facts emerge from this data. The first is that the initial impact of the coronacrisis (CC) during 2020 throughout the world was 115% worse for GDP growth than the initial global GDP impact of the GFC during 2009. Whereas many areas in the periphery and semi-periphery escaped a deep GFC crisis because they did not have sophisticated financial systems subject to large speculative bubbles and crashes, these areas were not so able to escape the deep impact of the CC on GDP. In this sense CC uncertainty was much more global than that of the GFC. Areas hit worst by the pandemic were small-island and coastal tourist states (and some tax havens) such as The Maldives, Fiji, Panama, Babados and the Bahamas, which were severed by the lockdowns and airline closures that were typical of the CC. South Asian and Latin American peripheral and semi-peripheral areas were the hardest hit of all the (sub)continents of the world during the coronacrisis of 2020.

Being a global pandemic, few major continents or specific areas could eschew the pandemic's 2020 initial negative impact on GDP. The CC hit the Americas, Europe, the Middle East, Central Asia and sub-Saharan Africa hard as lockdowns, travel bans, business closures and un(der)employment escalated in most areas. One crucial factor instigating the initial crisis and deepening of the pandemic was the cavalier

Table 4.5 Real GDP growth rate, 2008–2010, 2019–2021

	2008	2009GFC	2010	2019	2020CC	2021^p
World	1.86	−1.67	4.31	2.34	−3.59	6.00
South Asia	3.24	7.13	7.70	4.02	−6.58	11.00
LAC	3.92	−1.87	5.84	0.95	−6.31	4.60
EU	0.64	−4.33	2.21	1.56	−6.20	4.40
Europe & Cent. Asia	1.05	−4.42	2.65	1.59	−5.70	3.90^b
MENA	4.50	0.50	4.98	0.49	−3.66	2.50
North America	−0.02	−2.58	2.61	2.13	−3.67	6.10
SSA	5.35	3.10	5.57	2.31	−2.45	3.40
East Asia & Pacific	3.54	1.39	7.07	3.61	3.66*	7.30^a

Source: Adapted from the raw data at World Bank (2021) and IMF (2021: 4)
p Projection (Real GDP Growth) IMF (2021), * IDA & IBRD nations. *SSA* sub-Saharan Africa, *MENA* Middle East & North Africa, *LAC* Latin America & Caribbean, *a* Asia & Pacific, *b* Eastern Europe

attitude of many of the politicians, as mentioned above, and the anti-masks and anti-lockdown groups that spread myths about the pandemic, the virus and the vaccines.

Secondly, the nations and areas that managed to evade recessions during the pandemic in 2020 were mainly in East Asia, an area that also eschewed many of the negative impacts of the GFC. Notably, China, and Vietnam (initially), were able to use their centralized power structure to institute early lockdowns, social isolation norms and masks to prevent major infections and fatalities long before vaccinations became available. Other nations that evaded recessions in 2020 were, for instance, Ireland, Ethiopia, Bangladesh, Turkey, Tajitstan and Egypt.

Thirdly, initial crisis recoveries during late 2020 and 2021 were robust and intense. While the vast majority of nations failed to control the virus and recessions during 2020, they were able to instigate economic and health policies that prevented, so far, the recessions from being depressions, as most also did during the aftermath of the GFC. A critical factor was, as *The Economist* (2021e) noted, that 'neoliberalism has gone out of fashion', in the sense that functional finance, printing money to finance spending on business and workers, and reducing interest rates to low rates, have become the norm during crises. Use of Keynesian crisis-management policy has become institutionalised, and even financial experts appear to (unwittingly) think the economy operates according to aspects of modern monetary theory (MMT) (*Economist* 2021e).

Estimates for uncertainty for 2020 are higher for advanced nations and lower for emerging and lower-developed nations. These estimates also exhibit higher *volatility* for advanced nations as uncertainty declined majorly from the crisis of 2020 to recovery in late 2020 and 2021. But for numerous 'underdeveloped' nations, especially in Africa, Latin America and South Asia, core elements of coronavirus uncertainty remains, if not for economic activity then for infections and fatalities. While global GDP growth has expanded majorly during 2021 and early 2022 (haltingly in many places, especially due to the invasion of Ukraine), infections and deaths have increased or stayed high for numerous peripheral and semi-peripheral nations due to difficulties in getting enough quality vaccinations, tests, drugs, and health infrastructures. Advanced nations with *relatively high* immunity rates that have opened-up have seen major infection *rates*, as well as large *aggregates* of deaths for especially the unvaccinated and those with pre-established conditions. Over time in advanced nations infection rates and aggregate deaths may decline if no new major variants of concern impact, and if the unsure and those with major ailments are fully inoculated.

4.7 Preparedness Policies, Uncertainty and the Future

Here we look at the principles of uncertainty, innovation and policy/governance linked to lack of preparedness for the pandemic, and policies that can be instituted to reduce uncertainty by preparing adequately for the next socioeconomic-health crisis. Prior to the coronacrisis there were several specific policies and institutions used by authorities throughout the world to prepare for biological pandemics/attacks to reduce uncertainty and crises. These pre-established preparedness structures were critically scrutinised by the 3 year (2017–2019) global research initiative associated with the Global Health Security Index (GHSI), undertaken jointly by the *Economist Intelligence Unit*, the John Hopkins University Bloomberg School of Public Health, and the Nuclear Threat Initiative (EIU, JHU, NTI 2019). The GHSI was finalised in late 2019 and sought to assess the potential for the world and its areas and nations to tackle *biological risks* that are likely to impinge on areas in the near future, especially pandemics or epidemics, terrorist attacks and accidental (e.g., laboratory) leaks. The timing and nature of this GHSI exercise was perfect for assessing preparedness for the SARS-CoV-2/COVID-19 anomaly, given that it was done with an emphasis on the ability of areas to respond to a biological crisis, and was published a month or two before the first COVID-19 case was officially detected in China. The six areas studied include [1] prevention of the release of a pathogen, [2] detection and reporting, [3] rapid response, [4] robust health system, [5] compliance with international norms, and [6] overall risk environment (EIU, JHU, NTI 2019: 65).

Table 4.6, below, summarises the GHS Index for major areas of the world.

A core result of the GHSI exercise was that the world as a whole was unprepared for a global catastrophic biological risk, since "at least 75% of countries received a low score in biosecurity, oversight for dual-use research, emergency response operations, linking of public health and security operations, and medical countermeasure dispensing" (EIU, JHU, NTI 2019: 42). The average for all six indicators was 40.2 out of 100 for the 195 countries in aggregate (population weighted). Overall the GHSI group concluded that "national health security is fundamentally weak around the world. No country is fully prepared for epidemics or pandemics, and every country has important gaps to fill" (EIU, JHU, NTI 2019: 12).

More specifically, as Table 4.6 indicates, the advanced capitalist economies of North America (NA), Europe (EU) and Oceania (Australia and New Zealand) were mostly 'somewhat prepared', though many were 'not very prepared'. The countries of Asia were mostly 'not very prepared', although some were 'somewhat prepared' and 'unprepared'. Those from the Middle East and North Africa (MENA) were mostly 'not very prepared', though others were 'somewhat', 'badly' and

Table 4.6 195 Nations in regions: GHS Index, pandemic preparedness, 2019

GHS Index	Degree prepared	EU & NA	ASIA	MENA	Latin America	Sub-Saharan Africa	Oceania
0–50	Somewhat prepared	28	8	4	6	1	2
51–100	Not very prepared	15	11	10	11	7	0
101–150	Unprepared	4	9	4	14	17	2
151–195	Badly unprepared	1	3	6	6	17	11

Source: Based on the data in EIU, JHU, NTI (2019: 20–29)
NA North America, *EU* Europe, *MENA* Middle East and North Africa

4.7 Preparedness Policies, Uncertainty and the Future

'unprepared'. Latin American nations were usually 'unprepared', though a lot were 'not very prepared'; and a few 'somewhat' and 'badly' prepared. With some exceptions (such as South Africa), nations of Sub-Saharan Africa were mostly 'unprepared' and 'badly prepared', while small island states in the Pacific, Oceania, were almost entirely 'badly prepared' for the pandemic.

Even for the advanced capitalist economies of North America and Europe, that were 'somewhat prepared', major gaps existed, which led to much uncertainty. For instance, in the USA, which was top of the list (1/195) for preparedness, there was no exercise of rapid response plans, major defects in the emergency response operation, serious deficiencies in access to medical care for many citizens, and a low level of responsible science culture for many people (EIU, JHU, NTI 2019: 303). The UK (2/195) was documented as having problems with biosafety prevention, detection and reporting, emergency response operations, and access to health care for numerous citizens.

China, where the virus first manifested itself, overall came 51/195 for the GHS Index, with a score of 48.2/100. This is higher than the average score of 40.2, but not epidemiologically optimistic for the future of COVID-19 once it became active in the human population. Indeed, China got abysmal results especially for dual use research and culture of responsible science; data integration between human, animal, and environmental health sectors; exercising rapid response plans; linking public health and security authorities; communication between healthcare workers during an emergency; aspects of compliance with international norms; and emergency rapid response operations (EIU, JHU, NTI 2019: 152). It is thus not surprising that China failed to share epidemiological data on the very first cases of COVID-19, and to prevent the disease from ultimately becoming national and transnational in scope and transfer.

Although the Index has been criticised, it does appear to have calculated quite well the capabilities of certain nations to respond to an emergency. As mentioned, it documented several limitations, even for top-scoring nations, such as the US and UK; and what is a capability may not transfer to action if the politicians and administrators do not adequately activate and communicate properly with health care workers and citizens. Indeed, critics of the index often centred on these differences between technical preparedness and the broader political and social determinants of pandemic response, especially for the leading nations (e.g., see Manjari Mahajan 2021).

Critics have also attacked the GHSI (as well as the Economic Preparedness Index, and the National Health Security Preparedness Index) for failing to predict *specific national rates* of COVID-19 mortality (Mark Keim and Alex Lovallo 2021; Fran Baum et al. 2021). These critiques argue that, now and into the future, we need broader social and political indicators of how policies and institutions adequately deal with pandemics. For instance, Baum et al. (2021) put forward eight such factors necessary to consider for adequate pandemic preparation and prevention dynamics, which should assist policymakers dealing with present and potential future such crises. The first is the need to consider globalisation, geography and global governance. For instance, larger island states, such as Australia and New Zealand, were able to isolate from global forces, for a long time, instituting lockdowns, social distancing, contract tracing, limits on overseas (and domestic) arrivals, facemasks, and the like, and reduce deaths to a minimum, even before vaccines became widespread. The second is participatory rather than just authoritarian governance: they argue it is necessary to include civil society groups and decentralised factors to ensure community participation in governance. This helps explain some individuals and groups attacking government mandates and rules where communities required integrating into policy. The third is the need for universal, publically well-funded health systems that are not privately outsourced; which they say help to explain some of the *initial* success of policy in Thailand and Vietnam; plus Australia and New Zealand more generally.

The fourth factor is political leadership and ideology, which helps explain why populist forces underlying nations, such as the US, Brazilian, Indian and UK responses led to high rates of mortality in these nations. Fifthly, the importance of *context,* including the unevenness of sub-national structures, help explain some regional differences in Federations such as the US, India, South Africa, Belgium and Australia. The sixth factor critiques the indices' obsession with GDP levels being (indirectly) a major determinant of pandemic preparation and performance. They point to, for instance, the effectiveness of the Rwandan and Vietnamese (initially) solid pandemic response despite being poor nations. The seventh factor is heterogeneous agents and groups, as marginalised groups within nations have tended to suffer most from the pandemic, yet this inequality was not analysed in the indices (at least not directly).

The eighth factor required for pandemic preparedness and low levels of uncertainty in the present and future is the use of government support for households and business in the form of furlough schemes, unemployment benefits, income support schemes, interest rate decreases, ad hoc handouts to people, business lockdown payments, accelerated investment depreciation schemes, extended sick leave allowances, and the like. These schemes have been accelerated majorly, especially in the advanced nations of the EU, USA, UK, Australia, Japan, Canada and New Zealand, primarily because they have sophisticated financial and budget systems. Neoliberalism is also declining majorly in these nations, especially in light of the GFC and the pandemic, which helps to explain the quick implementation of functional finance, handouts and monetary easing. The least developed nations are generally unable to utilise these schemes effectively due to their underdeveloped technological, financial and budget systems. It is also important for policies not to revert back to neoliberal priorities so as to inhibit proper preparation for the next major crisis, as has often happened in the past.

One core additional factor for reducing uncertainty now and into the future, vis-à-vis the principle of innovation, is the ongoing role of vaccinations, in the defence of the population from COVID-19 and other infections. Many advanced nations, while not *consistently* emphasising lockdowns, social distancing, facemasks, and so on, have managed to institute an effective global system of science and manufacturing, for the production and distribution of effective vaccines.

They are pinning their hopes on opening up the economy while having a large proportion of their population with sufficient antibodies through vaccinations and previous infection to achieve herd immunity. The US, UK, EU and others are likely to eventually have such immunity but at the cost of large numbers of infections and substantial numbers of deaths.

As mentioned, most less developed economies have difficulty getting access to vaccines to reach 80–90% immunity and activating sophisticated functional finance and discretionary fiscal and monetary policies to prevent major dislocation, if recovery fails to become sustained. Two other anomalies may generate renewed uncertainty and dislocate global and national political economies in light of the coronacrisis. The first is the emergence of *newer strains of the virus* that are even more capable of evading immune system/vaccine protection, some of which are already in motion. And the second is *major inflationary/stagflationary forces* precipitating higher interest rates that dislocate the circuits of capital, in the light of high levels of international debt, supply-side anomalies and demand forces. Both factors operating forcefully may lead to another global or regional crisis, perhaps being worse than that of 2020.

In relation to the principles of innovation and policy/governance, the pandemic has had some crucial political and health impacts, which will affect the world majorly into the future. For instance, it led to the creation in a short period of several effective vaccines, sharpened the scientific edifice of virology and immunology, and laid the policy foundations of potential pandemic reactions, that will likely put the world (or at least certain areas) in good stead for future such crises. Secondly, it led to Donald Trump's defeat in the US Presidential election, and reduced majorly the popularity of several other populist-nationalist politicians, especially in Brazil, India and some other nations. Thirdly, it taught and is still teaching the world about the limitations of austerity and neoliberalism, and also about the need to speed up reactions to potential pandemics, and for assistance to the poorest nations to make available sufficient vaccines through global assistance.

Also, one cannot ignore climate change in the context of the coronacrisis as well as future policies and practices (Dieter Helm 2020; Samuel Sarkodie and Phebe Owusu 2020). The pandemic crisis led to moderated carbon emissions during the 2020 recession phase while the 2021 recovery increased emissions. The pandemic crisis also crowded-out climate change endeavours to some degree as the world concentrated on the 'immediate pandemic tasks', even while extreme events such as wildfires, floods and droughts become ever-more evident in reality. All this as the IPCC (2021) documented the greater speed and intensity of climate events now and into the future. Multiple simultaneous crises can lead to some of them, such as climate change, being underplayed, which happened during both the GFC and the coronacrisis. Also, it was found that coronacrisis demand policies that focussed on labor-intensive green projects were good for the environment, employment and recovery, while those green policies that were capital-intensive and large-scale helped climate change but not so much employment and recovery (Gustav Engstrom and Spiro 2020). Whether or not the coronacrisis descends into history sooner rather than later, climate change policies should be kept in full view and deepened now and into the future.

4.8 Conclusion

The purpose of this chapter has been to investigate the coronavirus pandemic crisis through the prism of some core principles of institutional and evolutionary political economy. We started with the principle of historical specificity and evolution, as the pandemics of the last 100 years were surveyed and the coronavirus crisis was situated as critical but not as major as the 'Kansas flu' of 1918–2021 or the AIDS-HIV malady. We surveyed the evolution of the crisis from its origins in Wuhan to the international spread around the world and its impact. Then we scrutinized the principle of heterogeneous groups and agents, noting the peculiarities of gender, class, age and ethnic group with respect to infections and deaths; as well as the key viral agents and vaccines that have impacted, thanks to bio-innovators and COVID-19 macro policy-makers. Next we explored the principles of circular and cumulative causation, contradiction and hegemony/uneven development, paying special attention to viral-human antimony, neoliberal-embedded double movements, hegemony-development conflicts, and science/technology versus disinformation trends.

The principle of uncertainty explained how the circular and cumulative contradictions manifested in varying levels of uncertainty regarding the future, which closely tracked demand and growth anomalies. Relevant to the principles of innovation and policy/governance, the chapter then examined how technical and general preparedness for pandemic-type events was uneven throughout the world as the pandemic started, leading to substantial uncertainty in the global political economy, especially during 2020, although there was significant unevenness between core, periphery and semi-periphery. Further investments into various preparedness and prevention measures can reduce uncertainty and provide insurance against such crises now and into the future.

The principles were useful for gaining information about the nature and evolution of the coronavirus crisis and for providing insights into how it has been dampened and hopefully contained as the world tentatively survives yet another major global crisis. We have collectively learned some important lessons. Major ones are preparedness and prevention, especially the need for more developed health care systems that cope quickly with such bio-emergencies in the future. We have also learned the core role of functional finance, whereby government policy reacts positively to potential simultaneous crises, be they financial, economic, health, climate, war, and other forms of major instability. We also focussed on the need to protect the global common good, which means ensuring protection and adequate policy responses to assist the less developed and not just the emerging and advanced nations. Certain microorganisms have major power over humans and hence someday humanity may disappear from the Universe in the same way that they have destroyed other species, if we don't learn and act on principle and governance lessons to improve our preparation, prevention and responses to crises into the future.

Acknowledgements I wish to thank Ian Kerr and Kosta Josifidis for feedback and inspiration, regarding an earlier version of this paper, which was published as O'Hara (2021a); and Michael Dillon for technical advice.

References

Ahir, Hites, Nicholas Bloom, and Davide Fercuri. 2019. *The World Uncertainty Index*. Stanford Mimeo. https://siepr.stanford.edu/research/publications/world-uncertainty-index.

Al-Qahtani, Ahmed. 2020. Severe Acute Respiratory Syndrome Coronavirus 2 (SARS-CoV-2): Emergence, History, Basic and Clinical Aspects. *Saudi Journal of Biological Sciences* 27 (1): 2531–2538. https://doi.org/10.1016/j.sjbs.2020.04.033.

Atlig, David, Jose Maria Borrero, Nicholas Bloom, Steven J. Davis, Brent Mayer, and Nicholas Parker. 2020. Surveying Business Uncertainty. *Journal of Econometrics*. https://doi.org/10.1016/j.jeconom.2020.03.021.

Bar-On, Yinon, Yair Goldberg, Micha Mandel, Omri Bodenheimer, Laurence Freedman, Nir Kalkstein, Barak Mizrahi, Sharon Alroy-Preis, Nachman Ash, Ron Milo, and Amit Huppert. 2021. Protection of BNT162b2 Vaccine Booster Against Covid-19 in Israel. *New England Journal of Medicine* 385: 1393–1400. https://doi.org/10.1056/NEJMoa2114255.

Baum, Fran, Toby Freeman, Connie Musolino, Mimi Abramovitz, Wim De Ceukelaire, Joanne Flavel, Sharon Friel, Camila Giugliani, Philippa Howden-Chapman, Nguyen Thanh Huong, Leslie London, Martin McKee, Jennie Popay, Hani Serag, and Eugenio Villar. 2021. Explaining COVID-19 Performance: What Factors Might Predict National Responses? *BMJ* 372: n91. https://doi.org/10.1136/bmj.n91.

Boettke, Peter, and Benjamin Powell. 2021. The Political Economy of the COVID-19 Pandemic. *Southern Economic Journal* 87 (4): 1090–1106. https://doi.org/10.1002/soej.12488.

Brennan, Andrew John, and Jaslyn Kaur Kalsi. 2015. Elephant Poaching & Ivory Trafficking Problems in Sub-Saharan Africa: An Application of O'Hara's Principles of Political Economy. *Ecological Economics* 120: 312–337. https://doi.org/10.1016/j.ecolecon.2015.08.013.

Cai, Yongfei, Jun Zhang, Tianshu Xiao, Christy L. Lavine, Shaun Rawson, Hanqin Peng, Haisun Zhu, et al. 2021. Structural Basis for Enhanced Infectivity and Immune Evasion of SARS-CoV-2 Variants. *Science* 2021 (June): 1–14. https://doi.org/10.1126/science.abi9745.

Carcer, de Daniel, Alberto Lopex-Bueno, David A. Pearce, and Antonio Alcami. 2015. Biological Diversity and Distribution of Polar Freshwater DNA Viruses. *Science Advances* 1 (e1400127): 1–9. https://doi.org/10.1126/sciadv.1400127.

Chen, Nanshan, Min Zhou, Xuan Dong, Jieming Qu, Fengyun Gong, Yang Han, Yang Qiu, Jingli Yang, Ying Liu, Yuan Wei, Jia'an Xia, Ting Yu, Xinxin Zhang, and Li Zhang. 2020. Epidemiological and Clinical Characteristics of 99 Cases of 2019 Novel Coronavirus Pneumonia in Wuhan, China: A Descriptive Study. *The Lancet* 395 (10223): 507–513. https://doi.org/10.1016/S0140-6736(20)30211-7.

Chen, Jiahui, Rui Wang, Nancy Benovich Gilby, and Guo-Wei We. 2022. Omicron (B.1.1.529): Infectivity, Vaccine Breakthrough, and Antibody Resistance. *Journal of Chemical Information and Modeling*. Available Online https://pubs.acs.org/doi/pdf/10.1021/acs.jcim.1c01451.

Chinnadurai, Rajkumar, Onesi Ogedengbe, Priya Agarwal, Sally Money-Coomes, Ahmad Z. Abdurrahman, Sajeel Mohammed, Philip A. Kalra, Nicola Rothwell, and Sweta Pradhan. 2020. Older Age and Frailty Are the Chief Predictors of Mortality in COVID-19 Patients Admitted to an Acute Medical Unit in a Secondary Care Setting – A Cohort Study. *BMC Geriatrics* 20: 409. https://doi.org/10.1186/s12877-020-01803-5.

Condon, Roderick. 2020. The Coronavirus Crisis and the Legitimation Crisis of Neoliberalism. *European Societies* 23 (sup1): S805–S816. https://doi.org/10.1080/14616696.2020.1839669.

ECDPC. 2021. *SARS-CoV-2 Variants of Concern as of 3 June 2021*. European Centre for Disease Prevention and Control. https://www.ecdc.europa.eu/COVID-19/variants-concern.

Economist. 2021a. The Quest to Quit QE. *The Economist*, 10–16 July, 57–59.

———. 2021b. The Lab-Leak Hypothesis: Possible, But Far from Proven. *The Economist*, 29 May–4 June 2021, 51–52.

———. 2021c. COVID Drugs: Antibody of Evidence. *The Economist*, 19–25 June, 71–72.

———. 2021d. Something Ventured: America's Roaring Recovery Might Teach Economists More About Recessions. *The Economist*, 7–13 August, 56.

———. 2021e. The Origins of COVID-19: Putting It All Together. *The Economist*, 21–27 August, 41–43.

———. 2022. *COVID-19 Data: The Pandemic's True Death Toll: Our Daily Estimate of Excess Deaths Around the World*, 21 March. https://www.economist.com/graphic-detail/coronavirus-excess-deaths-estimates.

EIU, JHU, NTI. 2019. *GSI Index: Global Health Security Index: Building Collective Action and Accountability*, October. Economist Intelligence Unit, John Hopkins University, Nuclear Threat Initiative. https://www.ghsindex.org.

Engstrom, Gustav, Johan Gars, Niko Jaakkola, Therese Lindahl, Daniel Spiro, and Arthur A. van Benthem. 2020. What Policies Address Both the Coronavirus Crisis and the Climate Crisis? *Environmental and Resource Economics* 76: 789–810. https://doi.org/10.1007/s10640-020-00451-y.

Evanega, Sarah, Mark Lynas, Jordan Adams, and Karinne Smolenyak 2020. *Coronavirus Misinformation: Quantifying Sources and Themes in the COVID-19 'Infodemic'*. Cornell Alliance for Science, Department of Global Development, Cornell University, Ithaca, USA, 21 September. https://allianceforscience.cornell.edu/wp-content/uploads/2020/10/Evanega-et-al-Coronavirus-misinformation-submitted_07_23_20-1.pdf.

Flecknoe, Daniel, Benjamin Wakefield, and Aldan Simmons. 2018. Plagues & Wars: The 'Spanish Flu' Pandemic as a Lesson from History. *Medicine, Conflict, and Survival* 34 (2): 61–68. https://doi.org/10.1080/13623699.2018.1472892.

Gauttan, Priya, Bawa Singh, and Jaspal Kaur. 2020. COVID-19 and Chinese Global Health Diplomacy: Geopolitical Opportunity for China's Hegemony. *Millennial Asia* 11 (3): 318–340. https://doi.org/10.1177/0976399620959771.

Gertz, Geoffrey, and Homi Kharas, eds. 2019. *Beyond Neoliberalism: Insights from Emerging Markets*. Washington, DC: Brookings Institute.

Grabner, Claudius, Philipp Heimberger, Jacob Kapeller, and Florian Springholz. 2021. Understanding Economic Openness: A Review of Existing Measures. *Review of World Economics* 157: 87–120. https://doi.org/10.1007/s10290-020-00391-1.

Harapan, Harapan, Naoya Itoh, Amanda Yufika, Wira Winardi, Synat Keam, Heyhpeng Te, Dewi Megawati, Zinatul Hayati, Abram L. Wagner, and Mudatsir Mudatsit. 2020. Coronavirus Disease 2019 (COVID-19): A Literature Review. *Journal of Infection and Public Health* 13 (5): 667–673. https://doi.org/10.1016/j.jiph.2020.03.019.

Harvey, David. 2014. *Seventeen Contradictions and the End of Capitalism*. London: Profile Books.

Harvey, William, Alessandro M. Carabelli, Ben Jackson, Ravindra K. Gupta, Emma C. Thomson, Ewan M. Harrison, Catherine Ludden, Richard Reeve, and Andrew Rambaut. 2021. SARS-CoV-2 Variants, Spike Mutations and Immune Escape. *Nature Reviews. Microbiology* 19 (July): 409–424. https://doi.org/10.1038/s41579-021-00573-0.

Helm, Dieter. 2020. The Environmental Impacts of the Coronavirus. *Environmental and Resource Economics*, Advance Online Publication, 7 May 2020. https://doi.org/10.1007/s10640-020-00426-z.

IMF (International Monetary Fund). 2021. *World Economic Outlook Update*. Geneva: IMF.

IPCC (Intergovernmental Panel on Climate Change). 2021. *AR6 Climate Change 2021: The Physical Science Basis*. United Nations: Working Group 1 Contribution to the 6th Assessment Report. https://ipcc.com.ch.

Izurieta, Hector, David J. Granham, Yixin Jian, Man Hu, Yun Lu, Yue Wu, Yoganand Chillarige, Michael Wernecks, Mikhail Wernecke, Douglas Pratt, Jeffrey Kelman, and Richard Forshee Richard. 2021. Natural History of Coronavirus Disease 2019: Rick Factors for Hospitalisations

References

and Deaths Among >26 Million US Medicare Beneficiaries. *Journal of Infectious Diseases* 223 (6): 945–956. https://doi.org/10.1093/infdis/jiaa767.

Kaldor, Nicholas. 1972. The Irrelevance of Equilibrium Economics. *Economic Journal* 82 (328): 1237–1255. https://doi.org/10.2307/2231304.

Kaplan, Scott, Jacob Lefler, and David Zilkerman. 2021. The Political Economy of COVID-19. *Applied Economic Perspectives and Policy*, Published Online 23 March 2021. https://doi.org/10.1002/aepp.13164.

Keim, Mark, and Alex Lovallo. 2021. Validity of the National Health Security Preparedness Index as a Predictor of Excess COVID-19 Mortality. *Prehospital and Disaster Medicine* 36 (2): 141–144. https://doi.org/10.1017/S1049023X20001521.

Keynes, John Maynard. 1936. *The General Theory of Employment, Interest and Money*. London: Macmillan, 1990.

———. 1937. The General Theory of Employment. *Quarterly Journal of Economics* 51 (2): 209–223. https://doi.org/10.2307/1882087.

Knight, Frank. 1921. *Risk, Uncertainty and Profit*. New York: Cosimo Classics, 2005.

Krause, Philip, Thomas Fleming, Richard Peto, Ira Longini, J. Peter Figueroa, Jonathan Sterne, Alejandro Cravioto, Helen Rees, Julian Higgins, Isabelle Boutron, Hongchao Pan, Marion F. Gruber, Narendra Arora, Fatema Kazi, Rogerio Gaspar, Soumya Swaminathan, Michael J. Ryan, and Ana-Maria Henao-Restrepo. 2021. Considerations in Boosting COVID-19 Vaccine Immune Responses. *The Lancet*, Published Online 13 September 2021. https://doi.org/10.1016/S0140-6736(21)02046-8.

Kupferschmidt, Kapi, and Meredith Wadman. 2021. Delta Variant Triggers New Phase in the Pandemic. *Science* 372 (6549): 1375–1376. https://doi.org/10.1126/science.372.6549.1375.

Lerner, Abba. 1943. Functional Finance and the Federal Debt. *Social Research* 10: 38–51. https://www.jstor.org/stable/40981939.

Levine-Tiefenbrun, Matan, Idan Yelin, Hillel Alapi, Rachel Katz, Esma Herzel, Jacob Kuint, Gabriel Chodick, Sivan Gazit, Tal Patalon, and Roy Kishony. 2021. Viral Loads of Delta-Variant SARS-CoV2 Breakthrough Infections Following Vaccination and Booster with the BNT162b2 Vaccine, 1 September. *medRxiv preprint*. https://doi.org/10.1101/2021.08.29.21262798.

Liu, Yen-Chin, Rei-Lin Kuo, and Shin-Ru Shih. 2020. COVID-19: The First Documented Coronavirus in History. *Biomedical Journal*. 43 (4): 328–333. https://doi.org/10.1016/j.bj.2020.04.007.

Liu, Lihong, Sho Iketani, Yicheng Guo, Jasper F.-W. Chan, Maple Wang, Liyuan Liu, Yang Luo, Hin Chu, Yiming Huang, Manoj S. Nair, Jian Yu, Kenn K.-H. Chik, Terrence T.-T. Yuen, Chaemin Yoon, Kelvin K-W. To, Honglin Chen, Michael T. Yin, Magdalena E. Sobieszczyk, Yaoxing Huang, Harris H. Wang, Zizhang Sheng, Kwok-Yung Yuen, and David D. Ho. 2021. Striking Antibody Evasion Manifested by the Omicron Variant of SARS-CoV-2. *bioRxiv: The Preprint Server for Biology*. https://doi.org/10.1101/2021.12.14.472719.

Mahagan, Manjari. 2021. Casualties of Preparedness: The Global Health Security Index and COVID-19. *International Journal of Law in Context* 17 (2): 204–214. https://doi.org/10.1017/S1744552321000288.

Mahase, Elizabeth. 2021. Delta Variant: What Is Happening with Transmissions, Hospital Admissions, and Restrictions? *British Medical Journal* 373 (n1530): 1–2. https://doi.org/10.1136/bmj.n1513.

———. 2022. Covid-19: What Do We Know About Omicron Sublineages? *BMJ* 376: o358. (Published Online 11 February 2022). https://www.bmj.com/content/bmj/376/bmj.o358.full.pdf.

Mair, Simon. 2020. Neoliberal Economics, Planetary Health, and the COVID-19 Pandemic: A Marxist Ecofeminist Analysis. *The Lancet: Planetary Health* 4 (12): e588–e596. https://doi.org/10.1016/S2542-5196(20)30252-7.

Marx, Karl. 1857–58. *Grundrisse: Foundations of the Critique of Political Economy (Rough Draft)*. Harmondsworth: Penguin, 1973.

Mathieu, Edouard, Hannah Ritchie, Esteban Ortiz-Ospina, Max Roser, Joe Hasell, Cameron Appel, Charlie Giattino, and Lucas Rodés-Guirao. 2021. A Global Database of COVID-19 Vaccinations. *Nature Human Behaviour* 5 (July): 947–953. https://doi.org/10.1038/s41562-021-01122-8.

Myrdal, Gunnar. 1968. Appendix 2: The Mechanism of Underdevelopment and Development and a Sketch of an Elementary Theory of Planning for Development: 1. Circular Causation. In *Asian Drama: An Inquiry into the Poverty of Nations*, ed. G. Myrdal, vol. 3. Harmondsworth: Penguin.

New Scientist. 2021. Special Report: Long COVID. *New Scientist* 3340 (26 June): 7–14. https://www.newscientist.com/issue/3340/.

Nidadavolu, Lolita, and Jeremy Walston. 2021. Underlying Vulnerabilities to the Cytokine Storm and Adverse COVID-19 Outcomes in the Aging Immune System. *Journals of Gerontology: Medical Sciences* 76 (3): E13–E18. https://doi.org/10.1093/gerona/glaa209.

Novak, Mikayla. 2021. *Entangled Political Economy of the COVID-19 Pandemic*. Paper Presented at the November 2020 Entangled Political Economy Research Network Network. Seminar. https://www.entangledpoliticaleconomy.org/virtual-seminars.

O'Hara, Phillip Anthony. 2001. Contradictions. In *Encyclopedia of Political Economy*, ed. P.A. O'Hara, vol. 1, 140–143. London/New York: Routledge. Paper Edition. https://www.routledge.com/Encyclopedia-of-Political-Economy-2-volume-set/OHara/p/book/9780415241885.

———. 2006. The Contradictory Dynamics of Globalization. In *Globalization and the Third World: A Study of Negative Consequences*, ed. B.N. Ghosh and Halil M. Guven, 17–35. New York: Palgrave Macmillan.

———. 2007a. Principles of Institutional-Evolutionary Political Economy: Converging Themes from the Schools of Heterodoxy. *Journal of Economic Issues* 41 (1): 1–42. https://doi.org/10.1080/00213624.2007.11506993.

———. 2007b. The Global Spread of AIDS and HIV. *Journal of Economic Issues* 41 (2): 350–360. https://doi.org/10.1080/00213624.2007.11507034.

———. 2008. Principle of Circular and Cumulative Causation: Fusing Myrdalian and Kaldorian Growth and Development Dynamics. *Journal of Economic Issues* 42 (2): 375–387. https://doi.org/10.1080/00213624.2008.11507146.

———. 2009. Cultural Contradictions of Global Capitalism. In Chapter 2 of P.A. O'Hara, *Growth and Development in the Global Political Economy: Social Structures of Accumulation and Modes of Regulation*, 34–48. London/New York: Routledge. Paper Edition. https://www.routledge.com/Growth-and-Development-in-the-Global-Political-Economy-Modes-of-Regulation/OHara/p/book/9780415547659.

———. 2010. After Neoliberalism: A Social Structure of Accumulation or Mode of Regulation for Global or Regional Performance? *Journal of Economic Issues* 44 (2): 369–384. https://doi.org/10.2753/JEI0021-3624440209.

———. 2011. International Subprime Crisis and Recession: Emerging Macroprudential, Monetary, Fiscal and Global Governance. *Panoeconomicus* LVIII (1): 1–17. https://doi.org/10.2298/PAN1101001O, https://doi.org/10.1080/07360932.2018.1467332.

———. 2021a. Global Coronavirus Pandemic Crisis and Future Crisis Prevention. *Panoeconomicus* 68 (5): 587–623. https://doi.org/10.2298/PAN2105587O.

———. 2021b. Objectives of the *Review of Evolutionary Political Economy*'s 'Manifesto' and Editorial Proposals on World Problems, Complex Systems, Historico-Institutional and Corruption Issues. *Review of Evolutionary Political Economy* 2 (2): 359–387. https://doi.org/10.1007/s43253-021-00040-9.

———. 2022a. Integrating Dugger's Concepts with O'Hara's Principles to Advance Social and Institutional Economics. *Forum for Social Economics* 51 (1): 9–40. https://doi.org/10.1080/07360932.2018.1467332.

———. 2022b. AIDS and HIV. In *International Encyclopedia of Public Policy: Volume 1: Global Governance*, ed. P.A. O'Hara, 1–18. Perth: GPERU. http://pohara.homestead.com/Encyclopedia/Volume-1.pdf.

References

———. 2023. *Long Wave Institutional Dynamics and Political Economy Crises of Capitalism: Principles, Social Structures of Accumulation and Empirics*. Geneva: Springer.

ODNI (Office of the Director of National Intelligence). 2021. *Unclassified: Key Takeaways [On the Origins of SARS-CoV-2]*. Washington, DC: National Intelligence Council.

OWID (Our World in Data). 2022. *Coronavirus (COVID-19) by Country and Region*. Coronavirus Pandemic (COVID-19)—Our World in Data.

Pedreañez, Adriana, Jesus Mosquera-Sulbaran, and Nelson Muñoz. 2021. SARS-CoV-2 Infection Represents a High Risk for the Elderly: Analysis of Pathogenesis. *Archives of Virology* 166: 1565–1574. https://doi.org/10.1007/s00705-021-05042-w.

Phillips, Howard. 2014. The Recent Wave of 'Spanish' Flu Historiography. *Social History of Medicine* 27 (4): 789–808. https://doi.org/10.1093/shm/hku066.

Pouwels, Koen, Emma Pritchard, Philippa Mathews, Nicole Stoesser, David Eyre, Karina-Doris Vihta, et al. 2021. *Impact of Delta on Viral Burden and Vaccine Effectiveness Against the New SARS-CoV-2 Infections in the UK*. mimeo, 13 August. University of Oxford. https://doi.org/10.1038/s41591-021-01548-7.

Primrose, David, Robin Chang, and Rodney Loeppky. 2020. Pandemic Unplugged: COVID-19, Public Health and the Persistence of Neoliberalism. *Journal of Australian Political Economy* 85 (Winter): 17–28. https://www.ppesydney.net/content/uploads/2020/06/JAPE-85-complete.pdf.

Riediker, Michael, Leonardo Briceno-Ayalab, Gaku Ichiharac, Daniele Albanid, Deyan Poffete, Dai-Hua Tsaia, Samuel Ifff, and Christian Monn. 2022. Higher Viral Load and Infectivity Increase Risk of Aerosol Transmission for Delta and Omicron Variants of SARS-CoV-2. *Swiss Medical Weekly* 152: w30133. https://doi.org/10.4414/SMW.2022.w30133.

Roser, Max, and Hannah Ritchie. 2021. *HIV–AIDS Historical Online Data*. https://ourworldindata.org/hiv-aids.

Samudro, Bhimo Rizky. 2012. *A Political Economy Analysis of Uneven Global, Regional, National and Subnational Performance 1950–2010*. PhD Thesis. School of Economics and Finance, Curtin University, Perth, Australia. https://library.curtin.edu.au/find-resources/theses/.

Sarkodie, Samuel, and Phebe Asantewaa Owusu. 2020. Global Assessment of Environmental, Health, and Economic Impact of the Novel Coronavirus (COVID-19). *Environment, Development and Sustainability* 23: 5005–5015. https://doi.org/10.1007/s10668-020-00801-2.

Sen, Sunanda. 2020. Investment Decisions Under Uncertainty. *Journal of Post Keynesian Economics* 43 (2): 267–280. https://doi.org/10.1080/01603477.2019.1571927.

Shackle, G.L.S. 1972. *Expectations, Enterprise and Profit*. London: Allen & Unwin.

Stanfield, James Ronald. 1986. *The Economic Thought of Karl Polanyi*. London/New York: Macmillan/St Martins Press.

Sumonja, Milos. 2021. Neoliberalism Is Not Dead: On Political Implications of Covid-19. *Capital & Class* 45 (2): 215–228. https://doi.org/10.1177/0309816820982381.

Tang, Jujun, Jiajia Liu, Dangyi Zang, Zhenghao Xo, Jinjung Ji, and Chengping Wen. 2020. Cytokine Storm in COVID-19: The Current Evidence and Treatment Strategies. *Frontiers in Immunology* 11 (1708): 1–13. https://doi.org/10.3389/fimmu.2020.01708.

Terry, Mark. 2021. *Comparing COVID-19 Vaccines: Timelines, Types and Prices: Updated*, 28 July. https://www.biospace.com.

Tool, Marc. 2000. *The Discretionary Economy: A Normative Theory of Political Economy*. 2nd ed. New Brunswick/London: Transaction Publishers.

Veblen, Thorstein Bunde. 1919. *The Vested Interests and the Common Man*. New York: Augustus M. Kelley, 1964.

WHO. 2021a. *Update on SARS-CoV-2 Variant Nomenclature*. World Health Organization. Available Online at http://worldheathorg.shinyapp.io/covid/.

———. 2021b. *Coronavirus Disease (COVID-19) Advice for the Public*. https://www.who.int/emergencies/diseases/novel-coronavirus-2019/advice-for-public.

———. 2022. *COVID-19 Explorer: Stock of Data on the Pandemic*. Available Online at http://worldhealthorg.shinyapps.io/covid/.

WHO-China Joint Mission. 2020. *Report of the WHO-China Joint Mission on Coronavirus Disease 2019 (COVID-19)*, 40. Geneva: WHO.

WHO-China Joint Report. 2021. *WHO-Convened Global Study of Origins of SARS-CoV-2: China Part*, 6 April, ed. David FitzSimons, 120.

Wikipedia. 2021a. Variants of SARS-CoV-20. *Wikipedia Encyclopedia*. Online. Accessed 2 Sept 2021.

———. 2021b. COVID-19 Vaccine. *Wikipedia Encyclopedia*. Online. Accessed 2 Sept 2021.

Wise, Jacqui. 2021. COVID-19: The E484K Mutation and the Risks It Poses. *British Medical Journal* 372 (359): 1–2. https://doi.org/10.1136/bmj.n359.

World Bank. 2021. *World Development Indicators: Real GDP Growth Rate Per Annum*. Washington, DC. http://worldbank.com. Accessed 23 Sept 2021.

WWF (Worldwide Fund for Nature). 2020. *Living Planet Index: Bending the Curve of Biodiversity Loss*, ed. R.E.A. Almond, M. Grooten, and T. Petersen. Gland: WWF. Available Online at https://livingplanet.panda.org/.

Zhou, Weilin, and Wei Wang. 2021. Fast-Spreading SARS-CoV-2 Variants: Challenges to the New Design Strategies of COVID-19 Vaccines. *Signal Transduction and Targeted Therapy* 6 (226): 1–6. https://doi.org/10.1038/s41392-021-00644-x.

Climate Change 5

Abstract

The purpose of this chapter is to analyse climate change and ecological destruction through the prism of the some core general principles of institutional and evolutionary political economy. The chapter starts with the principle of historical specificity, and the various waves of climate change through successive cooler and warmer periods on planet Earth, including the most recent climate change escalation through the open circuit associated with the treadmill of production. Then we scrutinise the principle of contradiction associated with the disembedded economy, social costs, entropy and destructive creation. The principle of hegemony and uneven development is then explored through core-periphery dynamics, ecologically unequal exchange, metabolic rift and asymmetric global (in)justice. The principles of circular and cumulative causation (CCC) and uncertainty are then related to climate change dynamics through non-linear transformations, complex interaction of dominant variables, threshold effects, and tipping points. This introduces the principles of innovation and policy/governance, relating to the concept of shared socioeconomic pathways, and specifically the Green Road to Sustainability. The current path is inconsistent with solving the climate change conundrum, while the Green Road requires deepening plus more stringent structural changes in institutions and systems to reduce emissions more rapidly, in addition to adaptation to tipping points that emerge.

Keywords

Political economy · Principles · Climate change · Historical specificity · Ecological destruction · Greenhouse gasses · Contradiction · Hegemony & uneven development · Circular & cumulative causation · Uncertainty · Tipping points · Innovation · Policy & governance

5.1 Introduction

For decades the 'global warming' hypothesis has been a contested terrain, and even after the conclusive scientific reports of the late 2000s (Gore 2006; IPCC 2007b; Stern 2007; UNDP 2007; Garnaut 2008), vested interests and politicians have been trying still to downplay the science, especially with populist-nationalistic political arguments. Now it seems many of these groups have found it difficult to question the science of climate change, especially in the light of more recent evidence, such as the latest IPCC (2021), UNDP (2020) and WMO (2021) reports. A crucial argument is that less developed countries (LDCs) have not caused the problem, so advanced nations should compensate them for past and present climate damage plus future adaptation and damage costs; while advanced nations especially should ensure limited future global greenhouse gas (GHG) emissions and climate change.

The recent 2021 COP26 climate summit in Glasgow demonstrated some nations are determined to reduce GHG emissions to keep to the 1.5 °C mean global temperature increase by 2100 vis-à-vis preindustrial times, and some small island nations are feeling the pinch of destruction of their land and livelihood. But most especially big nations are not really committed to achieving the changes necessary to save the planet. In fact, GHG emissions (flows) have been increasing in the past decade, leading to heightened GHG concentrations (stocks), greater land and ocean temperatures, rising sea levels, and more extreme climate events such as flood, drought, wildfire, hurricane and temperature emergencies. The world will likely need to adopt a Green Road/Sustainability Pathway for temperature rises to be at or below 1.5 °C by 2100, but even this temperature is subject to relatively extreme climate events, with some areas experiencing extreme heat due to uneven climate patterns throughout the world, as well as likely tipping points.

In climate research, it has now become common to take a multi-disciplinary, even perhaps a transdisciplinary, approach to climate change. The sort of changes we are viewing are quite major, and there are deep uncertainties involved in every aspect of the problem. These uncertainties do not challenge the general idea of climate change, but indicate that threshold effects such as major ice-sheets melting or shifting in the Arctic region, Greenland and the Western Antarctic are likely happening sooner than later, while coral bleaching is already upon us. Much of the methodology of these reports (IPCC 2021; UNDP 2020; WMO 2021) is similar to the concerns of ecological economists and political economists. However, it is likely that these reports *underplay* critical concepts and processes, including structural changes in social organisation (rather than simply technology, 'policy issues', adaptation, mitigation, and pathways); the social costs embedded in the treadmill of production (rather than resolution through market valuation policies); the structural connection between the costs imposed on the periphery and benefits directed to the core nations; ongoing entropic degradation of energy-matter (rather than sustainable production and development); and the likely early onset of destructive tipping points.

Here I utilise core principles to understand climate change and environmental destruction, Special emphasis is given to work within and between the fields of institutional and evolutionary political economy. The chapter starts with the principle of historical specificity, which states that history is an important starting point in a political economy perspective. Here climate change is embedded into the historical process, including the evolutionary transformation of capitalism. Then the chapter examines the principle of contradiction, which states that core anomalies must be studied and acted upon in order to moderate the crisis of climate change; including the disembedded economy, social costs, entropy and the accumulation of capital that link to the destruction of environmental resources and climate patterns. The principle of uneven development then reveals serious conflict between core and periphery, and why policy may fail to change the world for the better; unless these uneven developments are examined and acted upon. The principle of circular and cumulative causation states that we need to identify the major causes of greenhouse gas emissions and their impact on climate, due to major accelerated and magnified impacts. The principle of innovation and policy/governance introduces the concept of shared socioeconomic pathway, as the Green Road to Sustainability requires more structural changes to solve the climate change problem. This is closely associated with the principle of uncertainty, as several deep ambiguities necessitate an evolutionary and non-linear analysis of threshold effects and cumulative impacts, and we scrutinise these uncertainties to understand how to adopt certain pathways, but especially structural changes in organisation, to moderate the anomalies.

5.2   Historical Specificity of Climate Change

One of the defining characteristics of political economy is its historical foundation, since it relies on history to assist in comprehending evolutionary processes. Grand political economists such as Karl Marx, Thorstein Veblen, John Maynard Keynes and Joseph Schumpeter (and their followers) embedded history in their political economy approaches. Numerous more recent scholars, such as Michael Howard and John King (1985) and Geoffrey Hodgson (2004) specifically cite the principle of historical specificity as being crucial for science. According to this principle, we must be cognizant of how history provides a corpus of knowledge concerning stages and phases of evolution, life cycles, changing habits, institutions and technologies, and path dependent patterns. Without history, political economy would be a mere formality, lacking in operational, social and organisational content. This is especially the case with climate change, as it is necessary to situate it within the framework of past phases of change and metamorphosis as we look towards the future.

It helps to comprehend in broad terms the waves and patterns of climatic change through the millennia. Several waves and changing patterns of climate have been apparent through the life-history of the world (Moberg et al. 2005: 616). There were

100–140 m-year long waves of climate change during the Phanerozoic eon (0–540 m years BP; 'before the present'; the current *geological* eon), and 70,000–115,000 year long waves during the Pleistocene era (12,000–2.6 m years BP; often called the 'Ice Age'). The two eras were characterised by recurring hot and cold waves, usually culminating in successive glacial or ice ages during the cold periods, followed by periods of much warmer weather. Less regular long patterns have been operating during the Holocene period when human beings *settled most of the areas of Earth* (0–12,000 years BP). For instance, just before and during the early years of the Holocene "human era" there was a period of sudden and very deep cooling and glaciation between 12,700 and 11,400 BP, then rapid change from glacial to warm conditions more suitable for human habitation between 11,000 and 10,000 BP (2–3 °C warmer than before). This was followed by a somewhat cooler period from 9300 to 8000 BP (0.5 °C cooler than normal), and then a warmer period from 8000 to 6500 BP (0.0–0.3 °C warmer than normal). The next 2000 years from 6500 to 4250 BP was fairly stable around the norm.

The period from 4250 to 150 BP looks decidedly like a transition to colder temperatures until industrialisation commenced in Britain. When examined more narrowly, 0–800 AD exhibited a stable cold tendency (0.2–0.6 °C cooler than normal), followed by a medieval warm*er* period from 975 to 1425 AD (0–0.2 °C *below* norm), a little ice-age (especially in Europe) from 1440 to 1710 AD (0.4–0.9 °C below norm), and then since 1850–1900 a progressively warmer era (1.07–1.2 °C above mean) to 2020.

None of these waves or periods before 1850 were *anthropogenic*; i.e., caused specifically by humans (or other animals). They were caused by things such as changes in the tilting of the Earth's axis, volcanic forcing, or solar irradiance. The more recent trends concerning climate are the first to be precipitated by human beings or 'non-natural' forces. The current period of expansion of greenhouse gasses, during the era of the anthropocene, commenced at a low base during the industrial revolution from the mid-1850s, but did not noticeably increase until the 1950s and 1960s, thereafter showing upward warming from the 1970s through to the 2010s (UNDP 2020; IPCC 2021). The 'anthropocene' refers to the era since the mid-1900s, when the activities of human beings started markedly affecting the planet. The warming trend became especially noticeable in the mid-1900s, but did not become a serious threat until the oceans became a less efficient sink in the 1970s onwards. Since then the signs have been there in abundance for serious CO_2 emissions, rising temperatures, further expansion in sea levels, modified precipitation and wind patterns, greater extreme events, plus the melting of ice-sheets.

The reason for the rising greenhouse gas levels is the rapid expansion of a new economic system that commenced its industrial phase in the mid-1800s, especially in Europe and North America. This system of "industrial capitalism" was based around different class processes of capitalists and workers, coal-and-later-oil-fired engines, production of steel, technological expansions and productivity increases. It also gradually began to penetrate the market for consumer goods, and the so-called

5.2 Historical Specificity of Climate Change

'first phase of globalisation' ('concerted imperialism') began in earnest in the 1880s–1910s as it was 'exported' to many further areas of the world. Capitalism is a class system based on deep capital structures, with often complex input-output linkages and changing production processes, products, corporate systems, markets, and raw materials.[1] During the 1950s to the 1970s a new phase of evolution of capitalism started, neo-Fordism and the Keynesian welfare state, generating the highest rate of global growth since records began, adversely affecting the biosphere. Globalisation and neoliberalism matured during the 1980s–2000s, while neoliberalism waned 2008–2022. But commodification and profit-making activities continue to effect the environment much more than even the earlier era.

Capitalism in the contemporary world is a mixed system of private enterprise and government, along with non-capitalist institutions such as the family and community. The system revolves around business processes, such as innovation, markets and finance. Marx's (1885) circuit of money capital (CMC), when expanded and situated as an *open system* linked to social and environmental processes, is useful to understanding its operational dynamics.[2] Initially see Fig. 5.1 below for this extended circuit, which we call the *systemic circuit of social capital* (SCSC):

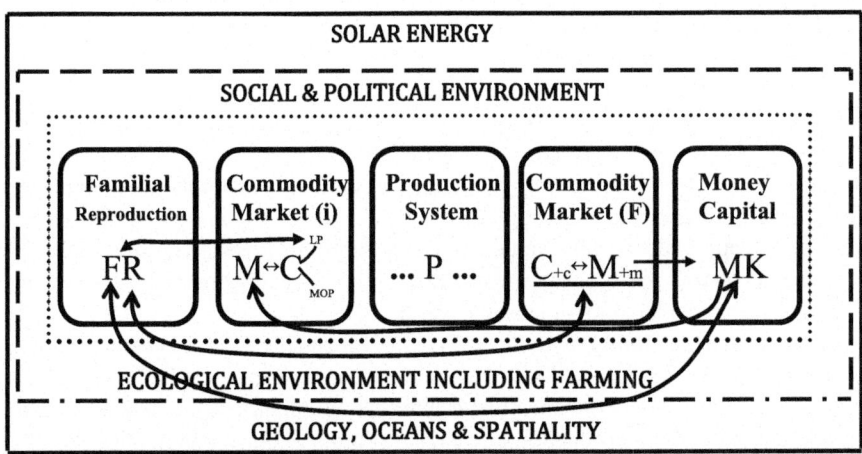

Fig. 5.1 Systemic circuit of social capital, or extended circular treadmill of production. (Source: Adapted from O'Hara, 2004)

---

[1] According to Resnick and Wolff (2002), capitalism emerged in Central and Eastern Europe in the late 1800s, especially as state capitalism during the 1920s–1980s as the bureaucrats expropriated the surplus normally distributed to private owners or managers.

[2] We need to deepen the open nature of the circuit of money capital. While Marx does link the circuit to both labor and nature contributing to use-values, and the processes of metabolic rift, making the circuit (or the treadmill) a more explicitly open system does help embed the environment and ecology into the capitalist process more specifically.

This (open) circuit as a whole has the logic of the "treadmill of production", which many sociological political economists have been using to describe the ongoing dynamics of capitalism. John Bellamy Foster (2009: 48) defines the treadmill of production as "an unstoppable, accelerating treadmill that constantly increases the scale of the throughput of energy and raw materials as part of its quest for profit and accumulation, thereby pressing on the earth's absorptive capacity." Within this open-circular treadmill, familial reproduction (FR) of labor power; and finance (money capital, MK = new debt + new equity + reinvested undistributed profits) are added to the usual flow of processes, while the circuit is set within a wider system including solar energy, ecological environment, systems of geology, oceans and spatiality, as well as the social and political environment.

In this context, the family (plus the community and state) can contribute negatively or positively to the reproduction of labor power, while it can also contribute through enhancing market exchange as non-market activities become marketised. Money (M) is then used to buy commodities (C), both labor power (LP) and means of production (MOP), including machines, buildings, factories, animals, seeds, plus non-renewable resources such as oil, natural gas, coal, nuclear energy, minerals and metal-ores. The system of production (... P ...) then comes into play with the transformation of matter-energy from low to high entropic processes (Georgescu-Roegen 1971). Out of this production process emerges commodities (including services), with a value equal to the inputs (C), plus usually a surplus product (c) over costs of production.

Then the Keynesian problem emerges concerning selling goods and services for money, including a surplus value (m) (profits; interest and rent). Here consumption demand becomes a core concern. After that it is crucial that the capitalist instinct be sufficiently developed to re-invest the sales money, along with credit, bond money or the original selling of shares through the financial system. The faster this circuit turns over the greater is the surplus value that can be used for investment, dividends and managerial salaries, or other purposes. But as this happens the resources become increasingly unavailable in an entropic sense.

This circular treadmill of production is thus dependent upon expanding markets to transform non-market relations into new means for profit. Cheap ecological resources are required, below their renewable cost, to enhance profit; as is the turning of non-market familial production into capitalist production; expanding the world in search for new markets; and generating new needs and wants, with the credit system for expanded accumulation. Turning things into commodities is thus the way to generate new profits, especially if their cost of production is low due to cheap methods of exploiting resources and other inputs. The circuit as a whole also requires government to provide a system of laws and property rights to protect systems of profit and accumulation; plus fiscal and monetary policy to ensure renewal of the circuit through time. It is assisted by consumers in the habit of buying and selling as means of reproducing everyday life, expanding credit usage and engaging in Veblenian conspicuous consumption and emulation to enhance the circuit. Preferences have endogenously eschewed sustainability in the pursuit of profit and consumption, affected by social and business norms (Sabine O'Hara 2001a, b,

5.2 Historical Specificity of Climate Change

2002), while "the earth remains in large part a "free gift to capital"" (Foster 2002: 11) as the circular treadmill accumulates and profits from the motion.

Extending these processes even more to the ecological and social system implies the existence of an integrated (open and partly uni-directional) circuit of human-ecological greenhouse gas emissions (GHGE) and climate change, as shown below in Fig. 5.2.

This integrated (open) circuit shows the linkages between the circular treadmill of money capital (MCM + m), land use clearing (LUC) plus emissions (EM) of carbon dioxide equivalents (CO_2-e) or GHGs, including the process of radiative forcing (RadForc) after a lag, and associated climate sensitivity parameters (λ), producing changes in temperatures, rising sea levels and changes in current, wind and rain patterns. These can feedback through to other aspects of the climate system (with lags), along with other (feedback) impacts on various systems in the physical, biological and human domains (with further lags).

Thus far the observed warming (+) in global mean temperature (GMT) for Planet Earth, up to 2010–2020, relative to 1850–1900, is a net +1.07–1.2 °C, contributed by greenhouse gasses warming of between +1.0 and +2.0 °C and anthropogenic cooling (−) of between −0.0 and −0.8 °C (IPCC 2021: TS, 29; *draft* report). Natural sources of GHG over the long-term horizon are generally balanced by sinks such as photosynthesis and the activities of marine plankton. The predominant greenhouse gas contributions to rising (+1.0 to +2.0) temperatures to date include: carbon dioxide (CO_2) (42.80% of total), methane (CH_4) (28.70%) (estimates have nearly doubled in recent years), halogenated gasses (CFC + HCFC+HFC) (5.41%), nitrous oxide (4.95%), other gasses (including carbon monoxide) (11.90%), black carbon (4.95%), and aviation contrails (0.83%). The predominant contributions to reductions (−0.0 to −0.8 °C) in temperatures over this period include sulphur dioxide (SO2) (−61.77%), nitrogen oxides (NOx) (−17.43%), land-use reflectance and irrigation (including albedo) (−10%), organic carbon (−8.84%), and ammonia (−1.82%). (CEDA 2021.) (See also IPCC 2021: Table TS14, Tech Sum, pp. TS-129.)

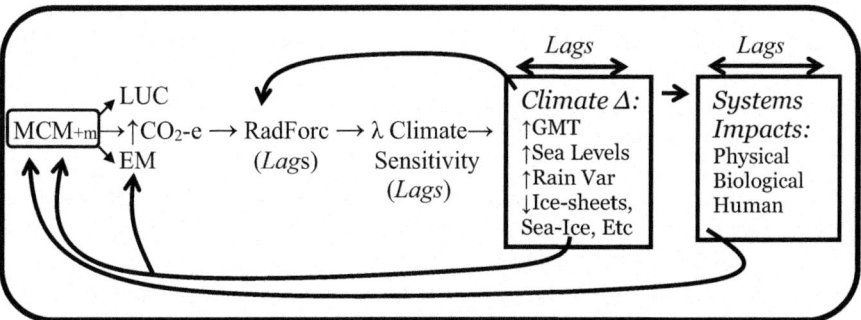

Fig. 5.2 Integrated circuit of business-consumers, ecology & climate. (Source: Adapted from Stern, 2007: 10)

In terms of global sectoral contributors to GHG, the major sources, during 2016 were energy use, which constitutes 73.2% of total GHG emissions. These include energy used in industry (24.2%), transport (16.2%), buildings (17.5%), agriculture and fishing (1.7%), fugitive functions (5.8%), plus other fuel combustion uses (7.8%). The other major emitter of GHG is 'agriculture, forestry and land-use' (18.4%), which comprises livestock & manure (5.8%), soils (4.1%), crop burning (3.5%), deforestation (2.2%), crop/grasslands (1.5%), and rice cultivation (1.3%). Further contributors are *direct* industrial activities (5.2%) and waste (3.2%). (Ritchie and Roser 2021).

During the 1970s there was no clear convention about Earth's maximum desired climate change by 2100. Some thought the Earth would cool, possibly due to aerosols (IPCC 2007a: 98). William Nordhaus (1977) estimated that over the past 100,000 years the range of Earth's temperature changes did not exceed 2 °C, and that this did not cause catastrophic results. Often he argued capping climate change at 2 degrees would be too costly (e.g., Nordhaus 1991); but since then has changed his mind (Nordhaus 2008). Consistent global plans suggesting "below 2 °C" or "maximum 2 °C" started in the 1990s (e.g., Vellinga and Swart 1991), and were alluded to by EU and IPCC studies. "2 °C maximum" targets continued into the 2000s, usually with uncertainty limits added (see Randalls 2010) and became a policy convention, though some unofficial analysts broke with the convention down or upwards.

This official convention was broken more recently, as the Paris Agreement (2016) limited rises at "well-below 2 degrees C". Fairly suddenly this convention has changed as several official reports now posit a target limit rise to 1.5 °C (with uncertainty levels added). As part of its sixth assessment cycle, the IPCC (2018) produced a 'Special Report': *Global Warming of 1.5 °C,* in which it examined the impact of 1.5 °C on natural and human and human systems, mitigation strategies for 1.5 °C, and ways of strengthening the global response to achieving sustainable development, poverty eradication and reducing inequalities. This special report indicates that a 1.5 °C instead of 2 °C rise could limit global water stress to vulnerable populations by 50% (p. 9), and lessen the impact of sea-level rises by 100 mm (or 10 cm), thereby reducing the incidence on 100 million people.

But even a rise to 1.5 °C by 2100 is not going to prevent multi-metre rises in sea-levels in the very long-term due to instability/irreversible loss of ice sheets in Antarctica and Greenland (p. 7). Coral reefs are estimated to decline by an additional 70–80% with the 1.5 °C increase and 99% for the 2 °C regime. One robust model shows a decline in global fishery catch of 1.5 m tonnes at 1.5 °C and 3 m tonnes at 2 °C. The IPCC predicts critical thresholds, one major one of which is said to likely start around 1.5 °C. Achieving 1.5 °C by 2100 requires the world generating net zero CO_2 emissions by 2050 and much greater reductions in methane emissions. It requires pronounced and rapid reductions over the next one, two and three decades.

Already at 1.07–1.2 °C increase in global mean temperatures, relative to the 1850–1900 mean, the world is experiencing much more major flooding, droughts, wildfires, and hurricanes, plus species extinction and critical threats, in numerous areas of the world. Some have said that perhaps the current temperature increase is high enough, or too high, especially given that it impacts regions unevenly, and

5.2 Historical Specificity of Climate Change

already poses numerous emergencies that were not present 20 years ago. Examples include the more intense droughts in parts of Africa and the Middle East, the critical wildfires in California, other states, as well as in Australia, the more extreme floods in Europe, China, Australia and elsewhere, the threatened state of coral reefs in several areas, and the disintegration of ice sheets in the Arctic, Greenland and Antarctica. A 1.5 °C increase will see events become much more severe, and any higher will eventually generate further critical thresholds and thus many more extreme events.

One could reasonably make a prediction that in 10 years the conventional wisdom will be a desired cap equal to the current mean rise of 1.07–1.2 °C, especially given the uneven climate change impacts throughout the world: affecting small island nations, the periphery, and more northerly regions more than other areas.

Current trends of 1.07–1.2 °C and rising cannot lead to optimism about the chances of reaching 1.5 °C, or even 2 °C, by 2100, after the COP26 conference in Glasgow, Scotland, during late 2021. The Glasgow Climate Pact, signed by 197 nations, includes a number of pledges, including reducing dependency on coal (rather than phasing it out), phasing out fossil fuel subsides, financial assistance for mitigation and adaptation; while special agreements were signed by over 80 nations to cut methane emissions, with many attendees committing to net zero carbon emissions by 2050 or 2070 (C2ES 2021). The philosophy of self-regulation underlying the event, pledges not being mandatory, not all nations signing the various agreements, many nations not attending (such as China, the biggest emitter) and having no fines for failure to achieve targets, do not auger well for climate change mitigation and adaptation into the future.

It is, therefore, unlikely that the basic scenarios established will change, for long-term mean temperature rises, based on certain policies, pledges and targets, into the near future at least (see CAT 2021). CAT Scenario 1, with no climate policies, is said to likely lead to 4.1–4.8 °C (uncertainty range) rise in average global temperatures by 2100. Scenario 2, with current policies, is likely to result in 2.7–3.1 °C rise in temperature by 2100. Additional pledges and targets will likely lead to a 2.4 °C rise in temperature by 2100; this is where COP26 enters, but much uncertainty surrounds its agreements, targets and pledges.

In this context, it is possible to use the *concept of shared socioeconomic pathways* (SSPs), for assessing potential progress in reducing temperature declines by 2100. SSPs is used by the IPCC to assess the nature and likelihood of policies and practices into the future. There are further details on this concept below in Sect. 5.4, but for the moment we can broadly say that we would likely need SSP_1 devoted to "Sustainability: The Green Road" (O'Neill et al. 2017: 4–5) for the 1.5 °C (1.0–1.8 °C uncertainty limits) mean global temperature increase to potentially come into play by 2100. This is where human well-being, lower growth, lower resource and energy intensity, reliance on renewable energy, proper accounting of environmental costs, and high levels of transborder collaboration and cooperation on climate change are presumed to come into play. SSP_2, where temperatures rise by potentially 2.7 °C (2.1–3.5 °C uncertainty limits) by 2100, would probably be the most likely optimistic outcome for the world, what is called the "Middle of the

Road" SSP. But for the Green Road (SSP_1) to come into play will likely require substantial organisational social and political change to transcend the circular treadmill of accumulation, which we discuss in the next section.

5.3 Contradictions of Climate Change

The principle of contradiction states that there are numerous interrelated contradictions associated with the open circuit of money capital, which have been variously documented by the grand political economists of the past, including Marx, Veblen, Keynes, Schumpeter and their followers, and which need to be scrutinised closely. These contradictions include, for instance, that between capital and labor, finance and industry, monopoly and competition, men and women, and so on (see O'Hara 2001a, b, 2023). Some that specifically relate to climate change are the contradictions between ecological resources and profit, and the related one between core and periphery, which are examined in this and the next section.

The principal general contradiction is that of the disembedded economy (Brennan 2008); namely, Karl Polanyi's (1944) idea that capitalism undergoes the process of destructive creation, variously destroying socio-ecological resources in the very process of creating market value, with many of these destructions not being included in the market valuation of goods and services. These things which orthodox economics calls externalities are actually endogenously necessary "social costs" for business enterprise to generate a sustainable profit. The disembedded economy is based on the notion that there are various "fictitious commodities" involved in the treadmill which tend to be under-reproduced if markets are left to their own devices. These include labor power, money and the environment, all of which require for their proper maintenance many more resources than the free market is likely to provide. Extra resources need to be generated for these spheres, even for the long-term functioning of capitalism, and even more resources for systems of lower community and entropic degradation (e.g., SSP1). Hence we see the operation of the double movement, that capitalism variously moves between complex systems of insufficiently providing such resources (on the one hand), while the state and community (and even corporations) respond in certain historical junctures with many more resources for their reproduction (on the other hand). Capitalism as a whole thus moves through cycles and waves of insufficiently and over-sufficiently providing these resources, which is a prime dynamic of the system generating instability and motion (see Chap. 8, below, for details).

Through such motion, the double movement of the market versus more embedded relationships evolves through varying degrees of stability and instability. 'Formal exchange' (buying and selling commodities) promotes capitalism and market relations, activities designed for private profit. The other, more integrative transactions or relationships, such as redistribution, reciprocity, householding and informal exchange (community buying and selling) promote the reproduction of human labor power, central banks/lender of last resort facilities and environmental protection requirements and institutions. The three quasi-commodities of labor

5.3 Contradictions of Climate Change

power, money and environmental resources are in need of special protection due to market capitalism insufficiently providing for the system-requirements of complex socioeconomic processes. Hence market capitalism is perpetually being limited by the dynamics of individual capitals (which limit protective resources), capitalism as a whole (which also limit them by community standards), and community requirements (which exceed the limits of capital). The core contradiction of capitalism in the disembedded economy is that private and public capitals seek to secure the services of labor power, credit-money and land/seas (including natural resources) in ways that generate periodic and tendential underconsumption, overindebtedness and overexploitation of resources, respectively, and hence crisis/uncertainty anomalies.

Key specific insights into aspects of this disembedded economy can be gained from the work of political economists such as Karl William Kapp, Nicholas Georgescu-Roegen, James O'Connor and John Bellamy Foster. These four scholars, in particular, teach us that social and environmental costs of growth and profit require us to go beyond market valuation in determining solutions to resource preservation and utilisation.[3]

Kapp's (1978: 31–37, 42–46) theory of social costs drew some inspiration from Polanyi, since he saw Polanyi's work as "an illustration of what can be done in rewriting history if ... social costs are kept in view" (p. 45). He also drew heavily from Marx, especially in relation to "Capitalist production ... sapping the original sources of all wealth—the soil and the labourer" (p. 36), and Veblen (along with "some his followers") who "analysed a wide variety of social costs which arise primarily in connection with technical progress, depressions and monopolistic practices" (p. 44). In his magnum opus, *The Social Costs of Business Enterprise* (various editions, e.g. 1978), Kapp saw the institution of business enterprise (whether privately or publically owned) to be based on the permanent revolution of technology and accumulation in the interests of the corporation. Such a revolution generates non-linear and cumulative changes that variously abstract from numerous socio-ecological costs.

Kapp was especially concerned with the category of renewable resources vis-à-vis ecological balance between the land and its vegetative "cover" (along with waterways and fish stocks). With non-renewable resources such as petroleum, coal, natural gas, and other minerals his concern is with the finite stock as the business system expands cumulatively (and with volatility) through historical time. With the human factors in production he is concerned with the inability of the business system to suitably reproduce the conditions of fullness of life in the working population; along with duplication, obsolescence, and misallocated

---

[3] Kapp's work developed in the interface between institutional and ecological economics (Kapp 1974) (see also Elsner et al. 2006; Berger 2008a), while the most important reference for Georgescu-Roegen on energy is Georgescu-Roegen (1975). Kenneth Boulding's (1945, 1949–50) analysis is also important, since for him the objective of economics is to stimulate the continuation of durable structures that provide services, and not consumption ("destruction") since this wastes resources. Boulding (1981) links the entropy process to "the law of diminishing potential" as resources are consumed rather than maintained. (See also Boulding 1966.)

resources as forms of waste. These conceptually linked but heterogeneous, quantitative and qualitative social costs, are said to impair the socio-ecological environment, in a cumulative and irreversible manner.

Kapp's core thesis is that as renewable resources are increasingly exploited they are subject to a "critical zone" of cumulative "irreversible depletion and exhaustion", likely long before the supply of such resources reach zero. This is especially the case with soil, forests, wildlife such as fish and many other natural assets. Non-renewable resources are also subject to a cumulative process of exploitation which competitive forces tend to exhaust so that they can move onto other more remunerative sources. Competitive forces lead to "unnecessary duplication of capital outlays" and "premature depletion" of many reserves to the dis-benefit of future generations. Similar types of processes are said to impact on labor in terms of conditions of work, wages and unemployment. These cumulative socio-ecological processes are exacerbated by other competitive conditions such as cyclical trends, excess capacity, obsolescence and misallocation of resources inherent in the business system. He posits the need for a theory of social valuation in a modern system of "political economy" (Kapp 1978: ch 15) that includes the social control of business, a recognition of the heterogeneous nature of these costs, and the "broadening of the scope of economic investigation" (p. 284) especially into quality of life issues and processes.

Georgescu-Roegen, with a "degree from Universitas Schumpeteriana" (the same class as Nicholas Kaldor and Oscar Lange at Harvard), developed a system of "dialectics" and "process" (Georgescu-Roegen 2000: 221, 223). He started his ecological political economy from two propositions, one gained from Marx, that the economy is not an isolated system, and the other from Marx and Veblen (and others), concerning more interest in distribution than in the efficient allocation of resources. Embedding political economy in an open system concerned with distribution, he was able to situate the industrial system as having a relatively short life cycle of perhaps only a few hundred years. In his works, there is a core contradiction of the industrial treadmill involving thermodynamic systems.

The first law of thermodynamics states that energy and matter can be neither created nor destroyed, but they can change their form from (for instance) sunlight to terrestrial forms to minerals to waste. The second law thermodynamic contradiction is that in a closed system the energy-matter being worked on tends towards greater levels of unavailability or entropy (the entropy law). The industrial system, moreover, draws much of its free energy-matter from existing forms such as minerals, oil and established forests and fields, and comparatively little from the ever-present source of energy from the sun (in an open system). Industrialism thus uses energy to produce structured products and waste which through successive rounds of usage and recycling are increasing unavailable for use as 'bounded' forms expand. Such a system, therefore, must necessarily access free energy directly from the sun or face a very limited lifetime as the resources become used up and/or generate extreme climate events that destroy human and ecological potentiality.

Traditional economics ignores this purely physical limit to production, consumption and distribution, since it assumes that while resources are relatively scarce, there are always substitutes and trade-offs that ensure sustainability in the long-run. Georgesscu-Roegen teaches us that an economic system based on accumulation and growth cannot continue to generate unlimited entropy in the long-run because resources will be used up producing masses of bounded waste and hence unavailability of energy-matter. The entropy from products produced is lower than that of the inputs into production only because of waste, and when the products are consumed the waste accumulates further. Thus a purely circular process is impossible because the entropy is a leakage from the system, which gathers momentum along with growth and consumption. The circular economy needs to build from the individual to the group level (Frank Figge et al. 2021), and then from the group to the macro, and from the macro to the global levels: for emergent and complexity non-linear circularity to be fully contextualized. Free energy is limited by the use of established terrestrial stocks of minerals, soil, plants and animals which become bounded as human population and industry expand, generating a depletion of low entropy. The core contradiction becomes one of the present system generating industrial and consumption advances to the exclusion of future generations of human beings and other species (Georgescu-Roegen 1973: 57–58) at the global level. During the 1980s and 1990s, Georgescu-Roegen grew "tired of trying to convince the champions of 'sustainable development' that this plank is even more foolhardy than 'steady state'; that even a steady state needs a constant flow of resources that are continuously and irrevocably degraded into waste as the entropy law requires" (2000: 224).[4]

These contradictions of the disembedded economy, social costs and entropy are closely linked to certain neo-Marxian ecological views of political economy, especially the work of James O'Connor (1991), John Bellamy Foster (2005) and Paul Burkett (2004). O'Connor's analysis of the *second contradiction of capitalism* was partly inspired by Polanyi's analysis, while Foster and Burkett's work is broadly consistent with that of Polanyi, Kapp and Georgescu-Roegen. O'Connor argued that the first contradiction of capitalism is associated the capital-labor conflict and the tendency to overproduction and underconsumption crises. His second contradiction is associated with the conflicting forces of accumulation and production conditions; the latter including urban space and infrastructure, labor power, and the natural environment.[5] In this context, climate change is specifically linked to the conflict between accumulation and ecological resources (O'Connor 1991, 1994). The key point O'Connor makes is that the "social costs" of these conditions of production will increase crisis tendencies for capital as they impinge on businesses either

---

[4] Georgescu-Roegen (1973: 53, 59) further argued that "the true economic output of the economic process is not a material flow of waste, but an immaterial flux: the enjoyment of life", and that the "discovery" of being able "to transform solar radiation into motor power directly" will "represent the greatest possible breakthrough for [the human] entropic problem."

[5] This critical analysis of the "second contradiction" is a brief review of some of the arguments in the literature, since space considerations limit a detailed investigation. For a somewhat fuller coverage of the material, see the references mentioned in the text of this chapter plus the cyberbook published by the Centre for Political Ecology (CPE 2000).

directly through greater private costs, or through the efforts of state intervention and new social movements such as the environmentalists, community activists, and feminists. These trends have also penetrated corporate boards as many corporations become committed to reducing their carbon footprint; though not enough to constitute a structural limit on accumulation, profit and environmental destruction.

Many scholars have made the point that the relationship between accumulation and environmental destruction and hence climate change is closely linked to the first contradiction of capitalism (as is labor power and space). They argue that it is perhaps more likely that capital will continue to accumulate in large measure "free" of these social costs as the treadmill of production continues in a business-as-usual manner since climate change (and ecological) governance is likely to fail to reach global accord in an effective manner. Capital is also benefitting from the destruction of natural resources through marketization of ecological problems and waste (see Spence 2000; Foster 1992, 2009; Burkett 2006). In this perspective, there is a first-order relationship between the accumulation of capital in the treadmill, plus the anomalous reproduction of labor power, public space, and natural environment. In addition, according to Burkett (2006), more emphasise should be given to organisational and systemic 'qualitative forms' of eco-human reproduction, 'human beings co-evolving with other species and the entire biosphere', 'alternative forms of waste management and prevention', plus the 'environmental requirements of human development', rather than *merely* internalising costs into the current system of market valuation, profit and accumulation.

But how have accumulation contradictions affected the natural environment per se? The real foundations for the contradictory link between environmental destruction, climate change and the dynamics of business are certain opportunity costs ("unpaid costs" Foster 2009: 207) associated with building human resources, such as durable fixed business capital, physical infrastructure and commodity capitals within the open circuit. These opportunity costs include the continual over-use of non-renewable minerals and resources; the emergence of various critical zones of destruction of renewable resources; and the encroachment of human populations and industry that reduce species numbers and genetic quality as well as increasing the stock of greenhouse gasses.

These are reflected in various anomalous ecological processes that are interlinked, and which will be getting much worse over time. For instance, consider these trends from *1970 through to 2016–2020*. As global real GDP rose (2015 prices) from [a] US$18,049 trillion to US$81,749 t (353% increase); [b] human populations increased from 3.68 billion to 7.76 b (111% increase); [c] global flows of CO_2 *emissions* expanded from 15.27 Gt to 34.04 Gt of CO_2 (112% increase), [d] global CO_2 *stocks* (concentrations) rose from 325.68 ppm to 414.24 ppm (27.29% increase), [e] CO_2-eq flows rose from 25.06 t kt to 45.87 t kt (83.04% increase) [e] CO2-eq stocks (concentrations) from 290 ppm (1970) to 467 ppm (61% increase), the global stock of fauna and flora, indicated by the [g] Living Planet

Index (LPI),[6] declined from 100 to 32 (68% decrease), the [h] global ecological footprint[7] increased from 0.6 to 1.3 (117%) (from 1.0 to 1.75 Earths being needed to absorb the extra pollution), [i] global ocean heat content anomaly rose from -7.910^{22}J to $+17.310^{22}$J (compared to 1900–2000 average), and [k] global mean sea levels rose by 129 mm (relative to 1900–2000 average).[8] Land and ocean temperatures consistently increased more in the northern hemisphere than in the southern hemisphere.

Most of the climate change reports emphasise adaptation and mitigation policies to respond to climate change problems, including regulations, taxes, permits, agreements, subsidies, incentives, technological changes, informational instruments, and pricing (IPCC 2022; UNDP 2020). These changes are unlikely to see sufficient systemic changes to reduce the intensity of these contradictions, and many now see an eventual required stabilisation level of 300 ppm for CO_2 or 400 ppm for CO_2-e, especially (but not just) in view of the evidence of the past few years that more extreme events are happening earlier than expected. Political economy teaches us that on current trends (even before the recent upscale assessments) a more embedded socio-ecological future looks unlikely unless we are able to replace the contradictions of the circular treadmill of production with a system with much lower social costs and entropic degradation. The more recent IPCC terminology of adopting green or environmentally sustainable *shared socioeconomic pathways* is in fact major terminological progress, but little in the way of *substantive organisational and structural change,* in addition to systemic changes in habits and customs, have accompanied such terminological innovation (more on this in Sect. 5.5, below).

5.4 Uneven Development of Climate Change

The principle of hegemony and uneven development states that the political economy is embedded in the asymmetrical influence of geopolitics, geography, industrial development and culture. Empirical evidence reveals various forms of uneven processes on a global scale, including some nations and areas developing hegemonic trends while others have inferior levels of political-economic power. Periodic

---

[6]LPI is based on 3600 populations of more than 1300 vertebrate species around the world, subdivided into 695 terrestrial species, 274 marine species and 344 freshwater species. The Earth's surface is divided into 14 terrestrial habit types and 8 biogeographic habitat covers. Numerous data sources, including scientific journals, NGO literature and Internet. Plants and invertebrates were excluded due to lack of data. (WWF et al. 2008.)

[7]The ecological footprint "measures humanity's demand on the biosphere in terms of the area of biologically productive land and sea required to provide the resources we use and to absorb our waste". "A country's footprint is the sum of all the cropland, grazing land, forest and fishing grounds required to produce the food, fibre and timber it consumes, to absorb the wastes emitted when it uses energy, and to provide space for its infrastructure." (WWF et al. 2008: 14).

[8]Data in this paragraph is based on Worldbank (2022); Statistica.com (2022a, b); EEA (2021, 2022); WWF (2021); GFN (2022); NORR (2022); NCDC (2022).

convergence may emerge from time to time, but the uneven distribution of world power is a core trend. Most of this research examines the relationship between core, semi-periphery and periphery within the world-system, including applications, for instance, to climate change and ecological destruction. These ecological and climate debates (linked to broader questions of metabolic rift) have been ongoing in such journals as *Organization and Environment,* the *Journal of World-Systems Research,* the *International Journal of Comparative Sociology, Journal of Economic Issues, Human Ecology Review* and *Monthly Review.* Hopefully this trend will come to appear regularly in the recently commenced *Review of Evolutionary Political Economy,* which has close links to the European Association for Evolutionary Political Economy (EAEPE).

A core fact is that the circular treadmill of production generates unequal global, regional, national and local power relations and material-labor flows through historical time (Smith 1984; Harvey 2001). Some areas are able to develop articulated linkages through production networks, commodity chains and supply chains manifesting in high technology processes and expanded market production. Power and accumulation change through historical time as, for instance, 'Dutch' hegemony evolved eventually to British hegemony and later to US hegemony and beyond. At present advanced capitalist economies are undergoing the process of maturation while East Asian economies, particularly China, have been undertaking a remarkable industrial transformation; including potential global hegemony into the future. Concurrently, many parts of Sub-Saharan Africa, Latin America, the Middle East and South Asia have been unable to significantly advance the relative living standards of their populations (with some exceptions in the semi-periphery).

These forms of uneven development impact on climate change and human development. Generally, over the long-term, most areas of the periphery are stalling relatively speaking in the treadmill of production while contributing less to climate change than those of the core. On the other hand, especially nations in the semi-periphery have been making up for lost time in the degree to which they are industrialising and hence contributing to major GHG emissions. There are differentials according to per capita and total emissions of greenhouse gasses (UNDP 2020). In terms of absolute and per capita emissions, the US leads the pack, along with other Western capitalist areas (such as the European Union). China has joined the major polluters in *absolute* terms, since its level of capitalist development has been expanding rapidly, but its level of per capita emissions is lower than the core (but rising rapidly). Sub-Saharan Africa and most other peripheral areas have contributed a low absolute and per capita level of emissions, along with several semi-peripheral areas. Generally speaking, accumulation and growth are positively linked with emissions and greenhouse gasses, but the social and environmental costs of climate change are being felt disproportionately in the periphery.

Some empirical dimensions of this uneven development and asymmetric climate change impacts are mentioned in the major reports (IPCC 2021; UNDP 2020). The UNDP report (especially) emphasises that the 'less developed nations' will be relatively less able to cope with problems of rising sea levels and major climate catastrophes. They are said to lack the resources that the advanced capitalist nations have to respond to such problems. They are also more severely subject to climate catastrophes and excesses than the advanced nations. The severest forms of climate change are emerging, and will continue to emerge at a faster rate in and around the tropics and sub-tropics (along with high latitudes). Less developed nations are thus impacted through climate crises in a manner inversely related to their relative contribution to greenhouse gas accumulation (compared with industrial nations). Recent figures for extreme climate disasters demonstrate similar trends, and also some complexity in the results, as shown in Table 5.1, below.

These data, from the World Meteorological Organization (2021), show that, firstly, over successive decades during 1970–2019 the number of reported climate disasters have generally increased, though with slightly smaller numbers for 2010–2019 compared with 2000–2009. Such climate disasters include major floods, droughts, severe winter conditions, cyclones and tornados, heat waves, cold waves, and forest fires. The data show, secondly, that economic losses (financial losses often covered by insurance) have progressively increased over these decades, with the losses for 2010–2019 being 7–8 times more extreme than for 1970–1979. The third result is that deaths have been highly unequal, with 82% of them occurring in low and lower-middle income nations, compared with 18% being in high and upper middle income.

In the developing areas there are fewer resources to adapt through dikes and other means of (for instance) physically reducing the impact of rising sea levels; and they are affected far out of proportion to their contribution to climate change. These factors, the UNDP Report (2020) recognises, are going to continue to adversely impact on their relative and absolute levels of human development. Major climate impacts will retard health infrastructure, increase the incidence of diseases such as Malaria, and reduce levels of government finance for education and nation-building. In essence, this is a problem of circular and cumulative causation (see next section), since less human development leads to even less human development, sometimes in unpredictable ways. In the future this impact will get worse, as Cline (2007) shows, since while most areas of the world will get much hotter, it is primarily the 'developing' areas in the tropics and sub-tropics which will have much less precipitation as well, generating low agricultural output.

Table 5.1 Extreme climate events, 1970 to 2019; economic losses, deaths, regions

	1970–1979	1980–1989	1990–1999	2000–2009	2010–2019
Reported disasters (cases)	711	1410	2250	3536	3165
Reported economic losses (US$b) ($\sum = 3.6b$)	175	289	852	942	1381
	High income	Upper middle income	Lower middle income	Low income	
Deaths from climate extremes (%) (2019)	6	12	53	29	

Source: Adapted from parts of the WMO (2021: 19, 21)

However, the climate change reports mentioned have not adequately explored the extent to which these contradictory core-periphery forces are structurally related. (They are also relatively indifferent to the fate of non-human species.) In discussing 'developing' and 'developed' areas the reports fail to recognise the strong network, power and corporate relationships that link varying degrees of underdevelopment of the periphery and overdevelopment of the core, with differential results in the semi-periphery. The core nations are the most powerful, the periphery includes the weakest, while the semi-periphery has intermediate power relative to the rest. There are strong connections between the social and environmental costs being felt in the periphery and the relatively lower costs borne by the core. To comprehend these relationships we need to situate climate change and environmental destruction within the global circular treadmill of production which generates ecologically unequal forms of exchange, several forms of metabolic rift, and serious injustices.

The core–periphery contradictions associated with climate change are multiple yet dialectically interrelated, since they are associated with the social and environmental costs of the treadmill of production. Capitalism is a system built on accumulation, expansion, innovation and profit. It 'naturally' seeks to caste aside barriers to its powerful motion through expanding on a world scale, destroying pre-capitalist systems, introducing new methods of production, creating new needs and wants, and discovering new forms of energy and minerals to enhance its circular and cumulative motion of reproduction (Schumpeter 1911; Marx 1857–58). In the process it generates new forms of competition as well as changing concentrations of economic power. It exploits resources as much as possible, including labor power, soils, trees, animals, minerals, forms of energy, winds, weather patterns and anything else that will stimulate accumulation and profit. It generates new forms of credit and finance to stimulate this creative pattern of destruction. It seeks out new areas and populations to exploit in its incessant drive for growth and expansion.

In the process, however, it generates numerous social and environmental costs, as Polanyi, ("disembeddedness"), Kapp ("social costs") and Georgescu-Roegen ("entropy") point out. Indeed, these costs are structurally linked to the search for profit, since if the costs were internalised into accounting techniques and prices, it is unlikely that the system could generate sufficient profit and investment for expansion. But the costs cannot always be easily calculated, and certainly not in market prices, since the market is imbued with numerous forms of power and authority which mask the costs and destructions inherent in such motion. Core elements of these costs are linked to the concept of metabolic rift. As Foster (2000, 2009) has argued, Marx used this notion based on his research which drew on various forms of exploitation emanating from the social and spatial unevenness of its motion. One element of this metabolic rift is the recognition that the generation of wealth and use value is dependent upon the creative exploitation of labor power through transforming it into labor exertion in the production and reproduction of goods and services. There is thus a transformation of use-values in the circuit made possible by the exertion of human potential, through stimulating the creative force of human beings as they live, sleep, eat, and yet return back to earn their keep in the circuit. Capital can exploit labor unrepentantly if a continual supply is forthcoming, such as when the reserve army is large, or with the movement of 'surplus' labor from the countryside to the town and cities, or when low-wage workers are mobilised for capital through the global system. But otherwise there is a limit to capital since it must 'enable' labor power to be suitably replenished so that it can be exploited every day through the treadmill of production.

Metabolic rift also applies to capital gaining material resources from the periphery for use in the core. Here there is a continual process of exploiting soil, energy and resources from the countryside and producing capital and consumer goods in the towns and cities. This transfer of materials and energy tends to develop the core while it exhausts the periphery through soil degradation, exhaustion of minerals and energy, biomass depletion of fish, cattle and wildlife, and modification of climate. Soil degradation of the countryside is inextricably linked to the pollution of the towns and cities, the extraction of scarce natural fertilisers in the periphery is necessary for replenishment of soils in the core, and the importation of cheap natural resources and food from the periphery has historically enhanced the industrial development of the core. The metabolic rift of dead and deteriorating workers when the reserve army is high is analytically similar to the degradation of the soil and terrain for the benefit of imperial countries, which constitutes the transfer of high-quality energy and materials from the periphery to the industrial centres of the core and semi-periphery. In short, the uneven global and regional impact of climate change and ecological destruction is structurally linked to the accumulation requirements of powerful business interests, and without these critical social and ecological costs, accumulation and profit would likely cease to operate as required (see Hornborg 2006; Napoletano et al. 2019).

Sociological political economists have also been developing the notion of ecologically unequal exchange to help explain these global contradictions and injustices. Jorgenson et al. (2009: 263), for instance, demonstrate that the "vertical flow of exports is a structural mechanism allowing for more-developed countries to partially externalize their consumption-based environmental impacts to lesser-developed countries." The terms of trade plays a role here in tending to undervalue minerals, agricultural output and to some degree mass production manufactures from the periphery while enhancing the value of high-technology goods and high-skill output from the core and semi-periphery. What has been called the 'ecological Prebisch-Singer hypothesis' postulates that the periphery provides materials, labor power and energy to support the development of the core and semi-periphery. In the process the periphery suffers the negative social and ecological costs of soil degradation, deforestation, and the entropic unavailability of resources. This also negatively impacts on industrial development potential, standard of living and quality of life. The core is simultaneously saved many of these social and environmental costs through cheap resources from overseas, lower levels of domestic ecological waste, and being able to protect their own environmental space.

The structure of international trade, foreign direct investment, and commodity chains thus generate a contradictory series of processes as resource and labor exploitation of the periphery contribute to the material advancement and quality of life of the core nations and areas.[9] Jorgenson (2009) demonstrates how unequal power relationships encourage the use of foreign direct investment in the periphery in ways that enhance polluting and ecologically inefficient processes such as deforestation and water pollution (which negatively influence human health). Hornborg (2009) argues that the use of international market prices hides the unequal flow of biophysical resources in the form of embodied labor, land, matter and energy, as the social and environmental costs of the global system of production and trade are hidden from view. A zero-sum game is seen to be in operation as this system of power largely supports business and consumers in the core at the expense of the periphery. (See Dorninger et al. 2021.)

James Rice (2009) scrutinizes the role of agency in these structural forces as powerful corporations enhance their accumulation and profit, core workers seek higher wages and better conditions, and strong states try to accommodate workers and corporations through the treadmill of production. Formal transnational agreements and organisations also play a role through the World Trade Organisation, the numerous Free Trade Agreements, and the International Monetary Fund. Asymmetric power relations are thus institutionalised into these institutions and agreements through the drain of surplus labor and energy/natural resources from the periphery to the core. The semi-periphery plays an important role as it "possess [es] international exchange advantages over peripheral countries ... even as semi-peripheral countries are subject to unequal exchange in relation to the core" (p. 223).

The climatological and ecological significance of the circular treadmill generating metabolic rift through ecologically unequal exchange is considerable. For instance, after the second-world war global imbalances started to become significant as the core consumed more resources than it produced. This tendency has continued into the present. John Shandra et al. (2009) provide empirical evidence that poor nations exporting masses of raw materials to core nations have higher levels of mammals under threat of extinction or unsustainably low levels of supply, while core nations with higher income levels per capita have lower levels of threatened mammals. Jorgenson (2009) found that transnational corporate FDI in less developed countries stimulates total and per unit carbon dioxide emissions, and is thus relatively less ecoefficient. Meanwhile core and semi-peripheral nations are expanding their domestic consumption through grander lifestyles and conspicuous emulation that speed up the transformation of low into high entropy.

In a series of articles and books, J. Timmons Roberts and Bradley C. Parks have examined the significance of these asymmetric power relations for questions of justice and new social movements. At the core of their argument in *A Climate of*

---

[9] Clark and Foster (2009) study an example of unequal exchange enhancing the primary accumulation of capitalism, as labor and resources were exploited unsustainably through Guano and nitrate imperialism, which promoted global metabolic rift. Complex relationships between Peru, Chile, Britain, China and the US saw long-term transfers of economic value in the nineteenth century through exploitation of accumulated bird droppings (Guano) and labor. Core nations were thus able to replenish their supply of soil nutrients through unequal exchange of materials and labor from the periphery to the core.

Injustice (Roberts and Parks 2007) is the empirical fact (cited above) that mostly it is the core advanced nations that have the highest *per capita* levels of greenhouse gas emissions, while the nations of the periphery have the lowest emissions but the highest incidence of extreme climate events and catastrophes. Some emerging nations have high absolute levels of greenhouse gasses (such as China) but lower (but majorly rising) per capita emissions. These inequalities and contrasting power relations generate differential visions and distrust among the players involved in global climate change policy. Inequality thus engenders non-cooperation as those with the most power eschew responsibility and those with the greatest extreme events have rising but still less relative bargaining power; plus major social costs and entropy degradation. (Newell et al. 2020.)

The death and destruction in the periphery are ongoing while the core and parts of the semi-periphery continue to benefit through cheap materials and labor power from the periphery. Global resentment is garnished as the south expects the north to reduce their consumption, while the north expects the south to make adjustments to reduce the extreme events and greenhouse gas emissions. Distrust generated by inequality, power differentials and divergent worldviews is a major reason Parks and Roberts (2008) indicate major problems in creating a coherent, workable and effective global climate accord during the first quarter of the twenty-first century. The north will necessarily have to massively assist the periphery (and semi-periphery) in any effective global accord, if sufficient reciprocity, trust, shared worldviews and negotiated forms of justice are to succeed in generating agreement. Central to the vision of Roberts and Parks (2009), still relevant now, is the core thesis of the ecologically unequal exchange theory that the core owes the periphery (and semi-periphery) an ecological debt for the environmental damage embodied in energy and materials transferred to the north from the south, which is the cause of much of the inequality underlying global distrust and the lack of an effective climate change regime. The recent COP26 conference in Glasgow provides evidence that this is even more relevant in the current environment, as the periphery and semi-periphery step up efforts for compensation from the core.

5.5 CCC and Uncertainties of Climate Change

Every aspect of climate change and ecological destruction through the treadmill of production and metabolic rift involve numerous processes of circular and cumulative causation (CCC). It is now time to introduce this concept formally, and to relate it specifically to the social and environmental costs of business. The principle of CCC is a critical one for political economy, drawing from (among many others) the traditions linked to Thorstein Veblen, Gunnar Myrdal, Nicholas Kaldor, K William Kapp and Nicholas Georgescu-Roegen. CCC includes two processes, the first being the interaction between *multiple variables*; and the second being the tendency for the variables to interact in a *cumulative manner* generating dynamic motion, periodic instability and irreversibility through historical time. (See Berger 2008b, 2009 for details.) The principle of CCC states that we must analyze the world's major problems, including climate change, through the use of such instability, disequilibrium, accelerating and magnified effects of the processes involved; since anomalies always involve tipping points, threshold effects, hysteresis and path dependence.

In a CCC fashion, we examine the linkages between three interrelated (open) sub-systems of habitat and species; human activities (including the circular treadmill); and climate change. These are shown below in Fig. 5.3.

Several main factors involved in the circular treadmill have adversely impacted the ecological environment since the industrial revolution, and especially during the 1970s–2020s, within the anthropocene era of human dominance. Livestock activities, energy use, land-use clearing, chemical fertilisers/insecticides, and pollution, associated with *agriculture and forestry*, contributed 20.1% of GHG emissions. *Industrial* energy use, direct industrial pollution, land clearing and related activities contributed 29.4% of GHGs. The supply chain activities of *transportation*, and also *building*, contributed another 33.7% of GHGs. *Fugitive energy*, other fuel *combustion*, as well as *waste*, contributed the remaining 16.8% of GHGs. Overall, energy use—comprising electricity, heat and transport—contributes a massive 73.2% of total greenhouse gas emissions worldwide.

These commercial and consumption activities reduced the stock of ecological resources, especially flora for photosynthesis and oxygen production, and fauna, which provided useful fertiliser and seed-distribution for the reproduction of life. Atmospheric systems were also changed. These factors coevolved into climate change trends. As this occurred entropy expanded and thus reduced the energy and matter available *for use* by human beings and other animals and plants.

Historical evidence demonstrates that these CCC effects generated anomalous climate events, such as greater unevenness of climate tendencies, increased heavy

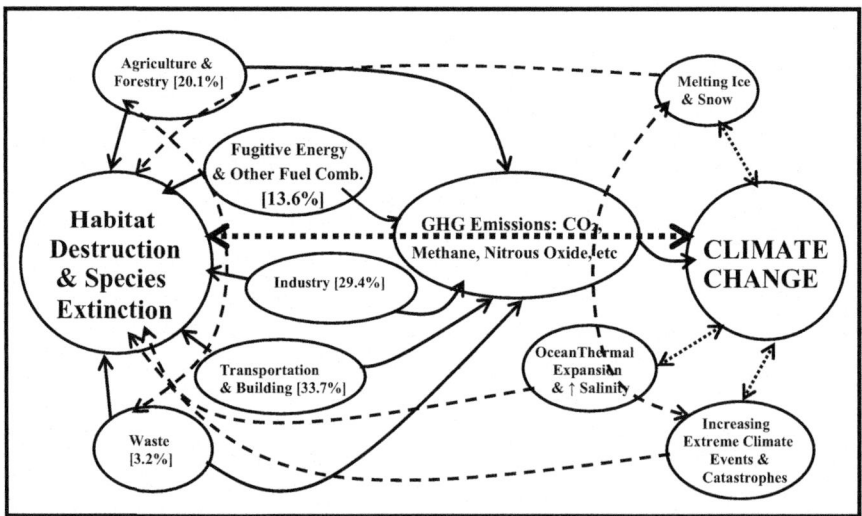

Fig. 5.3 Multi-factor CCC model of species extinction & climate change, 2016. (Source: Figures are adapted from the raw data of Ritchie and Roser (2021))

5.5 CCC and Uncertainties of Climate Change

precipitation events, more regular heatwaves, increasing tropospheric water vapour, declining glaciers in the Arctic region and Greenland, more acidic oceans, and rising sea levels (IPCC 2021). Looking to the future, various scenarios have been formulated depending on the likely levels of temperature change. Some of the more obvious changes link to likely successive increases in temperature from 1 °C through to above 5 °C, bearing in mind uncertainty levels and uneven changes throughout the world.

The major climate reports of the late 2000s did acknowledge some micro-meso non-linear processes happening in the Earth's climate system above 2.0 °C (since 'preindustrial' times). For instance, while some extremes are already happening, these *were* thought to be much more pronounced beyond, say, a 2 °C increase in global temperatures (*above* 450–550 ppm CO_2-e concentrates). These threshold effects include major increases in global temperatures, major variability of temperature (including many more heatwaves and frosts), heavy rainfall events, major droughts and flooding, more tropical cyclones, major bushfires, and extreme winds (Garnaut 2008: 40). Another threshold point was said to possibly emerge at increases of above, say, 3 °C, so that any success in mitigating these higher excesses would be crucial for reducing the even more catastrophic impacts. The IPCC (2007b) also discussed the possible increase from 4 to 5 °C (since pre-industrial times) as being "much greater than the consequences of moving from 2 to 3°C" since, for example, "hurricane damage increases as a cube (or more) of wind-speed, which itself scales closely with sea temperatures" (p. 59).

The earlier Stern Review (2007: 60) demonstrated these CCC effects in terms of heightened costs as climate change accelerates (especially beyond 450–550 ppm CO_2-e). For instance, it discusses floods and droughts increasing *exponentially*; a small increase in temperature accelerating the frequency of extreme events (a *convex* curve); passing into the threshold effects propelling "increasingly negative" impacts on crop growth (*an inverse parabolic "hill function"*); a "sharp increase in mortality once human temperature tolerances are exceeded"; infrastructure damage from storms *"increas[ing] as a cube of wind speed"*; and "costs of sea-wall construction *increas[ing] as a square of defence height*" (emphases added).[10] It is now thought that these threshold effects will happen (or are happening) much sooner than earlier expected.

Things have thus changed markedly since the major climate reports of the late 2000s (Stern 2007: 66–67; IPCC 2007b: 66) argued that with average global temperatures of 2.1 °C (uncertainty ranges of between 1.4 and 3.1 °C) by 2100, with CO_2-e around 450 ppm, that there would be 'minimum' damage to the environment. This then 'optimistic' outcome was even then fraught with anomalies as likely the Greenland ice sheet will have begun irreversible melting, between 15%

---

[10] All four of the studies (IPPC, Stern, UNDP and Garnaut) assume equilibrium analysis in terms of the eventual calming down of impacts, when mitigation is effective (see also US NSTC 2009). However, this equilibrium terminology is questionable due to "pervasive" uncertainty built into the systems; a medium-term (pragmatic) view shows that no equilibrium of CO_2-e occurs in any of the scenarios; and the assessments make very strict assumptions about the parameters, which are unlikely to prevail. Usage of circular and cumulative causation is a better framework of analysis.

and 40% of species face extinction, 40–60 m people are likely to be exposed to malaria in Africa, there is likely to be a 20–30% cut in precipitation to certain areas, a major drop in crop yield is probable in tropical regions, and around possibly 10 m people are predicted to be affected by coastal flooding. On the other extreme, with no attempt to mitigate greenhouse gas emissions, average temperatures were expected to rise by between 3.2 and 7.8 °C, leading to around 700–900 ppm of CO_2-e by 2100. At this level all major ecosystems were said to be likely be in crisis, mass extinction is probable, catastrophes common, the Himalayan glaciers destroyed, fish stocks seriously diminished and dozens of major cities under water.

The recent IPCC Reports (2018, 2019, 2021 [draft]) underplay the *global* CCC processes that are likely to occur contemporaneously, soon or on the pathway to a 1.5 °C temperature rise relative to preindustrial times. First they differentiate between transient, short-term and long-term 1.5 °C situations on planet Earth, and treat the long-term as an *equilibrium process* (e.g., IPCC 2018: 184). Second, they treat most responses of temperature to GHG emissions or concentrations as being (near-)linear, even though a few non-linear feedbacks are mentioned, although often these are negative feedbacks (IPCC 2021). And thirdly, they underplay the CCC interdependencies between the dominant tipping points, and often tend to treat them in isolation (IPCC 2018: ch 3). This third factor is especially crucial, as the micro-meso (usually regional) approach of the IPCC, severely understates the potential for major climate change at or below 1.5° (transient or short term) relative to preindustrial times; or even current levels of 1.07–1.2 °C.

The principle of uncertainty is critical to these CCC effects. The work of Frank Knight (1921), J.M. Keynes (1921, 1936), and G.L.S. Shackle (1970) have laid the ground-rules of this analysis, and some environmental experts have taken this further. Risk is where a challenging element is calculable and fairly determinate, such as the throwing of a dice, or the chance of being hit by a car in an automobile accident. But uncertainty is where there is relative ignorance, or concerns the distant future when knowledge is lacking or ambiguous. The less weight of evidence we have for a specific phenomenon, the greater the uncertainty associated with a specific probability, and the earlier we have to respond to the problem. The informational anomalies associated with greenhouse gas emissions and climate changes generate deep uncertainties. These uncertainties are exacerbated by CCC dynamics generating complex dynamics, social costs, entropic irreversibilities, and periodic instabilities along the lines drawn by Kapp (1978: ch 4), Georgescu-Roegen (1971: 121–122) and Foster (2009: ch 10).

CCC necessarily leads to greater uncertainty. This is because the greater the number of factors considered the more uncertain is the result. For instance, Keller et al. (2008) describe climate change as being "deeply uncertainty" due to the complexity of the phenomena. Complexity is due to the involvement of models used, ecological processes and behavioral variables. Modular uncertainty involves initial conditions, boundary conditions, parameters, structural factors and subjective factors. Ecological uncertainties include radiative forcing, ocean heat uptake, winds and currents, climate sensitivity, and complex feedbacks. Behavioral uncertainties involve investment, technology, social relationships, population, consumption and

5.5 CCC and Uncertainties of Climate Change

governance. With all these mostly unknown variables, uncertainty increases, heightening the degree that GHGs need to be reduced in the immediate future. With deep uncertainty the main factor promising to reduce uncertainty is timely decreases in greenhouse gasses. Thus the more circular and cumulative the processes the greater the uncertainty and the more urgent is the need for changes in social behavior and organization to limit climate change.

The more circular and cumulative the processes become also the more problematic becomes the relationship between stocks and flows of GHG. This is because once the stocks of emissions rise to a higher plateau due to multiple processes the longer it will take for reductions in flows to affect stocks. As Knutti et al. (2008: 5) recognizes, the "temperature response of the system is determined by the stock of atmospheric greenhouse gasses, rather than the flows represented by annual emissions". Knutti emphasizes the importance of ignorance about core processes such as climate sensitivity, cloud formation, and absorptive capacity of the seas leading to "intractable uncertainty".

5.5.1 Shared Socioeconomic Pathways (SSPs)

The IPCC (2021), for instance, in its draft-version of *Climate Change 2021: The Physical Science Basis,* volume one report, has adopted a dual pathway approach to analyzing future possible climate change plus socioeconomic scenarios. Throughout the whole volume, various scenarios of socioeconomic forms are associated with various pathways of greenhouse gas/aerosols/other gasses/land-use and land-cover to provide an integrated framework of analysis. This framework includes both shared socioeconomic pathways (SSPs) and Representative Concentration Pathways (RCPs), what one might call the SSP-RCP paradigm, to scrutinize the various ways we can go forward with potential socioeconomic forms appropriate for various GHG concentration levels in the trajectory up to 2100 (and beyond). This SSP-RCP paradigm is also used in the other volumes associated with the IPCC's Sixth assessment Report (AR6) (e.g., IPCC 2022).

This is linked to the principles of innovation and policy/governance. The shared socioeconomic pathways (SSP) paradigm scrutinizes a scholarly scenario approach to governance, lifestyle and environment required to analyze various pathways of GHG concentrations and land-use, along with temperature increases for the planet. Specifically, it is closely linked to the work of Brian C. O'Neill and his teams of researchers (e.g., O'Neill et al. 2014, 2020), and analyses the type of socioeconomic processes and behaviors, also including mitigation and adaptation, that are capable of providing various structured scenarios for the planet. Each of the pathways involves demographics, economy and lifestyle, human development, technology, environment, natural resources, plus policies and institutions. It involves groups of experts providing advice on an array of practical and realistic conditions that may operate in various places and to varying degrees throughout the world.

It is the trajectories and the long-term concentrations of GHGs etc. to reach the outcome in 2100 and beyond that are of interest with RCPs. Some of the core RCPs used in the IPCC (2021) draft volume are, RCP 2.6, where radiative forcing peaks at 3 W m^{-2} and declines to 2.6 W m^{-2} by 2100; another is an intermediate scenario where radiative forcing is eventually limited to 4.5 W m^{-2} by 2100; and a third is a high pathway leading eventually to greater than 8.5 W m^{-2} by 2100 (IPCC 2021: Glossary). For instance, some of the core dual scenarios studied by the IPCC involve [a] SSP1-RCP1.9; [b] SSP2-RCP4.5; [c] SSP3-RCP7.0; and [d] SSP5-RCP8.5. Assessments for these pathways are summarized in Table 5.2 below.

Of the various scenarios included in the IPCC report, only one has an estimated 1.4 °C (1.0–1.8 °C) global mean temperature by 2100, SSP1, associated with low concentrations RCP1.9. SSP1 is termed *Sustainability: Taking the Green Road* (O'Neill et al. 2017: 2), and includes advancing the state of sustainability to a relatively high degree, promoting environmentally sensitive technology, declining inequality, low carbon footprint, an emphasis on quality of life rather than growth, and highly productive land. It could be said that this is the road precisely not taken at present by the global community at large, and also not taken by the dominant power brokers of the world economy. Perhaps the EU could be seen as having certain members with an interest in this pathway, but certainly not a general philosophy working in this direction. So far the IPCC has discussed no specific *structural changes* in habits, institutions *and* cultures to promote identified SSP1 objectives.

SSP3, with an estimated 3.6 °C (2.8–4.6 °C range) (along with RCP 7.0; high concentrations) is based around *Regional Rivalry*, high inequality, with rising nationalism, ineffective global institutions, declining investment in education and

Table 5.2 SSP-RCP contribution to global temperature increase °C

Scenario	2041–2060		2081–2100		CO_2	Non-CO_2 GHGs	Aerosols & land-use
	Estimate	Range	Est.	Range			
SSP1—RCP1.9 Green Road	1.6 °C	1.2–2.0 °C	1.4 °C	1.0–1.8 °C	1.15	0.45	−0.2
SSP2—RCP4.5 Middle of Road	2.0 °C	1.6–2.5 °C	2.7 °C	2.1–3.5 °C	2.15	0.75	−0.2
SSP3—RCP7.0 Regional Rivalry	2.1 °C	1.7–2.6 °C	3.6 °C	2.8–4.6 °C	2.80	1.30	−0.5
SSP5—RCP8.5 High GDP Road	2.4 °C	1.9–3.0 °C	4.4 °C	3.3–5.7 °C	3.45	1.20	−0.25

Source: Adapted from IPCC (2021: SPM-16 to SPM-18) (*Draft* Report)

5.5 CCC and Uncertainties of Climate Change

technology, strong environmental degradation, population decline in core and rise in periphery, fossil fuel dependency, and low levels of sustainability. SSP2, at 2.7 °C (2.1–3.5 °C by 2100), RCP of 4.5, with medium concentrations, is a *Middle of the Road* scenario in between SSP1 and SSP3, where historical patterns continue in many areas, including vis-à-vis technological developments; uneven development; global institutions working slowly towards sustainability; heterogeneous national and regional progress towards mitigation and adaptation; and slowly declining dependency on fossil fuels.

SSP5, with an estimated 4.4 °C in 2100 (3.3–5.7 °C), and RCP 8.5, which is very high, is an interesting case of *High GDP Growth*, competitive economies, a globalizing trend, with rapid technological developments, rising levels of education, but concentration on fossil fuels with little or no sustainable development. There is little mitigation and a strong emphasis on adaptation to severe climate change. (Scenario SSP4 was underplayed in the report because it was likely considered as not providing sufficient additional information for analysis.)

The fact that SSP1, The Green Road, is considered effectively the only viable pathway to 1.5 °C by 2100, and the trajectory leading to 2100, does not auger well for the future of the planet. This is because at present few of the leading powerful nations and regions are taking the green road seriously, and indeed, from a global perspective, it does not appear to be the leading global philosophy of governance at present or in the near future. Continuing historical trends would likely lead to, at best, around 2.7 °C, or if we accept the mostly weak promises of COP26, perhaps 2.3 °C by mid-to-late century, and any significant improvement is not likely, if at all, until the 2030s, by which time GHG concentrations will likely be too high for any major change in emissions to impact temperatures majorly towards mean global increases of 1.5 °C or even 2.0 °C (relative to 1850–1900 mean) by 2100.

There is also significant probability of major climate changes already impacting planet Earth, leading to cascading tipping points in the near future or even now at 1.07–1.2 °C above 1850–1900 levels. We examine this in the next section.

5.5.2 Cascading Tipping Points

As mentioned, climate change uncertainties relate to the lack of knowledge about key ecological, behavioural and modular relationships as they change through historical time. The extreme weather events and catastrophes linked to threshold impacts ("tipping points") are the greatest source of uncertainty. At these crucial tipping points rapid escalations will occur in critical environmental processes that radically upset the climate, producing a whole series of catastrophes (IPCC 2007c: chs 6, 19; IPCC 2007d; Keller et al. 2008; Lenton et al. 2008; Lenton 2019, 2021). The key idea underlying threshold effects is that a small change can have major impacts, in a circular and cumulative fashion. Some of the tipping points are already happening, such as with coral bleaching, but we can also see current major anomalies occurring with West Antarctic and Arctic ice-sheet disintegration, and Greenland ice-sheet melting, among others.

All of the threshold effects have some element of nonlinearity, hysteresis and irreversibility as feedback processes change parameters, thereby producing cumulative effects. The uncertainty relates to the timing or states (multiple) when the changes and effects manifest *suddenly*. The complexities involve a multifarious linking of numerous variables that are difficult to predict. Threshold effects are important because they challenge the idea that climate change with bring linearly related impacts on the system. Threshold effects are likely to happen sooner than linear models predict, and Keller et al. (2008: 5) argue that "only subtle warning signs" are likely in many cases "before climate thresholds have been crossed" due to "multiple parameter" interaction (see McInerney and Keller 2008: 29).

Cascading tipping points are the most important CCC processes likely to lead to severe breakdown of the Earth's climate system, systemic non-linear changes in climate, and even more severe climate events such as major droughts, floods, hurricanes, heat waves, cold snaps, and sea level rises. These cascading tipping points are caused by multiple interacting breakdowns involving some of the dozen or more regional climate systems that constitute the basis of the Earth's ability to resist major temperature rises. These multiple structural interacting crises are of significant probability at 1 °C, and a high chance of happening at 1.5 °C, more so at 2.0 °C temperature rises, relative to 1850–1900 mean levels.

The individual tipping points that are potentially culminating in cascading interacting tipping points, involve an array of core Earth systems. These include the [1] collapse of the west Antarctic ice sheet (WAIS); [2] disintegration of the Greenland ice sheet (GIS); [3] transformation of the Atlantic meridional overturning circulation (AMOC); [4] dieback of the Amazon rainforest (AMAZ); [5] thawing of the northeast permafrost (NEP); [6] death of the tropical coral reefs (TCR); [7] major shifts of the northern boreal forests (NBF); [8] thawing of the northern permafrost (NPF); [9] collapse of the Arctic summer sea ice (ASSI); [10] destruction of the alpine glaciers (APG); [11] a major shift in the West African monsoonal system (WAMS); [12] chaotic instability of the Indian monsoonal system (IMS); [13] collapse of the eastern Antarctic ice sheet (EAIS); [14] more persistent El-Nino regime (ENR); and [15] major instability of the Arctic winter ice sheet (AWIS). *Individual* tipping points for these ecological systems are a function of linear *or* non-linear increases in mean global temperatures, extreme northern hemisphere mean temperatures rising well above most other areas, and land mean temperatures rising more than ocean temperatures. (Cai et al. 2016.)

When temperatures and extreme events impact simultaneously on several of these individual tipping elements the process transforms into an interacting series of cascading tipping points for whole earth and regional systems. The reason for this is that the different tipping point elements experience interacting influences which heighten, magnify and accelerate the individual elements into an emergent novel major system crisis of symbiotic processes (in emergent and complexity fashion). For instance, we know that there has been major melting of sea ice and ice sheets in the Arctic, Antarctic and Greenland regions; and that Greenland ice (GIS) tipping contributes to changing patterns in the Atlantic meridional (AMOC) by increasing the flow of freshwater into the region. A tipping of El-Nino increases the likelihood of Amazon rainforest dieback by increasing temperatures and reducing rainfall. Melting of ice sheets and sea ice tipping points due to rising temperatures increase the likelihood of permafrost thawing and boreal forest dieback. Through time the growing number of tipping elements, and the increasing interconnected nature of their transformations, amplifies the process of temperature rises, extreme events and evidential global crisis in a CCC fashion (Cai et al. 2016).

Already numerous individual elements have likely begun tipping, or are on the cusp of doing so, including parts of the west Antarctic, Greenland, Arctic summer and Alpine glaciers/ice sheets plus coral reef systems (Schellnhuber et al. 2016: 650). With five systems in varying degrees of interactive synchrony 1.0 °C looks more like the upper boundary temperature limit than 1.5 °C, and future arguments will likely generate 'one degree' being the preferred objective, relative to the 1850–1900 mean. This is especially the case as current rises of 1.07–1.20 °C have not yet impacted the relatively *slower-moving processes* which will escalate even at current rates as the full impact escalates.

In this context we can do little better than quote James Hansen's famous statement of *2008* (Hansen 2008: 228–229):

> Humanity today, collectively, must face the uncomfortable fact that industrial civilization has become the principal driver of climate change. … Paleoclimiate evidence and ongoing changes imply that today's CO_2 [concentrations], about 385 ppm, is already too high to maintain the climate to which humanity, wildlife, and the rest of the biosphere are adapted. … Continued growth of greenhouse gas [concentrations], for just another decade [to 412.5 ppm in 2020; NOAA 2021], practically eliminates the possibility of near-term return of atmospheric composition beneath the tipping point for catastrophic effects.

Within this context of rapid cumulative causation and multiple feedback between processes that are often not included in the models (loss of Arctic sea ice, extinction of interdependent species and ecosystems) there is the likelihood of very rapid changes towards not only *tipping points* but also *points of no return* (path dependence). In this context, it is timely to embed in the analysis the contradictions elaborated by Karl Polanyi, K.W. Kapp, Nicholas Georgescu-Roegen and John Bellamy Foster concerning the disembedded economy, social costs, treadmill of production, metabolic rift, entropy and cumulative causation and uncertainty. In relation to the principles of innovation and policy/governance, this reinforces the importance of systemic changes in replacing the circular treadmill of production with more embedded social, political and economic practices, in 'solving' the climate change conundrum.

5.6 Conclusion

This chapter has related core principles of political economy to the problem of climate change. It started with the principle of historical specificity to situate patterns of climate change through the history of planet Earth, paying special attention to waves of warming and cooling during the Phanerozoic, Pleistocene, Holocene and Anthropocene eras. The most recent history of climate change is the only one generated by anthropogenic influences, and it is likely to have even more catastrophic impacts into the future. The principle of contradiction showed that market capitalism has been reproducing the circular treadmill of production at the expense of the ecological environment through disembedded tendencies of escalating social costs, entropy and destructive creation. Major changes in social and ecological organisation are required to prevent path dependent destruction of ecological resources and processes becoming too extreme.

In this context, the principle of uneven development is instructive, since the periphery (which is not contributing to major climate change) is being and is likely to continue to be much more affected by climate change than the core (and semi-periphery) into the future. This is because most of the periphery lies in the tropics and sub-tropics and because of the structural linkages between unequal exchange of resources and labor between periphery and core. These unequal forces generate distrust, divergent visions of justice and lack of accord between core and periphery, while the circular treadmill of production exacerbates the inability to resolve climate change problems.

The principle of circular and cumulative causation centres on the interaction of multiple variables and feedback loops that magnify the atmospheric extremes. These cumulative results also relate specifically to the principle of uncertainty, since the major uncertainty is how quickly climate change will destroy/upset core elements of ecological resources (including atmospheric patterns and ocean currents). Deep uncertainties generate problems especially when tipping points are scrutinized. Likely major threshold effects will emerge suddenly, with only subtle warning signs, hence earlier than expected, which will necessitate more serious efforts at environmental preservation, even while entropy continues to generate waste even in a steady state system. Currently, even at 1.07–1.2 °C mean temperature rise (relative to the mean for 1850–1900) we are likely in the process of multiple individual tipping points which have major non-linear impacts on climate change when impacting in unison at the global level. Vis-à-vis the *principles of innovation and policy/governance,* this will likely make a 1.5 °C rise by 2100 too high as the Green Road to sustainability requires us to institute several critical structural changes to organizations, habits and cultures now and into the near and distant future.

The principles of political economy enable one to gain a holistic (broader, more comprehensive) vision of the climate change problem. It seeks to explain the historical origins of the problems, the role played by institutions in its perpetuation, the core impact of contradictions involving the vested interests against the commons, uneven developments between core, periphery and semi-periphery, the role of multiple factors and cumulative effects, as well as uncertainty and sudden impacts. Political economy can be seen as a critical part of an ecological economics perspective, albeit broader than the usual one applied to the problem.

Acknowledgements I wish to thank, for the original version of this chapter (O'Hara 2009), two anonymous referees from Ecological Economics; Greg Hayden for comments (at AFIT conference in Albuquerque, New Mexico); Fred Lee, Mathew Forstater & Erik Olsen when presented at UMKC, Kansas City; and Andrew Brennan for help with sourcing of information. This chapter is dedicated with much love to my mother, Rhoda Adelaide O'Hara (1915–2008), who died while I was researching the earlier version. The earlier version of this chapter won two awards for "Journal Article of the Year", one from the European Association for Evolutionary Political Economy (EAEPE) and the other from Curtin Business School.

References

Berger, Sebastian. 2008a. K. William Kapp's Theory of Social Costs and Environmental Policy: Towards Political Ecological Economics. *Ecological Economics* 67: 244–252.

———. 2008b. Circular Cumulative Causation (CCC) A La Myrdal and Kapp—*Political* Institutionalism for Minimizing Social Costs. *Journal of Economic Issues* 42: 357–366.

———, ed. 2009. *The Foundations of Non-Equilibrium Economics: The Principle of Circular and Cumulative Causation*. Oxon/New York: Routledge.

Boulding, Kenneth. 1945. The Consumption Concept in Economic Theory. *American Economic Review* 35: 1–14.

———. 1949-50. Income or Welfare. *Review of Economic Studies* 17: 77–86.

———. 1966. The Economics of Coming Spaceship Earth. In *Environmental Quality in a Growing Economy*, ed. Henry Jarrett, 3–14. Baltimore: John Hopkins Press.

———. 1981. *Evolutionary Economics*. Beverly Hills: Sage Publications.

Brennan, Andrew John. 2008. Theoretical Foundations of Sustainable Economic Welfare Indicators—ISEW and Political Economy of the Disembedded Economy. *Ecological Economics* 67: 1–19.

Burkett, Paul. 2004. Marx's Reproductive Schemes and the Environment. *Ecological Economics* 49: 457–467.

———. 2006. Two Stages of Ecosocialism? Implications of Some Neglected Analyses of Ecological Conflict and Crisis. *International Journal of Political Economy* 35 (3): 23–45.

C2ES (Centre for Climate Change and Energy Solutions). 2021. *Outcomes for the UN Climate Change Conference in Glasgow: COP26*. C2ES.

Cai, Yongyang, Timothy M. Linton, and Thomas S. Lontzek. 2016. Risk of Multiple Interacting Tipping Points Should Encourage Rapid CO2 Emission Reduction. *Nature Climate Change* 6: 520–525.

CAT (Climate Action Tracker). 2021. *Five Scenarios for Annual Global Greenhouse Gas Emissions*. Https://Climateactiontracker.Org/. Accessed 21 Dec 2021.

CEDA (Centre for Environmental Data Analysis). 2021. *Summary for Policymakers of the Working Group I Contribution to the IPCC Sixth Assessment Report.* https://Data.Ceda.Ac.Uk/Badc/Ar6_Wg1/Data/Spm/Spm_02/V20210809/Panel_C.

Clark, B., and John Bellamy Foster. 2009. Ecological Imperialism and the Global Metabolic Rift: Unequal Exchange and the Guano/Nitrates Trade. *International Journal of Comparative Sociology* 50: 311–334.

Cline, W.R. 2007. *Global Warming and Agriculture: Impact Estimates by Country*. Washington, DC: Peterson Institute for International Economics.

CPE (Centre for Political Ecology). 2000. *The Second Contradiction of Capitalism*. Santa Cruz: Centre for Political Ecology.

Dorninger, Christian, Alf Hornborg, David J. Abson, Henrik Von Wehrden, and Hanspeter Wieland. 2021. Global Patterns of Ecologically Unequal Exchange: Implications for Sustainability in the 21st Century. *Ecological Economics* 179 (January).

EEA (European Environmental Agency). 2021. *Global and European Sea Level Rise*. Https://Www.Eea.Europa.Eu/Ims/Global-and-European-Sea-Level-Rise.

———. 2022. *Global CO_2-Eq Concentrations*. Https://Www.Eea.Europa.Eu/Ims/Atmospheric-Greenhouse-Gas-Concentrations.

Elsner, Wolfram, T. Frigato, and Paolo Ramazzotti. 2006. *Social Costs and Public Action in Modern Capitalism: Essays Inspired by Karl William Kapp's Theory of Social Costs*. Oxon/New York: Routledge.

Figge, Frank, Andrea Stevenson Thorpe, and Jason Good. 2021. Us Before Me: A Group Level Approach to the Circular Economy. *Ecological Economics* 179 (January).

Foster, John Bellamy. 1992. The Absolute General Law of Environmental Degradation. *Capitalism Nature Socialism* 3 (3): 34–40.

———. 2000. *Marx's Ecology: Materialism and Nature*. New York: Monthly Review.

———. 2002. Capitalism and Ecology: The Nature of the Contradiction. *Monthly Review* 54: 6–16.

———. 2005. The Treadmill of Accumulation. *Organization and Environment* 18: 7–18.

———. 2009. *The Ecological Revolution: Making Peace with the Planet*. New York: Monthly Review.

Garnaut, Ross. 2008. *The Garnaut Climate Change Review: Final Report*. Cambridge/New York: Cambridge University Press.

Georgescu-Roegen, Nicholas. 1971. *The Entropy Law and The Economic Process*. Cambridge, MA: Harvard University Press.

———. 1973. The Entropy Law and the Economic Problem. In *Economics, Ecology, Ethics: Essays Toward a Steady-State Economy*, ed. Herman E. Daly, 49–60. San Fransisco: W.H. Freeman.

———. 1975. Energy and Economic Myths. *Southern Economic Journal* 41: 347–381. Reprinted in: Nicholas Georgescu-Roegen, *Energy and Economic Myths: Institutional and Analytical Essays*, 3–36. New York: Pergamon Press.

Georgescu-Roegen, N. 2000. Nicholas Georgescu-Roegen (1906-1994). In *A Biographical Dictionary of Dissenting Economists*, ed. Philip Arestis and Malcolm Sawyer, 217–226. Aldershot/Northampton: Edward Elgar.

Global Footprint Network. 2022. *Ecological Overshoot: World Footprint*. Https://Www.Footprintnetwork.Org/Our-Work/Ecological-Footprint/.

Gore, Albert Arnold. 2006. *An Inconvenient Truth*. A Film Directed by Davis Guggenheim. Produced by David, Laurie; Bender, Lawrence, and Scott Z. Burns. Hollywood: Paramount Classics and Participant Productions.

Hansen, James. 2008. Tipping Point: Perspective of a Climatologist. In *2008–2009 State of the Wild: A Global Portrait of Wildlife, Wildlands and Oceans*, ed. Eva Fearn. Boston: Island Press.

Harvey, David. 2001. *Spaces of Capital: Towards a Critical Geography*. New York: Routledge.

Hodgson, Geoffrey. 2004. *The Evolution of Institutional Economics: Agency, Structure and Darwinism in American Institutionalism*. London/New York: Routledge.

Hornborg, A. 2006. Footprints in the Cotton Fields: The Industrial Revolution as Time-Space Appropriation and Environmental Load Displacement. *Ecological Economics* 59: 74–81.

———. 2009. Zero-Sum World: Challenges in Conceptualizing Environmental Load Displacement and Ecologically Unequal Exchange in the World-System. *International Journal of Comparative Sociology* 50: 237–262.

Howard, Michael C., and John E. King. 1985. *The Political Economy of Marx*. 2nd ed. New York: New York University Press.

IPCC. (Intergovernmental Panel on Climate Change). 2007a. *Climate Change 2007—The Physical Science Basis*. Contribution of Working Group I to Fourth Assessment Report, ed. Susan Solomon, Dahe Qin, Martin Manning, Melinda Marquis, Kristen Averyt, Melinda Tignor, Henry Miller Jr, and Zhenlini Chen. New York: Cambridge University Press.

———. 2007b. *Climate Change 2007—Impacts, Adaptation and Vulnerability*. Contribution of Working Group II to Fourth Assessment Report, ed. Martin Parry, Osvaldo Canziani, Jean Palutikof, Paul Van Der Linden, and Clair Hanson. New York: Cambridge University Press.

———. 2007c. *Climate Change 2007—Mitigation of Climate Change*. Contribution of Working Group III to Fourth Assessment Report, ed. Bert Metz, Peter Bosch, Rutu Dave, Ogun Davidson, and Leo Mayer. New York: Cambridge University Press.

———. 2007d. *Climate Change 2007: Synthesis Report*. IPCC.

———. 2018. *Global Warming of 1.5°C: An IPCC Special Report on the Impacts of Global Warming of 1.5°C Above Pre-industrial Levels and Related Global Greenhouse Gas Emissions Pathways*. Cambridge: IPCC. https://www.ipcc.ch/reports/.

———. 2019. *Special Report: The Ocean and Cryosphere in a Changing Climate*. Cambridge: IPCC. https://www.iecc.ch/reports/.

———. 2021. *Climate Change 2021: The Physical Science Basis*, Working Group 1 Contribution to the Sixth Assessment Report of the IPCC. Cambridge: IPCC. https://www.ipcc.ch/reports/.

———. 2022. *Climate Change 2022: Mitigation of Climate Change*, Working Group III Contribution to the Sixth Assessment Report. IPCC. https://www.ipcc.ch/reports/.

Jordenson, Andrew K., K. Austin, and C. Dick. 2009. Ecologically Unequal Exchange and the Resource Consumption/Environmental Degradation Paradox: A Panel Study of Less-Developed Countries, 1970-2000. *International Journal of Comparative Sociology* 50: 263–284.

Jorgenson, Andrew. 2009. The Transnational Organization of Production, the Scale of Degradation, and Ecoefficiency: A Study of Carbon Dioxide Emissions in Less Developed Countries. *Human Ecology Review* 16: 64–74.

Kapp, Karl W. 1974. *Environmental Policies and Development Planning in Contemporary China and Other Essays*. The Hague: Mouton Press.

———. 1978. *The Social Costs of Business Enterprise*. Second Revised Edition. Nottingham: Spokesman Books. Preface By Michael Barratt Brown.

Keller, K., G. Yoke, and M. Schlesinger. 2008. Managing the Risks of Climate Thresholds: Uncertainties and Informational Needs. *Climatic Change* 91: 5–10.

Keynes, John Maynard. 1921. *A Treatise on Probability*. New York: Rough Draft Printing, 2008.

———. 1936. *The General Theory of Employment, Interest and Money*. London: BN Publishing, 2008.

Knight, Frank H. 1921. *Risk, Uncertainty and Profit*. New York: Cosimo Classics.

Knutti, R., M.R. Alen, P. Friedlingstein, J.M. Gregory, G.C. Hegeri, G.A. Meehi, M. Meinshausen, J.M. Murphy, G.-K. Plattner, S.C.B. Raper, T.F. Stocker, P.A. Stott, H. Teng, and T.M.L. Wigley. 2008. A Review of Uncertainties in Global Temperature Projections Over the Twenty-First Century. *Journal of Climate* 21: 2651–2663.

Lenton, Timothy M. 2019. Climate Tipping Points: Too Risky to Bet Against. *Nature* 575 (29 November): 592–595.

———. 2021. Tipping Points in the Climate System. *Weather* 76 (10): 325–326.

Lenton, Timothy M., H. Held, E. Kriegler, W. Lucht, S. Rahmstorf, and H.J. Schellnhuber. 2008. Tipping Elements in the Earth's Climate System. *Proceedings of the National Academy of Sciences* 105: 1786–1793.

Marx, Karl. 1857–58. *The Grundrisse*. Harmondsworth: Penguin, 1973.

———. 1885. *Capital, Volume 2: The Process of Circulation of Capital*. Harmondsworth: Penguin, 1978.

Mcinerney, D., and K. Keller. 2008. Economically Optimal Risk Reduction Strategies in the Face of Uncertain Climate Thresholds. *Climatic Change* 91: 29–41.

Moberg, A., D.M. Sonechkin, K. Holmgren, N.M. Datsenko, and W. Karlen. 2005. Highly Variable Northern Hemisphere Temperatures Reconstructed from Low- and High-Resolution Proxy Data. *Nature* 433: 613–618.

Napoletano, Brian M., John Bellamy Foster, Brett Clark, Pedro S. Urquijo, Michael K. McCall, and Jaime Paneque-Gálvez. 2019. Making Space in Critical Environmental Geography for the Metabolic Rift. *Annals of the American Association of Geographers* 109 (6): 1811–1828.

NCDC. 2022. *Global Climate Data: Time Series, Relative to 1900–2000*. https://Www.Ncdc.Noaa.Gov/Cag/Global/Time-Series Relative To 1900-2000.

Newell, Peter, Shilpi Srivastava, Lars Otto Naess, Gerardo A. Torres Contreras, and Roz Price. 2020. Towards Transformative Climate Justice: Key Challenges and Future Directions for Research. *Institute of Development Studies Working Paper* 2020 (540): 150.

NOAA (National Oceanic and Atmospheric Association). 2021. *Despite Pandemic Shutdowns, Carbon Dioxide and Methane Surged in 2020*, 7 April. Research News. https://Research.Noaa.Gov/Article/Artmid/587/Articleid/2742/Despite-Pandemic-Shutdowns-Carbon-Dioxide-and-Methane-Surged-In-2020.

Nordhaus, William M. 1977. Economic Growth and Climate: The Carbon Dioxide Problem. *American Economic Review: Papers and Proceedings* 67 (1): 341–346.

———. 1991. To Slow or Not to Slow: The Economics of the Greenhouse Effect. *Economic Journal* 101: 920–937.

———. 2008. *A Question of Balance: Weighing the Options on Global Warming Policies*. New Haven: Yale University Press.

NORR. 2022. *Ocean Heat Content Anomaly: Global Climate Change*. Https://Www.Climate.Gov/News-Features/Understanding-Climate/Climate-Change-Ocean-Heat-Content.

O'Connor, James. 1991. On the Two Contradictions of Capitalism. *Capitalism Nature Socialism* 2 (3): 1–5.

———. 1994. Is Sustainable Capitalism Possible? In *Is Capitalism Sustainable? Political Economy and the Politics of Ecology*, ed. Martin O'Connor, 152–175. New York: Guilford Press.

O'Hara, Phillip Anthony, ed. 2001a. *Encyclopedia of Political Economy*. London/New York: Routledge.

O'Hara, Sabine U. 2001b. The Challenges of Valuation: Ecological Economics Between Matter and Meaning. In *The Economics of Nature and the Nature of Economics*, ed. Cutler J. Cleveland, David I. Stern, and Robert Costanza, 89–208. Cheltenham/Northampton: Edward Elgar.

———. 2002. Endogenous Preferences and Sustainable Development. *The Journal of Socio-Economics* 31: 511–527.

O'Hara, Phillip Anthony. 2004. A New Family-Community Social Structure of Accumulation for the United States? *Forum for Social Economics* 33 (2): 51–80. https://doi.org/10.1007/BF02745496.

———. 2009. Political Economy of Climate Change, Ecological Destruction and Uneven Development. *Ecological Economics* 69: 223–234. https://doi.org/10.1016/j.ecolecon.2009.09.015.

———. 2023. *Long Wave Institutional Dynamics and Political Economy Crises of Capitalism: Principles, Social Structures of Accumulation and Empirics*. Springer.

O'Neill, Brian C., Elmar Kriegler, Keywan Raihi, Kristie L. Ebi, Stephane Hallegatte, Timothy R. Carter, Ritu Mathur, and Detlef P. Van Vuuren. 2014. A New Scenario Framework for Climate Change: The Concept of Shared Socioeconomic Pathways. *Climate Change* 122: 387–400.

O'Neill, Brian C., Elmar Kriegler, Kristie L. Ebi, Eric Kemp-Benedict, Keywan Riahi, Dale S. Rothman, Bas J. Van Ruijven, Detlef P. Van Vuuren, Joern Birkmann, Kasper Kok, Marc Levy, and William Solecki. 2017. The Roads Ahead: Narratives for Shared Socioeconomic Pathways Describing World Futures in 21st Century. *Global Environmental Change* 42 (1): 169–180.

O'Neill, Brian C., Timothy R. Carter, Kristie Ebi, Paula A. Harrison, Eric Kamp-Benedict, Kasper Kok, Elmar Kriegler, et al. 2020. Achievements and Needs for the Climate Change Scenario Framework. *Nature Climate Change* 10 (December): 1074–1084.

Parks, B.C., and J.T. Roberts. 2008. Inequality and the Global Climate Regime: Breaking the North-South Impasse. *Cambridge Review of International Affairs* 21: 621–648.

Polanyi, Karl. 1944. *The Great Transformation*. Boston: Beacon Press.

Randalls, Samuel. 2010. History of the 2°C Climate Target. *WIREs Climate Change* 1 (4): 598–605.

Resnick, Stephen, and Richard Wolff. 2002. *Class Theory and History: Capitalism and Communism in the USSR*. London/New York: Routledge.

Rice, J. 2009. The Transnational Organization of Production and Uneven Environmental Degradation and Change in the World Economy. *International Journal of Comparative Sociology* 50: 215–236.

Ritchie, Hannah, and Max Roser. 2021. *Emissions by Sector*. Our World in Data. Https://Ourworldindata.Org/Emissions-By-Sector.

Roberts, J.T., and B.C. Parks. 2007. *A Climate of Injustice: Global Inequality, North-South Politics, and Climate Policy*. Cambridge, MA: MIT Press.

———. 2009. Ecologically Unequal Exchange, Ecological Debt, and Climate Justice: The History and Implications of Three Related Ideas for a New Social Movement. *International Journal of Comparative Sociology* 50: 385–409.

Schellnhuber, Hans Joachim, Stefan Rahmstorf, and Ricarda Winklemann. 2016. Why the Right Climate Target Was Agreed in Paris. *Nature Climate Change* 6 (July): 649–653.

Schumpeter, Joseph Alois. 1911. *The Theory of Economic Development*, 1964. Oxford: Oxford University Press.

Shackle, George L.S. 1970. *Expectation, Enterprise and Profit*. London: Allen & Unwin.

Shandra, J., C. Leckband, L.A. Mckinney, and B. London. 2009. Ecologically Unequal Exchange, World Polity, and Biodiversity Loss: A Cross-National Analysis of Threatened Mammals. *International Journal of Comparative Sociology* 50: 285–310.

Smith, Neil. 1984. *Uneven Development: Nature, Capital and the Production of Space*. Oxford: Blackwell.

Spense, M. 2000. Capital Against Nature: James O'Connor's Theory of the Second Contradiction of Capitalism. *Capital & Class* 72: 81–109.

Statistica.com. 2022a. https://www.statista.com/statistics/1091926/atmospheric-concentration-of-co2-historic/ (CO_2 stocks global).

———. 2022b. *Divergence of Ocean Temperatures from 20th Century Average*. https://www.statista.com/chart/19418/divergence-of-ocean-temperatures-from-20th-century-average/

Stern, Nicholas. 2007. *The Economics of Climate Change: The Stern Review*. Cambridge: Cambridge University Press.

UNDP (United Nations Development Program). 2007. *Human Development Report 2007/2008: Fighting Climate Change: Human Solidarity in a Divided World*. New York: Palgrave Macmillan. Available on the Internet.

———. 2020. *Human Development Report 2020: The Next Frontier: Human Development and the Anthropocene*. New York: United Nations.

US NSTC (United States National Science & Technology Council). 2009. *Scientific Assessment of Effects of Global Change on United States*. Committee on Environment & Natural Resources, Washington, DC, 261.

Vellinga, P., and R. Swart. 1991. The Greenhouse Marathon: Proposal for a Global Strategy. In *Climate Change: Science, Impacts and Policy*, ed. J. Jager and H.L. Ferguson, 129–134. Cambridge: Cambridge University Press.

WMO (World Meteorological Organization). 2021. *WMO Atlas of Mortality and Economic Losses from Weather, Climate and Water Extremes, 1970–2019*, WMO-No. 1267. Zurich: WMO. https://library.wmo.int/doc_num.php?explnum_id=10902.

Worldbank. 2022. Worldbank Data Centre: https://data.worldbank.org/indicator/NY.GDP.MKTP.KD (global real GDP); https://data.worldbank.org/indicator/SP.POP.TOTL (total global population); https://data.worldbank.org/indicator/EN.ATM.CO2E.KT (CO_2 flows global); https://data.worldbank.org/indicator/EN.ATM.GHGT.KT.CE (CO_2-eq flows global).

WWF (Worldwide Fund for Nature). 2021. *Living Planet Report 2020*, ed. R.E.A. Almond, M. Grooten, and T. Petersen. Gland: WWF. https://livingplanetindex.org/home/index.

WWF/GFN/ZSL (World Wildlife Fund/Global Footprint Network/Institute of Zoology). 2008. *Living Planet Report 2008*. Gland/Oakland/London: WWF/GFN/ZSL.

Corruption 6

Abstract

The purpose of this chapter is to apply some core general principles of institutional and evolutionary political economy to corruption as a global, regional and national phenomenon. We start with the principle of historical specificity, where the known history of corruption processes and concepts are examined. We follow the classical scholars of ancient Greece and numerous others who had a systemic view of the matter; through to micro views of Roman law, Adam Smith and others who took an individualist view of corruption; and onto the reemergence of corruption discourse through the 1970s–2010s, initially with a micro perspective but increasingly taking a 'modern classical view' of systemic corruption. The principles of innovation and policy/governance are applied to an innovative corruption analysis for academic and policy purposes. The principle of contradiction presents corruption as the promotion of the vested interests against the common good in the form of bribery, fraud, embezzlement, state capture, nepotism, extortion, etc. The principle of heterogeneous groups and agents utilizes social dominance theory vis-à-vis dominant and subordinate groups, and the styles of corruption activated by elites are surveyed as they gain resources, favors and economic surplus against the interests of the common people. We also Lastly, scrutinize the principle of hegemony and uneven development vis-à-vis four stylized facts about corruption throughout the world in relation to [i] development patterns, [ii] corporate corruption, [iii] key sectors/nations and [iv] inequality. The fourth stylized fact [iv] inequality uses the principle of circular and cumulative causation (CCC) to analyze "internal uneven developments" within nations. The principles provide a framework for reducing systemic corruption and modifying the structure of power to benefit the common good, socioeconomic performance and functioning of institutions.

© The Author(s), under exclusive license to Springer Nature Singapore Pte Ltd. 2022
P. A. O'Hara, *Principles of Institutional and Evolutionary Political Economy*, Springer Texts in Business and Economics,
https://doi.org/10.1007/978-981-19-4158-0_6

Keywords

Systemic corruption · Principles · Historical specificity · Contradictions · Uneven development · Heterogeneous groups & agents · CCC · Innovation · Policy & governance

6.1 Historical Specificity of Corruption

The *first principle of institutional and evolutionary political economy is historical specificity*, the idea that economic theory and empirics should be embedded in a historical view of socioeconomic systems evolving through time.[1] Marx, Veblen, Keynes and Schumpeter, among others, all had this historical view, for without history, political economy would be nothing but abstractions divorced from the social and political fabric (O'Hara 2002). History reveals path dependency, namely, that the particular roads that economies and theories take will impact on their future trajectories. History also reveals various phases, stages, forms of social provisioning, evolutionary transformations and metamorphoses that are crucial for understanding the nature of the problems being studied. It also gives a richer picture of the phenomenon, compared with starting with current functioning, and hence provides a better, historical, view of the present and the future.

The history of corruption discourse typically starts with the classical texts of Ancient Greece, especially the ideas of Socrates (469–399 BC), Plato (427–347 BC) and Aristotle (384–322 BC). These scholars had a systemic view of corruption as being endogenous to human relationships, including the republican ideal of virtuous moral and political association. Corruption was associated with the decay, destruction and corrosion of the moral and political fiber of civil society, through abuse of positions of power against the common good. Corruption was also seen as dysfunctional in that it destroyed virtue and political association in the private interests of groups and individuals.

A comparison between the 'ideal' and the 'corrupt' was a core part of this classical method (Mulgan 2012). The ideal was a standard of judgment based around unqualified truth and goodness, wisdom and virtue, plus the common interest or good. A core aspect of Aristotle's analysis of truth and virtue is a citizen's ability to pursue an independent judgment to direct actions for the common good. The destruction of this ability and actuality is a critical aspect of the corruption of ethics as their actions become unsound, debased, infected, depraved and perverted for other

---

[1] These principles of IEPE have been explained in numerous articles and books, including for instance, O'Hara (2007, 2012a, b, 2023); Brennan and Kalsi (2015). An important part of the principle of historical specificity is the concept of culture: how every topic in IEPE needs to be situated in a cultural context embodying various norms, mores, institutions and systems of power.

than the public interest (Genaux 2004: 22). Thus the main concern became institutional structures and social norms which are variously ideal or corrupt, and then detailing the nature of the corruption and how to reduce it or change the style.

Polybius (c.203–c.120 BC) continued the classical view of corruption vis-à-vis systemic, endogenous, organizationally endemic, unjust, undemocratic and unproductive use of social resources for the benefit of the vested interests against the common good. Also drawing on this classical school was Augustine of Hippo (354–430 AD) who established an Augustinian tradition, which viewed earthly life "after the fall" (original sin and pride) as inherently corrupt. Helping to establish a Christian perspective on corruption that evolved at least until late medieval times, Augustine saw the role of the state as ensuring stable and predictable governance, which is nonetheless always corrupt in various ways and to varying degrees compared with God's city where pride and sin do not exist.

From the fourth to the sixteenth centuries AD varying degrees of conflict existed between the secular and church spheres in Europe, which increased through time, as variously church corruption was said to exist when its interference in the political sphere was seen by some to be too great, while secular corruption was said to exist when its power over church was seen by some as too great. This in itself is a testament to the 'stylized fact' (a term developed by Nicholas Kaldor) that the literature on corruption throughout its history amounts to a normative account of those corrosive elements of the political economy and civil society that are the subject of critical scrutiny based on the concept of the common good. The literature was influenced by an empirical and historical view of how various systems of political economy should be portrayed in a manner consistent with a 'progressive' view of socio-political institutions and morals.

These corrosive dysfunctional 'abuses of power' manifest themselves in various ways, such as through systemic bribery, embezzlement, extortion, fraud, nepotism, undue influence, and so on, 'to gain private resources against the common good'. To counter systemic corruption requires sufficient levels and types of *trust*, communication and justice consistent with the ongoing dynamics of the common good. In a neo-Aristotelian fashion, this 'systemic view of corruption' has continued through the ages, for instance, in the early-modern literature; where corruption is seen as dysfunctional, even if it is endogenous to the macro environment and inextricably engrained in institutions, behavior and habits. While corruption may be essential to the current system of arrangements and contributes therefore to its very structure and function, in a broader view and longer-term perspective a much better system is possible with core elements of structural change, and hence in this wider view the corrupting elements are unproductive of the common good.

For instance, Ibn Khaldun (1332–1406) wrote on the rise and decline of empires as dysfunctional corrosive practices escalate. Niccolò Machiavelli (1469–1527) made advances in understanding moral corruption, the occasional need for radical change to improve matters, and the need for checks and balances in the workings of healthy republican institutions. Henry St. John (1678–1751) contributed on the rise and decay of republics, and the importance of checks and balances being provided by an oppositional party. Montesquieu's (1689–1755) corruption discourse related to the separation of powers (balance) required between executive, legislature and judiciary; a study of institutional trends, material factors and classes; plus the importance of virtue. Jean-Jaques Rousseau (1712–1778) believed in the uncorrupted state of nature versus the stages of evolution of human society, and also the need for direct democracy to reduce corruption vis-à-vis inequality, vested interests and elites.

From Roman law (which influenced medieval and early-modern common law) at least, there has been a more micro view of corruption as pertaining to the bribery of public officials (e.g., judges, politicians, bureaucrats) for their private gain rather than public benefit (Genaux 2004: 18, 23). This legal tendency has delimited the view of corruption to bribery of public officials, and has close links to Thomas Hobbes (1588–1679) the rise of individualism and an economistic interpretation of corruption. Later Adam Smith played a role in being concerned with the public management of a market society, and how bribery can misallocate resources by supporting inefficient public officials. This micro view of corruption was more concerned with the health of markets, rather than a systemic view of morality, decay and disease *a la* the classical systemic view of corruption.

Scholars such as Adam Smith thus came to view corruption in what has been termed the 'modern liberal' view, where the state corruptly interferes with the natural laws of the market and discourages individual autonomy. The virtues Smith wants to nurture are private and commercial and not civic, including "prudence, justice, propriety, self-command, frugality, sobriety, vigilance, circumspection, temperance, constancy, firmness, punctuality, faithfulness, enterprise and industry" (Hill 2012: 102). He wishes to encourage the market economy set within an institutional structure of appropriate virtues and morals. Any corrupting of this so-called natural process through structures of power that constrain a market society can be broken up through appropriate policy or market action.[2]

Nonetheless the work of the classical neo-Aristotelian scholars on corruption continued; for instance, Smith's friend Adam Ferguson was a classicist. Ferguson's concerns are the same as those of contemporary communitarians, since, while being committed to progress, he was concerned with the negative costs of the rising commercial society in the form of deteriorating levels of virtue, fragile social bridging networks, *distrust* and weak civil society. The rising predominance of markets, commodities and profit saw the decay of community and social intimacy along with an increase in alienation. Thus the rising philosophy of individualism and

---

[2] There is a considerable amount of disagreement about Smith's contradictory dichotomy of benefits and disbenefits of markets, in relation to his work on *The Wealth of Nations* vis-à-vis *The Theory of Moral Sentiments*. Consider, for instance, the views of James Alvey (1998) and Lisa Hill (2012).

6.1 Historical Specificity of Corruption

private concerns saw the destruction of the common good—as Ferguson perceived it—as the costs were considerable in comparison with the benefits of change.[3]

While during the 1600s and 1700s the corruption of morals and the body politic were scrutinized throughout Europe, in other parts of the world scholars and officials were similarly worried about the corruption of virtue and institutions. Official corruption was emphasized by Chinese officials and scholars at least since 1600. During the Qing Dynasty (1644–1911) corruption was considered the "deviant use of public office to achieve private gain" (Park 1997: 968). Acts of corruption included the capital offenses of accepting a bribe in exchange for a favor, and extortion (obtaining resources through force or the threat of force); or the lesser offenses of influence peddling (e.g., accepting a large gift without specific quid pro quo) and soliciting unauthorized funds; and lastly offering, organizing or handling bribes (intermediaries were treated as seriously as those accepting a bribe) (Park, 970–974). Especially important here was the Chinese practice of differentiating between acceptable transactions, corrupt transactions, and ambiguous transactions.

The Chinese saw a continuum between smaller gifts to officials, which were acceptable; large gifts which were considered likely bribes (perhaps with a lag between receipt and exchange); and the ambiguous intermediate category of *gift-bribe*, which was difficult to either accept or criminalize. Similarly, there were customary modest fees for a service, which may be considered part of an official's rightful remuneration, and large extortionate fees which were considered corruption, plus the intermediate ambiguous title of *customary-extortion* which was neither legal nor an offence. Gifts and customary fees were seen as moral and consistent with the common good; bribes and extortion were considered corruption; while gift-bribes and customary-extortion were of ambiguous/borderline morality and legality. These subtle distinctions are useful ways of looking at current issues of corruption.

The success of the commercial republican model in Britain influenced events in the United States, where the literature emphasizes two *interrelated* types of corruption. The first is the generation of rent seeking behavior of the state in generating degrees of monopoly in business patronage, networks and resources; while the second is the issuance of bribes and other resources to influence public officials, politicians and judges. Gleaser and Goldin (2006) present data obtained from undertaking a fully searchable edition of the *New York Times*, for the number of times "corrupt" and "fraud" are used between 1850 and 1973 in the newspaper. They conclude that this indicates a major decline in corruption broadly alongside the trend in the figures, indicating that in the USA rent seeking behavior and bribery had fallen to very low levels by the 1970s (a conclusion reinforced by Wallis 2006).

---

[3] For more detail see Hill (2012). An alternative expression of this critical thinking is the need for the scholarly art of constructive criticism of existing society, ensuring the costs of the rise in the commercial society are adequately included in the analysis, even if there are difficulties measuring costs because of inadequate statistics. It may also be that the costs and benefits of the rising commercial society cannot be assessed in comparable units since they are complex (see Kapp 1978).

These studies have a relatively narrow, "micro" view of corruption as only occurring in the public sector, and the cut-off date of the early 1970s likely abstracts from increases in corruption during the 1980s through to the 2010s. They also likely mistake lack of use of the terms with lower incidence of corruption (see Myrdal 1968). The more recent figures analyzed by Dieter Zinnbauer give a better empirical account through the rise and fall and rise of the use of the word "corruption" in English-language books since 1800. Table 6.1, below, examines these waves of growth and decline and growth of the use of the word "corruption", along with the recent explosion of usage of the words "accountability" and "transparency", the latter two terms being core supplementary concepts associated with corruption:[4]

This data reveals that the usage of the term "corruption" in the West was quite high (comparatively) in the early nineteenth century, then it declined continuously until about 1920 when it leveled out for 20 years; then it increased during the 1950s and 1960s; followed by another bout of increase in the 1980s and 1990s; then a modest decline to 2010. The increasing discussion of 'accountability' (especially in the 1960s–1970s, 1990s and 2000s) and 'transparency' (1980s–1990s) in both private and public sectors is an indication of the interrelated set of processes associated with corruption through various abuses of power. Recent decades—notably the 1980s–2000s, with the 2000s being the highest levels ever for accountability and transparency—have thus seen an explosion of the "corruption industry" in terms of practitioners, scholars and policy-makers.

With the expansion of the corruption industry the literature has taken a decidedly pluralistic turn through several 'modern classical approaches', with innovative empirical assessments and interpretations. In this context, it is useful to investigate some of the core elements of this diversity of perspectives on corruption. Figure 6.1, below, presents a quadratic view of two continuums relevant to the literature on corruption, the first being a continuum of single process (bribery) through to multiple process (bribery, extortion, fraud, embezzlement, patronage, state capture, etc) views, and the second showing the continuum of micro, single sector (public) corruption through to systemic (general), multi-sector (private-to-public, private-to-private, non-profit-to-private, etc) corruption. Various examples of schools or specific authors are isolated along these two major continuums, including the 45° arrow of recent scholarly trends in corruption discourse.

For instance, typically a neoclassical scholar/policy analyst will take a narrow view of corruption as being services provided by a public official in exchange for a bribe. Many empirical papers assume that corruption only includes bribery via public officials abusing positions of power to gain private benefits (e.g., Belousova et al. 2011). Public choice theorists often are slightly broader by considering rent seeking efforts to enhance monopoly power through assistance to cronies in return

---

[4]This table is based on Google's archive of digitized books for the terms "corruption", "accountability" and "transparency". The figures used in the table are the percentage of all books analyzed using the respective terms somewhere in the text, multiplied by 1,000,000, so that the figure is a whole number rather than a very small fraction with lots of zeros (which would not fit onto the table).

6.1 Historical Specificity of Corruption

Table 6.1 Word use, "Corruption", "Accountability", "Transparency": English Language Books, 1800–2010

	1800	1840	1880	1920	1950	1960	1970	1980	1990	2000	2010
Corruption	3261	2640	1595	1010	1126	1253	1398	1240	1350	1712	1530
Accountability	00	128	57	71	73	75	240	462	510	980	1193
Transparency	187	191	87	162	170	181	240	204	396	670	680

Source: Adapted from Zimmbauer (2011)

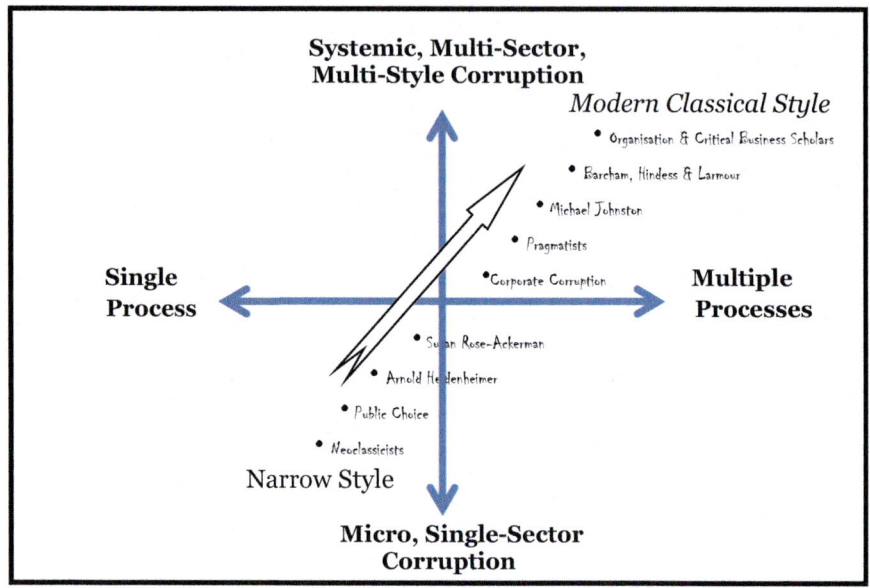

Fig. 6.1 Quadratic forces of corruption; diverse perspectives; recent trends

for bribery of public officials (Tullock 1996). Political scientists such as Arnold J. Heidenheimer (2002) offer a broad discussion of various types of transactions in different societies, yet still study only what they call "political corruption". Susan Rose-Ackerman takes public choice theory a step further by potentially including both public and corporate corruption, yet corporate corruption, while being discussed in one chapter, is underplayed in Rose-Ackerman (1978) and all her subsequent works.

Over the past two decades numerous schools and scholars/policy-analysts have implicitly or explicitly taken a much broader approach involving numerous sectors, heterogeneous agents and different styles of corruption. As the above arrow indicates, this has been the direction of much of the innovative work on corruption over the past decade. Numerous serious scholars scrutinize private-to-public corruption yet underplay the private element (e.g., Heidenheimer and Johnston 2002). Marshall Clinard (1990) was the first to seriously examine in detail the rising incidence of corporate (private-to-private) corruption. Pragmatic scholars such as Claire Fletcher and Daniela Herrmann (2012)—more interested in the empirical evidence than economistic theories—have generalized corruption as existing within and between private-to-private, private-to-public, public-to-public, not-for-profit and other sectors in a way that pushes them to the broader field.

The classical tradition of corruption has reemerged seeking a broader cultural analysis of corruption plus an endogenous and systemic view of its origins; epitomized by the remarkable series of papers in Barcham et al. (2012). This re-packaging of the classical view sees corruption as representing declining morality, justice and virtue causing various forms of decay and destruction within the institutions. Michael Johnston (2005) who for much of his career was close to the work of Heidenheimer on 'political' corruption, has come to take a systemic view of corruption as involving various complex styles and numerous complex sociopolitical processes. The 'modern classical trend' is also apparent in the work of numerous 'organizational studies' and 'critical business scholars' (see, eg, Blake Ashforth et al. 2008; Brown and Cloke 2011) in being systemic, cultural in outlook, critical of neoliberal policies, and concerned with the power of elites to extract resources against the common good through various networks of power and authority.

These innovative modern classical understandings of corruption enrich the literature immensely, through incorporating core aspects of the narrower views in a wider canvas of innovations concerning systemic and cultural power, habits, institutions, elites and structural change; where the narrower views become modified and widened substantially in the new edifice. Table 6.2, below, employing the principle of heterogeneous groups and agents, illustrates some of the multiple ways in which corruption can manifest itself, depending on circumstances, when these systemic/cultural pressures operate:

These six types of corruption employing different agents and groups include corporate-to-public bribery, corporate-to-corporate fraud, non-profit-to-corporate embezzlement, elite-to-family nepotism, business elite-to-public state capture, and mafia-boss-to-legitimate business extortion. The examples can be extended in many ways to enhance complexity and interdependency between sectors. The core thing about systemic corruption is that opportunities to promote the vested interests need multifarious ways of emerging, through different sectors, agents and styles. The next section outlines an institutional and evolutionary approach to systemic corruption through such sectors, agents and styles.

6.2 Contradictions of Corruption, Heterogeneous Groups and Uneven Development

The *principle of contradiction* posits the notion that there are certain processes in the economy which are in varying degrees of cooperation and conflict, depending on circumstances, and which should be a core part of political economic inquiry. They are usually in cooperation when the common good is in play; and in conflict when elites, moguls and other vested interests have enough power to advance their interests over the majority and other minorities, and when the common people seek to gain some power at the expense of the vested interests. The most general contradiction is Karl Polanyi's idea of the disembedded economy, where commercial forces have a tendency to promote formal exchange relations to the detriment of community relations of reciprocity, redistribution and informal markets (Stanfield 1987). More specific contradictions link to potential conflict between various forces—such as between capital and labor; finance and industry; competition and monopoly; capital and state; profit and the environment; men and women; nation(s)

Table 6.2 Six forms of systemic corruption in sectors through heterogeneous agents

Type	Example	Definition
$BC_m \leftrightarrow BP_{\bar{u}}$: Corporate-to-Public Bribery (**B**)	Corporate manager (Cm, supplier of monies) gives public sector worker ($P_{\bar{u}}$, demander of monies) a bribe for supporting contract	*Bribery* is "bestowing of a benefit in order to unduly influence an action or decision" (Langseth 2006: 10) (often disguised as commissions, success fees, expenses, presents, inflated prices or donations) (Fletcher and Hermann 2012: 120)
$FC_f \leftrightarrow FC_r$: Corporate-to-Corporate Fraud (**F**)	Corporate CFO (Cf) provides fraudulent assessment of quality of debt & ratings agency (company) (Cr) supports assessment	*Fraud* is false representation; deception, distortion, lies, misleading information and suppression of true facts (Fletcher and Hermann 2012: 6)
$EN_{Pa} \leftrightarrow EC_a$: Non-Profit Sector-to-Private Sector Embezzlement (**E**)	Non-profit accountant (NPa) embezzles money with support of auditing company agent (Ca), by siphoning for themselves wages of fictitious employees	*Embezzlement* is the "taking or conversion of money, property or other valuables for personal benefit…by someone to whom it has been *entrusted*" (Vargas-Hernandez 2010: 273; emphasis added).
$NE_g \leftrightarrow NF_a$: Elite Family Nepotism (**N**)	Ruling elite group head (Eg) intervenes to support relative/family (Fa) for managerial position.	*Nepotism* is undue favoritism by business, state, church etc agents to relatives/friends for promotion, employment etc without regard for merit and due process.
$SCB_e \leftrightarrow SCP_u$: State Capture (**SC**): Improper Political Funding	Ruling business elite (Be) fund political parties (Pu) in exchange for being on committees influencing rules, laws, regulations, etc	*State capture* is where business, unions, etc typically provide party funding in return for influence through the determination of laws, rules, regulations and decisions.
$XM \leftrightarrow XB_l$: Mafia (M) Extortion (X) against Legitimate Business (Bl).	Mafia boss threatens to takeover/destroy a legitimate business through force and violence if it fails to stop trading in the mafia boss's territory.	*Extortion* is the threat (instilling of fear/intimidation) of a negative action on certain victim(s) (person, group, institution, area or nation) if a specific or general demand is not satisfied usually within a certain time-period.

versus nation(s); plus ethnic group(s) versus ethnic group(s)—which are in varying degrees of opposition to each other, depending on time and circumstances (O'Hara 1999, 2002, 2023).

Contradictions are thus social pressures in which the forces of economy and society lead to the use of resources for one use rather than another; a type of social opportunity cost. Relating to corruption, it is mostly a power-generated pressure to promote the interests of elites rather than the common good. Narrow views of corruption often examine the *contradiction between principles and agents* (Groenendijk 1997). In this view, there are principals in the economy who must be served by agents; whether they be shareholders (principals) whose interests must be advanced by managers, CEOs and workers (agents); or citizens/electors (principals) whose concerns must be conditioned by politicians and public servants (agents). Thus when Chief Financial Officers (CFOs; agents) of companies seek to advance short-term shareholder value through fraudulent reports, and dubious assessments about risk and return which ultimately hurt company reputation, principals (long-term shareholders) are often harmed and in these cases corruption is in operation. Likewise when politicians (agents) sell their advice privately to the highest bidder, offer employment to family members ahead of others, and work through networks to advance their private interests, they are likely adversely affecting citizens and electors (principals) because jobs and money are not being rewarded/circulated according to merit and thus adversely impact on the performance of public entities. (There are also more complex forms of principal-agent theory.)

The 'standard argument' of corruption includes three main contradictions: the first relating to the forces of *monopoly versus competition*; the second being the forces of *market versus state*; and third total *state control versus democracy*. Susan Rose-Ackerman (1975, 1978) is the most eloquent 'economic' advocate of this approach. In her system, there would be no corruption in the economic realm if markets were all perfectly competitive and knowledge widely distributed.[5] Likewise, several conventional scholars have indicated that there would be no corruption in the political realm if there was perfect competition in this realm as well, through direct democracy (anarchism) and hence no need for (formal) politicians or public servants; or where checks and balances are effective (Heidenheimer 2002). Combining these 'orthodox' economic and political perspectives of corruption leads to the 'standard corruption equation', shown as $C = R + D - A$, where corruption (C) is said to be positively related to the degree of rent seeking (R) oligopolists in the private sector and discretionary (D) powers of the state, and negatively related to the degree of accountability (A) of corporations and states.[6] In this approach, reducing corruption often aims at changing incentives affecting agents and principals through channels

---

[5]To reduce corruption, Rose-Ackerman broadly advocates some sort of balance between market and state, and also between state and direct democracy; but while she advocates perfect competition, she realizes that moving *in the direction* of more deregulation may actually *increase* corruption (1978: 207–8). If we were to accept her argument, such was likely the case of the Russian experiment with privatization in the 1990s, and the deregulation experience in OECD nations/elsewhere during the 1980s and 1990s onwards.

[6]Corruption may exist, Rose-Ackerman recognizes, if there are scale economies; industries or products where there are uncertain qualities such as education, research and creativity; non-profit sectors; externalities such as information; or government regulation such as price controls and/or rationing. In the political realm, corruption may be encouraged by weak checks and balances between, for instance, the executive and the legislature; the judiciary and the executive; plus the 'public service' and the media.

such as personal honesty, institutional checks and balances, regulation, and market changes.[7]

This 'standard' approach is much narrower than the classical, more 'political economy', 'institutional-evolutionary', perspectives of corruption emanating from Plato, Aristotle, Polybius, Ibn Khaldun, Machiavelli, Bilingbroke, Montesquieu, Rousseau, Ferguson, and others discussed earlier. A series of modern classical approaches to corruption, as mentioned, have been developing in the last decade that seek to be pragmatic and policy-oriented while keeping the philosophical tradition of having a holistic approach, a systemic view of the problem, plus an 'immoral, unjust and dysfunctional' scrutiny of corrupt practices. The expanding empirical and theoretical work on public, corporate, non-profit, macro-micro, and organizational corruption etc has enabled this new modern classical view to evolve and become more sophisticated and empirically–based over recent years. Such an evolving view is really a form of institutional-evolutionary economics, or at least is easily grafted onto this political economy tradition.

The *first* main characteristic of modern classical approaches to corruption is that they tend to see the dominant contradiction as between the elite(s) who control the commanding heights of economy, polity and society and the common people who on average have barely enough to survive; with perhaps the middle class declining proportionately in numbers recently while some slip into the lower classes (in the Core) or alternatively increasing in relative size (e.g., in China; parts of the Semi-Periphery). Elites engage in grand corruption through the mechanisms of bribery, extortion, fraud, embezzlement, patronage, undue influence, lobbying, and so on, which enhances their share of economic surplus as well as other material/immaterial benefits that accrue to them through the systemic organization/distribution of power.

This modern institutional-evolutionary, classical view of corruption starts with the basic contradiction between the common good and corruption by sectional or selfish interests—or *The Vested Interests and the Common Man*, as Thorstein Veblen (1919) called it—illustrated below in Fig. 6.2:[8]

---

[7]Rose-Ackerman's research seems to support the private ruling elites. This is because in principal she accepts corruption emanating from any combination of private-public type agents or organizations (and other sectors), but she chooses mostly to only look at "public corruption" (similar to Heidenheimer, in this sense), even while we know that such a category usually operates in concert with the private sector (See Rose-Ackerman 1999, 2006; Rose-Ackerman and Soreide 2011).

[8]This diagram is similar to many I have included in other articles including, for instance, O'Hara (2012a, b, 2023: ch 7). The contradiction between the common good and the vested interests is also described in words in very similar ways (to my diagram) by several articles in Barcham et al. (2012): see especially papers by Mulgan (2012) on the common good v. sectional (or selfish) interests; Buchan (2012) on finance capital v. industrial or landowning capital; and Hill (2012) on social interests v. individual interests. The current writer is researching a paper on the common good versus the vested interests, dealing with various perspectives, such as the earlier and later classical schools; Veblen's (1919) analysis of *The Vested Interests and the Common Man*, in terms of waste of economic surplus etc; plus Chomsky (2002), Daly and Cobb (1994), Lutz (1998) and Williams and Houck (1987).

6.2 Contradictions of Corruption, Heterogeneous Groups and Uneven Development

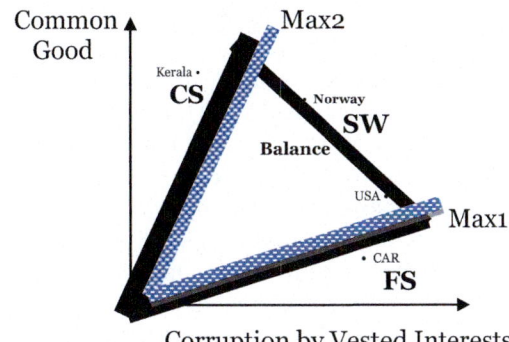

Fig. 6.2 Corruption by vested interests versus the common good. (*Source:* Adapted from O'Hara 2012a: 15, 2012b: 12, 2023: ch 7)

The principle of uncertainty has some relevance to the issue of the vested interest and the common good. This is because the figure has 'bars' rather than 'lines', the bars representing degrees of *uncertainty* or *informational anomalies* (indeterminacy). Information is thus usually imperfect about the precise distribution of resources, or social opportunity costs, involving the forces of the common good versus corruption by the vested interests. There are three bars traversing the triangular area. The first is a social wealth (SW) bar, where resources and economic surplus are distributed variously for the common good or corrupted by the vested interests. Expansions of social wealth push the SW bar outwards in the N/E direction; decreases pull it inwards in the S/W direction.

The second bar is the Max1 bar, which has a dotted bar of medium cyclical instability, and a black bar of great structural instability. As corruption increases from moderately large to extreme, instability thus increases through the dotted to the solid-black bar of Max1. Operating in the solid black bar of Max1 the common good is so lacking that structural socioeconomic crises set in due to a massive misallocation of resources from corruption; as corruption heightens, usually leading to a movement inwards of the SW bar (declining social wealth). The crisis may generate a worse result, promoting the vested interests more, moving beyond Max1 into the area of the "failed state" (FS). Possibly currently the Central African Republic (CAR) and North Korea are in this FS state. Or otherwise social and political change may reduce corruption back into relative balance. The United States and several other Core nations (among others), for instance, over the past several decades have likely periodically moved into the dotted Max1 bar through speculative bubble rises and crashes as fraudulent accounting techniques, tax havens (and influence politics) take hold during cyclical changes in the economy, especially during the GFC (2008–2010ff).

On the other hand, if social wealth is distributed to the common good away from the vested interests by major reductions in corruption (for instance, by movements along the SW bar to the N/W region), eventually this redistribution becomes so great that it is likely to generate a sociopolitical crisis of legitimacy as the vested interests fight to regain their presumed 'rightful place'; reaching bar Max2. A moderate crisis is likely when the less extreme dotted Max2 bar is reached; and a more intense one when the economy moves into the solid black Max2 bar. When such crises operate, the SW bar moves inwards since some degree of SW has been destroyed or its utilization reduced. Reducing the power of the vested interests to an extreme level in the short run at least will likely lead to socioeconomic instability, unless the common good can manage to emerge institutionally with few vested interests or new ones that accept the innovative change.

This is consistent with the *principle of minimal dislocation* (Bush 1983), namely, that a process that needs great attention in political economy is that sudden change can generate instability even if the changes are instrumentally dominant and consistent with the common good in the abstract. Thus, a major reduction in corruption through expansions of the common good need to provide alternative structures of collective power to satisfactorily substitute for the old elites and moguls; whereby a new communitarian system (CS) may emerge. Possibly the state of Kerala in India is currently in this CS area (though it is unlikely to have been inside the triangular area in recent history).

So long as political economies are operating not too close to the two crisis bars (Max1, Max2 x 2), and are relatively close to the SW bar (inside the triangle), they have at least a semblance of relative balance or dynamic stability. The reason for this large area of relative balance or dynamic stability is simply that all extant societies have elites and Moguls, and the purpose of 'conventional policy' is to get the quantitative and qualitative balance "right" between these forces, for the survival of current regimes.

Aside from during crisis periods, Norway is shown in Fig. 6.2 to be characteristically on the 'progressive' side of this triangle, since it tends to have a more instrumental workings of its institutions (supporting the common good more); while the US is on the 'regressive' side, since it tends typically to have a greater degree of ceremonial encapsulation of its institutions (invidious distinctions supporting elites).

Secondly, relevant to the principle of heterogeneous groups and agents, in the modern classical perspective, there is a heterogeneous geography of corruption, with differential patterns and processes occurring at the global, regional, national, subnational, systemic, institutional, local, micro, private, public and private-public levels; also involving non-profit institutions, civil society groups, families, elites, classes, ethnic groups, genders, associations, universities, and so on. *Social dominance theory*, an approach based on Sidanius and Pratto (1999), which seems similar to Dugger (1989, 1996), is useful for understanding the workings of elites and how corruption operates through hierarchical systems of power and authority within the regimes of accumulation through various styles of corruption. Organizational corruption is the 'misuse of power or position for personal or organizational gain' for the benefit of various elites and hierarchical agents. These organizations can include companies, states, groups, other institutions, and so on. As Valarie Rosenblatt (2012: 238) states, "institutional environments structured as hierarchies promoting power or status inequalities may compel individuals and organizations to get to the top by any means possible, in the process overlooking moral norms and values", or creating new ones through various niches or more generally. 'Cultures endorsing hierarchy

6.2 Contradictions of Corruption, Heterogeneous Groups and Uneven Development

and power inequality tend to have higher levels of corruption' (this is 'stylized fact four'; more on this in the next section).

Rosenblatt also argues that human beings "tend to organize their world around systems of group-based social hierarchies consisting of dominant and subordinate groups" (p. 238), and varying levels of dominance and subordinance within certain groups or institutions. People have social power based around membership of various groups or institutions. Engrained in the dynamic functioning of these groups or institutions are certain practices and relationships, which are variously thought necessary to the realization of their objectives and measured outcomes: such as profit, interest, rent, fees, output, contracts, revenue, salaries, bonuses, wages, costs, services provided, student numbers, research monies, position in 'league table', 'winning' a race or contract, etc.

Agents and institutions may abuse their power in the pursuit of these objectives or measured outcomes. This is 'corruption', which comprises various means of promoting outcomes, such as forms of bribery, fraud, extortion, embezzlement, nepotism, favoritism, and so on, against the common good but in pursuit of these objectives. Thus, 'socially dominant individuals, who believe that they belong to superior groups of people, are likely to be less aware of organizational corruption by feeling that they are more entitled to the use of power at the expense of others to get ahead and to maintain their dominant positions" (Rosenblatt 2012: 238). Rosenblatt further argues that "members of subordinate groups are also likely to have lower awareness of corruption when they show more favoritism and support for the members of the more powerful groups to increase their sense of worth and to preserve social order" (p. 238). Subordinates are not only subject to the negativities of the elitist actions of the dominant individuals and groups but also actively contribute to this subordination through their own elite-supporting beliefs and actions.

Corruption is thus a "dynamically integrating system", part of a mode of regulation, "coordinated by legitimizing beliefs, values, ideologies, rules and norms, which are jointly developed by individuals and institutions and mediate the relationship between the individual support of group-based hierarchies and the awareness of organization corruption" (p. 239). There are various social stratification systems: age groups, gender groups, classes, estates, tribes, ethnic groups, plus organizational-functioning groups. Within and between these groupings are various distortions such as stereotyping, discrimination, prejudice, favoritism and self-centered (group) behaviors. These distortions tend to influence decision-making behavior about the distribution of resources and positions, and often manifest as abuses of power that favor the vested interests against the common good. Objectives such as achieving a certain level or rate of profit, service provision, salary, productivity, etc are affected by these favoritisms and opportunisms.

Corruption is thus a form of unethical behavior and wrongdoing which is the outcome of abuse of power for individual or group benefit against the common good. It is usually an abuse or violation of *trust*, especially relating to the person who is entrusted to act in the interests of one party, but rather acts in another way to benefit the self or an(other) organization or person. Corruption is more common in certain sectors, such as energy-minerals-resources, military hard/software accounting, mutual funds, insurance, and the public-political sector (see 'stylized fact three' in the next section).

Thirdly, Michael Johnston's modern classical perspective enhances an understanding of systems of elite corruption through empirical work on the different *styles of corruption* throughout the world. Johnston's analysis of global differences in corruption styles provides critical knowledge of how elites generate their wealth and power through networks of corrupt relationships. Relevant to the principle of hegemony and uneven development, in his empirical study there are four major styles of corruption around the world that transcend individual continents and regions. However, since he has a strong intellectual link with Heidenheimer's analysis of so-called political corruption, Johnston has not generalized his view of systemic corruption, and therefore has a limited view of corporate corruption. For this reason, we have modified his first corruption style from simply "influence markets" to "influence, haven and speculative markets" corruption, as shown below in Table 6.3.

Corruption operates through various styles. Influence, haven and speculative markets corruption (e.g., USA, UK, Japan, etc) occurs especially in the advanced capitalist economies because money politics, tax havens and debt/fraud enable corporations to use their muscle to extract resources and influence politicians/market prices, where institutions (elections, judiciary, legislative, executive, markets, corporations) are strong. Elite cartels corruption (e.g., Botswana, Greece, Italy, etc) occurs where there is social stability, somewhat weaker institutions, but where elite cartels are able to gain resources through being insulated from broader social powers. Oligarch and clan corruption (e.g., India, Mexico, Russia, etc) occurs because rapid social change and often privatization enable resources to be captured through protection rackets, loans for shares, and racketeering for the benefit of those with elite power. Official Moguls corruption (e.g., China, Egypt, Nigeria, etc) exists even with sometimes high growth through officials having few checks and balances in the form of a relatively inactive civil society, undemocratic politics and undeveloped counterveiling private sector power.

Johnston recognizes that corruption involves various types of relationships between the private and public sectors (and civil society): some closely linked, some interfused, some more distant. His analysis also shows that corruption clearly exists in the private sector in all of these cases.[9] Styles of systemic corruption are thus not isolated, but open up a general discourse on the relationship between corruption, wealth and development, where "corruption is indeed a symptom of deeper and broader development problems and imbalances" (Johnston 1998: 94).

---

[9] Yet Johnston refuses to *explicitly* include as corruption that which operates in the private sector, for instance, in the wake of the corporate fraud and lack of due diligence exhibited through the corporate crises of the early 2000s and the subprime crisis of 2008–2010. He thinks this can easily be included as 'fraud' rather than corruption (yet we know that fraud is one form of corruption).

6.2 Contradictions of Corruption, Heterogeneous Groups and Uneven Development

Table 6.3 Four styles of elite corruption in the world, Circa 2000s

Style	Nations	Main features of corruption style
Influence, Haven & Speculative Market Corruption [ISMC]	US, UK, Germany, Japan, Costa Rica, Uruguay, etc.	1. Wealth is used for influence where institutions are strong; 2. System accommodates political/economic elites; 3. Political donations are less risky for favors to private interests; 4. Speculative fraud, bubbles and tax havens are engrained in the system; 5. Companies have too much power/influence. 6. Politicians do special favors in exchange for campaign contributors. 7. Public-private-legal access points proliferate for favors & fraud.
Elite Cartels Corruption [ECC]	Botswana, Greece, Italy, Poland, Portugal, South Korea, Spain, etc.	1. Centralized & stable ECC enriches top politicians, business people, bureaucrats, military & ethnic leaders; 2. ECC is a substitute for somewhat weaker institutions; 3. ECC benefits are insulated from electoral/social pressures; 4. Political parties embody elite followers rather than broad social groups.
Oligarchs & Clans Corruption [OCC]	Bulgaria, Columbia, India, Malaysia, Mexico, Pakistan, Philippines, Russia, etc.	1. OCC power is both private & public & links organized crime, officials & politicians; 2. OCC functions to protect and ensure predictability in very uncertain environments/very weak institutions; 3. Black markets, protection rackets, violence and electoral fraud are common; 4. OCC is a symptom of rapid change, low social *trust* & insecurity.
Official Moguls Corruption [OMC]	China, Egypt, Gabon, Iran, Kenya, Nigeria, Oman, etc.	1. OMC is caused by ultra-weak checks/balances against officials from democratic politics, civil society & private sector; 2. Often OMC coexists with high growth as it enhances corrupt windfalls; 3. Often strong anti-corruption agenda by state targeted at officials; 4. Usually OMC occurs under one-party rule.

Source: Based on Johnston (1998, 2005, 2008, 2012; modified due to ISMC)

Within each style there are often rather large differences in levels of corruption from nation to nation. This leads us below to the empirical section on different levels of corruption within and between Core, Periphery and Semi-Periphery.

6.3 Uneven Development of Corruption

IEPE throughout most of its history has been keen to analyze the complexities of socioeconomic performance through historical time, especially the asymmetric relationship between Core (C), Periphery (P) and Semi-Periphery (SP) through the world system (CPSP). The work of, especially, Paul Baran, Stephen Hymer, Andre Gunder Frank, Jane Rendall, Immanuel Wallerstein, Samir Amin, Beth Caniglia, and Amitava Krishna Dutt, has been crucial for investigating these uneven forces through the world. In the institutionalist tradition, the work of Thorstein Veblen (1915, 1917), plus James Street, Ilene Grabel, James Dietz, Dilmus James, Ha-Joon Chang, and James Cypher—has been at the forefront of these themes. The *principle of hegemony and uneven development* states that IEPE needs to emphasize that C-P-SP areas tend to undergo differential performance, due to unequal power relations involved in trade, production, finance and state; as the world economy is subject to uneven forces of elites, hegemons and subordinates due to centripetal processes, production networks, commodity chains, and value chains differentially affecting the various groups and areas.

The empirical literature on corruption is replete with examples of this unevenness as the process of wealth generation, distribution and exchange impact differentially on bribery, embezzlement, extortion, fraud, theft, nepotism, abuse of discretion, favoritism and improper political contributions throughout the world. Not only is the degree of systemic corruption quantitatively different globally, regionally, nationally and subnationally, but the way in which systemic corruption manifests itself qualitatively is substantially different through various styles of corruption in different areas (as we saw above). Also, very good time series data for corruption are lacking, since successive yearly Corruption Perceptions Index (CPI) levels are said to be *not comparable;* multiple year data for corporate corruption is very limited; and good data for other sectors is virtually non-existent.

The *first 'stylized fact'* about corruption throughout the world is that *perceived* 'political and public corruption' (shown as $P_{\ddot{u}}$) tends to be negatively related to the level of human development. Nations lower in human development tend to have higher levels of $P_{\ddot{u}}$ than those higher in development. Data for the CPI (where *perceived* corruption is lowest at 100 and highest at 0), compared with the Human Development Index (HDI; where development is highest at 100 and lowest at 0), from numerous nations of the world are shown below in Table 6.4 for 2012.

There is no *strict* correspondence between *apparently* similar figures for CPI and HDI (eg, CPI of 43 and HDI of 0.43). Core nations are defined as those with a HDI of 0.8 and above; Semi-Periphery includes nations with HDI between 0.6 and 0.79; while the Periphery refers to countries with a HDI of below 0.60. Core nations also tend to have levels of CPI of above 60; Semi-Peripheral nations tend to have CPIs between 30 and 60; while Peripheral states tend to have CPI levels below 30. The 36 nations thus have Core, Semi-Periphery and Periphery identified with both the HDI (the primary definition) and CPI (the secondary link).

The vast majority of nations included in Table 6.4 have close correspondence between CPI and HDI categories: e.g., if they are in the Core of HDI they also tend to

6.3 Uneven Development of Corruption

Table 6.4 CPI and HDI Correspondence, 2012, 36 Nations[a]

Country	CPI	HDI	CPI-HDI Corresp.	Country	CPI	HDI	CPI-HDI Corresp.
Denmark	90[C]	.90[C]	Yes	Italy	42[SP]	.88[C]	No
Singapore	87[C]	.90[C]	Yes	Serbia	39[SP]	.77[SP]	Yes
UK	74[C]	.88[C]	Yes	China	39[SP]	.70[SP]	Yes
Japan	74[C]	.91[C]	Yes	Greece	36[SP]	.86[C]	No
USA	73[C]	.94[C]	Yes	India	36[SP]	.55[P]	No
Chile	72[C]	.82[C]	Yes	Bolivia	34[SP]	.68[SP]	Yes
Qatar	68[C]	.83[C]	Yes	Albania	33[SP]	.77[SP]	Yes
Botswana	65[C]	.63[SP]	No	Russia	28[P]	.79[SP]	No
Lithuana	54[SP]	.82[C]	No	Kazakhstan	28[P]	.75[SP]	No
Georgia	52[SP]	.75[SP]	Yes	Iran	28[P]	.74[SP]	No
Turkey	49[SP]	.72[SP]	Yes	Honduras	28[P]	.63[SP]	No
Cuba	48[SP]	.78[SP]	Yes	Kenya	27[P]	.52[P]	Yes
Oman	47[SP]	.73[SP]	Yes	Nigeria	27[P]	.47[P]	Yes
Slovakia	46[SP]	.84[C]	No	C.Afric.Rep	26[P]	.35[P]	Yes
Kuwait	44[SP]	.79[SP]	Yes	Cambodia	22[P]	.54[P]	Yes
Saudi Arabia	44[SP]	.78[SP]	Yes	Zimbabwe	20[P]	.40[P]	Yes
South Africa	43[SP]	.63[SP]	Yes	Iraq	18[P]	.59[P]	Yes
Brazil	43[SP]	.73[SP]	Yes	Myanmar	15[P]	.50[P]	Yes

Source: Adapted from TI (2013a), UNDP (2013)
Note: The method for including nations is as follows: 36 nations were chosen; including 6 nations randomly chosen from each region (min. 2m. population):—(i) EU/W.Europe, (ii) E. Europe/Central Asia, (iii) Middle East & North Africa (MENA), (iv) Sub-Saharan Africa (SSA), (v) Asia Pacific, (vi) Americas
[a]CPI is calculated from 13 data sources (see TI 2013a), and TI (2013b) states that 2012 is the first year they have calculated CPI so that future years will be comparable with 2012 (hence previous years are not comparable with 2012 nor likely with other years). CPI is based on perceptions of corruption in the public sector (ignoring crucial links with the private sector), based on questions and interviews answered/given by 'corruption experts' and 'business analysts'. CPI is standardized so that the index runs from 0 (highest level of corruption possible) to 100 (lowest level of corruption possible) (TI 2013c, d). Data used (for 2012) must be 'trustworthy'; comparable between nations and likely to be available for future years; and a standard error and confidence interval are utilized/calculated (TI 2013e). The better known HDI, on the other hand, is a composite index of education, standard of living and health, based on a 'wide variety of international data providers'; with supplementary indices provided for the inequality-adjusted HDI, gender inequality index and multidimensional-poverty index (UNHD 2013)

be in the Core of CPI. It shows a very strong propensity for the Periphery to have higher levels of *perceived* public-political corruption than the Semi-Periphery; with the Semi-Periphery having higher *perceptions* of public-political corruption than the Core. This type of general tendency has consistently been observed in the empirical literature through numerous studies.[10] Thus we generally find high levels of

---
[10] E.G., see Jong-sung and Khagram (2005), McFerson (2009), Cockcroft (2010), and O'Connor and Fischer (2012).

perceived 'public corruption' in most Peripheral low-HDI nations of sub-Saharan Africa and South Asia; somewhat lower *perceptions* of corruption in Semi-Peripheral, medium-HDI areas of Eastern Europe (to some degree), the Middle East, North Africa, South/West Asia and South America; and comparatively low *perceptions* of public corruption in Core, high-HDI areas of North America, Western Europe and Japan.

Exceptions to this tendency exist, of course, for those nations with less correspondence between HDI and CPI. These exceptions include [i] higher levels of *perceived* public corruption (PPC) in Italy and Greece than expected for such 'Peripheral nations of the Core'; [ii] India which has lower levels of PPC than is usual for a Peripheral nation (although India is more of a 'dual nation' than most); [iii] some nations of Eastern Europe (such as Lithuania and Slovakia) which have HDIs corresponding with Core levels but CPIs more typical of the Semi-Periphery; [iv] some nations of Eastern Europe plus some nations of West Asia/Middle East and Central America (such as Russia, Kazakhstan, Iran and Honduras) that are in the Semi-Periphery of development but correspond to higher (Peripheral) levels of PPC; and [v] the special case of Botswana in sub-Saharan Africa, which is in the Semi-Periphery of development but has lower (Core) levels of PPC.

Typically, Peripheral areas per se have higher *perceived* levels of 'political-public' corruption due to 'grand corruption' on the part of elites, whether monarchs, military dictatorships or nepotistic families and networks, as they embezzle tens or hundreds of millions of dollars and receive bribes from powerful transnational corporations, with money being effectively laundered through Swiss banks in association with enabling corporate networks and friendly governments. As their heads of state are abusing their power by extracting the economic surplus for their own private benefit, the 'common people' of these nations tend to suffer from low wages, paltry standard of living and few effective public services such as education, health and infrastructure. This stimulates 'petty corruption' as bureaucrats, police and many others seek to have an adequate remuneration by supplementing their usually paltry income levels through bribes, fraud, extortion and any other means at their disposal.

Most of those interviewed for the 13 data sources used in generating the 2012 CPI were so-called senior private sector 'experts', 'business analysts' and 'executives' who would have interpreted 'corruption' in their own biased fashion. The CPI data for 2012, however, by no means necessarily provides a good proxy for *purely* public-political corruption. One reason for this is that many of the 13 data sources used include components dealing with dual *private*-public corruption. For instance, the 1st (African Development Bank Governance Ratings) and 11th (World Bank—Country Policy and Institutional Assessment) data sources used by TI, include questions dealing with "state capture by narrow vested interests" (e.g., elite families, business firms, transnational corporations). Most of the data sources deal with bribes paid by business for political-public benefits. The 9th data source (Political Risk Services Country Risk Guide) dealt with "close ties between politics and business", while the 12th data source (World Economic Forum Executive Opinion Survey) included "diversion of public funds to companies, individuals and groups" (p. 12).

6.3 Uneven Development of Corruption

Many of the papers critiquing the CPI have discussed these and other types of problems (See TI 2013b).[11]

While the CPI is problematic on public corruption, it is also not a good indicator of private corruption. The CPI underestimates the extent of *private*-to-public corruption and abstracts entirely from *private-to-private* (e.g., corporate-to-corporate) corruption. Corporations with head office in the Core have been notorious for playing substantive roles in the abuse of power, such that calling it 'political corruption' is really a misnomer as the complementary and coevolving sectors of state and corporation play interactive roles in its generation. The *supply of financially networked resources* (e.g., money) by companies is just as important as the *demand for financially networked benefits* (e.g., money) by political leaders and bureaucrats in this multi-sector process of corrupt redistribution.

This leads us to the *second stylized fact*, that corporate-financial corruption is currently quite high in the Core (and some other areas), especially North America and Europe; and likely been on the rise in recent decades. The 1980s–2010s period has been an era of financial, labor market and capital flow deregulation along with more flexible systems of production-distribution; in short, an increase in corporate power. Early signs of corruption involved the speculative excesses of the mid-to-late 1980s through to the stock market crash of 1987 onto the recession of the early 1990s. More extreme signs of corruption emerged with the speculative bubble and crash of the late 1990s and early 2000s, in the US especially with the corporate crises; and before and during the GFC and Eurodebt crises of 2008–2013ff. In Eastern Europe during the 1990s–2000s the experience of privatization and wholesale laundering/embezzling of citizens' bank accounts similarly saw a rise in corporate corruption, and a re-organization of public corruption.

Transparency International (TI) started collecting statistics in the mid-1990s on the results of questionnaires of mostly corporate experts and managers for corruption in the 'public sector'. As the literature expanded and knowledge grew it became more obvious that even this form of corruption included the private sector, e.g., often a corporate manager pays a public sector official or Head of State a bribe (*private*-to-public corruption). Critiques of TI data have become commonplace, which has made TI improve their methods, especially by including corporate corruption in their analysis, even if at this stage very imperfectly (see TI 2009). The earlier empirical and theoretical material on corporate corruption had taken a subtle form through the notion of 'business as a system of power' (e.g., Robert Brady 1943) and later work on 'corporate hegemony' (e.g., William Dugger 1989 who explicitly describes "corporate corruption"; p. 149), followed by detailed material on corporate corruption.

Marshall B. Clinard's (1990) *Corporate Corruption: The Abuse of Power* documented extensive abuse of power in car manufacturing, oil, drug manufacture

---

[11] Good critiques of the TI framework of corruption include the work of William De Maria (2008), Asad Zamon and Faiz-Ur-Rahim (2009), Maks Kobonbaev et al. (2009), Alan Doig (2011) and Jonathan Murphy (2011).

and defense sectors as well as by transnational corporations in the third world. The theoretical underpinnings of this book were underplayed while the emphasis was given to case study type evidence and examples. Antonio Argandona (2003) has done some good scholarly work on "private-to-private" (P_f—P_f) corruption, including bribery, fraud, extortion, nepotism, and so forth between private agents (e.g., within and between corporations). A lot of work has recently been done on private corruption in the wake of the boom and bust linked to corporate crises (1990s to early 2000s) and the foundations of the 'subprime crisis', GFC, Eurodebt crises, and their aftermath (2007 to mid-2010s) especially in the USA and Europe (e.g., Joseph LaPalombara 2004; Peter Fleming and Stelios Zyglidopoulos 2009; Judeen Bartos 2012; Stephen Arbogast 2013).

Some (only) of these dimensions of corporate corruption come under the umbrella of Daniel Kaufman's (2004) empirical study which was the first attempt to make detailed cross-sectional estimates of corporate corruption around the world. Table 6.5, below, summarizes elements of his data, corporate compared with public corruption. The indices move from 0 to 100; the closer to zero the higher the corruption; the closer to 100 the lower is corruption.

These data reveal several things about global corruption. Firstly, some Core economies perform badly on legal corporate corruption, and some perform badly on illegal corporate corruption. For instance, the US has substantial legal corruption (especially concerning political funding and undue influence) and not-so-good levels of illegal corruption (illegal political funding, state capture, banking fraud, procurement bribery). Secondly, Italy's levels of both corporate *and* public sector corruption

Table 6.5 Corporate Corruption (CC) & Public Corruption (PC), Circa 2003, 0–100

Region	Nation	A: Illegal CC Index	B: Legal CC Index	C: Legal Effect. Index	D: Public Sector Ethics Index
Core	Denmark	97	75	95	94
	UK	93	67	92	80
	USA	84	31	84	70
	Italy	47	34	41	34
Semi-Periphery	Botswana	54	47	60	56
	Brazil	51	20	42	35
	China	44	49	42	42
	Russia	20	21	16	20
Periphery	Zimbabwe	45	37	16	20
	Nigeria	23	29	27	15
	Pakistan	22	24	5	10
	Honduras	24	11	18	17

Source: Adapted from Kaufman (2004: Appendix)
Note:
A = Includes illegal political funding; state capture; banking; procurement
B = Includes legal political funding; undue political influence
C = Includes judicial independence; bribery; parliamentary effectiveness; police effectiveness
D = Includes honesty of politicians; procurement practices; bribery

are high and more in line with what one would expected of a Semi-Peripheral nation; while Russia's level of corporate and public corruption is very high, being more like what one would expect of a Peripheral nation, as even Zimbabwe has better levels of corporate governance.

While Kaufman's data does apparently include banking fraud in the illegal corruption category, as mentioned crucial variables linked to, for instance, the *causes* of the 'corporate crises' (of the early 2000s in the US etc.) and subprime crisis, GFC, Eurodebt crisis and their aftermath (2008–2014) are abstracted from. For instance, abstracted from are "private-to-private" (P_f—P_f) corruption through accounting fraud in industrial or service corporate sectors; CEO remuneration above the long term rate of profit or dividend rate (fundamentals) based on accounting fraud and bubbles; the rising rate of expansion of collateralized debt obligations where the debt to finance them is hidden in various corporate vehicles independently of the core business accounts; and the activities of accountants, lawyers, bankers and officials involved in tax havens that contribute to the laundering of third world grand corruption funds. These typical abuses of power and dysfunctional financial processes contributed majorly to the corporate crises and the subprime crises; which were against the common good in propelling unjust, immoral, and unaccountable practices benefiting the vested interests and classes that dominate the socioeconomic and political environment; or otherwise being reckless cases of "impropriety" and "dereliction of duty" (which are important to the Chinese vision of corruption, see Kilkon Ko and Cuifen Weng 2011; Park 1997; albeit for the public sector).

The Tax Justice Network (TJN 2012) estimates that between US$21 and US$32 trillion in unreported funds are sheltered through tax havens worldwide—the lower figure representing the combined GDP of USA and Japan. John Christensen (2011) demonstrates that with this huge unreported income in offshore accounts, the core economies, such as the UK, US, Switzerland and Singapore, would be counted among the top ten corruptors. The organization of such tax havens is said to be led by specialists from the World's largest banks, such as USB, Credit Suisse, Goldman Sachs, Bank of America and HSBC (TJN, p. 6). Tax havens contribute to fraudulent corporate and personal income, receipts, costs and tax reporting, playing a major role in the Special Purpose Vehicles' off balance sheet and other activities involved in the subprime crisis and GFC. Tax havens provide a platform for lax regulation, minimal taxation on income and capital, plus secret facilities whereby information is hidden from third party authorities. They enable extensive tax dodging, illicit political donations, insider trading, fraud, embezzlement, bribery and the commissioning of kickbacks. Their proliferation has been aided and abetted by neoliberal capital market liberalization, privatization, greater globalization and expansion of information and computer technology. They are dysfunctional for the efficient and equitable workings of global governance since they reduce tax receipts of governments, misallocate investment, inhibit social innovation, reduce public infrastructure, reward free riders and increase global inequality.

Tax havens and their associated global financial networks enable global and regional corrupt elites to operate more freely (Christensen 2011). They enable corporations engaged in fraudulent banking and accounting practices to hide their secrets and gain higher net profit. They enable international banks to launder monies embezzled by third world oligarchs, for instance, for buying expensive real estate in luxurious locations and amassing huge bank deposits. They enable whole industries of corrupt accountants, financiers, lawyers, influence peddlers, lobbyists, politicians and public servants to appear respectable and law abiding citizens. They finance governments and organizations committed to the free flow of finance to enhance their elite position in politics and business. They also undermine and corrupt the just, moral and equitable workings of business and government by reproducing hidden modes of regulation and power.

All this questions the *perceptions* behind stylized fact one that total corruption (public, private, non-profit, etc) is lower in the core than the periphery and semi-periphery, and that the core has a better governing structure to prevent corruption than the other areas.

This leads to the *third stylized fact* about corruption, namely, that certain sectors and nations/regions have become infamous for leading the charge of elite private-public grand corruption. These include especially (for the sectors) [i] extractive resources, [ii] military hardware/software (including aerospace), [iii] construction, and [iv] finance. These four sectors are big players in the corruption game because they involve huge sums of money, large capital investments and complex financial arrangements with large banks and other institutions. For instance, Hazel McFerson (2009) documents the 'resource curse' involving the expropriation of the oil and mineral resource surpluses as grand corruption by the ruling elites (and associated benefits to corporations) in Angola, the Democratic Republic of Congo, the Republic of Congo, Equatorial Guinea, Gabon and Nigeria. Such corruption is possible through an array of vertical power relations; transfers of resources from public sector asset to ruling elite properties; money laundering through corporate vehicles, including Western corporate assistance and Swiss banks; scholarships and medical amenities; ruling family business monopolies; and a massive misallocation of funds which inhibits industrial development.

The World Bank has developed a 'Grand Corruption Case Studies Database', associated with their publication *The Puppet Masters: How the Corrupt use Legal Structures to Hide Stolen Assets and What to Do about It* (de Willebois et al. 2011). In this study, a conscious effort was made to include cases from all regions to make it at least moderately representative of reality. This database is for 150 grand corruption legal cases that went before the courts, 112 of which were transnational schemes (where the bribe money supply-nation source was different from the demand-nation source), total funds 'laundered' being US$56.4 billion, with 118 people charged and/or convicted. All cases involved the "misuse of at least one corporate vehicle", where the origin of beneficiary was hidden to protect the main culprit or entity. The lowest threshold for inclusion was $1million (or 'equivalent'), 15 cases were less than $1m but equivalent; 67 involved between US$1m-US$20m, and 68 involving more than US$20m. Table 6.6, below, summarizes the nature of these corporate vehicles associated with the corruption case studies:

Two main conclusions emerge from this study. The first is a conclusion made by several empirical studies, namely, that most of the money laundered to hide the

6.3 Uneven Development of Corruption

Table 6.6 Corporate vehicles involved in grand corruption. jurisdictions, 1980–2010

	No. of corporate vehicles in jurisdiction of incorporation	No. of corporate vehicles in jurisdiction of bank account
US	102	107
Switzerland	7	76
UK	24	19
Nigeria	20	17
Bahamas	27	18
Cyprus	11	15
Hong Kong	24	14
Antigua & Barbuda	n.a.	11
Jersey	12	11
Leichtenstein	28	10

Source: Adapted from de Willebois et al. (2011: 121–122)

beneficiary through grand corruption is done via corporations with head office in powerful states such as the US and UK, even though a considerable number of small island/state tax havens are also involved. And secondly, some nations (such as Leichtenstein, in Central Europe) specialize in corporate vehicles in jurisdiction of incorporation, and rely on other nations to deal with the banking procedures required; while the opposite is the case for some nations (such as Switzerland), which specialize in jurisdiction of bank account rather than incorporation. The US has a large number of corporate vehicles in both jurisdiction of incorporation and bank account in these corruption cases.

The *fourth stylized fact* is linked to the *principle of circular and cumulative causation* (CCC; see Berger 2009). CCC states that political economy analysis should include two aspects of motion; the first being one of interdependency between factors, and thus a multi-variant investigation; and the second is that these interdependencies tend to generate multiplier and accelerator-type impacts through historical time. SF4 states that income inequality enables higher levels of corruption while corruption in turn stimulates (further) inequality, leading often to a vicious circle of poverty and corruption for many nations (and a virtuous circle in low corruption areas). Numerous studies support this. For instance, You Jong-sung and Sanjeev Khagram (2005) demonstrate that in highly unequal societies the rich will have more resources to buy influence through legal and illegal channels (high-end grand corruption) while the poor will have greater need to engage in petty corruption to enhance their paltry income. This reciprocal relationship between inequality and corruption holds for Core, Periphery and Semi-Periphery in their 129 nation sample; as "internal" uneven developments (between elite classes, ethnicities, genders, regions, institutions) are exacerbated within nations. Corruption produces outcomes preferred by the rich, whether it be poor nations subject to grand corruption by the elites and petty corruption by lower orders, or "skyrocketing CEO compensation in the United States, which was supposed to align the interests of CEOs with those of shareholders, [but which] not only increased income inequality but also stimulated corporate corruption as the recent scandals demonstrate" (p. 154).

Thus corruption is quite high in Core nations that have large income inequalities, such as the USA and parts of Europe (and elsewhere that inequality is high). Corruption fundamentally represents an abuse of position or role for private benefits (monetary or otherwise) against the common good. As the classical school argued, corruption is associated with problems of governance which manifest themselves and indeed are caused by insufficient virtue, unproductive activities, and unjust arrangements that have dysfunctional impacts on socioeconomic and political performance.

6.4 Conclusion

This chapter invoked the principles of innovation and policy/governance by developing a framework of systemic corruption by which to analyze and renew governance measures against such practices.

We started with the principle of historical specificity, examining the evolution of the concept of corruption from the classical scholars through to the theological view, and then going on to scrutinize developments occurring during the Enlightenment, the Renaissance, the emergence of liberalism, capitalism and socialism to the present day. We find that modern classical approaches have been developed with considerable attention to empirical and institutional evidence and theory; through linking systemic corruption to more empirical matters such as the rise of the modern state, corporate power, non-profit organizations, elite families and other institutions.

From there we scrutinized the principle of contradiction, including the contradictory nature of systemic corruption, including the trade-offs and relationships between the vested interests and the common good. Systemic corruption is thus defined as the abuse of power for private benefit against the common good through the actions of bribery, fraud, extortion, embezzlement, state capture, nepotism, etc.

The principle of heterogeneous groups and agents encapsulates social dominance theory to explain how elites manage grand corruption while subordinates support elites and practice petty corruption to promote their image/standard of living.

The principle of uneven development is applied to systemic corruption involving different styles depending on geopolitics, ranging from influence, haven and speculative market corruption (especially in the Core) through to elite cartels corruption (in the Periphery of the Core and other places), onto oligarch and clan corruption (in especially transitional and Semi-Peripheral nations), through to official Mogul corruption (in places like China, Iran and Egypt). A modern institutional-evolutionary view of corruption was outlined.

Lastly we explored a number of stylized facts (SF) about corruption throughout the world, also relevant to uneven development. The first SF is that *perceived* levels of "public-political corruption" tend to be inversely related to the degree of development. It is said to be higher in the Periphery than the Semi-Periphery, and higher in the Semi-Periphery than the Core. However, SF1 is a *misperception*. The second SF is that corporate–financial corruption has increased in the Core capitalist economies (plus numerous others) over the past few decades as privatization, deregulation, corporate crises and subprime crisis reveal a high degree of corporate fraud, state capture and influence politics. The third SF is that certain sectors and nations have been notably at the centre of recent corruption trends, including extractive resources, military hardware/software, construction and corporate–finance; plus the United States, UK, many other Core nations and some small nation states/islands. The fourth SF involves heterogeneous groups in that corruption engenders greater inequality in society while the greater inequality stimulates more corruption, and so on, consistent also with the principle of circular and cumulative causation.

Uneven development is also relevant to the evidence that corruption is shown to be a major world problem that is often hidden and undertaken at high levels, in the Periphery and also the Core and Semi-Periphery. There are structural linkages between the corruption styles in the CPSP inquiry. The origins of corruption are multifarious, with different sectors being involved, especially resources, military hard/software, construction, finance and the public sector. The main problem is systemic corruption, which is endogenously engrained in the institutions, behavior and habits of elites (grand corruption) and subordinates (petty corruption) against the common good. To reduce corruption, more research is required on its systemic, multisectoral and heterogeneous-agent origins; how the common good can be promoted through changing cultures that protect elites in their single-minded pursuit of objectives such as profit, sales and revenue; and how subordinate groups may reduce their support for elites as a way of enhancing their own quality of life.

Acknowledgements This chapter was presented as the Presidential Address at the annual meetings of the Association for Evolutionary Economics (AFEE) in Philadelphia (at the ASSAs), 4 January 2014 (O'Hara 2014). Many thanks to William Dugger (1989, 1996), Geoffrey Hodgson and Shuxia Jiang (2007); plus questions, comments and/or organizational assistance–by Philip Arestis, Chris Brown, Wolfram Elsner, Kosta Josifidis, Anna Klimina, John Marangos, Fatme Myuhtar-May, Steve Pressman, Eric Hake, and Teresa Rowell.

References

Alvey, James E. 1998. Adam Smith's Three Strikes Against Commercial Society. *International Journal of Social Economics* 25 (9): 1425–1441.
Arbogast, Stephen V. 2013. *Resisting Corporate Corruption: Cases in Practical Ethics from Enron through the Financial Crisis*. New York: Wiley.
Argandona, Antonio. 2003. Private-to-Private Corruption. *Journal of Business Ethics* 47 (3): 253–267.
Ashforth, Blake E., Dennis A. Gioia, Sandra L. Robinson, and Linda K. Trevino. 2008. Introduction to Special Topic Forum: Re-Viewing Organizational Corruption. *Academy of Management Review* 33 (3): 670–684.
Barcham, Manuhuia, Barry Hindess, and Peter Larmour, eds. 2012. *Corruption: Expanding the Focus*, 53–71. Canberra: ANU E Press.
Bartos, Judeen. 2012. *At Issue: Corporate Corruption*. Detroit: Greenhaven Press.
Belousova, Veronica, Rajeev K. Goel, and Likka Korhonen. 2011. *Causes of Corruption in Russia: A Disaggregated Analysis*, BOFIT Discussion Paper 31. Tokyo: Bank of Finland: Institute for Economies in Transition.

Berger, Sebastian, ed. 2009. *The Foundations of Non-equilibrium Economics: The Principle of Circular and Cumulative Causation.* Oxford/New York: Routledge.

Brady, Robert A. 1943. *Business as a System of Power.* New Brunswick/London: Transaction Publishers, 2001.

Brennan, Andrew, and Jaslin Kalsi. 2015. Elephant Poaching and Ivory Trafficking Problems in Sub-Saharan Africa: An Application of O'Hara's Principles of Political Economy. *Ecological Economics* 120: 312–337.

Brown, Ed, and Jonathan Cloke. 2011. Critical Perspectives on Corruption: An Overview. *Critical Perspectives on International Business* 7 (2): 116–124.

Buchan, Bruce. 2012. Changing Contours of Corruption in Western Political Thought. In *Corruption: Expanding the Focus*, ed. Manuhuia Barcham, Barry Hindess, and Peter Larmour, 73–95. Canberra: ANU E Press.

Bush, Paul Dale. 1983. An Exploration of the Structural Characteristics of a Veblen-Ayres-Foster Defined Institutional Domain. *Journal of Economic Issues* 17 (1): 35–66.

Chomsky, Noam. 2002. *The Common Good.* New York: Odonian Press.

Christensen, John. 2011. The Looting Continues: Tax Havens and Corruption. *Critical Perspectives on International Business* 7 (2): 177–196.

Clinard, Marshall B. 1990. *Corporate Corruption: The Abuse of Power.* New York: Praeger.

Cockcroft, Laurence. 2010. Global Corruption: An Untamed Hydra. *World Policy Journal* Spring: 21–28.

Daly, Herman E., and John B. Cobb. 1994. *For the Common Good.* 2nd ed. Boston: Beacon Press.

De Maria, William. 2008. Measurements and Markets: Deconstructing the Corruption Perceptions Index. *International Journal of Public Sector Management* 21 (7): 777–797.

de Willebois, Emile van der Does, Emily M. Halter, Robert A. Harrison, Ji Won Park, and J.C. Sharman. 2011. *The Puppet Masters: How the Corrupt Use Legal Structures to Hide Stolen Assets and What to Do About It.* Washington, DC: World Bank.

Doig, Alan. 2011. Numbers, Words and KYC: Knowing Your Country and Knowing Your Corruption. *Critical Perspectives on International Business* 7 (2): 142–158.

Dugger, William. 1989. *Corporate Hegemony.* Westport: Greenwood Press.

———, ed. 1996. *Inequality: Radical Institutionalist Views on Race, Gender, Class and Nation.* London/Westport: Greenwood Press.

Fletcher, Clare, and Daniela Herrmann. 2012. *The Internationalisation of Corruption: Scale, Impact and Countermeasures.* Farnham: Gower Publishing.

Fleming, Peter, and Stelios C. Zyglidopoulos. 2009. *Charting Corporate Corruption: Agency, Structure and Escalation.* Cheltenham/Northampton: Edward Elgar.

Genaux, Maryvonne. 2004. Social Sciences and the Evolving Concept of Corruption. *Crime, Law and Social Change* 42: 13–24.

Glaeser, Edward, and Claudia Goldin. 2006. Corruption & Reform. In *Corruption and Reform: Lessons from America's Economic History*, ed. E.L. Glaeser and C. Goldin. Chicago: University of Chicago Press.

Groenendijk, Nico. 1997. Principal-Agent Model of Corruption. *Crime, Law and Social Change* 27: 207–229.

Heidenheimer, Arnold J. 2002. Perspectives on the Perception of Corruption. In *Political Corruption: Concepts and Contexts*, ed. Arnold J. Heidenheimer and Michael Johnston. New Brunswick: Transaction Publishers.

Heidenheimer, Arnold J., and Michael Johnston, eds. 2002. *Political Corruption: Concepts and Contexts.* 3rd ed. New Brunswick/London: Transaction Publishers.

Hill, Lisa. 2012. Ideas of Corruption in the Eighteenth Century: The Competing Conceptions of Adam Ferguson and Adam Smith. In *Corruption: Expanding the Focus*, ed. Manuhuia Barcham, Barry Hindess, and Peter Larmour, 97–112. Canberra: ANU E Press.

Hodgson, Geoffrey M., and Shuxia Jiang. 2007. The Economics of Corruption and the Corruption of Economics: An Institutionalist Perspective. *Journal of Economic Issues* 41 (4): 1043–1061.

Johnston, Michael. 1998. Fighting Systemic Corruption: Social Foundations for Institutional Reform. *European Journal of Development Research* 10: 85–104.
———. 2005. *Syndromes of Corruption: Wealth, Power, and Democracy.* Cambridge: Cambridge University Press.
———. 2008. Japan, Korea, the Philippines, China: Four Syndromes of Corruption. *Crime, Law and Social Change* 49: 205–223.
———. 2012. Corruption Control in the United States: Law, Values and the Political Foundations of Reform. *International Review of Administrative Sciences* 78 (2): 329–345.
Jong-sung, You, and Sanjeev Khagram. 2005. A Comparative Study of Inequality and Corruption. *American Sociological Review* 70 (1): 136–157.
Kapp, Karl William. 1978. *The Social Costs of Business Enterprise.* Nottingham: Spokesman Books. Revised and Expanded Edition.
Kaufman, Daniel. 2004. Corruption, Governance and Security: Challenges for the Rich Countries and the World. In *Global Competitiveness Report 2004/2005*, ed. M. Porter, K. Schwab, X. Sala-I-Martin, and A. Lopez-Claros, 83–102. London: Palgrave-Macmillan.
Ko, Kilkon, and Cuifen Weng. 2011. Critical Review of Conceptual Definitions of Chinese Corruption: A Formal–Legal Perspective. *Journal of Contemporary China* 20: 359–378.
Kokonbaev, Maks, Donald Jacobsen, and Sharon Eicher. 2009. Critiquing the Indicators of Corruption and Governance. In *Corruption in International Business: The Challenge of Cultural and Legal Diversity*, ed. Sharon Eicher. Farnham: Ashgate Publishing.
Langseth, Petter. 2006. *Measuring Corruption.* In *Measuring Corruption*, ed. C. Sampford, A. Shacklock, C. Connors, and F. Galtung, 7–44. London: Ashgate Publishing.
LaPolambara, Joseph. 2004. Corporate Corruption and Other Pathologies. *Journal of Future Studies* 8 (4): 61–74.
Lutz, Mark A. 1998. *Economics for the Common Good.* New York: Routledge.
McFerson, Hazel M. 2009. Governance and Hyper-Corruption in Resource-Rich African Countries. *Third World Quarterly* 30 (8): 1529–1548.
Mulgan, Richard. 2012. Aristotle on Legality and Corruption. In *Corruption: Expanding the Focus*, ed. Manuhuia Barcham, Barry Hindess, and Peter Larmour, 97–112. Canberra: ANU E Press.
Murphy, Jonathan. 2011. Capitalism and Transparency. *Critical Perspectives on International Business* 7 (2): 125–141.
Myrdal, Gunnar. 1968. Corruption—Its Causes and Effects. In *Asian Drama: An Inquiry into the Poverty of Nations, Volume II*, ed. G. Myrdal, 937–958. New York: Twentieth Century Fund.
O'Connor, Seini, and Ronald Fischer. 2012. Predicting Societal Corruption Across Time: Values, Wealth, or Institutional? *Journal of Cross-Cultural Psychology* 43 (4): 644–659.
O'Hara, Phillip Anthony. 1999. Contradictions. In *Encyclopedia of Political Economy*, ed. P.A. O'Hara, vol. 1, 140–143. London/New York: Routledge.
———. 2002. The Contemporary Relevance of the 'Critical Economic Systems' Approach to Political Economy in the Tradition of Marx, Veblen, Keynes and Schumpeter. *International Journal of Applied Economics and Econometrics* 10 (1): 126–150.
———. 2007. Principles of Institutional-Evolutionary Political Economy—Converging Themes from the Schools of Heterodoxy. *Journal of Economic Issues* 41 (1): 1–42.
———. 2012a. Principles of Political Economy Applied to Policy and Governance: Disembedded Economy, Contradictions, Circular Cumulation and Uneven Development. *Journal of Economic and Social Policy* 15 (1): 1–38. http://epubs.scu.edu.au/jesp/vol15/iss1/.
———. 2012b. Core General Principles of Political Economy. *Journal of Economic Analysis* 3 (1): 1–24.
———. 2014. Political Economy of Systemic and Micro-Corruption Throughout the World. *Journal of Economic Issues* 48 (2): 379–307. http://users.ntua.gr/jea/contents.htm.
———. 2023. *Long Wave Institutional Dynamics and Political Economy Crises of Capitalism: Principles, Social Structures of Accumulation and Empirics.* Springer.
Park, Nancy. 1997. Corruption in Eighteenth Century China. *Journal of Asian Studies* 56 (4): 967–1005.

Rose-Ackerman, Susan. 1975. The Economics of Corruption. *Journal of Public Economics* 4: 187–203.
———. 1978. *Corruption: A Study in Political Economy*. New York: Academic.
———. 1999. *Corruption and Government: Causes, Consequences, and Reform*. Cambridge: Cambridge University Press.
———, ed. 2006. *International Handbook on the Economics of Corruption*. Cheltenham/Northampton: Edward Elgar Publishing.
Rose-Ackerman, Susan and Tina Soreide, eds. 2011. *International Handbook on the Economics of Corruption*. Vol. 2. Cheltenham/Northampton: Edward Elgar Publishing.
Rosenblatt, Valarie. 2012. Hierarchies, Power Inequalities, and Organisational Corruption. *Journal of Business Ethics* 111: 237–251.
Sidanius, Jim, and Felicia Pratto. 1999. *Social Dominance: An Intergroup Theory of Social Hierarchy and Oppression*. Cambridge University Press.
Stanfield, James Ronald. 1987. *The Economic Thought of Karl Polanyi: Lives and Livelihood*. New York: St Martins Press.
TI (Transparency International). 2009. *Global Corruption Report 2009: Corruption and the Private Sector*. Cambridge: Cambridge University Press. www.transparency.org.
———. 2013a. *Corruption Perceptions Index, 2012*. TI.
———. 2013b. *Corruption Perceptions Index 2012: Full Source Description*. TI. Available from www.transparency.org.
———. 2013c. *Corruption Perceptions Index 2012: Short Methodology Note*. TI. Available from www.transparency.org.
———. 2013d. *Corruption Perceptions Index 2012: An Updated Methology*. TI. www.transparency.org.
———. 2013e. *Corruption Perceptions Index 2012: Technical Methodology Note*. TI. Available from www.transparency.org.
TJN (Tax Justice Network). 2012. *Revealed: Global Super-Rich Has at Least $21 Trillion Hidden in Secret Tax Havens*. TJN.
Tullock, Gordon. 1996. Corruption Theory and Practice. *Contemporary Economic Policy* 14 (3): 6–13.
UNDP (United Nations Development Programme). 2013. *Human Development Report 2013*. UNDP.
Vargas-Hernandez, Jose G. 2010. *The Multiple Faces of Corruption: Typology, Forms and Levels*. Working Paper, University Centre for Economic and Managerial Sciences, University of Guadalajara, Mexico.
Veblen, Thorstein Bunde. 1915. *Imperial Germany and the Industrial Revolution*. Transaction Publishers, 1990.
———. 1917. *An Inquiry into the Nature of Peace and the Terms of its Perpetuation*. Tutis Digital Publishing, 2008.
———. 1964. *The Vested Interests and the Common Man* [1919]. New York: Augustus M. Kelley.
Wallis, John Joseph. 2006. The Concept of Systematic Corruption in American History. In *Corruption and Reform: Lessons from America's Economic History*, ed. Edward L. Glaeser and Claudia Goldin, 23–61. Chicago: Chicago University Press and NBER.
Williams, Oliver, and John W. Houck, eds. 1987. *The Common Good and U.S. Capitalism*. New York: University Press of America.
Zamon, Asad, and Faiz-Ur-Rahim. 2009. Corruption: Measuring the Unmeasurable. *Humanomics* 25 (2): 117–126.
Zinnbauer, Dieter. 2011. *Fighting Corruption in 1811 and 2011: What's New?* Transparency International.

Artificial General Intelligence and Autonomous Humanoid Robotics

7

Abstract

Relevant to the principles of innovation and policy/governance, the purpose of this chapter is to start a new research program, the neurobiological political economy of artificial general intelligence (AGI) and autonomous humanoid robotics (AHR). It is anticipated to contribute to both the expansion of new knowledge as well as to provide a framework for governance regarding robotic communication with humans (including the aged, the young, the infirm and many others). We use core general principles of institutional and evolutionary political economy to study the development of AGI-AHR and the philosophy and micro-meso design principles of traditional-old school and embodied cognition new school of artificial intelligence (AI). The (1–2) principles of innovation and policy/governance and the other six global-macro-meso-micro principles utilised for the task, and which collectively represent a type of complex-systems analysis, include also (3) heterogeneous groups and agents, (4) historical specificity and evolution, (5) hegemony & uneven development, (6) circular and cumulative causation (CCC), (7) contradiction and (8) uncertainty. In the first main section the principles of historical specificity, hegemony and uneven development, plus heterogeneous groups and agents, are used to situate the two schools, plus AGI and AHR, within the context of and, the history of AI, especially during 1950–2020. The second main section utilises the principles of CCC and uncertainty to situate and critically examine the principles of the two schools of AI, which are identified as 'philosophy' and 'micro-meso design' principles of AI political economy. The principle of contradiction is employed in the third main section to isolate whether the conflicts and antagonisms between the two main schools of AI may be potentially resolved. The fourth section seeks an alternative resolution by integrating the new school with neurorobotics through the creation of CCC-emergence-complexity brain-body-environment embodied cognition

AGI and AHR. A conclusion summarizes and presents areas for future research for policy and innovation purposes.

> **Keywords**
>
> Artificial general intelligence · Autonomous humanoid robotics · Old school AI · New school AI · Principles · Heterogeneous groups & agents · Historical specificity & evolution · Circular & cumulative causation · Contradiction · Neurobiological political economy · Innovation · Policy & governance

7.1 Introduction: *'hetero autonomia humanio roboto'*

Much has been written and discussed in recent decades in the media, academia, politics and industry about the emergence of a new phase of capitalism through the electronics and biomedical areas of innovation. Computer-engineering science led to the development of mainframe computers, then personal computers, followed by the Internet, and later smart phones, sophisticated electronic surveillance, electric cars, drones, industrial and consumer robots, plus the emerging autonomous vehicles and flying taxis. Concurrently with these innovations has been progress in replacement hearts and other organs, applications of stem cell research, chromosomal management of disease, plus the creation of new organisms, 'bots' and cells through genetic engineering. For decades and even centuries humans have speculated about creating entities that mimic or indeed do function like human beings, either mentally, physically or both. Artificial intelligence and robotics have become established areas of engineering, computer science, neurobiology and industry.

Relevant to the principle of heterogeneous groups and agents, in the area of A(G)I and humanoid robotics, some well-established personalities have emerged as heterogeneous groups of humanoid robots, including 'agents' such as Honda's "Asimo", "who" has undergone several generations of improvements, including having semi-autonomous capabilities, the existence of multiple Asimos that can work together, and having significant human-robot skills such as serving food, dancing and answering questions. Many other such humanoid robots exist, such as "Sophia", developed in Hong Kong by Hanson Robotics, "who" has artificial intelligence capabilities, such as facial recognition and visual data skills, and potential improvements through the use of OPenCog AI tools. Sophia is the first non-human to be awarded an honorary citizenship of a nation-state (Saudi Arabia).

Another "lifelike" humanoid robot, "Nadine", developed in Singapore at Nangyang Technological University, has been working as a customer service agent for an insurance company, where "she" acts as a social robot speaking several languages, having the capacity for various styles of emotional behaviour, with a 'brain' capacity to interpret different questions and environments. Also, several dozen iCub humanoid robots currently exist, supported by the EU Research Framework, and produced by the Italian Institute of Technology, based on open-source technology through the GNU free-document licence, enabling numerous AI hubs to develop collaborative embodied robot cognition systems, including visual guidance, 3D maze, emotional expression, torque sensors, collision avoidance and memory-brain systems.

These 'lifelike' humanoid robots will improve through time, and arguably they may eventually be almost human (hopefully without our follies) in the future, and perhaps even more intelligent (and empathetic) than humans in the long-distant future. The changing demography of especially advanced nations reveals rapidly aging populations requiring two things. First, it will require many more mechanical robots for industry, the supply of which will likely to be easily provided, given current trends. But secondly, it will require much more intelligent and empathetic autonomous humanoid robots to care for the aged (Acemoglu and Restrepo 2017), as well as the young, and those who are physically and/or mentally challenged, as well as many others, the supply of which is currently lacking due to insufficient technological progress in the areas of artificial general intelligence and autonomous humanoid robotics.

This chapter deals with the second of these areas—care for the aged, young and challenged, and so on; generally, robots who establish close physical, emotional, and/or intellectual associations with human beings—in relation to schools and processes advancing AGI and AHR. Innovations in these related areas of intelligence and robotics are likely to happen more effectively when the engineering and biotechnical elements of their construction are mixed with the intelligence and social interaction sides, whereby they become 'species' in their own right: '*hetero autonomia humanio roboto*'; or more likely, multiple groups of species, many with quite substantial differences. Then they will be able to provide not only a heterogeneous variety of care for the aged, young and challenged, but also more general human-robot relationships such as autonomous fellow workers, administrators, friends and even perhaps lovers.

Institutional and evolutionary political economy (IEPE), as the science of the organised use of power in the systems of production, distribution, exchange and socioeconomic reproduction, or the science of institutions and evolutionary processes engaged in the social economy, has not had anything much to say about these lifelike humanoid robots, from the point of view of AGI (nor has orthodox economics for that matter). Indeed, through a careful scrutiny of the literature I could find absolutely nothing about them from a political economy point of view. Some discussion in the literature is given over to a political economy analysis of *industrial robots* or *intelligent machines*, especially in relation to how important they are becoming for many areas of industry and consumers, and also in relation to (un)-employment and GDP issues. But this has not carried over into the more lifelike and intelligent entities that are emerging into the social economy. Even the promising title of Ryan Kiggins' (2018a) otherwise excellent edited book on *The Political Economy of Robots*, has nothing substantial on AHR or AGI, mainly being concerned with intellectual property rights, global value chains, machine AI, expert systems, military drones and associated technologies.

This chapter seeks to start the process of rectifying this oversight by applying some of the core (global-macro-meso) principles of IEPE to the philosophy and meso-micro design principles of the new AGI/AHR school (Rodney Brooks, Rolf Pfeifer, etc.) compared with the old A(G)I school (Nobel Laureate Herbert Simon, Allen Newell, Nils Nilsson, etc.). Combining macro-global with micro-meso dimensions we seek to contribute to the beginnings of a principled political economy analysis of AGI and AHR. Through textual content analysis we were able to ascertain certain specific principles of the old school of AI, while the new embodied school has already formulated their principles in some detail. These can be viewed as old and new school 'philosophy' and 'micro-meso design' principles of AI political economy, since they concern (to varying degrees) issues of efficiency, organisation, systems, values, power, emergence, complexity, information and knowledge, all crucial issues of political economy.

The (macro-meso-micro) principle of heterogeneous groups and agents is used in all sections, since it is of more general concern in areas of AI history, CCC and contradiction. This principle states that a core concern of political economy is to situate people and other species within the context of the institutional-cultural-physical environment in which they live. Core groups are the subject of investigation, especially various species, such as human beings, but also others such as birds, reptiles, other primates, and fish; as well as the myriad of plants and microorganisms that exist on planet Earth. Indeed, the planet and its ecology are core areas of concern for political economy, since it is the main habitat for such animals, plants and microorganisms, and is under threat from increasing concentrations of greenhouse gasses, which are generating more extreme climate change events such as heat stress, floods, rising sea levels, tornados, wildfires, and species destruction (O'Hara 2009a; Allen et al. Forthcoming). Human beings themselves include men, women, transgenders, various ethnic groups, classes, tribes, communities and nations. Classes are also differentiated into sub-classes, such as various types of workers, capitalists, rentiers and money managers, as well as micro workers such as household workers, accountants, teachers and bureaucrats (See O'Hara 2020). Questions are also being raised about how to class various types of machines and robots, especially those which are, to some degree, looking and acting like human beings (or other animals).

Through the principle of historical specificity and evolution, the first main section analyses the history of artificial intelligence within which the literature on AGI and AHR emerged and the old school evolved into the new. The principle of hegemony and uneven development is also used here to situate the major scholars and their innovations in the academic power structures of modern capitalism. Then in the second main section we scrutinize the principles of the old and new schools from the view of the principle of CCC, especially in terms of advances made by the Brooks-Pfeifer new school to comprehending how to promote AGI and AHR into the future. In the third main section we scrutinise the principle of contradiction associated with recent and likely future developments in A(G)I and (AH)R, and how these contradictions may potentially be resolved or otherwise vis-a-vis the old and new schools. The fourth main section uses a neurobiological political economy CCC-emergence-complexity framework for scrutinizing the option of reducing (or transcending) the contradiction by merging embodied AGI/AHR (Brooks and

Pfeifer, etc.) with neurorobotics (Edelman and Krichmar, etc.) through a community of such scholars; and thereby leaving the old school primarily in the field of expert systems, including possibly providing specialised services for intelligent robotic production, but not for the overall architecture.

7.2 Artificial Intelligence and Robotics in Historical Perspective

The (global-macro-meso) principle of historical specificity and evolution in IEPE states that every problem worth solving needs to be embedded and understood in its historico-cultural context (Brennan and Kalsi 2015). History enables one to comprehend the nature and context of any important problem or issue, because it reveals much about the dynamic emergence and evolution of the problem through historical time, vis-a-vis the various stylized facts, waves and cycles, norms, rules and principles of action and thought of the agents and groups involved. Such problems undergo historical changes which are important for understanding the phenomena in question. And so it is with A(G)I and (humanoid) robotics, that a comprehension of their history and evolution is critical not only for scrutinizing their operational dynamics but also for gaining information that is necessary for solving any research problem associated with them.

The history of AI and HR is a complex one, and so the objective of this section is to summarise and simplify it (where possible) as a prelude to linking it to other principles in due course. Since modern humanoid robotics and AGI emerged out of AI, and is part of it, we are interested in a schematic history of A(G)I and how it is intertwined with (AH)R through the twentieth and twenty-first centuries. It should be emphasised that every trend and area in AI has its own history, at least potentially, even if it hasn't been developed yet. For instance, expert systems have published material on the various waves of expert system-paradigms since the 1960s (e.g., see Li Deng 2018). We do not ignore this material in our history of AI, below, but merely embed the specialised history within a broader canvas of waves of innovation and cycles of activity concerning A(G)I and (AH)R. Expert systems can be very useful for the broader innovations, but for comprehending the broader arena we must be sure to see the forest without getting lost within the cluster of trees.

Historically, three core facts are crucial to understanding A(G)I/(AH)R. The first, linked to the principle of heterogeneous groups and agents, is that human beings have speculated about AI for a long time. Most of these speculators were men, since before the most recent feminist revivals, especially in the West, most women were engaged in household labor, or otherwise (and still now in some places) in the more female-centric areas, such as medicine, teaching, secretarial, and cleaning services. Engineering and 'natural' science (especially physics, chemistry, math and computer science), plus several other areas such as labouring and most apprenticeships were (and often still are) areas dominated by men. There are exceptions, such as that eight (out of 27) of Rodney Brooks' PhD students at MIT in the area of robotics during

1986–2007 were women, some of whom have achieved majorly in the area (such as Maja J Matarić at the University of Southern California).[1]

The second historical fact concerns the principle of hegemony and uneven development (see O'Hara 2019), namely, that the AI and robotics fields, including historians of the fields, are dominated by scholars from the US and Western Europe (more generally 'The West'). It is thus difficult to ascertain what role those from other areas may have played in these related fields (or what they might have played if they had more opportunities). Most of the material is on the US (see the histories by Nilsson 1989; McCorduck 2004), although some have attempted to balance this with material from the UK, Europe, the USSR/Russia (e.g., Bibel 2014) and Asia (especially Japan and South Korea; e.g., Takanishi 2019). The rise in AI and robotics since the 1940s coincided with the inception of US hegemony throughout the world (Wallerstein 1983), and generally this is reflected in the dominance of US scholarship, including in AI and robotics.

Thirdly, general historical *facts and trends* are necessarily crucial to IEPE, and so are A(G)I and robotic *waves and cycles*. Waves concern long term dynamics and the broader bunching of innovations and developments, whereas cycles usually refer to the rate of change or changes in absolute levels of A(G)I activity. A systematic political economy analysis of such AI stylized facts, trends, waves and cycles has not been undertaken in the literature, so this is a core area for future work in this new research program. In this section we merely review the general nature of these facts, trends, cycles and waves and how they may interact with the general history of AI schools.

Early modern influences, on what would later be called AI, include cybernetics (circular causation and multiple feedback loops), neurobiology (organisation and functioning of neural circuits and brains), engineering (machine technology) and information technology (computers). Two areas especially important to the later evolution of AI were robotics and digital machines.

For robotics, during the 1930s, William Grey Walter (1910–1977), a leading cyberneticist and neurologist, made numerous innovations in neuroscience, and in the 1940s he developed the first real functioning robots, with his multiple roaming 'tortoises'. He used these analogue machines to simulate certain neurological processes. Much later, Valentino Braitenberg (1926–2011) who also made advances in cybernetics and neurology, did thought experiments with virtual analogue machines called Braitenberg vehicles, and thereby made innovative analysis of actuators, sensors and analogue machines to advance robotic intelligence. Walter and Braitenberg were great innovators in 'embodied cognition' who influenced many others, including Rodney Brooks who transformed it into the new school of AI in the 1980s and 1990s.

---

[1] The ratio of 8/27 may appear, at first glance, to be a low figure, but when compared with similar scholars and departments, especially over the period of the 1980s–2000s, it is comparatively high indeed.

7.2 Artificial Intelligence and Robotics in Historical Perspective

As for digital machines, the 1930s–1950s saw progress in analogue and digital computers, but gradually hybrid machines and later digital ones started to edge ahead through innovative designs. Alan Turing (1912–1954) invented the principle of the modern computer in 1936, with its unlimited memory, use of symbolic representation, and the stored-program concept (Copeland 2017). The notion of the 'universal Turing machine' led to others exploiting the principle, including Konrad Zuse, Max Newman, Freddie Williams, Presper Eckert and John Mauchly. From early machines, such as the Atanasoff-Berry computer (1939), later conceptual developments included the so-called von Neumann architecture (1945), with its iconic use of Turing's stored program concept, the input → processor → output system, and the control unit with instructions and program systems. Military spending in various countries, especially the US, contributed to the development of mainframe computers and much later personal computers. The old school of AI utilised especially digital computers to promote their centralised systems of so-called intelligent machines and programs.

The mainly Western literature on the history of AI seems especially interested in the various AI 'Summers' and 'Winters' that have occurred over the mid-to-late twentieth, and twenty-first, centuries. This material is undertaken in a very general manner without distinguishing clearly between waves and cycles or rate of change versus changes in levels. Figure 7.1, below, maps the main waves, cycles, trends and schools associated with AI since the 1950s.

The first inkling of such a summer included the 'Turing Test' (1950) for 'human-type intelligence' in AI machines; the first conference on the subject, held in 1956; and the term 'AI' being coined (by John McCarthy) at the 1956 conference. The 1950s through to the mid-1970s, the 'first AI Summer', is temporally identical to the long wave upswing of the Fordist economic-technical expansion for the advanced capitalist economies and much of the rest of the world (O'Hara 2009b). At the 1956 Dartmouth Conference (in New Hampshire, US), organised by Marvin Minsky, John

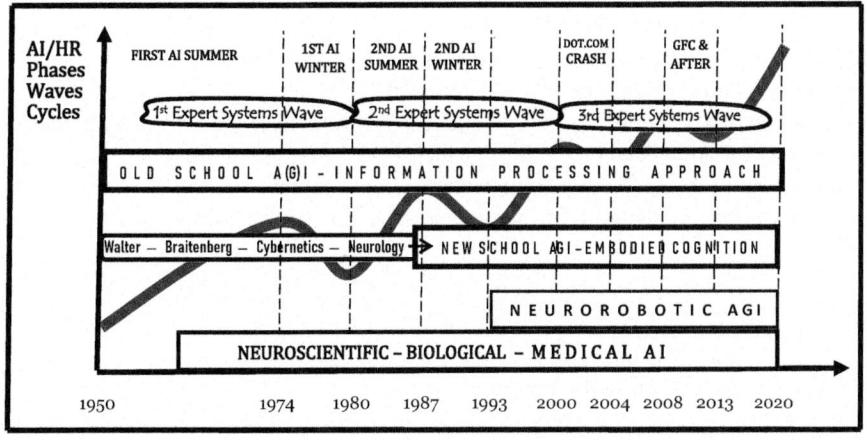

Fig. 7.1 AI innovation waves, expansion/contraction cycles & schools, 1950–2020 (stylized)

McCarthy, Claude Shannon and Nathan Rochester, ten scholars, including also Allen Newell, Herbert Simon, Oliver Selfridge, and others, illustrated and debated present and future AI trends. Here it was predicted that an intelligent machine on a par with human beings, i.e., AGI, would likely be operational in *less* than a generation.[2] Sixty five years later this is still an unlikely (short-to-medium-term) future occurrence.

Official and unofficial funding expanded from the 1950s to the early 1970s, especially for research into AGI. The classical-'old' school of AI was established, based on the information processing model, central control mechanisms, and symbolic systems. Even though the 'old school' (as it was later to be called, following, e.g., Simon, Newell, and Nilsson) was majorly concerned with general intelligence ('strong AI'), it had more influence on the emergence of the first wave of expert systems ('weak AI') into the 1960s and 1970s. Examples include "narrow domain dialogue systems and chatbots, chess-playing programs, traffic light controllers, optimization software for logistics of good[s] deliveries[,] ... early research and system design of speech recognition" (Deng 2018: 173), as well as medical diagnosis systems. Major advances were also made into humanoid robotics, for instance, through the WABOT (at Waseda University, Japan), the "first, full-scale anthropomorphic robot in the world—[which] was completed in 1973 with not only [a] static bipedal walking function for mobility but also stereo vision, speech recognition, and synthesis functions for communicating with humans" (Takanishi 2019: 35).

But because the results, especially in AGI, were not carried through to reality, optimism waned into the mid-to-late-1970s. Only "toys" were developed that mimicked elementary aspects of human intelligence; computing power was insufficiently advanced; and artificial neural network research was adversely affected, for a time, by Minsky and Papert's (1969) criticism of Rosenblatt's idea of 'perceptrons';[3] leading to the so-called 'first AI Winter' (1974–1980), which started at the same time as the first major global crisis of postwar capitalism. The winter was caused by the hype, by the excitement of the potential for IGA, receding, as the speculative bubble of excessive exuberance subsided. For AGI and expert systems, the old school of AI was unable to generate learning in their machines, nor to incorporate uncertainty, complex environments or general solutions to their algorithms.

The 'second AI Summer' started around 1980, as finance flowed for the second wave of expert systems, based on "shallow machine learning" into areas such as speech, facial and visual recognition, which were better at handling uncertainty and general solutions than during the first wave. Simple neural networks (connectionism) and backpropagation algorithms were especially prominent tools along with parallel

---

[2] As Herbert Simon said in 1965: "Machines will be capable, within twenty years, of doing any work a man can do" (Velik 2010: 13).

[3] It should rather be said that this involved mis-interpretations of Minsky and Papert's criticisms of Rosenblatt's conception of perceptrons, since it was single layered perceptrons where the anomaly existed, not multi-layered perceptrons (see Baum 1988).

distribution processes (Deng 2018). The Japanese government also spent almost a billion dollars on human-type (general) intelligence programs for computers.

The 'second AI Winter' that followed (1987–1993) was also closely linked to the wider economy, as the stock market bubble crash of 1987 was connected to the AI decline starting in the same year, and the recession of the early 1990s in many nations. The specialised AI hardware industry collapsed as personal computers became cheaper and more easily adapted to research purposes. The Japanese were disappointed with their AGI projects as they failed to progress as much as anticipated. And expert systems machine learning modules and algorithms were not powerful enough and had insufficient capacity for the huge amount of data analysis required.

Also during this downturn conceptual evolution was occurring as traditional-old-style AI (the information processing model) failed to fulfil its main promises: for instance, "robots designed according to the principles of classical A.I. failed to perform meaningful behaviour in the real world" (Boekhorst 2001: 97). New-AI emerged via the embodied-environmental robotics/AGI research of Rodney Brooks and associates;[4] plus the Internet (including the World Wide Web) became a general-use global communications system.

The next AI cycle upswing (summer) of 1993–2000, linked as well to the wider economy, led to an expanded trend of embodied AI (the new school), along with super computers (big data), systems of interacting intelligent agents, expert systems, and search (e.g., Google). In particular, Rolf Pfeifer and his group in Geneva were doing critical research into principles of the new school; applying these to a new generation of robots; and developing new networks of scholars not only in the US and Europe but also Japan and elsewhere. During the 1990s and 2000s, neurorobotics also started to evolve through the work of Nobel Laureate Gerald Edelman, Jeffrey Krichmar, and many others, who, like members of the new school, eschewed the computational approach, for the overall design architecture of robotics, in favour of a neurobiological perspective of intelligence.

Of the ten 'AI cycles/waves' sources I consulted, five were specific about the validity of the *first two AI summers and winters*, according to the record summarised above; and indicated that the period since 1993 was one of good AI performance (the 'third AI Summer', but no winters) (Kindberg 2017; Lim 2018; Schuchmann 2019; Morales 2020; Wikipedia 2020). This is the conventional wisdom. The other five were either fairly similar to the conventional wisdom but had somewhat different periodicity for one part of a cycle (e.g., Kellerman 2019), or else posited further cycles, especially a small AI Winter for 2000–2004 (e.g., Grudin 2009). I can,

---

[4]There is a heterogeneous grouping of embodied cognition scholars, including, for instance, the "enactivist approach", which emphasises the natural environment and social context within which AGI potentially operates (see, e.g., Varela et al. 1992; Froese and Ziemke 2009). I know of no practical robots or AGI machines developed by enactivists, as they tend to be philosophical and theoretical in their AI works. See also the work of Dreyfus (1997), who presented the best known early critique of the old school and especially its emphasis on disembodied information processing through use of computers, simplistic models and unrealistic methods.

however, find no one who has hypothesized possible AI relative downswings for the dot.com (internet) crash-impact of 2000–2004 *plus* the GFC and its aftermath of 2008–2012.

Yet there is some evidence to indicate these two temporary setbacks did adversely impact aspects of AI research and development. The Internet and dot.com crash of 2000–2002 majorly affected AI companies, especially in Silicon Valley, but also elsewhere, while the GFC and its aftermath led to relative shortfalls in AI activity (and other sectors). For instance, the UK Intellectual Property Office (UKIPO 2019: 11) shows a major *decline* in the percentage of AI patents compared with total patents, for the US during 1998–2001, from 0.56% (1998) to 0.27% (2001) associated with the dot.com crash (with weak patent activity continuing through 2002–2006); and a major drop in the *rate of increase* (2009–2010), as well as a modest *absolute decline* for the US from 0.50% (2010) to 0.47% (2012), in the afterthrows of the GFC; followed by a huge expansion to 1.56% by 2017, during the recent US cycle upswing. Australia and Canada also experienced these AI cycle downswings (though less intensely) plus a similarly expanding AI patents upswing during 2014–2017. The largest aggregate increases for the whole period 1998–2017 were in machine learning, neural networks and bio-inspired techniques (UKIPO 2019: 16), with expert systems undergoing their third wave of innovation via deep learning mechanisms in multiple areas such as web search, language processing, drug discovery and toxicology, medical informatics, robotics, and self-driving vehicles (Deng 2018).

Given heterogeneous groups, there also seems to be a *gender cycle* of recurring ups and downs linked to the dot.com crash and GFC plus its aftermath. While in many nations the proportion of female (compared with male) AI authors for published journal articles have been expanding over recent decades, this stalled in many nations, due to the 'dot.com crash' and 'GFC'-and-aftermath (Perrault et al. 2019: 201). As Perrault documents, in the US the female share of published AI papers declined from around 30% of the total in 1998 to 19.5% in 2001, and after increasing to 29.5% in 2008 it declined again to 24% in 2013. The Japanese *female AI Winters* are even steeper and more volatile. Here, while females represented 18% of AI authors in 2000, this decreased to 4% in 2002 and stayed low until 2005 when it was 3.5%. Then females rose to 24% of authors in 2009, but dropped rapidly during the GFC-and-aftermath recession to 9% in 2011, before rising again. Women thus continue to have a dominant role in home-keeping, and tend to reduce their emphasis on career (and/or have them reduced), especially during times of crisis and instability, even in some advanced capitalist economies, and notably in Japan.

These two crises have thus had a somewhat negative impact on the new school, and on the old school's ability to improve their methods and expert systems, as well as the ability of hybrid systems to develop. Nevertheless, much work in AI continued over the most recent cycle upswing (2013–2019), through expansions of expert systems, robotics, driverless cars, deep neural networks, and deep learning, as (potential) commercial forms were given priority. The coronavirus crisis has also led to expanded investment into automation and thus commercial robotics, as well as schemes to enhance aged-care through, for instance, relatively low intelligence robots. Some authors, however, have been alluding to major anomalies not only with expert systems, such as driverless cars, but especially artificial general intelligence and humanoid robotics. So much so that, for instance, the *Economist* (2020a: 12), has expressed this contradiction in terms of AI being, at present. "both powerful and limited [such that] [a]s that realisation spreads, some of the dreams of high summer will fade into the autumnal chill."

For instance, nowhere has AGI advanced anywhere near sufficiently for human-or-better levels of general intelligence. One can try to achieve human or higher levels of intelligence through artificial agents solving numerous complex problems, communicating through several means and networks, and achieving evolutionary goals by adapting to uncertain environments with limited resources (Pennachin and Goertzel 2007). One can also try to solve these problems devoid of human frailties of conflict, anger, jealousy, injustices (but having general empathy) embedded in its neurals. A most promising development in AGI, despite the setbacks, has been the hybrid system developing between the new school and neuroscience, through what is called embodied neurorobotics (as well as biological robots). This hybrid system is based on brain-body-environment embodied cognition through bio-inspired developments in robotics, evolutionary learning, and autonomous behaviour.

In summary, the 1950s started the ball rolling, so to speak, on issues associated with AGI, and indeed this was the core theme of the Dartmouth Conference of 1956. However, the decline in funding for AGI led to expert systems, industrial robots, and big data areas dominating the field. There was a gradual switch in AGI from traditional AI to the new embodied school in the late 1980s and 1990s, as Brooks and company changed the focus of AI to potential human-type embodied intelligence and hence AGI. This trend continued through the 2000s as Pfeifer and his colleagues developed specific principles of AGI and undertook research into robotics and their applications, which continued into the 2010s, while even traditional AI scholars are talking about pluralistic linkages between traditional and embodied, Brooks-Pfeifer (new AI) trends, as AI-robotics has taken a partially hybrid trend in research and experimentation. Meanwhile a distinct community of neurorobotics researchers has emerged and indeed become consolidated, also linked to the new school, as their brain-body-environment AGI work has blossomed.

7.3 CCC: Philosophy & Micro-Meso A(G)I Political Economy Principles

Now that the history of AI has been outlined, and the two main A(G)I schools situated, it is possible to examine differences between the principles of the two schools. In this section we study the causative processes involved in old and new AI schools, especially the (global-macro) philosophy and (micro-meso) design principles, and the interaction between variables. In the process we investigate whether eclectic linkages between the main approaches are feasible, given the principles of each approach, from the point of view of future advances in the political economy of AGI and AHR.

The (global-macro-meso) principle of circular and cumulative causation (CCC) states that IE political economy necessarily studies both the complex interaction between variables as well as the cumulative evolutionary forces associated with long-term change and metamorphosis. It involves multicausal processes, interdependent feedback between variables, non-linear changes, uncertainty, emergence, complexity, and the associated amplified dynamics of the real world. Following the CCC work of Veblen, Nobel Laureate Gunnar Myrdal (1898–1987), Nicholas Kaldor (1908–1986), and others (see Berger 2009 for details), we scrutinise the principles of each of the two schools, and whether they are, respectively, consistent with CCC motion. Table 7.1, below, succinctly states the main philosophy and micro-meso design principles of each school, as part of their respective architectures. This is followed by an explanation and analysis of the principles, how they differ, and afterwards how we may best move forward into the future vis-a-vis AGI and AHR:

There are thus two main A(G)I research programs with philosophy and micro-meso design principles of analysis and action, one from Traditional AI of the old school, best exemplified by Simon (1995), Newell (1963) and Nilsson (1982); and the other focusing on embodied agents, especially the work of Brooks (1999) and Pfeifer et al. (2005) of the new school. It should be mentioned, though, that only the latter, embodied approach, explicitly and repeatedly states precisely the nature of

Table 7.1 Architectures of old & new AI: 'Philosophy' & 'Micro-Meso Design' principles

Traditional old school architecture (e.g., Simon 1995)	Embodied-cognition new school architecture (e.g., Pfeifer et al. 2005)
A: *Global-macro philosophy principles*	A: *Global-macro philosophy principles*
1. Qualitative structure	1. Synthetic method
2. Physical symbol system	2. Emergence
3. Heuristic search	3. Diversity compliance
4. Complexity	4. Time perspective
5. Social unity of AI groups	5. Frame-of-reference
B: *Micro-meso design principles*	B: *Micro-meso design principles*
1. Information processing & computational methods	1. Three constituents (decentralisation)
2. Independent & dependent variables	2. Complete agents
3. Human-level intelligence: Expert systems or GI	3. Parallel loosely coupled processes
4. Input → [processor] → output problem solving	4. Sensory motor coordination
5. Toy tasks & highly controlled conditions	5. Dynamic ecological balance
6. Recognition software	6. Overlapping functions (redundancy)
7. Memory storehouse of knowledge	7. Cheap design
8. Hierarchical architecture	8. Value

their principles, whereas for writers such as Simon in traditional AI, these principles have to be extracted from complex textual analysis.[5]

Traditional AI (TAI) of the old school was interested in generating artificial machine capabilities to the level or greater than human beings, whether as expert systems, other micro-systems, computational-machine methods, or truly general human intelligence. It was thus not a sole concern for them to achieve the general level of human intelligence in their machines.

The *first global-macro philosophy principle* of the old school, enunciated by Simon (1995), is that of *qualitative structure.* This states that the principles of AI philosophy and design tend to be qualitative (rather than strictly *numerical*), because they involve complex and often vague processes, that cannot usually be optimised, and thereby require the second best solution of satisficing, due to bounded rationality. When designing programs, outlining strategy, and utilising learning and data, these qualitative concerns need to be at centre stage. The new school unwittingly agrees with this principle, even though the schools differ on the majority of the other philosophy and design principles.

The *second principle, physical symbol system* (PSS), is considered by Simon (1995) to be a "necessary and sufficient means for general intelligent action". He goes on to say that "A PSS is simply a system capable of storing symbols (patterns with denotations) and inputting, outputting, organising and reorganising such symbols and symbol structures, comparing them for identity of difference, and acting conditionally on the outcomes of the tests of identity. Digital computers are demonstrably PSSs, and a solid body of evidence has accumulated that brains are also" (p. 104). The neuroscience research by Gerald Edelman (2004a), Jeffrey Krichmar (2018), and many others, showed this not to be the case for brains.

The *third* principle of *heuristic search,* states that AI can be developed through searches that save time and money, since they are pragmatic and attempt to solve problems, rather than generating first-principles scientific discourse. Simons believes heuristic searches are qualitative processes involving reaching a goal through the search space of various algorithms, programs and micro-processes. They are designed to save resources by having certain rules, maxims and conditions to generate intelligence through solving certain problems. The new school recognises the use of techno-logical searches, but believes it just as important for agents to search for answers by asking questions and engaging in physical movement and social interaction within the environment.

The *fourth principle is complexity,* which states that in complex systems the whole is greater than the sum of the parts, because of systemic hierarchies, where a

---

[5] One might think that comprehending the principles of the old school would be easy from Nilsson's (1982) *Principles of Artificial Intelligence.* This, however, was not the case because, although the word "principles" is listed in the title, it is not listed anywhere in the main text of the book specifically linked to any such principles; although it is mentioned three times with reference to no specific principles in a "Prologue" (i.e., Preface). Hence it was much easier assessing the critical principles instead from a single paper (Simon 1995), which seemed to summarize the principles in a way that enabled one to specifically enunciate them.

system is comprised of interconnected subsystems, and these subsystems have their own sub-sub-systems, and so on until we reach the most micro of all subsystems (Simon 1962). Simon believed complex systems theory to be useful for understanding the vertical dimensions of AI from top through to lower levels of systems. The new school believes even more in complexity (and emergence), but observed the old school hardly ever putting this into practice due to their micro-view of processes and central controls that tend to ignore behaviour and the environment of the real world.

The *fifth principle of social unity between AI groups*, states that human agents involved in the AI groups Simon cited, such as various psychologists, cognitive scientists, computer analysts and engineers, need to have relatively close associations in order to advance the cause of AI. Fragmentation, he thought, would negate the processes of understanding and developing (general or specific) intelligent entities. The new school recognise that without fragmentation the hegemony of the old school would have prevailed, and thus they oppose such unity.

The *first global-macro philosophy principle* of the new school is *synthetic method*, which states that AGI scholars need to understand natural forms of intelligence, developmental principles of intelligent behaviour, and then build intelligent artefacts (Pfeifer and Bongard 2007: 78). The synthetic method uses the biological metaphor and builds artificial artefacts that may be similar, different or better than the natural forms. "Understanding by building" is the short-hand way of saying that the new school seeks to build artefacts, including, for instance, the main structures of the torso, legs, feet, arms, hands, head; sensors associated with vision, hearing, touch, smell, taste, pain, proprioception, and speech; plus whatever else is required to perform simple tasks that generate emergent behaviour in the organisational facilities of a robotic/AI department of a university or engineering company.

The new school's *emergence principle* states that behavioural properties of intelligent systems exist that are surprising and not fully understood; such system-properties are not contained in any of the parts; and such behaviour is not specifically pre-programmed, but arises from the interaction of body, environment and agent(s) (Pfeifer and Scheier 1999: 649). The *diversity-compliance principle* states that intelligent systems tend towards both flexibility and stability, since they must both fit into their niche(s) and also explore avenues for change and improvement (wittingly or otherwise).

The *time-perspective principle* states that three main time scales need to be considered: the present, lifetimes (generations of agents), and the evolution of species of intelligent agents. This is important for understanding intelligence since often it is necessary to start with simple, but still realistic, embodied systems of intelligence while progressively improving them or enabling such agents to evolve autonomously over time. The *frame-of-reference principle* states that since behaviours are emergent they are not a simple product of the designer-materials interface but rather emerge from the interaction of body, environment, agent(s) and designer. The behaviour of the robot is different when viewed as designer, observer or agent: for the observer sees the whole process in motion, which is quite a different reference frame to the designer or agent.

7.3 CCC: Philosophy & Micro-Meso A(G)I Political Economy Principles

A comparison between these two sets of philosophical principles reveals that traditional AI is not exclusively (or even majorly) concerned with AGI, since as time went by it came to specialise in machine-type, algorithmic AI, especially expert systems. The new embodied cognition school is primarily interested in AGI, whether in human, other biological and/or robotic forms. Traditional AI in principle thus develops expert systems or machines that can solve complex problems or even robots that mimic human or other animal forms. The new behavioural AGI, in contrast, defines general intelligence as necessarily assuming bodily form, working in an environment, including other agents, which itself affects learning.

The micro-meso design principles of the old school are, in general, qualitatively different from the new school. The *old school's first design principle is that of information processing and computational methods.* This states that AI should be studied through information processing programs, computational models and other tools that try to develop expert systems, general intelligence and/or human levels of intelligence (Simons 1995: 117). This should be undertaken through machine learning, robotics, and representation; representations taking the form of words, logic or mathematics, and pictures or diagrams; the use of control systems, proofs of theorems, rules of deduction, plus problem solving plans and goals. This is an overarching principle within which the other principles are embedded.

The 'new school' makes use of machines, actuators, batteries, programs and cables, but rather than taking a purely computational approach to intelligence it investigates the issues with a biological lens. It believes bodies, brains, environments and agents that are moderately realistic should be the basis on which intelligent design should proceed. In its *architectural global-macro-meso lens* (as distinct from some possible micro-tools) it eschews symbols, heuristic search, and computational models as the basic method of analysis, because of the biologically-oriented basis of new AI artefacts. While it agreed with the old school about qualitative, dynamic and complex systems analysis (Pfeifer and Bongard 2007: 64) it recognised that the old school itself mostly used simple input-output methods that typically eschewed micro → meso → macro → global, vertical complexity and emergence.

The *second design principle* of old AI is associated with scientific observation and experimentation, notably where Simon gives priority to differentiating between *independent and dependent variables*. The independent variables are the explanatory factors while the dependent variables are those to be explained as a result of changes in the independent variables. In contrast, the new, embodied school utilises a fully circular and cumulative method since all the major factors are interactively codetermined. For the new school there are no specifically a priori independent and dependent variables of behavioural action in a complex real environment.

The old school's *third design principle* concerns *human-level Intelligence,* since its prime concern is to generate AI to the level of or better than human beings, *whether as expert systems or general intelligence*. The new school, in contrast, mostly has AGI in mind and specifically seeks to advance the study of ultimately achieving full human or better levels of intelligence in their bionic machines, even though it is also interested in less advanced forms of embodied intelligence, and even expert systems, especially if it advances the interests of AGI directly or indirectly.

TAI's *fourth design principle* is that of *problem solving mechanisms*, especially the use of Input → [Processor] → Output problem solving. This I → [P] → O method of logical systems (e.g., programs) to solve problems, was used during the 1960s when Newell, Simon and Cliff Shaw developed the Logic Theorist and the General Problem Solver (GPS). The former was perhaps the first major AI program, for proving theorems of propositional logic, while GPS was used as a search mechanism for means-ends (initial- and goal-states) analysis. Later, Newell (1990) developed a theoretically similar SOAR so-called 'unified cognitive architecture'.

These examples of logicism performed merely at the level of "toy" tasks, simplified problems, and narrow puzzles, and were unable to develop general-level applications (Ohlsson 2012). SOAR's 'unified cognition' is an advance on logicism by including formal learning, but "shares with logicism the assumption that reasoning-like processes and conceptualization are central, and that it is methodologically acceptable to treat central processes in abstraction from perceptual and motor processes" (Kirsh 1991: 5). The new school, in contrast, does not equate these purely logical tasks with general intelligence; does not differentiate between means and ends (they are interrelated); and prioritizes real world problems affecting perceptual and motor issues over *purely* mental states.

The *fifth design principle of TAI* is to start with *small ("toy") tasks and highly controlled conditions*; check how the model and programs perform; before perhaps building it up to more real world conditions. The new school, in contrast, believes that AGI design must start with *core aspects* of the real world, since most AI programs that start with unrealistic assumptions seldom get extended to more real situations.

The *sixth design principle of TAI entails* the use of computer programs in the generation of *recognition software*. Simon was very clear on the need for developing expert systems, such as facial and voice recognition methods, or medical systems of recognising microbes, and he saw this as the development of potentially human-level intelligence (or better), at least at this micro level. In contrast, the new school is clear on the need to develop the whole global-macro (philosophy) micro-meso (design) AHR architecture as a clear priority, and not get diverted onto *purely* expert systems unless they advance the broader goals directly or indirectly.

The *seventh design principle of TAI* states that AI systems demonstrate their intelligence through utilising *specific stored knowledge* in memory of the concepts, models and heuristics of its core concerns, along with programs and computations, to achieve a specific or general goal, within a limited experimental task environment. The new school responds that knowledge needs to be built from embodied cognition operating in the real world of other agents, moving objects and 4-D situational dynamics. The knowledge of humans is not acquired, stored, and retrieved from memory in the mechanical way described by the old school, but is rather the ongoing dynamic workings of numerous complex processes involving neural spiking, synaptic weights and circuits of dense axonal connections.

Finally, the *eighth principle* of TAI states that systems have *hierarchical structure,* and analysts should utilise this hierarchy by working from top to bottom, minimising interaction between (sub-)systems, while long-run dynamics depend

7.3 CCC: Philosophy & Micro-Meso A(G)I Political Economy Principles 211

upon the higher-level structures. The new school, in contrast, believes that general intelligence does not require a central processing unit, since the body's sensors, motors, as well as environments, including observers/other participants, are all crucial to its sense of evolutionary and autonomous intelligence.

Overall, the principles of 'good old fashioned AI' (GOFAI), or traditional AI, as exemplified in, for instance, the work of Simon, Newell, Nilsson, etc. are a very narrow and over-simplified analysis of AI, imbued with logic, ceteris paribus assumptions, and few variables. While it can include AGI, at least potentially, and was originally started to work towards generating artificial human-type intelligence within a generation, mostly it is relevant to very simplified versions of logical inference, toy models, expert systems and chess games. The new school, inspired by previous work, such as Walter's 'tortoises' and Braitenberg vehicles, developed in practice by Rodney Brooks and others at MIT in the 1980s, started work on robots that was envisaged to likely eventually equate to high levels of autonomous intelligence. Through experiments at MIT, Brooks found that AI was necessarily based on the whole body, decentralised nodes, interaction with the environment, and endogenous learning. Such experiments involved a heterogeneous group of moving robots, such as those agents variously named 'Allen', 'Herbert', 'Seymour', 'Toto', 'Tito', 'Genghis', 'Squirt', 'Tom', 'Jerry' and 'Labnav', while he (and his colleagues) developed some basic principles of design for higher-order, dynamic, intelligent machines. Brooks (1999: 114) found that classic AI was based on simple principles that were "more and more biologically implausible".

This led Brooks to a model of higher general intelligence based on as much of the real world as possible: a model of reality more in keeping with CCC than classical AI. The multi-factor approach of Brooks/new school illustrated that "intelligence is an emergent property of certain complex systems—it sometimes arises without an easily identifiable reason for arising" (Brooks 1999:185). Included in his models and experiments were not only bodies, environments, agents, multiple behaviors, and emergence intelligence, but also multi-agents in social interaction, where learning and new behavior occurs through cooperation and even conflict. Believing that "Intelligence is determined by the dynamics of interaction with the world", Brooks (1999: 169) and his colleagues sought design principles that were at odds with traditional AI. These principles are more in keeping with the CCC tenets of multi-factorial, feedback processes, and magnified circular causation.

In a section of his book including the articles establishing the new school (Brooks 1999: 171–175), "6.1 Principles", he states that "All research goes on within the constraints of certain principles", and then summarizes these principles in simple prose. The first set of Brooksian principles "defines the domain of the work", including the goal of studying completely integrated and intelligent autonomous agents; agents that are embodied as mobile robots situated in unmodified worlds found around the laboratory; 'who' should operate comfortably with visitors, cleaners, changes in furniture, and changes in the environment; and with timescales commensurate with those of humans. Then he states his principles of computation, which include an asynchronous network of active computational elements in the form of augmented finite-state machines with *unidirectional connections*, sensors, affecters, and actuators, connected to circuits through asynchronous two-sided buffers.

This leads to Brooksian principles of organization where there is no central world model, no central control, few hierarchies, and an intertwining of perceptual, control and activation systems. The networks are *layered* and follow an *evolutionary* process, since behaviors are actuated, which at each stage of development are tested and if necessary debugged through further layers added or existing ones modified. The core principles of motion for the 'mobot lab robots' are that computation is done onboard the robots situated in the environment; model specifications can be easily compiled into a silicon circuit; electrical power utilized is proportionate to the size/complexity of the robots; and microprocesses can reduce wiring complexity by servicing local groups of sensors (e.g., for motion, vision, touch, hearing). Intelligence is thus a decentralized, ongoing, circular momentum, comprising network processes created sui generis through endogenous learning.

Brook's principles and robotic experiments at MIT provided the basis for a whole generation of scholars-engineers to progress the new school, not only in the US, but also in Europe, Japan and elsewhere. A major group was organized at the University of Zurich around the work of Pfeifer, and another in Japan at the Tokyo University of Science. Through PhD theses (e.g., Lungarella 2004) books (e.g., Pfeifer and Scheier 1999; Pfeifer and Bongard 2007; Lungarella et al. 2007) and dozens of scholarly journal articles, their principles and experiments have progressed further. Very technical engineering developments have been made as have refinements of the principles, with the long-term objectives of advancing artificial general intelligence equating with or even advancing beyond human processes. Apart from the philosophy principles, the following design principles have been especially crafted, with Pfeifer being the lead investigator of this material, which seeks to follow but improve on the work of Brooks. These principles are encapsulated below, within the CCC framework (see Table 7.1, above).

Of primary importance for the Pfeifer et al. framework (see e.g., Pfeifer et al. 2005) is micro-meso *design principle 1* (DP1), the *three constituents principle,* which states that general intelligence must be examined within the framework of the linkages between whole agents, environments and behaviours or tasks. This decentered totality is the core of the generation of emergent intelligence, which operates in a real world environment, as behaviour needs to be activated and modified in changing situations, both physical and social in nature. This view of complexity is indeed complex as it requires the totality of the context in which agents are operating in the world to be incorporated into the schema.

This leads to *DP2*, the *complete agent principle,* since the environment is more complex when encapsulating agents in embodied physical and mental dynamic structures in a complex environment (gaining information through their sensors), physically independent of other agents (they exist sui generis) yet also interdependent (behaviourally) with other agents, and self-sufficient (they can operate for a time without any help from scientists). This autonomy of the agents(s) is said to be crucial for the building of intelligent behaviour.

Critical to intelligence being emergent from an array of interactions is *DP3*, the *principle of parallel, loosely coupled processes*. This principle means that intelligence is the outcome of a complex interplay of skills and behaviours, in an environmental setting where physical bodies play core roles. For instance, movement of limbs can achieve various objectives, such as balance, movement, providing information, and interacting with others in the environment. Skills such as examining the environment *and* communicating *and* avoiding collision *and* getting to a specific place, are in a sense parallel (independent), but also interactively coordinated processes, so they are loosely coupled to achieve certain ongoing emergent behaviours, such as picking up empty cans, or giving tours of the MIT AI lab. The emergent display of practical intelligence is seen as *evolutionary* ongoing processes (means-ends-means) of all these interactions.

Closely linked is *DP4*, the *principle of sensory-motor coordination* (SMC), which was devised by Pfeifer and Scheier (1999: ch 12) under the influence of John Dewey, Jean Piaget and Gerald Edelman. There are numerous aspects to this principle, but the core one is that humans, and robots based on human biology, get their most obvious forms of sensory stimulation from moving about in the environment and interacting with other objects and subjects. This involves the fusion of moving, interacting, seeing, perceiving, categorizing, learning, modifying, memorizing, and getting stimulation within the agent's natural habitat or exploring other ecologies. More specifically, "through sensory-motor coordination a mobile agent can actively structure its own sensory input by manipulating the world" (p. 292). In this way, agents are able to "structure their own sensory input" and be able to categorize especially through the perceptual regularities of the environment.

Advances in neuroscience provide evidence for this *sensory-motor action thesis*, since as motor sensors in the legs, feet, hands, arms, etc. respond to worldly actions they send sensory messages via the ascending neural circuits to the spine and brain; while the eyes, ears, vestibular organ, mouth, skin and muscle senses in the head actively perceive the environment while sending messages directly through the cranial nerves to the brain. Since human and embodied robotic bodies are interdependent action systems, in response the brain-spine relays action signals back through the motor neurons to the muscles, joints, tendons, ligaments, and skin of the torso, organs, skin, legs, arms, feet and hands; with direct motor signals being relayed to the sensory organs in the head. With an active agent, there needs to be close sensory-motor coordination between especially the visual and vestibular sensors and the motion/touch sensors-motors, so that humans and robots can engage in locomotion quite speedily and without mishap. As sensory beings, humans and embodied robots need to respond to stimuli that enables continuous activation of the whole body and intelligence through synaptic weights and dense axonal circuits, in a circular and cumulative fashion through real time and place.

This leads to a core emergent principle, *DP5*, the *principle of dynamic ecological balance*, which includes two aspects. The first is that, for intelligent and workable agents, there needs to be a dynamic match between the complexity of the agent and the complexity of the task environment. The complexity of sensory, motor, and neural systems need to be dynamically matched by the nature of the tasks undertaken in the environment. Agents need to be able to behave in ways that are well adjusted to their surroundings. The second aspect is that there needs to be a dynamic distributional balance between materials, morphology, control and the task environment. This means that agents evolve better when their bodies are able to have a high degree of decentralized control with respect to materials and morphology, so that central control is relieved of much of the strain of processing within the dynamic task environment. The complex nature of these dual aspects lead often to intelligent behavior that is emergent (sui generis, cumulative), with respect to the various controls, materials, morphologies and environments.

There are three other design principles in Pfeifer et al.'s theoretical-practical systems of general intelligence. *DP6* is the *principle of overlapping functions,* which links to the principle of uncertainty, where intelligent systems must have some core elements of duplication of functions, which one can view as safety nets due to the riskiness and *uncertainty* of all the elements of the various systems in tandem with the environment. Every component requires that, in the event of damage to one sensory system, other parts can carry on some of the functions of the damaged system. For instance, if the vision system is impaired then other senses can be used to complement vision to help achieve ongoing behaviors. This is an active principle of animal (especially human) behavior where, for instance, complete blindness often leads to other senses being heightened which to some degree counteracts the impact of the visual damage; through compensatory increases in brain plasticity that helps in related ways; e.g., through more effective hearing, smell, and/or proprioception, propensities. The greater the uncertainty of the environment, where the future cannot be gauged, the more critical this element of what Brooks and Peifer call "redundancy" is for survival and intellectual development (technically some of the examples of what some authors call "redundancy" are really "degeneracy"; more on this later).

DP7 is the *principle of cheap design,* in which intelligent systems reduce the costs of physical-neural development vis-à-vis the ecological niche and levels of uncertainty. For instance, if the agent is moving around an environment that is level then wheels are likely a better option than legs. If the environment is slightly uneven then several sets of accommodating wheels and balancers may suffice. But if the terrain is uneven and involves trees, rocks and mountains then evolutionary forces generating legs and arms are likely better options. In the event of sudden attack by predators on runable surfaces, evolutionary mutations favoring Achilles tendons are likely useful. If the environment is highly uncertain, predators common, and innovations required then large, complex brains may evolve if survival is possible in the long-term.

Lastly, *DP8* is the *value principle,* which states that emergent behaviors are reinforced through the interaction of all the variables associated with the agent(s), which constitutes 'values-in-motion'. This principle is very similar if not identical with the neo-Veblenian normative theory of valuation developed by Marc Tool and Dale Bush (2003). Activities undertaken by agents indicate a valuation attributed to these behaviors, even though they are an emergent circular and cumulative outcome of interactive systems that may not include explicit goals. Such implicit goals are usually specified by designers, or if animals by the agents themselves. For instance,

7.3 CCC: Philosophy & Micro-Meso A(G)I Political Economy Principles

agents that kill or destroy other agents during war value death to enemies, or possibly broader values such as death to imperialists or invaders. Other values may involve looking after humans, cooking the dinner, or undergoing endogenous innovations (evolutionary or developmental learning). Such values are the result usually of Hebbian Learning, where multiple (artificial/natural) neurons are co-activated resulting in inter-association and thus implicitly valuation-reinforcing behaviors (we revisit Hebbian Learning later in this chapter).

As the embodied cognition model of intelligence develops, Pfeifer and coworkers anticipate further innovatory principles emerging, especially through evolutionary and collective system dynamics. Taking the basics of the new school into account we can now model, based on real world emergence, the CCC processes as they operate in motion; as shown by Fig. 7.2, below.

This figure illustrates that, for the new school, emergent behaviours and AGI are the ongoing means-ends-means processes associated with a complex set of interactive processes, including in part the plans of engineers-scientists, the environmental surroundings including agents, furniture, machines and so on, plus the layered neural systems, sensors and bodily schemas. None of these determine the ongoing processes completely or even majorly, but each contributes something to the whole by interacting with the other processes, and thereby affecting the behaviour of the agents. The behaviour is cumulative and emergent in that it represents an outcome quite different from the parts in isolation. Such behaviours are a complex outcome of

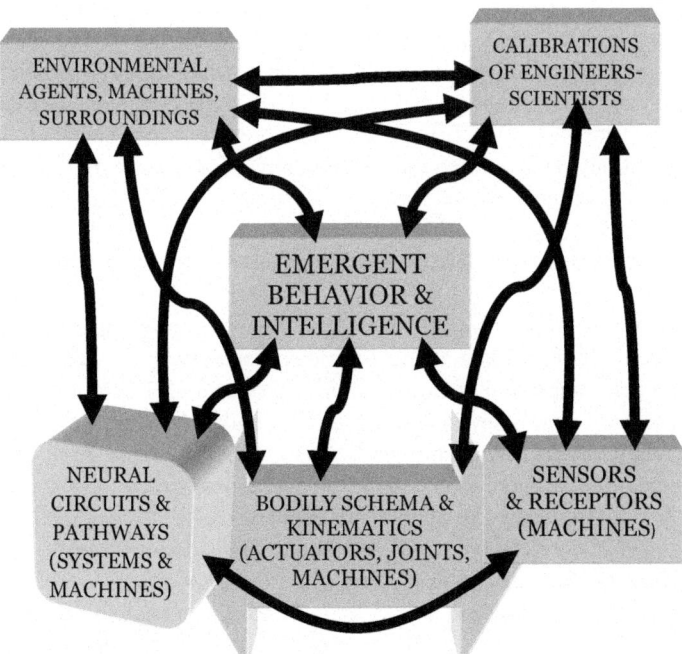

Fig. 7.2 New school CCC interactions of AGI and AH robotics

a multifarious set of interactions within and between the sub-processes. Behaviour cannot be completely or even majorly programmed at the central control system, as it is the result of this complex body-environment-other agent interaction.

Applying Fig. 7.2 to a real-world example, a PhD student of Brooks (co-supervised with Lynn Stein), Ian Horswill (1993), developed a vision-based robot called Polly, with an associative memory, to act as a tour guide for visitors to the corridors of the seventh floor of the MIT AI lab, during 1993. Polly moved very fast (1 meter per second), while its system operated at 15 Hz (15 cycles [hertz] per second), having a large behavioural repertoire, being specialized to its task and environment, using simple components, and costing about USD$20,000 (1993 prices). Horswill designed various layered, distributed rules for the robot, involving multiple strategies in parallel, which were loosely coupled. These included strategies such as (1) Move straight ahead, or to the right, or the left, or stop. (2) Avoid obstacles. (3) Recognise people (with the vision system). (4) Ask people whether they want a tour (using the voice synthesizer). (5) Tell visitors about specific parts of the lab as they come to them. It *appears* that the robot has a *goal* of specifically acting as a tour guide, but it does not. Rather, it is designed to undertake certain simple, parallel but also loosely coupled, multiple processes, which in *holistic view* are *emergent* as acting as a tour guide. A whole series of simple rules, sensors, actuators, alternators, motors, onboard computers and microprocessors enable this apparently complex behaviour to emerge from decentralised onboard systems (see also Brooks 2002: 53).

These two sets of philosophy and micro-meso design principles of AI/robotic political economy generate quite different dynamics, as the old school follows a logical, closed-system, simple input-output model, while the new school is consistent with macro-global emergent and complex CCC dynamics. Next we centre on the contradictions involving the two main schools of AI, and whether they may be partially or wholly resolved into the future to advance the cause of AGI and AHR.

7.4 Contradictions Between the Two Main Schools of A(G)I

The (global-macro-meso) principle of contradiction in institutional and evolutionary political economy states that there are many trade-offs involved in production, distribution, exchange and socioeconomic reproduction. These trade-off various dichotomies or forces, such as the power distribution between capital and labor, industry and finance, competition and monopoly, urban and rural, capital and ecology, men and women, ethnic group versus ethnic group, and so on (O'Hara 2001). The core general contradiction for modern capitalism is explained by Karl Polanyi's (1944) 'double movement' and the 'disembedded economy'. According to this, capitalism tends to promote disembedded forms of market exchange through commodification of ecological, social, knowledge, and human resources. But there are other forms of exchange, or other movements, that are more socially embedded, such as redistribution, reciprocity and householding. Market exchange is thus often undertaken through commodification in forms that crowd out redistribution, reciprocity and householding. But due to problems associated with such commodification, other movements ('double movements') involve agents historically and institutionally reacting to these so as to re-establish forms of redistribution, reciprocity and householding. (See Stanfield 1986 for more details.)

There are several contradictions uppermost in the minds of many who study recent trends involved in AI, three of which come readily to mind.[6] The first contradiction is the issue of human versus artificial intelligence, whether it be unemployment, underemployment, and skill obsolescence of humans as industrial robotics and AI take over a larger share of the economy's resources, or the longer-term issue of AGI competing with humans not only for jobs but also for power vis-à-vis broader issues of warfare, competitive intelligence, and citizenship. A large literature has evolved on the ethics and values of humanoid robotics, designed to protect humans and ensure they are user-friendly. These include, for instance, Isaac Asimov's (1942) three laws; the *Euronet Roboethics Atelier* ethical recommendations for commercial robots (see Veruggio 2006); and the BSI (2016) international guidelines for the ethical design of robots. (See Jim Torresen 2018 for details.) This ethical dimension is a core area of further analysis in political economy.

The second contradiction involves several AI summers/winters/cycles/crises and trends described in an earlier section of this chapter, and which usually track broader changes in the social economy and technology sectors. As mentioned earlier, this topic and related history and evolution, is a core area for serious development of the political economy of AGI and AHR into the near future. The third contradiction is associated with the two main forces discussed in this chapter, namely that linked with traditional AI versus the reactive movement of new embodied-cognition AGI. All three of these contradictions may be viewed from the perspective of the disembedded economy and the double movement. The third of these contradictions will be the main concern of this section of the section.

The two main AI worldviews involve fundamentally different perspectives of how intelligence can develop. The first, broadly following Simon, Newell, Nilsson, and colleagues, has a very simple vision of intelligence that involves logic, qualitative math, symbolic representation, plus centralised nodes and circuits. This type of formal (rather than actual) 'emergence' occurs when the micro systems are supposed to be different from the macro systems, but where the emphasis is given to micro processes, especially expert systems. Platforms include the Logic Machine, the General Problem Solver (another logic machine), chess machines, and expert systems. This tradition has failed to contribute majorly to AGI, the 'thing' that used to be uppermost in some of their minds: human-type general intelligence (or better). Hence, this is not complexity but simplicity, since the Logic Machine, etc. involve no emergent differences between parts and wholes, but purely

---

[6] While Ryan Kiggin's (2018a) edited book on *The Political Economy of Robots* has little detail on AGI or AHR, his introductory essay for the book (Kiggins 2018b) is excellent as a pragmatic and explanatory discussion of numerous AI contradictions; although he does not mention the word "contradiction". The book itself specifically cites the word "contradiction" (only) seven times throughout the entire volume.

logical-material-electrical processes from inputs to outputs, and few (if any) biologically plausible and embodied concepts.[7]

The new embodied-cognition AGI, on the other hand, is a more embedded 'movement', where complex processes, autonomous learning, holistic knowledge, and bodily forms are the essence of developing AGI. Complexity involves *real* emergence since the micro inputs are different from the emergent behaviour that in an ongoing fashion constitutes the crux of the CCC system. The whole is greater than the sum of the parts not only theoretically but also in practice. It is not a simple system since complexity is endogenous to decentralised intelligence where learning is activated within an agent(s)-environment-behaviour context. This decentered totality generates intelligence that cannot be centralised, nor programmed completely, since it is the outcome of a complex series of evolutionary processes involving learning, moving, parallel systems, and realistic environments.

We have presented this first contradiction in a moderately sophisticated fashion, but Arkoudas and Bringsjord's (2014: 56) "rough graphical depiction" of the main differences between the schools, illustrates the contradiction more starkly. Here the dichotomies are presented as old school v. new school; representational v. non-representational; individualistic v. social; abstract v. concrete; context-independent v. context-dependent; static v. dynamic; atomistic v. holistic; computer-inspired v. biology-inspired; and thought-oriented v. action-oriented. These dichotomies do perhaps exaggerate some of the differences, but the less-nuanced presentation help us recognise the type of paradigm shift that is occurring, not just in AI but in scientific practise more generally. It mirrors developments happening in other spheres too, such as with reference to variants of new institutional economics v. original institutional political economy; logical positivism v. pragmatism and constructivism; plus reductionism v. complexity in science and philosophy.

Many earlier histories of AI, written by those adhering to the traditional perspective, either mostly ignored the new, embodied school (e.g., McCorduck 2004), or treated it as just one approach among many (e.g., Nilsson 1989). More recently though, even historians of the mostly traditional view, such as Nilsson (2007), have come to realise how important the triadic architecture of agent(s)-environment-behaviour is, and even concludes that a better future may be one where the two traditions contribute in unison to advances in A(G)I. We have thus come a long way from the time when good old-fashioned AI dominated AI research.

---

[7] A good example of this is an attempt to develop what they call a "standard model of the mind" (following SOAR and similar methods) by Laird et al. (2017). This model does present some various architectures involving long-term memories, working memory, plus visual buffers for perception and motors. But no detailed biologically or neurobiologically realistic processes concerning the neural, peripheral, brain or motor-sensory systems are included in the model.

Even Brooks (1999) speculated that merging the two schools may be the way of the future; although he apparently discounted this speculation; but some disagree.[8] Nilsson agreed on the need to deepen the hybrid tendency. Pfeifer disagreed. A recent book by Arkapravo Bhaumik (2018: 114–122) agrees with Nilsson, based on a critique that embodied robotic systems, by themselves, are good for lower-level cognitive functions such as moving, touching, evading, grabbing, talking, and seeing, but lacking sufficient cerebral activities to engage in higher level cognitive functions such as conceptualisation, complex information processing, and other forms of advanced learning required for human-type intelligence.

Aaron Sloman's (2009) belief in the need for hybrid architectures, and hence his critique of a *purely* embodied approach as "holding up progress" in the development of "human-like robots", is more detailed and sophisticated than Bhaumik's analysis. He argues that the principles of 'nouvelle AI' are insufficient, in themselves, for the complex robotic behaviours of human companionship and social assistance; also for such robots to "grow, maintain and reproduce themselves" (p. 252); and especially for the robots to delve into philosophical issues, plus writing or reading books. He further argues that body morphology may well determine cognitive development in the early phases of human evolution, but that it needs to be scaled up to higher levels for social interaction, changing environments, studying ancient history, algebra, music or reading, requiring not only sensors and actuators but also symbolic representations. Human-level intelligence is thus said to require many different types of cognitive layers, representations and mechanisms to reproduce an ecosystem of multiple threads and feedback loops of many different kinds. Overall, we "require the two approaches to be brought together, along with a more general synthesis of research in different sub-fields of intelligence" (p. 273).

Sloman presented his paper at a conference also attended by Pfeifer. Sloman introduced and emphasised the work of Brooks, with no mention of Pfeifer in the main text. Pfeifer and Gomez's (2009) paper presented at this conference, the theme of which was (supposed to be) "Brain-Like Intelligence", discusses all sorts of robotic insects, birds, fish, and so forth, but nothing on the human brain. In discussing *crucial* embodied cognition aspects of, firstly, the ascending and descending neural pathways in specific non-humanoid robots; secondly, why concentrating on motor commands from the brain underplays the PNS in robotic dynamics; and, thirdly, why using local neural leg controllers rather than the spine-brain in robots are typically very effective and economical; Pfeifer and Gomex *by definition necessarily* include few *details* of brain dynamics (and no details of human brain dynamics). Had Pfeifer and Gomez's paper actually successfully dealt with the (human) brain in the manner indicated in the title—"Morphological Computation—Connecting Brain, Body, and Environment", it might have solved some aspects of the paradigmal contradiction.

---

[8] Sloman (2009: 248) believes Brooks has changed his mind about this; also Sloman says he has heard Brooks say at conferences that he believes there may be useful co-mingling between the two approaches.

The point to emphasize is that there is no reason why the brain should not be included, in the same general way as sensors, actuators, and decentralized nodes, in the generation of human-like intelligence and humanoid robotics. Indeed, a fully worked out system of embodied cognition, artificial general intelligence and human-like robotics, must necessarily link all the major cognitive systems and sub-systems together for comprehending and building intelligence 'life' forms (artificial or otherwise).

It is true that Pfeifer and Scheier (1999: ch 5) rightly treat the electrical circuits linking the sensors, actuators and motors of robots as forms of artificial neural networks, due to the connectionist principle associated with them. And it is true that the new school's work on *memory* does present some specific theses and hypotheses on the dynamics of 'acquisition, retention and retrieval' of information involving the decentralized workings of bodies and brains (Pfeifer and Scheier 1999: ch 15; Pfeifer and Bongard 2007: ch 10). But Pfeifer and company do not present *details* of the brain elements in the complete dynamic workings of memory. Perhaps inspired by this oversight, and the shortcomings of the 2009 paper, in the light of Sloman's critique, Pfeifer has more recently begun to recognize the importance of scrutinizing *specific brain areas* in the total embodiment of AGI and humanoid robotics.

For instance, in a coauthored paper (Hoffman et al. 2010), Pfeifer participates in isolating specific brain areas, especially regarding various parts of the parietal lobe, in the context of body schema and coordinated movements. Then Hoffman and Pfeifer (2018: 17) add a new principle to the embodied system, whereby "development under particular constraints in brain-body-environment coupling is crucial", and "by making the robot models more brain-like, we hope to inherit some of the desirable properties typical of how humans and animals master their highly complex bodies" (p. 16). Recognizing the importance of more thoroughly deepening the embodiment elements of brains in the full system of embodied AI is a step forward in AGI research. But still, as Sloman (2018) has emphasized, whether for embodied AI or the old school methods, there are ongoing major gaps between natural and artificial reasoning, that do not give us much confidence in reducing this gap markedly for AGI in the near-to-intermediate-term future.

A fully decentralized embodied system can incorporate all major elements in the totality of subsystems, including brains. And brains themselves constitute decentralized complex forms, since they include numerous lobes, segments, and cortexes, and are part of the body. In this context, it is crucial for a system of humanoid robotics to *emulate* (or transcend beyond) human intelligence and biology. There is no need to emasculate the principles of embodied AI by including some of the principles of old AI (except where the new school accords with them), since the old AI principles are insufficient for fully developed circular and cumulative intelligence. The new AI prototypes will likely need to be less-hybrid in principle and more taking the embodiment process to its logical conclusions. However, this does not prevent embodied cognition from utilizing some of the expert systems of the old AI in their robotic forms, if indeed it is possible to do so, so long as the overall architecture follows embodiment.

It is important to provide some elemental foundations for devising a totally embodied CCC model of AGI and robotics, where the brain is more contextually engrained in the total system of actuators, sensors, receptors, motors, neural circuits and pathways, environments and other agents. In the next section we seek to transcend or eschew the contradiction between schools, firstly, by outlining some brain-body-environment inspired AI CCC principles; secondly, by raising the issue of updating Pfeifer's principles on the basis of neuroscience; and, finally, by outlining the nature of the community of scholars that are working to enhance this emergent approach of neurorobotic embodied cognition.

7.5 Neurobiological Political Economy Design Principles of Brain-Body-Environment Interaction for Embodied Cognition AGI-AHR

Although much progress has been made in the neurosciences over the last several decades, the study of the nervous system is still a wide open area of research with many unresolved problems. This is not due to a lack of first-rate research by the neuroscience community, but instead it reflects the complexity of the problems. Krichmar and Edelman (2008: 157)

[N]euroscientists still do not understand what exactly brains do, or how they do it. *The Economist* (2020b: 10)

When Veblen (1898) castigated economists for not having an evolutionary science, he turned to biology for inspiration in his "post-Darwinian" evolutionary economics. He then mentions, "All this talk about cytoplasm, centrosomes, and karyokinetic processes, means that the inquiry now looks consistently to the life process, and aims to explain it in terms of cumulative causation" (p. 68). We follow his lead in looking to cumulative human action in context as the model to understand embodied cognition.

This section of the chapter endogenises CCC-emergence-complexity neurobiological dynamics into the embodied cognition, AGI-AHR, framework. This requires showing how the brain-spine is engrained in a neurobiological system that includes the so-called peripheral nervous and somatosensory systems, and is situated in an ecological environment of other agents, machines, and other entities. In the contemporary scene, most A(G)I and humanoid robotics or machine learning scholars deviate from this holistic view by concentrating either on the brain-spine (central control) or on the kinematics of movement (peripheral motion).

For instance, many of those who specialize in humanoid robotics, even those who do not specifically follow the Brooks-Pfeifer schema, tend to pay special attention to the Kinematics (classical mechanics) of the body, with only cursory attention to the brain-spine so-called central nervous system (and linkages to the PNS and the environment). For instance, the monumental, recently published, 2600 page (edited) work on *Humanoid Robotics: A Reference* (Goswami and Vadakkepat 2019), mostly ignores the so-called CNS in robots while detailing the theory and practice of bodily robotic motion, especially regarding the meso-micro architectures of the joints, sensors, and machanico-computational principles of control, structure and motion. Even Part II of this work which has a chapter on each the 14 most famous humanoid robots over recent decades, tends to follow this trend.[9]

On the other hand, numerous scholars (e.g., Nicola Kasabov 2019) detail brain dynamics devoid of full-body, environmental and other-agent processes and stimuli. An unfortunate norm is that most scholars (e.g., Huber 1993; Lexcellent 2019) explain memory and learning *in abstraction from* the whole environmental-body-brain systems of interdependency. They thus ignore the complex processes whereby environmental stimuli lead to the spiking of somatic/sensory organ synapses, followed by the flow of information along the axons and neuronal ascending pathways to the spine-brain and coactively back along the descending pathways to the somatic/sensory areas, ad infinitum through time.

Some scholars have provided basic general *philosophical* hypotheses to modify the brain-centered research habits and mores, such as the "peripheral mind hypotheses" of Istvan Aranyosi (2013). Pfeifer and coauthors have *detailed* the *theory and research hypotheses* of their "holistic" view of brain-body-environment (BBE) bases of memory and learning (Pfeifer and Scheier 1999: ch 15; Pfeifer and Bongard 2007: ch 10). The closest we get to a complete view of the *empirical* state-of-play, especially of memory, expressed in an embodied cognition framework (BBE), is that of the embodied (or grounded) psychology "action" scholars (e.g., Dijkstra and Zwaan 2014), and also that of Gerald Edelman and Jeffrey Krichmar from a bioneuroscience and neurorobotics view (Krichmar and Edelman 2006; Krichmar 2012a). There are, perhaps surprisingly, very thin network linkages between grounded "action" scholars (on the one hand) and Brooks-Pfeifer/Edelman-Krichmar and colleagues (on the other). Krichmar has, at least, attempted to merge his and colleagues' work with that of Pfeifer and Brooks, to provide more neurobiological foundations for the embodied cognition view of intelligence and robotics.

However, despite the impressive work of the grounded action, behavioral and neurobiological schools, there is no empirical or conceptual works that document comprehensively these complex body/PNS-spine/brain-environment processes. The Pfeifer et al. *theory-hypotheses* are the most promising, while the grounded psychology and bio-neurological schools seem to place too much emphasis on the brain, mostly decentralized as it is, even though they try hard to balance their account. We

---

[9]There are many papers from this book that are interesting, especially on humanoid robotic history (e.g., Takanishi 2019). On the question of papers on robotics and the brain/embodied cognition: one paper from this book of readings is a standout, while two others are interesting. The standout is by Yamane and Murai (2019) which includes material on Golgi tendon organs, muscle spindles and joint receptors, that are bundles of proprioceptor sensory receptors; linking crucially the descending and ascending pathways between the muscles/tendons/joints etc. and the spine-brain. Gelin (2019) examines the Softbank humanoid robot, Nao, paying special attention to the spine-brain, the robocup tournament, plus an array of position, proprioceptor, exteroceptor, and pressure receptors. Miller and Feil-Seifer (2019) analyse embodiment a la Brooks and Pfeifer, but still ignore the brain.

7.5 Neurobiological Political Economy Design Principles...

Table 7.2 Neurobiological political economy architecture: Body-spine/brain-environment design principles of embodied cognition (AGI-AHR)

Principle 1	Transfer neurobiological design principles to robotic design
Principle 2	Neurons involve embodied brain & embedded body in environment
Principle 3	Memory created by brain, motor-sensory systems, environment interaction
Principle 4	Functional specialization and integration
Principle 5	Overlapping functions (redundancy & degeneracy)
Principle 6	Hebbian learning
Principle 7	Spatial-spectral-temporal perception
Principle 8	Dynamic core & consciousness

develop in this section a coherent, balanced and holistic ("total") picture of the neurobiological political economy design principles of brain-body-environment embodied cognition (AGI-AHR), *to the extent possible in a chapter of a book, and given the need for much more research in the area*. Then we complete the chapter by *outlining* an embodied cognition-neurorobotics research-developmental platform for the future, based on current progress in the field.

Table 7.2 summarizes the architecture associated with the eight neurobiological political economy (NPE) brain-body-environment design principles of AGI-AHR, which are then explained.

Neurobiological Political Economy Design Principle 1 states that *"the goal is to work out principles of [neuro]biological systems and transfer those to robot design"* (Pfeifer et al. 2007) for the development of AGI. This is the foundation of all the principles stated here. This principle involves autonomous but also *developmental* humanoid robotics. This is well illustrated in the excellent survey by Asada et al. (2009), which presents evidence supporting the phases of human development from fetus to infant and onto adolescence, maturity and old age. Special reference is given to the typical social, motor, sensory, neural and brain developments that humans undergo during their life. The implication is that robots may have to undergo similar phases of evolution, especially for some of the earlier ones, to emulate human intelligence. Indeed, many others have also emphasized this point, that developmental robots (or androids) will likely undergo various phases of evolution as they learn and thus adapt to changes in their morphology, other agents, and the environment to enhance the quality of their experience (see e.g., Weng et al. 2001; Lungarella et al. 2003).

Krichmar (2012a) sequentially goes through Pfeifer's bionic design principles one-by-one vis-à-vis neurorobotics. He argues that neuroscience AI has traditionally underplayed the sensory-motor-environment-action factors while the new school failed to adequately include brain-mind dynamics in their analysis, and that these apparently disparate research communities need to come into balance more by learning from each other. In this way, the contradiction between the old and the new schools may be resolved somewhat (transcended) by merging the new school with neurorobotics, for a more coherent and holistic embodied paradigm with more biological rather than merely computational foundations.

Krichmar believes the first Pfeifer design maxim, the three constituents principle of 'ecological niche, defined behavior and agent design', can be extended to neurorobotics by adapting robotics to real world conditions, rather than simply the laboratory, and by ensuring experimental linkages between specific brain areas, sensory-motor action and the environment. The second Pfeifer design principle of complete agents, he argues, has been linked with neurorobotics operating in real time through complex real world behaviors, such as the Robocup—"Robot Soccer World Cup"—with fully autonomous humanoid soccer players performing complex skills and maneuvers. (Minoru Asada, one of the founders of Robocup, has close links to Krichmar; see Asada 2011).

The third Pfeifer design principle of parallel and loosely coupled processes is especially important since intelligent behavior requires independent skills and traits such as balance, movement, standing, conceptualization, social interaction and thinking, but these are also loosely coupled or interactive. Krichmar recognizes that purely brain-based logistics ignores this neural interdependency between environment, body and brain and thus underplays the extent to which traits can be added in a parallel fashion to the sensory-motor-brain neural pathways to simplify action. The fourth Pfeifer design principle of sensory-motor coordination is also relevant to the brain-body-environment system, since vision, hearing, touch, pain, smell, taste, proprioception (and related kinematics), plus navigation, provide sensory information that originates from the interface between body and environment, then is networked from the sensors through the neural pathways to the spine-brain, and then coactively back through neural pathways to motor, sensory, and environment-action systems. Those who limit their concern to spine-brain functioning underplay the role of peripheral neural sensors, receptors, motors, complex pathways and associated environments and agents in all areas of intelligence, such as association learning, conceptualization and creative self-direction.

The fifth Pfeifer design principle, of dynamic ecological balance between sensory, motor and neural systems, and between morphology and environment, is said to be crucial for neurorobotic learning and hence performance. Again, here 'brain-based machines' will likely underperform since they tend to ignore the complex workings of the neural circuits and pathways, linking the spiking of neurons in the sensory organs, motor areas and the spine-brain, plus the contextual environment within which this dynamic interplay of forces operates. The sixth Pfeifer design principle of redundancy was shown to be ideally suited to neuro-body-environment dynamics. Pfeifer probably should have called this principle, as I have, "overlapping functions", since it includes both redundancy and degeneracy. As we see later in more detail, redundancy is where the *same* process is duplicated in case of failure; whereas degeneracy is where a *different* process is included in case of failure. Kirchmar, drawing on Edelman, recognizes that "degeneracy" is much more important. For instance, he cites the Darwin XI robot (developed by Krichmar and colleagues) remaining stable even when neurons were damaged, by gaining sensory data from multiple sources that complement each other (e.g., through use of cameras, whiskers, compasses and laser range finders).

The seventh Pfeifer design principle of cheap design was argued by Kirchmar to be the hallmark of biological systems through exploiting the environment and energy minimization. Crucially, it enables neurorobots to offload some of their functions from expensive central control mechanisms to easier and cheaper body functions that exploit the environment. Lastly, Pfeifer's eighth design principle of intrinsic value states that robots are organized to perform along certain valuational lines. Biologically these include, linked to what Krichmar (2012b) calls 'principles of neuromodulation', the dopamine reward system where neurotransmitters reward motivated behavior, the serotonin system involving harm aversion, and the noradrenalin system dealing with unexpected events. Intertwined with these are the social and psychological habits of belief, principles of action, as well as pure reactions to events, concerning relational interactions such as empathy, sympathy, anger, sadness, as well as ideology, rules and norms. Valuation can only be fully understood by following the neural circuits along the entire brain-body system, leading to social action endeavors through space-time.

A corollary of this first NPE design principle is that "intelligent machines follow neurobiological rather than computational principles in their construction" (Krichmar and Edelman 2006: 40). For instance, long-term, working (short-term), sensory (from the receptors; very short-term), and other forms of memory, do not operate as logico-computational, static stocks/stores of symbols/representations, as per the old school. Rather, they are dynamic, flexible, evolutionary, emergent, flows of neuronal information, grouped together in complex bundles of spiked synapses, coordinated through various weights with other synapsian modules and neural circuits, glial cells, muscles, blood vessels, organs and sensors (NPE principle 3, below, provides more detail on memory). Hence the contradictions between human and computational methods: massively parallel yet interconnected (human) versus modular and serial mechanisms (computers); synapses that are very different from electrical logic-gates; human plasticity versus electronic-machine-algorithmic mechanisms; self-organization versus programmer plans; and brain-with-body-environment versus machine-with-cables-programs (Shanthi et al. 2015).

Whitworth and Ryn (2009) suggest that roboticists, firstly, should abstract from central control typical of the old school of logico-computation in favor of decentralized neuro-contextual innovations. Secondly, they should eschew serial and modular processing and promote instead massively parallel-interconnected processing. Thirdly, they are advised to renounce replacement when updating by emulating system-overlay updates. Fourthly, they should move from *static locational storage* of memory to *process-interconnected neural-complexity* types of dynamic retention. Fifthly, they can avoid linear input-(processor)-output types of content operators towards complex, circular, interactive context-driven systems that self-process. And sixthly, they should replace values that merely satisfy the rules of logic or have self-interested outcomes with more complicated values promoting the general good.

NPE Design Principle 2 states that "The brain is embodied and the body is embedded in the environment. That trio must operate in an integrated way. You can't separate the activity and development of the brain from the environment or the body.

There is a constant interplay between what is remembered and envisaged—an image—and what is actually happening in the senses" (Edelman 2004b: 85; emphases added). Applying this to the nervous system as a whole, Krichmar and Edelman (2006: 40), go on to say that "Higher brain functions depend on the cooperative activity of the entire nervous system, reflecting its morphology, its dynamics, and its interaction with its phenotype and the environment."

Traditionally in neuroscience there has been, for perhaps over one hundred years, the "neuron doctrine", which states that neurons are the fundamental functional and structural units of the circuits of spine-brain and body in association with environment. Numerous scholars have come to modify this thesis, especially due to the importance of *glial cells*. Research has only very recently, in the past two decades, been incorporating glial cells fundamentally into the edifice of neuroscience.

Glial cells are *usually* considered non-neural in substance, but they are at least as important as neurons in both the so-called PNS and spine-brain, and since another name for them is "neurglia", and they do much more than simply support neurons, they should be considered 'neural' in nature. There are over 100 billion glial cells in the average human body, about the same as neurons (it used to be thought there were ten times as many glials as neurons); but the ratio of glia to neurons differs markedly, especially in the brain. Glial cells have often been considered connective tissue (glia = "glue"), holding neurons in place, insulating them, promoting synaptic connections, helping to preserve the myelin sheath (Kettenmann and Verkhratsky 2013). Glial cells also perform numerous other functions, such as assisting neurons in the provision of nutrients, destroying pathogens, enabling memories, generating homeostasis, promoting brain blood flow, acting as neural stem cells, assisting neurogenesis and biodirectional communication between neurons, helping to repair the PNS, and stimulating informational flow.

There is also some argument about them promoting scarring and further destruction of damaged brain cells, even precipitating cancer and Alzheimer's disease (Allen and Barres 2009). I could find no evidence of glial cells being included in robotic theory or practice, but given their importance, especially in the building of intelligence (Morrens et al. 2012; e.g., neural plasticity, memory and information flow), glial cells are crucial to the neurorobotic and embodied cognition research program, and need to be included in the artificial neural network schema, which itself needs to become more complex and CCC in nature like the human neural systems themselves.

Neurons, on the other hand, are nerve cells that are connected through a series of circuits and pathways linking the environment with the peripheral nervous system and the latter with the spine-brain; as well as from the environment through to the sensors in the head and directly to the brain; plus from the organs of the body through to the spine-brain; which then provide information coactively from the spine and/or brain through motor neurons back to the body, organs and senses in the head. Neurons *typically* include dendrites, cell body, axons, axon terminals, and synaptic knobs; with a synapse utilizing chemo-neuro signals to transmit information to another cell's dendrites, which transmits signals along the cell via axons to the terminal and synaptic knobs, and then via neurtransmitters through to the next cell.

Synapses use neural chemicals such as dopamine, serotonin, acetylcholine, and glutamate to transmit signals from one neuron to another, and so on along the neural circuits (Saladin 2012: ch 12).

As Slavin (2016: 10) says: "In vertebrates, mammals, primates, and humans, the [so-called] central nervous system includes the brain and the spinal cord. ... *The [so-called] Peripheral Nervous System* ... is defined as the cranial nerves, spinal nerves, and peripheral ganglia [neurons] which lie outside the brain and spinal cord". *Sensory neurons* link information gained via environmental stimuli with touch, pain, sight, hearing, smell, taste, balance, movement, and navigation via sensory organs, especially through receptors in the skin, eyes, ears, nose, tongue, muscles and joints coactively to the brain-spine. *Motor neurons* carry signals from the brain and spinal cord to the muscles of the neck, legs, arms, head, torso, glands, etc. *Interneurons* assist in communication between motor neurons, sensory neurons and the spine-brain, and only exist within the so-called CNS. The cranial nerves associated with vision, hearing, balance, taste, smell and so on are functionally part of the so-called PNS but contextually they can be considered part of the so-called CNS.

While precise numbers are impossible to assess, it is likely that the average human brain has more than 80 billion neurons and over 100 trillion connections (Kasabov 2019: ch 3), that have evolved to this state, in different forms, for perhaps 200 million years on Planet Earth. The total number of neurons for the *whole body* is simply not known. Sensory neurons have receptors that respond to external and internal stimuli, including, for instance, proprioceptors (such as muscle spindles, Golgi tendon receptors, and joint receptors) that respond to and situate movement and position of the body in the environment; nocireceptors (in numerous areas of the body, such as the skin, muscles, bladder, mucosa) responding to internal and external threats to the body; photoreceptors (in the eyes: rods, cones, retinal ganglion cells) responding to changes in light conditions; and taste receptors (in the oral cavity, lungs, etc.), which interact with food and other chemicals.

Typically one differentiates between sensory neurons and receptors associated with the PNS around or below the spine (e.g., muscles, skin and organs below the head) and those that are in the head (e.g., for vision, hearing, taste; and the muscles and skin of the head). This is because the pathways for sensory neurons below the head typically include afferent sensory neurons leading to the spine and hindbrain, from which interneurons in the so-called CNS transmit information further to the specific sensory cortexes and other areas of the brain, and then to the motor neurons which relay messages back to the muscles, organs, and skin. This is in contrast to the sensory areas of sight, hearing, taste and so on in the head that have a more direct neural contact with the specific sensory cortexes and other areas of the brain (Goulding et al. 2002).

Consider proprioception, often called the "sixth sense", knowledge of which is still very much in process, as different authors have varying perspectives about it. The main source of difficulty seems to be how broad one examines the processes associated with it. Some authors delimit it to muscle, tendon and joint sensory, interneural and motor neuronal pathways; while others scrutinize it within the context of multisensory integration, comprising in addition the closely related senses of balance-hearing, vision and navigation (while some consider conscious and others unconscious mechanisms). In addition, Proske and Gandevia (2012) point out that numerous scholars, particularly of textbooks, encyclopedias and handbooks, ignore proprioception entirely, or underplay it; which often leads one to understate the importance of the PNS.

In a delimited view, proprioceptual neural pathways involve, for instance, Golgi tendon organs which respond to tension in the tendons; muscle spindles which monitor the length of muscles; and joint receptors which track the position, movement, speed and direction of body motion. For instance, the neural circuit of muscle spindles has been hypothesized to involve, firstly, the ascending pathway, including the flow of information from muscles to Clarke's column in the spinal cord, through to the dorsal spinocerebellar tract (DSCT); followed by two routes, one that flows to the anterior celebellum, and the other that flows to nucleus Z, the thalamus and the sensory cortex. In response to this information about muscle length, secondly, the brain responds through descending pathways, involving motor directions from the motor cortex to the anterior cerebellum, as well as through the spinal cord back to the muscle spindle (Proske and Gandevia 2012).

Especially in adults, information from the sensory organs is typically subject to integration via the neural circuits of the superior colliculus (in the midbrain), the intra-parietal sulcus, the superior temporal sulcus, and certain specific sensory cortexes (Calvert and Thesen 2004). Wallace et al. (2020) concluded that "bottom-up" factors such as complex sensory neural coding and "top-down" factors including levels of attention and decision-making coactively mediate such integration. From such bottom-up and top-down mediation, the "entorhinal-hippocampal circuit" is also able to promote integration and contribute to spatial navigation, learning and memory (Valeeza et al. 2019). Krichmar et al. (2005) have experimented with several Darwin robots, especially for the development of spatial navigation and episodic memory, with special emphasis on the modelling of the cortical-hippocampal interactions. They found in the early stages of navigation more complex neural pathways are used by Darwin robots, but afterwards "*short*-circuits" reduce the difficulty of the tasks as the pathways become quicker and more direct.

Such integration typically results from Gestalt wholes where the circular ongoing results are qualitatively different from the inputs. Such Gestalts also enhance specialized tool use, which has been crucial for human development, with evidence demonstrating that, remarkably, hand-held tools are incorporated into extended 'virtual neural networks', as the brain and hand work in tandem with other somatosensory and spinal neural networks to actuate tool spatial-temporal-behavioural dynamics (see Valyear et al. 2017; Hoffman et al. 2010).

The growth of new neurons, *neurogenic reproduction*, occurs not only before birth (mostly), but in some cases later, such as during adulthood. There is a likely lifelong emergence of new-born neurons, neurogenesis, in the subventricular zone and also the dentate gyrus of the brain in many vertebrates such as human beings (Kemperman et al. 2018). They form from neural stem cells that lie dormant, but under certain conditions start to proliferate, forming neuroblasts and eventually neurons. These new neurons can enhance plasticity of the brain and hence new learning, and their rate of development is affected by lifestyle factors associated with, among others, the health of the sensors, joints and motor systems in association with the environment (including other agents). Having an ecological environment that stimulates the motor-sensory systems and enables learning about the world reduces the potential for mental disease and deterioration in middle-to-old age. This is thus a core principle to incorporate into humanoid robot general intelligence dynamics.

NPE Design Principle 3 is that *"memory is embodied in the sense that it interacts with actions systems and shares a common neural basis with action"* (Dijkstra and Zwaan 2014: 301). This is a conclusion made by a survey of the *grounded psychology school,* presenting aspects of memory theory with empirical stylistic facts prominent in the literature. Of course, experts in brain functioning, especially those undertaking AI research on spiking neural networks, who have little interest in body-environment relationships to the brain, have been at the forefront of documenting specific brain areas assisting with learning and memory. Here we summarize some of this material, and then we discuss specifically how this links to the body and environment.

For instance, Nicola Kasabov, a brain-based AI scholar at the forefront of researching brain functions and how to incorporate them in machines, specifies the principle that time and space are deeply involved in learning and knowledge associated with brain systems. The evolution of species from single celled to more complex organisms, including plants, fish, reptiles, birds, mammals, primates, and humans, as the environment changed, led to the advanced learning complexity of the human brain. The three main types of memories are often said to be those of short term memory ('neuron memory potential'), long term memory (related to 'synaptic weights') and genetic memory ('in the nuclei of the neurons'), which link variously to temporal dimensions such as nanoseconds (quantums), milleseconds (neuron spiking), minutes (gene expressions), hours (synapse learning), and years (gene evolution). Deep knowledge is gained through a learning mechanism which generates 'long neural circuit connections' within and between brain modules (Kasabov 2019: ch 3).

Kasabov goes on to say that three quarters of the estimated 10^{11} to 10^{12} neurons in the brain form much of the substance of the cerebral cortex, said to be the seat of cognitive functions such as thinking, memory, perception, learning, and imagery; which communicates with other areas of the brain such as the mid-brain and brain stem. Kosabov is a *holist,* at least in relation to *brain functioning,* stating that memory acquisition, retention and recall is a holistic process of neural activation, often from fragmentary elements, to form a whole. These holistic mental Gestalts (forms and shapes), as Kasabov (2019: 96, 99, 103) calls them, emanate from certain verified rules/patterns such as the continuity and symmetry of acquisition, retention and retrieval of information. Certain synaptic weights help to generate the pattern of synchronous activity between brain areas involving perception of complex external stimuli and internal operations.

These stimuli and memory operations involve all the elements of the CCC process, beyond "Kasabov's brain areas". Sherrington (1906) famously differentiated sensory receptors based on location and source of stimuli: exteroceptors, interoceptors and proprioceptors. The external environment stimulates *exteroceptors*, associated with touch, vision, hearing, smell, taste, temperature, pressure, vibration, and pain, which link to neuronal circuits in the brain, with motor responses coactively being sent back to the sensory receptors. *Interoceptors* involve neuronal circuits linking the neurons of the internal organs, involved in reproduction, circulation, digestion, cardiovascular functioning, excretion and respiration, through to the spine and brain areas; with motor responses being sent back to the organs. And the sense of movement and positioning in the environment is linked to *proprioceptors*, outlined above, associated with the legs, feet, arms, hands, torso, which *variously* follow the peripheral-neuro ascending pathways, through to spino-brainal areas, with ongoing motor responses through descending pathways from the brain-spine to the so-called peripheral nerves, muscles, joints; as well as responses directly through the cranial nerves to the muscles in the head; to enable movement and positioning in the environment. (Tortora and Derrickson 2017.) Memory and informational recall is activated through these complex temporal-spatial circuits and cumulatively merged across the whole brain-spine and peripheral-internal-muscle-tendon-joint neural systems for position and movement in the environment, along with internal functioning.

Pfeifer and Scheier's (1999: ch 15) critique of the static "storehouse" concept of memory acquisition, storage and retrieval (ASR), alluded to above, demonstrates that it is not consistent with the emergent and ecological dynamics of memory and learning. The old-AI notion of ASR relates to the 'I → [P] → O' (input → [processing] → output) mechanistic workings of computers which eschews complexity, emergence and CCC. Rather than being a storehouse, memory is seen, by embodiment scholars, as a complex set of processes, a multifarious set of skills, including different types of memory, but all situated or contextualized in an ecological environment, and activated through the senses perceiving aspects in the environment, with neurons spiking as behaviour propels motor-sensory systems to undertake certain tasks in the process of learning and living in the real world. Neural plasticity thus encompasses but also goes beyond the brain-spine to include the peripheral nerves, the somato-sensory systems and the environment providing a *context* for systemic memory and learning to develop.

This ecological approach to memory explains context-dependent learning that interacts with all the systems of the 'body-brain' (in short) as behavior adjusts to environmental changes. Adaptability is the core process where behavior adjusts to modified perception resulting from new stimuli which impacts upon neural spiking, synaptic weights, and axonal circuits through the whole body-brain. Mostly these processes are unconscious or semi-conscious, although some degree of conscious behavior is included in the myriad of processes involved. But always the body, the brain and the environment are included in changes in memory and efforts to retrieve information. Whether it involves creative-concept work or habitual-retrieval, we are never simply dealing purely with our brain thinking these things out, and if we were, over time, our perceptions would gradually diminish due to a lack of external or internal stimuli to stir us into action.

Pfeifer and Scheier (1999: 525) agree with Edelman that memory is a form of categorization, and indeed usually recategorisation, as the memory changes with experience, which is always ongoing. These dynamic changes interconnect sensory with brain networks as well as motor activity through cumulative ongoing activity. Memory links sensory-motor coordination of the complete agent (or agents) in a complex environment of parallel but coupled processes. They also agree with Fuster that memories are "networks of interconnected neurons—with the connections formed by association" thus "increas[ing] the strength of the respective synapses ... [as] the weights are increased" (p. 525).

While it is true that "Learning involves making new connections between clusters of neurons in different parts of the brain" (Carter 2019: 157), the brain itself cannot function without the body, and requires the whole neural-circuits-system from the peripheral nerves, including the motor-sensory systems, the neck and the head (often ignored), through to the spine and the brain, to operate effectively. And as Kirchmar and Edelman (2006: 38) state, modeling for brain-based robotic devices are required at the single neuron, network, and synaptic levels, but, more importantly, at the "gross anatomic level", including especially for the "interaction between areas", which is often eschewed. As they say, "Brains are *defined* by a distinct neuroanatomy in which there are areas of special function, which are *defined* by their connectivity to sensory input, motor output, and to each other" (p. 38; emphases added).

In common with other animals, humans undergo learning via synaptic changes throughout the body-brain, leading to and interconnecting with ongoing emergent-novel neural activity and changes in behavior. Environmental stimuli lead to perceptual changes in the senses as motor activity is enervated while the brain shares memory processes with the sensory-motor systems. This circular and cumulative set of processes incorporating complex networks leads to ongoing advances in learning. Pfeifer and Bongard (2007: ch 10) note that this contextual expansion of life involving perception, bodily responses, and neural spiking with greater density of interconnecting circuits along with neurotransmitters, genetic markers and nutritional contributions, is a complex series of processes difficult to manage in the closed-circuit experimental setting of a laboratory. Until better, more appropriate settings are created for systemic, emergent experimentation, we are likely to continue to have quite a substantial amount of the empirical evidence centering on *human* memory in terms of brain areas.

However, Chen et al. (2020), using lateral thinking, have indicated that using *neurorobots* as a form of "neuroethology" is a useful way to comprehend deep convolutional neural networks in their "natural" environment, without the need for rigid laboratory conditions (often impossible with humans). In this way, ironically, *neurorobotic* experiments that link memory with spatial navigation, perception, and cognitive mapping can be used to help understand aspects of animal (including human) behavior. This, of course, presupposes that the neurorobots are based authentically on animal (and human) style architecture.

Embodied cognition "action" scholars, such as Dijkstra and Zwaan (2014), have attempted to provide as much grounding as possible for the 'memorial' empirical evidence, even given the limited laboratory conditions at play (to solve the 'grounding problem'). The limited laboratory conditions still give a *slightly* centralized flavor to their citing of empirical evidence. Their concept of grounded cognition states that "Mental representations need to be grounded in perception and action; they cannot be a free-floating system of symbols" (p. 296). Important is the "notion of interacting brain systems underlying memory retrieval and of memories being distributed across brain systems" (p. 297), which sounds like Edelman's concept of reentry. This process of integration operates via "convergence zones", "that bind ... features of a sensory or motor activity into single entities and then binds entities into events or sets of events" that assist with memorial and retrieval processes. For "retrieving an experience, neural states are reenacted from action, perception and introspective systems" (p. 298), including simulations of experience, which reenact, but *never* in an identical manner, not only the visual but also the motor and mental states that go along with the memory. Visual-motor-mental simulations are also used for preparation of action, linking the past with the future and also imaginary realms.

Some specific types of memories and brain areas are included in the grounded theory empirics of this cognitive psychology. For instance, they discuss issues of visual, body and mental memories, autobiographical and short-term memories, plus implicit and explicit memories. Also, they refer to the frontal lobe as playing a part in search and retrieval systems, the medial temporal lobe as being involved in explicit memory systems, and the hippocampus "and surrounding structures" as relevant for 'binding' aspects of memory. The body of course is crucially linked into these memory processes since, for instance, "motor fluency and expertise in complex motor movements can facilitate and enhance memory performance, but might also lead to memory errors when motor fluency overrides decision-making processes" (p. 298). They also mention body position (e.g., posture) as having an influence on memory both in terms of position per se and memory of position; and superior climbing experience (motor skills) is said to have a similar impact. Thus the evidence for body-spine/brain-environment codetermination of acquisition, retention and retrieval of these complex memory processes is considerable.

NPE Design Principle 4 is Functional Specialization and Integration. Some areas of the brain tend to have specialized functions, but always in an inter- and intra-associated manner. For instance, information from sense organs such as the eyes, nose, ears, skin and tongue are processed in the thalamus before being relayed to the cortex, with informational responses circulating back to the sense organs, in an ongoing fashion. The limbic system is the seat of emotions that influences and is affected by the sense organs, muscles and heart. The hippocampus facilitates the formation of new memories that are enabled by the reality of moving, talking and sensing the world around us. Preparation and anticipation of movement occurs in the premotor cortex, while the primary motor cortex signals voluntary muscle movements. Autonomous movements such as walking, driving and biking through the use of muscles, bones and blood vessels are coordinated interdependently with the peripheral neural system onwards to the cerebellum, with responses being relayed back to the peripheral nerves and motor systems. The initiation, tuning and degree of movement of motor outputs are associated with neural learning circuits that lead to the basal ganglia (at the base of the brain) and then to motor neurons that fire action potentials for contracting muscles.

However, some simple movements of the muscles, tendons and/or joints operate between local circuits and the spine (not the brain); with, for instance, sensory neurons firing from the hand to the spine, and motor neurons firing from the spine to the hand. Such is the case for a reflex arc where the hand touches something hot and responds almost immediately; and there is no direct link to the brain in that temporal moment.

Serrion et al. (2006) make the point that the old idea of the right side of the brain specializing in creative areas and left body movement while the left side concentrates more on logical reasoning and right body movement has some truth but is exaggerated. They argue the need to balance the *principles* of functional *specialization* with *integration*. Right brain functions tend to be linked to spatial memory, learning and orienting, right and left vision fields, global attention (holistic thought), and some experience-dependent left (and right) body movements; while the left brain functions correlate with spoken and sign language, skilled movement complexity, tool use, and some experience-dependent right (and left) body movements. Evidence is also said to exist for different sub-tasks of the same general motion being performed by different sides of the brain (depending on experience and genetics), and also for functions of both sides playing ancillary roles in both specialist and integrative functions. Both sides of the brain are coordinated through the workings of the corpus callosum. Neurogenetic potential can be enhanced through attentive exercise of the muscle, joint and sensory neurons, good diet, and management of stress (lifestyle factors associated with the somatosensory systems), which stimulates integration of both sides of the brain, and which in turn enhances systemic intelligence and memory (Hannaford 2005).

All parts of the brain are interconnected, directly or indirectly, with other parts of the brain, thus forming a large interdependent neural network. But some areas are more interconnected than others. For instance, Edelman and Gally (2013: 1) describe "reentry" (a notion first proposed by Edelman in 1977) in the nervous system as "the ongoing biodirectional exchange of signals along reciprocal axonal fibers linking two or more brain fibres", which "serves as a general mechanism to couple the functioning of multiple areas of the cerebral cortex and thalamus". Such integration promotes synaptic plasticity and assists with "categoris[ing] sensory input, remember[ing] and manipulate[ing] mental constructs and generat[ing] motor commands" (p. 5).

Furthermore, as Potter (2007) points out, while there are many micro-interactions within and between brain regions, the neurons feedback to and from all levels, including the body and indirectly the environment, so that it is fully situated and embodied. This is what Potter calls "circular causality" (part of CCC), involving the complex interconnections at many levels within the brain, and also with the sensory and motor systems, as well as the environment. Such complexity causes multiplier and emergent effects, such as behavior, memory, general intelligence and consciousness, as surprising results emanating from the ongoing cumulative impacts of all the interdependencies in dynamic motion through time and in social space. Typically, however, even sophisticated humanoid robots, including the 14 most famous documented in Goswami and Vadakkepat (2019), do not have an organ/machine one could call a brain, comparable to humans, and certainly not a left and right brain, although some do have a complex array of artificial neural networks (such as, for instance, for the humanoid robots iCub, ARMAR, ASIMO and NAO).

NPE Design Principle 5 is Overlapping Functions: Redundancy & Degeneracy. In biology, engineering, and other sciences, there is a necessary differentiation between the duplication of identical functions by more of the same entity, to prevent failure, which is called redundancy; and *different* structural elements producing the same (or very similar) function to prevent failure, termed degeneracy (as mentioned above). Examples of redundancy in engineering include having multiple motors in planes to guard against failures, and in biology reproducing duplicates of short genetic sequences for the same characteristic. An example of degeneracy in neurology is where there is an overabundance of *different* neurons which can be transposed to produce the *same* function.

Gerald Edelman and Joseph Gally (2001), as well as Paul Mason (2014), emphasize that degeneracy is a fundamental concept in biological and other complex systems, but which has been underrated and often ignored. Degeneracy is such a crucial concept since it is a "prerequisite for and an inescapable product of natural selection" (Edelman and Gally 2001: 13763). Their critique of applying the micro worlds of "logic and computation" to biological systems is based on degeneracy displaying none of this input-output, computational logic. Biological systems and their components have degeneracy built into them to enhance the plasticity, flexibility and adaptability of neurons, genes and synapses to enable the continuation of essential functions of life in a myriad of contrasting and often unpredictable ways.

Degeneracy is a remarkable example of CCC, including emergence and complexity working in full force, and should help shape advances in artificial intelligence and robotics, since it enables numerous systems and sub-systems to potentially continue functioning in the event of damage, failure, and hacking. It is more powerful than redundancy since the *different* tens of thousands of genetic markers, 100 billion neurons and several trillion synapses of human beings, lead to a myriad of ways in which the body and brain are capable of adapting to retain essential functions. For instance, humans have responded to changes in the environment throughout their history, by developing a "multitudinous [set] of complementary mechanisms" of adaptation, leading to literally hundreds or thousands of alternative potential processes interacting in ways that enhance life, usually in surprising and hence emergent ways (Edelman and Gally 2001: 13766). These different neuronal, synapse, genetic, protein and other structural-dynamic (sub)systems are thus capable of *innumerable methods* of communicating and replicating across body, brain circuits and networks, in response to environmental stimuli that require numerous potentially different changes for survival and development. Some currently operating humanoid robots, of course, utilize degeneracy, but at a very much lower level of sophistication than for humans. Much more experimental work is required to propel more sophisticated degeneracy robotic innovations into the future.

NPE Design Principle 6 is Hebbian Learning, named after the Canadian scholar Donald Hebb (1904–1985), which is a type of Pavlovian conditioned, unsupervised learning specified in neural terms. This principle is also used by the Pfeifer group, because it uses localized resources to stimulate association learning in robots and does not require central control. It is the most elemental form of learning, where the connections between neurons that spike (become activated) are simultaneously heightened. As Hebb (1932: 8) states in his Masters Thesis, "An excited neuron tends to decrease its discharge to inactive neurons, and to increase this discharge to any active neuron, and therefore to form a route to it, whether there are intervening neurons between the two or not. With repetition this tendency is prepotent in the formation of neural routes." Later in his famous book, *The Organization of Behavior* (1949: 62), he states more specifically that "When an axon of cell A is near enough to excite a cell B and repeatedly or persistently takes a part in firing it, some growth process of metabolic change takes place in one or both cells such that A's efficiency, as one of the cells firing B, is increased." This forms the basis of long-term potentiation and excitatory post-synaptic potentials (memory and plasticity). Generally, a normalized rule is needed to prevent unrealistic growth of the circular and cumulative synaptic strengths emanating from these processes (see Milner 2003 for details).[10]

Hebbian learning rules have been used in numerous humanoid robotic architectures and machines (see Bing et al. 2018 for a survey); including an innovative one for the iCub humanoid robot, using a spiking neural simulator to interface with a real iCub machine for undertaking proprioceptor functions with up to 100,000 neural points and one billion spikes per second (Gamex et al. 2012).

NPE Design Principle 7 is that of Spatial-Spectral-Temporal Perception. Perceptual information gained via the sensory organs associated with vision, hearing, touch, taste, smell, balance, proprioceptors, joints, and navigation is always associated with spatial, spectral and temporal typologies. Kasabov (2019: ch 3) notes that there are similar patterns, or as he calls them, principles, of neural oscillation between the sensory organs, and he concentrates on vision for examples. There are three main vision systems of perception: magno (space, movement, depth); parvo (shape recognition); and color. Processing at the sensory levels (such as the retina) is relayed to the so-called higher levels (such as the cortical neurons in the cerebral cortex). All perception (percepts being the singular) involves such synchronous neural oscillation, wherein sensory stimulation from the environment leads through the circuits to synapsian-spiking with the same frequency and the same phase, with frequencies of 40 Hz (40 cycles [hertz] per second) being notable in the cerebral cortex of humans, primates and other mammals. Such multisensory integration is thought to be a necessary but not sufficient condition for the emergence of consciousness in both humans and humanoid robotic models and machines.

---

[10]There are also processes, such as non-Hebbian learning (see Panda and Roy 2017) and anti-Hebbian learning (see Carlson 1990), associated with memory.

NPE Design Principle 8 is that of the Dynamic Core and Consciousness. Kasabov (pp. 100–102) goes on to posit evidence for the workings of conscious and sub-conscious neural connections. The conscious neural circuits correspond to the workings of a *dynamic core*, representing semi-global coherent activity involving transient interconnecting clusters of neural networks operating (continuously for a time) together at a time scale of several hundred milliseconds.

In the brain it involves reentry and degeneracy within and between primarily the cerebral cortex and the thalamus (the thalamocortical system), although other systems are also involved. The dynamic core emerges through extremely high complexity of recurrent interconnections between brain areas and perceptual actuators involving hundreds of thousands of dimensions of neural firing within specific groups. As Edelman (2004a, b: 69) has pointed out, the dynamic core "unifies" processes such as conceptual and memory maps; as well as value-category memory and perceptual categorization. This encoding of a given aspect of conscious experience can involve the temporary interfacing of an array of sensory-motor-perceptual areas, such as hearing, vision, touch, smell, taste; pain, proprioception; as well as thought and imagery; along several spatial-temporal-spectral conceptual spaces. Such self-awareness can occur during waking and also during rapid eye movement sleeping experiences.

Developing *artificial robots* with dynamic core forms of consciousness has not been undertaken in theory or practice, at least not specifically, and is likely one of the most difficult and contested areas of AGI. However, much work on parallel processes of multisensory integration and robotic perception of the environment and other agents with robots having cognizance of 'the self', has progressed at multiple levels and is a fruitful line of research. In this way we may be able to make inroads into the temporary interfacing of robotic awareness, perception, and self-image required for consciousness. Several of these themes are scrutinized in the literature, including, for instance, in a recent special issue of *Frontiers in Robotics and AI* (see Chella et al. 2019).

These eight NPE brain-body-environment design principles are an attempt to apply the principle of innovation, consistent with the developmental-embodied-robotic research and development program reviewed by Duro et al. (2014). Duro et al's comprehensive review of body-brain-environment robotic AGI starts off by accepting the basic Brooksian/Pfeifian principles, illustrates continuity with brain principles and outlines strongly correlated research platforms. Duro et al. also develop several evidence-based theses, and sketch critical issues for future progress of the embodied cognition—neurorobotics paradigm.

They show, firstly, that we are so very far away from generating human-type AGI, especially vis-à-vis the brain linkages to the system as a whole, that we must be reticent to speculate about what capacities we can generate, both as theory and through practical autonomous robotics, in the short to medium term. As they say: "current technology is not capable of coming even close to these [required] levels of performance" (p. 1020). This point necessitates continual reiteration.

Secondly, Duro et al. recognize the workings of circular and cumulative style robotic processes, wherein they note we must start, not with the old school, but rather

7.5 Neurobiological Political Economy Design Principles...

with *Brooks' principle of layering*, also non-linear systems, and complex bio-feedback processes between levels, where "the system [is] heterarchical [rather than hierarchical] in its conception and [which] make[s] it difficult to determine what is [a] higher or lower level in terms of control" (p. 1023). Thirdly, they argue that "when a system exhibits a large number of feedback interconnections, they can almost completely determine the behavior of the whole, making the details of the individual modules *almost* irrelevant", and thus it is "the architectures that can organize the computational contributions of the different modules, sensors, and actuators coherently and on how to harness these interactions[,] where the emphasis should be placed" (pp. 1023–4; emphasis added).

The fourth thesis of the survey is a foundational one in which the dynamic complexity of the body-brain-environmental interconnections and feedbacks form an emergent system where the whole is greater than the sum of the parts. Being able to conceptualize this, incorporate it in robotic behaviour, and progress further towards embedded, dynamic, autonomous, and conscious intelligent humanoids (or androids) are the core developmental tasks. Hence their fifth thesis that "through the instantiation of this brain view in artificial systems that include a body with sensors and actuators [we] can produce inputs for brain-like models [and] gain insight into this operation" (p. 1024). The authors see this "cognitive developmental robotics" paradigm as constituting the most promising field, where they "decided to break with the engineering tendency and started developing non-symbolic, dynamic and distributed architectures with the principles" (p. 1039). Succeeding in developing such versatile cognitive humanoid robots that assist humans with their everyday needs, such as general or specific knowledge, discussion, cooking, baby sitting, dressing, feeding, cleaning, fixing, shopping, emotional interaction, caring for the aged, young and the challenged, likely will require the following principles of processing.

First, agents should be "capable of learning from their embodied autonomous interaction with the real world, including other robots and people" (p. 1024). Secondly, these robots should have "the same functionalities that those brains show in humans or animals using the same operational principles and infrastructure (neurons and other underlying structures such as genes or proteins) as opposed to ... an engineering process, which was the traditional approach" (p. 1025). Thirdly, these humanoid robots should have suitable cognitive skills associated with the mental processes of knowing, reasoning, language, memory, consciousness, emotions and awareness. Fourthly, they should have a sensory memory (retention lasting less than a second; perception via the sensors onwards to the spine-brain and back to the sensors), with attention mechanism filters for information that is acquired and transposed to the working and potentially long-term, dynamic-processual memories.

We now update the CCC framework of Fig. 7.2 (above) to include a more complex brain-body-environment embodied, situated and cognitive system of AGI and AHR; see Fig. 7.3, below.

Here complexity is increased by situating embodied intelligence in the full array of brain-body-environment systems. It includes the complex brain, reflecting the

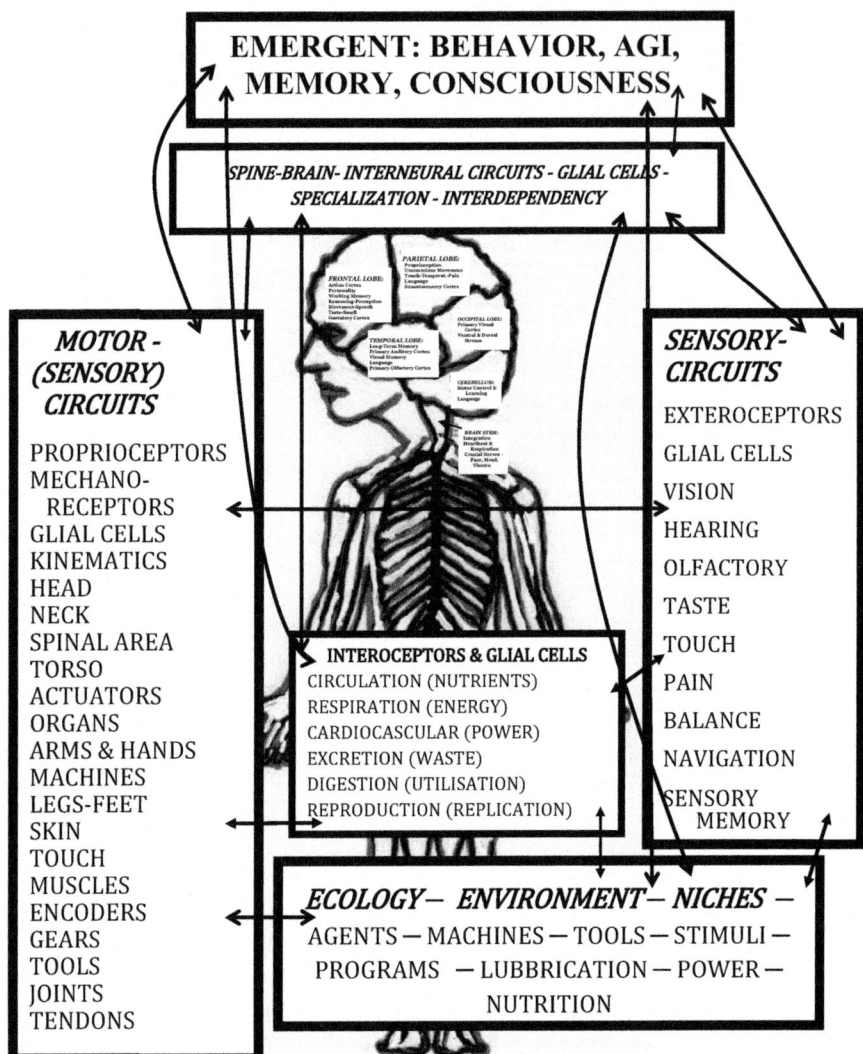

Fig. 7.3 Embodied cognition, body-spine/brain-environment, whole agents, CCC humanoid robotic, AGI architecture

human architecture of major lobes, neural circuits, glial cells, memories, specialization and interdependencies between sub-systems. It also reflects the full array of motor(−neural) systems, including the environment interacting with the receptors of the muscles, joints and tendons of the head, neck and body for position and movement (proprioception; e.g., muscle spindles, Golgi tendon receptors, joint receptors), along with the ascending and descending pathways to and from the spine and brain; glial cells; the environment impacting on the sensory-neural receptors via visual, auditory, touch, olfactory, taste, and pain senses (exteroception); the neural systems associated with circulation, respiration, excretion, digestion, reproduction, and caridiovascular activities (interoception); including the axonal circuits leading to and from the spine and brain, notably involving the cerebral cortex, cerebellum, midbrain and medulla oblongata. This complex array interacts with the ecology of the environment, external and extended stimuli, various niches, other agents, machines, sources of power, plus programs impacting on the system. These complexities codetermine emergent behavior, memory and consciousness which interactively promote the circuitous reproduction of agent general intelligence.

Veblen's (1899) concept of emulation is relevant here, of which there are two aspects to consider (O'Hara 2022). The first is the tendency of people to copy others, or compete to a higher level, in an attempt to ceremonially advance their relative status in the world ("keeping up with the Jones's"). The second is that emulation to some degree can instrumentally improve efficiency/joint stock of knowledge and thus potentially promote the common good. Neuro-embodied-contextual AGI scholars have been suggesting that other AGI-AHR scientists and developers *emulate* the body-neural structures and functioning of the human brain-body-environment in their work, rather than relying on logicalist-computational-machine methods, at least in regard to the overall architecture. Going forward via this evolutionary tendency will likely minimize the first aspect of emulation—the tendency to keep up with the Jones's for the sake of superior social standing per se—in favor of the second: "the repugnance to futility [which] to a good extent [potentially] coalesces with the incentive of emulation" for the common good (Veblen 1899: 27).

Important for the promotion of this common good-type of emulative CCC circuit is the relatively heterogeneous multinational community of scholars developing an array of robots, machines and publications seeking to further the cause of neurobiological-embodied intelligence. This community includes, for instance, former and/or current PhD students and colleagues of Brooks, Pfeifer, Edelman and Krichmar; potentially the current generation of grounded-cognition psychologists; the multiple generations of 'Darwin machines'; the European Union's iCub robot project (with many open-source components); the Japanese Cognitive developmental Robots initiative; as well as a group of new and established journals documenting advances in the field.[11]

The classic computational systems of Simons, Newell and Nilsson were the orthodoxy in the 1950s, 1960s and 1970s; while the new school of Brooks and Pfeifer was prominent in the 1990s and 2000s; and now a new, holistic and integrated body-brain-environment-social neurorobotics community of scholars is

---

[11] Duro et al. (2014) discuss promising cognitive embodied robotics systems or platforms that are currently being developed, according to the "fundamental premise...that... an organism's brain is closely coupled to its body, which actively interacts with the environment, and [where] cognition cannot be fully understood without taking into account that fact" (p. 1031). Three such platforms stand out as having high potential: ISAC, SASE, and iCub. iCub is perhaps the most ambitions and extensively networked global project.

developing, with a cutting edge upon which fully autonomous humanoid robots and AGI may emerge into the next several decades (see Krichmar 2018). Institutional and evolutionary political economics is now included in the embodied-cognition research network seeking to enhance artificial general intelligence and autonomous humanoid robotics.

7.6 Conclusion

This chapter utilises some of the core principles of institutional and evolutionary thought to examine the philosophy and micro-meso design principles of old and new schools of artificial intelligence. Consistent with the principle of innovation, it seeks to understand how artificial general intelligence and autonomous humanoid robotics has been advanced in the past, can be developed into the future, and how a fully-fledged neurobiological political economy research program can assist in understanding and advancing the core tasks.

The principle of heterogeneous groups and agents enables us to recognise the importance of groups of scientists-engineers (old and new schools, etc.), species (humans, various robots?), genders (e.g., men-women), ethnic groups (from the US, EU, UK, Japan, etc.), as well as individual agents themselves (e.g., Simon, Newell, Nilsson, Brooks, Pfeifer, Edelman, Krichmar, Asimo, Sophia, Polly, Darwin) in the generation of A(G)I and (AH)R. These heterogeneous groups and agents also manifest themselves as several groups of workers, be they automated manufacturing bots or the more humanoid types such as robocup players, human companions, or celebrities such as Sophia. The real question for the future is how far humanoid robots (or androids) will be seen as a type of species, such as *hetero autonomia humanio roboto* (or different species), and how far they will advance in this direction. The other option is that Rodney Brooks (2002) may be right as success comes (also?) through the merging of flesh and machines by artificial parts and organs improving the quality of life of human(oid)s or androids.

The principle of historical specificity and evolution follows the trend of various AI wave upswings and downswings over the past seventy years, while the principle of hegemony and uneven development showed that the inception of hegemonic forces played a large role in developing robotics and AI in the USA and to a much lesser extent the other advanced capitalist economies. We found four different upswings, the 'first AI Summer' associated with the computer, information processing model of the old school of science-scholars such as Herbert Simon, Allen Newell and Nils Nilsson, following the official inception of AI scholarship during the 1950s–1970s, when AGI (strong AI) was uppermost in their minds but most developments occurred in narrow AI fields (weak AI). As AGI failed to develop sufficiently, this led to the 'first AI Winter' during 1974–1980, which coincided with the breakdown of the Keynesian welfare state model in most advanced economies during this time. The 'second AI Summer' during the 1980s centred mostly on expert systems, but the Japanese government financed AGI research, and connectionism made a comeback, during this time. Again players

7.6 Conclusion

were disappointed with AI progress, leading to the 'second AI Winter', starting in 1987, at the time of the major stock market crash and the recession of the early 1990s in many nations. The old school (and connectionism) had again failed to advance the subject as much as the hype had anticipated, while the new school became active especially during this winter.

The 'third AI Summer' emerged during 1993–2000, as the high technology sector underwent a speculative bubble upswing and boom; the new school of embodied intelligence and robotics started to take off from the innovations of Rodney Brooks, Rolf Pfeifer and others; while neuroscience and neurorobotics started to make major inroads. Also during this time super-computers, expert systems and search-systems grew while the internet expanded majorly and set the scene for booming times for AI in critical areas of the world, until the crash came in high-technology sectors (and recession) during the 'third AI Winter' of 2000–2004. During the subsequent, 'fourth AI Summer' of 2004–2008, the computing, internet and biotechnology sectors went through high growth, and even managed to hold off another winter until the GFC and its aftermath of 2008–2012.

The GFC-and-aftermath 'fourth AI Winter' was the greatest crisis (along with the coronavirus crisis?) the world has seen since World War II and the Great Depression. Subsequent expansion, especially in AI, during 2012/2013–2019, saw a boom in expert systems AI, while robotics continued its progress in manufacturing systems and the toy world of small consumer items, such as vacuum cleaners and to a much lesser extent personal service robotics, especially for aged care.

The interest in AGI continued through this 'fifth AI Summer', despite slow progress, as the new school was assisted by advances in neurorobotics and biological systems of neural networks (while even some with less of an interest in embodied cognition still seek to advance artificial general forms of intelligence and even robotics; e.g., Goertzel 2014). The coronavirus crisis has expanded the use of AI and robotics in industry, trade and communications while aged (and other) care robotics and intelligence are somewhat muted (but progressing marginally) regarding genuine AGI and AHR.

The principle of contradiction isolated the core contradiction involved in developing A(G)I: the philosophical and design principles associated with the schism between the old and new schools. The old school followed the information processing model, central control and mostly disembodied systems, while the new school sought to link the body with the environment and later with the brain to develop a more general type of intelligence with real world context. Some sought to partially or wholly resolve the contradiction between schools through hybrid models that sought to merge information processing (input-output) models that were centralised and disembodied with aspects of embodied cognition and thus robotics; seeking the best of both schools. Others developed embodied cognition through linking the brain with the rest of the body and the environment, and thereby promoting human types of intelligence that are complex, interactive and emergent. The ongoing contradiction between these two schools of AI has been transcended somewhat as AGI/AHR is being advanced through embodied-neuroscience.

The principle of circular and cumulative causation was very helpful in comprehending the limitations of the old school, especially its emphasis on logical relationships, simple input-output models, the toy world of central control and hierarchical relationships. While these old AI traits failed to majorly advance AGI, they did lead to innovations in expert systems. The new school showed how decentralised control, parallel systems that are loosely coupled, and environment-body interaction with real world scenarios, can promote AGI and autonomous robotic innovations. Neurobiology highlighted the neuronal circuits, glial cells and pathways of the body, including the brain, in tandem with environment stimuli, using CCC processes such as re-entry and degeneracy, showing how emergence generates complex CCC systems of consciousness, memory, behaviour and intelligence.

The chapter innovates by presenting eight design principles of neurobiological political economy, and outlines a developmental robotic program likely to enhance this research program. Meanwhile expert systems continue their use of the classical style of centralised information processing, and where possible the neurobiological route to innovation, which does not prevent neuro-embodied cognition practitioners from utilising some expert systems if they are useful, without eschewing the overall architecture of embodiment. The future will tell if this partial resolution of the conflict through the two main schools taking different directions continues, though with some overlap, advances the state of play of artificial general intelligence and autonomous humanoid robotics.

Overall, the major principles of institutional and evolutionary thought provided a useful base from which to start a neurobiological political economy research program into artificial general intelligence and autonomous humanoid robotics, from which we have sought to innovate and provide a basis for policy to improve the care for the elderly, the young and other robotic-human communication now and in the future. Through this improved embodied-neuroscience approach hopefully we will come closer to achieving a more thoroughgoing artificial general intelligence and a more humanlike autonomous robotics foundation. This neurobiological political economy research program seeks to advance this state of affairs through analysis, publication, conferences and platforms promoting advanced cognition.

It is necessary to briefly outline a program/policy of innovative research for proactive institutional and evolutionary political economists, and others, for the improvement of artificial general intelligence and autonomous humanoid robotics. Some areas in need of immediate development in the area of neurobiological political economy include the following:

First: We need to apply the principles and concepts of institutional and evolutionary political economy to AGI and AHR in more detail, especially historical specificity and evolution; heterogeneous groups and agents; contradiction; circular and cumulative causation (linked to emergence and complexity); uneven development and hegemony; innovation and policy/governance; and uncertainty; We also anticipate applying other principles and concepts, such as social provisioning; the instrumental and ceremonial functions of institutions; culture, institutions

7.6 Conclusion

and instincts; emulation and conspicuous consumption; the disembedded economy; the joint stock of knowledge of the community; the common good; the circular economy; etc.

Second: CCC was especially helpful in comprehending body-brain-environment interdependencies, complexities and emergent processes. We highlight this principle as showing great promise specifically for generating further neurobiological-glial and robotic innovations via the complex circuits and pathways associated with redundancy, degeneracy, re-entry, as well as the mechanisms of healing, growing, and enhancing neural-glial, body-brain-environment interactions for learning and acting in the real world.

Third: The history and evolution of AI, AGI, AHR, robotics and the like need to be detailed from the 1700s or earlier onto more recent developments into the 1930s and 1940s, the onwards through the 1950s to the present. This should be done not only in terms of the principles of AI/AGI, but also the principles of computing, developments of machine learning and expert systems, as well as general and humanoid robotics and care for the aged, young, challenged, plus others. Special reference also needs to be given to the stages and phases of evolution, plus the waves and cycles of AI/robotics, and how these dynamics link to the general economy. From these historical foundations we need to assess what is being and can be developed into the future to enhance artificial general intelligence and the development of new species of robots and androids.

Fourth: More research is required into the old and new schools of artificial intelligence, hybrid tendencies, subschools within these and other schools, and how fresh perspectives can enhance the generation of neurorobotic and neurobiological political economy of AGI and AHR in terms of the *overall architecture* of principles and practices, and how expert systems may be utilised without negating the architectural foundations.

Fifth: Research is needed comparing the best dozen or so humanoid robots currently existing or emerging and writing survey papers examining the kinematics, as well as the proprioceptive, exteroceptive, interoceptive and glial aspects of these robots, for analysis of body-brain-environment social action potentials. Special attention should be given to the multitudinous circuits, spirals, loops and pathways linking the environment through the muscles, joints, tendons, various sense organs, and internal organs with the spino-brainal systems and back along the descending pathways to the peripheral nervous system, as well as to sensory-motor systems in the head, for activation of cerebral areas, senses, muscles, tendons and joints.

Sixth: Survey and reconstruction papers are required on memory in terms of humans and robots, concentrating on the environment-body-brain, and how sensory, short-term, long-term and other categories of memory link to the embodiment of the circuits and pathways of neurons, receptors, glial cells, synapses and axons, in addition to numerous brain areas, in a decentralised model of intelligence.

Seventh: Surveys of extant robots that provide care for the aged, young, and the physically and/or mentally challenged are necessary, including the extent to which the robots are able to care and talk with these agents and groups to stimulate their brains and bodies to function better as well as helping to care for them in an empathetic fashion to enhance their lifestyle. How can we develop this field so these groups and agents, plus many others, can benefit from intelligent and caring robots or androids in the intermediate to long-term future.

Eighth: Neurobiological political economists should use their principles and practical knowledge to start building robots that in the long-term engage in real world behaviours such as looking after the aged, the young, the physically and/or mentally challenged, and other persons, plus even providing political economy policy advice to politicians, activists and social movements. Turning our theory into practice can assist not only with robotic kinematics, but also general intelligence, memory, sensory-motor skills, and social interaction to help build a productive, caring and democratic robotic-human institutional and evolutionary political economy.

Ninth: We need to research deeply into the ethics of AGI and AHR, drawing on previous work and innovating with respect to new perspectives on robots for the aged and young, as well as the physically and mentally challenged, plus cooperation between humans and robots/androids in the workplace, the home and community. How can we stimulate the common good in this respect while developing practical principles to inhibit the use of robots and artificial intelligence for military, criminal and corrupt practices while enhancing uses that stimulate the robotic skills of providing empathy, sympathy, artificial general intelligence and physical assistance?

Tenth: We need to organise special issues of journals, edited and authored books, conferences, meetings with other embodied cognition as well as traditional AI scholars and practitioners, courses in educational institutions, lectures for the public, public-policy seminars, plus activities within international organisations that enhance neurobiological political economy.

It is also advisable to utilise collective social wealth of knowledge gained through neurobiological political economy to promote the general intelligence of members of the institutional and evolutionary community, as well as the general public; and also in the longer-term for political economists to utilise humanoid robots not only for assisting the community but also for developing political economy theories, empirics and policies to advance the interdiscipline itself.

References

Acemoglu, Daron, and Pascual Restrepo. 2017. Secular Stagnation? The Effects of Aging on Economic Growth in the Age of Automation. *American Economic Review: Papers and Proceedings* 107 (5): 74–79.

Allen, Nicola J., and Ben A. Barres. 2009. Glia: More Than Just Brain Glue. *Nature* 459 (February): 675–677.

Allen, M.R., O.P. Dube, W. Solecki, F. Aragon-Durand, W. Cramer, S. Humphreys, et al. Forthcoming. 2018: Framing and Context. In Global Warming of 1.5°C. Ch 1. of Global Warming of 1.5°C. *An IPCC Special Report on the Impacts of Global Warming of 1.5°C above*

References

Pre-Industrial Levels, ed. V. Masson-Delmotte, P. Zhai, H.-O. Portner, D. Roberts, J. Skea, P.R. Shukla et al. London: IPCC.

Aranyosi, Istvan. 2013. *The Peripheral Mind: Philosophy of Mind and Peripheral Nervous System*. Oxford: Oxford University Press.

Arkoudas, Konstantine, and Selmer Bringsjord. 2014. Philosophical Foundations. In *The Cambridge Handbook of Artificial Intelligence*, ed. Keith Frankish and William M. Ramsey, 34–63. CUP: Cambridge.

Asada, Minoru. 2011. Can Cognitive Developmental Robotics Cause a Paradigm Shift? In *Neuromorphic and Brain-Based Robotics*, ed. Jeffrey L. Krichmar and Hiroaki Wagatsuma, 251–273. Cambridge: CUP.

Asada, Minoru, Koh Hosoda, Yasuo Kuniyoshi, Hiroshi Ishiguro, Toshio Inui, Yuichiro Yoshikawa, Masaki Ogino, and Chisato Yoshida. 2009. Cognitive Developmental Robotics: A Survey. *IEEE Transactions on Autonomous Mental Development* 1 (1): 12–34.

Asimov, Isaac. 1942. Runaround. *Astounding Science Fiction* 29 (1): 95–103.

Baum, Eric B. 1988. On the Capabilities of Multilayer Perceptrons. *Journal of Complexity* 4: 193–215.

Berger, Sebastian, ed. 2009. *The Foundations of Non-Equilibrium Economics: The Principle of Circular and Cumulative Causation*. London/New York: Routledge.

Bhaumik, Arkapravo. 2018. *From AI to Robotics: Mobile, Social, and Sentient Robots*. Boca Raton: CRC Press (T&F Group).

Bibel, Wolfgang. 2014. Artificial Intelligence in a Historical Perspective. *AI Communications* 27: 87–102.

Bing, Zhenshan, Claus Meschede, Florien Rohrbein, Kai Huang, and Alois C. Knoll. 2018. A Survey of Robotics Control Based on Learning-Inspired Spiking Neural Networks. *Frontiers in Neurorobotics* 12 (July): Article 35.

Boekhorst, I. Renee J.A. te. 2001. Freeing Machines from Cartesian Chains. In *Cognitive Technology: Instruments of Mind*, ed. Meureg Baynon, Christopher Nihaniv, and Kirstin Dautenhahm, 95–108. Berlin: Springer.

Brennan, Andrew John, and Jaslin Kaur Kalsi. 2015. Elephant Poaching & Ivory Trafficking Problems in Sub-Saharan Africa: An Application of O'Hara's Principles of Political Economy. *Ecological Economics* 120: 312–337.

Brooks, Rodney. 1999. *Cambrian Intelligence: An Early History of the New AI*. Cambridge, MA: MIT Press.

———. 2002. *Flesh and Machines: How Robots Will Change Us*. 2003rd ed. New York: Vintage Books.

BSI (British Standards Association). 2016. *Robots and Robotic Devices: Guide to the Ethical Design and Application of Robots and Robotic Systems*. Vol. BS811.

Calvert, Gemma A., and Thomas Thesen. 2004. Multisensory Integration: Methodological Approaches and Emerging Principles in the Human Brain. *Journal of Physiology* 98: 191–205.

Carlson, A. 1990. Anti-Hebbian Learning in a Non-Linear Neural Network. *Biological Cybernetics* 64: 71–76.

Carter, Rita. 2019. *The Human Brain Book*, Revised New Edition. Penguin Random House.

Chella, Antonio, Angelo Cangelosi, Georgio Metta, and Selma Bringsjord. 2019. *Consciousness in Humanoid Robots*. A Special Issue and ebook Published by *Frontiers in Robotics and AI* (May 2019, 216).

Chen, Kexin, Tiffany Hwu, Hirak J. Kashyap, Jeffrey L. Krichmar, Kenneth Stewart, Jinwei Xing, and Xinyun Zou. 2020. Neurorobots as a Means Toward Neuroethology and Explainable AI. *Frontiers in Neurorobotics* 14 (October): Article 570308.

Copeland, B. Jack. 2017. The Modern History of Computing. In *Stanford Encyclopedia of Philosophy*, Edward N. Zalta (Principal Editor), 2017th ed. Stanford University. Online.

Deng, Li. 2018. Artificial Intelligence in the Rising Wave of Deep Learning. *IEEE Signal Processing Magazine*, January: 173–180.

Dijkstra, Katinka, and Rolf A. Zwaan. 2014. Memory and Action. In *The Routledge Handbook of Embodied Cognition*, ed. Lawrence Shapiro, 296–305. New York/London: Routledge.

Dreyfus, Herbert. 1997. *What Computers Still Can't Do: A Critique of Artificial Reason*. Cambridge, MA: MIT Press. Revised Edition. Fifth Printing.

Duro, Richard J., Francisco Bellas, and Jose A. Becerra Permuy. 2014. Brain-Like Robotics. In *Springer Handbook of Bio-/Neuroinformatics*, ed. Nikola Kasabov, 1019–1056. Heidelberg: Springer.

Economist. 2020a. "The Future: Autumn is Coming", Part of the "Technology Quarterly: Artificial Intelligence and Its Limits" (Special Section), *The Economist*, 13–19 June 2020, 12.

———. 2020b. "Computer Hardware: Machine Learning", Part of the "Technology Quarterly: Artificial Intelligence and Its Limits" (Special Section), *The Economist*, 13–19 June 2020, 10.

Edelman, Gerald M. 2004a. *Wider Than the Sky: The Phenomenal Gift of Consciousness*. New Haven: Yale University Press.

———. 2004b. When the Body Goes, We Go. *New Perspectives Quarterly* 21 (4): 83–86.

Edelman, Gerald M., and Joseph A. Gally. 2001. Degeneracy and Complexity in Biological Systems. *Proceedings of the National Academy of Science of the USA* 98 (24): 13763–13768.

———. 2013. Reentry: A Key Mechanism for Integrating Brain Function. *Frontiers in Integrative Neuroscience* 7: 1–6.

Froese, Tom, and Tom Ziemke. 2009. Enactive Artificial Intelligence: Investigating the Systemic Organization of Life and Mind. *Artificial Intelligence* 173: 466–500.

Gamex, D., A.K. Fidjeland, and E. Lazdins. 2012. iSpike: A Spiking Neural Interface for the iCub Robot. *Bioinspiration & Biomimetics* 7 (2): 025008.

Gelin, Rodolphe. 2019. Nao. In *Humanoid Robots: A Reference*, ed. Ambarish Goswami and Prahlad Vadakkepat, 147–168. Dordrecht: Springer.

Goertzel, Ben. 2014. Artificial General Intelligence: Concept, State of the Art, and Future Prospects. *Journal of Artificial General Intelligence* 5 (1): 1–46.

Goswami, Ambarish, and Prahlad Vadakkepat, eds. 2019. *Humanoid Robots: A Reference*. Dordrecht: Springer.

Goulding, Martyn, Guillermo Lanuza, Tamar Sapir, and Sujatha Narayan. 2002. The Formation of Sensorimotor Circuits. *Current Opinion in Neurobiology* 12: 508–515.

Grudin, Jonathan. 2009. AI and HCI: Two Fields Divided by a Common Focus. *AI Magazine* Winter: 48–57.

Hannaford, Carla. 2005. *Smart Moves: Why Learning is Not All in Your Head*. Salt Lake City: Great River Books.

Hebb, Donald. 1932. *Conditioned and Unconditioned Reflexes and Inhibition*. Unpublished Master of Arts Thesis. McGill University, Montreal.

———. 1949. *The Organization of Behavior: A Neurophysiological Theory*. New York: Wiley.

Hoffman, Matej, and Rolf Pfeifer. 2018. Robots as Powerful Allies for the Study of Embodied Cognition from the Bottom Up. In *The Oxford Handbook of Cognition*, ed. A. Newen, L. de Bruin, and Shaun Gallagher, 102–124. Oxford: OUP.

Hoffman, Matej, Hugo Marques, Alejandro Arieta, Hidenobu Sumioka, Max Lungarella, and Rolf Pfeifer. 2010. Body Schema in Robotics. *IEEE Transactions on Autonomous Mental Development* 2 (4): 304–321.

Horswill, Ian. 1993. Polly: A Vision-Based Artificial Agent. In *Proceedings of the Eleventh National Conference on Artificial Intelligence 1993*, 824–829. Washington, DC: AAAI.

Huber, Kay L. 1993. Memory Is Not Only About Storage. *New Directions for Adult and Continuing Education* 59 (Fall): 35–46.

Kasabov, Nikola K. 2019. *Time-Space, Spiking Neural Networks and Brain-Inspired Artificial Intelligence*. Heidelberg: Springer.

Kellerman, Travis. 2019. *What Happens When AI Is Let Out of Our Boxes? Another AI Winter Avoided*. https://medium.com/predict/what-happens-when-ai-is-let-out-of-our-boxes-8505e17ba00d.

References

Kemperman, Gerd, Fred H. Gage, Ludwig Aigner, Hongjun Song, Maurice Curtis, H. Sandrine Thuret, Georg Kuhn, Sebastian Jessberger, Paul W. Frankland, Heather A. Cameron, Elizabeth Gould, D. Rene Hen, Nora Abrous, Nicolas Toni, Alejandro F. Schinder, Xinyu Zhao, Paul J. Lucassen, and Jonas Frisén. 2018. Human Adult Neurogenesis: Evidence and Remaining Questions. *Cell Stem Cell* 23 (1): 25–30.

Kettenmann, Helmut, and Alex Verkhratsky. 2013. Glial Cells. In *Neuroscience in the 21st Century*, ed. D.W. Pfaff, 475–506. Heidelberg: Springer.

Kiggins, Ryan. 2018a. *The Political Economy of Robots: Prospects for Prosperity and Peace in the Automated 21st Century*. Cham: Palgrave Macmillan.

———. 2018b. Robots and Political Economy. In *The Political Economy of Robots: Prospects for Prosperity and Peace in the Automated 21st Century*, ed. Ryan Kiggins, 1–16. Cham: Palgrave Macmillan.

Kindberg, Tim. 2017. *The Third AI Winter*. https://matter2media.com/blog/the-third-ai-winter/.

Kirsh, David. 1991. Foundations of AI: The Big Issues. *Artificial Intelligence* 47: 3–30.

Krichmar, Jeffrey L. 2012a. Design Principles for Biologically Inspired Cognitive Robotics. *Biologically Inspired Cognitive Architectures* 1: 72–81.

———. 2012b. A Biologically Inspired Action Selection Algorithm Based on Principles of Neuromodulation. In *WCCI 2012 IEEE World Congress on Computational Intelligence*, 10–15 June 2012, Brisbane, Australia, 1–8.

———. 2018. Neurorobotics—A Thriving Community and a Promising Pathway Toward Intelligent Cognitive Robots. *Frontiers in Neurorobotics* 12: 1–9.

Krichmar, Jeffrey L., and Gerald M. Edelman. 2006. Principles Underlying the Construction of Brain-Based Devices. In *Adaptation in Artificial and Biological Systems*, ed. T. Kovacs and J.A.R. Marshall, 37–42. Bristol: Society for the Study of Artificial Intelligence and the Simulation of Behaviour.

———. 2008. Design Principles and Constraints Underlying the Construction of Brain-Based Devices. In *Neural Information Processing. ICONIP 2007. Lecture Notes in Computer Science*, ed. M. Ishikawa, K. Doya, H. Miyamoto, and T. Yamakawa, vol. 4985. Springer, Berlin, Heidelberg. https://doi.org/10.1007/978-3-540-69162-4_17.

Krichmar, Jeffrey L., Anil K. Seth, Douglas A. Nitz, Jason G. Fleischer, and Gerald M. Edelman. 2005. Spatial Navigation and Causal Analysis in a Brain-Based Device Modeling Cortical-Hippocampal Interactions. *Neuroinformatics* 3: 197–222.

Laird, John E., Christian Lebiere, and Paul S. Rosenbloom. 2017. Toward a Common Computational Framework Across Artificial Intelligence. Cognitive Science, Neuroscience, and Robotics. *AI Magazine* 38 (4): 1–19.

Lexcellent, C. 2019. *Human Memory and Material Memory*, 13–24. Geneva: Springer.

Lim, Milton. 2018. *History of AI Winters*. https://www.actuaries.digital/2018/09/05/history-of-ai-winters/.

Lungarella, Max. 2004. *Exploring Principles Toward a Developmental Theory of Embodied Artificial Intelligence*. Dissertation for the Doctorate in Natural Science. Faculty of Mathematics and Natural Science. University of Zurich.

Lungarella, Max, Georgio Metta, Rolf Pfeifer, and Giulio Sandini. 2003. Developmental Robotics: A Survey. *Connection Science* 15 (4): 151–190.

Lungarella, Max, Iido Fumiya, Josh Bongard, and Rolf Pfeifer, eds. 2007. *Fifty Years of Artificial Intelligence: Essays Dedicated to the 50th Anniversary of Artificial Intelligence*. Berlin: Springer.

Mason, Paul H. 2014. Degeneracy: Demystifying and Destigmatizing a Core Concept in Systems Biology. *Complexity* 2014: 1–10.

McCorduck, Pamela. 2004. *Machines Who Think: A Personal Inquiry into the History and Prospects of Artificial Intelligence*. Natick: A.K. Peters Ltd.

Miller, Blanca, and David Feil-Seifer. 2019. Embodiment, Situatedness, and Morphology for Humanoid Robots Interacting with People. In *Humanoid Robots: A Reference*, ed. Ambarish Goswami and Prahlad Vadakkepat, 2313–2336. Dordrecht: Springer.

Milner, Peter. 2003. A Brief History of the Hebbian Learning Rule. *Canadian Psychology* 44 (1): 5–9.
Minsky, M.L., and S.A. Papert. 1969. *Perceptrons*. Cambridge, MA: MIT Press.
Morales, Miguel. 2020. *Deep Reinforcement Learning*. Shelter Island/New York: Manning Publications.
Morrens, Joachim, Wim van den Broeck, and Gerd Kempermann. 2012. Glial Cells in Adult Neurogenesis. *Glia* 60: 159–174.
Newell, Allen. 1963. *A Guide to the General Problem-Solver Program GPS-2-2*. Santa Monica: RAND Corporation. Technical Report No. RM-3337-PR.
———. 1990. *Unified Theories of Cognition*. Cambridge, MA: Harvard University Press.
Nilsson, Nils J. 1982. *Principles of Artificial Intelligence*. San Francisco: Morgan Kaufman.
———. 1989. *The Quest for Artificial Intelligence: A History of Ideas and Achievements*. Cambridge: Cambridge University Press.
———. 2007. The Physical Symbol System Hypothesis: Status and Prospects. In *Fifty Years of AI: Essays Dedicated to the 50th Anniversary of Artificial Intelligence*, ed. Lungarella et al., 9–17. Berlin: Springer.
O'Hara, Phillip Anthony. 2001. Contradiction. In *Encyclopedia of Political Economy*, ed. P.A. O'Hara, 140–143. London/New York: Routledge. https://doi.org/10.4324/9780203443217.
———. 2009a. Political Economy of Climate Change, Uneven Development and Species Destruction. *Ecological Economics* 69: 223–234. https://doi.org/10.1016/j.ecolecon.2009.09.015.
———. 2009b. *Growth and Development in the Global Political Economy*. London/New York: Routledge. Paper Edition. 9780415547659.
———. 2019. History of Institutional Economics. In *Pluralistic Economics and Its History*, ed. Ajit Sinha and Alex M. Thomas, 171–190. Oxford/New York: Routledge. https://doi.org/10.4324/9780429278860-12.
———. 2020. *The Principle of Heterogeneous Groups and Agents in Political Economy*, GPERU Working Paper. Perth: Global Political Economy Research Unit.
———. 2022. Merging Dugger's Concepts with O'Hara's Principles to Advance Social and Institutional Economics. *Forum for Social Economics* 50 (1): 9–40. https://doi.org/10.1080/07360932.2018.1467332.
Ohlsson, Stellan. 2012. The Problems with Problem Solving: Reflections on the Rise, Current Status, and Possible Future of a Cognitive Research Paradigm. *The Journal of Problem Solving* 5 (1): 101–128.
Panda, Priyadarshini, and Kaushik Roy. 2017. Learning to Generate Sequences with [a] Combination of Hebbian and Non-Hebbian Plasticity in Recurrent Spiking Neural Networks. *Frontiers in Neurscience* 11 (Dec): 1–11.
Pennachin, Cassio, and Ben Goertzel. 2007. Contemporary Approaches to Artificial General Intelligence. In *Artificial General Intelligence*, ed. Ben Goertzel and Cassio Pennachin, 1–30. Berlin: Springer.
Perrault, Raymond (Coordinator), and Saurabh Mishra (Editor-in-Chief). 2019. *Artificial Intelligence Index: 2019 Annual Report*. Palo Alto: Stanford University.
Pfeifer, Rolf, and Josh Bongard. 2007. *How the Body Shapes the Way We Think A New View of Intelligence*. Cambridge, MA: MIT Press.
Pfeifer, Rolf, and Gabriel Gomez. 2009. Morphological Computation—Connecting Brain, Body, and Environment. In *Creating Brain-Like Intelligence: From Basic Principles to Complex Intelligent Systems*, ed. Bernhard Sendoff, Edgar Korner, Olaf Sporns, Helge Ritter, and Kenji Doya, 66–83. Heidelberg: Springer.
Pfeifer, Rolf, and Christian Scheier. 1999. *Understanding Intelligence*. Cambridge, MA: Mit Press.
Pfeifer, Rolf, Fumiya Iida, and Josh Bongard. 2005. New Robotics: Design Principles for Intelligent Systems. *Artificial Life* 11: 99–120.
Pfeifer, Rolf, Max Lungarella, and Fumiya Iida. 2007. Self-Organization, Embodiment, and Biologically-Inspired Robotics. *Science* 318 (5853): 1088–1093.

References

Polanyi, Karl. 1944. *The Great Transformation: The Political and Economic Origins of Our Time*. Boston: Beacon Press, 1968.
Potter, Steve M. 2007. What Can AI Get From Neuroscience? In *50 Years of Artificial Intelligence: Essays Dedicated to the 50th Anniversary of Artificial Intelligence*, ed. Max Lungarella, Fumiya Iida, Josh Bongard, and Rolf Pfeifer, 174–185. Heidelberg: Springer.
Proske, Uwe, and Simon C. Gandevia. 2012. The Proprioceptive Senses: Their Roles in Signaling Body Shape. Body Position and Movement, and Muscle Force. *Physiological Reviews* 92: 1651–1697.
Saladin, Kenneth S. 2012. *Anatomy & Physiology: The Unity of Form and Function*. 6th ed. New York: McGraw-Hill.
Schuchmann, Sebastian. 2019. *History of the First AI Winter*. https://towardsdatascience.com/history-of-the-first-ai-winter-6f8c2186f80b.
Serrien, Deborah J., Richard B. Ivry, and Stephan P. Swinnen. 2006. Dynamics of Hemispheric Specialization and Integration in the Context of Motor Control. *Nature Reviews. Neuroscience* 7 (Feb): 160–167.
Shanthi, D., G. Narsimha, and R.K. Mohanthy. 2015. Human Intelligence vs. Artificial Intelligence. *International Journal of Electronics Communication and Computer Engineering* 6 (5): 30–34.
Sherrington, Charles S. 1906. *The Integrative Action of the Nervous System*. New York: Charles Scribner's Sons.
Simon, Herbert A. 1962. The Architecture of Complexity. *Proceedings of the American Philosophical Society* 106: 467–482.
———. 1995. Artificial Intelligence: An Empirical Science. *Artificial Intelligence* 77: 95–127.
Slavin, Konstantin V., ed. 2016. *Stimulation of the Peripheral Nervous System: The Neuromodulation Frontier*. Paris: Karger Publications.
Sloman, Aaron. 2009. Some Requirements for Human-Like Robots: Why the Recent Over-Emphasis on Embodiment Has Held Up Progress. In *Creating Brain-Like Intelligence: From Basic Principles to Complex Intelligent Systems*, ed. Bernhard Sendhoff, Edgar Korner, Olaf Sporns, Helge Ritter, and Kenji Doya, 248–277. Heidelberg: Springer.
———. 2018. Huge, But Unnoticed, Gaps Between Current AI and Natural Intelligence. In *Philosophy and Theory of Artificial Intelligence 2017*, ed. Vincent C. Muller, 92–105. Geneva: Springer.
Stanfield, James Ronald. 1986. *The Economic Thought of Karl Polanyi: Lives and Livelihood*. New York: St Martins Press.
Takanishi, Atsuo. 2019. Historical Perspective of Humanoid Robots Research in Asia. In *Humanoid Robots: A Reference*, ed. A. Goswami and P. Vadakkepat, 35–52. Dordrecht: Springer.
Tool, Marc, and Dale Bush. 2003. *Institutional Analysis and Economic Policy*. Boston/London: Klewer Academic Publishers.
Torresen, Jim. 2018. A Review of Future and Ethical Perspectives of Robotics and AI. *Frontiers in Robotics and AI* 4: 75.
Tortora, Gerard J., and Bryan Derrickson. 2017. *Principles of Anatomy and Physiology*. 15th ed. Wiley.
UKIPO. 2019. *Artificial Intelligence: A Worldwide Overview of AI Patents and Patenting by the UK AI Sector*. London: UK Intellectual Property Office.
Valeeza, Guzel, Sona Janackova, Azat Nasretdinov, Veronika Rychkova, Roman Makarov, Gregory L. Holmes, Roustem Khazipov, and Pierre Pascal Lenck Santini. 2019. Emergence of Coordinated Activity in the Developing Entorhinal-Hippocampal Network. *Cerebral Cortex* 29: 906–920.
Valyear, K.F., A.M. Fitzpatrick, and E.F. McManus. 2017. The Neuroscience of Human Tool Use. In *Evolution of Nervous Systems*, ed. Jon H. Kaas, 2nd ed., 341–353. Oxford: Elsevier.
Veblen, Thorstein Bunde. 1898. Why Is Economics Not an Evolutionary Science. *Quarterly Journal of Economics* 12 (July). Reprinted in Thorstein Veblen, *The Place of Science in Modern Civilisation and Other Essays*, 56–81. New York: Russell & Russell, 1961.

———. 1899. *The Theory of the Leisure Class: An Economic Study of Institutions*. Boston: The Macmillan Company, 1968.

Velik, Rosemarie. 2010. Quo vadis, Intelligent Machine? *BRAIN. Broad Research in Artificial Intelligence and Neuroscience* 1 (4): 13–22.

Verela, Francisco, Evan Thompson, and Eleanor Rosch. 1992. *The Embodied Mind: Cognitive Science and Human Experience*. Boston: MIT Press.

Veruggio, G. 2006. The EURON Roboethics Roadmap. In *2006 IEEE-RAS International Conference on Humanoid Robots*, vol. 2006, 612–617.

Wallace, Mark T., Tiffany G. Woynaroski, A. Ryan, and Stevenson. 2020. Multisensory Integration as a Window into Orderly and Disrupted Cognition and Communication. *Annual Review of Psychology* 71 (15): 15.1–15.27.

Wallerstein, Immanuel. 1983. The Three Instances of Hegemony of the Capitalist-World Economy. *International Journal of Comparative Sociology* 24 (1–2): 22–38.

Weng, Juyang, James McClelland, Alex Pentland, Olaf Sporns, Ida Stockman, Mriganka Sur, and Esther Thelen. 2001. Autonomous Mental Development by Robots and Animals. *Science* 291 (5504): 559–606.

Whitworth, Brian, and Hokyoung Ryu. 2009. A Comparison of Human and Computer Information Processing. In *Encyclopedia of Multimedia Technology and Networking*, ed. Margherita Pagani, 2nd ed., 230–239. Hershey/New York: Information Science Reference.

Wikipedia. 2020. *History of Artificial Intelligence*. Online, 8 January.

Yamane, Katsu, and Akihiko Murai. 2019. A Comparative Study Between Humans and Homanoid Robots. In *Humanoid Robots: A Reference*, ed. Ambarish Goswami and Prahlad Vadakkepat, 873–892. Dordrecht: Springer.

Policy and Governance

8

Abstract

This chapter employs the principle of policy and governance to isolate key areas where IEPE informs socioeconomic policy; and this is continued especially in Chap. 9. We start with the concept of social provisioning; followed by the principles of the disembedded economy, uncertainty and historical specificity relating to cycles and waves of policy-making through the double movement relationship between markets, reciprocity, redistribution and householding. Then we study other aspects of the principle of contradiction, including capital-labor relations, finance-industry dichotomy, monopoly versus competition, profit and environment, plus individual versus society, etc. Thereafter the principles of circular and cumulative causation is linked to social and production aspects of complex systems of political economy which brings into focus the forces of emergence and complexity. Lastly, the principle of hegemony and uneven development is linked to global asymmetries of financial instability, climate change and wave dynamics, which brings into focus the principle of heterogeneous groups and agents. Core principles assist the policy process when activist governance measures are required to improve human and environmental provisioning.

Keywords

Principles · Policy and governance · Social provisioning · Disembedded economy · Historical specificity · Contradictions · Circular and cumulative causation · Uneven development · Uncertainty · Heterogeneous groups & agents

8.1 Introduction

In this book to date we have scrutinized numerous aspects of governance and policy innovation. These include, above, the progressive program of Chap. 3, the coronacrisis schemes of functional finance and preparing for the next such pandemic/crisis in Chap. 4, the importance of the Green Road shared socioeconomic pathway in Chap. 5, the broad corruption model of vested interests versus the common good of Chap. 6, and the embodied cognition approach to political economy from Chap. 7. Further chapters, below, examine governance issues relating to money, financial instability and crises in Chap. 9, those linked to anti-terrorism strategies in Chap. 10, policies linked to HIV-AIDS in Chap. 11, and suggestions for including more governance involvement in nurturance in Chap. 12.

To reduce duplication this chapter will concentrate on policies and governance issues more specifically linked to certain principles of IE political economy, and we shall try not to discuss issues analyzed in other Chapters (above and below [and in O'Hara 2023]) in detail. This current chapter, therefore, includes a very brief section on the concept of provisioning, which was mentioned in Chap. 3, but which we wish to bring to the fore here to show its significance for policy and governance in political economy.

The section after that highlights two principles in one: the first, principle of the disembedded economy, states that IEPE should put this issue, that historically capitalism tends to underplay transactions associated with community, family and environment in favor of those promoting formal markets, commodities and markets, at the core of the interdiscipline. This is inextricably linked to the principle of historical specificity: that IE political economy should place all its major concerns in a historical context and recognize transformations occurring through time. Here we introduce the *policy wave hypothesis*, which could also be called a principle: that governance agents can generate better policies if they investigate the economy operating through various waves of economic, social, political and environmental motion. The principle of uncertainty is inextricably intermeshed into this dynamic since we are discussing what in a slightly different context is called creative destruction.

The disembedded economy and uncertainty are also associated with the *principle of contradiction*, where political economy scrutinizes the conflicts between capital and labor, finance and industry, competition and monopoly, core and periphery, and so on. Contradictions link partly to the principle of heterogeneous groups and agents, where political economy is required to examine the roles played by groups and agents. At the broader level species, and vis-à-vis humans there are various classes, occupations, ethnic groups, genders, age groups, as well as different nationalities, and even more specific roles as we explore the institutions in detail. The trade-offs and movements between these realistic oppositions are critical to comprehending political economy processes, including the policy measures required for solutions to problems.

This leads us to two further principles, including the *principle of circular and cumulative causation*, that multiple factors are important for policy analysis and that they tend to magnify each other in the complexity of processes. Here we provide a brief example of a polycentric form of governance, which is likely more democratic and participatory than the usual forms. The *principle of hegemony and uneven development* is also crucial for IE political economy to investigate, because the world is subject to uneven forces, and policy needs to take into account these forces to properly represent the real forces impacting on the world. Examples of governance issues relevant to uneven development are briefly explored.

8.2 Science of Provisioning

Chapter 2 introduced the *concept of provisioning*, and here we show briefly its relevance to policy and governance. IEPE seeks to enhance the governance process through the principle of provisioning, that the purpose of governing institutions and their agents is to promote provisioning through contributing to the quality of life, standard of living, happiness, growth and development for the common good, while recognizing the cooperative and minimizing the conflicting interaction within and between classes, genders, ethnic groups, different ages, species, institutions, nations and regions.

A study of goods and services production-distribution within networks of people involved in social and economic life is a core part of the provisioning process. The provisioning process is heavily involved in ensuring that people and indeed other species have access to the basic needs of life and livelihood, including the provision of health services, a decent standard of living and quality of life, sufficient food and clothing, emotional bonding, childcare, housing, education, employment, transportation, and crucially protecting them from various crises and other difficulties that emerge throughout history.

Perhaps more important to the provisioning task is the commitment of governance processes and agents to providing a framework of services from before birth to even after death in trying to inculcate in the populace the need for them to learn to deal with life in an innovative fashion, and to seriously engage in the process of trying to solve their own, others, plus the community's, difficulties and needs, in a creative, democratic, sympathetic and trusting fashion. In this sense, we all potentially become part of the governance system, including individuals, groups, households, other institutions, states, and the like. This is a broad principle but nonetheless one required to state explicitly and generally for what follows in this chapter.

8.3 Disembedded Economy

Karl Polanyi in *The Great Transformation* (1944) developed the principle of the disembedded economy which posits a magisterial idea highly relevant to governance and policy. This principle posits the notion that a purely market economy is not possible because it requires a set of ancillary institutions, social support networks and public goods to protect the system from destructive creation. Being a more balanced version of Schumpeter's creative destruction, Polanyi established an idea that leads directly to major intervention. It posits that under a predominant market system policy requires the provision of safety nets to protect individuals from unemployment, on-the-job accidents, family and community breakdown, financial crises, and problems with the commons.

The disembedded economy signifies the core contradiction of the predominantly market system, namely, that it cannot exist as such; it operates through a whole series of institutions, habits, systems of knowledge, educational and social capitals, infrastructures and housing, plus the rearing of children (see O'Hara 2011a). In other words, markets have to operate in a complicated series of institutions which require resources from the collective wealth of the community, which itself contributes public goods for the system. Markets have a terrible tendency to become dislocated from the prevailing systems of economy, ecology and society. This contradiction tends to generate (unless unchecked) serious unequal distributions of income/wealth/power, major periodic financial instability, volatile business cycles plus short and long waves; alienation, social dislocation and familial destruction.

The disembedded economy posits three 'fictitious-commodities' that a market system insufficiently develops. These include labor power, money and common land. The market system fails to adequately reproduce the required amount and quality of labor power because this is a system function or public good largely outside of its jurisdiction. The business cycle, short and long waves, plus technological changes establish varying rates of economic activity, productivity and skills, usually at less than full employment. Thus various accords are required between groups and institutions, along with a sufficiently developed educational system and health apparatus, to contribute to this labor power reproduction outside normal markets (Block and Somers 2014; Seccareccia and Eugenia 2018; Lacher 2019).[1]

The second fictitious commodity is 'money'. 'Free banking' systems of monetary arrangements tend towards periodic instability and crisis, according to Polanyi (1944), because the stability mechanisms provided by the market do not operate effectively due to the failure of monetary provision. According to free bankers, purely free markets in money and banking are required, with the main stability mechanisms being too much credit being provided by some banks leading to a decline in specie, with the result of likely illiquidity and decline in reputation of the banks that are reckless with credit. A similar mechanism is said to operate when nations are over-lending inasmuch as they would have an outflow of specie and a similar decline in economic activity.

According to Polanyi (1944), free banking stability mechanisms are illusory since during most business cycle upswings a pure market system would lead to a general

---

[1] The disembedded economy (DE) is similar to the *concept of minimal dislocation*: where changes in the social economy are required to minimize long-term dislocative effects of changes (Bush 2001a: 736–737). Older important works on DE include, e.g., Neale (1976), Stanfield (1986), Ruggie (1982), Dale (2010), O'Hara (2000), Wolfson (2003) and Cangiani and Maucourant (2008).

expansion in lending in various markets, increasing the volatility of the business cycle, and leading to periodic crashes, recessions and depressions (especially during long wave downswings). Hence the need for an effective Central Bank to protect the system from these periodic credit over-expansions. The major cause of deep instabilities is the generation of over-and-under expansion of debt from the normal workings of the business system for endogenous money and credit through the innovations provided by banks and corporations. Public goods are therefore necessary in the form of lender of last resort facilities, prudential functions, deposit insurance, capital regulations and controls, to protect the system from periodic major instability and crisis.

The third fictitious commodity is 'land' or 'common property'. Polanyi believed that problems of land are not normally solved through the free market, since it produces too many private ownership certificates and fails to provide sufficient public lands. Under the free market, land use would tend to be over-exploited, including the resources, fish stocks and habitats, leading to destruction of critical species, atmospheric processes plus heritage sites and places of natural wonder. He therefore supported policy measures to protect the commons to ensure an adequate supply of natural resources, species and places of beauty for present and future generations.

Closely linked to this fictitious commodity approach to governance is Polanyi's recognition of the instabilities of the business cycle (see Sherman 1991; Sherman and Kolk 1996). It is not sufficient to provide adequate and effective monetary policies, but also activist fiscal policies are required. The system-needs for discretionary and automatic fiscal policy led historically to expansion of unemployment relief and demand management techniques. Polanyi (1944) would have accepted Abber Lerner's rules of functional finance, that tax, budget, money and other policies should be flexible according to ongoing changes in the state of the economy, without limits induced by ideology or conservative policy processes (see Wray 2018).

The disembedded economy also reveals the 'double movement' (Svetlana Kirdina-Chandler 2017), which is crucial for understanding the dynamic motion of governance practices. The double movement extricates from history that varying degrees of embeddedness and disembeddedness are historically ingrained in the evolution of state-market relations. Since a fully marketised economy is impossible, some degree of embeddedness is critical for its functioning. Thus, when disembeddedness leads to instability, socio-politico-economic pressures *tend to emerge* for greater levels of embeddedness. The new embeddedness is likely to last perhaps a few decades as the evolutionary contradictions within lead to necessary changes. As these contradictions come into play, along with economic difficulties, through time socioeconomic *pressures tend to emerge* for more disembeddedness (as the old system is 'blamed'), which in turn through time undergoes problems. The double movement of these ongoing waves is inherent in the motion of especially state-capitalist systems of production, distribution, exchange and reproduction.

If such recurring pressures are successful in these double movements, then short and long waves of disembeddedness tend to be followed by waves of embeddedness followed by waves of disembeddedness, and so on throughout history. This double movement is a powerful explanation for changes in systems of governance throughout the recent history of capitalism. This is related to the *policy wave hypothesis,* illustrated in Fig. 8.1, below.

Some examples relate to the history of policy since the 1870s/90s. In advanced capitalist economies, throughout the 1870s–90s there was overproduction in the key sectors, as large scale industry emerged while competitiveness was fairly strong, leading to low rates of profit and prices. This led to pressures for change, with several institutions emerging during the 1880s–1910s, including labor unions, banking and accounting institutions, European colonialism and business selling costs (Veblen 1923), which enhanced effective demand and balanced several contradictions, resulting in higher growth in the core economies during the late-1890s/1910s (Hobsbawm 1987).

The first-world war cut short this wave of (unbalanced) growth (van Duijn 1983) and prospects for progressive policy in many nations were dashed in the 1920s by the institutionalization of the 'Treasury View" in the UK, which "advocated monetary stabilization through the management of the bank rate, budgetary rigor, and the rejection of public investment, all of which became widely established goals among orthodox economic institutions, from the British Treasury to the Bank of England and the League of Nations" (Clara Mattei 2018: 490). Similar austerity measures were propounded in the US, although not quite as extreme, as "Conservative Republican supply-side ideas dominated fiscal policy actions, and conservative views promoted the deregulation of many government controls over business. Nevertheless, some aspects of the associative state – gathering economic statistics, promoting cooperation between government and business, and expanding the welfare system – were incorporated into the Federal government's activities" (Robert Keller 1987: 883).

In general the "pro-business" state throughout much of the world during the 1920s, characterized by unregulated financial markets, low taxes on business,

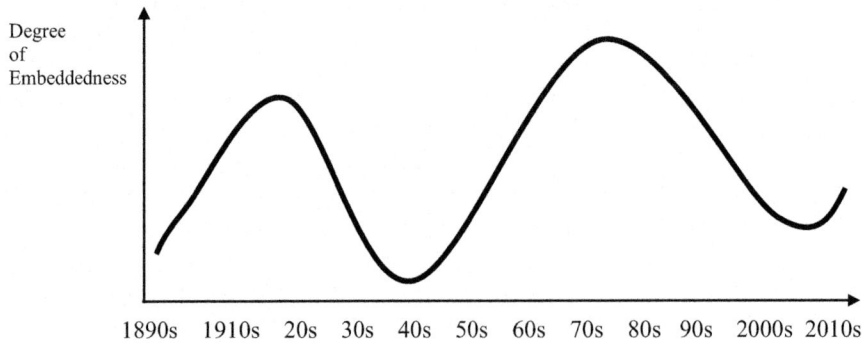

Fig. 8.1 Policy waves of embeddedness and disembeddedness (stylized)

declining fiscal power of the state, and relatively low real wages (and high debt), culminated in the Great Depression of the 1930s as disembeddedness intensified through crashing speculative bubbles, declining demand plus weak and inappropriate government short-medium term responses (Hobsbawm 1994).

It is well known that out of the Great Depression, Second World War and postwar reconstruction emerged central governments in many (especially Core) nations with relatively strong financial resources, automatic and discretionary policies, along with a working class mode of consumption that expanded demand. Pressures for change thus emerged, leading to institutions such as Fordism, the Keynesian welfare state (KWS), US hegemony, family formation, and regulated finance which enhanced demand, socioeconomic reproduction and general embeddedness during the 1950s through to the 1970s. The postwar boom saw long wave upswing in the vast majority of nations for two to three decades until the mid-1970s (Bowles et al.1990; O'Hara 2023).

Many see the contradictions of the KWS as representing too many or distorted forms of embeddedness, which contributed to the structural crisis of capitalism that emerged from the mid-1970s onwards (e.g. Claus Offe 1984). The key contradictions are seen as bureaucratization, disjointed incrementalism, and decreases in the 'cost of job loss', which contributed to low profit, investment and growth especially during the 1970s (O'Hara 2000: ch 12). The KWS was not the only institutional cluster contributing the anomalous performance. The deteriorating state of Fordism, the capital-labor accord, financial regulation, US hegemony and other institutions also played their roles. But both left and right wing economists saw a number of problematic tendencies in the KWS; while their policy reactions were quite different.

Out of the perceived failures of the form that embeddedness took into the 1970s emerged Thatcherism and Reaganomics, supply side economies and rational choice theory, along with the hegemony of neoliberalism into the 1980s−2000s. This new form of austerity, neoliberalism, was majorly informed by the earlier Treasury Views and related pro-business policies of the 1920s as the old "crowding-out" theses came back into vogue (Mattei 2018). This reversion back to a more disembedded form of governance was instituted with a view to improving economic performance. However it has failed to achieve this objective. Figure 8.2, below, compares the Stylized Long Wave (perfect) with the World Wave of GDP per capita real growth (decadal annual averages) for the period 1940–2020:

The World Wave (dashed line) is almost exactly the same as the (perfect) Stylized Wave (solid line). They both start at borderline growth (2.00–2.50%) in the 1940s; then undergo 20 years of long wave upswing in the 1950s–1960s (above 2.50% growth); followed by 20 years of long wave downswing (below 2.00% growth) in the 1980s and 1990s. The only difference is that the Stylized wave goes back to borderline during 2000–10, and then goes into upwave during 2010–20—thus completing a Full Wave from borderline-up to borderline-up, plus an upwave—whereas the World *continues* wave downswing into *secular* long wave downswing (40 years of downswing) during 2000–2010 and 2011–2020. The world has thus been suffering from a deteriorating regime of accumulation, including insufficient

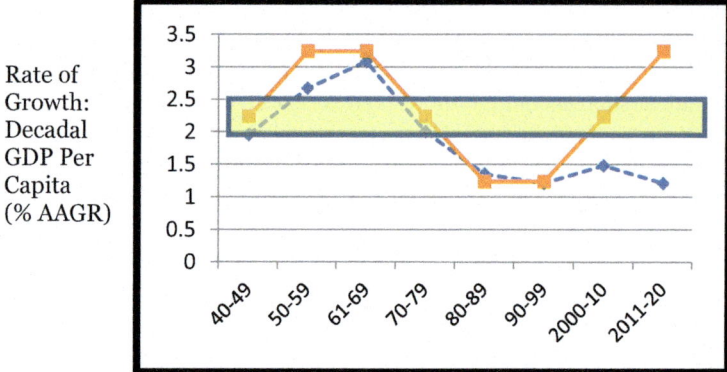

Fig. 8.2 Stylized wave, world wave; GDP per capita growth, 1940–2020. (*Source:* Adapted from O'Hara (2012b), World Bank (2022), Maddison (2006) & De Long (1998: 6). *Note 1:* Data are decadal AAGR (9–11 years; e.g., 1961–69, 2000–10). *Note 2:* The bar in the middle is the area of 'borderline' performance (2.00–2.50% growth) in between upswing and downswing.)

Table 8.1 Real GDP growth per capita, world, continents: 1950–2020

	World	NA	WE	CEE	LACA	MENA	SSA	Asia
1940–49	1.96	3.55	−0.71	1.24	2.06	n.a.	n.a.	−3.33
1950–59	2.68	2.09	4.03	3.68	2.03	3.49	1.82	3.82
1961–69	3.09	3.21	4.03	3.68	2.59	3.90	2.09	3.77
1970–79	2.01	2.60	2.94	3.26	3.19	5.77	1.30	3.39
1980–89	1.36	2.06	1.99	0.22	0.19	−1.63	−0.68	2.96
1990–99	1.22	1.91	1.88	−0.70	1.18	2.07	−0.60	2.87
2000–10	1.49	1.08	1.18	4.46ᵃ	2.35	2.42	2.34	4.32
2011–20	1.22	1.00	0.36◆	0.65∞	−0.08	0.21	0.23	3.65

Source: Adapted from O'Hara (2012b: 6), World Bank (2022), Maddison (2006), De Long (1998: 6)
NOTE: *NA* North America, *WE* Western Europe, *CEE* Central & Eastern Europe, *LACA* Latin America & Caribbean, *MENA* Middle East & North Africa, *SSA* Sub-Saharan Africa. ◆ Euro Area; ∞ Europe & Central Asia
ᵃ Based on growth for CEE5 (Russia, Hungary, Poland, Bulgaria, Czech Rep.; population weighted.)

demand, productivity and growth, through long wave downswing over the 1980s–2020.

Decadal annual average growth rates of GDP per capita are shown in Table 8.1, above; and then short, long and secular wave phases and periodicities are mapped in Table 8.2, for the World and its various continents/regions:

Neoliberal-neoclassical dominance of theory and policy over the past 40 years has been unsuccessful in restoring performance for wave upswing in the World economy and its major economies. The World and its Core, especially Western

8.3 Disembedded Economy

Table 8.2 'Map' of short, long & secular wave phases (Decadal GDP Per Capita Growth, AAGR), world, regions: 1940–2020: based on Table 8.1 & Fig. 8.2

	World	WE	NA	CEE	MENA	LACA	SSA	Asia
1940–49	B	SWD	SWU	SWD	n.a.	B	n.a.	SWD
1951–59	LWU	LWU	B	LWU	LWU		SWD	SECWU
1961–69			LWU			LWU	B	
1970–79	B						LWD	
1980–89	SECWD	SECWD[a]	B	LWD	SWD	LWD		
1990–99			LWD[a]		B-LW			
2000–10				SWU		B	B	
2011–20				SWD	SWD	SWD	SWD	

Source: Based on Table 8.1 & Fig. 8.2
Note: LWU long wave upswing, *B* Borderline, *LWD* long wave downswing, *SWU* short wave upswing, *SWD* short wave downswing, *SECWU* secular wave upswing, *SECWD* secular wave downswing
[a] *Main areas of Great International Crisis* (GFC and afterwards) *of 2008–2012*

Europe and North America, have been undergoing secular (>30 years) and long (20–30 years) wave downswing, respectively, over the past 30–40 years, culminating in the subprime crisis, the GFC, and the Eurodebt crisis of 2008–2014ff which affected mainly this Core. To the extent that the coronacrisis was conditioned by neoliberal traits, this can be seen to have had an downward impact on all areas. However, even without the coronacrisis in 2020 the same broad pattern emerges.

All the other areas of the World, mostly those deviating substantially from the neoliberal model, show some optimistic developments; including borderline results in Latin America (2000s), Middle East and North Africa (1990s–2000s) and sub-Saharan Africa (2000s); short wave upswing in Central and Eastern Europe (2000s); and secular long wave upswing for the past 70 years in Asia. However, for the period 2011–20 Latin America, Middle East & North America, sub-Saharan Africa and Central-Eastern Europe reverted back to short-wave downswing, with or without the results for 2020 (coronacrisis). Similarly, *the World* during 2011–2020 moved from long to secular wave downswing; the broad results are the same, with or without the data for 2020 (coronacrisis); as no borderline results appeared, although there was a *slight* pick-up for 2011–*2019* compared with 2000–2010 (when *2020* is included it is *worse*).

However, it should be stressed that economic performance is strongly linked to other institutions besides the state (and neoliberalism), including also the decline of the capital-labor accord, US hegemony and the industrial strength of the advanced capitalist economies (core relative to semi-periphery) (O'Hara 2023; Raffer 2011). In the periphery and semi-periphery (outside Asia), the failure to move from borderline to short wave upswing, or from short wave upswing to long wave upswing, during 2011–2020, is affected by several factors, including neoliberal policies, declining world income (declining exports), greater levels of corruption in numerous areas, increasing levels of autocratic rule in several places, and a whole series of wars, *jihadi* attacks and anomalous climate change events.

There are three (other) critical lessons for policy from these waves of embeddedness—disembeddedness and economic performance. The first is that governance structures—and the economy as a whole (World, continental, national and sub-national)—do tend to move from waves of varying levels of disembedded to more embedded and then onto more disembedded waves through time; as well as waves of high and low growth (plus other indicators). The *policy-wave principle* must be incorporated into practical policy analysis because there are wavelike-changes in the social economy that impact on government budgets, funding needs, social stability, financial crises, growth potential, labor supply issues, ecological changes and similar socio-politico-economic issues. Ignoring this principle leaves governance institutions and measures insufficiently prepared for the wave-like booms and busts as well as policy waves that affect all sectors of the political economy.

Secondly, it is useful to have different policy ideologies evolving at the same time as a foundation for changing levels of embeddedness, depending on the flow of institutions at the time. Many people have wondered why different groups of economists have so very different ideas about how to organize the economic system. The double movement indicates that without this pluralism and ideological diversity necessary reforms into the future would perhaps be difficult. Complicated systems of belief and ideology are required for public life and policy structures for any required changes to be instigated or evolved through time. The stock of knowledge in political economy needs to be fairly wide in scope given the complexity of the real world, and also since pressures long into the future can benefit from this variety as a stock of potential strategies, synergies and principles of action or inaction.

Thirdly, the double movement illustrates that we must transcend simple dichotomies of state and market to analyze socioeconomic waves of motion. As an evolutionary and institutional scholar Polanyi recognized the existence of several different yet related transactions impinging on political economy. State and market need to be supplemented with civil society, household, NGO, corporate, state and world economy institutions. The institutional structure and dynamics of capitalism or advanced societies is necessarily complex and policy processes need to be developed accordingly. The more advanced the society the more complex the structure and dynamics will be. Policy and governance should be cognizant of the polycentric diversity of arrangements in the real world, as households, communities, markets and production systems require safety nets to protect populations inhabiting/ surrounding them from wave-and-cycle-like dislocation.

8.4 Contradictions

The disembedded economy is a prime contradiction of capitalism, but others affect lives and fortunes of many. The principle of contradiction concerns prime movers of societies; forces that generate motion, potential conflict, endogenous sources of

8.4 Contradictions

change. The key is to illustrate their *concrete forms*, rather than delving into abstraction and uniformities. Contradictions need to be *brought down to the ground* and linked to the historical genesis of capitalism (and other systems). They have to do with opportunity costs or trade-offs between various forces, as indicated below in Fig. 8.3.

In Fig. 8.3 the DE bar-curve represents the social wealth of the community; the economic surplus (see Davis 1992), being a product of the skills, capabilities, institutions, capital structures and effective demands of the community. Economic surplus is variously distributed to capital or labor; finance or industry; competitive or monopoly forces; individuals or society; business or environment; gender A or gender B (or B/C); ethnic group A or ethnic group B; etc.. If too much is distributed towards any of the forces, combined or collectively, then this tends to generate systemic crises and deep recessions, including major financial crises. During such crises the *destruction of social wealth* occurs (the SW curve moves inwards) along either extreme (Crisis) bar-curves, CD or CE, as variously financial, economic, ecological and social instability, dislocation and fragmentation periodically become more extreme. Ideally these crisis bars are quite thick, due to problems with knowledge and also indeterminacy. The further the SW curve moves inward (reflecting destroyed social wealth or declining capacity utilization) along the periodic/structural crisis curves (CD, CE) the greater the depth of crises.

The core contradiction is that between capital and labor. Historically the relationship between workers and business has been a prime factor involved in the determination of production, distribution and exchange. This association has been at the forefront of the determination of wages and the rate of profit, influencing the lives and standards of living of families and communities. Capital represents the interests of business, including the means of production of machinery, buildings, implements, as well as the flow of finance into enterprises and the stock of inventories moving into shops and warehouses. The people who control these business assets may be

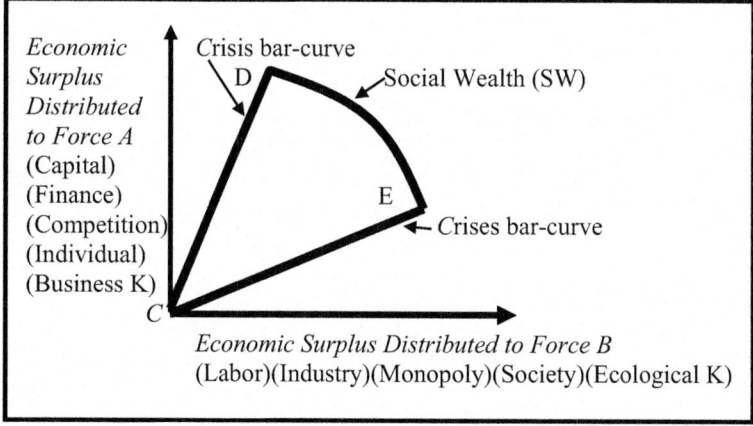

Fig. 8.3 Trade-offs between contradictory pairs. (*Source:* Adapted from O'Hara (2023: ch 7))

called capitalists, usually comprising CEOs, managers, small traders, financiers, and members of the Board of Directors. The people who work for these people, in return for a wage or salary, are the workers, those who depend upon their skills (or lack of) for a wage and have little controlling interest in business. Some of the workers may be deemed part of the Middle Class, which appears to be diminishing in relative numbers in the Core, plus the Lower Classes, including those working part-time, those in declining sectors, and the informal sector. Below these are the unemployed, the sick, and the homeless.[2]

Historically the institutions associated with capital and labor have been a critical part of policy-making. The difficulties of establishing viable wage levels, appropriate skills, cooperation in industrial relations, the free flow of commodities, and workplace conditions are at the core of policy-making. The capital-labor accord in the US (and many other Core nations), for instance, in the 1950s–70s was a system of full employment based on agreements between capital, labor and the state. The rise of Thatchism and Reaganomics, along with neoliberalism, into the 1980s–2010s was seen as a policy shift towards deregulating industrial relations, and increasing the power of capital vis-à-vis labor. The union movement has been in retreat over the past several decades which is part of the trend for credit to substitute for wages in the financing of consumer durables. Workplace agreements and on-the-job decisions have changed the focus of the debate somewhat to more decentralized institutions.

However, there are major problems when capital dominates labor, such as over the past 30 years in the Core nations and many others. These problems manifest themselves in major inequality between the high income achievers and the rest of the population. The dominance of capital over labor was influenced by the very structures of competition and uneven industrial development operating on a global and region scale. Lower real wages lead to more cyclical conditions due to financial instability, leading to greater financial crises through increases in debt for the middle and working classes, along with business; while increasing conspicuous consumption and waste of resources. A society based on consumption and social stratum is ceremonial since it increases competition and stress to keep up with the Joneses (Veblen 1899; Perez-Truglia 2012).

IEPEs tend to advocate moderating these contradictions between capital and labor through the implementation of accords, worker cooperatives, efficiency wages, social wages, worker participation programs, extended human capital schemes, community development initiatives and similar projects. These schemes seek to promote embeddedness and if their provisions become extreme may contribute to systemic crises for capitalism and/or help to generate the roots of a new communitarian system.

---

[2]Major debates on class relate to the literature of John E. Roemer (1982), Stephen Resnick and Richard D. Wolff (1987), Bowles et al. (2005), plus extensions to these perspectives. Resnick & Wolff, for instance, do not see classes as specific groups of people, but rather as multiple class positions based on the relationship to the production, distribution and exchange of surplus value (including households). See Steven Pressman (2008) on the global decline in the Middle Class.

8.4 Contradictions

The contradiction between monopoly and competition is another core issue of policy. Schumpeterian economists have established this dichotomy as a key area of analysis (Cantwell and Santangelo 2000). For them the ability of modern capitalism to generate ongoing innovations provides a foundation for short-term monopoly profit, followed by greater competition, further innovation and sectoral change, in an ongoing process of creative destruction. If this process proceeds unimpeded, it is said to generate continual growth and accumulation, employment and prosperity. The ability to reduce the incidence of patents and copyright somewhat is an important part of this process, as protecting vested interests is said to reduce the flow of innovation and competition through time, if they last too long.

'French' Regulation and social structure of accumulation scholars ('*SSA*') (e.g. Bowles et al. 2005) have a modified version whereby an evolutionary balance is required between monopoly and competition (O'Hara 2006, 2023). For them, too much competition produces too few profits and therefore insufficient accumulation and growth. A dynamic adjustment process of reasonable monopoly profits is said to balance the destructive powers of competition, without destroying it altogether. For instance, the postwar era of Fordism included this balance, whereas neoliberal globalization has been characterized by insufficient productive investment (financialization of the surplus). The differences between these schools (neo-Schumpeterian, '*SSA*') provide a fertile environment for active policy inquiry into the empirical evidence and how this dialectic relates specifically to industry policy (Elsner 2003) and competition policy (Gilbert 2020), as the economy moves through varying degrees of embeddedness and disembeddedness.

Recently another contradiction (linked also to the capital-labor contradiction, above) has come to the fore in the form of the industry versus finance conflict. Industry is the generation of knowledge, productivity, innovation and research and development. Finance is the provision of money, credit, bonds, equity, foreign exchange and other relatively liquid assets and liabilities. Closely linked to finance are the speculative sectors of domestic and commercial real estate. Often industry and finance work in cooperation, especially during the recovery and medium-boom of short cycles. This is also the case when finance is moderately regulated, such as during the postwar boom of the 1950s through to the early 1970s, especially in the Core nations. Some level of dynamic balance seems to be required for finance to support the interests of industry and society. When deregulation becomes too extreme, financial crises tend to become quite entrenched during long wave downswings. Such was the case in the 1920s and 1930s as well as during the 1980s to 2020s when finance has dominated industry.

As argued above, during the 1910s–20s finance was in the state of deregulation in many nations as it contributed to the speculative bubbles and crashes of the 1920s and 1930s. In the 1930s to the 1950s regulation was enhanced through more effective central bank activities, lender of last resort, separation of investment and commercial banking, deposit insurance, interest rate controls and qualitative directives (and beyond at least into the early 1970s). The (re)emergence of deregulation into the mid-late 1970s onwards saw the development of severe financial crises/recessions; including the early 1980s crises and recessions; the late 1980s/

early-late 1990s stock market crashes, recessions and Asian crisis; the corporate crises and recessions of the early 2000s; and the subprime, GFC and Eurodebt crisis of 2008-2014ff. As Aliber & Kindleberger say (2015: 347): "The three decades since the 1980s have been the most tumultuous in monetary history in terms of the number, scope and severity of banking crises". (See Chap. 9, below, on financial instability.)

The GFC (which affected especially the core) highlighted problems of initially US deregulation through 'innovations' that increase systemic risk through the distancing of mortgage arrangements from securitized mortgage bonds with increasing proportions of subprime assets in the portfolio. The deregulated environment failed to self-regulate as individual assessments of risk were often fraudulent and failed to recognize rising systemic uncertainty during the cycle boom of 2005–07. The circuit of money capital was thus subject to major dislocation of an uneven nature throughout the world, especially in the Core nations, as differential yet relatively deep levels of uncertainty, liquidity preference and recession prevailed over recent years. (See discussion of uncertainty and financial instability in Chap. 9, below.)

To prevent major depression on a global scale governments have seen the need for massive bailouts, in the form of trillions of dollars of lender of last resort bailouts, large interest rate discounts, bank nationalizations, increases in deposit insurance, and even bailouts of manufacturing companies (O'Hara 2011b). During the GFC many governments announced the official end of the neoliberal and deregulation experiment (e.g. USA, Australia). The first counter to neoliberalism was the Asian crisis of the late 1990s, when the IMF initiated major reforms such as quasi-lender of last resort facilities and protecting innocent bystanders (poverty relief), after deregulation in the early 1980s. The second was the corporate crisis of the early 2000s when the Sarbanes-Oxley Act took effect to counter corporate self-regulation.

The GFC, mostly blamed on deregulation, instigated the (re)emergence of a concerted embedded tendency for capitalism, which may become institututionalized, especially in the light of the coronacrisis, Brexit, 'leveling up areas', and other responses to deregulation: a modern balance between state and capital. There are now a number of scholarly, activist and policy movements against the rising inequality that has been impacting over several recent decades and adversely impacting socioeconomic performance as disembeddedness became relatively extreme (see Rohit 2011; Whalen 2011; Monteiro and Lima 2021).

A fourth contradiction that has recently become more obvious is that *between ecological capital and market capital*. If we compare global real GDP (as an indicator of market activity), even during a mostly secular wave downswing, as well as human population growth, with various ecological data we get a good idea of the trends. In this context, during 1970–2016/2020, as global real GDP and the human population grew by 353% and 111%, respectively (World Bank 2022), the global stock of fauna and flora declined by 68%, global CO_2 flows rose by 83% and global CO_2 stocks rose by 30% (IPCC 2021; WWF 2021). This inverse relationship between ecological resources and market activities, or the positive relationship between market activities and GHG flows and stocks, illustrates the contradictions

8.4 Contradictions

at play between markets (and human stocks) and their historically destructive impact on the natural environment (see Chap. 5, above, for details).

During 2007–2008 most of the major players agreed on the magnitude of the problem, although then it was thought a mean global temperature rise of 2 °C would be adequate by 2100, compared to the 1850–1900 mean. Since then, despite numerous COP climate summits, the most recent being COP26 in Glasgow (2021), global GHGs stocks and flows keep rising, and promises made by most nations are not backed up by stringent mandates. Meanwhile the accepted global temperature rise limit by 2100 (relative to the 1850–1900 mean) has changed to 1.5 °C, which is looking precarious as likely major global stocks of flora and fauna will have declined by over 80%, and major tipping points that are already noticeable will likely transform into cascades by that point (Lenton 2019, 2021). These likely cascading tipping point catastrophes only need to cumulate from merely a few of the more than a dozen likely/already upon us for it to lead to path dependent points of no return (see Chap. 5, above for details).

The only IPCC (2021) shared socioeconomic pathway (SSP) consistent with achieving 1.5 °C by 2100 is the Green Road of strong sustainability. But chances of this taking hold before stocks of GHGs rise to points of no return are small on current trends. The periphery and semi-periphery are still waiting for the core to commit on an ongoing basis to the annual $100b mitigation and adaptation fund, while core nations are slow to majorly develop the "loss and damage fund" in the light of the already escalating climate change costs of $290–580b to date (German Watch 2021).

The fact is that most nations have a low commitment to the process of reducing global mean temperatures to 1.5 °C or anything liked it, not to mention the more likely necessary 1.0 °C rise limit, with the failure of the Chinese President to attend the 2021 Summit and the openly cynical attitude of the Australian Prime Minister and his coalition government being merely attitudes common to most of the players.

Vested interests, including most national concerns, businesses, consumers, and governments, are the main opponents of change. The culture-institutions-habits nexus is a constraint on change. If there is success with these anti-GHGE technologies, accords and changing habits and institutions, alternative long waves of development and policy may emerge which are more ecologically embedded than the current regime of institutions. But this is unlikely to happen before it is too late.

Clearly these contradictions illustrate crucial current problems of the world. They involve various opportunity costs and trade-offs which need to be balanced by accords, agreements, new institutions/systems/habits rather than purely market forces.[3] Institutions, markets, governments, individuals, families and civil societies are important in the ongoing resolution of contradictions. They are always ongoing

---

[3] These contradictions, embody much of what Fagg Foster and Dale Bush—in a broad Marc Tooltype model of instrumental valuation—(FTB) scrutinise in the principle of ceremonial encapsulation, where progressive change is inhibited by ceremonial dominance of instrumental processes (Bush 2001b: 80–82), i.e., the *invidious use of power or knowledge* by the market system, capital or labor, finance or industry, monopoly or competition, core-periphery forces, and so on.

and being modified as history changes relationships and sudden metamorphoses emerge from time to time through varying degrees of embeddedness and disembeddedness.

8.5 Circular and Cumulative Causation

Probably the major challenge for any governance program is that the core problems of the world tend to be multi-causal. Rather than having singular origins they are complex, involving numerous interacting variables, and often cumulating multiplier impacts. Hence the orthodox idea of having one (or even two) instruments for each target seems very simplistic. Equilibrium models and ceteris paribus assumptions are hardly ever useful for investigating the causes and solutions to complex problems. Instead, the more realistic principle of circular and cumulative causation (CCC) can usefully be employed in governance issues. This model was developed by Gunnar Myrdal and Nicholas Kaldor to centre on monetary problems, ethnic issues, development, and growth issues (Lorentz et al. 2022). It has since been used by others to study urban and regional problems, AIDS and HIV, terrorism, subprime crisis, coronacrisis; and a host of other policy-issues (Berger 2009). At the higher reaches of theory/empirics CCC has evolved into complexity analysis and emergence (see Arthur 2007).

CCC includes five main features. The first is that the whole social system needs to be examined in relation to the problem at hand, or at least micro questions need to be linked into a macro, regional, and/or global framework. The second is that there is a degree of interdependency between variables, in the sense that most socioeconomic problems have a relatively large number of co-factors, usually of both a qualitative and quantitative nature. The third is that the variables tend to operate in a cumulative manner; that there is a multiplier effect with feedback processes involved. There may in fact be multiple cumulative effects, with some operating in different directions. The fourth is that there are contradictions (discussed above) usually operating as well, where there are various trade-offs and opportunity costs negatively impacting the system. These contradictions may either counter some of the cumulative impacts or impose dual cumulative movements (some in different directions). And finally, a core factor often intervenes into the complex mosaic: for Myrdal (1944, 1968) it was education; for Kaldor (1966, 1972) demand; for Amartya Sen (1999) capabilities and freedom; and for Dale Bush (1987), technological change (broadly conceived to include skills, knowledge and communication).

CCC models link well with modern perspectives that governance is more than simply 'government' or the 'state' (departments, executive, legislature and judiciary). Governance has more to do with the general provision of adequate levels of embedding processes that provide system-functions or public goods necessary to solve complex problems. The amount and nature of these embedded goods depend on the desired process of reform, whether social capitalism or a more communitarian system is considered proper in the current or future environment. Polanyi recognized that various institutions and individuals can potentially provide embedded goods that prevent or reduce the extent of problems, as indicated below in Fig. 8.4:

8.5 Circular and Cumulative Causation

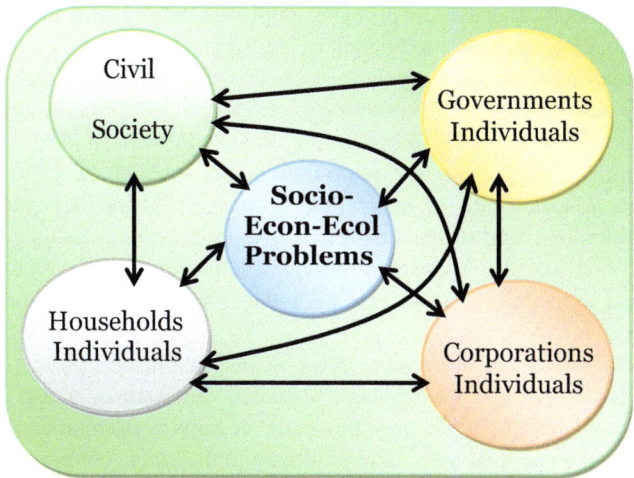

Fig. 8.4 Circuit-stock of institutional-ecological relations: quadratic elements of governance

This figure illustrates that all the dominant social institutions, groups and individuals, set in an ecological environment (background environment), influence the problem at hand; whatever it is: GFC, climate change, terrorism, AIDS-HIV, growth and development, corruption, HIV-AIDS, and so on. IE political economy and some modern progressive schools of governance believe that all sectors of society have a *responsibility* to provide elements of provisioning goods and services, including those that protect the global, regional, national and local communities from crisis and instability. The type of *potential* temporal, vertical and horizontal emergence emanating from the CCC interaction between these components of the Circuit-Stocks of Institutional-Ecological Relations can thereby become sui generis, a qualitative transformation from the past through instrumental interaction between agents, groups, institutions and ecologies.

During normal types of interactions between the parts, prior to the success of the innovations, or before they become highly effective, there tend to be waves of uncertainty that broadly follow the embedded—disembedded wave dynamic discussed above, due to three interrelated processes. First there is the *general insufficiency* of information, understanding, skills, knowledge, organization, coordination, capabilities and trust within core parts of the complexity of socioeconomic and political life. Secondly there is *asymmetric distribution* of information, understanding, organization, skills, knowledge, capabilities and trust between people in these activities. And thirdly, there are *differing geopolitical and socioeconomic distributions* of powerful systems of production, distribution and exchange throughout the World. Changes in these three variables through long historical time reveal waves of socioeconomic performance and phases of evolution. It is critical both to advance this theory and also to promote empirical inquiry into these areas for a proper system of governance and policy to emerge.

A core idea of IE political economists is that all of the dominant sectors and agents have a role to play in promoting such emergence through complexity, by balancing the conflicts through provisioning. Indeed, the critical need is to inculcate into the dominant institutions, including individuals, a belief and commitment to a wider vision, a social view of interaction – 'recognized interdependence' (Bush 1987). Corporations need to see themselves in a wider context, as do governments, households, civil society groups and individuals. The degree to which they seek a wider context for collective action is likely to be an indication of potential solutions to social problems.

This wider vision of governance views all institutions and groups as having a responsibility to various stakeholders; a social, environmental and governance (SEG) ethic. Under this ethic they moderate negative externalities; corporations and their agents go beyond their narrow domain to the whole community, including linkages to other communities; governments balance short and long term objectives through promoting the common good, including beyond its electoral, nation state, and local dynamics; and society's segments and their agents attempt to interact, comprehend, and improve the provisioning process.

Socioeconomic problems are thus caused by the inability of institutions and individuals to see beyond their own short-term vision to communicate and meaningfully seek resolution of ongoing problems with other groups and individuals. The extent to which they isolate themselves to their own functioning and ignore linkages and associations with other segments and individuals is likely to be positively associated with socioeconomic problems, or an inability to resolve them in a timely fashion. True democracy, in a political economy perspective, is not simply electing governments in every electoral cycle, but having people involved in matters that affect both themselves and the community as a whole. This decentralized form of political economy reveals the true anarchistic or 'republican' origins of its advocates and the underpinnings of its beliefs (Vanek 1975; Tool 2001). Still quite often we are left in the situation where rapid changes and asymmetric distributions of resources and knowledge lead to greater disembeddedness, and in this context the state is periodically under greater pressure to intervene where other processes have failed. The greatest challenge to anarchism is precisely this "left-over" thesis, namely: that in an individualist, creative destructive and mostly market-based system the state is usually the only entity to have the *potential* capabilities of dealing with these inequalities, at least in advanced nations.

The quadratic elements of governance represent a useful model not only for comprehending the ideological and policy beliefs of political economists, but also for understanding the sources of problems. In this model, governments are not only seen as a possible solution to the problem, but also as one of its causes. In like measure, the tendency in various quarters to blame governments for problems, either because they intervene when they should not, or because they fail to intervene when they should, seems a rather narrow view of governance. IE political economists tend not to assume that all critical problems should be solved by government, but they do believe governments can play a very useful role in a wider quadratic context.

8.6 Uneven Development

The principle of hegemony and uneven development has been a generic part of IE political economy for decades now. It has its roots in the desire to be realistic and follow the empirical process of growth and development throughout the global, regional, national and subnational political economies. Much of its edifice came from regional, development and international segments of political economy. The principle states that there are substantial inequities between nations and areas generating divergent quality of life and standard of living patterns and creating core, periphery and semi-periphery differentials which must be incorporated into theory and policy-making.

Key scholars contributing to the principle have been Stephen Hymer, Samir Amin, Immanuel Wallerstein, Andre Gunder Frank, Amitava Krishna Dutt and many others. Institutionalists have followed through on this work with contributions by (among others) Thorstein Veblen, James Street, Dilmus James, James Dietz and James Cypher. An area that used to be monopolized by male scholars has been emerging as a feminist issue-concern, thanks to the pioneering work of Joan Robinson (1979), Ha-Joon Chang and Ilene Grabel (2004), plus, e.g., Abjhijit Banerjee and Esther Duflo (2011), Naila Kabeer (2020), and many others.

The core idea is that the orthodox emphasis on convergence of nations towards the leading economies is highly abstract and ignores much of the empirical evidence. Some convergence trends operate, but usually the divergences and inequalities are more interesting and conspicuous. Therefore, governance theory and practices need to recognize this fact and incorporate it into development research and policy conventions and institutions.

There are many reasons for a combination of convergence and divergence, with critical elements of uneven development and inequality occurring in the regional and global economies. The first is that while knowledge is a public good and is difficult to privatize it can also be embedded in institutions, cultures, organizations and conventions that can prevent it from being distributed freely and widely. As Dale Bush (2001b) recognizes, knowledge can be ceremonially encapsulated by the vested interests, being also used to protect their power and authority from competition and open access. Hence the knowledge of the leading technological processes, technical solutions to specific problems and organizational ways of enhancing markets and sales are not open to use by the general population. They tend to be privatized through patents, copyright, inside information, tacit knowledge, and organizational capabilities.

The second is that knowledge that is easily bought and sold is subject to distribution through various commodity chains and production networks. These chains and networks are based on various forms of organization and communication within and between businesses mainly through the leading markets and economies.

For instance, the consumer-oriented value chains of leading sports shoes tend to operate between Asian producers and European and US consumers and distributors via transnational alliances. The producer value chains of mass production vehicles is based on Japanese and advanced capitalist economies linking to parts manufacturers in Asia and Central Europe plus consumers in the advanced economies. These productive, distributive, exchange and financial networks are very powerful modes of authority and business with cultural and organizational overtones (Dickens 2015).

Social networks are also important to the uneven distribution of social, cultural and human capital. Recent research has shown that economic development in the Core economies are not only based on physical capital but also intangible relationships underlying trust, institutions, organizations, and community relations (O'Hara 2009). Social capital has come to the fore as a crucial element in the development equation, since it is based on bonding and bridging within and between people and social groups. Bonding is important for communication and trust within small groups, but bridging is perhaps more critical in linking various groups together for core objectives. Often these forms of trust and sociality emerge within and between class, ethnic, gender, national and political groupings and networks.

For instance, historically in the US, the upper class mentoring and learning of subtle etiquette associated with the leading families and educational institutions of Harvard, Yale, Columbia, Stanford, Princeton and Cornell helped to create an elite group of powerful leaders of business and politics. John O'Hara in a whole series of novels, especially *Ten North Frederick* (1955, winner of the National Book Award), detailed the subtle nuances necessary for membership of these groups. In the UK a similar grouping of families was oriented around Cambridge and Oxford (Oxbridge). Networks of relationships linked to culture and knowledge promoted vested interests and class prestige. Veblen studied the distribution of power and institutional subtleties in an earlier era of capitalism (1890s–1920s), while C.W. Mills (1940s–1960s), later J.K. Galbraith (1950s–1980s), Ron Stanfield (1980s–2010s) and Bill Dugger (1980s–2020s) continued this tradition of scrutinizing the interface between culture, power, and lifestyle within and between the social institutions of capitalism.

In this context, IEPE incorporates the *principle of heterogeneous groups and agents*, wherein there are several layers of roles that impinge on socioeconomic and policy processes that should be at the centre stage of analysis. At the most general levels are roles played according to groupings of species, ethnicities, classes, ages, and genders. These are the key groupings, but there are several others as well, such as nationalities (linked to ethnicities to some degree), tribes, political alliances, families and interest groups. Within various institutions there are more micro groups such as within the economy there are different gradations of industrialists, bankers, traders, segmented workers, welfare recipients, politicians, civil servants and the unemployed. At a more micro level within the financial system there are layers of borrowers, lenders, speculators, underwriters, financial analysts, brokers, institutions

8.6 Uneven Development

and central bankers. These different roles are crucial to policy theory and practice. Political economy is thus in this wider sense a pragmatic science of provisioning and policymaking, where real people and other species are situated in groups in geopolitical, business, social and ecological environments.[4]

At the global, regional, national and sub-national levels, core–periphery–semi-periphery (CPSP) changes lead to varying margins of disparity between areas, especially between the advanced nations and sub-Saharan Africa, and to a lesser extent Latin America, Middle East, and parts of South Asia. As Fig. 8.5, below, indicates, there are various barriers due to a myriad of forces inhibiting certain areas and nations from moving from one level to another; such as from Periphery to Semi-Periphery and from Semi-Periphery to Core.

While over several recent decades, numerous nations in East Asia have managed to move from the periphery towards the semi-periphery, eventually (for some nations) moving towards the core; less success has been made by Sub-Saharan African (SSA) (mostly peripheral) and Latin American (LA) (semi-peripheral and peripheral) nations. As indicated in Table 8.1, above, in SSA and LA the 1980s–90s were decades of inadequate performance as structural adjustment policies and high US interest rates generated debt crises and deteriorating socioeconomic conditions. AIDS contributed to malaise in SSA throughout the 1990s, while a series of banking crises and collapses emerged in Latin America in the 1990s, and Eastern Europe underwent institutional destruction which set them back by decades in the 1990s. The optimistic results of the 2000s did not progress through to the 2010s in all these areas.

Recent decadal adjustments to the Human Development Index (HDI) have lessened the apparent degree of the crisis in SSA, but still their GDP levels are the lowest in the world, while their HDI levels are even worse, indicating major insufficiencies of human, organizational and health capital. The Middle East and North Africa managed respectable performance in the 1950s through to the 1970s, while in the 1980s growth rates dived in the light of declining oil prices and other

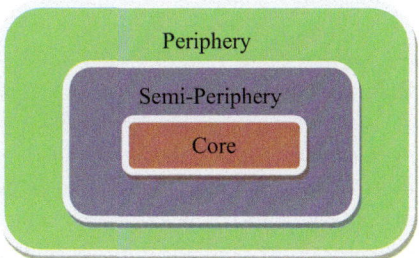

Fig. 8.5 Model of Core, Periphery, Semi-Periphery (CPSP)

---

[4]For instance, in the area of class the issue of cultural capital has helped to make the issue more practical and penetrable (Bourdieu 1986), as class relations are set in an institutional and habitual framework of the reproduction of relationships, objects and commodities; Irish social policy, for instance, has made advances here, despite their current terrible economic situation.

contradictions. The 1990s and 2000s saw stable if relatively mediocre rates. However the most recent decade, 2011–2020, has seen another dive as revolutions, counter-revolutions, wars, *jihadi* violence, corruption and authoritarian governments have adversely impacted performance. As a result, their ability to productively invest their oil and economic surpluses has been reduced severely.

The real challenge, however, is still sub-Saharan Africa, where problems have seemed irresolvable for some time now. The core problems have been a colonial heritage where artificial borders, unnatural elites, insufficient public social infrastructure, corruption and ethnic conflicts have proliferated. The colonial masters and their political offspring failed to provide an institutional order for the great mass of people. Power was held in the hands of colonial classes even after independence, and few successful transfers of power have occurred (Mensah 1997). Brain drain has played a crucial role in this equation (Ghosh and Ghosh 2001). Some apparent successes, such as Botswana and to a lesser extent Mozambique and Uganda, look promising in GDP growth terms, but their human development index demonstrate inadequacies. Problem nations, such as Zimbabwe, seem caught in a contradiction between the need for land reform and the minimal productiveness of the present mostly white property magnates.

Perhaps the greatest challenge of uneven development is environmental. As climate change reports noticed (e.g., UNDP 2020; IPCC 2021), a contradiction affecting the world is that major GHG generators are minimally affected while those least generating emissions are majorly impacted by climate change. This will likely exacerbate uneven global development by reducing agricultural productivity, income and health in the periphery and semi-periphery, while perhaps minimally promoting it in the core. Climate change is predicted to impact majorly on tropical and subtropical areas (mostly underdeveloped nations) as well as on upper-north latitudes. The major difficulty constructing a viable new environmental regime is structural linkages between differential impacts and abilities to tackle climate change between core, semi-periphery and periphery. Costs of climate change in the Periphery are linked to lower costs in the Core due to the structure of production and trade between the regions (see Chap. 5, above).

8.7 Conclusion

This chapter applies the principle of policy and governance to issues of IEPE, illustrating how PE principles can inform policy-makers and governance scholars of core elements of cycles-waves, contradictions such as capital-labor relations and capital-ecology conflicts, circular and cumulative production and social dynamics, and hegemonic-uneven forces of inequality, climate change, and development.

We started with the concept of provisioning and the principles of the disembedded economy, historical specificity and uncertainty. Generating goods, services, stimulating democratic governance and balancing various markets with governments, civil society groups and other potentially embedding agents in the double movement helps to explain otherwise uncertain waves of governance/

performance and different policy prescriptions over the past century and more. It also provides insight into future likely waves and cycles of policy-making that agents should be cognizant of for proper governance to be activated.

The principle of contradiction helps explain a series of related processes affecting socioeconomic performance. The degree of conflict and cooperation between capital-labor, monopoly-competition, industry-finance, ecological capital-market/population capital, men and women, and others, helps comprehend some core world problems.

The principle of circular and cumulative causation explains the complexity and emergence of socioeconomic problems as well as the multifarious sources of governance required for stability and provisioning. The principle of uncertainty also informs CCC since complex causation generates uncertainty in policy formulation and practices.

The principle of uneven development emphasizes diverging trends at the global, regional and local levels. Uneven development helps explain the differential performance of nations and regions as well as the climate change problem that is besetting the world. Linked to this is the principle of heterogeneous groups and agents which helps explain differentials on the basis of species, gender, class, ethnicity, age, and other groupings at the sub-national, national and regional levels.

Acknowledgements An earlier version was presented at the Association for Evolutionary Economics (AFEE) meetings of the the Allied Social Sciences Associations (ASSA), Denver, Colorado. I thank the anonymous referees, Dale Bush, John Hall, and Janice Peterson, plus Amanda Shoebridge and the Editor of the *Journal of Economic and Social Policy* [JESP], where it was originally published (O'Hara 2012a) for comments and encouragement. (JESP policy is for authors to have complete copyright ownership/control over their papers).

References

Aliber, Robert Z., and Charles P. Kindleberger. 2015. *Manias, Panics and Crashes: A History of Financial Crises*. 7th ed. New York: Palgrave Macmillan.
Arthur, W.B. 2007. Complexity and the economy. In *Elgar Companion to Neo-Schumpeterian Economics*, ed. H. Hanusch and A. Pyka, 1102–1110. Cheltenham, UK: Edward Elgar.
Banerjee, Abjhijit V., and Esther Duflo. 2011. *Poor Economics: A Radical Rethinking of the Way to Fight Global Poverty*. New York: Public Affairs.
Berger, S., ed. 2009. *The Foundations of Non-Equilibrium Economics: The Principle of Circular and Cumulative Causation*. New York/London: Routledge.
Block, Fred, and Margaret R. Somers. 2014. *The Power of Market Fundamentalism: Karl Polanyi's Critique*. Cambridge, MA: Harvard University Press.
Bourdieu, P. 1986. Forms of capital. In *Handbook of Theory and Research for the Sociology of Education*, ed. John G. Richardson, 241–258. New York: Greenwood Press.
Bowles, S., D.M. Gordon, and T.E. Weisskopf. 1990. *After the Waste Land: A Democratic Economics for the Year 2000*. Armonk: M.E. Sharpe Inc.
Bowles, S., R. Edwards, and F. Roosevelt. 2005. *Understanding Capitalism: Competition, Command and Change*. Oxford: Oxford University Press.
Bush, P.D. 1987. Theory of Institutional Change. *Journal of Economic Issues* 21 (3): 1075–1116.
———. 2001a. Minimal dislocation. In *Encyclopedia of Political Economy. Volume 2*, ed. P.A. O'Hara, 5736–5737. London/New York: Routledge.

———. 2001b. Ceremonial encapsulation. In *Encyclopedia of Political Economy. Volume 1*, ed. P.A. O'Hara, 80–82. London/New York: Routledge.

Cangiani, M., and J. Maucourant. 2008. *Essais de Karl Polanyi*. Paris: Seuil.

Cantwell, J., and G.D. Santangelo. 2000. Capitalism, Profits and Innovation in the New Techno-Economic Paradigm. *Journal of Evolutionary Economics* 10 (1): 131–157.

Chang, He-Joon, and Ilene Grabel. 2004. *Reclaining Development: An Alternative Economic Policy Manuel*. London: Zed Books.

Dale, G. 2010. *Karl Polanyi: The Limits of the Market*. Cambridge: Polity Press.

Davis, J.B., ed. 1992. *The Economic Surplus in Advanced Economies*. Aldershot: Edward Elgar.

De Long, J.B. 1998. *Estimates of World GDP, One Million B.C.–Present*. Berkeley: Mimeo. University of California, Department of Economics.

Dickens, P. 2015. *Global Shift: Reshaping the Global Economic Map in the 21st Century*. 7th ed. London: Sage.

Duin, van J.J. 1983. *The Long Wave in Economic Life*. London: Allen & Unwin.

Elsner, W. 2003. Global Industrial policies. In *Institutional Analysis and Economic Policy*, ed. M.R. Tool and P.D. Bush, 523–547. Boston: Kluwer Academic Publishers.

German Watch. 2021. *An Open Letter to World Leaders: Cop26 Must Deliver On Loss And Damage Finance*. (Signed by 301 organisations.) COP26 must deliver on Loss & Damage Finance | Germanwatch e.V.

Ghosh, B.N., and R. Ghosh. 2001. The problem of brain drain. In *Contemporary Issues in Development Economics*, ed. B.N. Ghosh. London/New York: Routledge.

Gilbert, Richard J. 2020. *Innovation Matters: Competition Policy for the High-Technology Economy*. Cambridge, MA: MIT Press.

Hobsbawm, Eric. 1987. *The Age of Empire 1875–1914*. London: Phoenix Press.

———. 1994. *Age of Extremes: The Short Twentieth Century 1914–1991*. Abacus: London.

IPCC. (Intergovernmental Panel on Climate Change). 2021. *Climate Change 2021: The Physical Science Basis*. Working Group 1 Contribution To The Sixth Assessment Report of The IPCC, UK: IPCC. https://www.ipcc.ch/reports/.

Kabeer, Naila. 2020. Women's Empowerment and Economic Development: A Feminist Critique of Storytelling Practices in "Randomista" Economics. *Feminist Economics* 26 (2): 1–26.

Kaldor, Nicholas. 1966. *Causes of the Slow Rate of Economic Growth in the United Kingdom*. Cambridge: Cambridge University Press.

———. 1972. The Irrelevance of Equilibrium Economics. *Economic Journal* 82 (328): 1237–1255.

Keller, Robert R. 1987. The Role of the State in the U.S. Economy in the 1920s. *Journal of Economic Issues* 21 (2): 877–884.

Kirdina-Chandler, Svetlana. 2017. Institutional Matrices Theory, or X- and Y- Theory: A Response to F. Gregory Hayden. *Journal of Economic Issues* 51 (2): 476–485.

Lacher, Hannes. 2019. Karl Polanyi, the "Always-Embedded Market Economy," and the Re-Writing of *The Great Transformation*. *Theory and Society* 48: 671–707.

Lenton, Timothy M. 2019. Climate Tipping Points: Too Risky to Bet Against. *Nature* 575: 592–595.

———. 2021. Tipping Points in the Climate System. *Weather* 76 (10): 325–326.

Lorentz, André, Tommaso Ciarli, Maria Savona, & Marco Valente. 2022. *Structural Transformations and Cumulative Causation Towards an Evolutionary Micro-Foundation of the Kaldorian Growth Mode*. Maastricht University—United Nations University, Working Paper Series. #2022–001. Maastricht Economic and Social Research Institute on Innovation and Technology (UNU-MERIT). Maastricht, The Netherlands.

Maddison, Angus. 2006. *The World Economy: Volume 1: A Millennial Perspective; Volume 2: Historical Statistics*. Paris: OECD.

Mattei, Clara. 2018. Hawtrey, Austerity, and the Treasury View, 1918-1925. *Journal of the History of Economic Thought* 40 (4): 471–492.

Mensah, J. 1997. Colonialism and Human Factor Degradation in Africa. *Review of Human Factor Studies* 3 (1): 48–64.

Monteiro, Cristiano, and Raphael Lima. 2021. Embeddedness and Disembed-dedness in Economic Sociology in Three Time Periods. *Sociologia & Anthropologia* 11 (1): 1–21.

Myrdal, G. 1944. *An American Dilemma: The Negro Problem and Modern Democracy*. New York/London: Harper and Row.

———. 1968. *Asian Drama: An inquiry into the poverty of nations*. Harmondsworth, UK: Penguin.

Neale, W.C. 1976. *Money in Societies*. Corte Madera: Chandler & Sharp Publishers.

O'Hara, J. 1955. *Ten North Frederick*. New York: Random House.

O'Hara, P.A. 2000. *Marx, Veblen and Contemporary Institutional Political Economy: Principles And Unstable Dynamics Of Capitalism*. Cheltenham/Northampton: Edward Elgar.

———. 2006. *Growth and Development in the Global Political Economy: Social Structure of Accumulation and Modes of Regulation*. New York/Oxford: Routledge.

———. 2009. Современные принципы неортодоксальной политической экономии. *Вопросы экономики* 12 (2009): 38–57. [In Russian].

———. 2011a. *International Encyclopedia of Public Policy* (4 Vols.). Global Political Economy Research Unit (GPERU). http://pohara.homestead.com/encyclopedia/volume-1.pdf, http://pohara.homestead.com/encyclopedia/volume-2.pdf, http://pohara.homestead.com/encyclopedia/volume-3.pdf, http://pohara.homestead.com/encyclopedia/volume-4.pdf

———. 2011b. International Subprime Crisis and Recession: Emerging, Macroprudential, Monetary, Fiscal and Global Governance. *Panoeconomicus* 58 (1): 1–17.

O'Hara, Phillip Anthony. 2012a. Principles of Political Economy Applied to Policy and Governance: Disembedded Economy, Contradictions, Circular Cumulation and Uneven Development. *Journal of Economic and Social Policy* 15 (1): 1–36.

———. 2012b. Short, Long and Secular Wave Growth in the World Political Economy: Periodicity, Amplitude and Phases for 8 Regions, 108 Nations, 1940-2010. *International Journal of Political Economy* 41 (1): 3–46. https://doi.org/10.2753/IJP0891-1916410101.

———. 2023. *Long Wave Institutional Dynamics and Political Economy Crises of Capitalism: Principles, Social Structures of Accumulation*. Empirics: Springer.

Offe, Claus. 1984. *Contradictions of the Welfare State*, ed. John Keane, London: Hutchinson.

Perez-Truglia, R. 2012, January. A Test of the Conspicuous Consumption Model Using Objective Well-Being Data. *Social Sciences Research Network*. (SSRN). https://papers.ssrn.com/sol3/papers.cfm?abstract_id=1934007.

Polanyi, K. 1944. *The Great Transformation*. Boston: Beacon Press.

Pressman, Steve. 2008. The Decline of the Middle Class: An International Perspective. *Journal of Economic Issues* 40 (1): 181–200.

Raffer, Kuni. 2011. Neoliberal Capitalism: A Time Warp Backwards To Capitalism's Origins. *Forum for Social Economics* 40 (1): 41–62.

Resnick, S.A., and R.D. Wolff. 1987. *Knowledge and Class: A Marxian Critique of Political Economy*. Chicago: Chicago University Press.

Robinson, Joan. 1979. *Aspects of Development and Underdevelopment*. Cambridge: Cambridge University Press.

Roemer, J.E. 1982. *A General Theory of Exploitation and Class*. Harvard: Harvard University Press.

Rohit. [sic]. 2011. Income Distribution, Irrational Exuberance, and Growth: A Theoretical Model of the U.S. Economy. *Review of Radical Political Economics* 43 (4): 449–466.

Ruggie, J.G. 1982. International Regimes, Transactions, and Change: Embedded Liberalism in the Postwar Economic Order. *International Organization* 36 (2): 222–248.

Seccareccia, Mario, and Correa Eugenia. 2018. Rethinking Money as an Institution of Capitalism and the Theory of Monetary Circulation: What Can Modern Heterodox Economists/Institutionalists Learn from Karl Polanyi? *Journal of Economic Issues* 52 (2): 422–429.

Sen, A. 1999. *Development as Freedom*. New York: Anchor Books.

Sherman, Howard J. 1991. *The Business Cycle: Growth and Crisis Under Capitalism*. Princeton: Princeton University Press.

Sherman, Howard J., and D.X. Kolk. 1996. *Business Cycles and Forecasting*. New York: Harper Collins.

Stanfield, James Ronald. 1986. *The Economic Thought of Karl Polanyi: Lives and Livelihood*. New York: St Martins Press.

Tool, Marc. 2001. *The Discretionary Economy: A Normative Theory of Political Economy*. New Brunswick: Transaction Publishers.

UNDP. (United Nations Development Program). 2020. *Human Development Report 2020: The Next Frontier: Human Development and the Anthropocene*. New York: UNDP. http://hdr.undp.org/en/reports/global/hdr2020.

Vanek, J. 1975. *Self-Management: Economic Liberation of Man*. Harmondsworth: Penguin.

Veblen, T.B. 1899. *The Theory of the Leisure Class*. London: Macmillan.

———. 1923. *Absentee Ownership and Business Enterprise in Recent Times: The Case of America*. New York: Transaction publishers.

Whalen, C.J., ed. 2011. *Financial Instability and Economic Insecurity after the Great Recession*. Cheltenham: Edward Elgar.

Wolfson, Martin. 2003. Neoliberalism and the Social Structure of Accumulation. *Review of Radical Political Economics* 35 (3): 255–226.

World Bank. 2022. World Bank Open World Development Data, 1961–2020. https://data.worldbank.org/.

Wray, L. Randall. 2018. *Functional Finance: A Comparison of the Evolution of the Positions of Hyman Minsky and Abba Lerner*. Annandale-on-Hudson: Levy Economics Institute. Working Paper No 900.

WWF. (Worldwide Fund for Nature). 2021. *Living Planet Report 2020* (ed. R.E.A. Almond, M. Grooten & T. Petersen). WWF: Gland. https://livingplanetindex.org/home/index.

Money and Credit Circuits, Cycles and Crises

Abstract

This chapter examines the nature of money, credit and finance under capitalism, paying special attention to the principle of innovation, involving IEPE scholars seeking to understand and change the system for the better, and the principle of policy/governance where they try and improve the theoretical tools of policy-making. The principle of historical specificity is used to situate money and finance in history since the political revolutions of the late 1700s, industrial revolutions of the 1800s, and the recent series of financial crises during the 1980s–2020s. We study the circuits, instabilities and crises that beset the major nations, especially over the past 50 years, and illustrate through the principle of contradiction how crises arose and forces leading to institutional-habitual changes generating phases of evolution.

Then we scrutinize the principle of uncertainty through an analysis of money, credit and finance in the circuit of social capital, endogenous money and credit, and the financial instability hypothesis (FIH). Hyman Minsky's FIH is explicitly related to the most intense period of financial instability and crises experienced by nations and regions, during the 1980s–2020s. We go on to examine reforms of the international financial architecture, especially in the context of the principle of hegemony and uneven development, vis-à-vis the role of the US dollar, plus the major tenets of modern monetary theory (MMT) as well as critics of this theory.

Keywords

Principles & concepts · Phases of financial capital · Money, credit & finance · Circuit of money capital · Endogenous money & credit · Financial instability hypothesis · Global money · Modern monetary theory · Fictitious capital · Financial crises

9.1 Introduction

An understanding of modern capitalism requires one to be cognizant of key elements of 'money, credit and finance', since they are crucial for workings of the system. This is especially the case for in a relatively deregulated environment where money and finance take on a life of their own. Previously businesses, the rich and governments were the principal agents of finance capital. More recently, lower middle class and working class households have become more involved in complicated questions of financial assets and portfolios. When speculative bubbles dominant the economy more people join the circus, and when they crash many people lose out as fewer households become involved in this risky business.

Institutional and evolutionary perspectives of money and credit are distinctive in that they seek to be realistic, institutional, historical and systemic in their methodology. They are realistic in that they try and develop a Wall Street perspective on the financial system, where cash flow and net worth are a critical part of the edifice (Dillard 1987). An attempt is made to embed successive institutional changes into the theory so knowledge becomes relevant to changes in the real economy (on the history of money see Neale 1976, and its theoretical history Vickers 1959). The principle of historical specificity is used to illustrate the different phases of evolution, hysteresis and path dependence impacting the political economy. The critical thing, relevant to the principle of contradiction, is to understand the financial-industry contradictions of capitalism, where 'capital' has three main pillars. The first is a system of classes, from workers and capitalists, to money and industrial capitalists, to venture capitalists and small businesses, and from lumpens to high-tech workers. The second is complex, long-term investments into productive structures of factories, warehouses, machinery, electronics, robotics, biotechnology, organisations and human capital. And the third is financial bundles and circuits of intangible capitals, including private and public capitals, debt instruments, electronic 'money', fintechs, and conventional banks and finance companies.

Consistent with the principle of heterogeneous groups and agents, several influences contribute to this institutional and evolutionary view of money and finance. These heterogeneous groups seek to inform the principle of innovation by making theoretical and empirical contributions to an understanding of financial capitalism, and also to the principle of policy and governance by the provision of theories and approaches to improving financial governance.

In this context, institutional neo-Marxian contributions centre on the circuit of money capital, social structures of accumulation, Regulation approach, fictitious capital and the break-up of the surplus value into profit, interest and rent (Nelson 1999; O'Hara 2000a). Schumpeterian evolutionary perspectives focus on the role of credit-money in financing innovation or variously being used for general accumulation or speculation (Schumpeter 2014; Perez 2007). Veblenian themes include the financial instability hypothesis, intangible capitals and business principles, while post Keynesian institutionalists recognize the importance of the principle of uncertainty, including the role of uncertainty in complex capital investments plus the nature of endogenous finance, the financial instability hypothesis and Modern

Monetary Theory (MMT) (Arestis and Eichner 1988). These traditions complement and overlap each other while they all centre on the core contradiction of industry versus finance, a monetary theory of production, and the need for a dynamic, circuitous vision of finance capitalism (Lavoie 2014).

9.2 Waves and Phases of Industrial-Financial Capitalism

The extent to which there are money-financial circuits, cycles, fragility and crises, depends on the nature and evolution of the institutions. Institutional and evolutionary perspectives of money and credit are based on the principle of contradiction, namely, that capitalism is forever variously subject to creative destruction and destructive creation (Aghion et al. 2021). This is the idea that capitalism has various tendencies within its emergent motion that upsets the prevailing mode of production, distribution, trade, circulation and reproduction. It seeks to expand in a seemingly unlimited fashion globally, creating new products, processes, markets, forms of competition, and types of raw materials. It seeks to innovate and in the process destroy numerous existing industries, products, skills, employments and towns. It castes asunder indigenous cultures, forests, fish stocks, plus existing habits of life and livelihood in the pursuit of new markets, processes and profits.

Evolutionary and institutional scholars, especially Schumpeterians, posit that this contradictory tendency to destroy and create simultaneously cannot be moderated for fear of undermining the inner dynamics of the system. However, they may agree with Schumpeter (1950) that a double movement against such contradictions will likely destroy this inner motion of capitalism. Other institutional and evolutionary scholars, especially neo-Marxists, institutionalists, post Keynesians and feminists, tend to agree that the economy should be *minimally dislocated* (Bush 2001), meaning that a degree of institutionalised stability is required, especially for a dynamic economy such as capitalism. This is similar to Karl Polanyi's (1944) idea that free market economies cannot exist in the long run because they propel instability due to inadequate levels of reciprocity, redistribution and householding. Deregulated monetary systems increase the volatility of the business cycle as endogenous finance escalates during cycle boom and diminishes radically during recession. Corporations suffer inadequate governance leading to periodic over-reporting of profitability and other accounting irregularities during cycle boom; and concentrations of economic power leading to higher levels of white collar crime, fraud, insider trading and corruption.

This section provides a mere outline of the role of money and finance in the evolution of industrial forms of capitalism, to provide a context within which more technical elements are then discussed. In a longer historical context, Asia was the centre of the world, especially China, from long before 1000 AD to sometime after 1500 AD. European powers started to evolve especially from the 1400s, became dominant into the 1800s and 1900s, and majorly declined from the 1980s through to the present. (Maddison 2006; Rojek 2018). Institutional and evolutionary political economy recognises that financial excesses vary over short business cycles and long waves. Long waves are important. These are long movements of the economy, characterised usually by particular *phases of capitalist development*, as well as typically *periods of relatively strong followed by relatively weaker/disjointed performance*, profit rates and often growth per capita.

Associated with the principle of historical specificity, the basis of these long phases of evolution and movements of socioeconomic activity is the shape of the culture and its institutions, habits and tendencies of its agents and groups. Cultures-institutions-habits undergo change and even transformation through long historical time. These changes can at a systemic level appear emergent in the sense of having a specific pattern, in which the parts fit together to varying degrees, although periodically and eventually these patterns change their qualitative nature, as some key elements transform more than others. Such changes also affect socioeconomic performance, as typically a period of relatively robust activity becomes reinforced by its successes, but also typically such positive elements (eventually) have negative impacts, and hence contradictions, which usually become greater through historical time as agents and groups continue to utilise the patterns of the regimes and exhaust their potential.

A schematic view of these long waves of phases of evolution for the advanced capitalist economies is presented in Table 9.1, below (see Mandel 1978; Mager 1987; Tylecote 1992; Freeman and Louca 2001; O'Hara 2023 for details), where the financial trends are outlined:

Central to an understanding of the evolution of capitalism is the principle of contradiction, which illustrates the endogenous forces of various opposing tendencies and vested interests in moving the system forward through time. In this context, during the late 1700s a host of political revolutions occurred that sought to variously emancipate the general population of an area or the bourgeoisie from the shackles of the past. The American and French revolutions are the most famous of these. The French Revolution had more of a long-term effect, but together the revolutions provided a foundation for radical-liberal movements of progress.

Table 9.1 Long waves/phases of capitalism and financial dynamics

	Long wave	Upswing?	Downswing?	Financial dynamics
1780s–1840s	Competitive capitalism	European rivalry	British consolidation	Evolving British hegemony & private banks
1850s–1890s	Industrial revolution	1850s–1870s	1870s–1890s	Equity capital and money capital in firms
1890s–1940s	Imperialism-finance capital	1890s–1910s	1910s–1940s	Investment banks and credit-money for finance capital
1940s–2010s	Fordism-welfare state to neoliberalism	1940s–1970s	1970s–2020s	Industry-finance balance → shareholder value economy
2020s–2050s?	Electronics & biotechnology	2020s–2030s?	2030s–2050s?	Predominant electronic & paperless economy

Drawing on these to some degree, the first long wave of industrial capitalism (1780s–1840s) involved the industrial revolution proper, in Britain and later in much of Europe and the so-called 'settler colonies', and later still in other continents. During this period, western economies constituted core elements of the industrial system, with other continents playing various peripheral roles in the structural system of capitalism. In this phase of evolution, the pre-eminent position of Amsterdam as a financial and industrial centre was well into decline, while London and Paris were vying for leadership, with London eventually eclipsing Paris, with Britain becoming the hegemonic nation by 1815 (Wallerstein 1983: 40) due to industrial, commercial, financial and (derivatively) military prowess.

Certain crucial heterogeneous groups and agents played key roles. Private bankers were the norm, usually small private ones, often based on partnerships with merchants ('merchant banks'), while the private Bank of England (BOE) had restricted functions, such as that of clearing house and some supervisory functions (Cassis 2006: ch 1). While London was the centre, Paris still played a key role through its familial and imperial networks and relationships, while lesser but important roles were played by Swiss, German, Dutch and Belgium agents. In response to serious banking crises during the mid-late 1830s in Britain, and several others throughout Europe and around the world, the British government instituted an inquiry to recommend measures to reduce instability.

Heterogeneous groups of scholars and policy-makers played key roles. The Currency School advocates, precursors to quantity theorists, and essentially Metallists, believed in the need for not simply convertability of bank notes into Bullion, but for there to be a strict ratio of bullion to notes, in order to reduce inflation, and for the Bank of England to be the main printer of bank notes, as a way of stabilising the system. The Banking School, essentially Chartalists, had a wider definition of money, including not only BOE notes but also other bank notes, cheques, bills of exchange, and so forth. The Banking School postulated that money is essentially endogenously generated, based on the demands of industry and consumers. The resulting Bank Charter Act of 1844 essentially instituted the demands of the Currency School, with some limited flexibility accorded by the Banking School, with the BOE becoming the main issuer of notes and regulator of banks, at least in England (Davies 2002).

The second long wave of capitalism, during the 1850s–1890s, saw the evolution of equity business finance and the incorporation of banks in many countries. One notable tendency was for the generation of long-term infrastructure assets, such as railways and electricity, financed by long-term share capital traded on stock markets (Toporowski 2020), which helped to generate successive booms and busts. Britain emerged as the hegemonic power, and large-scale production, including steam engines, became a dominant trend, during the so-called "Great Depression" of 1873–1996. However, despite several crises during the 'depression' years, *industry* enjoyed secular buoyancy during much of the 1850s–1890s, as large-scale production came to dominate the key sectors; while prices and profits fell substantially in many nations over 1873–1896 (Rostow 1938, 1940).

A core contradiction during this era of industrial dominance over finance required some resolution, due to the poor rates of return on capital, and pressure was mounting for institutional changes to re-establish some degree of financial power. Continuing from the latter years of the 'depression' through to the early years of the twentieth century, a new wave of "finance capital, imperialism and large corporations" (1896–1945) emerged, especially in the major economies. Key institutional elements of the 'New Era of Business' (Veblen 1923) involved concentrations of financial businesses and absentee owners controlling large segments of key industries; accounting principles advancing the cause of profitability; investment banking and credit-money organisations becoming growth industries; the scramble for Africa and other areas continuing unabated; and greater competition among the big powers, such as Britain, Germany and the USA. The first-world war put an end to the relative buoyancy of the markets, especially in Europe (van Duijn 1983), although not for the US and other nations not directly impacted by the war; and after the war/during the 1920s speculative bubbles developed, notably in the US, along with relatively low wages (except in Fordist industries). Another Great Depression emerged during the 1930s in the face of these anomalies of inadequate demand, speculative crashes and concentrated industries.

Heterogeneous groups and agents evolved through time. Intellectual and policy struggles were naturally occurring as the old quantity theorists and 'Treasury' officials battled with others who sought stability and development through public and private investment and the creative use of finance. J.M. Keynes was central to this latter movement as he and others tried to understand the workings of money and credit in a production economy. In particular these new scholars analysed the nature of the circuits through which money is used for expanding production, speculation and hoarding. Eventually the whole world became involved in these 'new' ideas, which of course went back to the Chartalists, the banking school and others, who recognised the importance of money velocity, shadow banking, and how to reduce hoarding and expand demand while minimising inflation.

In the context of the principles of innovation and policy/governance, a new phase of capitalism and long boom developed during the late-1940s through to the mid-1970s, including the New Deal between the state and capital/citizens (KWS), US hegemony in the world economy, Fordist relations of production-distribution, the accord between capital and labor, regulated finance, and familial households, in most significant economies of the world. During the long wave upswing of 1945–1973, well developed financial social structures of accumulation operated through central banking, credit creation, financial intermediaries and business-household savings and investment institutions (Wolfson 1994a; O'Hara 2002; Guttman 1994, 2001). These financial structures helped develop a viable system of industry and technology along with the rate of profit for business in most economies.

After 20–30 years of relatively high growth, the contradictions of the institutions started to manifest themselves, which led during the 1970s and 1980s to decline in the KWS, US hegemony, regulated finance, Fordism, and familial stability as recessions became deeper and financial crises more intense (O'Hara 2000b). This malaise was reflected in the breakup of the Bretton Woods system of fixed exchange rates, the emergence of Thatcherism-Reganomics, deregulated finance, monetarism, capital ruling over labor, and a loosening of familial ties. Finance came to dominate industry as the rate of industrial profit declined and financial motives majorly ruled business decisions.

During the 1980s–2020s, fictitious capitals periodically dominated industry with substantial misallocation of resources, throughout much of the world. Corporate finance led to debt financed unproductive speculative activity, leading to a major stock market crash of 1987, soon followed by a recession of the early 1990s; while debt crises became critical in much of the periphery. The 1990s led to excesses, especially in the internet and high-tech sectors, leading to a series of speculative bubble crashes and accounting crisis, which continued into the early 2000s. The mid to late-2000s also led to excesses, notably in the US sub-prime mortgage market which spilled over into the general and global economies through the GFC and the Eurodebt crisis of the late 2000s and early 2010s; and much later the coronacrisis, which many saw as a test of modern monetary theory (O'Hara 2023).

Meanwhile hegemonic forces and uneven development evolved as much of Asia, notably China, has since the 1980s been advancing the cause of state capitalism, through initially mass production techniques and later more sophisticated technologies and financial instruments. Expanding stock-markets, retail and commercial banks, derivatives, capital markets and electronic innovations have been useful in the transformation of Chinese industry and trade, with the emergence of numerous billionaires and the rising power of finance. Since 2021 the Chinese state has sought to address anomalies of financial power and rising inequality in addition to the desire for more domestic growth and development, while it has continued to challenge US hegemony often in association with Russia as conflict is increasing throughout the global political economy.

This era of financialization during the 1980s–2020s saw numerous periodic financial crises and recessions, notably during the Global Financial Crisis 2008ff as financial opaqueness, uncertainties and low levels of trust between agents led almost to systemic financial demise. On the back of functional finance, counter-cyclical fiscal and monetary policy, lender of last resort, and major intrusions of the state into economic and social life, a major catastrophe was averted, except during the Eurodebt crisis of 2010ff; while a decade later during the coronacrisis statist action was successful again in averting complete collapse. Historically, crises are getting worse, finance too powerful and financial innovations more radical (O'Hara 2023).

Electronic money, 'fintechs' (decentralised finance), venture capital firms and private capitals have become particularly crucial institutions of the new system. Globally the coronacrisis was worse than the GFC in the sense that the whole world was involved, whereas the GFC affected mainly the advanced nations but overall was more serious economically. The coronacrisis also advanced the cause of many sectors, such as financial and electronic capitals, which may see further major instabilities into the future, despite the double movement of functional finance, discretionary policy and state controls that provide buffers to protect the system from major collapse (see Chap. 4, above).

As Aliber and Kindleberger (2015: ch 15) demonstrate, the four global waves of stability-instability and banking crises during the 1980s–2010s were the most intense and critical in the whole history of capitalism; as the contradictions of deregulated international monetary networks became intense. Throughout this chapter we seek to illustrate why this was the case and how it might be rectified (for details see O'Hara 2013).

9.3 Dynamic Circuit of Money Capital

It is in this historical context that we should see issues of money and finance. Orthodox perspectives of money and credit, whether it be the currency school, metallism more generally, or the later (re)emergence of monetarism, are based on money as a static process of equilibrium, final-phase analysis. Here money is in a state of rest where nothing changes, information is well disseminated, and the economy undergoes no persistent counter-tendencies through time. In this equilibrium framework, money performs the tasks of buying and selling commodities. Money is a veil, in the sense that it has no long-term impact on output and employment, except under special circumstances, or sometimes in the short-run. In this scheme of things, money should not grow much faster than the rate of change of productivity, for if it does there will be inflation. The main objective of monetary policy is therefore to control the money supply to ensure that is does not stimulate inflation.

Challenges to orthodoxy, whether historically taking the form of Chartalism, the banking school, or more recently the circuit approach, have generated deviations from orthodoxy, under the impact of two things. More latterly, the recognition that different classes of people have different quantities and qualities of information has resulted in the development of a non-neoclassical theory of money and credit, under the impact of Joseph Stiglitz and Frederick Mishkin. The concept of asymmetrical information improves our understanding of the dynamics of the system, especially vis-à-vis creditors and debtors, the state and banking system, households and business, and capitalists and workers. Imperfect information means that we can never return to the perfect information situation where nothing changes and everyone is happy. As a result, we are potentially under constant threat of financial crisis, instability, and recession as moral hazard and adverse selection play critical roles in the institutions.

Heterogeneous groupings of IEPEs, notably Post-Keynesian institutionalists (PKI), institutional Schumpeterians, institutionalists and evolutionary neo-Marxists, are especially interested in the role of entrepreneurs in the creation of money and credit. According to Schumpeterians, entrepreneurs introduce dynamics into the system through innovation, which requires credit from money capitalists for long-term projects. For PKIs, entrepreneurs finance their innovations partly through various debt instruments, which enhances instability as decisions are

9.3 Dynamic Circuit of Money Capital

made concerning the future upon which we have little or no knowledge. Neo-Marxist institutionalists extend these views to the recognition that much credit is required for the production and realisation of surplus value, the basis of profit and capital accumulation.

Many of these institutional and evolutionary scholars link money and credit to the circuit of capital to comprehend the working of the system in dynamic motion. For instance, the circuit of social capital (CSC) illustrates the phases and stages involved in the general motion of money capital in the national, regional and global political economies (Palloix 1975; O'Hara 2006). All the phases of the circuit interlink in a complex cybernetic network of motion. One form of this CSC is illustrated below, the *circuit of money capital*, in Fig. 9.1:

Money and credit (M) are required to stir the production economy into action, via internal corporate revenue, financial institutions and central banks. These largely endogenous sources of funds, propelled by the demand for finance, activate local national, regional, and global sources of labour power (LP, payment of wages) and means of production (MOP, buying capital goods/materials). This enables regional and global production value chains to be formed (... ... P ... ...), thereby enhancing the process of valorisation, resulting in the production of surplus product (number of goods and services). Commodity value (C) and surplus product (c) must be sold on the market for value (M) and surplus value (m) to be realised via trade (which depend upon pricing strategies and demand). This resultant surplus value is distributed primarily between profit (π), interest (i)/dividends and rent (r) (as well as taxes and some 'salaries'). This is followed by a crucial process whereby capitalists inculcate the animal spirits to reinvest some of the profit (along with credit and/or equity financing) so that the circuit of money capital can reproduce itself, at a higher level, through long-historical time [$\rightarrow$M$\leftrightarrow$C].

Each of the five phases of the circuit—finance for investment, sourcing of labor power and means of production, production, sale, reinvestment (including debt)—

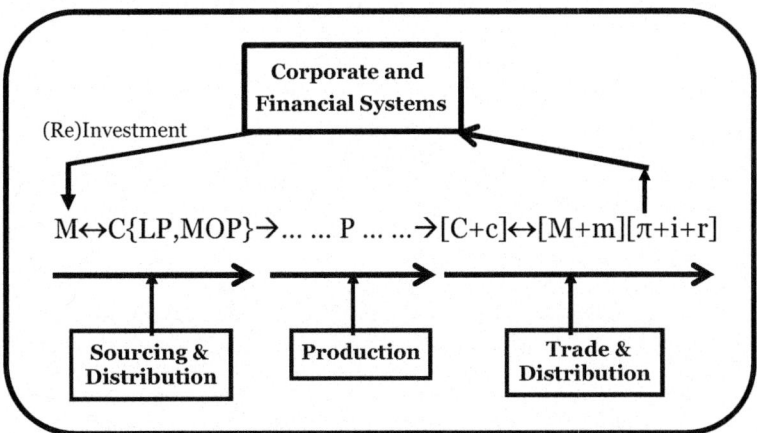

Fig. 9.1 Circuit of money capital

are institutionally linked through corporate, financial and governance structures and processes.[1]

This circuit approach recognises that money-credit-finance under capitalism is a dynamic force, one that is linked to investment, production, trade, and demand. This Monetary Theory of Production, as it is called, seeks to link money and credit to the critical forces of the system. Money cannot be conceived as a 'veil' because it finances much of the investment and consumption upon which growth and development is based. Any theory of money and credit, therefore, must be linked inextricably to the forces of enterprise, innovation, accumulation and speculation. As Marx, Veblen, Keynes and Schumpeter realised, capitalism could not exist without markets and credit. The ability of businesses to realise a profit depends partly on their ability to finance investments so the circuit can propel the stock of capital over long historical time. Anything that upsets this circuit will ultimately inhibit profit and capital accumulation, including disruptions to financial flows, inadequate demand, bottlenecks, insufficient inducement to invest, and conflict at the point of production. If the flows continue unabated value added is possible through the creation of *surplus value* (Marx, Schumpeter), *intangible value* (Veblen), and *prospective yield* (Keynes).[2]

9.4 Endogenous Versus Exogenous Money and Credit

Orthodoxy (quantity theory, monetarism) tends to assume that the money supply is exogenous in the sense that the 'government' has control over it and is able to effectively manage this power through the Reserve Bank and Treasury. Through being able to influence the money base—cash and coin—governments are able to control the rate of economic activity and demand, and therefore the rate of inflation. This is does through mainly open market operations, the buying and selling of government (and other) securities on the open market. Control of economic activity is made easier if the central bank has independence from an elected parliament to pursue inflation control as the primary target. Problems in controlling inflation are

---

[1] Earlier work on the financial circuit of money and credit, include French-Italian circuitists (e.g., Louis-Philippe Rochon 1999), endogenous finance (Alain Parguez 2001) plus linkages to the Marxian circuit of capital (Martha Campbell 1998), and the classic work of David P. Levine (1978, 1982).

[2] Surplus value is the value added from production, circulation and general reproduction manifesting in profit. The breakup of surplus value into profit, interest and rent reveals the money-finance aspects of surplus in a multi-capital framework (see Marx 1894). Intangible value is the term used by Veblen (1923) to describe the financial generation of value whereby finance capital generates profit and surplus. Prospective yield is the expected valuation of productive investment by entrepreneurs and capitalists that posits a return on their capital in the long-term horizon (Keynes 1936).

thus the fault of government, either not effectively undertaking its monetary duties or not giving the reserve bank adequate power to operationalise them.

Non-neoclassical alternatives to exogenous money and credit have been developing over the past few decades. One particularly influential trend is the new-Keynesian theory of broad money transmission mechanisms. The idea behind this is that governments cannot control money supply narrowly defined, but that they influence broad measures of economic activity through the credit process. This is a pragmatic perspective recognising economic activity being impacted by the financial system. Money and credit are thus not veils since they promote lending and borrowing through the financial system, which propels production and broad economic performance. This view thus realises that money and credit have a *critical element of endogeneity*, or in other words that they are influenced by and in turn promote economic activity.

Post-Keynesian, institutionalist and neo-Marxist institutional-evolutionary perspectives of money and credit are similar to this broad view, although they extend it in several directions (Arestis and Eichner 1988). The central hypothesis is that money demand stimulates money supply and credit, which in turn propels economic activity. The core idea here is that business cycle upswings generate their own momentum as the demand for finance stimulates supply. This is the essence of endogenous money and credit. Capitalist economies thus undergo relatively endogenous business cycles, where the upswings and downswings have a central element of self-reinforcing dynamics.[3]

When economic recovery takes hold businesses seek funds, and if they are not forthcoming from government then substitutes will emerge. This is the idea of *structural or innovative endogenous money and credit* (Rochone and Rossi 2017). In the absence of government accommodation, banks/firms will generate new forms of finance or expand existing means of finance that are not controlled by the central bank. This may variously take the form of bank bills, trade credit, negotiable certificates of deposit, overseas finance, and exotic options or swaps. It may also take the form of money and credit outside the formal circuits of governance, including illegal monies hidden in informal networks, finance evading authorities through offshore tax havens, and electronic forms of finance. This finance enables business cycle upswing to emerge through the normal workings of business. It is likely that this will overextend the system beyond fundamental variables and that speculative bubbles will eventually emerge in the high reaches of cycle prosperity. This structural endogeneity is perhaps the most important element of endogenous money and credit.

---

[3] For instance, the work of Howard Sherman (2003) applies endogenous business cycles to all the dominant institutions of contemporary capitalism, including financial capital; while Igor Matutinovic (2005) analyses the endogenous nature of cycles along the lines of Marx, Keynes, Schumpeter and Mitchell but with a more microeconomic foundation.

A second possible form of endogenous finance is through the government accommodating the demand for money through additional liquidity. If the government allows the greater (finance and transaction) demand for money to be realised in the system through expanding money and finance then this is another form of endogenous finance. Some have argued that it is normal for the government to legitimize the greater demand through enhancing system-wide liquidity. One such way is through open market operations (buying government and other bonds), or reduced reserve ratios. In the contemporary environment this normally means lower interest rates or failing to increase interest rates. Indeed, to the extent that the government can either control interest rates or money, and generally targets interest rates, endogenous government finance has become institutionalised into the system.[4]

The operation of endogenous-exogenous money and credit depends upon the shape of the money supply curve, and whether money-finance demand is satisfied through supply. Figure 9.2, below, illustrates some of the possible situations:

Ms_1 shows a state of affairs where money and credit are entirely endogenous as higher demand for finance expands supply. Ms_2 shows the exogenous situation where higher credit demand has no impact on supply. And Ms_3 is a middle of the road situation where sometimes finance is mostly endogenous, at other times it is exogenous and sometimes in between the extremes. Ms_3 indicates that the degree of endogeneity-exogeneity depends on the reality of the institutional situation of the time. Endogenous finance analysts would perhaps tend to support a combination of

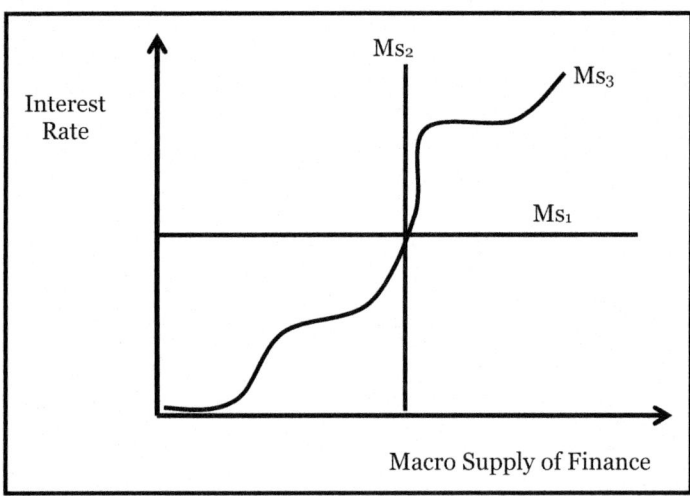

Fig. 9.2 Endogenous-exogenous finance

---

[4] Some of the classic studies, on structural and accommodative endogenous money, credit and finance include Basil Moore (1988), who tends to support accommodative approaches; Randy Wray (1990) who analyses the institutional complexities of endogenous money and credit; and Robert Pollin (1991), who empirically supports structural credit and finance.

9.4 Endogenous Versus Exogenous Money and Credit

Ms_1 and Ms_3, although they would add that the current institutional environment, where finance is mostly deregulated, supports structural endogeneity, while a system of interest rate targeting supports accommodative endogenous credit.

The analysis of structural endogenous money and credit *involves an institutional game* about the behaviour of economic agents and organisations through time. This dynamic game is about the conflict between systemic and individual interests of business and government. Business requires funds when business cycle upswing emerges, and usually the government provides liquidity to stimulate profit and investment, and business (including banks) often generates financial instruments to expand credit. This is the essence of endogenous funds, that both government and business may stimulate them. But as the higher points of the cycle emerge risk and especially uncertainty increases as inflation, speculative bubbles and recession loom. In this environment, the reserve bank may decide that the boom has gone on for too long and try and moderate it. If it does this, accommodative money and credit are not forthcoming and these funds become exogenous in the sense that they do not flow with the highs of the cycle. Instead, business may depend upon their own endogenous sources of funds, such as bank bills, overseas finance or certain exotic "innovations" such as mortgage-backed bonds, informal illegal finance, and electronic coins. The reserve bank may, however, try to limit the extent of these structural sources of endogenous finance by placing (higher) reserve requirements upon them (Rochon and Vernengo 2001).

But the reserve bank may not succeed in preventing the creation of structural endogenous finance as financial institutions and other businesses create ongoing alternative sources of funds. This cat and mouse game can continue through several runs, especially over successive business cycles, as Fig. 9.3, below illustrates:

This shows that if the reserve bank decides not to accommodate private sector finance during the high points of the business cycle upswing then private banks and other businesses will likely create their own instruments of finance. This will tend to heighten the business cycle, although government may intervene by introducing or increasing reserve requirements on these liabilities. In response, the private sector generates further innovative finance (or modifies existing ones) to stimulate financial capabilities. This game can continue through several runs, during a simple business cycle and over successive cycles. It thus demonstrates endogenous and exogenous money, credit and finance are variously impacting up the system, depending on the changes occurring in the institutions. However the reality of the situation is that some combination of accommodative and structural finance generates higher booms

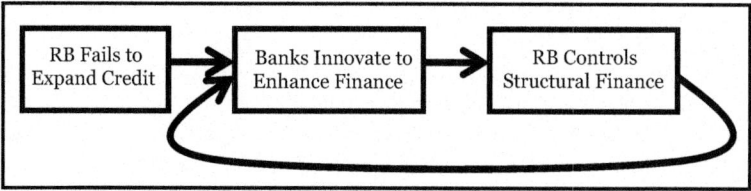

Fig. 9.3 Interactive game between central bank and private sector banks

in the cycle which thus leads generally to deeper recessions. This is because the highs of the booms, especially during long wave downswing, indicate the extent of the contradictory *unproductive finance, bubbles and overextended accumulation*. Marx, Veblen, Keynes, Schumpeter and most of their followers recognise the importance of endogenous cycles that emerge from an overextended economy during boom, especially under the influence of exaggerated confidence in the future, overexpanded debt, exuberance, and the bottlenecks of the high boom. This is where Hyman Minsky comes in.

9.5 Financial Instability Hypothesis

According to traditional neoclassical theory, financial stability is the normal state of a free market economy. If markets are deregulated and industry productive then the credit system will operate efficiently since value will be determined by fundamental variables such as long-term dividends or productivity. The financial system will be efficient since well developed markets enable resources to be distributed to those areas when they are required. In the extreme, free banking version of orthodoxy, it is necessary to have free markets in money and currency as well. There thus should be no state monopoly of central banking as this promotes instability and disarray in the markets. However, the dominant view amongst orthodox economists is that central banks are needed for promoting quality currency and inflation control, while prudential functions and even perhaps deposit insurance may promote stability into the system.

Institutional and evolutionary perspectives generally support the *financial instability hypothesis* (FIH), namely, that financial instability is endogenous to free market capitalist systems of production, distribution and exchange (Lavoie 2020). There are three main aspects to the FIH: uncertainly, endogenous money and credit, and the relationship between prospective yield and supply price. Hyman Minsky's FIH is an application of the industry-finance contradiction. The principle of uncertainty is critical because of the actions of entrepreneurs, who consider the viability of projects over a long time frame when knowledge of critical factors is lacking. Investment in capital projects with a life of 10 or 20 years into the future is based on a time frame that corporate planners know little about. They calculate prospective yield and supply price in an *uncertain environment when proper calculation is not possible*. It is simply that long-term (especially) future events are not known with any degree of certainty, or where the weight of confidence about future probabilities is very low. Making decisions about financing such projects in such a world of uncertainty is fraught with problems.

For this reason, as Minsky argues, vital business decisions are determined largely through institutions such as the prevailing business climate, accounting rules, and financial models. Without such conventions little action could reasonably be taken on critical business projects with a long gestation period. For this reason, instability is endogenous to the capitalist system since large credit-based projects run a high risk of failure as the business cycle moves from recovery to boom to financial crisis and recession. This is supported by evidence that most businesses fail in the formative stages of their development, with few firms incorporating such cycle dynamics into accounting systems (Mattingly and Kushev 2017).

Minsky differentiates between systems that tend towards instability periodically and others that do not tend to instability periodically. Capitalistic systems of finance tend towards instability, certainly over the course of the long wave downswing, and during short business cycles as well. The instabilities are greater during the highs of short cycle upswings (and associated recessions) during wave downswings (Minsky 1995), such as during the 1930s, and the 1980s-onwards (Wray 2002). He develops a model (Minsky 1974) to help explain the endogenous nature of this tendency towards instability, based on cash flow (income and contractual commitments) and capitalised values (of expected income and contractual commitments), plus degrees of safety. The model has two time periods, short and long, and a profit and loss account as well as a balance sheet. For the short run, cash flow is related to the difference between current income (Y) and current contractual commitments (CC) (related to debt); and for the long term, net worth is linked to capitalised income (or prospective yield) through many periods (K(Y)) compared with capitalised contractual commitments (or supply price) over the long-term (K(CC)). For business cycle phases when profit is at a relatively high level, with apparently little risk, "Hedge Finance" prevails:

Hedge Finance

$$Y > CC$$
$$K(Y) > K(CC)$$
$$Y = \delta CC$$
$$K(Y) = \beta K(CC)$$

Where δ and β represent margins of financial safety that are above unity (>1); in other words, income, on average, is greater than contractual commitments by a certain level of safety in every period. The recovery and moderate boom in the cycle are generally good for business since the rate of profit is relatively high while risk is low. Hyman Minsky (1982, 1986) and Martin Wolfson (1994a, b, 2000) argue that there are endogenous financial factors that lead from this safe type of finance (hedge finance) to those that are less secure (speculative and Ponzi finance).[5]

The generation of endogenous finance during the boom in the cycle normally overextends economic activity beyond fundamentals, since uncertainty about the future leads firms to depend on current levels of activity as a guide to investment. Firms thus generate massive investment when the business environment becomes euphoric during boom. Income rises to extraordinary highs relative to supply price or

---

[5] Some earlier studies on Minsky's hypothesis and related policies include, e.g., the destabilising influence of interest rate adjustments on investment by Greg Hannsgen (2005); the more selective policy developed by Thomas Palley of asset-based reserve requirements; and the relevance of the FIH to Asia (Lino Sau 2003).

contract commitments, even while interest rates may start to rise either as a result of higher demand for funds or monetary policy (modern parlance). These increases in interest rates do not upset upswing immediately since exuberant conditions still usually sustain prospective yield despite moderate increases in capitalised supply price. We thus have a slight deterioration in financial safety as, on average, cash flows become negative where income is often less than contractual commitments (short term) while capitalised income is still greater than capitalised contractual commitments (long-term). This is called "Speculative Finance", where long term conditions are still buoyant and credit demand high:

Speculative Finance

$Y < CC$

$K(Y) > K(CC)$

$Y = \delta CC \quad (\delta < 1)$

$K(Y) = \beta K(CC) \quad (\beta > 1)$

Lastly, buoyant conditions gradually stimulate instability and crisis (especially during long wave downswing) as a number of environmental conditions deteriorate, costs increase and bubbles crash. Because exuberant conditions push investment and stock prices beyond long-term fundamentals, decline is highly likely (Raines and Leathers 2000). In the age of neoliberalism and shareholder value during especially the 1980s–2020s in the US, UK and similar nations, the stock market gained relative autonomy from the real sector. A far greater proportion of credit went to finance equity expansion and new financial instruments, while a lesser proportion financed wages (hence declining inflation). Thus the crash in the share market prior to and during recession was far greater than average. A number of things stimulate these periodic crashes, including higher raw material prices, interest rates rises, corporate excesses and crises as profits are inflated and subsequently diminish as corporate bankruptcies escalate. All these factors lead to a deterioration in business climate, lower expected profits, declining investment, stock market crash and recession (especially during the mid-1970s, early 1980s, early 1990s, early 2000s, 2008, and early 2020 in most western nations).

This leads to a further decline in financial safety as a far greater number of firms move from Speculative to "Ponzi Finance", where cash flows are often negative through income being lower than contractual commitments and capitalised cash flows (prospective yield) being often smaller than capitalised contractual costs (supply price):

Ponzi Finance

$Y < CC$

$K(Y) < K(CC)$

$Y = \delta CC \quad (\delta < 1)$

$K(Y) = \beta K(CC) \quad (\beta < 1)$

Ponzi Finance is thus the worst form of financial condition for the economy as many firms are undergoing bankruptcy, the share market is crashing, corporate excesses are unsustainable, and deep recession emerges during long wave downswing (Dymski and Pollin 1994; Fazzari and Papadimitriou 1992). Due to intersectoral linkages these crises tend often to be regionally and internationally synchronised, although uneven, in similarly organised economies. Greater Ponzi positions thus tended to emerge during the financial and economic crises of 1974–1975, 1982–1983, 1990–1992, 2000–2001, 2008–2009, 2020 in many nations. The FIH has come into the mainstream of economic discourse, especially since its relevance for the GFC of 2008–2009ff is fairly evident (see Piero Ferri 2019 for details).

Aliber and Kindleberger (2015) argue that, on a global scale. "The three decades since the 1980s have been the most tumultuous in monetary history in terms of the number, scope and severity of banking crises" (p. 347). They go on to say that "The four waves of banking crises in the 30 years between 1980 and 2010 were more than any other comparable period" (p. 351). Not surprisingly, since the book's model of financial crises is based on Minsky's, they conclude that "The pattern of cash flows between lenders and borrowers in each [such] wave was Ponzian—the increase in the indebtedness of the borrowers was several times higher than their interest payments on their indebtedness" (p. 360) (See also Davidson 2008).

The endogenous force stimulating the movement from Hedge to Speculative Finance is a higher prospective yield as uncertainty seemingly declines while there are typically rising interest rates. On balance this is a positive environment, although hints of anomalies arise due to declining cash flow. The endogenous force moving the system from Speculative to Ponzi Finance is a crash in prospective yield, in a possible environment where input prices have risen considerably (increasing supply price). On balance this is a periodic system-crisis of finance and economics. Speculative bubbles tend to crash during these times of Ponzi finance, global flows of money and credit tend to be disrupted, corporate accounting crises are highly likely, and chains of bankruptcy are probable during these uncertain times. They are endogenously linked to the system dynamics of globalised state-capitalism throughout most advanced nations of the world, especially during the 1980s–2020s.

9.6 Global Money, Payments and Prices

I-E political economists tend to believe that capitalism is a global system, with centre-periphery uneven relations affecting growth and development. They also believe that economic power is central to its functioning, with money power being a critical aspect of this power equation. Market relations are imbued with power differentials because of certain centripetal and centralising tendencies of business. Money tends to be dispersed to those who are able to gain monopoly rents, be they individuals, organisations, firms, sectors, areas, nations or commodity chains. By-and-large, most of the rents go to those who are able to commodify the dominant technological, social and informational resources of society. In particular, those able to organise *global and regional networks of business* will gain the most profit and money (Grou 1985).

Power is linked to the principle of hegemony and uneven development, especially nations and areas that lead the world in production, commerce, and finance. Global power has shifted from Dutch hegemony in the seventeenth century through to British hegemony in the nineteenth century and on to US hegemony in the twentieth century; and possible Chinese hegemony by the 2040s. Most would likely argue the US has moved from *absolute* hegemony in the late twentieth century to *relative* hegemony in the early twenty-first century; and continuing a spiral downwards. The money-currency of the hegemonic power tends to be the world currency. At present the US dollar is the dominant currency in the world, although it is slowly losing power relative to the Euro and the Chinese Renminbi/Yuan. The problem is that asymmetric power leading to a dominant US dollar may inhibit global performance if the hegemon underplays critical system-functions or global public goods.

There is thus a *contradiction* between the US dollar performing a dual role of national and global currency (Vermeiren 2010). US monetary authorities often try to safeguard national objectives which are counter to the smooth workings of the global financial system. For instance, during the early-1980s US authorities doubled interest rates from 5% to 10% to moderate domestic inflation, which propelled debt crises in Latin America, since the latter's debt was denominated mostly in US dollars, US interest rates and "spot" contracts. This pushed many such nations backwards by a decade or more. Also, during the Asian crisis, most debt contracts were denominated in US dollars, US rates and often with US global banks. When US authorities raised rates in the light of the emerging speculative bubble of the late 1990s this had a major negative impact on Asian debt, leading to massive hot capital outflows and recession (Schmeister 2000).

Post Keynesian institutionalists tend to argue for a truly "global currency", that transcends national power relations, which they believe will eschew the hegemon's preferences and policies when it is otherwise typically abrogating global public goods. Having a truly global currency will likely make world monetary relations fairer and ensure more global stability. Balance of payments equilibria is thus better obtained through a new rule: Those nations experiencing persistent current account surpluses are obliged to increase demand for the goods and services of those nations experiencing current account deficits. Contemporaneously the opposite has tended to prevail, especially for developing or underdeveloped nations: BOP deficit developing nations are 'forced' by international institutions to reduce government spending, increase interest rates and reduce demand in the domestic economy to supposedly equilibrate payments imbalances. The opposite, 'new' rule, is said to likely rectify inadequate global demand and periodic financial instability.[6]

---

[6]Some of the earlier work on post-Keynesian institutionalist perspectives on global money and credit, and the link to global growth and development include Basil Moore (2004) on the need for a global currency, Paul Davidson (2004) on failures and policy potential in the international economy; Jan Kregal (2006) on international financial innovations for the developing nations; and Arestis et al. (2005) on the need for a single global reserve currency and global reserve bank.

9.6 Global Money, Payments and Prices

This view of global capital explains why I-E scholars advocate a Monetary Theory of Production through the principle of circular and cumulative causation (CCC), as shown in Fig. 9.4, below, which shows a pattern of eco-dynamic relations in the background, within which the institutions are situated:

It is critical to propel CCC dynamics in the global economy. The first is to enhance effective demand, ultimately to expand investment, both private and public (which includes much of so-called 'consumption' and 'state spending'). Where uncertainty is relatively low, private investment tends to be at a high rate, and when uncertainty is high public investment can help through crowding-in private investment in areas such as education, health, communications and infrastructure. Demand is in fact interdependent with supply, since demand can manifest in greater demand for capital which through economies of scope and scale plus embodied innovative investment will likely stimulate productivity. And when world income is relatively high—especially when governments do not impose austerity measures—this translates into higher demand for global exports. This in turn propels greater demand, and so on as the system works through this in multiple rounds of circular and cumulative action. If demand can be sustained productivity and profitability tend to increase, thus moderating financial crises and deep recession. However, this dynamic has not been strong for the neoliberal period for advanced capitalist economies, their client states, and the world economy.

It is necessary, though, to moderate levels of speculative and hot capitals, when they crowd-out investment, both private and public (Wincoop et al. 2000; O'Hara 2003). If speculative bubbles expand to great heights this indicates that finance dominates industry as resources transfer to relatively unproductive areas (Cypher 1998; Binswanger 1999, 2000; Stockhammer 2004; Muellerleile and French 2022). Rules need to be devised to moderate this dominance, so that real investment is

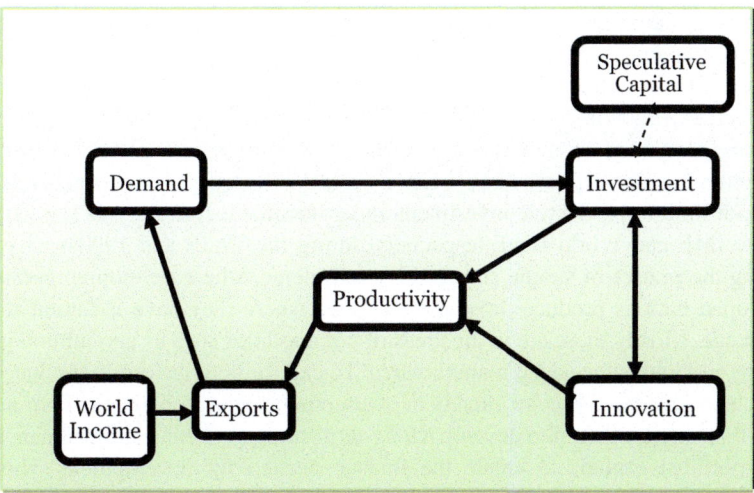

Fig. 9.4 Kaldorian dyamics of circular and cumulative causation

enhanced. Much of the force here is cultural and historical. But to some degree policy can help. For instance, the introduction of asset-based reserve requirements can be a way of moderating bubbles. If the authorities, for instance, believe that bubbles are rising rapidly in the stock, property and/or foreign currency markets, increasing reserve requirements on these specific bubble assets can redirect finance to more productive areas. This may relinquish the need for raising interest rates, which can be a very blunt tool, not discriminating between productive and unproductive areas (Mishkin 2001).

In a CCC fashion, the global financial instabilities of the 1990s and 2000s taught many financial analysts about the problems of hot capitals: e.g., incoming short-term: debt plus bond, equity and derivates purchases; borrowing funds from international banks for short maturity periods. Most countries linked to the Asian crisis of 1997–1998, for instance, saw an escalation of incoming loans before the crisis, followed by massive outflows during the crisis. It is not simply a problem of needing to develop a sound financial system prior to deregulation, since the US experienced similarly unstable finance in the early 2000s. Deregulating finance majorly is the major problem (Coggins 1998). Apart from the need for transparency, accountability, prudential regulation and speculative asset controls there is also a need for moderating hot capitals (O'Hara 2011). This can perhaps be done through the introduction of a Tobin Tax, with, say, a small 0.2% tax on international loans of less than 12 months duration. This may not only "put grains of sand into the wheels of international finance", but also perhaps be a way of financing some development projects for very poor nations, and providing funds for domestic governments (Deng et al. 2018).

IE perspectives of money and credit also recognise the often contradictory impact of the terms of trade on developing and underdeveloped nations. Probably the most important financial constraint on development is the inability of poor nations to produce and export goods and services with a high price that reflects a good income elasticity of demand and also the monopoly rents associated with the leading commodities and services. Empirical research shows the existence of two major problems. Firstly, there have been two periods of declining terms of trade for poor nations, the 1920s and the 1970s; and secondly, they tend to produce goods and services (particularly commodities) with a volatile price pattern. These two problems of low and variable prices have been a central limit on development, creating a financial limit to productive investment and government spending (O'Hara 2006).

The IMF and World Bank (especially during the 1980s and 1990s) have been singing the praises of simple comparative advantage, where developing and underdeveloped nations produce those commodities where they have a natural relative advantage. Mostly these are in the areas of commodities such as agricultural goods, timber, and low value added manufactures. To call for poor nations to produce more of such commodities that are already in over-abundance is problematic. Poor nations more than anything need to develop a long-term strategy of enhancing human, social and specialist capitals to create the finance needed for development. This will necessitate the use of intelligent industry policy to create relatively high value added goods and services; some degree of protection for infant industries; and a policy of generating human, social and network capitals for development. Development studies and international political economy have been isolating detailed measures along these lines for several decades now (e.g., Chang and Grabel 2004).

9.7 Chartalism and Modern Monetary Theory

Consistent with the principle of innovation, ultimately I-E political economy seeks to enhance social provisioning, standard of living, environmental sustainability and help to create a relatively efficient and equitable society. It especially seeks conventional rights where the rules of society promote less division on the basis of class, ethnicity, gender, age, nation and species. Special reference is given to a participatory social economy, where people have the right to a decent job, or alternative compensation, as well as the right to be included in decision making in the dominant institutions of business, state, community, family and environment. I-E political economy agrees that CEOs and business vested interests on average gain far too much remuneration compared with the underlings who often work harder and longer, or lack the resources for adequate inclusion in the social economy.

Financial considerations are primary to these concerns for greater participation and inclusion. I-E macro dynamics posits an investment-led growth program for social and environmental development. The orthodox theory assumes that savings stimulates investment through providing funds for productive projects, and encouraging the growth of a class of savers. Hence their concern with recent trends towards lower savings rates in especially advanced capitalist economies. Institutional-evolutionary scholars tend to have no such concern, since for them investment is the core variable for sustainable growth. The creation of an institutional apparatus for lower levels of uncertainty provides a business environment for higher levels of private investment, thus stimulating national income, and savings. Once effective demand is forthcoming long term progress is more likely.

Relevant to the principle of policy and governance, a method of encouraging inclusion, productivity and performance is long-term development of productive government investment in education, health, communications, infrastructure, and housing (Aschauer 1989; Chu et al. 2020). Extensive research in many nations has supported the case for public investment crowding-in private investment. Such productive investment is generally better than subsides for business and individuals which tend to crowd-out private investment.[7] However, especially during a socioeconomic crisis, using government spending as a general stimulus, including handouts, is crucial for preventing major slump or reversing the existing one (Liu 2022). This was shown especially during the GFC and the coronacrisis global crisis

---

[7] Some earlier IEPE studies on productive government spending point to the importance of education, health, infrastructure and communications; which are also detailed in O'Hara (2004), who argues that globalisation has not destroyed the potential for productive fiscal policy; Philip Arestis and Malcolm Sawyer (2004) on fiscal policy as an important source of demand; and Christian Weber (2000) on the lack of productive government spending in the US causing recent recessions.

of 2020–2022. In the long-term, a method of improving conditions of working people and others financially disadvantaged is to encourage them to *gain the skills and creative arts of a modern technological society* (Acemoglu and Autor 2011).

Recently a new form of an old theory of money and credit has emerged to support employment, inclusion and justice: the taxes-drive-money (TDM) approach; also called Chartalism and Modern Monetary Theory (MMT). It has been developed especially from scholars at the University of Missouri (Kansas City), Bard College (New York State), and the University of Newcastle, Australia, by a whole group of political economists, including Randall Wray (1998, 2015), Stephanie Kelton (2020), and Bill Mitchell (see Mitchell et al. 2019). This theory follows the Chartalist view that the core role of government is to sustain proper levels of aggregate demand, and that functional rules of public finance (Abber Lerner 1943) should prevail over rigid ideology. Along with Minsky's FIH it is another IEPE theory to have gained international recognition in recent years, in the light of the GFC and/or coronacrisis (Smialek 2022).

The major tenets of MMT are summarised in Table 9.2, below (compared with orthodoxy):

In MMT it is believed that usually budget deficits will be required by government to enhance private investment, especially when there is recession; while in the long run government spending will enhance aggregate demand and thus produce "balanced budgets" or even during booms "government surplus" (in the old-fashioned vocabulary). Balanced and surplus budgets tend to be generated during high points in the business cycle, but the government should spend adequately to reduce the depth of recession. Taxes do not finance central government spending; rather, taxes increase the demand for government money. Government spending is financed instead by money, since the Treasury writes a check to finance state spending, and does not need pre-existing taxes to do so.

The right of people to employment will only be achieved if pragmatic rules of finance are undertaken by government. It needs to spend more when demand is low and spend less when inflation looms. The role of government borrowing, on the other hand, is to activate monetary policy through open market operations. Government borrowing (bonds) from the public is done purely for interest rate targeting purposes. MMT thus argues that financing spending through deficits to prevent

Table 9.2 Modern monetary approach versus orthodoxy

	MMT function	MMT government finance	MMT purpose for government	Orthodox government accounting
Taxes	Drives demand for money	Does not finance G	Modifies demand	Revenue source for Gov spend
Money	Provides reserves for the system	Finances government spending	Government financing	Finances budget deficit
Bonds	Interest rate targeting	Does not finance G	Modifies demand	Finances budget deficit

recession does not crowd-out private investment via higher interest rates. This is because higher spending may increase rates but financing it from money reduces rates, the net effect likely being neutral. But if the spending is productive this has the added advantage of crowding-in private investment, as argued earlier.[8] Also, if interest rates are low this reduces the costs involved. Social justice may thus prevail as MMT encourages governments to stimulate social, regional and environmental development, and employment of last resort, especially if they can moderate the tendency to waste resources on major wars, military expansion and polluting sectors.

Criticisms have emerged of this MMT, TDM or Chartalist theory, especially since, in recent years, the theory has had a lot of media attention, and even Presidential candidates, such as Bernie Sanders, have been discussing it in the context of policy issues. First there are the fairly friendly critics. A neo-Keynesian, Gregory Mankiw (2020: 141–144) agrees with MMT on three things, but also has reservations on these same three things. He agrees with MMT that (1) "a currency-issuing government can always print more money when a bill becomes due"; (2) "the economy normally operates with excess capacity, in the sense that the economy's output often falls short of its optimum"; and (3) "in a world of pervasive market power, government price setting might improve private price setting as a matter of economic theory". While agreeing that MMT "contains a kernel of truth", on the other hand, Mankiw believes that printing money may be anomalous due to the payment of large interest amounts on the reserves in the banking system (hence the government budget constraint); reducing the difference between actual and optimum output is likely to lead to much higher inflationary forces; and he sees such government price setting historically as not usually working in practice.

Another friendly critique comes from Marc Lavoie (2013), who takes up the argument of MMT that orthodox monetary and fiscal theory does not adequately reflect the workings of the institutions, either in the USA or the Eurozone. He then turns the argument around by concluding that MMT is an improvement but that proponents also conflate theory and institutions through the "fictitious consolidation of government and the central bank" (p. 24). He adds that MMT does not reflect the complexity of the workings of the clearing, settlement and payment systems; plus their terminology is said to often confuse because they are redefining standard meanings of words. A similarly friendly critique comes from Thomas Palley (2004), who starts off by commending MMT for critiquing austerity theory and practice (neoliberalism). He then argues that MMT ignores, underplays and/or oversimplifies crucial issues such as the Phillips curve, real and financial sector stability, the open economy, political economy pragmatics and likely instability linked to MMT's interest rate policy.[9]

---

[8] Some studies support MMT, including, for instance, the work of Stephenie Bell et al. (2004) on a debt-based theory of money; and George Kadmos and O'Hara (2000) who discuss empirical material relating to MMT.

[9] Numerous others critique the MMT, including Warren Coats (2019), whose critique is mild-mannered; and Boris Begovic (2021), whose critique is rather caustic. Even Begovic is cognizant (as was Mankiw) of the matters of fact associated with MMT. His caustic manner seems to be

MMT does have a core of logical consistency, institutional realism and progressive governance in its edifice. Advocates will need to work on deepening these traits if they are to convince the friendly critics of its validity to be a force for policy action.

9.8 Conclusion

This chapter has sought to present the main contours of an institutional and evolutionary monetary approach to political economy. Firstly the principle of historical specificity is used to show that history matters and that a dynamic view of credit and finance is a core part of IEPE theory and policy. We surveyed the evolution of capitalism through phases of evolution and utilised the principle of contradiction to illustrate the periodic emergence of booms and bubbles as well as crises, crashes and recessions as the system underwent major institutional changes through time.

The chapter illustrated through the principle of heterogeneous groups and agents how different groups and agents pay core roles in the institutions of finance-industry as well in financial policy-making and scholarly circles. It made us cognizant of how the principle of contradiction and the principle of uncertainty helps to comprehend the tendency of capitalism to periodic and persistent instability since it depends upon prospective yield the knowledge of which is unstable due to the temporal mismatch between capital investment decisions and debt-financial considerations.

The future is unknowable, and conventions are introduced to deal with investment in the face of radical uncertainty. A model of Minsky's financial instability hypothesis was presented where financial conditions evolve periodically through hedge, speculative and Ponzi positions as business lacks the required knowledge for stability over time.

We went on to show that the principle of circular and cumulative causation implies that aggregate demand is a critical interdependent variable when finance funds productive investment and sustains industrial profit. The principle of policy and governance was used to illustrate effective governance is necessary to encourage spending through institutions and innovations that propel the circuit of money. It should stimulate industry, moderate speculative bubbles and aid the process of recreating financial social structures underlying accumulation.

The chapter showed how IE scholars recognise that policy responses to financialization should try and enhance the power of industry relative to finance. It should also ensure, vis-à-vis the principle of hegemony and uneven development, that hegemonic-inspired nations do not rule international money, creating contradictions between their national policy goals and the global system. A truly global currency is said to provide public goods benefits while current account surplus nations are encouraged to spend to stabilise international finance.

---

related, at least in part, to the more popular text of Kelton, which is self-consciously written for a very general audience. Probably Begovic should have included some of the other references in his book review (such as Wray 2015) as well.

Institutional and evolutionary approaches to money and finance embed financial theory in a pragmatic and realistic edifice based on endogenous processes. The institutions of business and government are potentially in periodic unity if the concepts of the monetary circuit, financial instability, money endogeneity, and hegemonic theory are put to service to sustain demand and stabilise liquidity preference. In the short to medium term (at least), the state needs to look to the common good rather than vested interests, while business is required to contribute some semblance of balance between industry and finance. Such are the lessons of the IEPE of money, credit and finance, aspects of which have gained international prominence in the light of the GFC and the coronacrisis, notably the financial instability hypothesis and modern monetary theory.

Acknowledgements An earlier version of this chapter was published as O'Hara (2009). I wish to thank the anonymous referees plus Jack Reardon for comments that improved the original version. The usual caveat applies. This chapter is an extensively updated version.

References

Acemoglu, Daron, and David Autor. 2011. Skills, Tasks and Technologies: Implications for Employment and Earnings. In *Handbook of Labor Economics*, ed. Orley Ashenfelter and David Card, 1043–1171. Boston: North-Holland.

Aghion, Philippe, Céline Antonin, and Simon Bunel. 2021. *The Power of Creative Destruction: Economic Upheaval and the Wealth of Nations*. Cambridge, MA: Belknap Press of Harvard University Press.

Aliber, Robert Z., and Charles P. Kindlberger. 2015. *Manias, Panics and Crashes: A History of Financial Crises*. 7th ed. New York: Palgrave Macmillan.

Arestis, Phillip, and Alfred S. Eichner. 1988. The Post-Keynesian and Institutionalist Theory of Money and Credit. *Journal of Economic Issues* 22 (4): 1003–1033.

Arestis, Philip, and Malcolm Sawyer. 2004. On the *Effectiveness* of Monetary Policy and of Fiscal Policy. *Review of Social Economy* 62 (4): 441–464.

Arestis, Philip, Santonu Basu, and Sushanta Mallick. 2005. Financial Globalisation, the Need for a Single Currency and a Global Central Bank. *Journal of Post Keynesian Economics* 27 (3): 507–532.

Aschauer, D. 1989. Is Public Expenditure Productive? *Journal of Monetary Economics* 23 (2): 177–200.

Begovic, Boris. 2021. The Deficit Myth: Modern Monetary Theory and How to Build a Better Economy. *Panoeconomicus* 68 (3): 405–414.

Bell, Stephanie, John F. Henry, and L. Randall Wray. 2004. A Chartalist Critique of John Lock's Theory of Property, Accumulation, and Money: Or, Is It Moral to Trade Your Nuts for Gold? *Review of Social Economy* 62 (1): 51–66.

Binswager, Mathias. 2000. Stock Returns and Real Activity: Is There Still a Connection? *Applied Financial Economics* 10: 379–388.

Binswanger, Matias. 1999. *Stock Markets, Speculative Bubbles and Economic Growth: New Dimensions in the Co-evolution of Real and Financial Markets*. Cheltenham/Northampton: Edward Elgar.

Bush, Paul Dale. 2001. Minimal Dislocation. In *Encyclopedia of Political Economy*, ed. P.A. O'Hara, vol. 2. 736–737. London/New York, Routledge. Paperback Edition.

Campbell, Martha. 1998. Money in the Circulation of Capital. In *The Circulation of Capital: Essays on Volume 2 of Marx's 'Capital'*, ed. Christopher Arthur and Geert Reuten, 129–158. London/New York: Macmillan/St Martins Press.

Cassis, Youssef. 2006. *Capitals of Capital: A History of International Financial Centres, 1780-2005*. Cambridge: Cambridge University Press.

Chang, Ha-Joon, and Ilene Grabel. 2004. *Reclaiming Development: An Alternative Economic Policy Manual*. New York: Palgrave Macmillan.

Chu, Tuan T., Jens Hölscher, and Dermot McCarthy. 2020. The Impact of Productive and Non-Productive Government Expenditure on Economic Growth: An Empirical Analysis in High-Income Versus Low-to-Middle-Income Economies. *Empirical Economics* 58: 2403–2430. https://doi.org/10.1007/s00181-018-1616-3.

Coats, Warren. 2019. Modern Monetary Theory: A Critique. *Cato Journal* 39 (3): 563–576.

Coggins, Bruce. 1998. *Does Financial Deregulation Work? A Critique of Free Market Approaches*. Cheltenham: Edward Elgar.

Cypher, James M. 1998. Financial Dominance in the US Economy: The Increased Relevance of Veblen's Analysis in a Post-Keynesian Structure. In *Institutionalist Theory and Applications: Essays in Honor of Paul Dale Bush*, ed. S. Fayazmanech and M.R. Tool, vol. 2. Cheltenham/Northampton: Edward Elgar.

Davidson, Paul. 2004. The Future of the International Financial System. *Journal of Post Keynesian Economics* 26 (4): 591–606.

———. 2008. Is the Current Financial Distress Caused by the Sub Prime Mortgage Crisis a Minsky Moment? Or Is It the Result of Attempting to Securitize Illiquid Non Commercial Mortgage Loans? *Journal of Post Keynesian Economics* 31 (1): 669–676.

Davies, Glyn. 2002. *A History of Money from Ancient Times to the Present Day*. Cardiff: University of Wales Press.

Deng, Yongheng, Xin Liu, and Shang-Jin Wei. 2018. One Fundamental and Two Taxes: When Does a Tobin Tax Reduce Financial Price Volatility? *Journal of Financial Economics* 130 (3): 663–692.

Dillard, Dudley. 1987. Money as an Institution of Capitalism. *Journal of Economic Issues* 21 (4): 1623–1647.

Dymski, Gary, and Robert Pollin. 1994. *New Perspectives in Monetary Macroeconomics: Exploration in the Tradition of Hyman P. Minsky*. Ann Arbor: University of Michigan Press.

Fazzari, Steven, and Dimitri Papadimitriou. 1992. *Financial Conditions and Macroeconomic Performance: Essays in Honor of Hyman P. Minsky*. Armonk/London: M.E. Sharpe Inc.

Ferri, Piero. 2019. *Minsky's Moment: An Insider's View on the Economics of Hyman Minsky*. Cheltenham: Edward Elgar.

Freeman, Chris, and Francisco Louca. 2001. *As Time Goes By: From the Industrial Revolution to the Information Revolution*. Oxford: Oxford University Press.

Grou, Pierre. 1985. *The Financial Structure of International Capitalism*. Heidelberg: Berg Publishers.

Guttman, Robert. 1994. *How Credit-Money Shapes the Economy: The United States in a Global System*. Armonk: M.E. Sharpe Inc.

———. 2001. Social Structure of Accumulation: Financial. In *Encyclopedia of Political Economy*, ed. P. O'Hara, vol. 2, 1061–1063. London/New York: Routledge. Paper Edition.

Hannsgen, Greg. 2005. Minsky's Acceleration Channel and the Role of Money. *Journal of Post Keynesian Economics* 27 (3): 471–489. https://doi.org/10.1080/01603477.2005.11051450

Kadmos, George Anthony, and Phillip Anthony O'Hara. 2000. The Taxes-Drive-Money and Employer of Last Resort Approach to Government Policy. *Journal of Economic and Social Policy* 5 (1): 1–22.

Kelton, Stephanie. 2020. *The Deficit Myth: Modern Monetary Theory and the Birth of the People's Economy*. New York: Hachette Book Group.

Keynes, John Maynard. 1936. *The General Theory of Employment, Interest and Money*. London: Macmillan.

Kregal, Jan. 2006. Can We Create a Stable International Financial Environment that Ensures Net Resource Transfers to Developing Countries? *Journal of Post Keynesian Economics* 26 (4): 573–590.

Lavoie, Marc. 2013. The Monetary and Fiscal Nexus of Neo-Chartalism: A Friendly Critique. *Journal of Economic Issues* 47 (1): 1–31.
———. 2014. *Post-Keynesian Economics: New Foundations*. Cheltenham: Edward Elgar.
———. 2020. Was Hyman Minsky a Post-Keynesian Economist? *Review of Evolutionary Political Economy* 1 (1): 85–101.
Lerner, Abba. 1943. Functional Finance and the Federal Debt. *Social Research* 10: 38–51. https://www.jstor.org/stable/40981939.
Levine, David P. 1978. *Economic Theory, Volume One: The Elementary Relations of Economic Life*. London/Boston: Routledge/Kegan Paul.
———. 1982. *Economic Theory, Volume Two: The System of Economic Relations as a Whole*. London/Boston: Routledge/Kegan Paul.
Liu, Siming. 2022. Government Spending During Sudden Stop Crises. *Journal of International Economics* 135 (1): 103571. https://doi.org/10.1016/j.jinteco.2022.103571.
Maddison, Angus. 2006. *The World Economy: Volume 1: A Millennial Perspective; Volume 2: Historical Statistics*. Paris: OECD.
Mager, Nathan H. 1987. *The Kondratieff Waves*. Westport, Connecticut: Praeger.
Mandel, Ernest. 1978. *Late Capitalism*. London: Verso. (Translated from the Original German Edition, Published by Suhrkamp Verlag in 1972, by Joris De Bres.).
Mankiw, N. Gregory. 2020. A Skeptics Guide to Modern Monetary Theory. *AEA Papers and Proceedings* 110: 141–144. https://doi.org/10.1257/pandp.20201102
Marx, Karl. 1894. *Capital, Volume Three: The Process of Capitalist Production as a Whole*. Harmondsworth: Penguin, 1981.
Mattingly, Eric Shaunn, and Trayan Kushev. 2017. Most New Businesses Fail, But Mine Won't...Right? *Journal of Entrepreneurship* 25 (1): 70–88.
Matutinovic, Igor. 2005. The Microeconomics of Business Cycles: From Institutions to Autocatalytic Networks. *Journal of Economic Issues* 39 (4): 867–898.
Minsky, Hyman P. 1974. The Modelling of Financial Instability: An Introduction. *Modelling and Simulation* 5: 44–49.
———. 1982. *Can "It" Happen Again? Essays on Instability and Finance*. Armonk: M.E. Sharpe. Reprinted by Routledge Classics, Oxford & New York, 2016 (with a Foreword by Jan Toporowsky).
Minsky, Hyman. 1986. *Stabilising an Unstable Economy*. New Haven/London: Yale University Press.
———. 1995. Larger Waves in Financial Relations: Financial Factors in the More Severe Depressions II. *Journal of Economic Issues* 29 (1): 83–96.
Mishkin, Frederick S. 2001. The Transmission Mechanism and the Role of Asset Prices in Monetary Policy. *NBER Working Paper 8617*, December. New York, National Bureau of Economic Research.
Mitchell, William, L. Randall Wray, and Martin Watts. 2019. *Macroeconomics*. London: Red Globe Press.
Moore, Basil. 1988. *Horizontalists and Verticalists: The Macroeconomics of Credit Money*. Cambridge: Cambridge University Press.
Moore, Basil J. 2004. A Global Currency for a Global Economy. *Journal of Post Keynesian Economics* 26 (4): 631–654.
Muellerleile, Chris, and Shaun French. 2022. Variegated Intersections of Neoliberalism and Financialization. *Economy and Space* 54 (1): 136–143.
Neale, Walter C. 1976. *Money in Societies*. San Francisco: Chandler & Sharpe Publishers Inc.
Nelson, Anitra. 1999. *Marx's Concept of Money: The God of Commodities*. London/New York: Routledge.
O'Hara, Phillip Anthony. (2000a) "Money and Credit in Marx's Political Economy and Contemporary Capitalism", *History of Economics Review,* 32(Summer): 83–95.
———. 2000b. *Marx, Veblen and Contemporary Institutional Political Economy: Principles and Unstable Dynamics of Capitalism*. Cheltenham: Edward Elgar.

———. 2002. A New Financial Social Structure of Accumulation for Long Wave Upswing in the United States? *Review of Radical Political Economics* 34 (3): 342–348.

———. 2003. Recent Changes to the IMF, WTO and FSP: An Emerging Global Money-Trade-Production Social Structure of Accumulation for Long Wave Upswing? *Review of International Political Economy* 10 (3): 481–519.

———. 2006. *Growth and Development in the Global Political Economy: Social Structures of Accumulation and Modes of Regulation*. London/New York: Routledge.

———. 2009. Money, Credit, and Finance in Political Economy: National, Regional and Global Dimensions. In *The Handbook of Pluralist Economics Education*, ed. Jack Reardon, 230–255. London/New York: Routledge.

———. 2011. International Subprime Crisis and Recession: Emerging Macroprudential, Monetary, Fiscal and Global Governance. *Panoeconomicus* 68 (1): 1–17.

———. 2013. Policies and Institutions for Moderating Deep Recessions, Debt Crises and Financial Instabilities. *Panoeconomicus* 60 (1): 19–49.

———. 2023. *Long Wave Institutional Dynamics and Political Economy Crises of Capitalism: Principles, Social Structures of Accumulation. Empirics*: Springer.

Palley, Thomas I. 2004. Asset-Based Reserve Requirements: Reasserting Domestic Monetary Control in an Era of Financial Innovation and Instability. *Review of Political Economy* 16 (1): 43–58.

Palloix, Christian. 1975. The Internationalization of Capital and the Circuit of Social Capital. In *International Firms and Modern Imperialism*, ed. H. Radice, 37–62. Harmondsworth: Penguin.

Parguez, Alain. 2001. Money Without Scarcity: From the Horizontalist Revolution to the Theory of the Monetary Circuit. In *Credit, Interest Rates and the Open Economy: Essays on Horizontalism*, ed. Louis-Philippe Rochen and Matias Vernengo, 69–103. Cheltenham/Northampton.

Perez, Carlotta. 2007. Finance and Technical Change: A Long-Term View. In *Elgar Companion to Neo-Schumpeterian Economics*, ed. Horst Hanusch and Andreas Pyka, 775–799. Cheltenham: Edward Elgar.

Polanyi, Karl. 1944. *The Great Transformation*. Boston: Beacon Press (1957 edition).

Raines, J. Patrick, and Charles G. Leathers. 2000. *Economics and the Stock Market: Speculative Theories of Stock Market Fluctuations*. Cheltenham/Northampton: Edward Elgar Publishing.

Robert, Pollin. 1991. Two Theories of Money Supply Endogeneity: Some Empirical Evidence. *Journal of Post Keynesian Economics* 13 (3): 366–396.

Rochon, Louis-Philippe. 1999. *Credit, Money and Production: An Alternative Post-Keynesian Approach*. Cheltenham/Northampton: Edward Elgar.

Rochon, Louis-Philippe, and Matias Vernengo. 2001. *Credit, Interest Rates and the Open Economy: Essays on Horizontalism*. Cheltenham/Northampton: Edward Elgar Publishing.

Rochone, Louis-Phillippe, and Sergio Rossi, eds. 2017. *Advances in Endogenous Money Analysis*. Chaltenham: Eward Elgar.

Rojek, Chris. 2018. The Longue Dure'e of Spengler's Thesis of the Decline of the West. *European Journal of Social Theory* 21 (4): 419–434.

Rostow, Walt W. 1938. Investment and the Great Depression. *The Economic History Review* 8 (2): 136–158.

———. 1940. Explanations of the "Great Depression," 1873–96. *The Economic History Review* 10 (1): 356–370.

Sau, Lino. 2003. Banking, Information and Financial Instability in Asia. *Journal of Post Keynesian Economics* 25 (3): 493–513.

Schulmeister, Stephan. 2000. Globalization Without Global Money: The Double Role of the Dollar as National Currency and World Currency. *Journal of Post Keynesian Economics* 22 (3): 365–395.

Schumpeter, Joseph A. 1950. *Capitalism, Socialism and Democracy*. 3rd ed. New York: Harper & Row.

———. 2014. *Treatise on Money*. Aalten: Wordbridge Publishing. Translated from the 1970 German Edition by Ruben Alvarado.

Sherman, Howard. 2003. Institutions and the Business Cycle. *Journal of Economic Issues* 37 (3): 621–642.

Smialek, Jeanna. 2022. Is This What Winning Looks Like? *New York Times*, 7 February. https://www.nytimes.com/2022/02/06/business/economy/modern-monetary-theory-stephanie-kelton.html.

Stockhammer, Engelbert. 2004. Financialisation and the Slowdown of Accumulation. *Cambridge Journal of Economics* 28 (5): 719–741.

Toporowski, Jan. 2020. Financialisation and the Periodisation of Capitalism: Appearances and Processes. *Review of Evolutionary Political Economy* 1 (2): 149–160.

Tylecote, Andrew. 1992. *The Long Wave in the World Economy*. London: Routledge.

van Duijn, Jacob Johan. 1983. *The Long Wave in Economic Life*. New York: Allen & Unwin.

Veblen, Thorstein Bunde. 1923. *Absentee Ownership and Business Enterprise in Recent Times: The Case of America*. New York: Augustus M. Kelley, 1964.

Vermeiren, Mattias. 2010. The Global Imbalances and the Contradictions of US Monetary Hegemony. *Journal of International Relations and Development* 13: 105–135.

Vickers, Douglas. 1959. *Studies in the Theory of Money, 1690–1776*. New York: Chilton Company.

Wallerstein, Immanuel. 1983. The Three Instances of Hegemony in the History of the Capitalist-World Economy. *International Journal of Comparative Sociology* 24 (1–2): 100–108.

Weber, Christian E. 2000. Government Purchases, Government Transfers, and the Post-1970 Slowdown in U.S. Economic Growth. *Contemporary Economic Policy* 18 (1): 107–123.

Wincoop, Eric van, and K.-M. Yi. 2000. Asia Crisis Postmortem: Where Did the Money Go and Did the United States Benefit?. *Economic Policy Review*, September, 51–70.

Wolfson, Martin H. 1994a. The Financial System and the Social Structure of Accumulation. In *Social Structures of Accumulation: The Political Economy of Growth and Crisis*, ed. D.M. Kotz, T. McDonough, and M. Reich. Cambridge: Cambridge University Press.

———. 1994b. *Financial crises: Understanding the Postwar U.S. Experience*. 2nd ed. Armonk/New York/London: M.E. Sharpe.

Wolfson, Martin. 2000. Neoliberalism and International Financial Instability. *Review of Radical Political Economics* 32 (3): 369–378.

Wray, L. Randall. 1990. *Money and Credit in Capitalist Economies: The Endogenous Money Approach*. Aldershot/Brookfield: Edward Elgar Publishing.

———. 1998. *Understanding Modern Money: The Key to Full Employment and Price Stability*. Cheltenham/Northampton: Edward Elgar.

———. 2002. What Happened to Goldilocks? A Minskian Framework. *Journal of Economic Issues* 26 (2): 383–391.

———. 2015. *Modern Money Theory: A Primer on Macroeconomics for Sovereign Monetary Systems*. 2nd ed. New York: Palgrave Macmillan.

Terrorism and the War on Terrorism 10

Abstract

This chapter applies principles of institutional and evolutionary political economy to the historical events and processes underlying the 9/11 attacks on New York and (near) Washington DC in late 2001, and examines policies that should be implemented to moderate the operational consequences of terrorism, as well as the war on terrorism. We start by addressing the principle of historical specificity, by situating the terrorist crisis, defining terrorism and its various types, and scrutinizing the dominant contradictions involved. The principle of contradiction is employed by analyzing four contradictions associated with jihadi terrorism and the war on terrorism. The first contradiction employs the principle of circular and cumulative causation (CCC) to ascertain how such attacks constitute relatively low risks of fatality for specific individuals compared with car accidents, suicide, murder and TB, but also a high apparently system (social) risk/uncertainty which often lead people to become fearful and intimidated in a CCC fashion. The second contradiction utilises the principle of innovation by recognising that the creative destruction of technology can both enhance the human condition as well as, when used by terrorists as a form of sabotage, substantially reduce the quality of life of the community. The third contradiction addresses the principle of hegemony and uneven development through the strategic use of such terrorists (such as the *Mujahideen*) by the United States to fight the Soviets leading to the emergence of a power vacuum which *Al Qaida*, the *Taliban* and other groups used to enhance their strategic ambitions. And the fourth contradiction is that global deregulation and neoliberalism led to greater uneven development throughout the world as well as lax regulations that enhanced the ability of terrorists to form financial and social networks to plan successful attacks on the west. Then I employ the principle of policy and governance by proposing policies relating to each contradiction to deescalate the power of such *jihadis*. These include public education programs on terrorism, and consequence management on the ground;

circuit breakers, supply buffers, microbe attack preparation, and alternative nodes to reduce the extent of technological centralization; the deepening of multilateralism, greater linkages to islamic cultures, and dialogue with islamic powers; a new balance between regulation and freedom to reduce cyber-terrorism, terrorist movement, and terrorist access to finance; plus the promotion of progressive counter-forces such as islamic political economy

Keywords

Terrorism · War on terrorism · Historical specificity · Contradiction · Circular & cumulative causation · Innovation · Hegemony & uneven development · Policy & governance

10.1 Introduction

The principle of historical specificity states that we should analyze the context within which our subject matter is embedded in politico-social time so as to comprehend its dynamic motion. In this context, over the past few decades, in particular, many planned attacks on civilians and others throughout the world have made terrorism a central concern in the global political economy. The vast majority of these attacks were agents of war. The 'event' that 'changed the world' was the 11 September 2001 attacks on the World Trade Center and the Pentagon in the United States, which killed around 3000 people. Since then there have been several other such attacks, such as the October 2002 suicide bombing in Bali which killed 202 people, and the May 2003 bombing in Casablanca which killed 43 people. These and others are said to be part of a wider, worldwide plan of attack by radical Islamic networks against US hegemony in the Middle East, the Persian Gulf and elsewhere (O'Hara 2008).

Drawing on the principle of hegemony and uneven development, of special concern to Osama bin Laden (1957–2011) and his *al-Qaeda* 'terrorist' network is the aggression they see the US as having wielded over Islamic nations. For instance, they complain the US has troops stationed in Saudi Arabia, a holy land of Islam. The US has historically strongly supported Israel – militarily and diplomatically – against the 'Palestinian people'. The US and its closest allies (the UK and Australia) are seen as having invaded Iraq with insufficient evidence of weapons of mass destruction. The UN – with the US at its head – disarmed and then stood by while some one hundred thousand ethnic Albanians were slaughtered in 1998. And an earlier 'ally' of the US, Russia, had been trying to defeat (or destroy) the Chechyan Islamic radicals in their bid for dominance in the area.

These actions and others have incensed bin Laden and his followers. He had earlier issued a *Fatwas* to all Muslims declaring a *jihad* or holy war on the US and its allies (bin Laden et al. 1998: 2):

> [W]e issue [t]he ... ruling [that] to kill ... Americans and their allies – civilians and military – is an individual duty for every Muslim who can do it in any country in which it is possible to do it, in order to liberate the al-Aqsa Mosque and the holy mosque [Mecca] from their grip, and in order for their armies to move out of all the lands of Islam, defeated

and unable to threaten any Muslim. This is in accordance with the words of Almighty God, [to] ... "fight the pagans all together as they fight you all together," and "fight them until there is no more tumult or oppression, and there prevail justice and faith in God."[1]

After around 3,000 people were killed in the 2001 attacks on New York and (near) Washington DC, George W. Bush ordered the Taliban to give bin Laden up to face a military or international tribunal. They refused and in the midst of sympathetic UN resolutions favoring anti-terrorist actions, the Afghan War started in November 2001. A new, more unilateralist policy has been instigated by the US, under the influence of the American Enterprise Institute and others, to rid the world of so-called renegade states and the "axis of evil". The combined air and ground forces of the US, NATO, other nations, plus the Northern Alliance managed to destroy most of the resistance put up by the Taliban, and a more broadly-based Afghan government was able to be installed by February 2002 (until 2021). Hundreds of captured Taliban and *al-Qaida* fighters are being held in Guantanamo Bay in Cuba for interrogation. The US and its strongest allies then went into Iraq in 2003 to defeat Saddam Hussein on the pretext of them having weapons of mass destruction and having association with Islamic terrorists.

What are we to make of the continuing political-economic significance of these conflicts for the world and its people? Does it represent, as Lawrence Freedman (2001–02) asks, the start of a Third World War that will impact greatly for some years to come? Does it represent, as Samuel Huntington (1996) believes, a major clash of civilizations, Islam and West, which will impact for many decades to come? Or could it be, as Charles Amjad-Ali (2001–02) proposes, a passing phase of the evolution of the world-system where the US seeks a meaningful form of dialogue with Islam? The aim of this chapter is to find out some of the answers to these and related questions.

10.2 Contemporary Terrorism: Nature and Trends

There are literally dozens of definitions of terrorism posited in the literature, which reveal its multifaceted nature, and lead to difficulties in obtaining consistent statistics. Close to the mark is M.V. Naidu's (2001: 2) perspective that:

---

[1] A 'personal message' from bin Laden (1996:2) to Muslims had specifically stated that: "It should not be hidden from you that the people of Islam had suffered from aggression, inequity and injustice imposed on them by the Zionist-Crusaders alliance and their collaborators; to the extent that the Muslims blood became the cheapest and their wealth as loot in the hands of the enemies. Their blood was spilled in Palestine and Iraq. The horrifying pictures of the massacre of Qana, in Lebanon are fresh in our memory. Massacres in Tajikistan, Burma, Cashmere, Assam, Philippine, Fatani, Ogadin, Somalia, Eritrea, Chechnya and in Bosnia Herzegovina took place, massacres that send shivers in the body and shake the conscience. All of this and the world watch and hear, and not only didn't respond to these atrocities, but also with a clear conspiracy between the USA and its' allies and under the cover of the iniquitous United Nations, the dispossessed people were even prevented from obtaining arms to defend themselves." (sic)

... terrorism is the phenomenon in which a community is subjected to fear and terror through threats to human well being, and/or through ... destruction of life, liberty and property of some individuals or groups [and where the] ... targets of these threats and/or attacks are essentially [the] civilian population, ... in pursuit of racist, religious, and ideological or political goals.

Usually when people talk of terrorism – as in this definition – they mean that certain actions have been taken by a group to kill, wound, threaten or infect civilians, and which propel fear and intimidation within the social-psychology of a wider population.[2]

Terrorism is unleashed on civilians in many forms. Michael Walzer (2002), for instance, differentiates between revolutionary terror, war terror and state terror; and I would add a fourth, namely 'cultural terrorism'. Of course, all four forms could be operating simultaneously, and are often closely related. *Revolutionary (or 'political') terrorism* includes the actions of a liberation movement (or its enemies) to force the hands of political leaders to yield on particular issues. Examples include the Irish Republican Army, the Palestine Liberation Organization, the Basque Separatist Movement, and the Algerian National Liberation Front. Recently, Islamic radicals are taking vague or very *general concerns at a global or regional level* as a basis of action. *War terrorism* is an attempt by a government or army to kill civilians in large numbers during a full-scale war in order to force the opposing army or government to surrender. The classic example is the dropping of atom bombs on Hiroshima and Nagasaki by the US during World War Two, resulting in the killing of over 100,000 civilians and the surrender of the Japanese government.

State terrorism usually includes war terrorism but is supposed to mean the targeting of civilians in peacetime, or the use of a state apparatus in one country to support an army that targets civilians in another. State terrorism in general (including the use of the state for war terrorism) is the most common form of terrorism – the greatest menace – and has elicited the greatest number of civilian deaths (see Sherman 2002). A good example is the destruction of native American culture and peoples by colonial and government armies during the 1700s and 1800s. Another is the attempted extermination of Aborigines in *Terra Australis* in the late 1700s and 1800s by the British and local authorities; especially through the introduction of smallpox viruses into the indigenous community (see Butlin 1983), and systematic shooting and other means. There is a fourth form of terrorism, what might be called *cultural terrorism*, where a dominant ethnic (or other) group kills or instills fear and

---

[2] The FBI's view seems to be problematic. They define terrorism as "the unlawful use of force or violence against persons or property to intimidate or coerce a government, the civilian population, or any segment thereof, in furtherance of political goals" (Sherman Jackson 2001a, b: 295). This has problems because it could include an army attacking the government or the military; and what is domestically "lawful" – according to state fiat – may still be terrorist, if the state legislates to allow state-terrorism.

intimidation into members of another group as part of the normal course of life. Usually, though, this requires the support of the state or other institutions such as the Church. Often those who are killed, intimidated or denied due process are looked upon as inconsequential, since they are 'no better than dogs'; 'savages', 'underlings', whose life is said to be 'worthless'. A good example is the lynching of African Americans by the Ku Klux Klan and their associates between the 1860s and the 1960s.

The new radical Islamic terrorism is closely related to other forms of terrorism. Specifically, it is a form of revolutionary terrorism; but it is also done within the context of a global war of radical Islam against the US and its closest allies. It is undertaken in response to what it sees as US state terrorism, war terrorism in Iraq, and the support of reactionary state and organized terrorism in Israel and elsewhere. In order to comprehend the causes of the war on terrorism and the war on US hegemony, it is necessary to study the conflicting tendencies and processes of modern terrorism and the global political economy. Such conflicting tendencies are not simple; they are complex. One has to examine the strategic nature of terrorism, and the major sources of conflict emanating within the global political economy (see Kennedy 1998). Why does *al-Qaida* want to engage in weapons of mass destruction? Why do they use modern forms of technology? Why are they against US hegemony? Why hasn't globalization led the whole world to successfully join the club of business networks establishing shareholder value? How can there be different interpretations of Islam? It is to these questions that we now proceed.

10.3 Terrorism: Low Fatality Risk, High System Risk

This chapter seeks to critically evaluate the recent terrorism issue on the basis of the political economy concept of 'contradiction'. Contradiction are positive and negative aspects of a phenomena that are inherently related to operational dynamics; aspects that cannot easily be separated from it. These inner contradictory dynamics are the forces that lead the phenomena to operate, but also the forces that lead to conflict and instability. The principle of contradiction states that it is critical for an understanding of political economy processes to analyze such contradictions, with a view to investigating whether they are capable of being moderated and if so how (See O'Hara 2001). Consistent with the principle of contradiction, this chapter examines four major contradictory dynamics of terrorism in the contemporary environment.

The first contradictory aspect of the inner motion of terrorism is this: for the type of terrorism typical of 9/11, it has a relatively low risk of death for specific individuals, yet it usually elicits a high level of social-psychological fear and uncertainty among the population. Historically, as shown by Table 10.1, below, compared with other risks of death – such as car accidents, suicide, murder, TB and meningitis – terrorism poses an insignificant threat to the lives of human beings in the United States and most other places on Earth. The risk of being killed by isolated

Table 10.1 Worldwide fatalities of various sources of death per 100,000 population, 1983–1997

Year	Car accidents	Suicide	Murder	Tuberculosis	Terrorism
1983	14.90	12.10	8.30	0.80	0.120
1987	19.12	12.71	8.30	0.70	0.003
1993	16.30	11.30	9.50	0.60	0.002
1997	15.80	10.80[a]	6.80	0.40	0.003

Source of raw data: Adapted from Falkenrath (2001: 170)
[a]1996

terrorist acts is infinitesimal compared with these other, major, causes of death (unless terrorists wage war, in which case it becomes 'war terrorism').

On the other hand, again historically, the political leadership and general public have a tendency to perceive terrorism as being a critical threat to their livelihood. People under the threat of isolated acts of terrorism tend to systematically overestimate terrorism as a threat to their life and livelihood. This is linked with the greater fear, intimidation, horror and indignity that terrorist actions – especially the new form bend on mass (but isolated) killings – tend to create in the collective social consciousness. As a result, terrorist threats may create mass uncertainty and fear as people become more inward-looking, or reduce their use of airline travel, or not go to certain strategic destinations. "According to opinion polling done by the Chicago Council on Foreign Relations in 1998–99 – before the 11 September actions – 84% of the general public identified international terrorism as a "critical threat" to the United States, more than any other issue. Sixty-one percent of "leaders" identified international terrorism as a "critical threat", putting it just behind nuclear proliferation (67%) and chemical and biological weapons (64%)" (Falkenrath 2001: 170). Yet a similar public concern (or campaign) against motor vehicle fatalities or suicide is nowhere in sight, despite the much higher fatalities from these sources.

A paradox, which is implicit in the contradictory 'multiplier' effects of terrorism, is that there appear to be an inverse relationship between the social psychological consequences of fatalities and its fatality probability or frequency, as shown in Fig. 10.1, below[3]:

---

[3]The "terrorist multiplier" equation includes a number of variables. The first is the number of fatalities; deaths and serious injuries, such as the 3000-odd deaths associated with the September 11 attacks. And the second is the ratio of the number of persons affected by – as well as the degree of - fear and intimidation. For instance, those directly affected by the 11 September 2001 attacks, in the form of fear and intimidation, could be defined as the population of the US (280 million); and the degree of fear and intimidation could be called "relatively high" (h). The multiplier effect (Sm) of the terrorist activities is a ratio of the population affected (p; 280 million), divided by the number of fatalities (f; 3,000 people), multiplied by the impact (i; high):

$$m = \frac{p}{f} \quad i = \frac{280m}{3000} \quad h = 9333(h)$$

For instance, fatalities of around 3000 people from the 11 September attacks being able to instill a relatively high level of fear and intimidation into a national population of around 280 m people in the US.

10.3 Terrorism: Low Fatality Risk, High System Risk

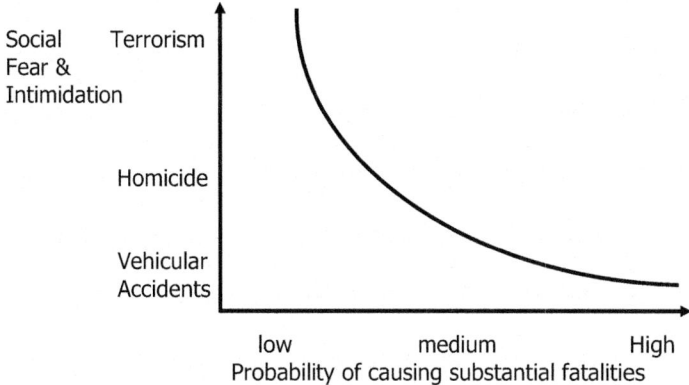

Fig. 10.1 Terrorism consequences-probability trade-off

There are many reasons for the fact that people are more fearful of isolated terrorist actions that are extremely unlikely to kill or maim them than they are of motor accident deaths, suicide and murder that are much more likely to affect them directly. The first is that people get more fearful from conscious acts of killing than from activities that kill as a by-product of something useful, such as driving a car. Secondly, people are more fearful of terrorist acts that seek to kill as a political statement, than they are from many killings that may be 'crimes of passion' or the isolated acts of psychopaths. Thirdly, people get scared more from a small number of critical fatalities spread over time in specific sites than they do from many more fatalities spread over a larger time period in many locations.[4] And fourthly, rarely does a government seriously stimulate community debate about the nature of so-called terrorism, because they are interested in their military or strategic response and their desire to exploit the short-term political advantages of being involved in patriotic fervor.

The general source of this dynamic is that there appears to be no real threat of fatality to the individual in the recent terrorist attacks, since anyone could have been hit, if they were near the source of the attacks. It is not a statistical problem for the individual, compared with other types of fatalities. But it surely is an attack on the system of (relative) US hegemony. Hence the general contradiction between individual and society: recent terrorism was unleashed so that there could be socioeconomic crises to upset the US and other economies. Individuals were not targeted, only people who happened to be in or near architectural and economic icons of US capitalism associated with trade (the WTC), finance (Wall Street) and military

---

[4]Even the 3000-odd deaths from the WTC and Pentagon etc. strikes represent a relatively low number of deaths per 100,000 population relative to car accidents, suicide and murder. For instance, per 100,000 population for the US as a whole, it represents 0.09 deaths per 100,000 population, compared with about 16 deaths per 100,000 for car accidents, 11 for suicide and 7 for murder.

dominance (the Pentagon); or tourist destinations and areas sympathetic to US interests.

Terrorists take advantage of this contradictory (or paradoxical) state of affairs: that terrorist acts pose a low risk to specific individuals, yet those same individuals feel fear and intimidation, nevertheless, due to social forces. Indeed, this is precisely the reason terrorists use such actions to advance their political or other objectives. It has a high impact action with a relatively low rate of fatality. Or more specific to *al-Qaida's* (and their allies') objectives, it creates massive fear and intimidation with relatively low cost for putting into operation. Hence *al-Qaida* were able to 'produce' a high cost of death and destruction ('social costs' to the US) ranging from estimates of $60 billion to $1 trillion (Homer-Dixon 2002: 58; Luke 2001:141).

These social costs are related to the principle of circular and cumulative vis-à-vis the circuits of modern terrorism. This shows how the terrorists use their belief system and *Jihad* as the principal stimulus to action. The action manifests itself in the creation of various terrorist networks, which plan and activate strategic attacks, using various technologies. This new radical Islamic terrorism tends to depend upon two sorts of networks. One is an internal network of committed comrades, linked to a loose collection of like-minded radicals, as well as being supported by a diverse group of sympathizers, in turn associated with various governments and businesses. The second is the total network, including the media, the fatalities and the population linked to the targeted group. The wider network is the source of its economies of scale and broad effectiveness, and is shown below in Fig. 10.2.

This multiplier effect is a product of the effective use of technology, media response and national sentiment. The governments of the affected population then respond to the situation. The combined influence of all factors creates a circular and cumulative impact on the whole process. Successful attacks reinforce fear and intimidation, greater media coverage, and so on in a circular and cumulative fashion,

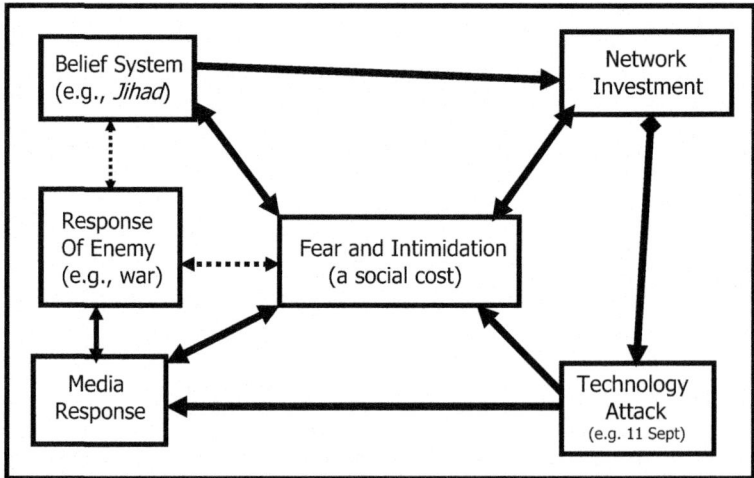

Fig. 10.2 Circular and cumulative network effects of terrorism

with the cycle perhaps continuing through several runs. Many variants of the process are possible, such as a further attack, pro-terrorist actions or war activated by the affected-population's government, and so on.

10.4 Technology Promotes Terrorism

Opposition religious groups against US capitalism and hegemony are much stronger, powerful, and more concerned with mass (isolated) casualties than just getting attention to their cause. They want to destroy US hegemony over Islamic nations and the Persian Gulf. They find that US power corrupts people, dominates whole nations, and that the cultural foundations of outside dominance are morally repugnant. Instead, they believe in a particular reading of the *Koran*, reestablishing certain Islamic values and practices. Ironically, though, they appear to be using the power of capital, and some of the methods of production and reproduction typical of capital, to enhance their cause.

We thus come to the second contradiction associated with the principle of innovation. The creative destruction of contemporary capitalism produces a massive technological infrastructure of machines, computers, airlines, weapons, buildings and roadways that enhances its creative regeneration, accumulation, profitability and systemic reproduction. But the very structures and dynamics of this technology are just as effectively used by terrorists to *sabotage* – as Thorstein Veblen (1921) called it – both the system of technology and the institutions and relationships of capitalism. Sabotage refers to the process whereby the technological and network processes that propel production and reproduction of institutions and material output are being destroyed or adversely affected through conscious decisions of classes and other groups. In the process, they are able to increase fear, uncertainty, and instability while reducing expected profit and accumulation for the system. This goes to the very heart of capitalism and US hegemony. A simple illustration of this contradictory relationship is shown below in Fig. 10.3:

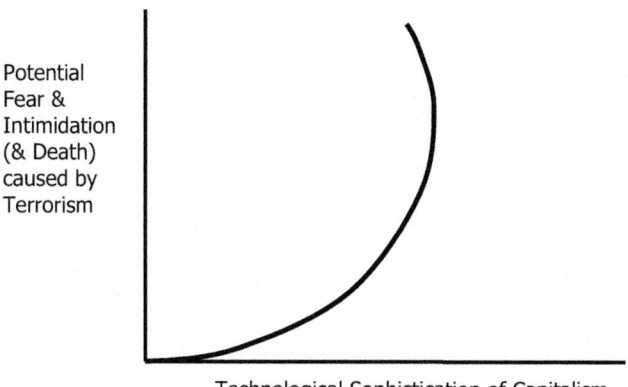

Fig. 10.3 Contradictions of technology

This shows that as the technological sophistication of capitalism increases, the potential for terrorists to utilize these structures of knowledge and technical competence to destroy such technology expands through historical time. The ability to sabotage is positively related to the degree of technological sophistication, at an accelerating rate; and a point may be reached where the fear and intimidation starts to inhibit technology. Hence sabotage could feasibly lead to a decline in technological sophistication through a sufficient acceleration of fear and intimidation. The fact is that the technological structures and dynamics of capitalism are becoming increasingly capable of being used against itself by this new form of terrorism committed to the overthrow of US hegemony in the region. Modern technologies make it possible for the effective use of cyber-terrorism and weapons of mass destruction in the pursuit of extreme political, religious and social beliefs that may completely disrupt society. The attacks on the World Trade Center and the Pentagon were not low tech-events, as some analysts have suggested. The *al-Qaida* network used simple objects such as box-cutters, knowledge of flying and physics to convert commercial planes and jet fuel into modes of mass destruction – or at least high-tech killing machines – capable of killing thousands of people and destroying icons or US power and capability. As Juan Corradi (2001:149) states:

> Contemporary societies make instruments of destruction possible as so many other commodities and make themselves, by that token, vulnerable. The more advanced and the freer the society, the greater the availability of do-it-yourself destruction. The means and opportunities have multiplied. The motives have evolved as well.... Technology makes it virtually impossible to distinguish between "peaceful" and "destructive" research and output. In a nutshell, contemporary violence, far from being a midwife of a new social system, is a state into which existing systems easily lapse.

The systems that are capable of being destroyed are networks or nodes of businesses, computer-information, highways, fiber-optic cables, railways, and defense arrangements that are interconnected and complex relationships between institutions and people. As Gunnar Myrdal (1978) realized in his theory of circular and cumulative causation, the closer and more complex the network of interrelationships that are generated by these systems, the greater potential uncertainty, instability and chaos that can result from their dislocation or destruction. An effective computer virus may destroy a whole network of business arrangements. A plane flown into a major building can reduce the perceived level of personal safety of a whole nation. A series of anthrax-laced letters has the potential to destroy a mail system. A nuclear device detonated in a series of major 'public' spaces simultaneously – such as Grand Central Station in peak period, Congress in mid-session, and a major league game in an exciting final quarter – can destroy the perceived security of a nation.

There are three main reasons or dimensions of technological vulnerability. First, modern technology has central nodes: critical sections, spaces, or areas that are the hub of the system, and that can be disrupted quite easily. For instance, the "root servers" of computers are of this type. Secondly, capitalism has historically undergone various forms of centralization and concentration in particular areas and specific businesses. This is because of economies of scale and scope, and the high positive externalities of geographic location. Tacit knowledge, for instance, is often best developed in specific areas; such as Silicon Valley; Wall Street; Parliament. And thirdly, these centers and networks do not simply affect physical reality, but also virtual reality; and, more especially, the psycho-social networks associated with national symbols, national-consciousness, and media outlets. The media is or has the potential to be the advertising agents of the terrorists - be they state-terrorists, religious terrorists or liberation-movement terrorists - either wittingly or unwittingly.

A critical factor enabling terrorists to "redirect the energies of our intricate societies against us" (Homer-Dixon 2002: 58) is their degree of tacit knowledge. Explicit knowledge is the information necessary for the operation of a machine or other system; the blueprint that needs to be codified, or the instructions that need to be put into practice. Much more difficult is the tacit knowledge, which includes the experience of the practitioner, or knowledge gained through intuition that cannot easily be copied, or the knowledge that effectively applies something in practice (Jackson 2001a: 187). It is this that the 11 September terrorists demonstrated to have an excellent grasp of.[5] They showed great novelty by using a plane hijacking in a completely different way; almost as a series of simultaneous bombing campaigns. In this they benefited from a sustained process of research and development and the existence of a sound, decentralized form of network capital.

10.5 Attempt to Reestablish Strategic US Hegemony Encouraged Terrorism

Relevant to the principle of hegemony and uneven development, during the 1950s–1960s the US enjoyed absolute hegemonic dominance in the world, with a caveat: there was also a relative *military* 'balance' between the US and the USSR (Wallerstein 1983; Bowles et al. 1992). In economic terms – production, commerce and finance – the US (in association with other Western nations) ruled the world, through the provision of leadership and at times coercion to establish public goods functions of stability and conflict resolution. Many authors concluded that, by the early 1970s, US hegemony had declined, reflected in defeat in Vietnam, declining productivity, plus global and financial instability. Deep recession and financial instability of a periodic nature were common during the 1970s–2000s. By the beginnings of the 1990s the Eastern Block variety of so-called communism – or what some Western Marxists called 'state capitalism' (Resnick and Wolff 1995) – was in absolute decline. The emergence of market socialism in China and Vietnam

---

[5] Some analysts, such as Jason Pate (2001: 13), believe that the 11 September attack "is a very, very low technology incident". However this is far from being the case. The attacks were part of a wideranging network of systems, including sophisticated internet communication, strategic use of multiple commercial planes, a high level of tacit knowledge and coordination, and the use of technological linkages between planes, buildings and other technologies.

furthered the worldwide belief in market systems and, by the beginning of the twenty-first century (or near the end of the last millennium), many thought US hegemony was becoming firmly re-established as a result of a series of military campaigns and the decline of the USSR; while others thought only *relative* US hegemony was established; or that it represented only US hegemony in the Middle East (not necessarily elsewhere).

During the 1980s the CIA did what it could to promote opposition to Soviet power and 'control' in Afghanistan (as well as to the power elite in Iran and Yugoslavia). In doing so, it established a *de facto* strategic alliance with radical Islamic groups in Pakistan, Iraq, Afghanistan and other nations. It supplied military, financial and strategic support, for instance, to the *Mujahideen*, enabling the Taliban to come to power in Afghanistan. It continued to supply strategic and logistic support for these groups through the 1990s and early 2000s. Congressional reports of these activities are providing substantial support to this, according to Michael Chossudovsky (2001: 35, 39; emphasis added), who says:

> The various [US] Congressional reports confirm that the U.S. government has been working hand in glove with Osama bin Laden's *al-Qaida*. ... The evidence amply confirms that the CIA never severed its ties to the "Islamic Militant Network"; the ties have become increasingly sophisticated. ... The role of the CIA in supporting and developing international terrorist organizations during the Cold War *and its aftermath* is casually ignored or downplayed by the Western media.

What this implies is a central, third, contradiction: the current power of the *al-Qaida* and many other Islamic terrorist networks is part and parcel of the decline of the Soviet system and the support the US and specifically the CIA provided for the radical Islamic groups in the fight against international communism and secular Islamic governments such as Iraq. As Michael Mann (2001: 66) says, "religious revivals have come to replace many socialist movements as self-proclaimed resistors of imperialism." In short, the US hired the Muslim radicals – 'combat fundamentalists', as Mann calls them – to fight secularity and communism, and in the process provided the foundation for the rise of international terrorism as a sophisticated network of worldwide groups and individuals. The World Trade Center and Pentagon terrorist actions were thus influenced by US strategic support for terrorist organizations right up until the new millennium to help in its quest for renewed hegemony. This is a critical form of conflict emanating within the global political economy.

It is not simply that the US supported terrorist organizations, but that it did so for purely *strategic* reasons, in order to promote the decline of Russian communism and the Iraqi state. It did not embrace the central concerns of the radical Islamic groups or attempt to include them in a durable set of diplomatic, military and economic institutions. As the *Mujahideen* mercenaries, bin Laden and later the Taliban realized, they were effectively being used in the interests of US foreign policy and military hegemony. No attempt was made to seriously and empathetically engage in theological debate on Islam, nor on the question of US influence in Saudi Arabia and support of a repressive administration there, and also not in relation to nationhood for Palestine (until very recently). US consumer capitalism and culture also symbolized the worst of sexual immorality, neocolonialism and lack of respect for Islamic customs.

Hence, the US not only encouraged terrorism but did it in such as way that that the terrorists involved would not support the US in the long-run; i.e., it remained a purely strategic and short-run alliance. The US abused any long-term, durable alliance with the radical groups by entrenching their power in the Middle East. American troops were stationed in Saudi Arabia in an agreement with that government after the 1990s Iraqi War; this humiliated bin Laden and his associates, being as it is, the holy land of Islam. American weapons and diplomatic support was also given to Israel against the Palestinians; Palestine being another holy land of Islam.

In response to what is perceived as US arrogance and dominance, radical Islamic groups retaliated by bombing the World Trade Center in 1993 (6 deaths, US$500 m damage); bombing US embassies in Tanzania and Kenya (1998, 220+ deaths); bombing the US embassy in Nairoibi in 2001; undertaking the 11 September 2001 attacks on the WTC and Pentagon (2001, 3000 deaths; $60b economic costs); plus more recent attacks mentioned earlier (Falkenrath 2001:165; Bergen 2001: 430; Burke 2001–2002:136; Luke 2001: 141). The attempt to reestablish US hegemony was thus undertaken in a crude fashion, without assessing the system-problems that emerge when the hegemonic power acts recklessly in regions such as the Middle East.

10.6 Global Deregulation Expands Terrorism and Radical Islam

This fourth contradiction has three aspects to it. The first is that the emergence of globalization and neoliberal deregulation over the past two decades has seen the freer movement of capital – money, production and goods – throughout most regions of the world; and that this has aided political terrorists by making it easier to build a global organizational terrorist network of human, social, financial, technological, advertising and strategic capitals. Deregulation of global capital makes it easier for the terrorists to build resources against such a system, and in the process help to (unwittingly) generate a new structure of governance with more regulation on private capitals.[6]

The second dimension of this contradiction is that neoliberal globalization has led to an increase in relative poverty and oppression (inequality) – particularly between the West and the Islamic world – which is a breeding ground for terrorism.[7] The

---

[6] As Therese Delpech (2001:11) says: "Terrorism's financial backers skillfully exploit the weaknesses of the international fight against financial crime, while at the same time benefiting from the globalization and deregulation of markets."

[7] However, as we suggest in many places, this is unlikely to lead to the inherent "clash of civilizations", posited by Samuel Huntington (1996), especially if policy and culture-response issues are handled well. Jonathon Fox's (2001) empirical research also casts doubt on the clash of civilizations thesis.

spread of deregulated globalization increases the degree of uneven development in the world, which promotes rebelliousness in some of those areas that suffer in relative terms (Alehabib 1999). An increase in the number of graduates who are unable to find employment or meaningful activities promotes the stock of those capable of being the leading cadres in the radical Islamic movement against all of the 'infidels' of the world.

This is linked to a third dimension of the contradiction: the double standard of the US and Western diplomats, who talk about the need for human rights, cultural sensitivities, peace and democracy – while at the same time seemingly showing little concern for the rights, cultural peculiarities, property and governance structures of Islamic people. Many see this as a double standard.[8] For instance, the US will often unilaterally decide to intervene in a country if it thinks it is in its best interests. It also has historically supported its own forms of "state terrorism" against the civilian population of various – especially Islamic – nations.

These three dimensions – (1) deregulation and terrorism; (2) globalization and uneven development; and (3) the double standards of the US – create various conflicts and instabilities. One particularly damaging result is the deep feelings in the Islamic world against the US. Evelin Lindner (2001), for instance, isolates the humiliation of Islamic peoples: when the US continues to support Israel against the 'Palestinians'; when it settles it troops in Saudi Arabia and supports a corrupt government (also in Egypt and the Sudan); when the US and its allies invade Afghanistan without (as they see it) direct material evidence about complicity in the 11 September attacks; and when it invades Iraq without adequate evidence of weapons of mass destruction. For instance, in March 1985 the CIA organized a car bombing in Beirut that killed 80 civilians and wounded 256 while they were attending Friday prayers at the Imam Rida Mosque; 'timed to kill the maximum number of people as they left' the service (missing their target, Shi'ite leader Sheikh Fadlallah) (Chomsky 2001). Also, over 100,000 civilians were killed in the US-led Gulf War of the early 1990s, and, according to Madeleine Albright, during 1991–2001 an estimated 500,000 children could have died as a result of US-inspired sanctions against Iraq (Editors 2001).

The lack of empathy by the US for Islamic ways and interests, and the inability of globalization and US power to positively influence the quality of life of many Islamic nations, has led many to engage in the "new" form of terrorism. Searching for roots of a better way of life for Islamic people's that transcend corrupt regimes and outside dominance, *al-Qaida* and their supporters represent a new generation of scholars, fighters and common people seeking to reestablish self-respect and

---

[8]E.g., Tim Luke (2001: 131) believes "the US slowly turned away from many larger internationalist responsibilities that befell it as the world's sole remaining superpower. Instead of continuing to stand resolutely for unshakable modern ideals, like democracy, equality, and freedom, the US ... permitted gangster capitalism to establish itself in places as varied as Russia, Columbia, and Rumania, and [did little] as horrendous civil strife racked areas in Africa, the Middle East, and Central Asia."

salvation for Islamic peoples. But they are just as much against so-called corrupt forms of Islam as they are in attacking the US. As Appleby and Marty (2002) state:

> Social context and the local or regional political culture have much to say about the directions that fundamentalism takes. Within the abode of Islam, nation states are either weak or failing, on the one hand, or dictatorial or repressive, on the other. Both contexts encourage violent variants of fundamentalism bent on replacing the state (as the Taliban did in Afghanistan) or overthrowing it (as the Shi'ites did in Iran and as radical Islamic groups have hoped to do in Egypt, Algeria, Saudi Arabia, and elsewhere).

10.7 Policy Issues and Measures

Here we center on the principle of policy and governance, concerning measures that directly link to each of the conflicting, contradictory tendencies. Some general points need to be mentioned first, though. A coherent global strategy needs to be formulated that deals with all levels of the problem, from prevention to deterrence to defense. Included here is a whole stream of dimensions, including the upgrade of intelligence work, homeland security, global cooperation, missile defense, conventional forces, consequence management, and nonproliferation agreements. Especially important is the building of global cooperation through institutions and relationships. Also critical is prevention and deterrence, because once a terrorist attack has been activated it may be difficult to ascertain precisely the source of the attack. Future attacks may be even more obscure and difficult to isolate. And lastly, it is not sufficient to devise strategies to minimize "political terrorism", since all dimensions of the problem from 'political', to 'war' and 'state', to 'cultural' terrorism are all critical to minimize in the global political economy. Quite often terrorism is inextricably linked to war and other forms of conflict, so this needs to be factored in as well.

In relation to the first contradiction, the vast majority of people have little knowledge of the statistics of relative fatalities and the ways in which terrorists use "big events" and the media to multiply and amplify their problems and concerns. The public needs to become more aware of these factors, while the media needs to be more responsible in not playing into the hands of terrorists in this fashion. Secondly, there needs to be a concerted effort to promote what William Perry (2002) calls "consequence management". This is the management of the human after-effects of terrorist tragedies, including the strengthening of the operations of firefighters, police, national guard, reserve units and the centers of disease control. It is critical to have sufficient reserves and an adequate system of activation against biological agents such as poisons and disease microbes. Sufficient stocks of antidotes, antiserums, antibiotics and inoculations may reduce the degree of fear and intimidation.

In response to the 'technology-terrorism' link of contradiction two, a potentially useful policy response can be 'circuit breakers' to reduce the circular and cumulative technological and system network effects and relationships linked to terrorism. They intervene in the negative feedback effects of terrorism, or promote additional buffers as alternative sources of supply. It is necessary to reduce the number and importance of "critical non-redundant nodes" – or central information centers – so that there are alternative sources of knowledge and data storage.[9] Decentralization of industry and the promotion of alternative sources of energy – as well as the creation of a alternative government 'in hiding' (which is in motion in the US) – can reduce the negative consequences of terrorism. Promoting local autonomy of food production can also help, in the case of national or transnational systems of supply being interrupted. Reducing the extent of just-in-time production methods can have the same effect. (Homer-Dixon 2002) Ensuring that there is a degree of decentralization of information through the Internet and institutional information systems is also important.

A national missile defense capability may provide an insurance policy against a sophisticated attack, although it does not help against the more likely attacks. An effective campaign against the proliferation of nuclear and biological weapons is necessary. Reenergizing the Nonproliferation Treaty, the Biological Weapons Convention, and the Strategic Arms Reduction Treaty (START), as well as activating treaties not yet formalized or implemented such as New Start II, those between the US and North Korea, the Comprehensive Test Ban Treaty, and the Trilateral Agreement between the US, Russia and the Ukraine, may help build cooperation (Perry 2002). Putting more resources into a conventional defense system makes sense – such as the modernization of aircraft carriers, modern information technology, and specialist battle troops. (This may stimulate state terrorism, which needs to be guarded against.)

There are many limits to the extent that 'political' terrorists can effectively use chemical, biological, radiological and nuclear (CBRN) means to generate weapons of mass destruction (WMD) (Hoffman 2001). Nevertheless, even if it were true that most sources of WMD are unlikely, there are plenty of other materials – chemicals, microorganisms, and nuclear energy – that could conceivably be effective, even if difficult to deliver on a mass scale. Examples include smallpox (formerly thought to be scarce), weapons-grade nuclear material (if not nuclear weapons), nerve gases such as sarin (used by Aum Shinrikyo in a Tokyo subway in 1995), and dozens of more freely available chemicals and toxins. The supply of microorganisms, nuclear material, nerve gas, and the like on the global black market poses grave problems of supply.

For contradictory tendency three, relating to US hegemony, a survey (March 2002) has shown that the Islamic world tends to view the US as an aggressive and arrogant imperial force. For instance, 53% of respondents from nine Muslim nations

---

[9]Thomas Homer-Dixon, for instance, believes that "the World Trade Center was not a critical, nonredundant node. At least it wasn't critical in the way most people (including, probably, the terrorists) would have thought. Many of the financial firms in the destroyed buildings had made contingency plans for disaster by setting up alternate facilities for data, information, and computer equipment in remote locations.... NASDAQ officials [for instance] later claimed that their system was so robust that they could have restarted trading only a few hours after the attack."

have a 'unfavorable' opinion of the US. 77% believe that US military action in Afghanistan is 'morally unjustified'. And 61% did not believe that the 11 September attacks were undertaken by Arabs. (Gallop Poll 2002) Clearly, the US has a terrible image in these nations, especially in Pakistan, Saudi Arabia, Iran and Jordan. The support for radical Islam is growing, and a critical way to reduce actual and potential conflict with the area is by having better cultural, political and economic linkages to those nations. In short, multilateralism needs to be deepened, expanded and rooted in effective participation and dialogue with Islam that goes way beyond questions of 'national interest'. As Jonathan Stevenson (2001: 44) says: "Constructive but cautious engagement with lesser evils – be they terrorist groups or their suspected state sponsors – is a price worth paying for the capacity to confront the greater evil without quarter."

In relation to an aspect of contradiction four, concerning deregulation and globalization, a new balance between security and freedom will be necessary, where the key to success will be close global cooperation against terrorist networks, including state terrorism. New governance measures will be necessary to regulate the global transfer of money, particularly to increase the level of transparency. Export controls will be required to check merchandise and supply chains. Suitable measures are in place at many airports for travelers, but these will need to be incorporated into the flows of money and capital as well. Certain basic regulations will be required on the global Internet, cyberways and computer systems.

Terrorists are currently working on *Offensive Information Warfare*, an example of which is *netwar*, a type of cyberterrorism, used to sabotage and gain information globally, nationally and regionally. However, there will be problems in applying these regulations, for instance, the difficulties in having a truly transatlantic (and beyond) system of governance in place (Bartsch 2001). Terrorists try and impair the trust that the public and corporations have developed in the use of the Internet and information technology. They are currently trying to corrupt strategic nodules in the system and infiltrate official networks to gain strategic information. *Al-Qaida* are known to be actively involved in cyberspace (Wheeler 2001), and many of their leading members have a considerable amount of technical knowledge and university training. The corruption of information technology nodules can potentially destroy the positive externalities associated with the Internet, due to the complex interdependencies involved. Sabotage of this type could disrupt whole global networks of business, causing a major recession or worse. It is thus critical to develop more alternatives nodules, a reduction in the tightness of the information fit, and alternative sources and storage of data. As Valery and Knights recognize (2000), this will require a radical increase in the level of priority given to information and systems security within and between companies and government departments. Evidence shows that company executives tend to be reactive (not proactive) vis-à-vis security breaches (Damphousse and Smith 1998).[10]

---

[10] Valeri and Knights (2000) believe that Islamic extremists are unlikely to try and sabotage the Internet or other information nodules because of their "established operational style" (p. 21). However, the 11 September attacks have taught us that they are quite likely and capable of taking risks and making innovatory changes in their strategies. This is also the message of the analysis done by Moorhead Kennedy (1998) and also Kelly Damphousse & Brent Smith (1998).

Islam has progressive elements in its thought, particularly well illustrated through the tenets of Islamic political economy.[11] But a "spectre is haunting the world – the specter of Muslim fundamentalism" (Hyman 1985: 3) – and as a result a crisis has existed within traditional Islamic thought and practice for some time now. The relative decline of Sufi spiritualism, and Islamic secular-nationalism, colonial domination, and the existence of certain demagogic notionally Islamic governments, left a spiritual vacuum that fundamentalism has sought to reconstruct along more activist lines. But there are alternatives to fundamentalism, and many scholars and officials have called for Islamic renewal – along traditional cultural lines – as a way of denting the impact of radical Islam and hence political terrorism. This is said to be in line with the tenets of Islam for a periodic renewal or revival of Islamic faith and the emergence of 'fresh impulses'.

Richard Bulliet (2002), for instance, believes that the foundations of this renewal are already in motion; for instance, in a revival of Sufism in Iran, Central Asia and other areas; the advocacy of participatory governing institutions by people such as Hezbollah leader Sheik Muhammad Fadlallah; and a series of progressive Islamic institutions such as the Institute of Islamic and Arabic Sciences in America. Murad Hofman (2001) puts forward a program of renewal, which has similarities with other programs, based around (a) the division of power, (b) female empowerment, and (c) general emancipation. Hofman suggests countering the influence of radical Islam and political terrorism through the promotion in Muslim nations of public participation, individual rights, female inclusion, institutional transparency, reduced inequality, plus increasing innovation, productivity and literacy.

He links these notions to Islamic tenets and philosophies, particularly stressing the need to eschew "Muslims [trying to] catch up with the Joneses in a consumerist spirit ... since Muslim life should never be dominated by economic considerations" (p. 303). Nevertheless, issues of livelihood, power and governance are critical to Islam. The advocacy of such principles and programs are needed in tandem with religious authorities "able to declare that the killing of innocents by terrorist attacks is contrary to Islam and ... Muslims can stand firmly against terrorism without seeming to embrace the United States and its policies" (p. 16). Jackson (2001b: 293) demonstrates philosophically the ways in which terrorism may be in contradistinction to Islam.[12] As a policy issue, the renewal of Islam in this fashion is critical to the fight against the killing of innocent civilians.

---

[11] For instance, IPE places emphasis on the Oneness of God linked to the stock of universal knowledge that augments cognition through institutions and social systems (Choudhury and Salleh 2001: 586–7).

[12] Sherman Jackson (2001a, b) shows how, in classic Islamic law, the promotion of *hirabab* – particularly if murder propels fear and intimidation (whether wittingly or not) among the population – is subject to major penalties.

10.8 Conclusion

The purpose of this chapter was to apply core general principles of IEPE to the issue of terrorism in the 9/11 environment; especially the dynamic contradictory tendencies that propel it as a tool of action, and policies that may be effective against various forms of terrorism. The principle of historical specificity helped situate 9/11 by explaining what terrorism is and who are the jihadis leading the US and its allies to start the war on terrorism. We used the principle of contradiction to examine four main tendencies of contemporary terrorism. The first inner contradictory tendency employs the principle of circular and cumulative causation to illustrate that terrorism has a low rate of fatality when compared to the major causes of death such as car accidents and murder; but that it manages to instill a relatively high rate of fear and intimidation into the population in spite of such low fatalities. The second contradictory tendency relates to the principle of innovation, whereby the very foundations of modern technology and knowledge in the advanced nations can be used by the terrorists as an attack on these foundations. The third dynamic tendency situates the principle of hegemony and uneven development with the attempt to reestablish US hegemony on the world against so-called communism which helped to create this new form of terrorism emerging from the power vacuum generated by Soviet demise. The fourth contradictory tendency is multifaceted. In general it relates to the forces of globalization and neoliberalism around the world that helped to create the terrorist networks.

The principles of innovation and policy/governance were used to develop strategies/policies/innovations against terrorism. The prime policy must be based on the recognition of the multifarious nature of terrorism: the main form is state terrorism; and it is difficult to address terrorism without addressing issues of war and conflict in general. The US and their allies should ensure that state terrorism is minimized, and that they reshape their strategies where they contribute to world conflict.

In relation to the policies corresponding to contradictory tendency one (fatalities and risks), it is necessary to put into practice policies that are able both to reduce fatalities – which should reduce the degree of fear and intimidation – and also to reduce the CCC multiplier effect between fatalities and fear. This includes measures such as an education process among the population about the nature of terrorism and how it works as well as the need to create a strategy through the mass media to reduce their level of complicity in the fear and intimidation process. Also important is a proper emergency and maintenance team that works on the ground to reduce the impact of attacks.

Contradictory tendency two relates to technology and knowledge. It is important to put in place a system of prevention, containment, and defense against both ordinary terrorist means and also weapons of mass destruction. The critical policy here should concentrate on the terrorist networks that are the life-blood of the attacks. This involves gathering intelligence about terrorist network membership and their circuit of money, goods and technology. WMD can also be targeted through strengthening existing agreements and policies – and developing new ones - against such proliferation.

Contradictory tendency three links to US hegemony and the need to form a multilateral alliance of states and interests against terrorism. To be effective, the US needs to moderate its periodic tendency to act in a unilateral fashion in support of its narrow interests. It needs to consolidate and strengthen multilateral alliances to include not simply its traditional allies; but also to act more in the interests of the common good, and build effective linkages with Islamic nations. Central to this policy is the need to think beyond the narrow interests of the US, and reinforce institutions, protocols and treaties that have a wider concern. Continuing to support the Kyoto protocol, the Ballistic Missile Treaty, and eschewing the Bush Doctrine about the "axis of evil" (Iran, Iraq and North Korea) will help build multilateralism.

Contradictory tendency four indicates that it would help to reduce terrorism by nations of the world being more proactive in the fight against what some see as the clash of civilizations. Measures need to put in place to moderate this *potential* clash. The West could participate through being more interested and concerned about Islam and the plight of the Arabs, encouraging the pace of reform in Iran and Libya, and being more proactive in support of a Palestinian homeland for Arabs. Islamic nations can contribute through developing forms of reinvention along lines of philosophy, gender and power. Perhaps the Islamic belief in a balance between economic and social/spiritual concerns can be a point of departure for policy makers in this respect. More than anything it is important to promote an ethical and just society and not simply one based on conspicuous consumption and material conditions. Policies that help promote such trends – in the long run – are best in the struggle against terrorism.

Acknowledgements I thank Hassan Bougrine, Jim Devine, Reynold Nesiba and Howard Sherman for comments on a previous version of this chapter. I also wish to thank seminar participants when presented at Loyola Marymount University, Los Angeles, and meetings of the Association for Social Economics as part of the Eastern Economic Association in Boston. This chapter is dedicated to the warmth, friendship and encouragement provided by Howard Sherman. Thanks are also due to the librarians at the Charles E. Young Research Library at UCLA who were of considerable assistance. It was originally published as O'Hara (2004), and I have decided to keep the original argument, as "9/11" was such an iconic series of events that had a major circular and cumulative impact on the world; also because I think the original version was very good, and has relevance to much that happened since.

References

Alehabib, Eshagh. 1999. The Role of Islamic Conference in Combating Terrorism. *The Iranian Journal of International Affairs* 11 (4): 524–540.

Amjad-Ali, Charles. 2001–2002. How Did We Get Here? Caveats and Encouragement from History. *Cresset*, Christmas/Epiphany, 9–13.

Appleby, R. Scott, and Martin E. Marty. 2002. *Fundamentalism*, 16–22. January/February: Foreign Policy.

Bartsch, Sabastian. 2001. Capitalizing Terrorism. *Internationale Politik: Transatlantic Edition* 2 (4): 13–18.

Bergen, Peter. 2001. The Bin Laden Trial: What did We Learn? *Studies in Conflict & Terrorism* 24: 429–434.

bin Laden, Shaykh Usamah Bin-Muhammed. 1996. "Declaration of war against the Americans occupying the land of the two holy places", reprinted (as Appendix 1A). In *Usama bin Laden's al-Qaida: Profile of a Terrorist Network*, ed. Alexander Yonah and Michael S. Swetnam. New York: Transnational Publishers.

bin Laden, Shaykh Usamah Bin-Muhammed, Ayman al-Zawahiri, Abu-Yasir Rifa'i Ahmad Taha, Shaykh Mir Hamzah, and Fazlul Rahman. 1998. "Jihad against Jews and crusaders: World Islamic statement", reprinted (as Appendix 1B). In *Usama bin Laden's Al-Qaida: Profile of a Terrorist Network*, ed. Yonah and Michael S. Swetnam. New York: Transnational Publishers.

Bowles, Samuel, David Gordon, and Thomas Weisskopf. 1992. *Beyond the Wasteland*. New York: Anchor & Doubeday.

Bulliet, Richard W. 2002. The Crisis Within Islam. *The Wilson Quarterly* 26 (1): 11–19.

Burke, Jason. 2001–2002. Portrait of the Terrorist as a Young Man. *Talk*, Dec 2001/Jan 2002: 90–95, 98–99, 138.

Butlin, Noel George. 1983. *Our Original Aggression: Aboriginal Populations of Southeastern Australia 1788–1850*. Sydney: Allen & Unwin.

Chomsky, Noam. 2001. The United States is a Leading Terrorist State. *Monthly Review* 53 (6): 10–19.

Chossudovsky, Michel. 2001. Osamagate. *Peace Research* 33 (2): 35–43.

Choudhury, M.A., and Muhammad Syukri Salleh. 2001. Islamic Political Economy. In *Encyclopedia of Political Economy*, ed. Phillip Anthony O'Hara, vol. 1, 585–586. London/New York: Routledge, paperback edition.

Corradi, Juan E. 2001. On Violence and Terror. *Telos* 120 (Summer): 147–153.

Damphousse, Kelly R., and Brent L. Smith. 1998. The internet: A terrorist medium for the 21st century. In *The Future of Terrorism: Violence in the New Millennium*, ed. Harvey W. Kushner, 208–224. London/New Delhi: Sage Publications.

Delpech, Therese. 2001. Embracing Death. *Internationale Politik: Transatlantic Edition* 2 (4): 9–12.

Editors. 2001. After the Attack ... The War on Terrorism. *Monthly Review* 53 (6): 1–9.

Falkenrath, Richard. 2001. Analytic Models and Policy Prescription: Understanding Recent Innovation in U.S. Counterterrorism. *Studies in Conflict & Terrorism* 24: 150–181.

Fox, Jonathan. 2001. Two Civilizations and Ethnic Conflict: Islam and the West. *Journal of Peace Research* 38 (4): 459–472.

Freedman, Lawrence. 2001–2002. The Third World War?. *Survival: The IISS quarterly* 43(4): 61–88.

Hoffman, Bruce. 2001. Change and Continuity in Terrorism. *Studies in Conflict and Terrorism* 24 (5): 417–428.

Hofman, Murad Wilfried. 2001. A Plea for Islamic Renewal. *Islamic Studies* 40 (2): 297–304.

Homer-Dixon, Thomas. 2002. January/February. The Rise of Complex Terrorism. *Foreign Policy* 128: 52–77.

Huntington, Samuel. 1996. *The Clash of Civilisations and the Remaking of World Order*. New York: Simon and Shuster.

Hyman, Anthony. 1985. Muslim fundamentalism. *Conflict Studies, 174*, 3–27. Reprinted in Yonah Alexander. In *Middle East Terrorism: Current Threats and Future Prospects*. New York \Toronto: Macmillan Publishing Company. 1997.

Jackson, Brian. 2001a. Technology Acquisition by Terrorist Groups: Threat Assessment Informed by Lessons from Private Sector Technology Adoption. *Studies in Conflict and Terrorism* 24: 183–213.

Jackson, Sherman. 2001b. Domestic Terrorism in the Islamic Legal Tradition. *The Muslim World* 91 (3 & 4): 293–310.

Kennedy, Moorehead. 1998. The 21ˢᵗ century conditions likely to inspire terrorism. In *The Future of Terrorism: Violence in the New Millennium*, ed. Harvey W. Kushner, 185–207. London/New Delhi: Sage Publications.

Lindner, Evelin Gerda. 2001. Humiliation as a Source of Terrorism: A New Paradigm. *Peace Research* 32 (2): 59–68.

Luke, Tim. 2001. On 9.11.01. *Telos* 120 (Summer): 129–142.

Mann, Michael. 2001, November–December. Globalization and September 11. *New Left Review*, no 12 (second series), 51–72.

Myrdal, Gunnar. 1978. Institutional Economics. *Journal of Economic Issues* 12 (4): 771–784.

Naidu, M.V. 2001. Anti-American Islamic Terrorism and War of Self-defense. *Peace Research* 33 (2): 1–34.

O'Hara, Phillip Anthony. 2001. Contradictions. In *Encyclopedia of Political Economy*, ed. Phillip Anthony O'Hara, 140–143. London/New York: Routledge.

———. 2004. The war on terrorism, political-economic contradictions and policy issues. In *Global Political Economy and the Wealth of Nations: Performance, Institutions, Problems and Policies*, ed. P.A. O'Hara, 302–324. London/New York: Routledge.

———. 2008. A new global military-terrorism-hegemony social structure of accumulation for long-wave upswing? In *Varieties of capitalism and New Institutional Deals: Regulation, Welfare and the New Economy*, ed. Wolfram Elsner and Hardy Hanappi, 159–180. Chaltenham: Edward Elgar.

Pate, Jason. 2001. Roundtable on the Implications of the September 11, 2001, Terrorist Attacks for Nonproliferation and Army Control. *The Nonproliferation Review* 8 (3): 11–27.

Perry, William J. 2002. Preparing for the Next Attack. *Foreign Affairs* 80 (6): 31–45.

Gallop Poll. 2002, February. Survey of Middle Eastern People in the Arabian Gulf on Attitudes to the United States and the War on Terrorism. *Gallop Poll*, 66.

Resnick, Stephen, and Richard D. Wolff. 1995. The end of the USSR: A Marxian class analysis. In *Marxism in the Postmodern AGE*, ed. Antonio Callari, Stephen Cullenberg, and Carole Biewener, 323–332. New York/London: The Guildford Press.

Sherman, Howard. 2002. *"Terrorism, War and Institutions", Mimeo*. Los Angeles: University of California.

Stevenson, Jonathan. 2001–2002. Pragmatic Counter-Terrorism. *Survival: The IISS Quarterly* 43(4): 35–48.

Valery, Lorenzo, and Michael Knights. 2000. Affecting Trust: Terrorism, Internet and Offensive Information Warfare. *Terrorism and Political Violence* 12 (1): 15–36.

Veblen, Thorstein B. 1921. *The Engineers and the Price System*. New York: Harcourt, Brace & World. 1963.

Wallerstein, Immanuel. 1983. Three Instances of Hegemony in the Capitalist World-System. *International Journal of Comparative Sociology* 7 (3): 77–93.

Walzer, Michael. 2002. Five Questions About Terrorism. Dissent, Winter, 5–16.

Wheeler, Deborah W. 2001. Beyond Global Culture: Islam, Economic Development, and the Challenges of Cyberspace. *Domes: Digest of Middle Eastern Studies* 10 (1): 1–26.

HIV and AIDS

Abstract

This chapter applies core general principles of institutional and evolutionary political economy to provide an interdisciplinary analysis of the HIV-AIDS epidemic that has befallen all parts of the world, especially Sub-Saharan Africa, and also more recently numerous other areas. We start with the principle of historical specificity and the social history of the acquired immunodeficiency syndrome (AIDS) and the human immunodeficiency virus (HIV), including the rise and fall of their incidence trajectory throughout the world, and the areas where it is currently rising. Then we deal with the natural history of HIV and the natural history of the condition in individuals, involving the principle of contradiction. This is followed by the contradiction involving various AIDS researchers, plus an investigation of cofactors involved in HIV and how it differs from AIDS, using the principle of circular and cumulative (CCC) to view the complex causal processes, and the principle of heterogeneous groups and agents to scrutinize the variants of HIV and human groups with differential rates of infection. Through the principle of uneven development the reasons why areas of Sub-Saharan Africa have been consistently so majorly impacted relative to other regions is analyzed. This is followed by a section on the principles of innovation and policy ('governance innovation'), where a five-pronged strategy is enunciated for keeping HIV-AIDS in check, and hopefully working towards successful vaccines and even better drugs into the future.

> **Keywords**
>
> HIV-AIDS · Principles · Historical specificity · Contradiction · Circular & cumulative causation · Socioeconomic impact · Governance innovation · Heterogeneous groups & agents · hegemony & uneven development

11.1 Introduction

We examine the HIV-AIDS problem by starting with the principle of historical specificity and how it links to the social and natural history of the virus and its life cycle through individuals and groups. Uneven development is explored through the differential impact of the condition throughout the world. Heterogeneous groups is scrutinized vis-à-vis the viruses and human beings that are involved. Contradictions are analyzed through investigating the way in which the virus infects people and how conflicts associated with different HIV scholars manifested. We then apply a circular and cumulative multifactor analysis of the reasons some groups and individuals are impacted by HIV-AIDS more than others. Finally we explore governance innovation (merging two principles) through a five-pronged strategy for the future.

11.2 Social History of HIV-AIDS

The principle of historical specificity requires that we study the history of HIV and AIDS, including both the social and natural history, over the course of the 1900s through to the 2020s. In this context, issues that would later be seen as involving AIDS were first brought to the attention of doctors in Los Angeles, New York and San Francisco in the late 1970s and early 1980s. The thing that perplexed medics was the existence of vague and specific diseases that normally were not serious suddenly manifesting in problematic ways. A Los Angeles general practitioner noticed an increase in mononucleosis-type symptoms such as high fever, swollen lymph glands, chronic diarrhoea, thrush and weight loss (opportunistic infections) among his young gay patients that never completely disappeared. Some were hospitalised with respiratory distress. Other LA medics had young gay patients coming down with pneumocystis carinii pneumonia (PCP) and candidiasis. The five cases of PCP were noted by the US federal government Centre for Disease Control (CDC) and documented in their weekly bulletin.

Other strange and unusually toxic infections were noticed in New York and San Francisco. A normally benign skin and mucosal cancer called Kaposi's sarcoma which tended to inflict the elderly, along with opportunistic infections, began causing serious problems and even death among young gays during 1980 and 1981. Other diseases that appeared were cryptococcal meningitis and serious cases of herpes. Over the next few years hundreds of young gay men came down with a combination of opportunistic infections, severe thrush and/or herpes, pneumonia, Kaposi's sarcoma, cerebral lesions and toxoplasia infection. By late 1981 the CDC reported 108 such patients and within a year half were dead. By April 1982, 248 cases were isolated, apparently at least 40 of them having had homosexual relations with one particular person, Gaetan Dugas, a French-Canadian Air Canada flight attendant. (He was nicknamed "Patient Zero" and died in March 1984.) By the end of 1984, 8000 people had been diagnosed with this syndrome in the US.

Soon it became apparent that the US was not the only nation with this affliction. A few cases were isolated in Europe and Haiti; while equatorial Africa soon became seriously involved. While AIDS patients in the West were predominantly homosexual, in Africa they were almost exclusively heterosexual (especially women). Many of the African cases seemed to have an earlier genesis to the US ones, going back to the mid-1970s, and having links with Europe. The French put forward the "African hypothesis": that the first (European) wave of the syndrome emanated from Africa, followed by a wave from the US. Some evidence then arose alluding to a Congolese patient going back to 1962 (Grmek 1990: 30).

The interconnected nature of the afflictions quickly became apparent, and by June 1982 the CDC had began to call it AIDS. Various other, equivalent, acronyms were used in non-English speaking nations. Early on AIDS was linked to lifestyle factors, such as drug use, sexual promiscuity and inadequate nutrition. Soon attention began to be focussed on a viral cause, thanks to the combined work of the French Pasteur Institute, the US National Institute of Health, and others. In 1984 it became apparent to many that a certain retrovirus with a propensity to destroy helper lymphocytes was the "ultimate cause" of the syndrome. During 1984–86 the mechanisms and processes of how the human immunodeficiency virus worked were better understood, at least in their basic form. Since then virtually all the attention has been given to how to fight this virus through drugs, vaccines and preventative measures such as condoms, better blood preparations, reducing needle exchanges and moderating promiscuous tendencies. UNAIDS, the World Health Organisation, national centres for AIDS policy, non-government organisations, and a host of community networks have all played their role in AIDS awareness, prevention and control.

In this chapter we follow the holistic method of Gunnar Myrdal (1944, 1968, 1974) in terms of circular and cumulative causation, imbedded in a historical and interdisciplinary fabric. A holistic approach to AIDS-HIV is not simply a question of theory, but, as Myrdal recognized, affects real people. A holistic analysis enables us to comprehend how AIDS and HIV arose, historically speaking. It leads us to take a broad view of "What causes the condition?" It provides multiple insights into "Why is it more extreme in Sub-Saharan Africa than elsewhere?" And it provides a coherent understanding of "what governance issues and conditions are relevant to reducing its incidence?"

This chapter starts with several sections on the natural history of HIV and AIDS in humans, individuals and also the empirics of the case. Then we examine cofactors and causal controversy, socioeconomic and political factors, plus several issues of governance.

11.3 Natural History of HIV

Figure 11.1 illustrates the natural history of SIV-HIV as it originated in western Africa and spread throughout the world.

It shows Phase A, the origins, starting around 1920–1930 with the transfer of two types of Simian Immunodeficiency Virus, SIV_{CPZ} (from chimpanzees [troglodytes]) and SIV_{SM} (sooty mangabeys) to humans, in the form of HIV-1 and HIV-2, respectively. Transmission occurred by sharing blood or mucosal tissue through dietetic, sexual and/or domestic relationships with simians. HIV-1 and HIV-2 parasites slowly became part of the pool of micro-organisms infecting human beings, and genetically evolving in the process through various sub-species of viruses. Phase B led to the initial spread of the viruses through the population from very small pockets to the wider society, as a result of rapid social change or dislocation. This includes, for instance, the end of colonial rule and wars of independence in western Africa in the 1950s (vis-à-vis, e.g., Portugal, France, Belgium); and the sexual and gay liberation movements as well as the explosion of recreational drug use and international travel, in the US (and Europe) in the 1960s and 1970s.

Phase C was the emergence of the virus in the medical and social consciousness as it gradually became a problem of epidemic proportions, at least in certain sub-populations or the population in general. From the 1980s it spread rapidly through homosexual populations in New York, Los Angeles and San Francisco; as

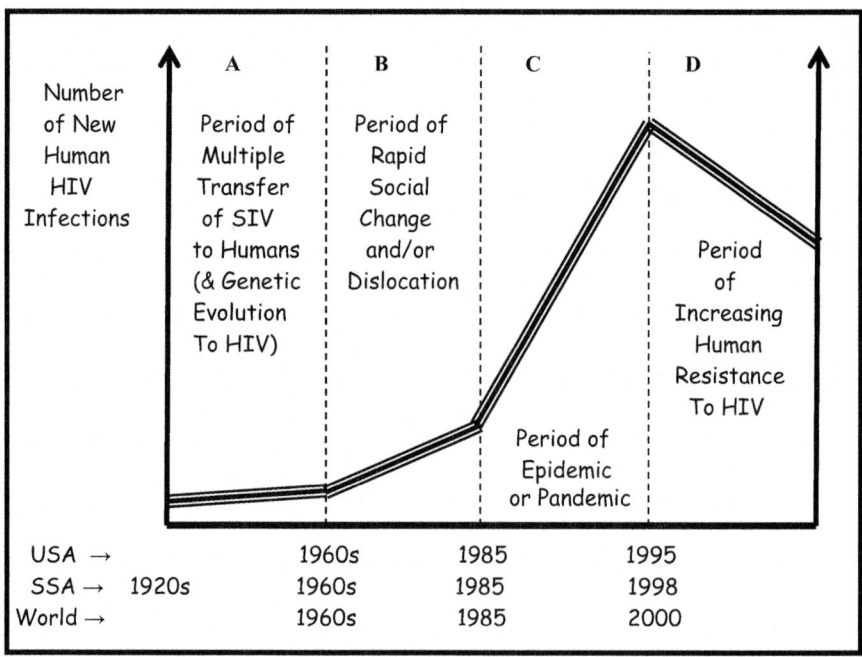

Fig. 11.1 Natural history of SIV-HIV among human beings

well as spreading through the general population in Sub-Saharan Africa; and more latterly in the Caribbean, Eastern Europe and parts of Asia (during the 1990s). Phase D, declining incidence of HIV and reduced deaths from AIDS, both emerged in the mid-1990s to early 2000s in most nations. As human beings began to increase their immunity to HIV-AIDS though natural or drug-enhanced measures, the declining incidence curve set in first in the Caribbean and the USA (1994), then in SSA as a whole as well as west-central SSA and the Asia-Pacific (1998), followed by the World and east-south SSA (2000). Two regions have not yet followed the declining trajectory curve, including Latin America (which has hovered around 100,000–110,000 new cases a year for the whole period of 1998–2020), and Eurasia (which reached its highest point of 0.14 m new cases during 2019 and 2020) (UNAIDS 2022).

11.4 Global Distribution of HIV-AIDS

Three ironies stand out in the history of AIDS-HIV. The first is that so much of its history and development has centred on the United States, as shown above, when Sub-Saharan Africa was both the place of origin of the virus and also the geographical area where incidence became most rampant. The second is that the earliest AIDS hypothesis was a multi-causal model, whereas the one that became dominant was a viral theory; despite the many interrelated factors impacting on the condition. And the third is that, in the face of all the scientific developments over the past century and more, scholars are generally unable to comprehend the multi-faceted dimensions of AIDS-HIV. Bringing to the fore a holistic approach reduces these ironies to understandable knowledge, since it is not Eurocentric, employs a multi-factor approach, and is interdisciplinary. But first we must start with the immediate facts of the case, relating to the global distribution of AIDS-HIV.

Major problems obtaining consistent statistics on HIV and AIDS are the changes in definition and testing methods over the decades. Comparable multi-regional cross-section data exist only since 1990. See Table 11.1, below, which report the mid-estimates of data (that exclude uncertainty ranges):

The principle of hegemony and uneven development is related to the first stylized fact that the *number of people living with HIV* has been increasing around the world at least since the early 1990s, and probably since the early 1980s. It now stands at nearly 38 million people, and has been increasing substantially since HIV was first diagnosed. The reasons for this state of affairs are multiple, including the fact that many people are still getting infected (at a decreasing rate generally) and fewer people are dying of AIDS. More than two thirds of HIV infections have centered in sub-Saharan Africa (SSA) since the disease was first diagnosed, and this state of affairs has not changed much. The *rate of infection* differs greatly throughout SSA, with much higher rates occurring in southern and eastern (especially south-eastern) SSA, and with some highly localized clusters in parts of the west, with far fewer cases generally in central and western SSA.

Table 11.1 Regional HIV & AIDS incidence-deaths, 1990, 2005, 2020

	Year	World	SSA	AsiaPac	LatAmer	EurAsia	EU-NA	Caribbean	MENA
Living with HIV	1990	8.0 m	5.8 m	0.88 m	0.34 m	3200	0.91 m	0.12 m	9500
	2005	28.6 m	19.4 m	5.6 m	1.2 m	0.5 m	1.5 m	0.29 m	0.16 m
	2020	37.7 m	25.3 m	5.8 m	2.1 m	1.6 m	2.2 m	0.33 m	0.23 m
New HIV cases	1990	2.0 m	1.49 m	0.39 m	0.07 m	980	0.09 m	30,000	2600
	2005	2.4 m	1.79 m	0.39 m	0.10 m	0.07 m	0.08 m	22,000	21,000
	2020	1.5 m	0.87 m	0.24 m	0.10 m	0.14 m	0.07 m	13,000	16,000
AIDS deaths	1990	0.32 m	0.24 m	16,000	19,000	<200	39,000	4200	<500
	2005	1.9 m	1.34 m	400,000	43,000	20,000	23,000	21,000	7400
	2020	0.68 m	0.46 m	130,000	31,000	35,000	13,000	6000	7900

Source: Adapted from various parts of UNAIDS (2022)

Secondly, the rate of *new HIV cases* has been declining in most places of the world for two decades or so (see below), especially in SSA, and also to some degree in the Asia-Pacific region, Europe and North America (EU-NA), the Caribbean plus the Middle East and North Africa (MENA). However, the number of *new cases* has been stable in Latin America, and rising in Eurasia, as the virus seeks out new geographical regions to spread more rapidly. In addition, AIDS *deaths* have been declining in most regions, especially in SSA, the Asia Pacific, Latin America, the EU and North America, plus the Caribbean. But deaths have risen markedly in Eurasia, and to some degree in North Africa and the Middle East.

Thirdly, overall, the incidence of HIV and AIDS in SSA far outweighs the experience elsewhere on Earth, both in terms of the absolute seriousness of the problem and the proportionate rates of mortality and those living with the virus. While AIDS patients in the West have been predominantly homosexual, in SSA they are almost exclusively heterosexual. Females constitute 53% of all HIV positive cases in SSA, while men comprise 47%. At the height of the HIV epidemic, medium estimates for newly acquired child (1–14 years) HIV infections in SSA were 460,000 per annum (1999 to 2003), but due to the improving HIV trajectory this has declined by more than 70% to 134,000 per annum (2019 to 2020). The vast majority of new SSA HIV cases are still from east and southern Africa, comprising 670,000 new cases in 2020, compared with those from west and central Africa of 200,000 cases. The highest proportionate annual cases are from South Africa (5/1000), Lesotho (5/1000), Iswatini (5/1000), Botswana (4/1000), and Mozambique (4/1000) (per 1000 uninfected pop.) (World Bank 2022).

11.5 Details of Natural History of HIV: Heterogeneous Groups

The principle of heterogeneous groups and agents requires that we scrutinize the different groups of HIV viruses and how they impact human populations, and also that we assess the different human groups that tend to be afflicted by the HIV virus and AIDS diseases (in this and the next section). In this context, there are two major strains of HIV, HIV-1 and HIV-2, both of which originated in sub-Saharan Africa. There are three groups of HIV-1, including M (major), O (outlier) and N. Within the major M group are numerous subtypes A-K, accounting for over 90% of all worldwide HIV infections. Group O origins are isolates from west-central Africa (Cameroon, Gabon and Equatorial Guinea), while N, which is rare, emanates from Cameroon. HIV originates from cross-species infections between monkeys and humans, specifically by simian immunodeficiency viruses (SIV) mutating into HIV.

Evidence points to at least three independent introductions of SIV_{cpz} from chimpanzees to humans. Zoonotic transmission of primate lentiviruses to humans is supported by SIV-HIV similarities in viral genome structure, phylogenic relationships, geographical linkages and plausible routes of transmission. The most likely subspecies involved is the common chimp (Pan troglodytes) through $SIV_{cpz\ (P.t.t.)}$ since they were kept as pets and eaten in west-eastern Africa (Gao et al. 1999).

SIVs do not cause diseases in monkeys as they have effective immunity to the viruses.

Samples of blood contaminated by HIV-1 have been collected as early as 1959. But the origins of zoonotic transmission are much earlier. Evidence points to a likely mean year of the most common ancestor of the O-subtype HIV virus (which *may* indicate the time of cross-species SIV infection) of around 1920–1930 (with a far lower probability of it occurring as early as 1850 or as late as 1950). It has been estimated that "group O infections have doubled approximately every 9 years since 1920" (Lemey et al. 2004: 1064).

Of the HIV-1 genus M there are 11 subtypes, A-K, the first five (A-E) having been studied closely. Korber et al. (2000) present evidence that "the last common ancestor of the HIV-1 [M] group point to the first half of the twentieth century", which could indicate the time of cross-species infection by SIV, specifically around 1930 (circa 1908–1950). A-J are found mostly in sub-Saharan Africa; B originated mainly in the US, Europe, and Haiti; a mix of A-C and D-G being common in central and eastern Africa (Uganda, Kenya, Tanzania and the DR Congo); while M subtype E is common in Thailand. Vassan et al. (2006) studied the degree of virulence of subtypes A, C and D (plus recombinants of these) in Tanzania, concluding subtype D to be the most deadly, followed by C, then A-C-D recombinants, and the least problematic being A. The African M-subtypes (A, C, D) are more virulent than the Thai subtype E, which in turn is more virulent than the B subtype common in the US, Europe and Haiti. This is one of the reasons AIDS-HIV diseases are more serious in Sub-Saharan Africa than elsewhere in the world. Korber argues that the B-subtype which became manifest in the mid-1970s, likely had a pre-epidemic period of evolution of 5–15 years, possibly beginning in 1960 (circa 1939–1972). Despite a large degree of regional specialization, all the M-subtypes exist globally, likely migrating from sub-Saharan Africa as a result of imperial pursuits, trading and wars of independence.

HIV-1 is significantly more virulent than HIV-2 (Jaffer et al., 2004), while the natural history of HIV-2 is more certain. HIV-2 has seven sub-types, HIV-2(A-G), with only HIV-2(A,B) being epidemic in nature. HIV-2 is restricted mainly to western Africa (especially Guinea-Bissau). It originated from cross-species infection between sooty mangabeys (monkeys) and humans through SIV_{sm} due to dietetic and social factors. Most recent common ancestors have been estimated at 1940 ± 16 (HIV-2A) and 1945 ± 14 (HIV-2B), which are possible upper limit proxy dates for cross-species transmission of SIV_{sm}, although a broader model gives 1889 ± 33 as a lower limit for cross-species transmission (Lemey et al. 2003).

For group A, after cross-species infection and mutation into HIV-2, there was a period of low endemicity (eg, 1940s–1960s) in this closely-knit, kinship-based society of Guinea-Bissau. This was followed by a period when the virus spread more widely (1960s–1970s) likely initiated by the war of independence from Portugal (1963–1974), when social dislocation and trans-migration were common. The *war hypothesis* is supported by epidemiological evidence of HIV-2 cases among Portuguese veterans who served in the colonial army during the war. The 1980s to around 2000 saw an exponential growth of infections, the principal source being the high rate of unsterilized injections.

11.6 Natural History of HIV-AIDS in Individuals: Heterogeneous Groups and Contradictions

Here we continue our discussion of heterogeneous groups from the previous section, as well as introducing contradictions associated with viral-human relations that led to the HIV-AIDS malady. In this context, one problem that has always plagued the HIV theory of AIDS is that it does not directly cause the syndrome. Rather, the usual proximate ailments that are part of the complex are all caused by other microorganisms. HIV is said to ultimately precipitate these ailments by destroying the helper white blood cells (CD4+ T-cells). When levels of such lymphocytes are at critically low levels – which could take 10 years or more – immunodeficiency sets in where any number of AIDS diseases can manifest themselves. The most common ailments are serious cases of skin cancer, tumors, pneumonia, thrush, herpes, and painful feet and legs.

What is called the "natural history" of HIV in the human body includes three main phases, as shown in Fig. 11.2, below:

The first phase is "acute" infection with the virus, whether through sexual contact, dirty needles, and/or blood exchanges. When the virus infects the body, "seroconversion" occurs as the body starts to produce antibodies to the parasite. Some people succeed in stopping the virus at this point, but in others there is a sudden increase in viral load in the cells and a sharp decline in helper T-cells below the normal level of

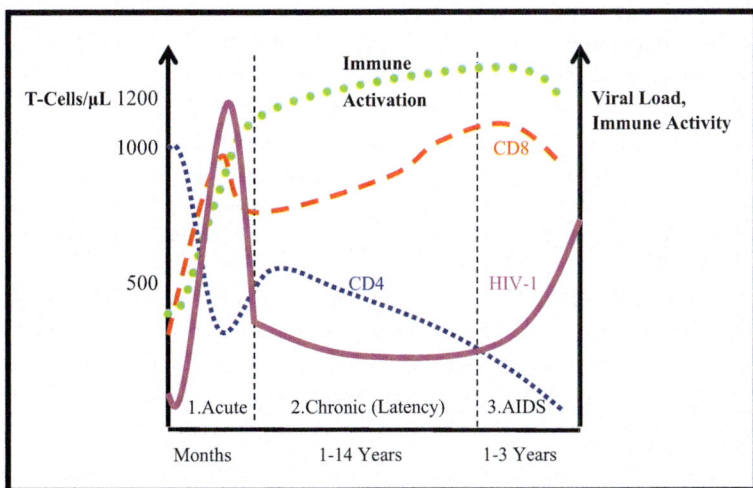

Fig. 11.2 Typical natural history of HIV-AIDS in individuals (Stylized). (*Source:* Variously Adapted from Grossman et al. (2006, p. 293); Joly and Pinto (2006, p. 858), Dornberg and Pomerantz (2000, p. 90); Feinberg (1996, pp. 241, 244))

1000/μL (1000 per micro-liter), especially in the mucus cells and to a lesser extent in the blood. A major immune response occurs as the body produces antibodies to the invading virus. Usually relatively minor symptoms emerge, including swollen lymph glands, fever, diarrhea, dry cough, numbness of the feet, and other vague symptoms. This phase may last a number of weeks or months, at the end of which the number of helper cells (CD4) stabilizes, as does the viral load and the immune response.

The second major phase is then reached in most HIV cases, the "chronic" stage, which lasts on average about 10 years, with variations mostly in the order of 3–5 years. Some call this the asymptomatic "latency" period, since the mortality-promoting (late-period) opportunistic diseases ("AIDS") have not yet appeared. In this slow moving phase major symptoms typically do not emerge. A number of patients never go beyond this stage and hence never get the typical AIDS diseases, with or without anti-viral drugs. Typically, after a number of years mucosal CD4 helper-cells decline moderately, while CD4 helper-cells in the blood decline slowly but significantly. At the end of this 10 year period CD4 helper T-cells typically decline from their normal level of around 1000/μL to the AIDS-defining level of <200/μL. Immune activation stays at a high level, while viral load increases only slightly.

The third phase of the condition then typically begins to manifest as AIDS around the 10 year (6–14 year) period as helper T-cells decline to very low levels (<200/μL), viral load begins to escalate, and immune activation declines somewhat. A combination of major diseases, caused by specific organisms, then begin to develop as the body's immune response is slow and ineffective. Some of the typical AIDS-defining diseases include pneumocystitis pneumonia, Kaposi's sarcoma, AIDS-related lymphoma, peripheral neuropathy, and opportunistic diseases.

It has to be said that HIV and AIDS reveals (or exploits) a *major contradictory limit* to the human immune system. This limit occurs in the chronic phase when CD4 T-cells decline while CD8 T-cells increase, in about equal proportions, while total T-cells remain about constant. CD4 and CD8 refer to a heterogeneous group of cell-surface glycoproteins on T-lymphocytes that enhance T-cell response to foreign antigens. In general, though, CD4s are called "helper" T-cells because they assist other white blood cells perform their immune function; while CD8 cells include "killer" T-cells that can destroy infected target cells (Mosier 1997). More specifically, CD4 cells provide helper functions for proper development of T-cell cytotoxicity and also for B-cells to produce immunoglobulin and lymphocyte populations. CD8 cells inhibit the proliferative response of infected cell immunoglobulin creation. CD4 and CD8 cells are more effective when working in tandem and their functions are somewhat interrelated, since killer CD4 cells and helper CD8 cells also exist (Parnes 1997).[1]

---

[1] The reference to CD4 and CD8 refers to different glycoproteins on the cell surface of T-cells. These lymphocytes have a cellular immune response capable of protecting individuals from microorganisms, cancer cells and foreign bodies. The proteins of CD4 and CD8 usually interact

The major contradiction that emerges between the virus and humans and which can lead to major diseases and even death is as follows. It is generally believed that CD4 functions are more critical than those of CD8 cells. The critical CD4 cells decline as HIV progresses, since they act as cell-surface receptors for HIV, and hence it is difficult to enhance their number because *CD4 cells are used by HIV to replicate more viruses*. This is the major limit or contradiction of human immunological function that HIV exploits. As a result, when CD4 cells are below 200/μL a combination of the following diseases tend to develop, while death usually follows CD4 levels of below 50/μL, as these diseases become more serious. HIV thus does not directly cause AIDS, but is said to eventually lead to a combination of infections when CD4 levels reach very low levels and the body is apparently unable to develop effective resistance to disease. These infections include:

Pneumocystis Pneumonia (PCP) PCP is the most common opportunistic HIV-related infection, occurring in up to 85% of AIDS cases. Historically it has been the most important cause of morbidity, associated with the fungus *pneumocystis jiroveci*. It is most common with CD4 cell counts of under 200/μL, and also for those with under 300/μL who have other opportunistic infections. It affects the lungs, typically causing recurring pneumonia, breathing difficulties, fever, dry cough, weight loss, and constitutional weakness. It can be treated now quite effectively with combination antibiotics TMP/SMX, Dapsome, Pentamidine, Atovaquone and antiretroviral therapy (ART).

Kaposi's Sarcoma This is a common ailment, caused by the human herpesvirus-8 (KSHV), affecting around 20% of AIDS cases. It usually takes the form of various lesions, tumors, and ulcers on the skin and sometimes in lymph nodes, mucosal surfaces, and internal organs (Cornelius et al. 2004). It can be localized, indolent, widespread or aggressive. KSHV typically evade recognition by T-cells by using human protein cell molecule xCT to reproduce itself (NIH 2006). Chemotherapy, radiation, retinoic acid, liposomal and anti-cancer drugs have been used against this disease; and increasingly through the effective use of highly active antiretroviral therapy (HAART).

AIDS-Related Lymphoma (ARL) This is the third most common immunodeficiency disease, being the cause of death for 12–16% of HIV patients, and including a heterogeneous group of AIDS-related lymphomas (ARLs) (Silvestris et al. 2002). The most common include cancers caused by the Epstein-Barr virus (EBV), HHV-8 and through other, genetic propensities. One interesting variety is PEL, associated with HHV-8 and EBV, manifesting as tumor masses, especially in the gastrointestinal tract. Systemic ARL attacks the immune system, blood stream and organs

---

with receptors to enhance T-cell activity. They tend to function as helper cells (CD4) or killer cells (CD8); although there can be a cross-over of functions. HIV viruses use CD4s to reproduce themselves (Parnes 1997).

simultaneously. While chemotherapy, azidothymidine and rituximab have proved toxic in the treatment of ARL, some success was found by minimal chemotherapy followed by HAART (Lim and Levine 2005) for patients with CD4+ cell counts of >100/μL. Prognosis is poor for those with <100/μL.

Opportunistic Infections (OIs) OIs are an array of diseases that in combination can contribute to morbidity in patients with low-CD4 levels. The most important of them, PCP, is important enough to be considered separately (above). The others can under some circumstances be critical, and include thrush (a fungal infection) of the mouth, throat, anus and/or vagina, even in high CD4 ranges; cytomegalovirus (a viral infection) that can cause blindness, especially in <50 CD4 cases; serious cases of herpes simplex (virus) of the mouth or genitals, at any CD4 level; mycobacterium avium complex, which causes recurring fever, digestion anomalies, general sickness, and serious weight loss, especially with CD4 counts of <75/μL; toxoplasmosis, a protozoal affliction of the brain, typically for those of CD4 counts of <100/μL; plus malaria and tuberculosis, which tend to be more severe with AIDS (NMAETC 2005).

Peripheral Neuropathy This is the most common neurological complaint associated with AIDS. It represents a whole series of neurological diseases, more commonly associated with sore feet, weak muscles, numbness and tingling in peripheral nerves, back pain, and bowel and bladder incontinence. It may become systemic to include gastrointestinal weakness, hepatitis, pneumonia, cervicitis and pancreatitis when associated with cytomegalovirus (CMV). A disturbingly high number of cases are precipitated by antiretroviral drugs, especially NRTIs, while the disease itself may predispose individuals to the neurotoxic effects of these medications. However, evidence seems to point to the positive influence of HAART in the prognosis of patients (Ferrari et al. 2006).

It is worth emphasizing that HIV develops into AIDS at different rates in different risk groups. For instance, hemophiliacs, older patients, those in lower socioeconomic groups, and those with synergistic infections and cofactors, develop AIDS much quicker than the average 10 years: 2–3 years is common. Quite a few HIV-positive people do not manifest symptoms or go on to develop AIDS (5%). Some are even repeatedly tested HIV-negative after being found seropositive. This is related to the concept of transient or incomplete infection where sero-reversion (from HIV-positive to negative) occurs in healthy individuals (Root-Bernstein 1996).

11.7 Cofactors and Causal Controversy: Contradiction and Heterogeneous Groups and Agents

Here we utilize the principle of circular and cumulative causation by studying the cofactors that precipitate people getting HIV-AIDS and that worsens their condition. In this context, early in AIDS research lifestyle factors were emphasized, such as sexual preference, sexual activity, drug use, nutrition levels, and so on. With the

11.7 Cofactors and Causal Controversy: Contradiction and Heterogeneous...

discovery of the HIV link to declining helper cells the viral factor became predominant. This is still the case today. However, evidence does support a multi-factor approach, and a substantial critique of the viral theory exists among a minority of researchers. The multi-factor approach looks at the link between a number of critical variables, as, for instance, shown below in Fig. 11.3.

Research indicates that the degree to which individuals are susceptible to the HIV virus depends upon an array of factors, including genetics, diet, stress, other infections, and the specific strain of HIV in question.[2] Similarly, the speed and magnitude to which initial and later AIDS symptoms and diseases progress depend on this complex pattern of lifestyle, genetics and socioeconomic position. Individuals are more likely to progress to AIDS with HIV-1(D) than HIV-1(A) or (B), and also with HIV-1 than HIV-2. The linkages are thus circular and cumulative; although negative feedback loops can lead to a declining incidence curve.

Individuals are also more likely to come down with AIDS-defining diseases if they (a) have a poor diet, especially if lacking zinc and vitamins A, C and E; (b) ingest substantial amyl or butyl nitrate; (c) undergo chemotherapy; or (d) take toxic anti-retroviral drugs (not HAART); (e) are older; and/or (f) are infected by critical microbes causing hepatitis, thrush or herpes. (Strathdee et al. 1996.) Many people are HIV-positive but fail to develop symptoms, others have symptoms but live for decades, while numerous others have AIDS-type diseases but are HIV-negative. Cofactors thus become critical to the mortality and well-being of individuals, acting as risk modifiers that impact on CD4 levels, viral load and disease manifestation.

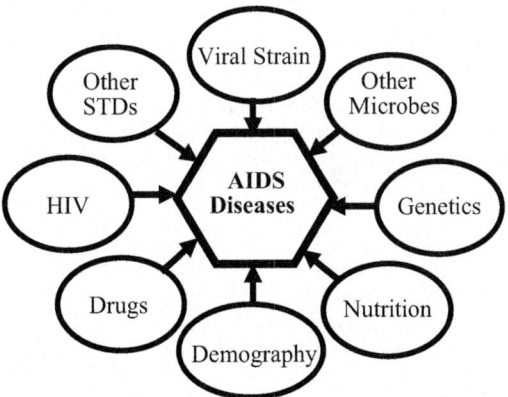

Fig. 11.3 Multiple factor approach to AIDS

---

[2] This aspect of the holistic method is perhaps the closest to that of Gunnar Myrdal (1944, 1968, 1974), since it clearly links to circular and cumulative causation. All the major factors are codetermined, and interact in a circular process. The interaction tends to generate a cumulative type of process, or (ultimately) a decumulative tendency (declining incidence curve). However, as Myrdal recognised, the degree of circular causation depends upon the coefficient of interdependency between variables, while the degree of (de) cumulative motion depends upon the extent to which they also are impacted by negative feedback factors such as policy, behaviour, drugs, etc.

Some researchers have an particular angle on cofactors, strongly attacking the mainstream emphasis on HIV. They either give priority to cofactors or deny the role of HIV altogether. Peter Duesberg and associates tackle the HIV theory critically, concluding that recreational and antiretroviral drugs are the major cause of AIDS in the US and Europe, and malnutrition in Africa and many other underdeveloped areas. Others may be less extreme, concluding that HIV may be neither necessary nor sufficient (or necessary but not sufficient) for the onset of typical AIDS-defining diseases such as Kaposi's sarcoma, AIDS related lymphoma, opportunistic infections and peripheral neuropathy (Koehnlein and Rasnick 2003).

'Duesberg arguments' against the "HIV-causes-AIDS" hypothesis are complex and multifarious (Papadopulos-Eleopulos et al. 1996). Many of his supporters argue, for instance, that HIV is an opportunistic or synergistic infection – or possibly just a "passenger virus" – that becomes manifest only in people predisposed to or in contact with agents that propel immune deficiency. AIDS is seen as primarily an immunodeficiency (not a viral) disease, where cofactors propel cumulative impairment of the immune system and leads patients to be predisposed to (passenger) HIV. It is seen as a multiple agent-induced series of conditions where cooperative infections create magnified destruction of the effective immune response. For instance, older hemophilia patients typically develop AIDS very rapidly, within 2–3 years, due to frequent use of clotting concentrates, transfusions, steroidal use, viral contamination, opiate drugs and joint injury treatment (Root-Bernstein 1996). Mono-causal models are seen as reductionist.[3]

Some critique the assumption of HIV-positive results necessarily linking to AIDS. It is argued that being HIV-positive simply means the body has produced antibodies against HIV in the past; it is not necessarily evidence that HIV is currently active. The best way to prove the presence of a virus is said to be through direct isolation and estimation of infectious particle numbers in immobilized cell culture. Correlation between HIV and AIDS may exist because of a combination of specious factors. These include the negative psychological impact of being found HIV-negative and of HIV drugs (including wide-spectrum antibiotics) on the immune system. Many HIV-positive people do not get sick, while others work off the virus.

Some HIV-negative patients have typical symptoms of AIDS, including a combination of low CD4-count, opportunistic infections, Kaposi's sarcoma, pneumonia, and so on. Also, there is a paucity of studies investigating patterns and processes involving CD4+ cell levels among HIV-negative people. Could the high level of CD8+ T-cells adequately compensate for the low level of CD4+ T-cells in typically

---

[3]While it may seem that Duesberg and his followers have a relatively deterministic method of concentrating on certain variables, the origins of their debate with orthodoxy was along the lines of a multi-causal model of AIDS. Within the context of this model, they then refined the analysis to concentrate on the principal factors. They are, though, better off emphasising the multi-causal processes, otherwise they run the risk of being reductionist in the same way as the orthodox argument. This analysis of interplay of various factors and the orthodox deterministic approach is well analysed by Resnick and Wolff (1987).

symptom-free HIV cases, since some research has indicated a cross-over of functions between CD4 and CD8 T-cells in some cases?

Ninety percent of AIDS patients emanate from high risk groups, such as homosexual or bisexual men; injecting drug users; recipients of blood and its components; sex workers; inhabitants of Sub-Saharan Africa; and sexual partners of injecting drug users. These groups have high risk of low CD4+ levels, cancers, lymphoma and opportunistic infections due to many (including lifestyle) factors, such as being inflicted with other venereal diseases, the impact of certain drugs on the immune system, malnutrition, and socioeconomic position (Koliadin 1995).

Some argue that the typical time taken from being HIV-positive to full-blown AIDS is excessive. The usual 6–14 years for the onset of typical diseases has been shown to be problematic on mathematical grounds, especially vis-à-vis the usual periodicity of viral toxicity. One such model predicts that the number of T-cells in a HIV+ person should have fallen by 84% in 2 years. As Mark Craddock (1996: 93) says: "it is very difficult to see why a large number of infected cells actively replicating takes so long to cause a disease. ... Such a virus should cause disease quickly or not at all."

A paradox of the HIV-AIDS hypothesis is said to be that a virus that is present in 1 out of 500 susceptible CD4+ T-cells could cause disease. But these T-cells are supposed to promote the reproduction of HIV viral load. Viruses are parasites that require a living host and cell to reproduce. CD4+ T-cells must, it is argued, therefore, be killed by other agents, such as recreational drugs, anti-retroviral drugs, chemotherapy, inadequate nutrition and opportunistic infections (Duesberg et al. 2003: 403).

A strange situation has arisen in the scientific community where the "Duesberg camp" is often given a limited space for their work, while also being excluded from publication. When government has taken their arguments seriously, such as President Thabo Mbeki in South Africa, they have been denounced by many in the international community, even by those who are not scientists or health professionals (e.g., Butler 2005). John Maddox (1995), the editor of *Nature*, states succinctly his understanding of the reason, namely, that if Duesberg and company are correct then most of the rest of the scientific community are wrong.

This conclusion is not quite true, since a multifactor analysis of AIDS comes close to allowing for both major groups being partially correct in their analysis. It is this multifactor approach of circular and cumulative causation, with potential negative loops, that this chapter utilizes as perhaps the best way to comprehend AIDS. With this in mind we turn to the socioeconomic impact and policy-responses of the pandemic from a holistic view.

11.8 Crisis in Social Reproduction During High Trajectory Period

The principle of uneven development states that IE political economists should study the global and regional forces that generate unequal performance throughout the world. In this context, the real AIDS crisis was in Sub-Saharan Africa, and to a much lesser extent in the Caribbean, the Americas, Europe and parts of south Asia, during the 1990s and the early 2000s. During this time AIDS constituted a core system-problem inhibiting the very function of the social, political and economic institutions of SSA. It therefore required core assistance from the international community. AIDS was an extension of the traditional problems of underdevelopment, poverty and malnutrition. No matter what theory of AIDS one adheres to, the challenge was to propel human development in SSA in particular as one critical co-solution to AIDS.

Anomalies of underdevelopment were reinforced by AIDS, although regional differences are important. Real economic growth *per capita* was less than 1 percent per annum in SSA during the 1990s and 2000s (O'Hara 2006a). In one study, the average rate of adult-prevalence of AIDS in SSA was shown to be about 8%, resulting in a decline in GDP growth of 0.5 per annum, or 27% over 20 years, as a result of declining human, physical and social capital (Freedman and Poku 2005: 671). However, the impact in many nations of SSA was much greater; especially in Botswana, Lesotha, Namibia, and South Africa, where GDP was likely to decline by 50–70% over 20 years due to AIDS (Haacker 2004: 71).

AIDS caused lower growth in SSA, especially during the 1990s and early 2000s, due to declining levels of productivity, increased absenteeism, loss of experience and skills, high labor turnover, and greater recruitment and training costs. Declining income reinforced this through deteriorating levels of demand and low multiplier and accelerator effects. AIDS especially impacted governance as public officials became sick, while education was severely impacted by high student-teacher ratios as the stock of knowledge declined or increased at a lower rate. Community trust and interaction diminished as networks were disrupted and bonds of sociality destroyed. Also, government spending was redirected from physical infrastructure, communications and education to the US$4.23 billion spent on HIV-AIDS projects per annum in low-income nations (Haacker 2004: 63).

Mortality was greatly increased in SSA as a result of AIDS. Life expectancy at birth with AIDS was markedly different than without it in many nations. For instance, the average life expectancy for a Botswanan was 34 years, and without AIDS it would have 76 years (2004). For South Africa the figures were 67 years without AIDS and 44 years with it; while for Zambia people would have on average expected to live to 56 years, while they actually lived an average 39 years. Crafts and Haacker (2004: 189) called this situation "catastrophic" and estimated the welfare losses involved. Using a "value of life" model, they estimated the aggregate decline in welfare (based on "discounted life expectancy") of 93% for Botswana, 77% for South Africa, 75% for Zambia, 44% for Cote d'Lvoire, and 30% for Ethiopia, at the height of the epidemic. These welfare losses were far greater than the narrower economic costs.

These large social costs of AIDS were due to magnified results of a multitude of factors, illustrated in Fig. 11.4, below.

The inability of certain African nations, in particular, to get beyond the epidemic phase of the disease until around 2000 was linked closely to centre-periphery dynamics. Many SSA nations adopted key planks of the neoliberal policy

11.8 Crisis in Social Reproduction During High Trajectory Period

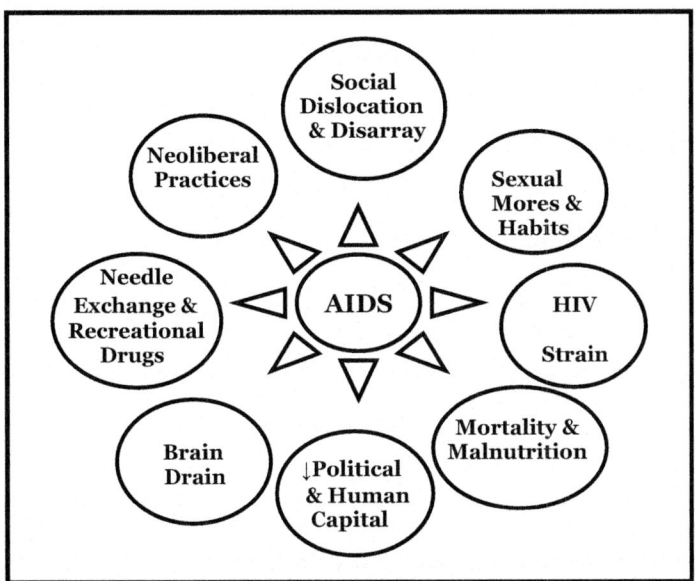

Fig. 11.4 Multiple factors magnified: AIDS in Sub Saharan Africa

framework, which contributed to declining emphasis on public capital such as physical infrastructure, education, health, and communications sector development. Partly for this reason, social resources had been severely limited in dealing with the AIDS crisis. In addition, high levels of poverty, malnutrition and death were perfect breeding grounds for immunodeficiency and the spread of HIV. High levels of brain drain sapped the energy of especially the business, health, education and governance sectors. Social instability linked to wars of independence, ethnic conflict, changes in sexual mores and habits, plus drought and famine led the virus to be spread more rapidly through the community. Inadequate political capital delayed and diminished the vital responses needed especially in the early-medium stages of the epidemic.

More generally, AIDS in SSA especially in the 1990s and early 2000s took the form of a *crisis in social reproduction* (Bujra 2004), precisely because the circular and cumulative linkages operated without effective negative feedback loops. The multiple factors associated with AIDS multiplied the extent of social dislocation since social support structures diminished, protective responses to AIDS were insufficient, and community resources exhausted. Development was inhibited as mortality rates were high, human capital levels in short supply, and networks of relations dislocated. Socioeconomic fragmentation promoted AIDS, especially HIV strains that are highly virulent, which further increased disarray and dislocation (Freedman and Poku 2005). AIDS and its cofactors were especially severely inhibiting the achievement of the New Millennium Goals by 2015 of eradicating extreme poverty and hunger, achieving universal primary education, promoting gender equality, reducing child mortality, improving maternal health and ensuring environmental sustainability (Whiteside 2006).[4]

11.9 Governance Policies and Innovation

The principles of innovation and policy-governance ('governance innovation') state that IE political economists should investigate ways of moderating the extent of global problems through various changes in the ways of doing things. In this context, HIV-AIDS has passed its high-trajectory point in many areas of the world, but for many the current costs of infection and disease are still considerable. And as shown, the incidence curve has been rising quite markedly in Eurasia while still not having reached the declining trajectory in Latin America. Throughout the world there are still 38 m people currently living with the condition, 1.5 m new HIV cases and 680,000 deaths per year from AIDS.

Five planks of policy are important for understanding and reducing the incidence of AIDS further, especially in Sub-Saharan Africa, but also other continents. The first plank is that a multi-factor approach needs to be utilized. This is one that recognizes the importance of cofactors, such as viral type/load, other microbes, drugs, genetics, socioeconomic status, nutritional and lifestyle factors, culture, prevention, and demography. Policies that incorporate these multiple contributors to the disease are more likely to impact than those that take a more reductionist approach. The cofactor method seeks to situate individuals within the social and economic context of their predicament. In this sense it takes into account their age, gender, cultural embeddedness, general health, infection status, habits and network relations. Any policy that seeks to promote behavioral change in individuals needs to recognize the multifaceted environment in which they operate.

The second plank is that policy-making in an AIDS environment needs to be multi-sectoral, including a high level of political commitment, with extensive community involvement. These seem to be priority areas for the most successful approaches, for instance those undertaken in Uganda, Senegal, Thailand and Brazil (Moran 2004). Being multi-sectoral involves decision-making across a wide range of actors and participants. The major sectors needing to be included are governments, NGOs, workplaces, families and civil society. It also helps if policy strategies can be gender-disaggregated to cater for different cohorts of HIV patients (Sherwood et al. 2017).

Governments can generate leadership, resources, coordination, communication and interaction, especially in a decentralized context (Haghighat et al. 2019). For instance, in Uganda where AIDS prevalence had declined since the early 1990s

---

[4] As Janet Bujra (2004: 637) says: "AIDS constitutes a stunning blow to processes of social reproduction, particularly of labour power, but also, by way of the politicisation of those affected and infected and their creation of innovative class alliances, to unbridled capital and the states that back it up." This of course is linked to Polanyi's analysis of the disembedded economy (O'Hara 2006b).

(rather than much later for most), President Museveni played a key role in stimulating debate and action among core community groups. Uganda has a decentralized system of governance where regional and community players have key roles (Allen and Heald 2004). In most successful AIDS policy environments, the Department of Health is crucial, being at the centre of education and awareness campaigns. An over-centralized approach will likely inhibit success by denying community input and participation (Butler 2005).

The third plank of governance needs to recognize the limitations of policy in a "long wave" environment where human resources are likely to be scarce.[5] In much of Sub-Saharan Africa the number of health workers, teachers and administrators are limited not only by low levels of development but also by AIDS itself. The majority of those who die from AIDS are in their prime sexual, reproductive and productive period of life. This loss of human capital is magnified by brain drain to more developed areas, and severely constrains policy measures to educate and equip societies for reducing AIDS (Moran 2004; Barnett 2006).

A fourth plank of successful policy relates to access to critical knowledge, technology and materials. Technology is a key aspect of any modern policy paradigm. In nations with high rates of AIDS it is difficult to access knowledge, products and processes that may help alleviate the condition. Promoting networks of access to products that are subject to patents can help with antiretroviral treatment, including drugs and potential vaccines. For instance, collaboration with NGOs and local companies enabled many poor countries to locally produce cheap generic AIDS drugs. Linkages to global health and medical research networks may in the future enable (poor) countries to access HIV vaccines (McMichael 2006). Recent coronavirus research has promise for a viable vaccine for HIV (Vasan and Pitisuttithum 2020), as well as for effective drugs, and there are lessons to be learned from HIV for the Corona experience (Granich and Gupta 2020).

The fifth plank of anti-AIDS policy recognizes that, ultimately, individual behavior modification is the key to success. This involves dissemination of knowledge, modification of habits, and implementation of preventative and prophylactic methods. This variously requires condom use, a reduction in the extent of needle sharing, declining sexual promiscuity, improved health, poverty reduction, and declining illiteracy. These measures link to both anti-AIDS measures and broader development goals. Ultimately, especially in developing nations, the fight against AIDS is also a fight against ignorance, bad habits, poverty and malnutrition (Kaufman et al. 2014).

---

[5] Research has been done into "long wave" AIDS-HIV processes, which are durable, long-term, and subject to wave type motion. AIDS has long-term impacts, lags, and systemic consequences (Barnett (2006), especially in Sub-Saharan Africa. Malnutrition, virulent microbes, neoliberalism and capital inadequacy are some of the core variables impacting in the long-run.

11.10 Conclusion

This article has applied some of the core IEPE principles to the AIDS and HIV predicament that has befallen humanity. Relative to the principle of historical specificity, it started by surveying the historical and natural origins and evolution of the condition in individuals and groups, as well as, relative to the principle of hegemony and uneven development, its global geographical incidence over the past 30 years. Special reference was given to the multi-factor principle of CCC capable of including apparently incompatible scientific perspectives on AIDS. The principle of heterogeneous groups and agents was utilized to ascertain the main strains promoting the condition and the major groups of humans being inflicted.

The multi-causal condition was linked to the policy/governance principle through a multi-sector approach. Such an approach recognizes the need to include governments, communities, NGOs and corporations in the strategy of modifying behavior. Central governments can provide leadership, Health Departments coordinate education and intervention, cultural values and habits need to be addressed, and corporations may assist in providing resources, drugs and hopefully vaccines.

While the crisis phase is over for the world at large, still large numbers of HIV and AIDS cases emerge every year, especially in SSA, increasingly in certain areas of Eurasia, at the same high rates in Latin America, and not in small numbers in most other areas. AIDS does not exist in a vacuum but is affected by and in turn impacts negatively on resources, human capital and institutions. Seen as a multi-causal process, both AIDS and development can be tackled as problems with interacting processes.

Acknowledgements This paper was originally published in the first edition of the 4-volume *International Encyclopedia of Public Policy*, (IEPP) edited by P.A. O'Hara, and subsequently revised for the latest edition of the encyclopedia (O'Hara 2022). Authors of the IEPP have copyright control over their works.

References

Allen, T., and S. Heald. 2004. HIV/AIDS in Africa: What Has worked in Uganda and What Has Failed in Botswana. *Journal of International Development* 1: 1141–1154.
Barnett, T. 2006. A Long-Wave Event. HIV/AIDS, Politics, Governance and 'Security': Sundering the Intergenerational Bond? *International Affairs* 82 (2): 297–313.
Bujra, J. 2004. AIDS as a Crisis in Social Reproduction. *Review of African Political Economy* 102: 631–638.
Butler, A. 2005. South Africa's HIV/AIDS Policy 1994–2004: How Can it be Explained?. *African Affairs, 104*(417), 591–614.
Cornelius, J.G., M. Sanders, R. Canninga-van Dijk, and J.C. Borleffs. 2004. Kaposi's Sarcoma. *The Lancet* 364: 1549–1552.
Craddock, M. 1996. Some Mathematical Considerations on HIV and AIDS. In *AIDS: Virus or Drug INDUCED?* ed. Peter H. Duesberg, 89–95. Boston\London: Kluwer Academic Publishers. Reprinted from *Genetica*, 95, Numbers 1–3.
Crafts, N., and M. Haacker. 2004. Welfare Implications of HIV/AIDS. In *The Macroeconomics of HIV/AIDS*, ed. Markus Haacker, 182–197. Washington DC: IMF.

Dornburg, R., and R.J. Pomerantz. 2000. Retroviruses. In *Encyclopedia of Microbiology*, ed. Josua Lederberg, 81–96. New York\London: Academic.

Feinberg, M.B. 1996. Changing the Natural History of HIV Disease. *The Lancet* 348: 239–246.

Ferrari, S., S. Vento, S. Monaco, T. Cavallaro, F. Cainelli, N. Rizzuto, and Z. Temesgen. 2006. Human Immunodeficiency Virus – Associated Peripheral Neuropathies. *Mayo Clinic Proceedings* 81 (2): 213–219.

Freedman, J., and N. Poku. 2005. The Socioeconomic Context of Africa's Vulnerability to HIV/AIDS. *Review of International Studies* 31: 665–686.

Gao, F., E. Bailes, D. Robertson, Y. Chen, and C. Rodenburg. 1999. Origin of HIV-1 in the Chimpanzee Pan Troglodytes Troglodytes. *Nature* 397 (6718): 436–441.

Granich, Rueben, and Somya Gupta. 2020. European Union, HIV, and Coronavirus Disease 2019 (COVID-19): Progress and Lessons Learned From the HIV Pandemic. *Clinical Infectious Diseases* 71 (11): 2917–2919. https://doi.org/10.1093/cid/ciaa689.

Grmek, Mirko D. 1990. *History of AIDS: Emergence and Origin of a Modern Pandemic*. Princeton: Princeton University Press. Translated by Russell C. Maulitz and Jacalyn Duffin.

Grossman, Z., M. Meir-Schellersheim, W.E. Paul, and L.J. Picker. 2006. Pathogenesis of HIV Infection: What the Virus Spares is as Important as What it Destroys. *Nature–Medicine* 12 (3): 289–295.

Haacker, M. 2004. HIV/AIDS: The impact on the social fabric and the economy. In *The Macroeconomics of HIV/AIDS*, ed. Markus Haacker, 41–98. Washington DC: IMF.

Haghighat, Roxanna, Janina Steinert, and Lucie Cluver. 2019. The Effects Of Decentralising Antiretroviral Therapy Care Delivery On Health Outcomes For Adolescents And Young Adults In Low- And Middle-Income Countries: A Systematic Review. *Global Health Action* 12 (1): 1–12. https://doi.org/10.1080/16549716.2019.1668596.

Jaffer, S., A. Grant, J. Whitworth, P. Smith, and H. Whittle. 2004. The Natural History of HIV-1 and HIV-2 Infections in Adults in Africa: A Literature Review. *Bulletin of the World Health Organization* 86 (6): 462–469.

Joly, M., and J.M. Pinto. 2006. Role of Mathematical Modelling on The Optimal Control of HIV-1 Pathogenesis. *American Institute of Chemical Engineering Journal* 52 (3): 856–884.

Kaufman, Michelle R., Flora Cornish, Rick S. Zimmerman, and Blair T. Johnson. 2014. Health Behavior Change Models for HIV Prevention and AIDS Care: Practical Recommendations for a Multi-Level Approach. *Journal of Acquired Immune Deficiency Syndrome* 66 (Suppl 3): S250–S258. https://doi.org/10.1097/QAI.0000000000000236.

Koehnlein, C., and D. Rasnick. 2003. The Chemical Bases of the Various AIDS Epidemics: Recreational Drugs, Anti-Viral Chemotherapy and Malnutrition. *Journal of Biosciences* 28 (4): 383–412.

Koliadin, V. 1995. Critical analysis of the current views on the nature of AIDS. In *AIDS: Virus or Drug Induced?* ed. Peter H. Duesberg, vol. 1996, 69–88. Boston\London: Kluwer Academic Publishers. Reprinted from *Genetica*, 95, Numbers 1-3.

Korber, B., M. Muldoon, J. Theiler, F. Gao, R. Gupta, A. Lapedes, B. Hahn, S. Wolinsky, and T. Bhattacharya. 2000. Timing the Ancestor of the HIV-1 Pandemic Strains. *Science* 288 (9): 1789–1796.

Lemey, P., O. Pybus, B. Wang, N. Saksena, and Anne-Mieke Vandamme. 2003. Tracing the Origin and History of the HIV-2 Epidemic. *Proceedings of the National Academy of Sciences* 100 (11): 6588–6592.

Lemey, P., O. Pybus, A. Rambaut, A. Drummond, D. Robertson, P. Roques, M. Worobey, and A.-M. Vandamme. 2004. The Molecular Population Genetics of HIV-1 Group O. *Genetics* 167: 1059–1068.

Lim, S.T., and A.M. Levine. 2005. Recent Advances in Acquired Immunodeficiency Syndrome (AIDS)-Related Lymphoma. *CA: A Cancer Journal for Clinicians* 55 (4): 229–241.

Maddox, J. 1995. Letter to Peter H. Duesberg (2 March). In *AIDS: Virus or Drug Induced?* ed. Peter H. Duesberg, 120–121. Dordrecht\London: Kluwer.

McMichael, A.J. 2006. HIV Vaccines. *Annual Review of Immunology* 24: 227–255.

Moran, D. 2004. HIV-AIDS, Governance and Development: The Public Administration Factor. *Public Administration and Development* 24: 7–18.

Mosier, D.E. 1997. Acquired immune deficiency syndrome, T-cell subsets. In *Encyclopedia of Human Biology*, ed. Renato Dulbecco, 43–47. London\New York: Academic Press.

Myrdal, Gunnar. 1944. *An American Dilemma: The Negro Problem and Modern Democracy*. Vol. 2. New York. isbn:Pantheon Books. 1962.

———. 1968. *Asian drama: An Inquiry into the Poverty of Nations, 3 vols*. New York: Twentieth Century Fund.

———. 1974. What is Development? *Journal of Economic Issues* 8 (4): 729–736.

NIH. (US National Institute of Health). 2006, April 6. *Landmark Discovery of a Kaposi's Sarcoma-Associated Herpesvirus Receptor Provides New Perspectives on Disease Associated with HIV/AIDS*. US Department of Health and Human Services.

NMAETC. (New Mexico AIDS Education and Training Centre). 2005. *Opportunistic Infections – AIDS InfoNet*. Fact Sheet 500. NMAETC: New Mexico.

O'Hara, Phillip Anthony. 2006a. *Growth and Development in the Global Political Economy: Social Structures of Accumulation and Modes of Regulation*. London/New York: Routledge/Taylor & Francis.

———. 2006b. The contradictory dynamics of globalization. In *Globalization and the Third World*, ed. B.N. Ghosh and H.M. Guven, 17–35. New York: Palgrave Macmillan.

———. 2022. AIDS and HIV. In *International Encyclopedia of Public Policy: Volume 1, Global Governance and Development*, ed. P.A. O'Hara, 1–16. Perth: Global Political Economy Research Unit (GPERU). http://pohara.homestead.com/Encyclopedia/Volume-1.pdf.

Papadopulos-Eleopulos, E., V. Turner, J. Papadimitrior, D. Causer, B. Hedland-Thomas, and B. Page. 1996. A critical analysis of the HIV-T4-cell-AIDS hypothesis. In *AIDS: Virus- or Drug Induced*, ed. Peter H. Duesberg, 3–22. Boston/London: Kluwer. Reprinted from *Genetica*, 95, Numbers 1-3.

Parnes, J.R. 1997. CD8 and CD4: Structure, function, and molecular biology. In *Encyclopedia of Human Biology*, ed. Renato Dulbecco, 455–465. London/New York: Academic.

Resnick, S., and Richard Wolff. 1987. *Knowledge and Class: A Marxian Critique of Political Economy*. Chicago/London: University of Chicago Press.

Root-Bernstein, R.S. 1996. Five myths about AIDS that have misdirected research and treatment. In *AIDS: Virus or Drug Induced?* ed. Peter H. Duesberg, 185–206. Boston\London: Kluwer Academic Publishers. Reprinted from *Genetica*, 95, Numbers 1−3.

Sherwood, Jennifer, Alana Sharp, Bergen Cooper, Beirne Roose-Snyder, and Susan Blumenthal. 2017. HIV/AIDS National Strategic Plans of Sub-Saharan African Countries: An Analysis for Gender Equality and Sex-Disaggregated HIV Targets. *Health Policy and Planning* 32 (10): 1361–1367.

Silvestris, N., E. Crucitta, V. Lorusso, T. Gamuccia, and M. de Lena. 2002. AIDS-Related Non-Hodgson's Lymphona: Clinico-Pathological Characteristics and Therapeutic Strategies (Review). *International Journal of Oncology* 20: 611–615.

Strathdee, S., R. Hogg, M. O'Shaughnessy, J. Montaner, and M. Schechter. 1996. A Decade of Research on the Natural History of HIV Infection: Part 2. Cofactors. *Clinical and Investigative Medicine* 19 (2): 121–130.

UNAIDS. 2022. *HIV Estimates with Uncertainty Bounds: UNAIDS 2021 estimates.* Accessed 11 Jan 2022. https://www.unaids.org/en/resources/documents/2021/2021_unaids_data

Vasan, Sandhya, and Punnee Pitisuttithum. 2020. Vaccine Development Lessons Between HIV and COVID-19. *The Lancet: Infection* 21 (June): 759–761.

Vassan, A., B. Renjifo, Ellen Hertzmark, B. Chaplin, G. Msamango, M. East, W. Fawzi, and M. Hunter. 2006. Different RATES of disease Progression of HIV Type 1 Infection in Tanzania Based on Infecting Subtype. *Clinical Infectious Diseases* 42: 843–852.

Whiteside, A. 2006. HIV/AIDS and Development: Failures of Vision and Imagination. *International Affairs* 82 (2): 327–343.

World Bank. 2022. *World Bank Global Databank.* Accessed 12 Jan 2022. https://data.worldbank.org

Love Capital and the Nurturance Gap   12

Abstract

This chapter seeks to activate the principle of (scholarly) innovation by critically evaluating the forms of love capital being accumulated by people in capitalist economies. We situate love, according to the principle of historical specificity, in the neoliberal culture, and then examine the principle of heterogeneous groups and agents through the six love styles and the five critical factors, especially involving the principle of circular and cumulative causation due to multifactors and magnified processes. Then we apply the principle of contradiction vis-à-vis neoliberal capitalism undergoing the nurturance gap, disembedded economy and freedom constraint that inhibit holistic love capital. The principles of path dependence and uncertainty are then connected to instabilities, especially involving serial monogamy in the United States. Some of the core principles of IEPE provide a vantage point for scrutinising the problems involved in stimulating holistic love capital in the contemporary environment.

Keywords

Historical specificity · Circular and cumulative causation · Contradiction · Innovation · Uncertainty · Heterogeneous groups & agents · Path dependence · Love capital · Nurturance gap · Disembedded economy · Neoliberalism · Hegemony & uneven development

12.1 Introduction

Panoeconomics has published a long and productive discourse recently on the nature of neoliberalism, especially in relation to the generation of the GFC and Eurodebt crises of 2008–2014ff. Howard Stein (2012), for instance, writes about the nature of and reasons for the continuation of neoliberalism even though it is implicated in the generation of these instabilities. Gary Dymski (2011) recognizes that the 30 year-strong neoliberal policies of increasing the power of capital, especially finance capital, has not had a positive influence on global performance. Kosta Josifidis et al. (2011) argue that the GFC (and associated Eurocrisis) is not simply cyclical but also structural, and they posit certain policy parameters for renewal, some desirable and others not. Phillip O'Hara (2013) puts forward a policy framework for moderating deep recessions, debt crises and financial instabilities. Alpar Lošonc (2006) scrutinizes neoliberal environmental policy, especially relating to water resources, which he critiques for ignoring community property rights that are essential for public goods provision.

Timur Han Gür et al. (2011) generalize the opposition to neoliberalism by introducing Karl Polanyi's thesis of the disembedded economy, in which neoliberalism is seen as a radical response to the Keynesian welfare state of the 1950s–1970s. Having gone too far in the "deregulation" and rule-of-capital direction, neoliberalism needs to be replaced by a more embedded set of institutional and policy practices where, at the very least, the "fictitious capitals" of land, money and labour are suitably reproduced in the long run.

But one area not studied in detail in these *Panoeconomicus* papers is the social cement of the family, friendships, community and work environments, which have been eroded not only by the GFC and the Eurodebt crisis but also by neoliberalism in general. As certain feminists and social economists have recognized, part of Polanyi's embedded system involves transactions such as reciprocity and redistribution, which are alternatives to the market. The *concept of trust* is a crucial part of this equation, as is distributional equity, wise counselling (social, financial, personal), community governance, children's security and play, unemployment benefits, skill upgrading, and the provision of pensions.

At a wider level these questions involve what sort of society we want as we go forward with policy measures for long-term stability and progress. Do we want to encourage competition to the exclusion of cooperation in social life, or have some balance between the two? Do we want to encourage *reciprocity and redistribution* and/or *markets* or some balance between the two? Do we want love or hate to inspire institutional rebuilding and personality development? With the international conflicts, wars and military-industrial complexes that we see in motion, it is clear that hate does impact upon people's lives significantly. What policies would we put into practice to stimulate love?

If changing experiences of love, hate or indifference involves changes in utility, happiness, social provisioning, economic activity, social welfare, power, distribution of income, quality of life and productivity then they are essentially economic questions or have economic dimensions. For instance, love is likely to have declined

12.1 Introduction

in direct proportion to the depth of crises in various areas during the 2008–2014 instabilities; and neoliberal policies since the 1980s have likely impacted negatively on love where these policies have affected community and familial life.

Love (or the lack of it) is, in fact, a critical aspect of human life, but statistical bureaus and governance analysts have so far failed to devise adequate time series and cross-section data on these practices to inform social and economic policies. Political economists and economic sociologists have also given the subject little attention. It has mostly been left to sociologists and psychologists to do the necessary empirical and theoretical work to help understand the nature and tendencies of these practices.[1] But this work is comparatively recent, and while we have some cross-section data for some nations and areas, there is not a great deal for serious policy work, and very little historical data to inform debate. Nevertheless, some basic stylized facts about love are capable of being delineated from a careful mining of the literature, which are discussed in this chapter.

The purpose of this chapter is to present the core stylized facts, research results and metadata about love within the framework of the edifice and hypotheses of IEPE. A social science that purports to comprehend the workings of contemporary human practices should provide important insights into the nature of love. This is especially the case for IEPE, since various trends within its thought seek to understand the reproduction of everyday life, including the dominant institutions, such as the family and community. One could, therefore, assess the usefulness of IEPE according to the extent that it is capable of providing useful insights into love. This chapter seeks to advance this objective. Special reference is given to how some of the core general principles of IEPE (a) help to contextualize the data, research results and stylized facts on love; and more generally (b) in the process help to comprehend the nature, significance and limitations of love and intimacy in the contemporary environment of neoliberal capitalism.

IE political economy is an emerging field of study drawing from the various tendencies of political economy. It is somewhat of a hybrid or mutation that has sprung from these schools as an evolving, integrative framework of analysis. It has sought to transcend narrow allegiances towards a more inclusive frame of reference. Its boundaries are open and receptive to pluralistic influences. IEPE is not restricted in its field of vision, but is rather an emerging *method* (or series of methods) of analysis, with some core general and also lesser principles to guide analysis. The core principles examined in this chapter include historical specificity, circular and cumulative causation, innovation, contradiction, uncertainty and path dependence.

Some of the institutional and evolutionary works have made attempts to understand love, the most important being the work of James Ronald Stanfield and Jaqueline B. Stanfield (1997). Drawing from the social and institutional schools,

---

[1] A problem with some of the literature is that it seeks to study love but instead investigates sex. Anthony Giddens (1992) tries to reinvent the wheel in that he ignores the major literatures on love and thereby passes over some potential insights (despite the subtitle to the book). Eva Illouz (1997, 2007) similarly tends to ignore much of the theoretical and empirical work on love, although she has an interesting discussion of "contradictions".

they examine the lack of nurturance in contemporary US capitalism as being a product of insufficient reciprocity in interpersonal lives and the dominance of exchange and self-interest. This is a magisterial paper, the main results of which we integrate into the current analysis. Feminist IE scholars have tended to examine love in terms of caring labor, such as Julie Nelson (2006) who links it to the interface between work and nurturance; while Nancy Folbre and Nelson (2000) recognise the problems of trying to substitute more impersonal paid carers for loving care. Frederic Jennings (2009) views love from a Kaldorian perspective of being a complementary good where "[r]ewards and losses are mutual and these social effects are aligned, not opposed." He rightly seeks to transcend equilibrium theory and recognizes that systems and organizations need to be re-designed to favour cooperation and reciprocity.

Kenneth Boulding (1969) explores a Christian ethic through Agape or universal benevolence, indicating that this can be developed through exchange, reciprocity and redistribution (see also Neibuhr 1949). He then seeks to stimulate debate about how this may be applied to various social problems, such as war, development, discrimination, education and alternatives lifestyles. Various other attempts have been made within political economy to understand love, such as Romesh Diwan's (1982) exploration of love through a Gandhian economics, which lies exclusively in the social domain with little explicit attention to interpersonal love. Jean Thison (1987) develops a 'universal theorem' of love where it reaches a peak "at a 50–50 per cent profitability level" (p. 36), including a series of equations concerning reciprocity, a Jesus Christ "law", and an examination of wedding markets. Margaret Stout (2010) outlines a program to develop a public economy based on collaboration, self-governance within institutions, and social bonds between people. This new system is meant to affect people in their multiple walks of life, including the personal. A more recent 'political economy' paper by Freddy Cante (2013) treats love as a moral value, also as a form of power, and recognises it can dissipate when privatisation and/or monopolies emerge; but he evades all the literature on the subject of love except that of Boulding, and looks more at the social rather than personal aspects of love.

Various streams of political economy have thus mostly sought to comprehend the *social* dimensions of love, whereas, applying the principle of innovation, a comprehensive political economy of love exhorts us to analyse the interface between interpersonal *and* social dimensions of love. In seeking to utilise the principles of the broader mutation of IEPE to these multiple dimensions of love, therefore, we need to scrutinise some of the core cultural, social, and psychological literatures on the subject. For this reason the study applies the principle of historical specificity where culture and other factors are linked to love, and where the dominant contemporary neoliberal system is situated. We then connect the principles of circular and cumulative causation and heterogeneous groups and agents to the core empirico-theoretical social and psychological perspectives of love, especially the notions of love styles, triadic love, social spread and freedom. From this we develop the concept of holistic love capital, after which, using the principle of contradiction, the limitations of neoliberalism are evaluated based on the problems of individual versus society, markets versus nurturance, and freedom versus constraint; where the principle of hegemony and uneven development comes into play. The principle of uncertainty is applied to various aspects of love, especially involving the difficulty generating sufficient trust to sustain a relationship through time. The final major section examines the principle of path dependence through various phases of relational development and instability. Special attention is given to how the styles of love and the major factors evolved through time in neoliberal-based systems of political economy.

12.2 Historical Specificity of Love: Collectivist and Individualistic Economies

Core elements of the IE political economy literature argue that history is an important part of its edifice. Every aspect of political economy needs to be embedded in historical context, since history is linked to culture, and culture changes through time and space. The *principle of historical specificity* (see e.g., Howard Sherman 1995: 62) recognises the need to situate human relationships through the process of change, as well as revealing *path dependence*, namely, that the past matters for the present because it sets up structures that change through time and are commonly irreversible. Changes are thus unlikely to move from one equilibrium point to another since the past affects change and the process of moving affects human evolution.

This is critical to an understanding of love, since an analysis of intimate relationships needs to be embedded in the historical culture in question. The current state of love in the world is multifarious, affected by different cultural relationships—Western, Islamic, tribal, Christian, atheist, and so on. One can generalise through these cultural differences and reveal commonalities; and these generalities are important for comprehending the biological, genetic, species and cross-cultural foundations of love processes (see Elaine Hatfield and Richard Rapson 2005; Helen Fisher 1992, 2004). We can also scrutinize love within different cultures through the contemporary world-system. Most scholars who study this isolate two main processes at play, those of *individualism* and *collectivism.*

Hatfield and Rapson (2005: ch 2) argue that there are transcultural elements of love embedded in current societies, and that the similarities are often more important than the differences. For instance, in a cross-cultural study they explored it was shown that the first four traits in mate selection tend to be similar across societies, ethnic groups and genders. These include 'mutual attraction', 'having a dependable character', 'emotional stability and maturity' and 'having a pleasing disposition'. In general, regardless of sexual orientation, there were only very slight gender differences, with men only marginally preferring (relative to women) their mates to have good looks and cooking skills, while women (relative to men) only marginally preferring ambition and financial prospects among their partners. While pan-European cultures have over the past several hundred years variously been under the influence of the enlightenment, the Renaissance, Western science and technology, more latterly the sexual revolution, and even more recently the Internet and cell phone culture, more collectivist cultures have often been affected by elements of these influences over perhaps only the past several decades.

Despite these similarities, Hatfield and Rapson also find cultural differences more important than gender differences. Typically individualist cultures value romantic love between two people, with passion often playing a core role, whereby people tend (especially in their younger years) to assume the relationship should dissolve if and when they fall out of love. Individualist cultures, such as the US, UK, Australia and Western Europe, tend to put rights and individual goals at the forefront, whereas collectivist cultures, such as Venezuala, Indonesia, South Korea and West Africa, more usually put duties ahead of rights. Cultures in between the extremes, such as Japan, India, Turkey and Greece, tend to fuse the values of individualism and collectivism. Collectivist cultures may generate love more socially through families, friends and others in the community, since they value the fundamental connectivity between people. Individualist ones may generate friends more easily along a broader spectrum of interests yet find difficulty maintaining close and/or long-term relationships. For these reasons, Anne Bealle and Robert Sternberg (1995: 427) believe that "cultures define the beloved, the thoughts, the feelings and the relations that should accompany love and therefore implicitly define how people should think about, feel and relate to one another."

Despite some similarities between cultures and the process of US cultural hegemony, there is thus a core degree of cultural heterogeneity. Even in the model of love commonly associated with western capitalist societies differences remain. This is especially the case between Scandinavian-style capitalism where social cohesion remains fairly high as a degree of collectivism still operates, and classical neoliberal economies such as the US, UK and Australia, where cohesion has been diminishing as collectivism has been on the wane (O'Hara 2009). This chapter therefore applies much more to the neoliberal styles than the Scandinavian. The chapter presents a critical analysis of the increasingly market-based style of governance associated with these neoliberal economies, where the cash nexus tends to rule most institutions, women represent an increasing proportion of the labor market, and sex (especially female sexuality) is displayed with all its grandeur in advertisements, films, television shows, the Internet and everyday life. The state plays a secondary role compared to markets and corporations, while elements of collectivism (beyond the state) still operate in the crevices and beyond, perhaps within religious activities, family gatherings, friendly relationships, *certain specific* corporate networks and social movements.

We continue historical specificity by scrutinising the principle of circular and cumulative causation, which compels political economists to analyse the dominant theoretico-empirical studies of love within capitalist societies. Then we scrutinise the contradictions of intimacy within neoliberal systems, which both inhibit holistic love and also direct it into specific paths. Finally we examine the evolution and transformation of love in relationships, including path dependent processes, particularly in the Unites States, and how this manifests through interpersonal dynamics.

12.3 Circular and Cumulative Causation: Love Styles and Core Factors

The *principle of circular and cumulative causation* (CCC) is a critical one in political economy, drawing especially from the work of Gunnar Myrdal (1898–1987) and Nicholas Kaldor (1908–1986). The long tradition of CCC includes two main processes (see Sebastian Berger 2009), the first being the need to comprehend the *interaction between multiple variables* in the social economy; and the second being the *tendency for the variables to interact in a cumulative manner* generating instability and dynamic motion through historical time. The literature on love generally recognises the interactive feedback between variables, the multicausal nature of the love process, and the magnified and unstable impact through time.

While embedded relationships, nurturance and the social spread of *trust and intimacy* are limited in relationships under (neoliberal) capitalism, certain forms of love do emerge. John Alan Lee (1973, 1978, 1988), for instance, developed the first fully-formed multicausal and cumulative theoretico-empirical analysis of love, based on his PhD, and extensive applied research in Western capitalist economies (UK, Canada and the USA). He has become what could be called the 'guru' of love studies, since dozens of empirical papers have followed his schema (see Clyde Hendrick and Susan Hendrick 2006; Lee 1988, 2000). Lee and his followers reveal that there are six basic styles of love, but the critical thing is that these styles are often mixed, changing through time, and can adapt to the dynamics of different people through time. Understanding the six basic typologies is just as important as scrutinizing their interdependencies and how the same people can utilise variations of love styles through time with different people.

The six styles (or "love ideologies" as Lee also calls them) include three generic styles of Eros, Ludic and Storge plus the derivative styles of Agape (said to link Eros with Storge), Pragma (linking Ludic with Storge) and Manic (linking Eros with Ludic). Most empirical studies do not following the distinction between generic and derivative styles, but evidence points to concrete styles being combinations of influences. The co-linkage and interdependency between styles is shown below in Fig. 12.1.

It is important to comprehend the nature of the styles before the concrete linkages can be understood. Note here the importance of the principle of heterogeneous groups and agents, since love styles are indicative of various groups adopting certain love ideologies and practices, either as dominant single styles that people adopt or as variants that merge various parts of several styles.

Eros Love is the first style discussed by Lee, which is oriented around the idea and practices of physical beauty, which depends upon initial attraction, an ideal type of physical perfection, and revealing unashamedly the bodily aspect of interaction. Eros love often links to "love at first sight", and is portrayed in films such as *The Blue Lagoon* (Randall Kleiser 1980). The powerful physical attraction need not be purely sexual, as there may be a core element of artistic beauty, and such relationships often develop and become quite successful. Nevertheless, a desire for early sexual union is typical of this style. Intense and open feelings of love are core elements, as is usually

Fig. 12.1 Interdependent co-linkages between love styles

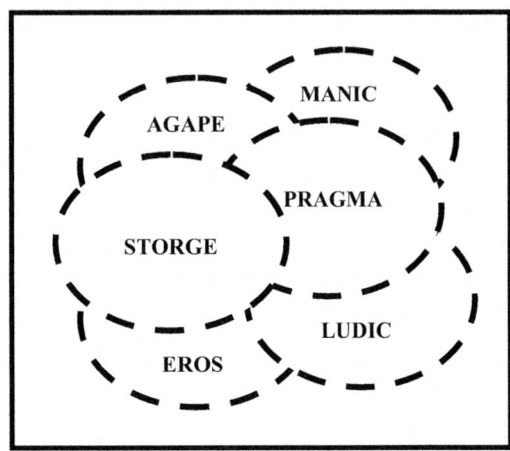

the search for 'one true love'. Long absence is a risky element here as tactile contact is crucial for love development. Both genders tend to engage in Eros-type styles, although there was some apparently conflicting evidence about Eros vis-a-vis gender and culture.

Superficially similar to Eros is the *Ludic Love* style, where love is seen as a game, and numerous simultaneous lovers (or at least short-term serial lovers) is central to this style. The Ludic style is immortalised in the movie, *Adventures of Don Juan* (Vincent Sherman 1948; and the many versions of the Don Juan theme over hundreds of years). Fair rules of the game, low levels of dependence, and a willingness to relate freely to multiple lovers are key characteristics of the Ludic "ideology" (see Russell Vannoy 1980). Strategies may include flattery, playing the field, low levels of psychological intimacy, and not revealing information about the other lovers. Ludic lovers may also exploit asymmetric intensity of feelings if one of the partners makes the mistake of falling in love deeply with a typical ludic. Casual meetings, basic levels of respect, and the idea that love should be fun are core elements of a ludic ideology. The ludic lover depends on meeting people for a continual supply of lovers, and often has a supply of good opening lines. It is more common among youth and males (including gays) in Western societies (see Lee 1978: 67; Hendrick et al. 1984; Marilyn Montgomery and Gwendolyn Sorell 1997).

Of some similarity to Ludic is *Storge Love,* or love as friendship, since both typically exhibit a lack of passion. Mama Cass Elliott's (1969) song, *It's Getting Better* (written by Barry Mann and Cynthia Weil), about a relationship that starts slowly and builds into a meaningful form of intimacy, is characteristic of this style. Affection, strong friendship and natural affinity are the primary traits of Storge love. In many cases Storge develops from living together in the same suburb, being a member of the same class, and most especially associating in rural areas. Durable companionship, building up a reserve of stability, having both empathy and sympathy with the loved one are primary elements of this form of love. Historically, Storge was quite common centuries ago during feudalism in Western Europe, when social customs, family, church and locality played a much stronger role in people's lives. But this style is common even now, ironically as social customs enable people to be more relaxed about lifestyle. Lee's (1978: 79) empirical research shows that this style is somewhat more common among women (especially lesbians) (see also Hendrick et al. 1984; Gregory Morrow et al. 1995).

Pragma love has some similarities with Storge, the main one being a tendency to downplay passion and intensity. *Pragmatic love* is one that seeks out relationships with people based on compatibility and satisfying practical needs. In literature, it is characterised by the behaviour of Charlotte in Jane Austen's (1813) novel, *Pride and Prejudice*. Dating agencies and computer mating techniques use such pragmatic methods of finding common interests and habits between people. Like the Eros lover, pragmatic love has an ideal image, but it is wider in scope than Eros since it considers not simply physicality but also (or instead) "qualities of character, social standing and social attitudes" (Lee 1978: 126). Pragma is level-headed and typically seeks someone with a certain level of college education, a specific type or level of profession, having, for instance, basic social skills, a particular ideology or religion, and a certain appearance. Pragmatic lovers are searching for "the possible", someone to fit into their lifestyle, and perhaps seeing love as an investment in the future, considering the broad calculations of profit and loss through time (computation). Women have a marginal partiality to this style (Morrow et al. 1995; Rachel Lacey et al. 2004).

Quite different from Pragma are the final two styles of Manic and Agape. *Manic love* is based on obsession; being concerned primarily with being with the loved one, thinking about the loved one, and planning for the future with the loved one. Obsessional love is illustrated in the film, *Fatal Attraction* (Adrian Lyne 1987). The Manic lover exclusively concerns herself with the partner, or desired partner, and her whole life is obsessed with the role of The Other. It is a form of love many believe not to be love: "demonic ... [,] narcissistic, neurotic and pathological" (Lee 1978: 86), including extreme jealousy, tragedy, and potential conflict. Manic is common among those who are stressed, unsure of themselves, and unhappy. The tendency to Manic is often linked with dissatisfaction with life as the Manic lover sees rivals in every crevice as jealousies abound, forever seeking reassurance, and worrying continually (Susan Forward and Craig Buck 1991). These relationships are often short-lived, expressing the contradictory similarities between love and hate, as one can easily turn to the other (Sternberg 2003). Empirical research indicates a tendency for youth to be influenced by this style, and also (marginally) women (Judith Fenney and Patricia Noller 1990; Kurt Frey and Mahzad Hojjat 1998).

Lastly, there is *Agape Love,* which feminists (bell hooks [*sic*.] 2000), socialists (Eric Fromm 1957) and numerous religions (John Templeton 1999) believe to be the most authentic form. Agape love occurs when there is unconditional love, where the lover is deeply altruistic and compassionate, in "complete disregard for personal gain of any kind" (Lee 1978: 142). Agape lovers typically are concerned with the fate of humanity, and loving whoever is at hand, often spreading beyond one person to a group or community. The archetypical example would be the life of Jesus of Nazareth. He was committed to treating others with compassion, mercy and understanding, while advocating the Golden Rule: "In everything ... treat people the same way you want them to treat you" (Tod Lindberg 2007: 237). Obligation, passion and commitment dominate over egotism and the self. In modern (especially neoliberal) capitalist economies, at least, it is difficult to sustain altruistic love (except perhaps by parents for children), as the demands of a selfless association are too difficult to nurture (and are seen as undesirable) in an environment of conspicuous consumption, "being all one can", and competing with others for jobs, lovers and friendships. In such a system, most people are concerned instead with costs and benefits, individual achievement, and quid pro quo (or at least reciprocity or dual-enjoyment). Perhaps surprising, when controls were present for gender, age and culture, men had a slightly greater tendency towards Agape compared with females (Li-Wein Lin 2005). However, as Fromm recognises, this form in its ideal type is almost completely lacking in market-capitalist economies, and the empirical studies are exclusively concerned with altruism *within* couple relationships.

It may well be, as Lee stated, that Pragma has links to Storge and Ludic, depending as it does on friendship and lack of passion or compassion. Perhaps also Manic links with Eros and Ludic, since there is a general passion without specific links to compassion and intelligence. Agape may also link with Storge and Eros since it tends to include compassion, empathy and intelligence. Whether these are strong associations supporting Lee's specific generic—derivative forms has not been empirically scrutinised in detail. What does appear likely from much of the evidence is that mixed typologies (of various combinations) tend to predominate. However, much of the empirical work underplays the circular and cumulative aspect of love styles, since the methods used are relatively new and the reality of mixed-changing styles through time are often hard to link to the interview schedules and statistical tests.[2] These schedules and tests also tend to underplay the richness of Lee's analysis, for instance, by often reducing Agape to couple-concern and empathy rather than also involving communal love at the social level.

Gender differences in love styles are modest in this heterogeneous groups framework. In many studies of advanced neoliberal economies, especially the US, males have shown a (slight) tendency to be more Ludic and Agape than females. Some studies linking women to Agape (in couples) have been reversed once allowance is made for age, education, satisfaction and religion. Li-Wen Lin (2005) shows (for the general population of a US Midwestern agricultural state) that those who are male, older, religious, having less education and more relationship satisfaction tend to exhibit 'couple-Agape'. Some studies show men scoring somewhat higher than women in Eros (e.g., Hatkoff and Lasswell 1979), while some others show women scoring higher than males (e.g., Hendrick and Hendrick 1991, 1992). It does appear to depend on circumstances and specific populations. Felix Neto (2007),

---

[2] The most common interview schedules are (short and long forms) of the love attitude scales (LAS) and the most common statistical tests are correlation, intercorrelation matrices and cluster analysis. (See e.g., Hendrick et al. 1984.) But note some criticisms Lee (1988) makes of some of the tests.

12.3 Circular and Cumulative Causation: Love Styles and Core Factors

comparing British, Indian and Portugese students, sought to make more general conclusions that there are no discernable differences in Eros on the basis of gender or culture.

Apart from John Alan Lee's theory, which has been specifically applied to neoliberal-style economies such as the UK and US (as well as several other capitalist economies), the other theory which has elements of multicausality, cumulation, empirical, and heterogeneous groups/agent application is Robert J. Sternberg's triangular theory of love (see Sternberg and Michael Barnes 1988; Sternberg and Karin Weiss 2006). Sternberg's theory is complementary to that of Lee, and enhances the multi-causal, cumulative and heterogeneous nature of the love factors. We have added to Sternberg's theory two critical factors: Eric Fromm's emphasis on Social Spread; and the notion of Freedom from Jean-Paul Sartre (1956), plus the associated emphasis on the principle of novelty-innovation discussed by Thorstein Veblen (1914) and Joseph Schumpeter (1911). These factors seem necessary to add to Sternberg's theory, and indeed, his analysis of *hate* (Sternberg 2003) does link specifically to the search for *freedom* and *social spread*, in addition to the other three factors (for terrorists etc.). We have thus developed a five factor theory of love which exhibits circular and cumulative dynamics. This is shown in Fig. 12.2, below. We illustrate later that the CCC dynamics of love can link Lee's styles to these core factors.

This circuit has many forms, and we start with the basic form of P↔i↔C, Passion↔Intimacy↔Commitment (Sternberg 1988), linked to additional factors Freedom (F) and Social Spread (S). This basic circuit shows that a significant degree of Passion in interpersonal relationships often leads to a degree of Intimacy, which through time may stimulate a short term feeling of love, followed by a long-term Commitment. If this basic circuit is well developed then "consummate love" (Sternberg's term) may emerge. But to evolve further requires a degree of Freedom and Social Spread. If all five elements coevolve in a durable fashion (love capital) then a degree of "holistic love" can emerge. Holistic love, of varying degrees, is the most evolved form, since all five elements are transforming the lives of people.

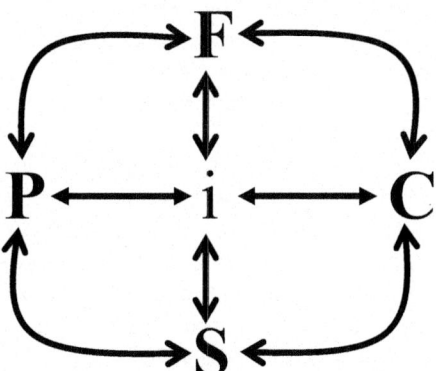

Fig. 12.2 Love circuit of cumulative interdependency: Five core factors

Freedom (Sartre 1956) and novelty-innovation (Veblen 1914; Schumpeter 1911) are the elemental components of love; dynamic factors enabling love to grow-develop into new areas and experiences. Love often requires dynamic processes to enhance the experiential metamorphosis required for higher forms of consciousness and excitement. There needs to be an endogenous stimulus embedded in the structure of a human relationship that generates new knowledge and experience. Without this, love will often die or form a vicious circle of mediocrity. In a closed system eventually deterioration occurs, but with an open system (characteristic of political economy systems) new stimuli can enhance the love process and propel new phases of metamorphosis over the long term through transcendental freedom.

Social spread is Eric Fromm's (1957) idea that holistic love cannot exist between two people only, but requires a suitable social environment to stimulate progressive habits and values. He says that "love" purely between two people is more an addiction, and that 'true love' concerns loving people in an environment of community. The degree of social spread is thus important in the wider equation of holistic love, because if love can spread beyond two people to a wider sphere then the two-people process can become more meaningful, and the social dimension is critical to heightened love experiences.

The next three factors emanate from the triadic theory of love developed by Sternberg (1986, 1987): Passion, Intimacy and Commitment. Passion is an intense feeling of connection between people (and/or other animals, places and things). It involves a high degree of arousal, stimulation and longing for union. Passion often develops quickly, and in sexual relationships often precedes Intimacy and Commitment. Excess Passion by itself can lead to addiction, so it is important that some of the other elements balance Passion for holistic love to develop.

Intimacy is a core of love (as Sternberg 1998a, b recognises), since without it most of the essential feelings and processes of love cannot be reproduced. Intimacy includes the sharing of knowledge, life history, and goals. Meaningful communication is often a critical element, as are close bonding, trust, emotional support, and respect. Intimate linkages enable the development of feelings of attachment, and often lead to Passion and Commitment. Sternberg believes that relationships include both latent and manifest levels of Intimacy, the more successful ones having increasing levels of hidden Intimacy through time and declining levels of manifest Intimacy; while the failed relationships have major declines in hidden Intimacy and lower manifest levels than successful relationships. The latent Intimacies provide potential stores of trust, knowledge and shared interests that can be retrieved when required.

The *principle of uncertainty* states that one should be cognizant of the importance of informational anomalies (asymmetry and insufficiency), opaque behaviour, instability, precariousness, unreliability and unpredictability of relationships in the generation of world problems. This is especially the case with intimate relationships, since a lot happens in this realm that is not discussed, especially concerning the future, and is forever subject to varying degrees of suspicion and ambiguity. The *concept of trust* is especially critical here for "uncertainty reduction" since "trust is an exchange of actions or messages that gradually reduces uncertainty and increases mutual assurance that the relationship will endure" (John Holmes and John Rempel 1989: 190, 193). Trust provides a store of potential reciprocity in the future which reduces the instabilities of everyday life, and increases the potential for dealing with conflict. The durable bonding of trust enhances temporal changes in life situations, and moderates negative reactions to the other's behaviour. Paul Miller and John Rempel (2004) demonstrate that trust generates a "tendency to charitably evaluate the motives underlying a partner's behaviour" (p. 695), promoting a cooperative, caring, considerate, responsive, tolerant, concerned, friendly and forgiving attitude. This strongly suggests that some minimal elements of Agape and/or Storge (along with Passion) are crucial for dynamic and successfully relationships. Commitment has short and long term components. In the short-term one may conclude that 'love is in the air', while in the longer-term one may consciously or subconsciously commit to a person.[3] Generically, Commitment means that there is a durable bond that enables the reproduction of the key elements of love. Sometimes Commitment may be the only thing enabling survival of the relationship, when hard times emerge, while at other times it may coevolve with the other factors.

The principle of circular and cumulative causation is relevant to the interaction between these five coevolving factors which generate a non-equilibrium process of covariant amplification and transformation. CCC creates phases of development as holistic love is never an equilibrium process. Change, amplification and metamorphosis are critical to love. Indeed, love is a critical part of life, and life is always in the process of evolving and becoming. People generate different relationships through life, which change and become modified through action. Habits, norms and mores evolve through time; and because of this love also undergoes phases of evolution.

The five core CCC factors involved in love styles can be examined via a series of Venn Diagrams, as shown in Fig. 12.3, below (the six styles can also be scrutinized in this way):

This figure represents *one example* of the *combined* activities within a couples' lifestyle, including two main sets, the first being activities (or qualities) exerted within the "Relationship" per se (within the hexagon); and the second being activities (or qualities) within their "Social Environment" (within the rectangle), which includes the relationship per se as well as activities of the five factors outside their relationship. Three things stand out in these particular Venn Diagrams. The first is that the most dominant activity or quality within the relationship is Passion. This Passion, however, is of the most general kind, with only slight links to Intimacy and Commitment. Secondly, there are modestly good degrees of Intimacy, Commitment, Social Spread and Freedom exerted in this relationship. And thirdly, some of the

---

[3] This refers to the obvious fact that love can be not only for human beings but also other animals, cars, plants and other entities. There is of course the love of knowledge, non-animal-human substitutes and love on the Internet. The Japanese experiment with virtual love (or is it sex?) on the Internet and associated technologies (especially among youth) is especially instructive (see Dominic Pettman 2009 on "virtual" boyfriends and girlfriends in Japan).

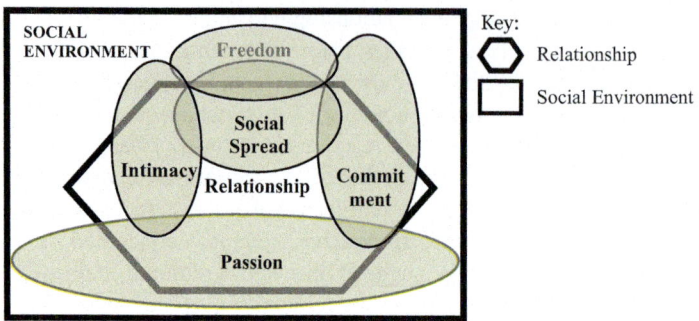

Fig. 12.3 Five elements of holistic love in relationships

Table 12.1 Types of love capital: 5 factors, sets

Type of love capital	Sets of factors	Description of love capital
Holistic love =	{I, P, C, F, S}	5 factors operate to *significant degrees* [TSD] within relationship
Dynamic interpersonal love =	{I, P, C, F}	Sternberg's 3 factors + freedom operate TSD within relationship
Consummate couple love =	{I, P, C}	Sternberg's 3 factors operate TSD within relationship
Romantic love =	{I, P}	Intimacy & passion operate TSD within relationship
Companionship =	{I, C}	Intimacy & commitment operate TSD within relationship
Fatuous love =	{P, C}	Passion & commitment operate TSD within relationship
Liking/friendship =	{i}	Intimacy dominates
Empty love =	{C}	Commitment dominates
Infatuation =	{P}	Passion dominates
Experiential–yet–empty =	{F}	Freedom dominates
Personally–empty love =	{S}	Social spread dominates

Freedom-seeking is generated by the couple together, but most is individually in their social environment (outside the relationship). Overall, it seems like a fairly healthy relationship except for one thing: there are few intersections between the sets in the relationship diagram, indicating a high degree of separation or fragmentation of activities or qualities. (More complex diagrams are possible with different structures of activities and qualities; and variations of the above figure.)

Table 12.1, provides metadata for the various types of love, where the different types differ in their degree of love capital. The *sets* of love characteristics refer to those happening *within* relationships, as shown in Table 12.1.

12.3 Circular and Cumulative Causation: Love Styles and Core Factors

These different types and degrees of love have much real world application, as the various empirical studies demonstrate. While most of the studies tend to concentrate on specific styles, the reality is combined styles and core factors. The types of love actually experienced in reality quite often start with some of the less holistic factors, while gradually building a greater stock of durable elements. While many may rise to the level of consummate couple love, dynamic interpersonal love and to a much lesser degree holistic love, the extent to which these types are experienced is usually at the lower levels of intersection and union. In particular, in neoliberal economies, high levels of balanced-factor development of dynamic interpersonal and holistic love are rare, although certainly possible in the *crevices* where very special people or arrangements are able to eschew or "manage" neoliberal ideology and institutions.

Merging John Alan Lee's "Love Styles" and the "Five Critical Factors" (Sternberg's "Three Factors" along with Freedom and Social Spread) enables one to scrutinise the notion of holistic love. Holistic love is associated with the higher dimensions of love where the core factors are well developed. This requires the effective reproduction of human relationships (set in a suitable geographical and ecological environment) where understanding and communication are well developed, and where the core factors of Social Spread, Freedom, Passion, Intimacy and Commitment are highly evolved. The stock of love is a form of capital, "love capital", while the flow is a form of investment, "love investment", but unlike most forms of capital using it does not destroy it but rather enhances it (much the same as with social capital). There are thus degrees of love capital, from low to medium to high levels.

Table 12.2, below, provides metadata for the Index of Love Capital (ILC) according to the various styles and core factors. The table seeks to scrutinise the typical degree of love possible with a high level of development of each specific style of love. It is based on groups of people engaging in each respective style of love together, and the typical degree of development of the core factors associated with each style, after a typical period of "successful" development of the respective style. Each of the "ideal type" dimensions is given a scale of 1–10, with a possible maximum of 50 points:

Overall, Agape lovers typically have the highest level of love capital, including a high level of durability and a good balance between the various components of the index. However, it is difficult for Agape love to develop in a market economy, in

Table 12.2 Index of Love Capital (ILC)

	Social spread	Freedom	Passion	Intimacy	Commitment	ILC	ILC position
Eros	3	4	8	6	6	27	2nd
Ludic	5	8	2	1	1	17	5th
Storge	5	5	3	5	6	24	3rd
Pragma	4	4	3	5	5	21	4th
Manic	1	1	6	4	4	16	6th
Agape	8	5	5	4	6	28	1st

terms of Social Spread. The second highest level of love capital is typically exhibited by Eros lovers, since they are generally mentally positive and have a good balance of all the major components, once they develop. Close behind them are Storge lovers, who are historically more likely to survive than Agape lovers, in terms of quantity of people rather than the individual love capital index, and have a good balance of all factors except Passion. Pragma lovers perform less well since they tend to lack Passion and have high ratings in none of the variables; yet they tend to have good levels of Intimacy and Commitment. The two styles comparatively lacking in love capital are Ludic and Manic, with Ludics being high in Freedom but very low in three major variables, and Manics having no variable at a high level, although Passion is at a good level.

Each of the love styles has a competitive advantage and also a limit. For instance, Agape excels in Social Spread (notably in liberal-communitarian systems) and is good in all other variables. In reality, in market economies it mostly exists in its underdeveloped form as Agape behaviour between lovers pure and simple. Eros is especially high on Passion (general, bodily, personal) but is typically not well garnered on Social Spread. Storge has a good balance of measures but excels in none. Pragma has a good balance of variables but is very low in Passion. Ludic excels in a *certain type* of Freedom and is good on Social Spread, but is the lowest of all in Intimacy and Commitment. Manic has a moderately good balance of three variables but virtually no Social Spread nor Commitment to Freedom.

Generally, each style works well (except Manic and Ludic) with someone of the same style. The Index of Love Capital provides a good general understanding of the stock of love for people associating with others of the same love style. To investigate further why the styles often require linkages between styles and changes through time, we scrutinise the contradictions within and between them. While some styles may work well with someone of the same style, they are likely to operate better when linked to certain other styles as well.

For instance, Timothy Levine et al. (2006) undertook an empirical study of love styles for undergraduate students in upper-division studies at a western US university. They found that Agape was linked to factors such as 'humour' and being 'smart', as well as the usual ones such as being 'understanding', 'compassionate' and 'sensitive'. While the most important characteristics of Eros lovers are 'looks' and 'sex', very close behind are variables normally linked to Agape or Storge, namely 'compassion' and 'caring', which were much more important than 'romance'. Storge lovers relied on typical factors such as 'communication', 'compassion' and 'personality', but also on another characteristic not usually necessarily linked with any of the styles, namely being 'smart'. Pragma was linked not only to factors common to itself, but also some linked to other styles, such as 'romance' (usually associated with Eros) and 'honesty' (linked to Agape or Storge).

Perhaps the reason why typically Ludic is difficult to reproduce in the long-term is the fact that, in this study by Levine et al. (as with most), it was shown to be a strongly negatively correlated, especially with being 'smart', 'sensitive', 'romantic' and having 'personality'. Manic is also a similarly negative style. However, Manic is much more widespread than the ideal type would indicate simply because it usually links into other styles such as Eros, individual-Agape, Storge, Pragma and even possibly a little Ludic. This seems to support our hypothesis that the least widespread styles are those which are either incompatible with neoliberalism (social-individual Agape) and/or those which fail to effectively link with other styles and factors to enhance its reproducibility through long historical time (especially Ludic; occasionally Pragma).

While Lee's love style approach is largely complementary to Sternberg's triangular theory, one specific criticism that Lee has of Sternberg's analysis needs to be mentioned. This is "Sternberg's acceptance of the bias towards some kinds of relationships as more truly love than others[.] ... The very names adopted–fatuous, empty, consummate–signal the bias. For Sternberg, manic is "infatuated love gone berserk"" (Lee 1988: 65). A similar criticism is made of the work of Fromm (1957) and C.S. Lewis (1960) by Lee. Given the empirical evidence gained (referenced throughout this current chapter), it would appear that Sternberg has good reason to be somewhat critical of Manic and Ludic love styles in their extreme form; and hence the current chapter uses the phrases "fatuous, empty, consummate" (as well as "holistic", etc.) in Table 12.1 (etc.), to recognise lower and higher-order love experiences. But this current chapter *does go out of the way* to situate Manic and Ludic in love dynamics in as sympathetic a form as possible, given the evidence available.

12.4 Contradictions of Love Styles: General and Within Neoliberal Capitalism

The *principle of contradiction* states that every phenomenon has its internal dynamics that generate positive and negative processes that are forever in motion, and which periodically manifest in anomalous outcomes. Examining contradictions reveals the inner dynamics of the phenomenon and how change, conflict and instability are core elements of every real thing through time (O'Hara 2012, 2023). In this context, it is true that some love styles are relatively compatible with others, while some are more conflicting or fundamentally contradictory. All of the styles are inherently contradictory, in the sense of being unlikely to lead to durable long-term association in themselves. Styles thus require linking together, co-evolving and changing through time, in order to stimulate successful relationships.

Table 12.3 below generates metadata for the Index of Contradiction between love styles. The matrix is based on empirical studies and assesses the *typical* extent to which each style is in contradiction with each of the styles. Each is given a possible 6 points, with the index being out of 36. Because we are here interested in the linkages, we develop this Index at the margin, assuming 50% development of the specific individual styles. In other words, once each of the love styles has been developed to a (say) 50% level with another person of the same style, what are the contradictory relationships beyond this level, for the same style as well as the others?

This table provides an understanding of the styles that are complementary and also helps comprehend the contradictions between the styles. The Table shows that

Table 12.3 Index of Contradiction between Love Styles (ICS) beyond 50%

	Eros	Ludic	Storge	Pragma	Manic	Agape	∑ICS
Eros	6	4	2	3	5	1	21
Ludic	2	6	3	4	5	1	21
Storge	2	5	6	3	4	1	21
Pragma	2	4	3	6	5	1	21
Manic	2	5	3	4	6	1	21
Agape	1	4	2	3	5	6	21
∑ICS	15	28	19	23	30	11	
Position	5th	2nd	4th	3rd	1st	6th	

beyond a certain level of development of each style, diminishing (marginal) returns set in, thus requiring elements of the characteristics of other styles to develop a greater quality of the love experience. For instance, while Agape has the highest potential for holistic love, beyond a certain point of its development (say, 50 percent) it is enhanced by acquiring the characteristics of other styles. This is especially true in market capitalist societies where Agape is difficult to sustain, and may require other styles to be more consistent with the surrounding socioeconomic conditions. Beyond this level, it would benefit most by some influence from Eros, thereafter from Storge, some point after from Pragma, then Ludic and finally Manic. The exact point at which the other styles require movement from one to another style probably depends upon specific circumstances. It is likely possible to transcend diminishing (marginal) returns if Eros, Storge and Pragma are introduced into the situation at an early phase of evolution.

Agape is thus shown to have the lowest degree of contradictions with the other styles, and indeed requires a degree of Eros (followed by other styles) to be successful, since without interpersonal passion and intimacy it tends to lack an internal process of development. Agape can also benefit from elements of Storge, since friendship builds practical forms of trust and intimacy necessary for success. Pragma has an inner contradiction in itself, namely the two elements of its motion—similar class, values or background versus concern for money and success—since while class, values and background may be positive up to a point, too much of a concern for money and success may limit its viability. Nonetheless, Agape may benefit by certain values in common and background factors—as well as money and success, especially in a market-capitalist economy. Combining Agape with Eros, Storge and Pragma may be sufficient for a high level of Holistic Love, while certain additional minimal elements of Ludic and Manic may assist in the process.

Eros has the second lowest contradictions with the other styles, and is in fact the dominant style, but usually requires some other elements for success. It usually requires some elements of Agape, Storge and possibly Pragma to become dominant. The style with the third lowest degree of contradiction with other styles is Storge. Many of the empirical studies downplay Storge as a style being utilised in reality, because it is necessary for most styles while it may not be the dominant element in most. Pragma has the fourth lowest degree of contradictions, since it tries to link to commonalities associated with class, cultural habits and tendencies. However these positive traits of similarities are moderated by the negatives of concern for money and success. These two dialectical twins help explain why in many empirical studies Pragma is relatively less common than otherwise may be envisaged. In modern capitalist economies, the 'common habit and interest' side of it may be dominated by concern with money and success, which may lead often to dissolution. Hence, if Pragma is moderated at a certain stage by elements of Agape, followed by Eros and then Storge, holistic love may develop considerably. Afterwards some minimal level of Ludic or Manic may assist.

The highest level of contradictions is evident for Manic, followed by Ludic. Ironically, the empirical literature often shows that while Ludic is mostly linked with youth and declines through the other stages of life; Manic is actually quite common, certainly more so than might otherwise be thought possible. The typical life cycle of relationships in neoliberal economies often show Ludic tendencies in young people suddenly declining when relationships become more durable. Males tend to be more Ludic (especially when young), and perhaps surprisingly more 'couple-Agape'. The reason why Manic is quite common in reality, although never discussed in this context in the literature, is simply that it can benefit from elements of Social Spread, Freedom and Intimacy. Hence when Manic links with Agape, then Eros and Storge and even a little Pragma and possibly Ludic, the problematic levels of jealously, instability and uncertainty can be moderated to enhance durability. This is likely why some empirical studies show Manic to be almost as common as Storge and Pragma, especially among young women (Hendrick et al. 1984: 193; Morrow et al. 1995: 383); and it is sometimes able to moderate 'the obsession' through elements of friendship, intelligence and compassion.

It is understandable, then, why life cycles of people in advanced capitalist economies tend to be higher in Ludic (especially for males) and to some degree Manic (especially for women) in the younger years, and as this evolves towards greater durability Eros and couple-Agape often become more important. An element of Pragma and Storge may evolve as marriage and parenting start to impact. In somewhat older ages friendship often starts to become stronger (in relative terms), and a some Ludic may even impact when children move on.

An increasing tendency over the past few decades is for 'money and position' (one of the two core elements of Pragma) as well as individual objectives (rather than the supposed 'organic family' of the 1950s–1960s) to take precedent in *relationships*, and as a result serial monogamy has become increasingly institutionalised in the United States (to a much lesser extent in Europe). According to Andrew Cherlin (2010), serial monogamy is 'the US way' of trying to resolve the contradiction (as he calls it) between their *belief in ongoing relationships* and their *emphasis on personal goals*, despite the inherent fragility of the arrangement.

Love in neoliberal political economies is thus affected not only by the specific contradictory relationships between the different love styles and core factors, but also by the more specific contradictions of neoliberalism. The contradictions of neoliberalism affect love in such societies in specific ways, directing its motion and inhibiting its development. The core contradictions of neoliberalism are the inner tendencies that enable it to grow and develop. There are primary and secondary contradictions at play, which have a dynamic interdependency of linkage. Through time these contradictions become modified, and the degree of conflict changes (see O'Hara 2001, 2023). The core such contradictions are markets versus nurturance, individual versus society, and love freedom versus constraint, discussed below.

12.4.1 Contradiction Between Markets and Nurturance

The general contradiction of the disembedded economy states that market capitalism has a tendency to destroy non-market institutions in the process of destructive creation (Polanyi 1944; James Ronald Stanfield 1986). In so doing it transforms these institutions into market forms of remuneration for relatively quick monetary gain. This, indeed, is how capitalism works to stimulate the propensity for innovation and accumulation. The problem is that these non-market relations of reciprocity, redistribution and householding are critical for long-term socioeconomic reproduction in the form of public goods.

Consequently, market capitalism has a double movement, whereby it creates markets out of these non-market opportunities, while at the same time variously having to create public goods that protect the system. When it moves too much in the market direction periodic financial instability and low growth are highly likely. Governance and institutional changes respond eventually by recreating mostly government redistribution schemes to ensure reasonable reproduction. These include lender of last resort facilities, discretionary and automatic fiscal and monetary policies, sickness and health insurance for workers, accords between capital and labor, employing caring labour, foster homes, and unemployment insurance. Periodically it encounters too many of these protective responses to the market which may reduce profit and accumulation. Hence market capitalism undergoes waves of deregulation followed by regulation and/or welfare/civil society that is a critical part of its momentum (see O'Hara 2012; Ch. 8 above).

These processes impact on love, intimacy and friendship. The destructive creation of market capitalism progressively substitutes market relations for personal relations; wage labour for non-market relations of intimacy and love. It also creates conspicuous consumption, including the 'trophy' wife/husband, in place of authentic instrumental functions of institutions. It stimulates competition between people in the realm of intimate relations, in place of caring, sentiment, and sociality. It turns human relationships into alienated experiences based on money, quid pro quo, and equal exchanges. It transforms love into sex, sex into commodities, and leaves little time for people to regenerate their intimate connections. In short, it generates a perpetual nurturance gap, with likely cyclical, wave-like and geographical differences, in the extent of the problem.

The double movement ensures that *many* non-market relations of intimacy are transformed into commodity production. And when protective responses are called into play the state plays a major role. The state, however, while critical in the provision of these protected responses, is no substitute for protection based on family, community and friendship. At best we are left with a bureaucratic embeddedness, and at worst people are left to exist in an array of market-based regulations and requirements, or to fend for ourselves. The nurturance gap is a perennial problem of societies based on accumulation and competition when exchange (especially) substitutes for intimate reciprocity (Stanfield and Stanfield 1997).

The market process, both in creative destruction and protective response, drives a wedge between love and sex by destroying the former while stimulating the latter. To use a useful hyperbole, 'love is transformed into sex, sex into orgasm, and orgasm into number of times.' As household activities decline, communities disappear, extended families evaporate, global economic relations escalate, human relationships become superficial, external beauty and sex is emphasised, and people have little time for intimacy. These indeed are core tendencies imbued in its motion.

Relevant to the principle of hegemony and uneven development, cultural differences propel uneven levels of uncertainty, as the nations of northern Europe still experience a degree of embeddedness as community, sociality and trust remain quite high. Scandinavian style social-capitalism has managed to protect society and love against the ravages and destruction of creative destruction to some degree. American and UK-style capitalism, on the other hand, is bearing the relatively full brunt of a disembedded economy through market destruction (O'Hara 1995, 2004). Neoliberalism has pushed both styles of capitalism further into disarray, but the Scandinavian-style has managed to protect itself much more than average.

12.4.2 Contradiction Between Individual and Society

The concept of holism says that every person needs to have a good knowledge and experience of an array of political, economic, social, psychological and technical processes for personal development. It also says that a well-rounded personality requires a holistic lifestyle, including work, play and emotional bonding. Love thus involves knowledge and experience, but also both a loving person and a caring society. A prime contradictory process, especially under neoliberal capitalism, is for two people to project their love onto another person without a strong social element. Eric Fromm (1957) emphasised that love needs to be a dominant tendency in both person and society. Thus emerges the notion of a "loving person" who relates empathetically with others, in tandem with a culture that generates a positive environment for people to enhance trust and genuine intimacies with others (Social Spread).

In Fromm's perspective, as market-capitalism advances the potential for love declines, both because individuals exist qua individuals, and also since the culture eschews caring, intimacy and spiritual oneness. Thus the individualist form of love stimulated by market capitalism is inauthentic and tends to privatise the experience rather than link it to the common good and the community. Love in most capitalist societies is seen as intimacy between two persons, often spreading to parents and children and sometimes to extended families and a few good friends; whereas "real love" resides in the oneness of the individual with those around them, including the community as a whole. These community externalities—including social trust, extended friendship, and concern for strangers—tend to be sporadic under neoliberal capitalism due to the social alienation that is pervasive.

Agapic-Eros-Storgic love is inhibited in neoliberal societies due to the materialistic culture, trends that eschew ethics beyond the market, and emphasis on work and money. People increasingly specialise, both in education and work. Specialisation is seen as stimulating a comparative advantage, whereas the costs of doing so are not including in the analysis. Work and money are seen as more important than sharing and giving. A large number of loving people are unlikely in this psychological, social and cultural state of alienation based on exchange and *quid pro quo*. Nevertheless, certain niches or pockets of *expansive Agapic-Eros-Storgic love* may be feasible in the crevices where these oppressive forces have less impact, or where special people strive energetically to generate wholeness out of existential desperation. However, these pockets are very restricted, while the empirical research into capitalist economies otherwise following Lee's work, (as mentioned) completely ignore Agape love in its *combined* individual *and* social context, defining it purely as concern and compassion for *the* (singular) loved one.

None of the empirical studies examine Agape love in the individual *and* social context discussed by Lee in his many works. More troubling, none of them even discuss this disparity between Lee's view of Agape and their own 'evidence' of 'Agape' love. Lee (1988: 48) argued, for instance, that "the agapic lover in a relationship is likely to see the partner as only one of many people in need. The partner may have to be content with a small portion of the lover's time and energy, for so many others are in need." Some examples of empirical studies that ignore this perspective include the following. Lacey et al. (2004) argue that "Agapic individuals tend to put *their partner's* needs and wishes above their own" (emphasis added). Hendrick and Hendrick (2006: 153) say that "This [Agapic] style is sacrificial, placing *the loved person's* welfare above one's own" (emphasis added). Also, Levine et al. (2006: 466) argue that "Agapic is also characterized by gentle caring and tolerance for *one's partner*"; (emphasis added). Lin (2005) recognised Lee's emphasis on the social individual yet strangely centred the empirical work on "their *current* partner" (p. 36, emphasis added). This reinforces Fromm's crucial point about the decline in *real* Agape (and Lee's point about what Agape 'actually is'), as even the scholars cannot (bother to) find any evidence of it, given the divergence between the theory and the stunted real loves of people within neoliberal capitalism.

12.4.3 Contradiction Between Love Freedom and Constraint

A primary contradiction of love draws from the existentialist work of Jean-Paul Sartre (1956), the most well-known French philosopher, who sought to comprehend concrete human relations of the type with which love is a supreme example. These contradictions emanate from the conflict between the ontological principle of love as freedom and the concrete form it takes as structure and capital.

12.4 Contradictions of Love Styles: General and Within Neoliberal Capitalism

In principle, love is the seeking of freedom; searching for the realisation of one's potential in an environment of liberality, expression, and wholeness. In love we seek to express our humanity, to generate creative endeavours, and delve into the pleasures that are denied us elsewhere. Here we exist in the nakedness of intimacy, sexual interaction, and a caring attitude. The love that we create must be free from constraint for it to blossom in a natural fashion. This opening up of human potential is the basis of the feeling of freedom. This is what we seek and feel which reveals our inner potential. Being-for-Other reveals things about us that we are unable to realise when Being-for-Self. In it we achieve varying degrees of transcendence from the mundane reality of everyday life.

There is a conflict between this ontological freedom and the structures with which we try and embed, maintain and develop the potentiality of this freedom. We invest resources into making the love process durable, pinning it down, putting constraints on it; trying to maintain the process in a bounded environment. We link the love process to Being-for-Other people who are geographically bounded and of a particular nature (friends, relations, work colleagues). Love has to deal with the constraints of an individualistic society based on *work and business/human capital*; which does not recognise the anarchistic needs of a creative love process. We demand that our lover commits to us, becomes engaged to us, marries us, lives with us; shares our habits and tendencies; plans children with us; invests in household capital with us.

The creative love process setting freedom in motion is in conflict with the process of investing in "real life love capital"; the durable structures of freedom are *often* in conflict with the durable structures of everyday habits, work and association. We try and link the freedom of love into the alienated existence of structured lives in a capitalist society. The freedom of love can never completely actualise in the reality of bodies, geographies and everyday lives because love has the principle of spontaneous generation. Thus the real question arises about the notion of "freedom in structure": how do we maintain some of the creative freedoms of love in society, more particularly a neoliberal "weak society". As Sartre (1956: 478–479) said of this contradiction, "the lover can not be satisfied with that superior form of freedom which is a free and voluntary engagement. ... Thus the lover demands a pledge, yet is irritated by a pledge. He wants to be loved by a freedom but demands that this freedom as freedom should no longer be free. He wishes that the Other's freedom should determine itself to become love ... and at the same time he wants this freedom to be captured by itself, to turn back upon itself, ... so as to will its own captivity."

We thus have a dual contradiction. The original contradiction between the ontological principle of love and the reality of different bodies, Others and stresses of everyday life; and the additional contradiction between love in real *society* and love in neoliberal capitalist *economy*. Being under the influence of these multiple contradictions (in the concrete they multiply), as Sartre alludes to, we are more likely to "awaken" from the transcendence of the love dream into the reality of a life of stresses and strains; gender, class and ethnic divisions; competitive struggles; and other problems in the world of *business*. In some respects, therefore, the love honeymoon that some people awaken from is not the superficial one of passion versus intimacy, but often love freedom versus the alienated reality of everyday life. We may thus keep in mind the romantic ideal of our early months and years together, in contradistinction to the reality of awaking from it and never being able to bring it back. Love in a complex individualistic society is thus unlikely to be holistic or ongoing as people perpetually awaken from their dream as alienated beings existing in real life. Durable transcendence is not often possible under current conditions.

In a closed system love will gradually decline and become subject to less potential, until the energy dissipates entirely. Relevant to the principle of innovation, only when relationships are open in the sense of being subject to continual Agapic-Eros-Storge forces can love be sustained. It needs ongoing negentropic energy as time-dependent novelty (an aspect of 'Freedom'), which is embedded in nurturance, compassion, intelligence and passion. These forms of novelty generate love energy, taking the form of new cooperative experiences, holidays, friends, shared knowledge, trust, and sociality. The combined effects of these processes may sustain and develop a degree of holistic love. Stephen Mitchell (2002) recognises how strong the contradictions are between 'freedom and safety', indicating again how important it is to link commitment and intimacy with passion, freedom and social spread.

Sartre's notion of freedom linked to love, surprisingly, has been almost completely ignored in the vast literature reviewed for this chapter. The only references to his analysis that I came across (while scrutinizing the theoretical and empirical material on love) were a few short papers, such as those by Susan Linich (2001), Chris Stevens (2008) and Christina Smerick (2009). This is perhaps surprising since Sartre's view of love is different and important. Numerous empirical papers make similar points to Sartre, and a number of important books adopt his core thesis without any reference to him. For instance, the interrelated contradictions between security and adventure, passion and friendship, and static versus dynamic lifestyles are the core of Mitchell's (2002) neo-psychoanalytical view of love. Laura Kipnis's (2004) remarkable book about "enforced compliance rather than a free expression of desire" explores similar territory.

12.5 Love Phases Through Path Dependence, Evolution and Instability

We briefly noted earlier in the chapter that love, being of a relational nature, is subject to the effects described by the *principle of path dependence*. The principle of path dependence states that history matters, and that practical factors impinge on relationships which are difficult to abstract from through historical time. Good relationships are not equilibrium processes, but are forever changing and moving forward, being modified and evolving through phases of metamorphoses. Good relationships need to be continually moving, being reformed, and subject to new forces and complexities. While good relationships require Social Spread and Freedom beyond the basic elements of Passion, Intimacy and Commitment, recognising the deficiencies in these core elements in neoliberal economies, and scrutinising the more stunted forms of love, can be a useful exercise for recognising the specific forms of change and evolution experienced in reality.

Path dependence implies that many practical things in a relationship are difficult to erase from its motion. This gives rise to greater complexity, often a richer experience, and ways of learning and transforming. Sometimes these are good and sometimes these have negative effects on the relationship. For instance, something one party does which the other party does not like may lessen the degree to which the second party "loves" the first party. This may include the first party having sex with another, having a bad habit such as snoring, or forgetting a meeting date. Practices such as these are forever negatively impinging on people in relationships, often resulting in relational dissolution.

Path dependence can also have a positive effect, such as a series of enjoyable and enriching experiences together that are never forgotten, and that stimulate durable bonding, intimacy, passion, trust and hence love. This may also include having a good holiday together, good friends for enjoyment, and investing in a property that stimulates bonding and intimacy. Path dependence is really the thing which makes for a richer, loving relationship when it is of a positive nature. When the net balance of positives and negatives is itself positive and growing love is developing and becoming more durable through time.

Path dependence often generates *lock-in relationships*. People regularly have a preference for stability in their lives, for it is from stable relationships that they are able to plan and commit for the future. It is common for people to accept a partner when the first reasonable one comes along. This is especially the case if they are lonely, and also if they are able to "get along well". The desire to reduce uncertainty and thereby enhance lock-in associations, may well contribute to stability, regularity and predictability in certain aspects of life. It also leads to having a stable partner, and reduces the need for continual searching and experimenting with others.

Relational lock-ins can have many quite different consequences. If the choice of the lock-in is a good one, then positive results are likely to follow (Agape, Storge and Eros), at least for a time. But if the lock-in is premature, resulting from bad choices or unanticipated changes, then the relationship may well be negative (Ludic, Manic). Even negative relationships can be hard to break if the parties are addicted to each other, and habits are not easily changed. This can lead to unhappy times, conflict, disagreements, and especially complicated dynamics if children are involved.

Research shows that relationships change through time, and that there are various uncertainties that impact on intimacy. For instance, many relationships within neoliberal economies undergo a series of typical evolutionary changes and instabilities. Figure 12.4 provides a stylised view of some of the major ones. A pre-relationship stage (not shown) is that of being an acquaintance, where people get to know each other and develop knowledge about their 'fit' for each other (White 2005). The honeymoon phase is a common characteristic of many early-phase relationships, especially for Manic and Ludic (and to some degree Eros) lovers. Here sexual intercourse is typically very regular, perhaps every day or two, people often tell each other "I love you", and the physical (Ludic, Manic, Eros) and emotional (Manic, Eros) passion for each other is very strong.

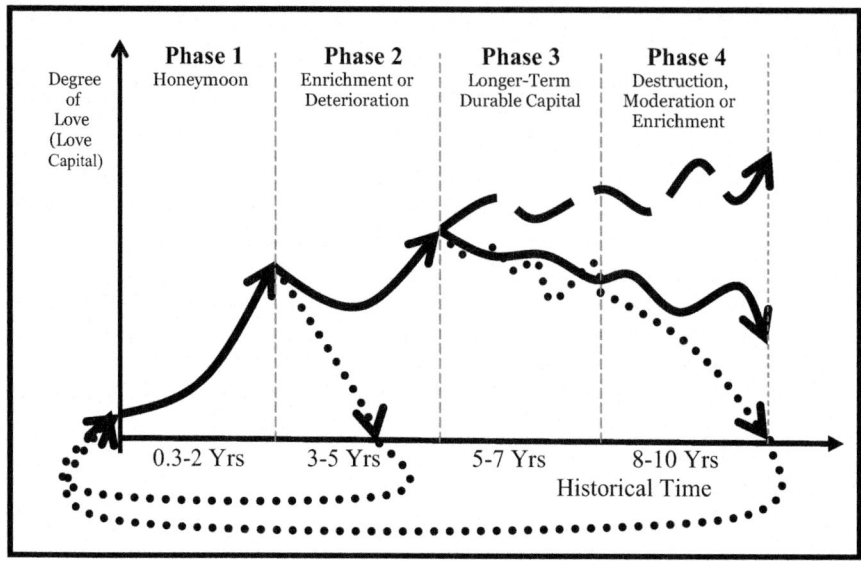

Fig. 12.4 Typical phases of 'love capital' evolution and instabilities within neoliberal economies (esp. USA) (Stylized)

The real test of a relationship is whether people can successfully undergo a positive transition when the "in love" feeling dissipates (although such feelings are unlikely for Ludics), and the bodily chemicals settle down to a more normal experience. It is at this point that most relationships break down, especially Manic and Ludic (and to some degree Eros) ones. Indeed, increasingly in the disembedded economy people go through serial bouts of termination at this stage, especially in youth but often throughout their whole life. In this way, relational instability is a normal part of life for such people; and we call it the *Relationship Instability Hypothesis* (adapting Hyman Minsky's [1986] term to relationships). Terminating relationships in this phase may also be due to incompatible styles or the stress of everyday life. Often it is due to insufficient investment in holistic love, as other activities (such as work) take precedence, or participants having few love skills. All styles have the potential to deteriorate in this phase since love is mostly a trial and error process, and often requires the building of appropriate love skills.

Figure 12.4, llustrates the typical phases of evolution of certain love styles through historical time, after an initial phase of attraction:

If there is more to the relationship than sex or passion, and people have an emotional affinity with each other, things in common, and the experiential process continues somewhat, then Phase 2 (Enrichment or Deterioration) may come into play. This is especially likely for those who manage to variously link Eros, Storge, Agape and possibly an element of Pragma. This is the phase of "developing durable bonding", which, if it lasts beyond a year or two, often leads to 3–5 years of close association. Early on in this phase people often get involved in a de facto situation

12.5 Love Phases Through Path Dependence, Evolution and Instability

and possibly marry. Children regularly emerge on the scene in this phase, and a period of familial development and fulfilment often follow. During this second phase love may evolve; experiential discovery and learning may enhance holistic love. Successful investment in love capital during this phase may be due to compatible styles, a good mix of styles, and the development of appropriate skills.

During Phase 3 (Long-term Durable) a number of possible scenarios emerge in advanced capitalist economies. Firstly, the building of familial and love capital continues to grow, usually where the bringing up of children generates positive forms of reciprocity, Freedom, Passion, trust and sociality. The life process can be enhanced as relative stability and development stimulate new knowledge and experiences. However, often the love and family environment begins to perpetuate mediocre results characterised by conformity and sameness. In this phase, the relationships may continue but at a lower trajectory. Long-term relationships often tend to lack Freedom, Social Spread and innovation due to entrenched habits, pressures of work, marriage, children, and incompatible styles. Entropy may thus settle in to some degree.

Even for those relationships with children which seem to be working well, Shoshana Grossbard and Sankar Mukhopadhyay (2012: 2) present research findings from their studies on the USA (longitudinal data, 1997–2008) that "(a) presence of children is associated with a loss of spousal love; (b) loss of spousal love is associated with loss of overall happiness; but (c) presence of children is not associated with significant loss of overall happiness. If children reduce feelings of being loved by the spouse but do not reduce reported happiness even though spousal love induces happiness, then it must be the case that children contribute to parental happiness by providing other benefits. These other benefits from children could be either material or emotional (what economists have called 'psychic benefits')". This indicates that there may be trade-offs between love and other phenomena (such that overall happiness is not diminished). This is what we found in general, as love may be traded-off for money, safety, stability or any other activity which gives "happiness". But are these "other-forms of happiness" a suitable substitute for love in a neoliberal world that is losing love at an escalating rate; especially if the trade-off is not a specific choice made by people but is primarily inspired by the culture in which they live and are brought up (the neoliberal economic environment)?[4]

Phase 4 (Destruction, Moderation or Enrichment) shows three trajectories: growing love capital, moderate decline, and destruction of the relationship. Some few especially dynamic or loving persons may find their love expanding. Most are not so lucky. Quite a few find satisfaction falling off only modestly as they engage in novelty, freedom, changing styles and so on. Many eventually self-destruct. Here sexual intercourse drops off rapidly, time invested in developing close bonds decline, and often they stay together (for a time) "for the children", eventually realising the failure of their project. As mentioned earlier, a recently growing

---

[4] In this context, could the decline in love from a spouse be balanced by an increase in love for/from the children?

trend, especially in the United States, is serial monogamy with each major relationship lasting about 8–10 years (e.g., see Shawn Haley 2000). Serial relational instability thus often becomes embedded in the process of change in an individualistic society as entropy becomes institutionalised in relationships.

With serial monogamy, one or both partners have new intimate connections, yet they often stay in touch, mainly due to their desire to see the children (if they are present). Their new relationship thus potentially undergoes one or more of the earlier phases, and the family connections become quite complex. For children, if there are any, they now have more time with a main single parent, in between relationships, and through time possibly three (or four) parents, probably much geography to traverse in the process of keeping up with the (other) biological parent (usually the father), and a more complex life. This can be a positive thing for the children as they likely are relieved at the decline in familial conflict (since the separation), and it may set them up to learn how to survive in a complex environment. On the other hand, multiple separations can lead to a difficult environment, likely fewer resources, and more ephemeral linkages to people (O'Hara 2009: ch 9).

The contradictions of relationships in neoliberal economies are also manifest in other ways. Marriage is being deinstitutionalised. Fewer people are marrying, and if they do it is later in life. Divorce rates are more than double what they were in the 1960s. More people are living alone, and in de facto relationships (O'Hara 1995, 2004). As serial monogamy becomes institutionalised, the 'individualized family' is becoming more common. What Elisabeth Beck-Gernsheimi (1998) describes as a 'post-familial family" is in process, where its members have 'individually designed lives', 'lives of their own', lives 'scattered between several different locations', where its members "confront each other as individuals eager to assert their own interests and pursuits, their own wishes and rights" (p. 64), with uncertainty and weaker bonds.

In the current environment of neoliberal capitalist economies, relationships are becoming more complex. Single parent families (especially women) are very prevalent, homosexual and polyamorous relationships are also common in some nations. Even among these relationships, change and periodic instability are the norm as partners try to juggle all of life's challenging roles of partner, parent, worker, capitalist, student, consumer, uncle, aunty, grandparent, friend, and so on. Serial monogamy is more common, especially in the US, not only in and out of marriage, but also in and out of cohabitation; as people put more emphasis on individualised rewards and personal development, rather than group rewards.

Andrew J. Cherlin (2005, 2010) argues that there are now greater numbers of children, in the US at least, having to bear the brunt of serial relationships and marriages, through lives that are more unstable and more uncertain. Changes in economic conditions and greater numbers of single parent families (many being in-between serial marriages) have led to three classes of children: the well-off, the not so well off, and the under-resourced; with the extremes having increased in relative numbers over recent decades. Thus the greater proportion of people having concern for their own individualised preferences, in an economic environment that is more unstable, has led to a decline in love capital in the US, and a lesser potential for children in their adult years also having fulfilling long-term love experiences.

In most neoliberal democracies these different roles have created more challenges and potential instabilities during the 1970s–2020s, through several severe financial crises and deep recessions; and this fact of change and instability is a critical aspect of love and sex in neoliberal society. The GFC and Eurocrises, for instance, the worst systemic crises since World War 2 and the Great Depression (along with the coronacrisis), placed limits on the ability of people to promote holistic love, while necessitating greater love in the uncertain environment (Catherine Hartford 2010). Neoliberal policies and practices have been negatively affecting familial life while at the same time putting extra pressure on households to solve their own problems (Harriet Fraad et al. 1994; David Ciscel and Julia Heath 2001). Love under neoliberal economies tend to undergo several phases of evolution, the social dimension usually fails to emerge, intimacy is inhibited by work, study, unemployment and other pressures, while competition and individual concerns limit the generation of freedom. Current institutional arrangements tend to limit compassion, friendship and intimate connections that would enhance the life experience of people, thus stunting the growth of holistic love.

12.6 Conclusion

We found in this chapter that some of the core principles of IE political economy provide a window through which love can be viewed and critically scrutinised in a neoliberal context. These principles include historical specificity, circular and cumulative causation, heterogeneous groups and agents, contradiction, innovation, uncertainty, hegemony/uneven development and path dependence. Through historical specificity and uneven development we were able to situate love culturally by recognising the forces of individualism and collectivism throughout the world. Using circular and cumulative causation and heterogeneous groups and agents, love styles are linked with core factors and degrees of holistic and other forms of love developed by various people. The styles and core factors were then explained in the light of the contradictions of neoliberalism, including markets versus nurturance, individual versus society, and freedom versus constraint. These contradictions help to explain why love takes the form it does under market systems of capitalism, through high levels of uncertainty, especially undermining nurturance, compassion and intimacy. Path dependence provided insights into the different phases of metamorphosis that relationships take through time. The recent trend towards serial monogamy, through greater levels of uncertainty, putting self above group, and the post-familial family have led to more flexible, ephemeral, and unstable relationships.

Overall, vis-à-vis the principle of innovation, this chapter seeks to contribute towards love being a core area of analysis in political economy. Seeing IEPE as an emerging mutation from the existing schools of thought, this chapter adds weight to the importance of a transdisciplinary field of inquiry that represents more a series of methods and principles than fields of content. Love is perhaps the most important quality of human endeavour, which is often left out of the theoretical, empirical and policy issues that IE political economy investigates. This is a great shame since there is much to offer from a political economy view of the matter. Seeking to incorporate love into the corpus of inquiry enables one to recognise that the costs of taking a crude economic view of social phenomena include not only environment destruction and financial instability but also insufficient nurturance, intimacy and freedom. Love should be a core part of people's lives, but under neoliberal conditions holistic love is unable to develop sufficiently, resulting in stunted personalities and psycho-cultural malaise. Efforts need to be taken to establish love as a core component of IEPE theory, empirics and policy, for otherwise this area of human endeavour will continue to be stunted by the power of the vested interests and the restricted experiences of people as they go about their work, study, leisure and networks of often ephemeral relationships.

Acknowledgements This chapter was presented at the ASE at ASSA meetings in San Francisco, and at a New Political Economy Club meeting. Thanks are especially due to the Fred Jennings, Caitriona Jones, Ian Kerr, Andrew Brennan, Judy Cockburn-Campbell, Wolfram Elsner, Kosta Josifidis, Rob McMaster, Ryan Walter, plus Ron and Jackie Stanfield. It is dedicated to Dr Suzanne Ng. It was published as O'Hara (2014). It came to my attention too late to be included in the analysis of this chapter, but an author has published a book during late 2021, translated and published in English during 2022, in which she explicitly discusses my concept of "love capital", and uses it as the title of her book, as well as investigating my analysis of "holistic love" (see Jennifer Guerra 2022). She then goes further and discusses love ideologies, love under neoliberalism, love and community, and the transformative and even revolutionary potential of love.

References

Austen, Jane. 1813. *Pride and Prejudice*. London: Penguin, 1994.
Bealle, Anne E., and Robert J. Sternberg. 1995. The Social Construction of Love. *Journal of Social and Personal Relationships* 12 (3): 417–438.
Beck-Gernsheim, Elisabeth. 1998. On the Way to a Post-Familial Family: From a Community of Need to Elective Affinities. *Theory, Culture and Society* 15 (3–4): 53–70.
Berger, Sebastein. 2009. *The Foundations of Non-Equilibrium Economics: The Principle of Circular and Cumulative Causation*. London/New York: Routledge.
Boulding, Kenneth. 1969. The Fifth Meaning of Love: Notes on Christian Ethics and Social Policy. *Lutheran World* 16 (3): 219–229.
Cante, Freddy. 2013. Economía Política del Amor. *Cuadernos de Economia* 32 (59): 43–66.
Cherlin, Andrew J. 2005. American Marriage in the Early Twenty-First Century. *The Future of Children* 15 (2): 33–55.
———. 2010. *The Marriage-Go-Around: The State of Marriage and the Family in America Today*. New York: Vintage Books.
Ciscel, David H., and Julia A. Heath. 2001. To Market, to Market: Imperial Capitalism's Destruction of Social Capital and the Family. *Review of Radical Political Economics* 33 (4): 401–414.
Diwan, Romesh. 1982. The Economics of Love: An Attempt at Gandhian Economics. *Journal of Economic Issues* 16 (2): 413–433.
Dymski, Gary A. 2011. Limits of Policy Intervention in a World of Neoliberal Mechanism Designs: Paradoxes of the Global Crisis. *Panoeconomicus* 58 (3): 285–308.

Elliott, Cass. 1969. *It's Getting Better*. Single Record (Also Available in an LP). Written by Barry Mann and Cynthia Weil. Issued as an MP3 Digital audio Recording 11 February 1997. Geffen Records.

Fenney, Judith, and Patricia Noller. 1990. Attachment Style as a Predictor of Adult Romantic Relationships. *Journal of Personality and Social Psychology* 58 (2): 281–291.

Fisher, Helen. 1992. *Anatomy of Love: A Natural History of Mating, Marriage, and Why We Stray*. New York: Fawcett Columbine.

———. 2004. *Why We Love: The Nature and Chemistry of Romantic Love*. New York: Henry Holt & Co.

Folbre, Nancy, and Julie A. Nelson. 2000. For Love or Money—Or Both. *Journal of Economic Perspectives* 14 (4): 123–140.

Forward, Susan, and Craig Buck. 1991. *Obsessive Love*. New York/London: Bantam Books.

Fraad, Harriet, Stephen Resnick, and Richard Wolff. 1994. *Bringing It All Back Home: Class, Gender & Power in the Modern Household*. London/Boulder: Pluto Press.

Frey, Kurt, and Mahzad Hojjat. 1998. Are Love Styles Related to Sexual Styles? *The Journal of Sex Research* 35 (3): 265–271.

Fromm, Erich. 1957. *The Art of Loving*. London/Boston: Allen & Unwin.

Giddens, Anthony. 1992. *The Transformation of Intimacy: Sexuality, Love and Erotism in Modern Societies*. Stanford: Stanford University Press.

Grossbard, Shoshana, and Sankar Mukhopadhyay. 2012. Children, Spousal Love, and Happiness: An Economic Analysis, IZA Discussion Paper 7119. Bonn: IZA. Available Online.

Guerra, Jennifer. 2022. *Love Capital: A Manifesto for Political and Revolutionary Eros*. Milan: Bompiani Publishers. Translated from the Italian by Alice Kilgariff.

Gür, Timur Han, Naci Canpolat, and Hüseyin Özel. 2011. The Crisis and After: There Is No Alternative? *Panoeconomicus* 58 (1): 113–133.

Haley, Shawn. 2000. The Future of the Family in North America. *Futures* 32 (8): 777–781.

Harford, Katherine. 2010. 'When Poverty Flies in the Window, Love Walks Out the Door': Recessionary Times for People Experiencing Poverty. *Irish Journal of Public Policy* 2 (1): 178–184.

Hatfield, Elaine, and Richard L. Rapson. 2005. *Love and Sex: Cross-Cultural Experiences*. Boulder/New York: University Press of America.

Hatkoff, T., and T.E. Lasswell. 1979. Male-Female Similarities and Differences in Conceptualising Love. In *Love and Attraction: An International Conference*, ed. M. Cook and G. Wilson, 221–227. Oxford: Pergamon.

Hendrick, Clyde, and Susan Hendrick. 1991. Dimensions of Love: A Sociobiological Interpretation. *Journal of Social and Clinical Psychology* 10: 206–230.

———. 1992. *Liking, Loving and Relating*. 2nd ed. Monterey: Brooks/Cole Publishing Company.

Hendrick, Clyde, and Susan S. Hendrick. 2006. Styles of Romantic Love. In *The New Psychology of Love*, ed. Robert J. Sternberg and Karin Weis, 149–183. New Haven/London: Yale University Press.

Hendrick, Clyde, Susan S. Hendrick, Franklin H. Foote, and Michelle J. Slapion-Foote. 1984. Do Men and Women Love Differently? *Journal of Social and Personal Relationships* 1 (1): 177–195.

Holmes, John G., and John K. Rempel. 1989. Trust in Close Relationships. In *Clyde Hendrick*, ed. Close Relationships, 187–220. London: Sage.

hooks, bell. [sic.]. 2000. *All About Love: New Visions*. New York: Perennial.

Illouz, Eva. 1997. *Consuming the Romantic Utopia: Love and the Cultural Contradictions of Capitalism*. Berkeley: University of California Press.

———. 2007. *Cold Intimacies: The Making of Emotional Capitalism*. Cambridge: Polity Press.

Jennings, Frederic B., Jr. 2009. *The Economics of Love*, Working Paper. Centre for Ecological Economics and Ethnical Education Ipswitch, MA, USA.

Josifidis, Kosta, Alpar Lošonc, and Novica Supić. 2011. Neoliberalism: Befall or Respite? *Panoeconomicus* 57 (1): 101–117.

Kipnis, Laura. 2004. *Against Love*. New York: Vintage Books.
Kleiser, Randall. 1980. (Director) *The Blue Lagoon*. Sony Pictures. DVD Released 5 October 1999. Writers: Douglas Day Stewart, Henry De Vere Stacpoole. Producers: Randal Kleiser, Richard Franklin. Main Actors: Brooke Shields, Christopher Atkins and Leo McKern.
Lacey, Rachel Saul, Alan Reifman, Jean Pearson Scott, Steven M. Harris, and Jacki Fitzpatrick. 2004. Sexual-Moral Attitudes, Love Styles and Mate Selection. *The Journal of Sex Research* 41 (2): 121–128.
Lee, John Alan. 1973. *The Colors of Love*, 1976. Englewood Cliffs: Prentice-Hall.
———. 1978. *Lovestyles*. London: Abacus.
———. 1988. Love-Styles. In *The Psychology of Love*, ed. Robert J. Sternberg and Michael L. Barnes, 38–67. New Haven/London: Yale University Press.
———. 2000. Appendix 1: Validation Studies by Researchers in 14 Countries, Testing my Theory of Love Styles (Up to 1999). In *Love's Gay Fool*. Autobiography of John Alan Lee. http://www.johnalanlee.ca/contents.html.
Levine, Timothy R., Krystyna Strzyzewski Aune, and Hee Sun Park. 2006. Love Styles and Communication in Relationships: Pertner Preferences, Initiation and Intensification. *Communication Quarterly* 54 (4): 465–486.
Lewis, Clive Staples. 1960. *The Four Loves*. New York: Harcourt, Brace & Co.
Lin, Li-Wen. 2005. Agape Love in Couple Relationships. *Marriage & Family Review* 37 (4): 29–48.
Lindberg, Tod. 2007. *The Political Teachings of Jesus*. New York: HarperCollins.
Linich, Susan. 2001. *Love and freedom*. Philosophy at St. Olaf College. Online.
Losone, Alpar. 2006. Vodeni svet, ili neoliberalizam na probi: da li je voda javno dobro ili privatna svojina? *Panoeconomics* 53 (2): 161–178.
Lyne, Adrian. 1987. (Director) *Fatal Attraction*. Hollywood: Paramount. Writer: James Dearden. Main actors: Michael Douglas and Glenn Close. DVD Version 2002.
Miller, Paul J., and John K. Rempel. 2004. Trust and Partner-Enhancing Attributes in Close Relationships. *Personality and Social Psychology Bulletin* 30 (3): 695–705.
Minsky, Hyman. 1986. *Stabilizing an Unstable Economy*. New Haven: Yale University Press.
Mitchell, Stephen A. 2002. *Can Love Last? The Fate of Romance Over Time*. New York/London: W.W. Norton & Co.
Montgomery, Marilyn, and Gwendolyn T. Sorell. 1997. Differences in Love Attitudes Across Family Life Stages. *Family Relations* 46 (1): 55–61.
Morrow, Gregory D., Eddie M. Clark, and Karia F. Brock. 1995. Individual and Partner Love Styles: Implications for the Quality of Romantic Involvements. *Journal of Social and Personal Relationships* 12 (3): 363–387.
Neibuhr, Reinhold. 1949. *The Nature and Destiny of Man*. New York: Random House.
Nelson, Julie. 2006. *Economics for Humans*. Chicago/London: University of Chicago.
Neto, Felix. 2007. Love Styles: A Cross-Cultural Study of British, Indian, and Portugese College Students. *Journal of Comparative Family Studies* 38 (2): 239–254.
O'Hara, Phillip Anthony. 1995. Household Labour, the Family and Macroinstitutional Instability in the United States: 1940s-1990s. *Review of Social Economy* 53 (1): 89–120.
———. 2001. Contradictions. In *Encyclopedia of Political Economy*, ed. P.A. O'Hara, vol. 1, 140–143. London/New York: Routledge.
———. 2004. A New Family-Community Social Structure of Accumulation for Long Wave Upswing in the United States? *Forum for Social Economics* 34 (2): 51–80.
———. 2009. *Growth and Development in the Global Political Economy: Social Structures of Accumulation and Mode of Regulation*. London/New York: Routledge. Paper Edition.
———. 2012. Principles of Political Economy Applied to Policy and Governance: Disembedded Economy, Contradictions, Circular Cumulation and Uneven Development. *Journal of Economic and Social Policy* 15 (1): 1–38.
———. 2013. Policies and Institutions for Moderating Deep Recessions, Debt Crises and Financial Instabilities. *Panoeconomicus* 60 (1): 19–49.

———. 2014. Political Economy of Love: Nurturance Gap, Disembedded Economy and Freedom Constraints Within Neoliberal Capitalism. *Panoeconomicus* 61 (2): 161–192.

———. 2023. *Long Wave Institutional Dynamics and Political Economy Crises of Capitalism: Principles, Social Structures of Accumulation.* Empirics: Springer.

Pettman, Dominic. 2009. Love in the Time of Tamagotchi. *Theory, Culture and Society* 26 (2–3): 189–208.

Polanyi, Karl. 1944. *The Great Transformation.* Boston: Beacon Press.

Sartre, Jean-Paul. 1956. *Being and Nothingness.* New York: Pocket Books.

Schumpeter, Joseph. 1911. *The Theory of Economic Development.* Oxford: Oxford University Press, 1966.

Sherman, Vincent. 1948. (Director) *Adventures of Don Juan.* Warner Brothers. DVD Released 2008. Story by Herbert Dalmas. Produced by Jerry Wald. Main Actors: Errol Flynn and Viveca Lindfors.

Sherman, Howard J. 1995. *Reinventing Marxism.* Baltimore/London: John Hopkins University Press.

Smerick, Christina. 2009. The Failure of Hate: Love, Hate, and Hope in Jean-Paul Sartre. *Philosophy Today* 53 (4): 386–394.

Stanfield, James Ronald. 1986. *The Economic Thought of Karl Polanyi.* New York: St Martin's Press.

Stanfield, James Ronald, and Jaqueline B. Stanfield. 1997. Where Has Love Gone? Reciprocity, Redistribution, and the Nurturance Gap. *Journal of SocioEconomics* 12 (1): 106–129.

Stein, Howard. 2012. The Neoliberal Policy Paradigm and the Great Recession. *Panoeconomica* 59 (4): 421–440.

Sternberg, Robert J. 1986. A Triangular Theory of Love. *Psychological Review* 93 (2): 119–135.

———. 1987. Liking and Loving: A Comparative Evaluation of Theories. *Psychological Bulletin* 102: 331–345.

———. 1988. *The Triangle of Love: Intimacy, Passion, Commitment.* New York: Basic Books.

———. 1998a. *Love Is a Story: A New Theory of Relationships.* New York/Oxford: Oxford University Press.

———. 1998b. *Cupid's Arrow: The Course of Love Through Time.* Cambridge: Cambridge University Press.

———. 2003. A Duplex Theory of Hate: Development and Application to Terrorism, Massacres, and Genocide. *Review of General Psychology* 7 (3): 299–238.

Sternberg, Robert J., and Michael L. Barnes, eds. 1988. *The Psychology of Love.* New Haven/London: Yale University Press.

Sternberg, Robert J., and Karin Weis. 2006. *The New Psychology of Love.* New Haven/London: Yale University Press.

Stevens, Chris. 2008. Critical Discussion of Sartre on Love. *Stance* 1 (April): 1–7.

Stout, Margaret. 2010. Back to the Future: Toward a Political Economy of Love and Abundance. *Administration and Society* 42 (1): 3–37.

Templeton, John. 1999. *Agape Love: A Tradition Found in Eight Religions.* Philadelphia/London: Templeton Foundation Press.

Thisen, Jean K. 1987. A Theory of Love in the Contemporary World. *International Journal of Social Economics* 14 (12): 31–53.

Vannoy, Russell. 1980. *Sex Without Love: A Philosophical Exploration.* Buffalo: Prometheus Books.

Veblen, Thorstein Bunde. 1914. *The Instinct of Workmanship.* New York: Augustus M. Kelley, 1964.

White, Tony. 2005. *Serial Monogamy.* Available Online.

Conclusion 13

This volume introduces the issue of institutional and evolutionary principles in two chapters, one on the history (Chap. 2), and a second a general view of principles for use in this book (Chap. 3). The purpose of these Chaps. 2 and 3 is to outline the conceptual edifice to lay the groundwork for later chapters on the application of the principles. The main conclusions of Chaps. 2 and 3 are that there is a set of *core general principles* (associated with *core general concepts*), what we call "O'Hara's principles of political economy", including (1) historical specificity and evolution, (2) hegemony and uneven development, (3) heterogeneous groups and agents, (4) circular and cumulative causation, (5) contradiction, (6) uncertainty, (7) innovation, plus (8) policy and governance. There are also an even larger set of institutional and evolutionary *specific concepts* that variously lay under the umbrella of these core general principles/concepts; and the sets (as a whole) could be rearranged with perhaps alternative sets of core principles and concepts under various umbrellas (see Chap. 3 for details).

Relative to the *ensemble* of "O'Hara's core principles" the architecture could be summarised as follows (see Chap. 3). Under the umbrella of the core *principle of historical specificity and evolution* are the more specific concepts (and potential principles) of historical time, realism, culture-institutions-habits-individuals nexus, phases of evolution, social provisioning, blind drift, path dependence and stylized facts.

The second core principle of hegemony and uneven development, includes other concepts/principles such as capitalist world-system, absolute & relative hegemony, hegemonic stability hypothesis, core-periphery-semi/periphery (CPSP), production, commercial & financial (PCF) dominance, international regimes, trust-cooperation-conflict, and hard-soft power.

Under the umbrella of the core general *principle of heterogeneous groups and agents* (inextricably linked to trust) are the more specific concepts/principles of agency-structure, gender, class, ethnicity, age, species, nationality, other agents/

classes, emulation/conspicuous consumption, inequality of income, wealth and power, and enabling myths.

Associated with the core general *principle of circular and cumulative causation* are specific concepts of multifactor approach, circular economy, interdependence, magnification/amplification, emergence, complexity, uneven development, effective demand, economic surplus, and positive (& negative) feedbacks.

Under the heading of the core general *principle of contradiction* (K) are the concepts of power and authority; plus the general contradictions of vested interests vs. common good, instrumental and ceremonial functions, disembedded economy; plus more specific Ks such as capital-labor, finance-industry, state-capital, ecology-capital/consumers, core-periphery, urban-regional, men-women, ethnicity-ethnicity, species-species, and so on.

The *principle of uncertainty* is associated with the specific concepts/principles of the circuit of money capital, prevailing business climate, cycles-waves-crises, recoveries-booms-recessions-depressions, endogenous money-finance, financial instability hypothesis, modern monetary theory (MMT) and tipping points.

The *principle of innovation* is closely associated with the specific concepts of the community's joint stock of knowledge, creative destruction, information-skills-intelligence, products-processes-materials-etc, monopoly-competition, artificial intelligence, overproduction, social innovation, mutation-variation-selection, and intellectual property.

Under the canvas of the core general *principles of policy and governance* are the specific concepts/principles of social provisioning, standard of living, quality of life, participatory democracy, community health, functional finance, social-ecological-community (SEC) governance, agreements-accords-contracts, and climate change mitigation & adaptation.

Depending on one's objective, one can rearrange any hierarchy of general and specific principles and concepts to suit one's focus. The hierarchy just outlined pertains especially to my own ensemble of principles, but one could rearrange it, as well as modify it, to emulate the concerns of other institutional and evolutionary analysts, such as those who emphasise other aspects or ensembles associated with broad areas of gender, innovation, class, effective demand, social provisioning, and so on.

The main point is that these core general concept and principles (plus others where relevant) have been put to the use of critically analysing central problems of the social, political and ecological economy; indeed, this is the main reason why institutional-evolutionary political economy exists. As Mario Bunge (2014) and many others believe, examining core problems of the world necessitates adopting interdisciplinary, multidisciplinary and/or transdisciplinary methods and scope. There is effectively no limit to the scope of political economy in this context, since it can adapt concepts and principles to the core problems in view. This is the case when one wants to, as we have in this book, understand and moderate the core problems of the coronavirus pandemic (Chap. 4), climate change (Chap. 5), corruption (Chap. 6), AI-robotics (Chap. 7), policy and governance (Chap. 8), financial instability and crises (Chap. 9), terrorism and the war on terrorism (Chap. 10), HIV-AIDS (Chap. 11) and the nurturance gap (Chap. 12).

These global problems are the central focus of this volume. We sought not only to study the causes and context within which the problems emerged, but also to moderate the problems now and into the future. All of the concepts/principles can be useful in this context, but especially the core general principles of innovation and policy-governance and their umbrella concepts/principles.

The question then arises: where to from here? There are two main avenues available to us. The first lies within the international scholarly community. This being the first volume of *specific* institutional and evolutionary concepts/principles and problems, it will require critical analysis and enhancement in the scholarly journals, further books, teaching and policy-making. The book will thus need to be reviewed extensively in the journals, where it should also be improved upon, extended and modified. I look forward to seeing such work in motion.

The second avenue is through further volumes of books where institutional and evolutionary concepts and principles are developed and extended, through this book (second edition; and related volumes by others), and further volumes, with a view to analysing other issues and world problems. Two such volumes are in process at the moment. The second volume on institutional and evolutionary principles and concepts will be published soon, entitled, *Long Wave Institutional Dynamics and Political Economy Crises of Capitalism: Principles, Social Structures of Accumulation, and Empirics* (O'Hara 2023).

In this volume I deepen the application of the concept/principle of historical specificity and evolution by scrutinizing wave-like dynamics and crises of capitalism from the 1780s to the present, with special reference given to details on the 1940–2020s and 1980–2020s periods. We then study the four greatest global socioeconomic crises since the second-world-war: namely, the recent geo-political conflicts in Eastern Europe and elsewhere; the GFC and related Eurodebt crises of 2008–2013ff; the coronavirus pandemic crisis of 2020–2022ff; and the climate crisis (cascading tipping points); including policy issues to reduce the severity of such crises into the future. We also deepen our understanding of social structures of accumulation (SSAs) underlying crises for China and the USA. We finalise the book by comparing the contradictions of China and the USA during 1980–2022 affecting long waves and SSAs, and the outlook for these two nations as they battle with each other for hegemony into the immediate future.

The third such volume of principles and concepts applied to current global problems is ongoing and will emerge later. Its title is *Advances in Political Economy Principles: Applied to Current World Problems* (O'Hara Forthcoming). This volume has full-length chapters on core general concepts and principles, including historical specificity, heterogeneous groups and agents, circular and cumulative causation (linked to complexity and emergence), contradiction, uneven development and hegemony, economic surplus and effective demand, uncertainty, innovation, and policy. Within the context of these general principles we encapsulate other concepts, such as power, habits and institutions, instrumental and ceremonial functions, social provisioning, plus others. This list may be modified according to the world problems

I investigate, constructive analysis in the literature, and my own innovations relating to problems and principles.

Then this third volume includes full-length specific chapters on core general problems of the world, including a global survey of the state of the world in historical context, to situate such problems; population settlement on other planets and (inter-)galactic travel; global and regional inequality and uneven development; business cycles and financial crises, AI and humanoid robotics (e.g., memory), innovation and development; global trust, sociality and community; policy and governance; crime and injustice; plus chapters on a number of global crises in the near-future.

After this volume is complete I will be finalising a related project of mine on *A Global History of the World*, where the principles are integrated into a story of the emergence and evolution of life on Earth and other planets.

I look forward to an energetic response to this first volume, and the second emerging soon, so that I can learn more from others and move forward conceptually and empirically to scrutinize principles and applications. In this way we can improve our comprehension of how to moderate core problems of the world and see this understanding being put into practice to enhance the quality of life and social provisioning for all life forms on planet Earth and beyond, and thereby enhancing the efficacy of political economy.

References

Bunge, Mario. 2014. *Memoirs of a Philosopher-Scientist*. Springer.
O'Hara, Phillip Anthony. 2023. *Long Wave Institutional Dynamics and Economic Crises of Capitalism: Principles, Social Structures of Accumulation, Empirics*. Springer.
———. Forthcoming. *Advances in Political Economy Principles: Applied to Current World Problems*.

Correction to: Principles of Institutional and Evolutionary Political Economy

Phillip Anthony O'Hara

Correction to: P. A. O'Hara, *Principles of Institutional and Evolutionary Political Economy*, Springer Texts in Business and Economics, https://doi.org/10.1007/978-981-19-4158-0

This book was inadvertently published with the following incorrect information:

In the About the Author section on page XV, the expansion for the abbreviation GPERU was incorrectly published as Global Political Economy Political Economy. This has been corrected to "Global Political Economy Research Unit."

In Chapter 1, page 4, the word "laws" was incorrect in the sentence "These three 'laws', what we may call 'Kerr's laws of concepts and principles', have been incorporated into the concepts/principles in this chapter and the book as a whole."

It has been corrected as follows:

"These three 'rules', what we may call 'Kerr's rules of concepts and principles', have been incorporated into the concepts/principles in this chapter and the book as a whole."

On page 5, the citation to Fig 3.1 was incorrect, it has been corrected to Table 3.1.

On page 9, the text "(Acknowledgements for each chapter are included as the first footnote to the respective chapters.)" was incorrect. This has been corrected as follows:

"(Acknowledgements for each chapter are included as a note just before the "References" section.)"

The updated version of the book can be found at
https://doi.org/10.1007/978-981-19-4158-0

© The Author(s), under exclusive license to Springer Nature Singapore Pte Ltd. 2023
P. A. O'Hara, *Principles of Institutional and Evolutionary Political Economy*, Springer Texts in Business and Economics,
https://doi.org/10.1007/978-981-19-4158-0_14

In Chapter 2, page 32, the sentence "And the third is a the concept of the irrational system..." has been updated as follows:

"And the third is the concept of the irrational system, where B&S argue that utilising the surplus involves much waste, militarism and useless commodities-services that question the legitimacy of capitalist dynamics."

On page 36, the sentence "New institutionalists tend to emphasise exogenous preferences rather endogenous preferences a la Veblenians." was incorrect and has been corrected as follows:

"New institutionalists tend to emphasise exogenous preferences rather than endogenous preferences a la Veblenians."

In Chapter 3, page 86, the reference "————. 2023. Long Wave Institutional Dynamics and Political Economy Crises of Capitalism: Principles, Social Structures of Accumulation. Empirics: Springer.", has been corrected as follows:

"————. 2023. Long Wave Institutional Dynamics and Political Economy Crises of Capitalism: Principles, Social Structures of Accumulation. Empirics. Singapore: Springer."

In Chapter 9, page 303, the additional "B" reference "Mattingly, Eric Shaunn, and Trayan Kushev. 2017. Most New Businesses Fail, Bbut Mine Won't...Right? Journal of Entrepreneurship 25 (1): 70–88.", was incorrect and has been corrected as "Mattingly, Eric Shaunn, and Trayan Kushev. 2017. Most New Businesses Fail, but Mine Won't...Right? Journal of Entrepreneurship 25 (1): 70–88."

In Glossary, page 406, the sentence "The first is that the whole is greater than the parts ('emergence'), and hence the whole is magnified, novel, different, from the parts.", has been corrected as follows:

"The first is that the whole is greater than the sum of the parts ('emergence'), and hence the whole is magnified, novel, different, from the parts."

On page 408, the number "five" mentioned in the sentence "The literature on love involves..." was incorrect and has been updated as six.

The correct sentence is "The literature on love involves various combinations of six styles of love and five core processes."

On page 431, the term "principle of innovation" in the index has been removed.

Glossary

This glossary is not intended to be exhaustive, simply indicative of some terms relevant to institutional and evolutionary political economy (IEPE) and certain world problems. For more detail on many of the political economy concepts, principles and terms mentioned here see the *Encyclopedia of Political Economy,* edited by P.A. O'Hara (Routledge, 1999; 2 vols; paper edition 2001; Chinese Translation 2010). These terms are often written from the point of view of "understanding and solving world problems", the subject-matter of this book.

9/11 On 11 September 2001, four planes were hijacked in the United States, with the plan to hit hi-profile building/person-icons of US trade, finance, government and defence. Two of the planes hit the twin towers of the World Trade Centre, at the time the tallest building(s) in the world, near Wall Street, New York, and the building(s) collapsed. A third plane hit a wing of the Pentagon, US military headquarters, near Washington DC; and a fourth hit a field in the countryside after passengers intervened and stopped a likely plot to hit the White House or other icons in Washington DC. Direct casualties were about 3000 deaths, plus around 25,000 injured. Of the 19 hijackers 15 were from Saudi Arabia. The Al Qaeda terrorist network was responsible for the attacks. The attacks contributed to the depth of the 2001 recession in the US, and led to the invasion of Afghanistan and Iraq by US-supported allies. "9/11" is certainly one of the most significant events of the twenty-first century, due to the factors leading to it, the nature of it, and the impact on the world. It will likely lay claim to being associated with one of the most defining issues of world history [See Chap. 10].

Age Age is a concept that refers to how old one is, and indirectly relates to how one looks, one's closeness to death, and also usually how healthy one is likely to be. In the social economy, age is very important, since in most societies age has certain privileges and some disadvantages. People are often treated differently depending upon whether they are looked on as a child, an adolescent, or an adult; and also whether one is young, middle aged or old. Generally, depending on the society, people usually more easily get certain diseases if they are very young or very old.

The coronavirus, however, tended to afflict the aged much more severely (although some variants differ from this somewhat). The human population of planet Earth is getting older, not just in the core but also much elsewhere, which is likely increasing the saving rate of most nations and regions [See esp. Chap. 4].

Al Qaeda The name Al Qaeda was originally a general reference to Bin Laden's "base camp" in Afghanistan, and was not a specific organisation. Bin Laden himself re-stated this numerous times that Al Qaeda was a general concept or base from which he and his fellow Islamic *jihadis* conducted strategic operations, initially against the Soviets and also against the US and its allies. From such a concept or base it has magnified its significance many times in a CCC fashion. The general concept has become a reference from which it has often generated self-styled movements throughout the whole world, who claim to be affiliated to the concept or the movement, and in this sense it can be considered a network of Salafi-jihadi Islamists, under the influence of Sayyid Qutb (1906–1966), a member of the Muslim Brotherhood who critiqued western egoistic individualism, its alienating culture, superficial interactions and support for Israel. Those who subscribe to Al Qaeda doctrine are Sunni Muslims who wish to return to the traditions of the first generation of believers around the life and teachings of the Prophet Muhammad, including subscribing to the *Koran* (core religious text of Islam), the *Sunnah* (practices and traditions of Muhammad), and *Ijmā* (a type of Islamic Law). Politically Al Qaeda is committed to the global destruction of foreign and particularly Western influences on Islamic countries. This is in contrast to Islamic State's (IS, ISIS) emphasis on the region, especially Iraq, Syria and related areas; and also Al Qaeda objected to the sectarian violence and what they considered to be the 'gruesome extremes' of Islamic State [See Chap. 10].

Artificial Intelligence (AI) Schools: Old and New The old school of AI, also known as the information processing school (e.g., Herbert Simon, Allen Newell), sought to develop artificial intelligence (AI) through computational methods, symbols, heuristics, and information processing. It also uses an input → (processor) → output method of analysis, a hierarchical control system, and treats memory as a storehouse concept. It anticipated developing AI to the level of human beings by 1985, but failed. It is still very active, especially in developing weak AI (expert systems). The new school of AI, also known as the embodied-cognition approach (e.g., Rodney Brooks, Rolf Pfeifer), believes that intelligence is about moving and acting in the real world, engaging in communication and responding to challenges as they come. Hence it is necessarily embodied in its approach: moving and communicating are necessary parts of its model of intelligence. It uses the principles of emergence (the whole is greater than the parts, intelligence can arise unexpectedly from an array of interactions), complete agents (body and mind), overlapping functions (several components that generate similar/alternative functions), sensory-motor coordination, and decentralised components (many onboard the robots). Several analysts believe linking the two schools to be the way of the future, but others prefer the new school, but are willing to utilise the computational approach for expert systems embedded in bodies and brains, using the embodiment architecture. The new school also includes neuroroboticists such as Nobel Laureate Gerald Edelman and Jeffrey Krichmar, who have been inculcating neurological authenticity into the literature and also into robotic design [See Chap. 7].

Artificial General Intelligence (AGI) AGI is also known as 'strong AI', and seeks to emulate the intelligence of human beings. The information processing approach to AI (e.g., Herbert Simon, Allen Newell) seeks to emulate human activities through either strong or weak AI, whereas the embodied intelligence school (e.g., Rodney Brooks, Rolf Pfeifer) seeks to emulate regular animal behaviour, whether it be human or other (insect, etc) animals. Members of the information processing approach thought in the 1950s that they could successfully emulate human behavior within a generation. The reason they failed, according to the embodied approach, is that general intelligence has to do with dealing with real world processes and adapting to changing ecosystems through historical time. In other words, they argue it is not sufficient to have a brain, but that AGI must necessarily be embodied in the sense that there has to be movement and social interaction, which means having some form of locomotion and ability to communicate with others. There are several tests of AGI, such as the Turing Test, where a machine and a human are performing unseen in a room, while a person(s) in the other room must conclude that the computer is a human (to pass the test) [Chap. 7].

Autonomous Humanoid Robotics (AHR) AHR is a research area committed to developing robots that are fully autonomous in functioning, in the sense of being able to move, communicate and undertake various tasks in the ecological environment. Historically the research area started with non-human agents, such as artificial insects, but the area was always generally committed to extending that to artificial human functioning as advances were made. Some AHRs look like humans but cannot engage in much cognitive thinking, but may be useful for working, e.g., in a warehouse storage and package facility (like Agility Robotics' 'Digit') or providing routine functions in the home (like 'Walker' from UBTECH Robotics). But serious AHR researchers seek to develop humanoid robots that can interact meaningfully with other humans, perhaps in an age care facility, educational institution or as a customer service representative (such as Sophia, who can talk, walk, draw, sing and express feelings) [Chap. 7].

Bribery Bribery is a form of corruption in which an agent or group pays or claims monies to influence decisions and distort due processes. These bribes may be hidden by calling them success fees, donations, commissions or prices for goods or services. Bribery is institutionalised into many corporate and government activities in numerous nations. Sometimes it takes the form of grand corruption when a Head of State demands millions of dollars for mineral rights to important resources, and at other times it takes the form of petty corruption when public officers demand some extra percent payment for entry into a restricted area or for a license. It is common in all nations when a party in power allocates grants mainly in their (marginal?) electorates to bribe voters to favour them in elections [Chap. 6].

Capitalism Capitalism is a socioeconomic system where the means of production, distribution and exchange are owned or controlled privately or through shareholdings, and where the inner motion generates new products, processes, markets, raw materials and skills that are forever upsetting the prevailing structures of humanity and ecology (creative destruction). Most of the productive work is undertaken by workers and also the middle class, although managers and others do often coordinate the work and value-chain processes. Capitalism is forever changing, with new products, processes, markets, materials, resources and forms of competition on a global scale. Periodically the changes are so great as to constitute a qualitatively evolution to a new phase of metamorphosis. Hence phases of evolution, from mercantilism to industrial capitalism and onto imperialism, the Keynesian-welfare state, neoliberalism and beyond; and also through numerous varieties of capitalism, such as neoliberal capitalism, state capitalism, embedded capitalism, authoritarian capitalism, and so forth. State capitalism is where the dominant means of production, distribution and exchange are owned or controlled by governments, but where the basic processes of creative destruction are undergone nevertheless [All chapters].

Circuit of Social Capital The Circuit of Social Capital (CSC) is a model developed by Karl Marx in volume two of *Capital* (the sphere of circulation), whereby the money (M) invested (exchanged) by capitalists into 'commodities' (C), such as labor power (LP) and means of production (MOP) (M↔C), is then followed by the hidden abode of production (...P...), leading to the generation of output (C+c) in the form of commodities (including services) with a potential value greater (c) than that originally invested (M, C). This extra value is called surplus product (or service). Then the Keynesian problem of effective demand needs to be put into practice so that the potential value (surplus product, c) can be transformed into an actual surplus (s), in the form of surplus value ([C+c]↔[M+s]), which is represented as m or in this case 's'. In this case the commodity value (C+c) is exchanged (↔) for M+s. The 's' may be smaller or equal to 'c' after the effective demand phase of the circuit. The 's', surplus value, can then be called (net) profit, p, also paying bank fees (i = interest), shareholders (d=dividends) and monies to owners of property (r=rent): $s = p+i+d+r$. Hence : CSC = M ↔ C(LP, MOP)...P...[C + c] ↔ [M + s] ∥ $s = p + i + d + r$∥.

Then the process of reinvestment can be activated, where part of the profit (p', retained earnings, reinvested), plus possibly bank credit (bc) and monies from issuing new shares or equity [e] is invested into the circuit of money capital, viz.: $p' + bc + e$ → $M' ↔ C'(LP, MOP)...P'...[C' + c] ↔ [M' + s]$: Then the circular process can be set in motion to a new higher (or lower) level, through repeated circuitries. There can be interruptions to the circuit at any point which usually lead to crises if they are major. Taxes and government spending, as well as monetary policy, may be included in the circuit. In devising the CSC Marx was influenced by the physiocrats and especially the *Economic Tableau*. Essentially the CSC is a circular flow-stock diagram illustrating the major transactions/interactions of the process whereby the investments of capitalists are potentially able to eventually make a profit. In a wider schema the CSC can be transformed into the *Systemic Circuit of*

Social Capital (SCSC) which includes the ecological, environmental, social and political processes linked to the CSC; there is also an international circuit of social capital [Chaps. 5 and 9].

Circular and Cumulative Causation (CCC) CCC is a concept in political economy, drawing especially from Gunnar Myrdal and Nicholas Kaldor, comprising two main movements. The first involves interdependency. Political economy involves processes that are intertwined. Problems tend to be caused by multiple factors that interrelate (multifactor approach). The second involves magnification. When problems and processes involve multiple factors that interrelate they tend to produce an accelerating impact. This involves positive feedback between multiple variables. Gunnar Myrdal, for instance, examined the interrelated factors that cause poverty on the one hand and riches on the other. Differential skills, (un)employment, (un)-education, and remuneration, as well as discrimination, produce differential outcomes. He suggested, for instance, more extensive, accessible and free education to help moderate the differential and increase the outcomes for the disadvantaged. Nicholas Kaldor examined CCC from the point of view of regions and productivities. Aggregate demand tends to provide the source of funds for investment and consumption, and with economies of scale and innovation these funds can generate high productivity, which in turn may expand exports, and thereby world income. But areas with low levels of aggregate demand, low economies, and modest productivity tend to be relatively worse off. These differentials can thus become exacerbated. The principle of CCC states that one needs to apply the method of CCC to comprehend socioeconomic problems and processes. CCC usually involves emergence and complexity. (One also may need to take into account backward (negative-feedback) effects) [Every chapter of this book deals with CCC].

Circular Flow Model (CFM) & Circular Stock-Flow Model (CSFM) The circular flow model (CFM) is perhaps the most powerful tool in political economy, but more so when we extend the model and include stocks as well (particularly institutions). A major inspiration for the model was the "blood-flow" analysis of William Harvey. The CFM was developed variously by Richard Cantillon, François Quesnay, Karl Marx, J.M. Keynes, Richard Stone and others to analyze the circular movement of financial, physical and service activities that contribute to political economic dynamics. In this one can use between 2 and 6 sector models. An expansive model uses (1) households, (2) business, (3) finance/banking, (4) state, (5) world economy, and (6) ecology/environment. The circular economy model comes to life more when also including stocks, and especially dynamic structures of institutions. Thus when we include the physico-historical institutions of the household, business, finance, state, world economy, and ecology/environment we can analyze the evolution of the institutions/organizations, along with the flow of resources, services and labor, as well as the stock of inventories, money, savings, knowledge, routines, governance measures, habits and conventions [Chaps. 3, 5 and 9].

Class Class is a concept that relates to the socioeconomic position of people in society; where they stand compared with others. It is in this sense an invidious distinction, but it also does often relate to 'real' standing, while often it links to perceived standing. There are different theories of class. One theory depends upon the class position of people vis-à-vis income and/or wealth; here there are upper, lower and middle classes. Another relates to people's position vis-à-vis their relationship to surplus value production, distribution and exchange. In this context people may be a member of the working class, the capitalist class, or the subsumed class necessary for the others to reproduce. In this context, people can undertake different class roles. Class can also be conceived as one relating to property control/ ownership, such as the means of production; or power, how much power one wields in multifarious ways. Often to solve a world problem one needs to examine classes, genders, ethnicities, species, intelligent machines and other heterogeneous roles played in world/regional/national/subnational processes [Most chapters of this book deal with 'class'].

Community's Joint Stock of Knowledge [CJSK] The concept of the CJSK is a communitarian perspective of the origins of property, knowledge and wealth, that places emphasis on the collective generation process. In contemporary social economies wealth and property are seen as produced in unison, by various individuals within groups, institutions and organisations. But the perspective goes further than this by indicating that knowledge is a social process, residing in the general dynamic processual stock of brains, journals, books, cultures, practices and institutions in motion throughout the community. Even in capitalist political economies it is argued that wealth and property is generated primarily by the cultural transmission of skills, techniques, appliances, knowledge, practices, designs and plans of a multitude of actors, groups, institutions, nations and world processes. But the community's joint stock of knowledge can be encapsulated by certain vested interests through numerous networks of control, institutions, patents, takeovers, legal challenges, monopoly powers, and classes. The principle of the CJSK states that one should recognise this collective social wealth and study its ongoing generation, as it can be a useful source for alleviating global problems. Since knowledge, property and wealth are collectively generated it should be fairly evenly distributed throughout the community not only as income, but also as a source of collective investment into public goods such as education, health, infrastructure, public policy initiatives, ecological sustainability and climate change mitigation and adaptation [Elements of this concept permeate every chapter].

Complexity The principle of complexity states that one needs to situate the problems of the world in their historical, relational, and situational context to comprehend how they emerged and how we may reduce their impact. The temporal (historical) emergence of problems needs to be understood. The relational networks and interdependencies associated with the horizontal emergence of the problems need to be scrutinized. And the way in which the vertical emergence of the problems as they link individuals with groups and institutions, as well as nations and the whole world, need to be comprehended. This involves concepts such as path dependence, lock-in, non-equilibrium, uncertainty, evolutionary metamorphosis and blind drift. Only on the basis of examining the contradictory circular and cumulative nature of the behaviour of heterogeneous groups and agents through an uncertain and evolutionary path of emergence can innovations potentially be enacted to tackle these complex world problems [Every chapter deals with elements of this].

Concept A concept in political economy is an idea, based around a realistic process/thought, which seeks to comprehend the process/thought in more detail. For instance, the concept of historical specificity states that historical time, phases of evolution, social provisioning and transformational processes are important in the generation/resolution of world problems; while the principle of historical specificity states that one must be cognizant of these historical changes and processes in understanding as well as in ameliorating the intensity of world problems. The concept of heterogeneous agents and groups states that world problems involve different agents and groups often in different ways, both in the generation of the problem and the myriad of potential forms of resolution; while the principle of heterogeneous agents and groups states that one must be cognizant of these agents and groups in the process of both understanding and trying to ameliorate the world problem [Every chapter of this book deals with concepts; see Chap. 1 for details].

Contradiction The concept of contradiction is the idea that everything exists in a potential conflict, trade-off, opposition, dichotomy and so on, with other things, that operates at all levels of the political economy, including practices of groups and agents, as well as theories, concepts and principles. These contradictions are important to analyse because they usually majorly impact on the problems and processes investigated. Some of the dominant contradictions include that between (a) the vested interests versus the common good, (b) the instrumental and ceremonial functions of institutions, (c) the disembedded economy and the double movement, (d) plus the usual oppositions between capital and labor; industry and finance; monopoly and competition; state and capital; urban and regional; nation/region versus nation/region; capital/consumption and the environment; men and women (gender); ethnic group versus ethnic group; consumers versus producers/advertisers; industrial capitalists versus money capitalists; innovators versus existing routine-makers; and so on. The principle of contradiction states one should analyse the contradictions associated with a problem or a process in order to comprehend its complex workings, including for innovation and policy purposes to ameliorate the problem [All chapters].

Coronacrisis The coronacrisis is a global health and socioeconomic crisis involving a viral infection that started in China during late 2019 and spread throughout the whole world during 2020, thus becoming a Pandemic in the sense of having widespread infections and deaths around the globe. There have been numerous variants and subtypes of the SARS-Cov-2 virus during 2019–2022 that have been of concern which has led to Coronavirus disease 2019 (Covid-19), as it is called, undergoing various waves of several hundred million infections and so far more than 20 million "excess-deaths" throughout the world. Governance health principles put in place to limit the spread of the disease have been variable from region to region, including personal protective measures (e.g., masks), case and contact tracing, social distancing, isolation and management, vaccines, a degree of international collaboration, lockdowns, etc. Political economy innovation and governance measures to ameliorate the anomaly have included functional finance and private innovation/investment to generate and distribute vaccines, public health infrastructures, informational communication, discretionary fiscal and monetary policies, and public health principles put into action [Esp. Chap. 4].

Corruption Corruption is the abuse of power by the vested interests to exploit the common wealth to the detriment of the community. Usually the dominant vested interests include agents who have more power than other classes, and this provides them with various roles to expropriate wealth or other benefits without much violence or other heavy-handed approaches. The roles of those involved in grand corruption include chief financial officers, CEOs, members of parliament, Presidents, members of the board of directors, legal experts, judges, Secretaries of companies, and so on. Through use of these roles they are able to engage in corrupt acts such as nepotism, state capture, fraud, extortion, bribery and embezzlement. Often they think these are not unjust acts on their part, but that they deserve the benefits because of their important role in the system. Examples of corruption include activities of tax havens; money laundering; bribes to officials; nepotism to provide university places and other benefits for their children; in-house benefits of many organisations; and mores enabling them to gain corrupt benefits without undue pressure. In response to these obvious (to others) abuses of power, other classes and groups often seek to engage in petty corruption to obtain lower-level gains through similar means, or through pressure and even threats, since they have less power and have to often be more aggressive, or assertive, in order to gain these lesser benefits. Both groups can often multiply to form cartels and criminal groups, where the activities are still corrupt, but even more illegal involving killings and abductions, etc. [Chap. 6].

Crises A crisis is a turning point for the worse for an area or sector of a political economy. During a crisis uncertainty rises, trust declines, and asset prices usually start to fall. There are several types of crises. The first is associated with a business cycle peak when boom turns to recession, speculative bubbles usually burst, and exuberance turns to panic. These are typical of the recessions in many nations during 1974–75, 1980–82, 1990–92, 1997–98, 2000–2001, 2008–2009ff, and 2021. The second type of crisis is a financial crisis, which is usually closely linked with business cycles, but may appear before or during recessions. For instance, the stock market collapse of 1987 was not directly linked to the recession of 1990–92 in many nations. Usually a financial crisis occurs once the upper turning point of the business cycle has been reached, and it has already turned into recession. In other words, it is caused by the business cycle recession, and recedes once lender of last resort and associated policies provide liquidity to the system. There are many other types of crises, such as crises of legitimacy, governance, climate, finance, distrust, as well as those caused by wars and pandemics [Chaps. 4, 5, 9, 10, 11 and 12].

Cytokine Storm (CS) A CS is a hyper-inflammatory series of processes that produce major disease in humans, and which generates a typical circular and cumulative type of causation (CCC) linked to, e.g., COVID-19. Most of those in intensive care for COVID-19 and those who die of SARS-Cov-2 have been suffering from a cytokine storm. The CS is a typical out-of-control, non-equilibrium, magnified, exaggerated response of the body to an invading microorganism, drug or other substance. The CS can be triggered by chronic disease (e.g., diabetes), environmental risk factors (such as smoking), SARS-Cov-2 specific factors (e.g., higher levels of cytokines), and old age (e.g., additional inflammatory cytokines). Inflammation is a normal process of reaction to infection, but under CS it becomes hyper-activated and itself causes disease [Chap. 4].

Economic Surplus The roots of the concept of the economic surplus go back to the classical economists and Marx. In modern times, it was specifically resurrected by Paul Baran as a term by which to analyse development and underdevelopment (potential and actual). An economic surplus is defined in numerous ways, but usually it is thought of as net income over costs (Y-C). It can be examined from the point of view of society as a whole, general capital, and individual capital. It is usually a macroeconomic term, so this net income is for the whole economy, or at least a sector. Sometimes it is defined for the whole political economy as income minus necessary social costs (Y-NSC), or actual or necessary consumption (Y-Con). It is actually a rather flexible term that can be modified according to one's concern. If one defines it as the net output/income of society minus the historically necessary costs of living (consumption) $(Y_n - C_h)$, then the surplus can be viewed as a fund for social change, or discretionary income of society. Viewed in this way, depending on how the political economy is structured, people could vote on how to use the surplus by, for instance, investing specific proportions into health, education, technology, ecological projects, housing, pensions, national parks, and so on. There is also the notion of potential economic surplus, or what it could be under specified ideal conditions [Various chapters].

Embezzlement Embezzlement is a form of corruption associated with the "taking or conversion of money, property or other valuables for personal benefit...by someone to whom it has been entrusted" (Vargas-Hernandez 2010: 273; see Chap. 6 References). For instance, an accountant embezzles money with support of auditing company agent, by siphoning for themselves wages of fictitious employees. Or a departmental head redirects money earmarked to certain public amenities to her bank account through the use of fraudulent accounting practices [Chap. 6].

Emergence Emergence is a concept that refers to features that make certain entities different or novel from others that they may be closely related to. For instance, at the very micro level human beings exist as individuals, yet when they cooperate together they generate a reality quite different from the reality of the individual. In this sense we have the emergence of cooperation and group practices. Also, individual groups have certain characteristics, but when they cooperate with other groups, they, again, can generate a reality of practices that are emergent or novel. And when these different groups within nations cooperate with other groups in other nations, they often generate practices that are more novel still than the macro outcomes. In the near future, different groups from different planets or galaxies may cooperate in such a way that they generate even newer, novel arrangements and practices. Generally one refers to horizontal, vertical and temporal emergence. Horizontal refers to the linking of entities at the same level; vertical to entities at different levels; and temporal processes at differing levels of time or durability. Emergence is important to political economy especially because it helps to provide a realistic ontology as to how the world and its problems emerge and operate, as well as to how to ameliorate these anomalies. Emergence is inextricably related to complexity and CCC [All chapters deal with this to varying degrees].

Emulation and Conspicuous Consumption These concepts emanate from Thorstein Veblen, who in *The Theory of the Leisure Class* (1899) set out to constructively critique the society in which he lived. Most societies have a powerful leisure class with lots of wealth from business or inheritance, usually educated at ivy-league universities, and characteristically living or searching for a trophy wife/ husband to display. The leisure class have advantages not provided to underlings of the class system, since they can engage in conspicuous consumption on large properties, famous-make cars, extravagant dinner parties, elegant garb, and sophisticated etiquette. Lower classes emulate them by buying items outside their income range, thus increasing their propensity to consume to greater than average levels. Members of society under emulative pressure often become unhappy when it fails to impress; or they fail to succeed in the conspicuous consumption and emulation game; or when people realize how destructive and wasteful the whole game can be. This can lead to alcoholism, junk food, bad sleep, depression, suicide and ailments such as heart disease and diabetes. But when they realise how wasteful the whole thing is it may lead to greater quality of life. Periodically there are movements against such social anomalies as emulation and conspicuous consumption, which attempt to promote progressive change and better lifestyles. The double movement of following the habits and institutions of the privileged and challenging it to promote better institutions continues throughout history. Institutional and evolutionary science is part of this double movement.

Ethnicity The concept of ethnicity refers to a shared set of characteristics that usually unites people together as part of a culture. For instance, a tribe may operate together as a group, eating, living, hunting and cooking together. A group of people living in a nation may have elements of togetherness and feel as one group. A group of people who have similar looks may cooperate together, intermarry and eat together. These cultural traits of tradition, nation, interbreeding, looks and customs are what makes (or breaks) ethnic groups. This concept is important for political economy because one's ethnicity often has ramifications for one's standard of living. Some ethnic groups are discriminated against, others may be disadvantaged, and some may have surmounted discrimination and developed much cultural and economic capital. Others may live in specific areas which imposes climatic costs or benefits. Some ethnic groups are more subject to certain diseases than others. Ethnicity can be used to promote contradictions, such as inter-ethnic conflict, divide and rule tactics, ethnic hate groups such as the Ku-Klux Klan (KKK), Nazi Parties, and ethno-nationalist extremist governments. Religious similarities and differences can be a factor promoting cooperation and conflict. For instance, some terrorist groups are religious fundamentalists wanting to return to the practices of an earlier age when perceived norms were seen as pure, and who see contemporary Western society (especially) as corrupt, immoral and decadent (e.g., Al Qaeda, the Taliban, IS) [Chaps. 3, 4, 10 and 12].

Eurodebt Crisis The Eurodebt crisis hit numerous nations of Europe during and after the Global Financial Crisis (GFC), especially Greece, Italy, Spain and Portugal (GISP), part of what is (or was) often called the periphery of the EU (or the 'South'). It hit these nations because the GFC exposed several key anomalies both in the structural workings of the EU and the differential trends of southern and northern EU states. The GFC impacted since the South increased debt, and when problems hit the EU they could not devalue their currency (since they used the Euro dollar). Banks and other financial institutions also suffered in the light of the GFC, and this particularly hurt the South (as well as other nations such as Iceland) which was financially rather weak. Dealing with problems of unemployment and low growth continued for many years, especially for Greece (2009–2016ff), which has only recently started to recover somewhat [Chaps. 8 and 9].

Evolution The concept of evolution states that the world and its constituents, indeed probably the whole universe and its parts, is subject to change involving mutations, modifications and various adaptations that change some of its elements, and that when significant enough become qualitatively different. For instance, capitalism undergoes changes to its institutions and the habits of individuals and groups that generate various phases of evolution through time. Capitalism is said to evolve through several phases of development (not necessarily implying progress), from mercantilism to industrial capitalism, then to imperialism, the Keynesian-welfare state, neoliberalism and beyond. The principle of evolution states that political economists and others must situate world problems within specific phases of evolution in the process of understanding and ameliorating such problems [All chapters deal with aspects of evolution].

Extortion Extortion is a form of corruption where a person or group poses a threat (instills fear/intimidation) in the form of a negative action on certain victim(s) (person, group, institution, area, nation) if a specific or general demand is not satisfied usually within a certain time-period. For instance, a mafia group may demand protection money from a business by a certain date or otherwise the business owner will be shot, or her business set on fire. Often in certain countries an authoritarian government will demand that a certain ethnic group leave an area by a certain date otherwise their property will be demolished, burnt, or they will be imprisoned or killed [Chap. 6].

Feminist Political Economy (FPE) Many FPEs are institutional and evolutionary scholars. In this they apply various theories and methods to institutional and evolutionary topics. What makes a political economist a feminist likely varies from scholar to scholar. But three things stand out. The first is they tend to place *gender issues* at the forefront of their analysis. The reason for this is that, historically and still in many cases, women have been placed lower down than men in the power stakes of society. Some may have had some limited power in the household, and in typical female jobs such as cleaning, child-rearing, secretarial, teaching and medical areas, but in the broader areas of power they have had limited authority, until more recent decades in the advanced nations.

These broader areas of power include geopolitics, national politics, CEOs, science, and criminal areas (gangs). More recently in several nations, women have increased their power in several areas, including politics, science, business, medical and computing areas. But several trends in some areas of the world have gone backwards, such as with the Taliban in Afghanistan, the military junta in Myanmar, and in the USA with declining abortion rights in several states (and more conservative Supreme Court judges). In virtually all nations women still do not have equality with men in areas of wages, salaries and superannuation.

The second thing that some women claim to be a feminist issue is their method of analysis, namely, that they tend to have a more *holistic method*, in that it often is interdisciplinary or transdisciplinary. This trend to making institutional and evolutionary issues more holistic is in keeping with the main principles of IEPE, and therefore, in this context and more, feminist themes and IEPE are very much complementary. The third, related thing that makes FPEs evolutionary-institutional is their emphasis on *social provisioning*. In this they are interested in the ways in which humans and other beings are provided for vis-à-vis nurturance, sustenance, food, clothing, shelter, and the cultural ways genders, classes, ethnicities, nationalities and species interact, and how identity is formed through these roles and norms [Relevant to most chapters].

Fictitious Capital The concept that certain forms of 'capital' are fictitious revolves around the idea that capital proper is something real rather than merely intangible or non-fundamental. When Marx in volume 3 of *Capital* discusses "fictitious capital", he is referring to the idea of speculative bubbles, intangible capitals that do not reflect fundamentals, and shadow banking that is a sideshow to industrial capital. Hence when these fictitious capitals are growing stronger than industrial capital it is an indicator that the economy is not operating effectively. There may be excess debt, equity prices beyond real value, and real estate valuations artificially inflated by excess demand. This occurs when fictitious capitals are a sideshow to the goods and services that people depend upon for their standard of living, and whose valuation does not move linearly with productivity plus real output and services. It can also refer to various forms of new financial instruments that do not often directly correlate with the valuation of real goods and services. However, declining prices for fictitious commodities can also decrease prices of real capital through declining confidence and greater uncertainty in the wider political economy [Chaps. 8 and 9].

Fictitious Commodities When Karl Polanyi wrote about fictitious commodities he was referring to labor (or labor-power), land and money not being commodities in the sense that they do not operate like an automobile in the motor market. One cannot get hold of labor, land or money in the same sense that, under capitalism, one can buy a vehicle. This is because labor-power is human and therefore cannot be exploited to death in the same way that an automobile can, at least not in normal circumstances. Land similarly can have the soil destroyed and minerals extracted but the land itself cannot be alienated or destroyed entirely. Similarly money does not have a use-value in itself, since one cannot reasonably be said to be able to eat it, or use it to produce some commodity. These three commodities are sui generis, public goods, that need special attention for if privatised they may lead to destruction at prices less than their social cost. Labor, land and money need to be considered from the point of view of the system as a whole. For instance, what is the state of the labouring classes in Hong Kong? How much has the soil been degraded through overuse, and how does this contribute to climate change? To what extend does the government need to provide liquidity to the system to protect markets via lender of last resort? These public goods type questions are crucial to Polanyi's vision of the common good where special attention is given to the state of labor, land and money through the various types of transactions such as reciprocity, redistribution, exchange and householding [Relevant to most chapters].

Financial Instability Hypothesis (FIH) The FIH is a term created by Hyman Minsky to describe a theory and also a series of empirical stylized facts about the cyclical and wave-like dynamics of capitalism. It appears to be influenced by Marx, Veblen, Schumpeter and Keynes; their view of financial capitalism. Basically it concerns the dynamic movement of capitalism over cycles and waves. When recovery happens in a socioeconomic cycle or wave, confidence starts to build which leads capitalists to invest more in complex durable structures such as machinery, buildings, hardware, software, workers, robots, knowledge and land. They also tend to finance this capital investment from internal funds, shares or equity in their firm, borrowing, or other often complex financial instruments. As confidence in the prevailing business climate increases they engage in more financial vehicles, eg, debt instruments. Minsky would say most firms would be in "Hedge Finance" position at this point, where cash flow and net worth are positive. They tend to get exuberant as their animal instincts grow cumulatively and in a circular fashion. However, eventually the cycle upward dynamic starts to turn down somewhat, due to a possible variety of factors often endogenous to the upswing, such as rising interest rates, wages, material costs, supply bottlenecks, conflict, strikes and so on. During these times Minsky would likely argue that many firms are moving to "Speculative

Finance", where cash flow has declined majorly (possibly negative) but still net worth is positive. Then usually some major event happens, a "Minsky moment", such as a sudden collapse of a famous company (e.g., Enron, Lehman Bros), or some other endogenous yet unexpected process, which reduces business confidence majorly and leads to a crash in the markets, and eventually likely to recession. Many firms then move to "Ponzi Finance", where cash flow is very low or negative and also net worth is negative. If this is a major economy, such as a hegemon, these instabilities will likely affect much of the rest of the world. During these crises likely reserve banks will have long intervened, or extend intervention, to try and stabilise matters. Eventually, depending on numerous lags, the economy eventually readjusts towards at least some semblance of 'recovery' (unless Depression occurs), and the cycle or wave continues again [Chap. 9].

Fraud Fraud is a form of corruption in which some agent or groups claim to be "A" but are in fact "B", and where the deception is implicated in some form of gain, whether institutional, personal, or business related. For instance, a group of money launderers may claim to be operating a legitimate business whereas the so-called business is mostly a front for illegitimate activities. A rich person may claim income of $50,000 in tax returns, but has hidden $5 m of income in secret overseas accounts. Organised criminal business agents often use fraud—deception, lies, suppression of true facts— to cover their illegal activities [Chap. 6].

Functional Finance This is a political economy principle of governance initiated by Abba Lerner, which states that policies to tackle socioeconomic problems should be concerned with the state of the economy and how to improve it rather than, e.g., conservative principles of balanced budgets and budgets being equal to a maximum percent of GDP. Hence if there is a lot of uncertainty throughout the political economy then policy should be pointed to reducing this over time. Under these circumstances, governments should be concerned with reducing this uncertainty through, for instance, automatic and discretionary fiscal and monetary policy. Taxes and government spending, in this context, should be seen as aggregate demand facilitators, rather than means of public accounting. Other such governance measures should be seen in this light as well. Functional finance is seen as crucial for dealing with all forms of socioeconomic crisis, recession/booms, depressions and financial crises; as well as day-to-day issues of governance [Chaps. 4, 8 and 9].

Gender Gender is a complex concept that relates to, partly, ones physical, genetic and/or social behaviour or structure; secondly, ones identity; and thirdly, one's relationship to sex. For some it is entirely a matter of social role, for others it links to genetics, and for others it is concerned with identity. In aggregate it concerns all these factors. One's gender could be male, or female, or transgender, or some other category. Recently there has been a tendency for gender to refer to one's identity, whether one is male, or female or transgender, and so on. Increasingly the literature differentiates between gender in terms of role, identity and behaviour; and sex, which concerns biology, sexuality and physicality. Gender role and identity has implications for all questions of IEPE and is hence related to the distribution of economic power, remuneration, and role played in the social economy. It is also closely associated with class, ethnicity, nationality, age and species through the concept of heterogeneous groups and agents [Most chapters deal with gender, esp. 2, 3, 4, 7, 11 and 12].

Global Financial Crisis (GFC) The GFC (2008–10) was, at the time, the greatest economic and financial crisis since the Great Depression of the 1930s (and the subsequent second world war of 1939–1945). It started out as the subprime crisis in the United States during 2008–2009, which was caused by rising uncertainty and debt that was not sufficiently embedded in risk assessments for companies, clients and nations. Many sub-standard mortgage arrangements were bundled together with other mortgages and sold as prime assets (or at least reasonable ones) or securitized mortgage bonds. It took the market time to realise that these bonds were substandard and that they were closely linked to predatory lending, opaque information, underpricing of risk and high debt. Once the market priced some of the risk and uncertainty into securities it affected profits of many firms and triggered declining equity prices in the US. There were many inter-sectoral linkages between the US and Europe, in particular, and the effects of US instability soon impacted other especially advanced nations, as well as many parts of Asia. Other factors also intervened which made it an international crisis, such as the move from conservative to market accounting, increasing distance between underlying assets and instruments, calculative risk models ignoring systemic risk and uncertainty, the use of structured investment vehicles, abuse of credit default swaps, and securitized mortgage bonds infecting global circuits of finance. International disarray especially impacted Iceland and soon the periphery of Europe was undergoing a Eurodebt crisis which lasted several years. Many economists and policy-makers blamed the GFC on neoliberalism and it led to the latter's relative demise. This helped policy-makers deal with the next crisis, the coronacrisis during 2020–2022, as functional finance was used to reduce the degree of crisis affecting the macro and global economies [Chaps. 4, 7, 9 and 12].

Global Political Economy [GPE] GPE is a field of political economy involving the dynamic interplay of power, production, trade, money and conflict involving corporate, state and other actors with the concern being the functioning of the circuit of social capital throughout the world. GPE especially involves power and conflict but also cooperation and agreement through which institutions and agents seek to achieve their objectives of profit, control and power over resources. It especially links to the relative power of nations and regions and their seeking of various types of hegemonic dominance throughout the world, as they have varying capacities in areas of production, commerce, finance and military prowess. The circuit of social capital reaches the global economy as capitalism seeks to caste-aside all barriers to its growth and development through the creation of new products, processes, markets, raw materials and other means while simultaneously destroying established jobs, institutions, cultures, and ways of life. International politics is often used as a vehicle for the expansion of capitalism, but also for other concerns such as terrorism, human rights activities, corruption, warfare, and so on. Currently the GPE is mostly concerned with the rise of China and the relative decline of the US, plus the nations and interests that are variously supporting each party, and those who are caught in the middle or playing off both parties for their greatest gain. A double power block is forming with China-Russia and other nations versus the US-EU-Australia and others dealing with issues such as trade, finance, production, military and diplomatic issues that are evolving into extreme forms of potential and actual violence, confrontation and war [Chaps. 4, 5 and 8].

Hegemony The general concept of hegemony is that a culture, region or nation tends to hold much of the power in the global economy, or in certain nations or regions. Usually this power has varying degrees of legitimacy, due to the material benefits some gain from the power relations, and/or from the enabling myths that validate the prevailing system of arrangements, and/or from the very concepts the hegemonic power develops and the agents it employs to market these concepts. Within this general concept are two types of hegemonies which are sometimes differentiated from the general view. The first is one of hegemonic culture, where the prevailing norms, mores and habits of the individuals and groups tend to help reproduce a certain type of social ecology. The second refers to the forces of global or regional hegemony, where a certain area or nation dominates other areas or nations. With the latter, there is a large literature documenting the rise and demise of various hegemonic nations, such as the Dutch states of the 1700s, British hegemony during the 1800s, the United States hegemony during the 1900s, and possible Chinese hegemony later in the twenty-first century [Chaps. 2, 3, 4, 7, 8 and 10].

Heterogeneous Groups and Agents The concept of heterogeneous group and agents in political economy states that the dominant roles that people play in groups are important for comprehending any major problem or process in the political economy. These roles include those based around gender, class, ethnicity, species, age, but also more technical roles that people play in institutions, and skills and attributes that they have when interacting with others in social life. People and other species always perform multiple roles in the political economy, even when one role is dominant, and they also have various traits based around gender, class, ethnicity, species, age, technical roles, that make them heterogeneous in these multiple respects. This concept is increasingly also including intelligent machines as playing roles that have been attributed to human beings, and even mechanical robots and similar machines should be included in the analysis. The principle of heterogeneous groups and agents states that one should utilise this concept to comprehend any problem or issue in the political economy, including for innovation and policy purposes to ameliorate the anomaly [Most chapters deal with this].

Historical Specificity The concept of historical specificity states that knowledge of the history of a problem, practice or a theory is important for comprehending the nature of it, and the way in which it can be useful for improving the performance of the political economy. The principle of historical specificity states that one should examine all problems historically in order to provide a better and more complex understanding of how to improve matters through innovation and policy into the future [All chapters].

HIV-AIDS There is a fundamental difference between HIV and AIDS. HIV is a viral infection that reduces the ability of people to reproduce their CD4 white blood cells effectively to fight disease because the HIV virus is using CD4 cells to reproduce itself. Getting HIV leads initially to usually mild symptoms, then a latency period of few symptoms, followed by AIDS diseases when CD4 cells are below 200 µL, with death occurring if and when CD4 cells decline to 50 µL and below. AIDS, on the other hand, refers to the diseases one gets when CD4 cells decline majorly, such as below 200 µL, including specific types of pneumonia, cancer, TB, opportunistic infections, and peripheral neuropathy. Thus HIV does not directly cause AIDS, but rather HIV reduces the ability of the body to fight infections, and often when this happens patients can die of these various ailments, unless they recover somewhat through natural immunity, drugs and/or other means (diet, exercise, lifestyle) [Chap. 11].

Holism The concept of holism has a long history and is subject to many versions and traditions. Some of these traditions are especially relevant to institutional and evolutionary political economy. One tradition states that holism is the principle that people should try and develop a lifestyle that includes an array of stimulating, developmental and innovative activities. People should try always to be learning something new, being on the lookout for new experiences, while also being able to relax and absorb these experiences, so that one undergoes dynamic transformation and renewal, but never extreme instability and disarray that could lead to death or disability. This should include a balanced diet that is nutritious and developmental in its effects on the mind and body. It should also include activities that stimulate the affective domain of emotions and feelings, so that one develops emotional as well as mental intelligence; in fact the two become intertwined when enabled.

This principle is used by political economists to advise governments, corporations and individuals to enhance the body-mind experience of all of us. The principle of holism can also be extended further into the socioeconomic and political domains, by suggesting that political economy should be interdisciplinary in the sense of including an array of social, economic, political and environmental elements together to solve complex world problems. World problems go beyond single disciplines, and therefore one necessarily scrutinises anomalies such as world poverty, inequality, insufficient trust and nurturance, Pandemics, financial crises and recessions, un(der)employment, inflation and other problems such as terrorism, corruption and artificial intelligence, by looking at these issues through a wide-scope and depth of vision. Political economists are likely to be able to do this more effectively if they have developed a holistic lifestyle that enhances the functioning of their body and mind.

More technically, holism in IEPE refers to four things about political economies. The first is that *the whole is greater than the sum of the parts* ('emergence'), and hence the whole is magnified, novel, different, from the parts. This may be because of interaction between the parts, communication, reproduction of a new thing, innovation, and a host of other factors. Second, quantitative change among the parts can become so great than *a qualitative change* operates within the whole (e.g., a new phase of evolution of capitalism, a new innovation). Third, the parts interact continuously so that *the whole is forever in the process of becoming*; i.e., evolving and changing through historical time. And fourthly, some of the parts interact in processually contradictory ways that generate endogenous movement, transformation, unfolding, often through *serious crises, wars, conflict*; but also often these contradictions encourage/require cooperation, coordination, *collaboration and other types of synergies* [All chapters].

Holistic Love Holistic love is a concept that involves a combination of styles of love and a major degree of development of the five core factors involved in its development. These five core factors include a considerable degree of passion, intimacy, commitment, social spread and freedom. The evidence supports the notion that holistic love, i.e., the five core factors, can only develop when various styles of love are employed in unison to promote one's quality of life. The three most important styles which collectively can help generate varying degrees of holistic love include (real) Agape, Eros and Storge, while some minimal elements of Pragma, Ludic and/or Manic may assist from time to time to generate a developmental path. From the concept emerges the principle of holistic love, that to develop it one needs to consciously work to improve one's relational loving experience through means to merge passion with intimacy and commitment, and these qualities with freedom and social spread. Successfully developing the major styles of love and the crucial factors involve new modes of enrichment with core elements of reflection and living in the moment to reap the benefits of holistic experiences [Chap. 12].

Innovation The concept of innovation states that there are numerous ways of contributing to solving world problem, and one can do this by innovating, which means doing something different in socioeconomic life, which contributes to the solution of these problems. Some of the methods include purely technical or material innovations, some concern changes in organisation, others relate to changes in ideas, while others concern knowledge and its application to concrete issues. Invariably they concern promoting the instrumental workings of core elements of the social, political, economic, engineering and ecological systems in dynamic motion. Some innovations may be 'things' in the past that have been resurrected, others concern principles that are applied, while some concern quite different elements from the past. The principle of innovation states that one should promote innovations to contribute to solving anomalous world problems [All chapters].

Institution There are various ways of looking at the concept of an institution. One is to see an institution is a structured way of organising group behaviour, comprising various routines, roles and behavioural norms to undertake some important social practice(s). Some differentiate between behavioural, organisational and theoretical institutions, so that an institution can variously comprise, for instance, the gendered division of labor, the organisations of the state, and double entry bookkeeping. Some scholars delimit the concept to the organisational institutions, such as households, corporations, financial institutions, government departments or ministries (and parliament), plus the world institutions such as the United Nations, the IMF and the World Bank. In scholarly discourse, the institutions associated with neoclassical economics dominated economics for a long time, but has always been the subject of double movements, such as institutional and evolutionary political economy [Most chapters].

Institutional and Evolutionary Political Economy (IEPE) IEPE is a form of political economy that seeks to understand the dynamic and institutional nature of groups and agents as they interact and thereby form the basis of the roles that potentially enhance socioeconomic performance. Many of its adherents seek to improve performance by advocating innovations to enhance social provisioning, community, skills, learning, communication, trust, productivity, capacities and capabilities. These innovations especially seek to instrumentally promote the common good and also seek to eschew institutional characteristics that promote ceremonial discrimination, distrust, conflict, war, and extremes of inequality. There are various traditions of IEPE, and some of them are trying to work together to generate a relatively common discourse for solving critical world problems. But the process will take some time and requires much innovation and invention to succeed. This book attempts to start (or continue) the process of doing just that [All chapters].

Liberal Democracy A liberal democracy is usually thought of as a socioeconomic system where capitalism is the dominant mode of production, distribution and exchange, but where the political system is subject to well-organised and respected parliamentary elections, usually where parties alternate in power, sometimes as various coalitions and often through the two dominant parties, one being centre-left and the other centre-right. The idea of liberal democracy is where elections have a high degree of legitimacy, where the rule of law is generally respected, and where people have various civil rights to freedom of expression, congregation and movement (except during pandemics and wars). A liberal democracy usually has a fairly strong state, where the state constitutes a dominant player in providing education, health, infrastructure, plus bureaucracy, military, parliament, and legal-justice systems. Examples include the United States, the UK and Australia.

Long Waves Long waves is the concept that most economies, particularly capitalist economies, undergo phases of evolution and transformation, characterized by alternating upward and downward motion of socioeconomic and political performance, and rising and collapsing patterns of institutional and technological metamorphosis. Modern wave analysts typically seek to comprehend the complexity of the motion, and to embed this multifarious dynamics into theory and empirics. Often they use the ideal-type wave motion as a standard with which to compare the empirical dynamics of specific nations, regions and the world. Usually one would expect differential but structurally linked wave patterns between core, periphery and semi-periphery (CPSP), and indeed within and between all nations and regions. Undertaking a global analysis of waves incorporating all the regional and CPSP complexities into the investigation would be the ideal method of approaching the subject. The principle of long waves states that one must include long patterns of evolution and socioeconomic and political performance into political economy to be cognizant of some of the core dynamics of the system, which is useful for innovation, policy and governance purposes for solving world problems [Most chapters; esp. Chaps. 5, 8 and 9].

Love Love is a multifarious process of developing intimacy between various parties and sometimes physical objects and even plants. One can, for instance, love virtually anything, but probably it requires at least one animal, or possibly in the future robots. The literature on love involves various combinations of six styles of love and five core processes. The styles of love include Eros, Agape, Storge, Pragma, Ludic and Manic. Eros relates to physical beauty and passion; Agape centres on empathy and sympathy; Storge is associated with friendship; Pragma involves commonalities and workability; Ludic concerns multiple partners; and Manic illustrates jealousy and obsession. There are also five major processes relating to love: intimacy, passion, commitment, social spread and freedom. Intimacy generates the sharing of knowledge and trust; passion produces intensity and lust; commitment reproduces ongoing associations; social spread includes others; and freedom creates innovation and new experiences. In practice, at least some of the love styles tend to interlink, and the more holistic the love is the greater is the mixture of intimacy, passion, commitment, social spread and freedom; plus elements of Eros, Storge and Agape. Love typically undergoes phases of evolution, for instance involving meeting and assessing the 'fit' (many finish there); the honeymoon phase (many finish there); enrichment or deterioration; longer-term durability; followed by destruction, moderation or enrichment. Serial relationships are common, often involving 7–11 year cycles [Chap. 12].

Love Capital The stock of love is a form of capital, "love capital", while the flow is a form of investment, "love investment", but unlike most forms of capital using it, at least up to a point, does not destroy it but rather enhances it (much the same as with social capital). There are five co-determinants of love capital, including passion, intimacy, commitment, freedom and social spread. If all five elements are coevolving in a durable fashion (love capital) then a degree of "holistic love" can emerge. There are trade-offs between love capital and other phenomena, as love capital may be traded-off for money, safety, stability, etc. The tendency for a greater proportion of people having concern for their own individualised preferences, in an economic environment that is unstable, has led to a decline in love capital in many nations over recent decades, and a lesser potential for children in their adult years also having fulfilling long-term love experiences. Under these conditions, love is unable to develop sufficiently, resulting in numerous stunted personalities and psycho-cultural malaise. [See Chap. 12].

Marxian Institutional and Evolutionary PE [MIEPE] Marxian political economy (MPE) has a tradition of including institutional and evolutionary aspects into its theoretical and empirical edifice. This does not include all Marxian traditions, but certainly it has been a major trend in some forms of Marxian analysis. It is especially noticeable in Marxian economic history (e.g., Eric Hobsbawm), Marxian archaeology (e.g., V. Gordon Childe), social structures of accumulation, the Regulation Approach, and some other approaches (e.g., *Rethinking Marxism*). Often the term 'Marxian' seems redundant when writing Marxian IEPE since the important thing is the quality of the analysis rather than the category of the approach. Indeed, MIEPE has influenced so many traditions and scholars that isolating one element of the totality seems unnecessary. Marx himself was influenced by a myriad of scholars and his IE elements; including, for instance, historical investigations into capitalism, its origins and evolution; the circuit of social capital, including the details on the production system, the sphere of circulation, and effective demand; plus investigations into the monetary system, fictitious capitals, competition, centralisation, technological change, labor market and world economy. There is a lot in Marx to stimulate one's interest in institutional and evolutionary themes. Contemporary IEPE has used many aspects of his analysis, including innovations thereof, to investigate the dynamic motion of capitalism and its alternatives [Most chapters].

Metabolic Rift Metabolic rift is the Marxian idea that capitalism historically sets up major rifts (contradictions) not only between capital and labor but also between capital and ecology, core and periphery, city and countryside, plus industry and agriculture. Most of the rifts of capitalism are caused by capital's need to exploit not only labor but also nature. Capital will try and exploit labor to the hilt, treating them like commodities and slaves where possible, and replacing them when they die, like a piece of earth discarded when not needed; but labor may develop effective countervailing powers to challenge this exploitation and subordination through a double movement. The exploitation of nature is usually looked on as the crux of metabolic rift. Capital will exploit the powers of the soil, waterways and hills so as to gain a surplus devoid of the costs of reproduction of these soils, waterways and hills. Hence it will seek out fish stocks until they dissipate and then turn to other fish stocks until they dissipate, in a circular and cumulative fashion. It will seek out rural or peripheral areas to provide resources until they dissipate, and then turn to other areas to exploit them until they dissipate, in order to propagate city-urban commodification, again in a CCC fashion. It will annex and colonise islands and areas rich in guano (bat and bird droppings), high in nitrogen, protein, phosphorus, calcium and magnesium, to support its depleted agricultural areas, using exploited labor to extract the resources until they collapse, until sources dry up, upsetting the ecological habitats that depend on these resources. Each phase of capitalism develops new avenues for exploitation of labor and nature, to adapt and transform systems for profitable investment. Again, effective ecological counterveiling powers may counter the exploitation and destruction by capital through effective double movements [Chap. 5].

Modern Monetary Theory [MMT] The four main principles of MMT are (a) state money symbol, (b) functional finance, (c) taxes drive money and (d) bonds are interest rate control mechanisms. MMT is an approach to money, production and employment that follows the Chartalist tenet that money is a mere *symbol*, established by the state, for purposes of promoting sustainable socioeconomic performance. It has historically been institutionalised by states as fiat money, and *taxes* have been imposed by states to ensure demand for state money. Functional finance is the main tool of state policy, namely, that the state policy should be directed to ensuring full employment and price stability. Taxes and government spending are demand-moderating devices, while government bonds are used for moderating interest rates to regulate levels of demand. The coronacrisis period (2020–2022ff) has been described by some commentators as MMT put into practice; a scientific test of the efficacy of MMT [Chap. 9].

Neoliberalism Neoliberalism is system of thought and a socioeconomic system of governance. The system of thought is based around small government, strong and free markets, well-developed police and military (possibly privatised), state providing legality and electoral systems and a relatively small public sector. It is committed to deregulating industrial relations, the financial system, corporations, foreign capital flows, plus the health care system and education. The basic philosophy of neoliberalism is that a deregulated economy (often undertaken by a strong state) is the only form of socioeconomic organisation possible for promoting high levels of productivity, profitability and economic growth. It seeks to privatise as many public functions as possible, institute self-regulation by the business sector, and leave people free to choose commodities they prefer. Historically, neoliberalism is seen as a strong global force since the late 1970s through to the 2000s; still strong, but having less legitimacy in the light of the Global Financial Crisis, Eurodebt crises of 2008–2014, and the coronacrises of the early 2020s [Chaps. 3, 4, 8, 9 and 12].

Neo-Schumpeterian IEPE Neo-Schumpeterian political economy is a contemporary trend in IEPE that draws liberally on the insights of Joseph Schumpeter but also incorporates many of the (other) advances in science that have emerged since Schumpeter's time. Especially relevant in this respect is the general emergence of IEPE, as well as complexity theory, notions of uncertainty, bounded rationality, qualitative novelty, meso-innovation, a perspective on development, change and long waves, in addition to the heterogeneity of agents, systems theory, new knowledge, industrial development, and innovative finance. In addition an important role is given to public goods provision, especially education, health, infrastructure and fiscal and monetary policy. Neo-Schumpeterians tend to try and balance over- (socialism) and under- (excess privatization) provision of public goods through some type of the mixed economy [Chaps. 2 and 3].

Nepotism Nepotism is a type of corruption where unfair favouritism is given to people who do not deserve it by any unbiased assessment. Usually in these cases due process has not been undertaken. Typical instances include where someone has been given undue privilege in support of a job, tender process, research grant, position in a football team, inclusion in a ballot, due to friendship, relationship, or other forms of attachment to the person. Nepotism historically is one of the means whereby the upper classes have retained their privileges by promoting networks of privilege, including relatives, friends and colleagues [Chap. 6].

Path Dependence The concept of path dependence states that the future of political economies depends upon the path they take through time, and that these paths cannot easily be broken, although recognition of this fact can help establish a new trajectory for the future. Path dependence is closely associated with the concepts of hysteresis and lock-in. Macro and global economies do not easily tend to equilibrium because the trajectory of evolution is complex, often involves blind drift, and subject to the impacts of multiple processes. Non-equilibrium processes, or multiple equilibria, involve complex movements and often major crises; periods of boom and crash. For instance, a major period of institutional dissonance, debt crises, depression, crisis, may generate substantial unemployment, and the longer the unemployment continues the higher the unemployment rate (hidden plus actual). Also, the establishment of a productive, investment-generating capitalist class, along with a generation of skill-upscaled working people, and a forward-looking middle class, can help promote a long period of sustained socioeconomic performance that may last a generation, until its potential declines markedly. Similarly, an economy unable to generate substantial investment, consumption and productive government spending cannot easily eschew this trend as the institutional conditions underlying this underperforming economy continue into the foreseeable future. People often start relationships that are hard to break because of habits, institutions, emotions, and lock-ins. The principle of path dependence states that one needs to analyse these processes to comprehend and ameliorate world problems [Chap. 12].

Policy and Governance The principle of policy and governance states that we should seek to improve the conditions of all species of life on planet Earth (except maybe certain viruses, bacteria, etc.), since many forms of variety improve our knowledge and experience of life and thereby enhance the common good. In this context, it also involves the process of social provisioning, enhancing the quality of life, standard of living and participatory democracy while protecting the community from conflicts, wars and other forms of violence. It also includes functional finance, automatic and discretionary fiscal/monetary policy, accords and agreements, plus climate change mitigation and adaptation. In theory, governance can and should be provided by all institutions, organisations and agents, but only if they seek to enhance the common good rather than their own self-interest. Self-regulation by business is sometimes a good objective but too often is undertaken out of self-interest rather than the concern being the whole society. Too often also states are captured by corrupt interests, through various actions including bribery, fraud, embezzlement, nepotism, extortion, and numerous conflicts of interest [Most chapters, esp. Chap. 8; also Chaps. 4, 9, 10 and 11]

Political Economy Political economy has many meanings, but a core one is that it is an interdisciplinary study of the evolution, development, organisation and contradictory reproduction of the processes of social provision, production, distribution, and exchange of material and immaterial means of life on planet Earth and beyond. Often accompanying this is the notion that it is a study of the structured use of power by the various vested interests to control the economic surplus for their own benefit, and also the use of governance processes to provide the legitimacy required to continue to reproduce this asymmetric distribution of resources to benefit the hegemonic cliques and nations. It is often also recognised that one can use political economy to provide a theory and framework for potentially challenging this hegemonic dominance to distribute and control resources more equitably and enhancing social provisioning for the benefit of the community. This is what IEPE seek to do [All chapters].

Post-Keynesian Institutionalism [PKI] PKI is a term to formalise the notion that Keynes and specifically many of his followers are institutionalists in the sense that the historical and institutional environment of capitalism and its alternatives (and antecedents) are core parts of their analysis. They also usually recommend institutional changes to improve the functioning of capitalism or modify it towards a more social democratic or democratic socialist direction. Some of the more well known PKIs of recent decades include Hyman Minsky, J.K. Galbraith, Victoria Chick, Philip Arestis, L. Randall Wray and Stephanie Kelton. These PKIs have always had a strong linkage with Veblenian institutionalists, and also to some degree those other IEPEs who share an interest in their concepts of aggregate demand, uncertainty, monetary theory of production, endogenous money and credit, financial instability hypothesis and also modern monetary theory [Chap. 9].

Power Bertrand Russell (1938) in his book *Power*, defined power as the "ability to produced intended effects", and argued that rather than sex being the motive force of human energy (as in Freud), and rather than economic self-interest being the core motive for human action (as in economists), it actually resides in power. People seek to increase or sustain their power, in the sense of producing intended effects to their actions. William Dugger believes that in contemporary political economies power lies in the various roles that people play, e.g., as parent, employed personnel, citizen, participant in public affairs, stakeholder, environmental activist, CEO, etc; and that business has most power compared with states, families and civil society groups. E.L. Wheelwright thought corporate power was executed through the corporate domination of the world, regions and nations; market concentration; restrictive trade practices; interlocking directorates; and linkages with political-power networks. Power also resides in largescale aggregates, such as nations in the world economy, as with hegemonic power, that evolved from, e.g., Dutch (1700s) to British (1800s) to Unites States (1900s) to potentially Chinese (mid-2000s) hegemony (viz. Wallerstein) [All chapters].

Glossary 413

Principle A principle in political economy is a rule of action based on a concept. For instance, the principle of historical specificity states that one should examine all problems within an historically specific context to understand them more fully, and that this concept of historical specificity will assist in developing innovations and policies for moderating problems [All chapters; see Chap. 1 for details].

Radiative Forcing Radiative forcing is the process where the sun's rays on Earth has an influence on Earth's temperature; the influence can be positive, negative or in balance. If it is in balance the net incoming and outgoing radiations are equal to zero. If it is positive the net incomings are greater than zero, and Earth's climate warms. And if it is negative the net figure is less than zero, and Earth's climate cools. Much depends upon what happens when the incoming radiation is affected by natural and human activities. For instance, if trees are cut down to be replaced by concrete buildings then there is more carbon dioxide relative to oxygen in the 'transaction', which usually results in warming. If wild animal habitats are destroyed and replaced by coal fired power stations, there is again more carbon dioxide produced in the transaction, and temperatures rise. A reduction in glaciers and ice-sheets will likely reduce the degree of reflection of radiation to the outer atmosphere and result in warming and rising sea levels. However, a certain increase in radiative forcing, due to higher levels of GHG, may take time for the full impact to manifest itself, resulting in, e.g., rising mean temperatures. *Through historical time* (in the future), a specific extant increase in Earth's mean temperature takes time to fully impact crucial tipping points such as ice sheets, glaciers, monsoonal systems, coral reefs, ocean currents, and meso/macro-climate systems such as El Nino. Mean Earth atmospheric temperatures in 2020 have risen by 1.07–1.2 °C since 1850–1900 but the full impact of this increase lies in the future. Impacts will continue to increase even if temperatures fail to rise further; but the fact that mean atmospheric temperatures are still rising majorly means we have cascading cumulative escalating back-logs of impacts to deal with. In other words, cascading tipping points of no return are happening with the current 4–5 tipping points being impacted due to magnified, amplified and CCC-type expansions of these contradictions. The change in surface temperature (T_s) caused by increases in radiative forcing (F) can be calculated using the formula: $\Delta T_s = \lambda \Delta F$, where λ is typically valued at 0.8 K/(W/m^2) [Chap. 5].

Schumpeterian A Schumpeterian institutional and evolutionary political economist (IEPE) is one who follows the method and/or terminology of Joseph Alois Schumpeter (1883–1950). This often involves looking at capitalism through the lens of socioeconomic dynamics, such as product, process, market, raw material and corporate clusters of innovation. It includes scholars who examine, as Schumpeter did, multiple forms of fluctuations, cycles and/or waves, such as 'Kitchins, Juglars and Kondratieffs'. It includes scholars who use Schumpeter's method of starting with the circular flow of economic activity in equilibrium, which includes perfect competition, workers and landlords, and money functioning only as a means of simple circulation. Then we can introduce entrepreneurs and money capitalists that start the process of metamorphosis, borrowing to finance innovation, which generates a 2-phase cycle of recession and recovery. We will want to make the analysis more realistic by introducing credit that finances also general accumulation, which produces a four-phase cycle of upswing, boom, recession and depression. In addition, a Schumpeterian will be cognizant of capitals of different durabilities impacting on the macro economy in different ways and through differing time periods, potentially generating cycles/waves comprising different periodicities, volatilities and mechanisms/processes. A Schumpeterian IEPE will also deal with issues associated with creative destruction, as the motivate force of capitalism generates major changes and new ways of doing things, it destroys cultures, firms, jobs, industries, ecologies and institutions, with the need to deal with the ramifications of these creations/destructions [Chaps. 2, 3, 5, 8 and 12].

Shared Socioeconomic Pathways (SSP) A SSP is a concept used by ecological economists and the IPCC to describe specific types of responses to the environmental crisis of climate change. One pathway used to help solve climate change anomalies is called the Green Road to Sustainability (SSP1), where quality of life is given priority over GDP growth, GHGs are replaced by technologies such as wind and solar power to reduce emissions, and electric cars as well as bicycles and walkways assist in temperature rises to up to 1.0–1.8 °C (uncertainty differentials) by 2100, relative to 1850–1900 mean. Another SSP, the High Road of Growth (SSP5), emphasises adaptation while promoting GHG emissions, high GDP growth and rising levels of consumption, where the global mean temperature may rise by up to 3.3–5.7 °C by 2100, compared to 1850–1900 mean; thereby not really solving the climate change problem. There are various other SSPs in between these extremes that lead to temperature increases of between 2.1 °C and 4.6 °C by 2100 compared with the 1850–1900 mean. Discussing SSPs in terms of pathways is an innovation in thinking about climate change, but usually they are not analysed in terms of the degree of structural change required, nor with respect to the likely fact that the 2020 rise in global mean temperature to 1.2 °C, relative to the 1850–1900 mean, is probably the highest we could go before 4–5 tipping points lead to 'points of no return' [Chap. 5].

Social Democracy Especially over the past 100 years, social democracy has been seen as a sociopolitical system, or a political party, which balance the forces of socialism with the forces of capitalism, usually where most of the means of production, distribution and exchange are controlled by private or public (shareholder) corporations, but where there is a very strong state, and also usually a very strong sense of civil society (social trust). The social democratic state has a strong interest in education, health, infrastructure and social protection such as pensions, unemployment benefits, as well as often a commitment to some form of participatory democracy in business. It also has well-organised and legitimate electoral systems, police-justice systems and at least a moderately well equipped military. Historically, the Scandinavian countries have been classed as social democracies, possibly also, at times, the Netherlands, Germany and France. In the UK the Fabian Society has been the major bearer of social democracy principles. Following the lead of these nations many others have embraced social democracy.

Socialism There are many models, theories and practices of socialism. They comprise arrangements such as worker controlled enterprises; state control of many leading enterprises; the socialisation of much of education, health, infrastructure development, housing, social security, child care and functional finance; involvement of the community in decisions which affect their lives in business and government; promotion of community trust, interaction, and sociality; the development of producer and consumer cooperatives; and the development of the joint stock of community knowledge and skills. Generally, political economists talk about socialism when there is a high(er) degree of community involvement, control, ownership or sharing of economic and social resources. The objectives of socialism are related to enhancing the role of the lower classes in social, political and economic life; and reducing alienation and subjugation of all classes. Socialism also links to the development of more trust, bridging social networks and voluntary association between all the genders, ethnic groups, classes and ages of people plus other species involving the ecology of planet Earth.

Social Provisioning IEPE is the science of provisioning in the sense that its main concern is to provide a framework where the vast majority of inhabitants on planet Earth can survive and develop. It seeks to provide a principled architecture for providing the material and immaterial needs and wants of the all life forms on Planet Earth and beyond. In other words, it seeks to devise ways in which life forms have access to adequate habitats, ecosystems, communities, and repositories of food, clothing and shelter. It also seeks to provide a framework for promoting development of these assets for the common good. It does recognise that the system we live under, capitalism in its various forms, is subject to the dynamics of opening up all cultures to the ravages of mining, production, innovation, transport and markets. In this context, it tries to moderate the excesses of creative destruction by financing the updating of skills, knowledge and tacit understandings of the changes in ecosystems that require adaptation and modification of behaviour to survive in a constantly changing environment. It also seeks to protect species and classes that are subject to the most devastating forms of destruction and decimation through safety nets and action plans. Since the forces of capitalism are rampant, and even governance measures to protect species and classes are usually modestly ameliorative at best, it is likely that we will need other planets to colonise to continue life in other places. But hopefully the governance measures implemented on other planets will learn from past mistakes and promote a more embedded system for all species and classes. IEPEs should seek to provide a framework for that as well [All chapters].

Species The concept of a species is one of the most complex notions in political economy, since there are so many ways of categorizing living organisms. But generally, a species is a set of 'living' organisms that share some critical traits, whether they are genetic, reproductive, evolutionary, or behavioural in nature. For instance, some define a species as those living organisms that can successfully breed together. Then of course there are those that undergo non-sexual reproduction. Species are important in political economy because they link to world problems, such as the coronavirus pandemic, declining biodiversity, HIV-AIDS, AI-robotics, and climate change [Chaps. 4, 5, 7 and 11].

State Capitalism State capitalism is a socioeconomic system comprising two things. First, it is a system whose inner motion is driven by the continual changes in products, processes, markets, raw materials and organisations such that skills, lifestyles and ecologies are forever being modified and ravaged in the interests of productivity and growth (creative destruction). Secondly, control of such a system is directed by a group or series of agents who call themselves the government or the state. State capitalism is a hybrid of private capitalism and state, where the inner motion of capitalism is given full sway, but where the state or its representatives control much of the material and immaterial base. Currently, the Chinese system could be called state capitalism; possibly also that of Russia; numerous others as well.

State Capture State capture is a form of corruption where business, unions, etc typically provide party funding in return for influence through the determination of laws, rules, regulations and decisions. Historically in many nations, for instance, 'liberal' or 'conservative' parties have been entrapped by business interests, where such governments provide support for commerce when the party is in power, and also at other times, while business provides funding for the party. Also in many nations, 'labor' parties have historically been entrapped by unions, which expect support in government, while the unions also provide funding for the party. Business now provides much funding for both types of parties. State capture has also occurred in some countries where criminal gangs, mafia groups and militias have control or undue influence over governments [Chap. 6].

Terrorism Terrorism can be defined as those practices associated with the planning and executing of attacks on civilians for purposes of making political, ideological, theological and/or related statements on behalf of the attacker or more usually a group of like-minded activists or state apparatus. Usually the purpose of such attacks is to bring a core issue to the mind of the public and state or other actors, and often to instil fear and intimidation into the minds of the community. Examples include the atom bombs dropped on Hiroshima and Nagasaki during the latter stages of the second world war; the strikes on many cities and towns of Britain by the Germans during the second world war, and later on Germany by the British; the many attacks by, for instance, Al Qaeda, Islamic State, Al Shabaab, Mujahadeen, and so on, against the US, its supporters, and national governments in the Middle East, North Africa, and elsewhere (plus US terrorism against Arabs, etc); Israel and Palestinian attacks on civilians over the past 70 years; the IRA, Unionists and UK Police/Army in their many skirmishes; and Russia in its invasion of Ukraine, where it purposefully targets civilian suburbs, hospitals and emergency accomodation to pressure the government to adhere to its terms [Chap. 10].

Thing A 'thing' is an important part of the vocabulary of any science. Without it one would have to be more or *too* specific about what is written about. Mario Bunge, for instance, a major "philosopher-scientist", includes "thing" as part of his *Philosophical Dictionary* (NY: Prometheus Books, 2003). For him, a "thing" is "an object other than a construct" (p. 294). For IEPE a thing is somewhat wider in meaning, since it can also include a construct (as well as an object), eg, an idea or concept. Writers often try and avoid the term, usually for ceremonial purposes; i.e., to appear more intelligent or sophisticated (than they are). Here we use the term often because it is instrumentally useful in introducing specific items, such as objects, concepts, and so on.

Tipping Points Climatic tipping points are when changes occur in the climate systems that are sudden, and represent a qualitative change where the future is more uncertain and subject to potential irreversibilities. Cascading tipping points relate to the emergence of multiple tipping points, where they interdependently emerge through multiplier and accelerator forces leading to major increases in radiative forcing and temperature increases to the point where catastrophic climate crises emerge. There are at least 15 areas/forces of planet Earth where tipping points would coalesce resulting in points of no return. Currently we are already undergoing the early phases of tipping points relating to the destruction of (a) west Antarctic ice-sheets, (b) Greenland ice sheets, (c) Arctic summer sea-ice, (d) Alpine glaciers, and (e) coral reefs. Cascading tipping points relate not only to higher temperatures but also the effects of current temperatures that are relatively slow moving. Currently, at rises in mean temperatures of between $1.07\,°C$ and $1.20\,°C$ (2020), relative to the 1850–1900 mean, with rises in the Arctic region (and some other areas) being great than this, we are likely already past the point of no return for many of these interdependent tipping points [Chap. 5].

Treadmill of Production The treadmill of production (TOP) concept uses the circuit of social capital (CSC) apparatus to explain ecological problems and climate change under capitalism. Capitalism is based on complex capital processes to reduce the input of labor as much as possible to make higher profits. This means producing machines, robotics, buildings, packaging, and transportation as well as warehouses, shops and roadways, in addition to using iron, coal, steel, timber, oil, gas and other minerals and materials. These items of constant capital (fixed and circulating capital) produce much pollution, waste, destruction of habitat and oxygen vis-à-vis carbon absorbing plants and sinks. Waterways are destroyed by constant destruction of fish species and conglomerations of waste in the form of plastics, other containers and wrappers. GDP growth generates GHGs and waste. Generating capital uses materials cheaper than their reproduction costs. The treadmill of production needs replacing through structural changes to emasculate the laws of capital by promoting social provisioning, quality of life and preservation of nature [Chap. 5].

Uncertainty Institutional and evolutionary political economists [IEPPs] tend to differentiate between risk and uncertainty. Risk is something fairly determinate in the sense that it is relatively easy (given current knowledge and techniques) to calculate quantitatively. Examples include the weather, housing prices, stock market fluctuations, insurance costs, equestrian performance, unemployment, and inflation. The concept of uncertainty posits the notion that there are core elements of opaqueness, futurity, ignorance, complex lags, and lack of information and/or knowledge in the political economy. Risk often relates to current events and things in the not-to-distant future. Uncertainty links to the long-term future, tipping points, and very complex processes. Marx and Schumpeter, for instance, saw capitalism as having an inherently uncertain character, because it was based around seeking out new areas, new products and processes, new skills and knowledge, and new markets and corporate arrangements. In the process it generates obsolescence, unemployment, bankruptcy, poverty, decimated environments, and species extinction. For Keynes the dominant uncertainty about capitalism was the long-term generation of complex capital goods and short term debt, with these different time dimensions creating heightened instability and crisis. Institutions are often created to moderate uncertainties in the system, such as through lender of last resort facilities, deposit insurance, unemployment benefits, climate control strategies, and poverty-reducing policies [Chaps. 2, 3, 4, 5, 9 and 10].

Uneven Development The concept of hegemony and uneven development states that global capitalism tends to generate uneven forces throughout the world, where some states or regions benefit majorly from the system of socioeconomic and political arrangements, but numerous others fail to achieve high rates of growth, investment, social provisioning and standard of living. The areas that tend to benefit from the global system of arrangements include the highly advanced capitalist economies, and possibly some newly emerging states from the semi-periphery. Areas that benefit less from global arrangements are usually from the periphery, providing agricultural, market garden and raw material commodities, as well as ecological sinks for global corporations and the core; whose commodity prices tend to be low and volatile but play a positive role in highly advanced nations' standard of living and social provisioning [Chaps. 4, 5, 6, 8 and 11].

Veblenian A Veblenian is a institutional and evolutionary political economist who is influenced by or follows the method or analysis of Thorstein Veblen (1857–1929). Firstly this involves being an interdisciplinary, multidisciplinary and/or transdisciplinary scholar, who studies world problems involving an array of economic, social, political, ecological and psychological elements. Secondly, such a scholar may adopt and utilise some of the core concepts of Veblen, such as conspicuous consumption, emulation, cumulative causation, community's stock of knowledge, instrumental versus ceremonial functions of institutions, common good versus the vested interests, instincts, relative income, Veblen goods, intangible value, absentee ownership, the New Era of Business, sabotage, the Great Union of Vested Interests, blind drift, and the gendered social economy [Relevant to most chapters].

Name Index

A
Acemoglu, D., 197, 298
Ahir, H., 115
Aliber, R.Z., 52, 264, 284, 293
Amin, S., 182, 269
Anderson, K.L., 23
Aranyosi, I., 222
Arestis, P., 72, 279, 287, 294, 297
Argandona, A., 186
Aristotle, 11, 166, 176
Arthur, W.B., 37, 66, 266
Asada, M., 223, 224
Asimov, I., 217
Austen, J., 359
Ayres, C., 9, 20, 28, 29, 33, 38

B
Banerjee, A., 269
Barcham, M., 176
Barnes, M., 361
Barnett, T., 347
Bealle, A., 356
Beck-Gernsheimi, E., 378
Bell, S., 299
Belousova, V., 170
Berger, S., 25, 61, 139, 149, 189, 206, 266, 357
Berle, A.A., 24
Bhaumik, A., 219
Bin Laden, Shaykh Usamah Bin-Muhammed, 308, 309, 318, 319
Binswanger, M., 295
Bloom, N., 115
Boulding, K., 139, 354
Bourdieu, P., 54, 271
Bowles, S., 57, 76, 262, 263
Brady, R.A., 185

Brennan, A.J., 3, 59, 80, 93, 138, 166, 199
Brooks, R., 198–200, 203, 205, 206, 211, 212, 214, 216, 219, 221, 222, 237, 239–241
Buck, C., 359
Bujra, J., 345, 346
Bulliet, R.W., 324
Bunge, M., 14, 24, 63, 66–68, 386
Bush, P.D., 4, 6, 34, 70, 77, 178, 214, 254, 265, 266, 268, 269, 279
Butlin, N.G., 310

C
Campbell, M., 286
Cante, F., 354
Cantwell, J., 263
Carter, R., 231
Chella, A., 236
Chen, N., 102
Cherlin, A.J., 369, 378
Chomsky, N., 176, 320
Chossudovsky, M., 318
Choudhury, M.A., 324
Christensen, J., 187
Ciscel, D., 379
Clinard, M., 172, 185
Commons, J., 9, 20, 28, 33, 36, 38
Condon, R., 93
Correa, E., 254
Cypher, J., 33, 182, 269, 295

D
Davidson, P., 12, 293, 294
De Long, J.B., 258
de Willebois, Emile van der Does, 188, 189
Delpech, T., 319

Deng, L., 199, 202–204, 296
Dewey, J., 33, 213
Dickens, P., 270
Dillard, D., 34, 114, 278
Diwan, R., 354
Dorninger, C., 148
Dreyfus, H., 203
Duesberg, Peter H., 342, 343
Duflo, E., 269
Dugger, W. (Bill), 4, 24, 34, 35, 70, 74, 178, 185, 270
Dutt, A., 182, 269
Dymski, G., 293, 352

E
Edelman, G., 199, 203, 207, 213, 221, 222, 224–226, 231–234, 236, 239, 240
Elliott, C., 23, 358
Elsner, W., 13, 33, 34, 37, 66, 70, 139, 263
Engels, F., 7, 74
Engstrom, G., 121
Evanega, S., 113

F
Fenney, J., 359
Ferguson, A., 168, 169, 176
Ferri, P., 293
Figart, D., 58
Figge, F., 141
Fisher, H., 355
Fletcher, C., 172
Folbre, N., 354
Forward, S., 359
Foster, F., 34, 37, 265
Foster, J.B., 134, 135, 139, 141, 142, 146, 148, 152, 157
Fraad, H., 379
Frank, A., 182, 269
Freeman, C., 73, 280
Fromm, E., 359–362, 367, 371, 372
Furceri, D., 115
Fusfeld, D., 4

G
Galbraith, J.K., 9, 20, 24, 28, 30, 38, 270
Garnaut, R., 130, 151
Genaux, M., 167, 168
Georgescu-Roegen, N., 77, 134, 139–141, 146, 149, 152, 157

Gertz, G., 110, 111
Ghosh, B.N., 272
Ghosh, I., 55
Gilbert, R.J., 263
Gilman, C.P., 5, 9, 20, 30, 38, 50
Goertzel, B., 205, 241
Gordon, D., 31, 50, 70, 73
Gore, A., 130
Goswami, A., 221, 234
Grabel, I., 33, 182, 269, 297
Grabner, C., 111
Greenwood, D.Y., 36, 74
Grossbard, S., 377
Grou, P., 294
Guttman, R., 282

H
Haley, S., 378
Hanson, J., 196
Hanusch, H., 74, 75
Hartford, C., 379
Harvey, D., 63, 68, 104, 108, 144
Hatfield, E., 355, 356
Hayek, F., 36
Heath, J., 379
Hebb, D., 235
Hegel, G.W.F., 6, 68
Heidenheimer, A.J., 172, 173, 175, 176, 180
Hendrick, C., 357–360, 369, 372
Hendrick, S., 357, 359, 360, 369, 372
Henry, J.F., 168
Herrmann, D., 172
Hill, L., 168, 169, 176
Hobsbawm, E., 52, 256, 257
Hobson, J., 27
Hodgson, G., 28, 34, 49, 56, 131
Holmes, J., 363
Holt, R.P.F., 36, 74
Horswill, I., 216
Huntington, S., 309, 319
Hymer, S., 182, 269

I
Izurieta, H., 103

J
Jennings, F., 354
Johnston, M., 172, 173, 180, 181
Jong-sung, Y., 183, 189

Name Index

K
Kabeer, N., 269
Kadmos, G.A., 299
Kaldor, N., 9, 20, 29, 31, 34, 50, 62, 66, 73, 108, 140, 149, 167, 206, 266, 357
Kalecki, M., 34
Kalsi, J.K., 80, 93, 166, 199
Kaplan, S., 92
Kapp, K.W., 34, 38, 64, 66, 139–141, 146, 149, 152, 157, 169
Kasabov, N.K., 222, 227, 229, 235, 236
Kaufman, D., 186, 187
Keller, K., 152, 155, 156
Kelton, S., 298, 300
Kerr, I.A., 4
Kerr, P., 22
Keynes, J.M., 5, 8, 12, 20, 21, 27–32, 38, 50, 71–73, 114, 131, 138, 152, 166, 282, 286, 287, 290
Khagram, S., 183, 189
Khaldun, I., 167, 176
Kharas, H., 110, 111
Kiggins, R., 197, 217
Kindleberger, C., 12, 50, 52, 264, 284, 293
Kipnis, L., 374
Kirdina-Chandler, S., 34, 255
Knight, F., 71, 72, 114, 152
Kregal, J., 294
Krichmar, J.L., 199, 203, 207, 221–226, 228, 239, 240
Kuznets, S., 33

L
Lacey, R., 359, 372
Lavoie, M., 57, 279, 290, 299
Lee, F., 23
Lee, J.A., 357–361, 365, 367, 372
Lenton, T.M., 155, 265
Lerner, A., 110
Levine, D.P., 286, 340
Levine, T., 366, 372
Lewis, W.A., 33
Lin, L.-W., 360, 372
Linich, S., 374
Louca, F., 280
Lungarella, M., 212, 223

M
Machiavelli, N., 167, 176
Maddison, A., 258, 279

Mager, N.H., 280
Mair, S., 92
Malthus, T., 23, 27
Mandel, E., 280
Marx, K., 3, 5–8, 12, 20, 21, 23, 25, 27, 28, 31, 32, 38, 49, 50, 68, 69, 74, 77, 108, 131, 133, 138–140, 146, 166, 286, 287, 290
Mattei, C., 256, 257
Mayhew, A., 34
McCarthy, J., 201
McFerson, H., 183, 188
Means, G.C., 24
Mensah, J., 272
Mensch, G., 37
Metcalfe, J.S., 37, 74
Mills, C.W., 8, 49, 270
Minsky, H., 34, 71, 73, 290, 291, 293, 298, 300
Minsky, M., 201, 202
Mishkin, F., 284, 296
Mitchell, S., 374
Mitchell, W., 9, 20, 28, 33, 38
Montesquieu, 176
Montgomery, M., 358
Moore, B., 288, 294
Mukhopadhyay, S., 377
Myrdal, G., 3, 9, 316, 331, 341

N
Naidu, M.V., 309
Neale, W.C., 254, 278
Nelson, A., 278
Nelson, J., 354
Neto, F., 360
Newell, A., 149, 198, 202, 206, 210, 211, 217, 239, 240
Nilsson, N., 4, 198, 200, 202, 206, 207, 211, 217–219, 239, 240
Noller, P., 359
North, D., 36

O
O'Connor, J., 139, 141, 183
O'Hara, J., 270
O'Hara, P.A., 2–4, 8–15, 23, 24, 33–35, 37, 48, 50, 51, 53–55, 61, 62, 64, 66, 68, 70, 74, 77, 80, 93, 95, 108, 110, 133, 134, 138, 166–191, 196–244, 252–273, 278, 280, 282–285, 295–297, 299, 308, 311, 326, 344, 346, 352, 356, 367, 370, 371, 378, 387

O'Neill, B.C., 137, 153, 154
Offe, C., 257
Olgen, F., 36
Olsen, M., 36
Ostrom, E., 36

P
Palley, T.I., 291
Palloix, C., 285
Parguez, A., 286
Park, N., 169, 187
Parks, B.C., 148, 149
Pauls, R., 73
Perez-Truglia, R., 262
Peterson, J., 58
Peterson, W., 114
Pfeifer, R., 198, 203, 205, 206, 208, 209, 212–215, 219–225, 230, 231, 235, 239–241
Piaget, J., 213
Plato, 11, 166, 176
Polanyi, K., 21, 37, 49, 69, 77, 138, 139, 141, 146, 157, 253–255, 260, 266, 352, 370
Pollin, R., 288
Posner, R., 36
Potts, J., 37
Power, M., 35
Pratto, F., 178
Pressman, S., 262
Primrose, D., 111
Pyka, A., 74, 75

R
Raffer, K., 259
Rapson, R., 355, 356
Rempel, J., 363
Resnick, S., 57, 133, 262, 317, 342
Restrepo, P., 197
Rice, J., 148
Roberts, J.T., 148, 149
Robinson, J., 9, 20, 30, 31, 34, 38, 269
Rochon, L.-P., 72, 73, 286, 289
Rose-Ackerman, S., 172, 175, 176
Rosenblatt, V., 178, 179
Rossi, S., 72, 287
Rostow, W.W., 52, 281
Rousseau, J.-J., 168, 176
Ruggie, J.G., 254
Rutherford, M., 34, 37

S
Salleh, M.S., 324
Samuels, W.J., 24, 34
Santangelo, G.D., 263
Sartre, J.-P., 361, 362, 372–374
Schotter, A., 36
Schumpeter, J., 5–8, 12, 20, 21, 27–32, 38, 50, 69, 73, 74, 131, 138, 146, 166, 254, 278, 279, 286, 287, 290, 361, 362
Seccareccia, M., 254
Sen, A., 64, 266
Shackle, G.L.S., 71, 72, 114, 152
Sherman, H., 29, 70, 73, 255, 287, 310, 324, 326, 355, 358
Sherrington, C.S., 229
Sherwood, J., 346
Sidanius, J., 178
Simon, H., 198, 202, 206–211, 217, 240
Sloman, A., 219, 220
Smerick, C., 374
Smith, A., 22, 144, 168
Socrates, 11, 166
Sorell, G., 358
St. John, H., 168
Stanfield, J.B., 353
Stanfield, J.R., 30, 34, 36, 69, 108, 173, 217, 254, 270, 353, 370, 371
Stein, L., 216
Stern, N., 130, 135, 151
Sternberg, R., 356, 359, 361, 362, 364, 365, 367
Stevens, C., 374
Stiglitz, J., 284
Stockhammer, E., 295
Stout, M., 354
Street, J., 182, 269
Sumonja, M., 110
Sweezy, P.M., 9, 20, 31, 32

T
Takanishi, A., 200, 202, 222
Tang, J., 110
Terry, M., 106
Thison, J., 354
Tilman, R., 23, 34
Tool, M., 6, 24, 34, 70, 76, 77, 108, 214, 265, 268
Toporowski, J., 281
Tullock, G., 172

V

Vadakkepat, P., 221
Valyear, K.F., 228
van Duijn, J.J., 52, 256, 282
Vannoy, R., 358
Veblen, T., 3, 5, 6, 8, 11, 12, 20, 21, 23–33, 35–38, 50, 52, 65, 74, 80, 108, 131, 138–140, 149, 166, 176, 182, 206, 221, 239, 256, 262, 269, 270, 282, 286, 290, 315, 361, 362
Vickers, D., 278

W

Waller, W., 33, 65
Wallerstein, I., 50, 182, 200, 269, 281, 317
Weber, M., 74
Weiss, K., 361
Whalen, C.J., 264
Wheeler, D.W., 323
Wheelwright, E.L., 412
White, T., 375
Wilber, C., v, 64
Williamson, O., 36
Wolff, R., 57, 133, 262, 317, 342
Wolfson, M., 73, 254, 282, 291
Wray, L.R., 255, 288, 298, 300
Wrenn, M., 34, 70

Z

Zinnbauer, D., 170, 171

Subject Index

A
Absentee Ownership, 26
Accords and agreements, 81
Accountability, 170, 171, 175, 296
Adaptation, 7, 22, 37, 48, 55, 71, 78, 130, 137, 143, 153, 155, 234, 265, 386
Age, 6, 15, 34, 48, 57, 59, 64, 68, 81, 102, 103, 106, 107, 122, 132, 179, 223, 229, 252, 273, 292, 297, 346, 360, 385
Agency and structure, 56
Agents, v, 6, 10, 14, 23, 25, 37, 46–48, 57, 60, 68, 74, 79, 81, 91–93, 101, 103–105, 120, 122, 172–175, 178, 179, 186, 196, 199, 203, 205–218, 221, 223, 224, 229, 231, 236–240, 243, 244, 252, 253, 267, 268, 272, 273, 278, 280, 281, 283, 289, 300, 308, 317, 321, 342, 343, 361, 385
Alpine glaciers (APG), xvii, 156, 157
Al Qaida, 13, 309, 311, 314, 316, 318, 320, 323
AI summers and winters, 203
Amazon rainforest, xvii, 156, 157
Amplification, 6, 48, 65, 363, 386
Arctic summer sea ice (ASSI), xvii, 156
Arctic winter ice sheet (AWIS), xvii, 156
Artificial general intelligence (AGI), xvii, 196–244
Asimo (robot), 234
Association for Evolutionary Economics (AFEE), vii, viii, xv, 11, 20, 33
Association for Institutional Thought (AFIT), 33
Atlantic meridional overturning circulation (AMOC), xvii, 156
Australian PM, 97
Austrian political economy, 91

Authority, 6, 48, 81, 90, 92, 96, 97, 117, 119, 146, 173, 178, 187, 269, 270, 287, 294, 296, 310, 324, 386
Autonomous humanoid robotics (AHR), xvii, 196–244

B
Banking School, 281, 282, 284
Base and superstructure, 29
Behaviour, 24, 36, 93, 113, 196, 203, 205, 208, 212, 213, 215, 216, 218, 219, 230, 237, 242, 244, 289, 359, 362, 363, 366
Biology, 13, 213, 220, 221, 234
Blind drift, 5, 48, 81, 385
Bounded rationality, 36, 37, 47, 57, 74, 80, 207
Brain, vi, 196, 200, 207, 209, 213, 214, 219–234, 236–239, 241–244, 272, 340, 345, 347
Braitenberg vehicles, 200, 211
Bretton Woods System (BWS), xvii, 33, 282
Bribery, 35, 60, 167–170, 172–174, 176, 179, 182, 186, 187, 190
British hegemony, 51, 144, 280, 294
Business cycles, 27–29, 72, 81, 108, 254, 255, 279, 287, 289–291, 298, 388

C
Capabilities, 21, 24, 28, 35, 36, 58, 64, 65, 76, 92, 119, 196, 207, 261, 266–269, 289, 316, 322
Capital and ecology, 216
Capital and labor, 6, 108, 138, 173, 216, 252, 261, 262, 282, 370

Capitalism
  capitalist development, phases of, 280
  evolution of capitalism, 25, 50–55, 133, 280, 300
Central banks, 12, 138, 255, 263, 285–287, 289, 290, 299
Central nervous system (CNS), 221, 227
Ceremonial, 26, 29, 48, 71, 108, 262
Ceremonial encapsulation, 70, 178, 265
Chartalists, 281, 282, 298, 299
China, 2, 11, 33, 51, 53, 54, 95–97, 104, 106, 112, 113, 115, 117–119, 137, 144, 149, 176, 180, 181, 183, 186, 190, 279, 283, 317, 387
Chinese hegemony, 294
Circuit of money capital (CMC), 7, 12, 48, 71, 79, 133, 138, 264, 278, 284–286, 386
Circuit of social capital (CSC), 10, 23, 133, 285
Circuits, 13, 22, 35, 57, 61, 65, 69, 73, 121, 133–135, 142, 146, 200, 210, 212, 213, 217, 220, 225–236, 238, 239, 242, 243, 278–301, 314, 321, 325, 361
Circular and cumulative causation (CCC), v, xvii, 2, 5, 6, 9–15, 21–23, 28, 29, 38, 48, 57, 60–68, 73, 79, 81, 91, 93, 108–110, 113, 114, 122, 131, 145, 149–158, 189, 191, 198, 205–216, 218, 221, 226, 229, 230, 233, 234, 237–239, 242, 243, 252, 266–269, 273, 295, 296, 300, 316, 325, 331, 340, 341, 343, 348, 353, 354, 356–367, 379, 385–387
Circular economy, 6, 13, 28, 29, 37, 48, 60, 141, 243, 386
Classes, 4, 6, 10, 22–26, 35–37, 48, 54, 56, 57, 59–61, 64, 65, 68, 70, 74, 81, 102, 106, 122, 132, 133, 140, 168, 176, 178, 179, 187, 189, 198, 252, 253, 257, 262, 270, 272, 273, 278, 284, 297, 315, 358, 368, 369, 373, 378, 385, 386
Classical economists, 8, 20, 22, 25, 38
Climate change, vi, vii, ix, xvii, xviii, 2, 3, 7, 8, 10–13, 22, 34, 38, 46, 48, 53, 55, 63, 68, 69, 71, 73, 75, 77–79, 81, 82, 90, 108, 109, 111, 121, 122, 129–158, 198, 260, 265, 267, 272, 273, 386
Collective social wealth, 244
Collectivist cultures, 356
Colonialism, 256
Community, v, 2, 3, 7, 12–15, 24, 26, 30, 32, 34–36, 38, 47–50, 55, 57, 65, 74–77, 92, 97, 112–114, 120, 133, 134, 138, 139, 142, 154, 168, 173, 198, 199, 205, 221, 223, 239, 243, 244, 252–254, 260–262, 267, 268, 270, 297, 310, 313, 331, 343–348, 352, 353, 356, 359, 362, 371, 372, 386–388
Community's joint stock of knowledge (CJSK), 7, 9, 25, 35, 386
Competition and monopoly, 38, 173, 216, 252
Complexity, v, 6, 9, 11, 25, 34, 36–39, 48, 64–68, 70, 74, 75, 79, 108, 111, 141, 145, 152, 156, 173, 182, 198, 206–209, 212, 213, 217, 218, 221, 229, 230, 233, 234, 236, 237, 239, 242, 243, 253, 260, 266–268, 273, 299, 374, 375, 386, 387
Concepts, v, vi, ix, xv, 1–9, 12, 14, 20–28, 31, 32, 34–39, 46–49, 51, 54–57, 60, 61, 65, 67–74, 77–81, 91, 101, 108, 114, 130, 131, 137, 146, 149, 167, 170, 190, 201, 210, 218, 230, 232, 234, 239, 242, 252, 253, 272, 284, 301, 311, 340, 352, 354, 362, 371, 385–387
Confidence, 64, 65, 91, 220, 290
Consciousness, 11, 67, 223, 233, 235–237, 239, 242, 312, 332, 362
Conspicuous consumption, 24, 26, 35, 48, 65, 134, 243, 262, 326, 360, 370, 386
Contradictions, v, viii, 2, 5, 6, 8–15, 21, 23, 25–28, 30, 31, 35–38, 46–48, 59, 64, 66, 68–71, 73, 74, 79–81, 91, 93, 108–114, 122, 131, 138–143, 146, 147, 157, 158, 173–181, 190, 198, 205, 216–221, 223, 225, 241, 242, 252, 254–257, 260–266, 271–273, 278–280, 282, 284, 290, 294, 300, 311, 313, 315, 318–321, 323, 325, 330, 337–343, 353, 354, 356, 366–374, 378, 379, 385–387
Core, periphery, semi-periphery (CPSP), 5, 48, 182, 191, 271, 385
Coronacrisis, vi, xvii, 2, 3, 9, 10, 12, 13, 34, 52–55, 59, 68, 73, 78, 79, 82, 101, 108–117, 121, 252, 259, 264, 266, 283, 297, 298, 301, 379
Coronavirus, vii, ix, 8, 10, 55, 59, 60, 90–102, 105, 110, 113, 115, 117, 122, 204, 241, 347, 386, 387
Coronavirus disease 2019 (Covid-19), xvii, 91–93, 96–100, 102, 103, 105, 107, 109–112, 114, 118–120, 122
Corporations, 22, 24–26, 28, 30, 31, 33, 39, 54, 55, 57, 67–69, 74, 76, 77, 138, 139, 142, 148, 175, 180, 184–189, 255, 268, 279, 282, 323, 348, 356

Corruption, vi, ix, 2, 3, 8, 11, 46, 54, 55, 60, 68, 69, 71, 75, 77, 79, 82, 100, 108, 111, 166–191, 252, 259, 267, 272, 279, 323, 386

Corruption Perceptions Index (CPI), xvii, 182–185

COVID-19 Vaccines Global Access (COVAX), xvii, 100, 112

Creative destruction, v, 6, 7, 9, 21, 27, 28, 37, 48, 69, 73, 81, 252, 254, 263, 279, 315, 371, 386

Credit, 23, 48, 52, 61, 71, 72, 79, 90, 134, 146, 187, 254, 255, 262, 263, 278–301

Crises, vi, vii, ix, 2, 3, 6–10, 12, 15, 23, 26–28, 46, 48, 52, 53, 55, 57, 68, 70, 72, 73, 80, 82, 90, 91, 93–101, 110–112, 114–122, 131, 139, 141, 145, 152, 156, 157, 177, 178, 185–187, 191, 202, 204, 217, 241, 252–255, 259, 261–264, 266, 267, 271, 278–301, 313, 324, 343–346, 348, 352, 353, 379, 387, 388

Cultures, v, 7, 13, 15, 20, 21, 34, 35, 39, 47–49, 54, 56, 57, 61, 75, 81, 106, 119, 143, 154, 158, 178, 191, 242, 269, 270, 279, 280, 310, 319, 321, 342, 346, 354–356, 358, 360, 361, 371, 372, 377

Currency School, 281, 284

Cyber-terrorism, 13, 316

Cytokine storm (CS), 109, 110, 178

D

Dartmouth Conference of 1956, 205

Davidson Proposal, 12

Deaths from Covid-19, 97, 99, 100, 103, 112, 115

Decentered totality, 29, 212, 218

Degeneracy, 214, 223, 224, 234, 236, 242, 243

Demand, v, 3, 6, 7, 23, 26–28, 31, 36, 37, 48, 52, 61–63, 69, 72, 74, 92, 105, 111, 114, 121, 122, 134, 174, 185, 255–257, 261, 266, 281, 282, 285–288, 292, 294–298, 300, 301, 344, 360, 373, 386, 387

Destructive creation, 67, 76–77, 138, 158, 254, 279, 370

Determinism, 29

Discrimination, 32, 39, 64, 68, 179, 354

Disembedded economy, v, viii, 6, 11, 15, 48, 69, 71, 77, 79–81, 108, 131, 138, 139, 141, 157, 173, 216, 217, 243, 252–260, 272, 346, 352, 370, 371, 376, 386

Double day, 58

Double movement, v, vi, 6, 12, 27, 54, 55, 69, 122, 138, 216, 217, 255, 256, 260, 272, 279, 283, 370

Dutch hegemony, 294

E

Eastern Antarctic ice sheet (EAIS), 156

Ecological capitals, 62, 264

Ecologically unequal exchange, 147–149

Ecologies, 6, 7, 13, 24, 35, 38, 39, 48, 61, 66, 67, 77, 93, 135, 144, 198, 213, 239, 254, 267

Economic surplus, v, 2, 6, 21–24, 26, 31, 32, 35, 48, 60, 61, 176, 177, 184, 261, 386, 387

Economies of scale and scope, 69, 317

Economist, The, 90, 96, 100, 117, 118

Education, viii, xv, 13, 26, 30, 35, 36, 39, 57, 64, 65, 70, 74, 75, 111, 145, 154, 155, 184, 253, 266, 295, 297, 325, 344, 345, 347, 348, 354, 359, 360, 372

Egalitarian framework, 36

Electronic money, 283

El-Nino, xvii, 156, 157

Embeddedness and disembeddedness, 255, 256, 263, 266

Embezzlement, 35, 60, 167, 170, 173, 174, 176, 179, 182, 187, 190

Embodied cognition, 11, 75, 200, 203, 205, 206, 209, 210, 217–241, 244, 252

Emergence
   horizontal, 267
   temporal, 11, 66, 267
   vertical, 267

Emotional development, 64

Empirics, 2, 3, 34, 49, 50, 114, 166, 232, 244, 266, 331, 380, 387

Emulation, 6, 48, 65, 134, 148, 239, 243, 386

Enabling myths, 6, 48, 70, 386

Endogenous money and credit, 7, 63, 72, 255, 287–290

Entropy, 13, 71, 77–78, 131, 140, 141, 146, 148–150, 157, 158, 377, 378

Equality, 346

Ethnicities, 6, 10, 48, 56–60, 70, 81, 102, 106, 189, 270, 273, 297, 385

Eurodebt crises, 53, 54, 185–187, 259, 264, 283, 352, 387

European Association for Evolutionary Political Economy (EAEPE), xv, 3, 10, 20, 21, 31, 33, 37, 91, 144

Evolutions, v, 2, 5, 8–10, 12–14, 20–25, 29, 30, 32–34, 36–39, 47–55, 64, 70, 71, 75, 79–81, 90, 93–101, 105, 122, 131, 133, 168, 190, 198–200, 203, 208, 217, 219, 223, 229, 240, 242, 243, 255, 267, 278–281, 300, 309, 336, 348, 355, 356, 363, 368, 374–379, 385, 387, 388
Excess deaths from Covid-19, 95, 100, 101, 114
Extortion, 35, 60, 167, 169, 170, 173, 174, 176, 179, 182, 184, 186, 190
Extreme weather events, 155

F

Familial (in)stability, 282
Family, 14, 24, 25, 30, 34, 55–58, 67–69, 73, 74, 76–78, 113, 133, 134, 174, 175, 178, 184, 188, 190, 252, 254, 257, 261, 265, 270, 297, 346, 352, 353, 356, 359, 369–371, 377–379
Feedback loops (positive and/ negative), 341, 345
Feminist/feminism, 5, 9, 20, 21, 30, 32, 34, 35, 38, 39, 76, 142, 199, 269, 279, 352, 354, 359
Fictitious capitals, 7, 71, 278, 283, 352
Fictitious commodities, 138, 254, 255
Finance, 21, 133, 173, 202, 252, 278, 313, 352, 386
Finance and industry, 6, 38, 73, 108, 138, 173, 252
Finance capital, 23, 26, 52, 278, 280, 282, 352
Financial crises, vi, ix, 26, 34, 38, 46, 50, 52, 60, 69, 73, 78, 80, 81, 108, 254, 260–263, 282–284, 290, 293, 295, 379, 388
Financial instability hypothesis (FIH), xvii, 7, 15, 48, 73, 79, 278, 290–293, 298, 300, 301, 386
Financialization, 263, 283, 300
Fintechs, 278, 283
Fordism, 52, 257, 263, 282
Fraud, 35, 60, 70, 167, 169, 170, 173, 174, 176, 179–182, 184, 186, 187, 190, 191, 279
Freedom constraints, viii, 15
Functional finance, 7, 12, 39, 48, 54, 73, 75, 81, 90, 91, 110, 111, 117, 120–122, 252, 255, 283, 386

G

GDP per capita real growth rate, 257, 258

Gender cycle, 204
Genders, 6, 10, 25, 30, 31, 38, 48, 50, 56–60, 64, 68, 70, 81, 102, 106, 108, 122, 178, 179, 189, 240, 252, 253, 261, 270, 273, 297, 326, 345, 346, 355, 356, 358, 360, 361, 373, 385, 386
General Problem Solver (GPS), 210, 217
Genetics, 14, 57, 101, 109, 142, 196, 229, 231, 233, 234, 339, 341, 346, 355
Glial cells, 225, 226, 238, 242, 243
Global economies, 269, 283, 295
Global financial crisis (GFC), vi, xviii, 2, 3, 34, 53–55, 73, 78, 90, 93, 110, 111, 115–117, 120, 121, 177, 185–187, 204, 241, 259, 264, 267, 283, 293, 297, 298, 301, 352, 379, 387
Global injustice, 146, 147, 388
Globalization, 3, 55, 79, 110, 187, 263, 311, 319, 320, 323, 325
Global money, 79, 293–297
Global New Deal, 29
Global political economy, v, viii, ix, xv, 3, 51, 81, 90, 122, 283, 285, 308, 311, 318, 321
Global Political Economy Research Unit (GPERU), viii, xv, 3
Governments, 22, 55, 59, 62, 63, 65, 75, 76, 78, 91, 92, 100, 111, 116, 120, 122, 133, 134, 145, 184, 187, 188, 203, 240, 256, 257, 260, 264–266, 268, 269, 272, 278, 281, 286–289, 294–299, 301, 309, 310, 313–315, 318–320, 322–324, 330, 343, 344, 346, 348, 370
Great Depression
  1870s-1890s, 52, 281
  1930s, 26, 52, 53, 116, 257
Great Union of Vested Interests, 26, 35
Greenhouse gas emissions (GHGE), 69, 131, 135, 149, 150, 152
Greenhouse gasses, xviii, 68, 132, 135, 142, 144, 149, 153, 198
Greenland ice sheet (GIS), xviii, 151, 156
Green Road, 76, 78, 130, 131, 137, 138, 154, 155, 158, 252, 265
Grounded psychology school, 229

H

Habits, v, 20, 21, 24, 36, 38, 48, 61, 65, 74, 76, 80, 81, 101, 113, 131, 134, 143, 154, 158, 167, 173, 191, 222, 225, 254, 265,

Subject Index

279, 280, 345–348, 359, 362, 363, 369, 373, 375, 377, 387
Hebbian learning, 11, 215, 223, 235
Hedge, speculative and Ponzi finance, 12, 291
Hegemony
  British, 51, 144, 280, 294, 404, 412
  Chinese (potential), 294
  Dutch, 51, 144, 294
  US, 33, 51, 71, 144, 200, 257, 259, 282, 283, 294, 308, 315–319, 325, 326
Heterodox political economy, 91
Heterogeneous groups and agents, v, 2, 5, 6, 8–10, 14, 21, 25, 38, 56–60, 67, 81, 90, 101–107, 122, 173, 178, 190, 196, 198, 199, 240, 242, 252, 270, 273, 278, 281, 282, 300, 335, 340–343, 348, 354, 357, 379, 385, 387
High GDP Road, 154
Historical schools, 23, 25
Historical specificity, v, 2, 5, 8–11, 14, 20, 22–24, 32, 35, 36, 38, 48–55, 79–81, 90, 93, 122, 131–138, 157, 166–173, 190, 198, 199, 240, 242, 252, 272, 278, 280, 300, 308, 325, 330, 348, 353–356, 379, 385, 387
Historical time, v, 5, 8, 20, 22, 24, 25, 27, 29, 31, 32, 36, 47–49, 51, 59, 66, 75, 81, 108, 111, 114, 139, 144, 149, 155, 182, 189, 199, 267, 280, 286, 316, 357, 367, 374, 376, 385
HIV and AIDS, 330–348
Holistic love, 15, 68, 354, 356, 361–365, 368, 369, 374, 376, 377, 379, 380
Holistic method/holism, 2, 29, 63, 331, 341, 371
Households, 14, 30, 35, 54, 57, 58, 61, 65, 77, 120, 198, 199, 253, 260, 268, 278, 282, 284, 371, 373, 379
Huanan Wholesale Seafood Market, 96
Human-level intelligence, 206, 209, 210, 219
Humanoid robotics, 2, 71, 75, 196, 199, 202, 205, 217, 220–223, 235, 238, 243, 388
Hysteresis, 20, 78, 81, 150, 156, 278

I

Imperialism, 20, 23, 27, 52, 133, 282, 318
Indian monsoonal system (IMS), xviii, 156
Individualist cultures, 356
Inequality, 6, 15, 29, 32, 48, 54, 55, 59, 61, 68, 69, 120, 136, 149, 154, 168, 178, 179, 187, 189–191, 262, 264, 268, 269, 272, 283, 319, 324, 386, 388

Information processing approach, 203, 390, 391
Information, skills and intelligence, 7, 48
Innovation and competition, 73, 263
Innovations, v, 2, 5, 7–9, 11–13, 21, 26–29, 31, 32, 35–37, 39, 46, 48, 52, 60–64, 69, 70, 72–75, 79–81, 91, 93, 105, 113, 117, 120–122, 131, 133, 143, 146, 153, 157, 158, 173, 187, 190, 196–201, 204, 214, 215, 225, 234, 236, 240–243, 252, 255, 263, 264, 267, 278, 282–284, 286, 289, 294, 297, 300, 315, 324, 325, 330, 346–347, 353, 354, 370, 374, 377, 379, 385–388
Instincts, v, 24, 80, 134, 243
Institutional and evolutionary political economy (IEPE), ix, xviii, 1, 2, 5, 9, 20–22, 29–39, 46–51, 56, 57, 60, 61, 63, 65, 66, 68, 69, 71, 73, 75–77, 80, 81, 90, 91, 93, 122, 131, 166, 182, 197, 199, 200, 216, 242, 244, 252, 253, 270, 272, 279, 298, 300, 301, 325, 348, 353, 354, 379, 380
Institutions, v, viii, 2, 3, 6, 10, 12, 14, 20–26, 28–34, 36–38, 46–53, 55–58, 60–62, 64, 66–70, 74–78, 80, 81, 92, 108, 111, 117, 119, 131, 133, 138, 139, 148, 153–155, 158, 167–169, 173, 174, 178–181, 188–191, 197, 242, 244, 252–254, 256, 257, 259–262, 265–270, 279, 280, 282–285, 289, 290, 294, 295, 297, 299–301, 311, 315, 316, 318, 321, 324, 326, 344, 348, 353, 354, 356, 365, 370, 387
Instrumental and ceremonial functions, 2, 6, 69, 77, 242, 386, 387
Intangible capital, 12, 278
Intellectual property, xviii, 7, 48, 197, 204, 386
Intelligence Community (IC), 97
Interdependency (principle of), 38
Interdisciplinary, v, 13, 29, 47, 68, 331, 333, 386
Intergovernmental Panel on Climate Change (IPCC), 78, 121, 130, 132, 135–137, 143, 144, 151–155, 264, 265, 272
International Monetary Fund (IMF), xviii, 3, 33, 53, 114, 116, 148, 264, 296
Investment, 6, 22, 27, 28, 31, 34, 39, 62, 63, 72, 105, 111, 116, 120, 122, 134, 146–148, 152, 154, 187, 188, 204, 256, 257, 263, 278, 280, 282, 285, 286, 289–292, 295–300, 359, 365, 376, 377

Irreversibilities, 66, 74, 149, 152, 156
Islam, 308, 309, 311, 318–321, 323, 324, 326
Islamic political economy, 13, 324
Islamic State, 53

J

Jihadis, 13, 53, 68, 71, 260, 272, 325
Journal of Economic Issues, vii, viii, 9, 14, 21, 33, 144

K

Kansas flu, 122
Keynesian revolution, 27
Keynesian-welfare state (KWS), xviii, 33, 257, 282
Kinematics, 221, 224, 243, 244

L

Labor power, 69, 112, 134, 138, 139, 141, 142, 146, 147, 149, 254, 285
Laws of thermodynamics, 77
Lesbian, gay, bisexual, and transsexual (people or movement) (LGBT), xviii, 58
Living Planet Index (LPI), xviii, 109, 142
Logic machine, 217
Long COVID, 107
Long waves, 2, 12, 14, 15, 28, 37, 50, 53, 70, 72, 73, 132, 201, 254–259, 263, 265, 279–282, 290–293, 347, 387
Love, 2, 14, 15, 352–380
Love capital, viii, 15, 46, 60, 71, 75, 79, 352–380
Love styles, 15, 354, 357–374, 376, 379

M

Market capital, 264
Markets, 7, 11, 12, 21–23, 26, 27, 30, 36, 52–55, 59, 61–63, 69, 71, 72, 74, 77, 79, 91, 92, 96, 110, 112, 130, 132–134, 138, 139, 142, 144, 146, 148, 158, 168, 173, 175, 176, 180, 181, 185, 187, 190, 203, 216, 241, 252–256, 260, 264, 265, 269, 272, 279, 281–283, 285, 286, 288, 290, 292, 293, 296, 298, 299, 317, 318, 322, 352, 354, 356, 365, 366, 368, 370–372, 379
Marxism, 23
Means of production (MOP), 134, 261, 285

Memory, 11, 201, 206, 210, 216, 220, 222, 223, 225, 226, 228–233, 235–239, 242–244, 388
Metabolic rift, 144, 146–149, 157
Metallists, 281
Micro-meso-macro-global, 65
Middle of the Road, 137, 155, 288
Minimum dislocation, 78
Misinformation, 10, 71, 113
Mitigation, 7, 22, 48, 55, 69, 78, 92, 130, 136, 137, 143, 153, 155, 265, 386
Modern monetary theory (MMT), v, xviii, 7, 12, 39, 48, 73, 79, 117, 278, 283, 298–301, 386
Monetary and fiscal policy, 255
Monetary theory of production, 27, 279, 286, 295
Money, credit and finance, viii, 3, 12, 278, 289, 301
Money laundering, 11, 188
Monopoly capital, 26
Monopoly *vs.* competition, 12, 48, 175
Moral, 22, 55, 166–169, 178, 188, 284, 354
Mores, 133, 197–200, 202–204, 208, 210–214, 216–229, 231, 233–235, 237, 240–243, 345, 385, 386, 388
Multifactor approach, 6, 68, 108, 343, 386
Multiplication, 6, 48
Mutation, variation & selection, 7, 48

N

Nadine (robot), 196
Nationalism, 34, 111, 154
Nationality, 6, 48, 252, 270, 385
Neoclassical synthesis, 27
Neoliberalism, 3, 10, 13, 15, 34, 53–55, 71, 78, 90, 92, 93, 110, 111, 113, 114, 117, 120, 121, 133, 257, 259, 262, 264, 280, 292, 299, 325, 347, 352, 354, 367, 369, 371, 379
Neo-Schumpeterian, 39, 263
Neo-Veblenian, 214
Nepotism, 35, 60, 167, 173, 174, 179, 182, 186, 190
Neural circuits and pathways, 221, 224
Neurobiological political economy (NPE), 68, 198, 221–240, 242–244
Neurobiology, 196, 200, 242
Neurorobotic AGI, 199, 205, 239, 241, 243
Neuroscience, 2, 34, 200, 205, 207, 213, 221, 223, 226, 241

Subject Index

New deal, 20, 28, 29, 282
9/11, 12, 13, 53, 55, 68, 311, 325
Nobel Laureates, 33, 36, 63, 198, 203, 206
Nonlinear, 10, 63, 65, 66, 74, 131, 139, 141, 151, 152, 156, 158, 206, 237
Northeast permafrost (NEP), xviii, 156
Northern boreal forests (NBF), xviii, 156
Northern permafrost (NPF), xviii, 156
Nurturance gap, v, vi, viii, ix, 2, 3, 8, 15, 46, 55, 60, 77, 82, 352–380, 387
Nutrition, 14, 64, 110, 331, 340, 343

O

Occupations, 25, 57–59, 252
Ontology, 24, 67
Organizations, 50, 57, 58, 61, 62, 68–70, 74, 76, 144, 145, 153, 158, 176, 178, 179, 187, 188, 190, 212, 235, 267, 269, 270, 310, 318, 354
Oxford Dictionary, 4

P

Pandemic, vii, 8, 9, 14, 46, 54, 55, 59, 60, 68, 69, 75, 81, 90–97, 100, 103, 111, 112, 114, 116–122, 252, 343, 386, 387
Participatory democracy, 7, 48, 75, 76, 81, 386
Path dependence, v, 5, 10, 20, 32, 36, 37, 48, 66, 74, 79–81, 150, 157, 278, 353, 355, 374–379, 385
Peripheral nervous system (PNS), 219, 221, 226–228, 243
Phases, 2, 5, 15, 20, 23, 28, 30, 32, 34, 38, 48, 50–52, 64, 72, 79, 81, 98, 105, 121, 131–133, 166, 196, 219, 223, 235, 243, 258, 259, 267, 278–285, 291, 300, 309, 332, 333, 337, 338, 344, 348, 355, 362, 363, 368, 374–379, 385
Physiocrats, 8, 20, 22
Policy and governance, viii, ix, 2, 5, 7, 9, 11, 22, 26, 35, 39, 46, 75–78, 80, 81, 252–273, 278, 297, 300, 321, 385, 386, 388
Policy waves, 46, 252, 256, 260
Political economy, v, vii–ix, xv, xvii, xviii, 1–6, 9, 11–15, 21, 23, 25, 28, 31–33, 35, 38, 39, 46, 49–51, 53, 55, 57, 59, 63, 65, 70, 75, 80, 90–93, 110, 114, 121, 131, 140, 141, 143, 149, 158, 166, 167, 176, 178, 189, 197, 198, 200, 205–218, 244, 252, 253, 260, 267–269, 271, 278, 297, 299, 300, 311, 353–355, 357, 362, 369, 379, 380, 386–388

Polly (robot), 216, 240
Polycentric systems, 36
Post-Keynesian, xviii, 9, 21, 30, 32, 34, 38, 39, 71, 72, 76, 114, 278, 284, 287, 294
Power, 325
Pragmatism, 23, 218
Prebisch-Singer hypothesis, 63, 147
Prevailing business climate, 7, 8, 48, 290, 386
Principle(s), 1, 20, 90, 131, 166, 196, 252, 278, 308, 330, 353, 385
Principles of AI, 198, 207, 216, 243
Principles of neuromodulation, 225
Principles of political economy, v, vi, viii, ix, 2–4, 11, 15, 23, 80, 157, 158, 385
Principles of public health, 75, 97, 109
Problems, vi, viii, ix, xv, 1–3, 5–15, 20, 22, 26, 27, 29, 30, 32, 34, 37, 47, 49–53, 56, 60, 64–66, 69–73, 75, 78–82, 92–94, 100, 107, 110, 113, 114, 119, 130, 131, 134, 142–145, 149, 152, 157, 158, 166, 176, 180, 185, 190, 191, 199, 205–207, 209, 210, 217, 221, 232, 252, 254, 255, 261, 262, 264–269, 272, 273, 286, 290, 294, 296, 313, 321–323, 330, 332, 333, 335, 337, 344, 346, 348, 354, 370, 371, 373, 379, 386–388
Production, 3, 5, 10, 12, 20, 23, 24, 26, 27, 34, 35, 39, 47, 48, 58, 60, 61, 63, 71, 74, 76, 77, 90, 110, 111, 120, 130, 132–134, 139–144, 146–150, 157, 158, 182, 197, 199, 216, 255, 260, 261, 267, 269, 270, 272, 279, 281–283, 285–287, 290, 294, 315, 317, 319, 322, 370, 385
Productive and unproductive activities, 26, 296
Productivity, 26, 62, 69, 73, 132, 179, 254, 258, 263, 272, 284, 290, 295, 297, 317, 324, 344, 352
Proprioception, 208, 214, 224, 227, 228, 236, 238
Prospective yield and supply price, 290
Provisioning, 12, 35, 92, 252, 253, 267, 268, 271–273
Public goods, 39, 54, 55, 61, 69, 70, 74, 254, 255, 266, 269, 294, 300, 317, 352, 370

Q

Quality of life, 7, 11, 13, 22, 29, 36, 48, 56, 58, 59, 65, 69, 74, 77, 140, 147, 154, 191, 240, 253, 269, 320, 352, 386, 388
Quantity theory of money, 286
Quesnay, F., 22

R

Racism, 32
Radiative forcing, 135, 152, 154
Reaganomics, 257, 262
Realism, 5, 64–66, 300, 385
Recessions, 7, 23, 26, 28, 38, 46, 48, 63, 70, 72, 90, 116, 117, 121, 185, 203, 204, 241, 255, 261, 263, 264, 279, 282–284, 289–295, 297, 298, 300, 317, 323, 352, 379
Reciprocity, 12, 37, 55, 69, 138, 149, 173, 216, 217, 279, 352, 354, 360, 363, 370, 371, 377
Recognized interdependence, 70, 268
Redistribution, 12, 36, 37, 55, 58, 69, 138, 173, 177, 185, 216, 217, 279, 352, 354, 370
Redundancies, 26, 206, 214, 223, 224, 234, 243
Reganomics, 283
Regional rivalry, 154
Regulation Approach, 70, 278
Regulations, 3, 9, 13, 33, 34, 36, 54, 62, 70, 77, 90, 92, 143, 174, 176, 179, 187, 188, 255, 257, 263, 296, 319, 323, 370, 371
Relative income, 65
Reproduction, 25, 32, 35, 38, 46, 47, 60, 65, 68, 69, 71, 79, 80, 134, 138, 142, 146, 150, 228, 230, 239, 254, 255, 271, 279, 315, 343–346, 353, 363, 365, 370
Review of Evolutionary Political Economy, xv, 21, 33, 144
Revolutions, 10, 29, 30, 38, 50–53, 132, 139, 150, 272, 280, 281, 355
Ricardo, D., 23
Risks, 13, 50, 71–73, 103, 110, 114, 118, 152, 175, 184, 264, 289–291, 311–315, 325, 340, 341, 343
Robotics, vi, ix, 2, 11, 13, 35, 55, 79, 196–244, 278
Routines, 25, 37, 62, 76

S

Sabotage, 13, 26, 315, 316, 323
SARS-Cov-2, 96, 97, 100, 103–107, 109, 110, 112, 113, 118
Schumpeterians, 9, 31, 39, 74, 263, 278, 279, 284
Science and technology, 75, 113, 355
Scientific realism, 48, 63, 66
Scramble for Africa, 52, 282
Sensors and receptors, 221, 224
Serial monogamy, 15, 369, 378, 379
Shared socioeconomic pathways (SSP), xviii, 73, 75, 78, 137, 138, 143, 153–155, 265

Skills, 21, 24–26, 29, 35, 36, 38, 39, 57, 61, 64, 65, 67, 68, 72, 74, 78, 196, 213, 217, 224, 230, 232, 237, 244, 254, 261, 262, 266, 267, 279, 298, 344, 352, 355, 359, 376, 377
Social balance, 30
Social capital, 13, 54, 55, 65, 254, 270, 344, 365
Social conditions of innovation, 7, 48
Socioeconomic reproduction, 14, 20, 197, 216, 257, 370
Socialism, 27, 33, 38, 47, 69, 91, 190, 317
Social provisioning, v, 5, 7, 8, 20, 22, 32, 35, 38, 39, 48, 49, 71, 75, 79–81, 166, 242, 297, 352, 385–388
Social structures of accumulation (SSA), xviii, 2, 3, 34, 70, 116, 183, 258, 259, 263, 271, 278, 282, 333–335, 344, 345, 348, 387
Social wealth, 177, 261
Sophia (robot), 196, 240
Soviet Union, 52, 200, 317, 318
Spanish flu, 52, 54, 94
Species, 6, 10, 25, 38, 48, 57, 59, 61, 68, 81, 101, 108, 109, 122, 136, 141, 142, 146, 150, 152, 157, 197, 198, 208, 229, 240, 243, 252, 253, 255, 270, 271, 273, 297, 355, 385
Speculative bubbles, 26, 52, 53, 72, 90, 114, 116, 177, 185, 202, 241, 257, 263, 278, 282, 283, 287, 289, 293–295, 300
Stages, 2, 5, 20, 39, 48, 100, 111, 131, 166, 168, 185, 207, 212, 228, 243, 270, 285, 291, 338, 345, 369, 375, 376
Standard corruption equation, 175
Standard of living, 7, 22, 26, 36, 48, 53, 59, 63, 69, 74, 147, 183, 184, 190, 253, 269, 297, 386
State and capital, 264, 282
State capture, 35, 60, 170, 173, 174, 184, 186, 190, 191
States, xviii, 2, 5–7, 12, 14, 15, 21, 22, 24–26, 30, 32–36, 38, 49, 51, 54, 56, 61, 63, 68, 70, 74, 75, 77, 78, 81, 93, 96, 101, 110, 114, 116, 119, 131, 133, 134, 137, 138, 140–143, 148, 149, 154, 156, 158, 167–169, 173–175, 177, 178, 181, 182, 184, 185, 189–191, 198, 199, 206–212, 214, 216, 223, 225–227, 231, 232, 235, 240, 242, 252, 253, 255–257, 259, 260, 262, 263, 266, 268, 269, 280, 283, 284, 288, 290, 295, 297, 298, 301, 308–312, 314, 316–318, 320–326, 333, 343, 346, 352, 355, 356, 360, 362, 367, 369, 370, 372, 374, 378, 388

Structural changes, 130, 131, 143, 154, 158, 167, 173
Structural crises, 2, 26, 27, 37, 257, 261
Styles of Covid-19 waves, 99
Stylized facts, 5, 31, 37, 48–50, 80, 92, 116, 167, 179, 180, 182, 185, 188–190, 199, 200, 333, 353, 385
Surplus value, v, 12, 23, 27, 134, 278, 285, 286
Sustainability, 36, 75, 77, 78, 92, 130, 131, 134, 137, 141, 154, 155, 158, 265, 297, 346
System dynamics, 63–65, 215, 293
Systemic corruption, 35, 69, 167, 173, 174, 180, 182, 190, 191
Systemism, 29, 66

T
Taliban, 13, 53, 309, 318, 321
Tax evasion, 11, 55
Tax havens, 116, 177, 180, 181, 187, 189, 287
Tax Justice Network, 187
Technology, xviii, 13, 32, 37, 51, 53, 61, 66, 67, 71, 79, 111, 122, 130, 131, 139, 144, 152–154, 187, 196, 197, 200, 217, 236, 241, 265, 282, 283, 311, 314–317, 322, 323, 325, 347, 363
Terrorism, vi, ix, 2, 3, 8, 12, 13, 35, 38, 46, 55, 68, 71, 73, 75, 78–82, 266, 267, 308–326, 387
Thatcherism, 257
Threshold effects, 10, 130, 131, 150, 151, 155, 156, 158
Tipping points, 10, 48, 63, 73, 81, 102, 130, 150, 152, 155–158, 265, 386, 387
Transaction costs, 37, 65
Transactions, 28, 36, 37, 69, 138, 169, 172, 252, 260, 288, 352
Transparency, 170, 171, 185, 296, 323, 324
Tropical coral reefs (TCR), xviii, 156
Trump, D., 93, 112, 113, 115, 121
Trust, 2, 3, 6, 15, 22, 36, 48, 50–57, 61, 65, 73, 76–77, 80, 149, 167, 179, 181, 267, 270, 283, 323, 344, 352, 355, 357, 362, 363, 368, 371, 372, 374, 375, 377, 385, 388

U
Uncertainty, v, 2, 5–10, 21, 27, 28, 31, 37, 39, 46, 48, 62, 63, 65, 66, 69–74, 78–81, 91, 93, 101, 111, 112, 114–122, 130, 131, 136, 137, 139, 149–158, 177, 202, 206, 214, 242, 252, 264, 267, 272, 273, 278, 283, 289–291, 293, 295, 297, 300, 311, 312, 315, 316, 333, 353, 355, 362, 369, 371, 375, 378, 379, 385–387
Unemployment and underemployment, 64
Uneven development, v, vii, viii, 2, 3, 5, 8–13, 21, 25, 29, 31, 32, 39, 46, 48–55, 59, 69, 71, 79–81, 90, 91, 93, 114, 122, 131, 143–149, 155, 158, 173–191, 198, 200, 240, 242, 253, 269–273, 283, 294, 300, 308, 317, 320, 325, 330, 333, 343, 348, 355, 371, 379, 385–388
US President, 97

V
Vaccines, xvii, 10, 60, 75, 90, 91, 95, 97, 100, 101, 103, 105–107, 109, 112, 117, 120–122, 331, 347, 348
Variants of SARS-Cov-2, 106
Varieties of capitalism, 33, 34, 47, 54
Varieties of Coronavirus, 94
Veblenians, 9, 20, 21, 32, 34, 36, 37, 134, 278
Venture capital, 283
Vested interests *vs.* common good, 48, 69, 71, 74, 79, 252, 386
Vietnam War, 32, 52

W
War on terrorism, vi, viii, ix, 3, 12, 13, 80, 308–326, 387
Waste, 26, 28, 30, 32, 65, 78, 136, 140–142, 147, 150, 158, 262, 299
Waves of Covid-19 cases and infections, 99
West African monsoonal system (WAMS), xviii, 156
West Antarctic ice sheet (WAIS), 156
World Bank, xviii, 53, 116, 184, 188, 258, 264, 296, 335
World development, 29, 33, 75
World economy, 14, 25, 34, 35, 51, 52, 58, 154, 182, 258, 260, 282, 295
World income, 259, 295
World problems, v, vi, ix, 1, 2, 5, 7–10, 14, 15, 39, 46, 47, 49, 51, 53, 55, 60, 66, 68, 71, 73, 75, 79–82, 93, 101, 108, 191, 210, 273, 362, 387
World-system, 5, 48, 144, 182, 309, 355, 385
World Trade Organisation (WTO), 3, 93, 148
Worldwide Fund for Nature (WWF), 109, 264
Wuhan, China, 96, 97, 102, 104, 105, 112, 113, 122

The manufacturer's authorised representative in the EU is Springer Nature Customer Service Centre GmbH, Europaplatz 3, 69115 Heidelberg, Germany. If you have any concerns regarding our products, please contact ProductSafety@springernature.com

Printed and bound by CPI Group (UK) Ltd, Croydon, CR0 4YY

23/03/2026

02076651-0001